Snapshot

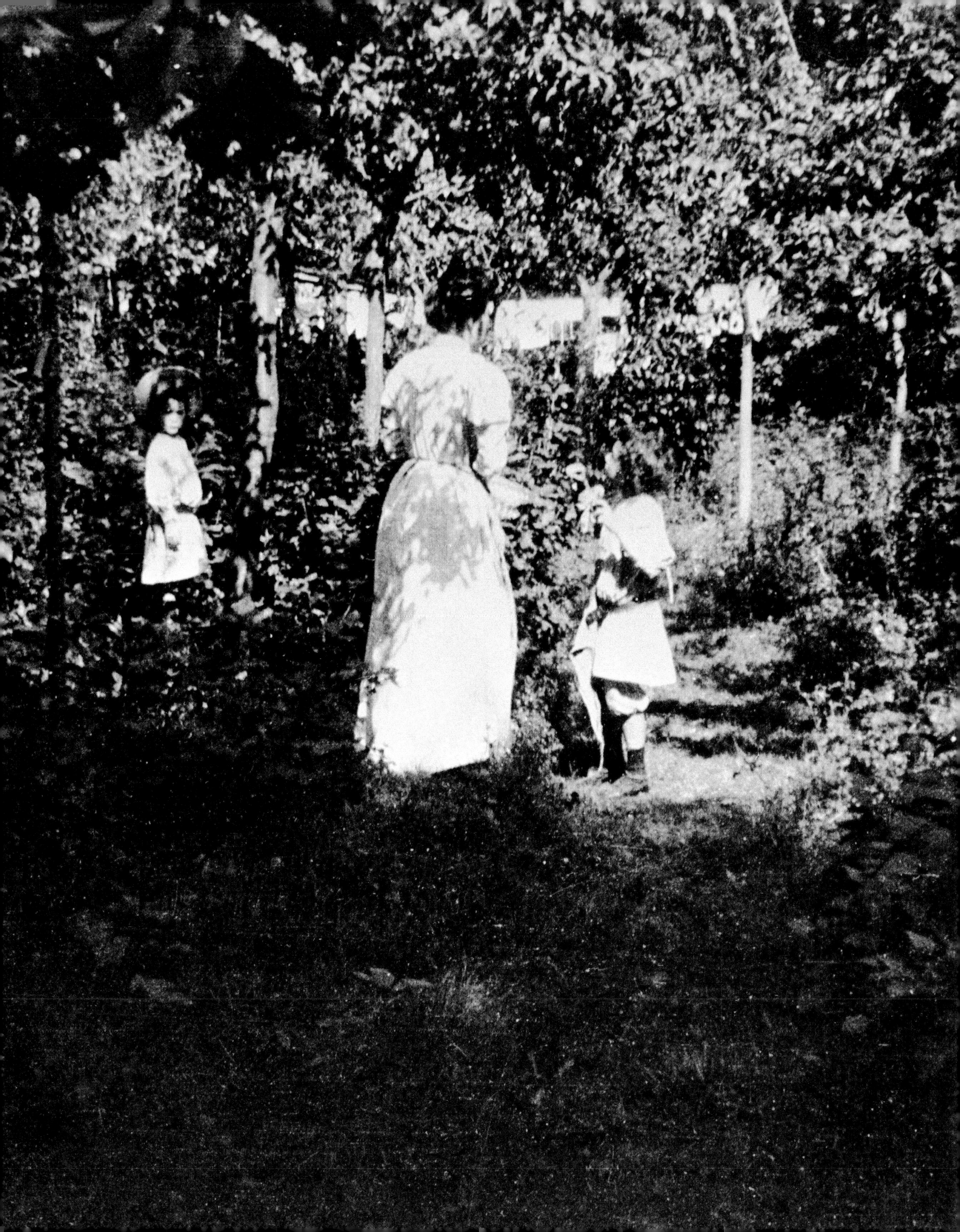

Snapshot

Painters and Photography, Bonnard to Vuillard

Edited by Elizabeth W. Easton

With contributions by Clément Chéroux, Michel Frizot, Todd Gustavson, Françoise Heilbrun, Ellen W. Lee, Anne McCauley, Saskia Ooms, Katia Poletti, Eliza Rathbone, and Hans Rooseboom

Published by Yale University Press, New Haven and London

IN ASSOCIATION WITH

Indianapolis Museum of Art

The Phillips Collection, Washington, D.C.

Van Gogh Museum, Amsterdam

Published on the occasion of an exhibition at the following institutions:

Snapshot. Schilders en fotografie, 1888–1915 | *Snapshot. Painters and Photography, 1888–1915*
Van Gogh Museum, Amsterdam
October 14, 2011–January 8, 2012

Snapshot: Painters and Photography, Bonnard to Vuillard
The Phillips Collection, Washington, D.C.
February 4–May 6, 2012

Indianapolis Museum of Art
June 8–September 2, 2012

This exhibition was realized with the curatorial collaboration of and exceptional loans from the Musée d'Orsay.

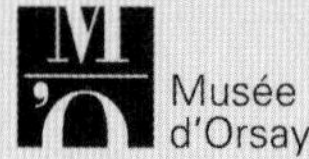

www.yalebooks.com/art

Designed by Rita Jules, Miko McGinty Inc.
Set in Fournier and The Sans type by Tina Henderson
Printed in Italy by Mondadori

LIBRARY OF CONGRESS CATALOGING-IN-PUBLICATION DATA
Snapshot : painters and photography, Bonnard to Vuillard / edited by Elizabeth W. Easton ; with contributions by Clément Chéroux . . . [et al.].
p. cm.
Includes bibliographical references and index.
ISBN 978-0-300-17236-2 (cloth, Yale)—ISBN 978-90-79310-28-9 (cloth, Van Gogh Museum)
1. Photography—France—History—19th century—Exhibitions. 2. Art and photography—Exhibitions.
I. Easton, Elizabeth Wynne. II. Chéroux, Clément. III. Van Gogh Museum, Amsterdam. IV. Phillips Collection.
V. Indianapolis Museum of Art.
TR71.S63 2011
779.0944'074—dc23
2011012326

A catalogue record for this book is available from the British Library.

The paper in this book meets the requirements of ANSI/NISO Z39.48-1992 (Permanence of Paper).

10 9 8 7 6 5 4 3 2 1

Jacket illustrations: ISBN 978-0-300-17236-2 *(front)* detail of cat. 1; *(back)* detail of cat. 140;
ISBN 978-90-79310-28-9 *(front)* detail of cat. 83; *(back)* detail of cat. 33
Frontispiece: detail of cat. 5
Endpapers: *(front)* detail of cat. 105; *(back)* detail of cat. 103
Pages 58–59: detail of cat. 48

Contents

Directors' Foreword

Caught up as we are in the digital age, it seems natural for the transmission of images to be easy, instantaneous, and potentially ubiquitous. We are habituated to a world in which images operate on a vast spectrum, from titillating to banal. Notwithstanding the routine manipulation of digital images with computer desktop tools, we are prepared to accept as fact photographic representations of people, places, and events that have no accompanying seal of approval — and which may be wholly inventions, with mischievous or fraudulent intent. A chance snapshot can change the course of national policy or our collective psyche, as did the Abu Ghraib photographs, or it can upend the fortunes of the privileged, as with security camera evidence of shoplifting by Hollywood stars.

Today's floating sea of images has its ancestral roots in the subject of the present exhibition: the formative years when amateur photography was introduced, thanks to technological advances of an earlier sort. Until the invention of the Kodak camera in 1888, the representation of the world had been the province of professional artists and photographers. The need for painterly talent or access to cumbersome photographic equipment limited the universe of widespread imagery, and the publication of photographs was in the hands of those with printing presses or professional darkrooms.

The pre-digital dawn of widespread photographic documentation had a sudden and profound impact on painters in the late nineteenth century, in particular the group of artists in the Parisian avant-garde known as the Nabis. Photography changed the course of the visual arts by fomenting an existential dilemma: If representation by a machine could be faster and more accurate than representation by a painter, the whole enterprise of painting was called into question. The resulting question articulated in Walter Benjamin's 1936 essay "The Work of Art in the Age of Mechanical Reproduction" continues to roil the creative enterprise up to this moment: What do we mean by an authentic creative gesture?

The Van Gogh Museum, the Phillips Collection, and the Indianapolis Museum of Art are proud of the collaboration that has resulted in this exceptional exhibition and scholarly publication. Under the curatorial leadership of Edwin Becker, head of exhibitions at the Van Gogh Museum, Eliza Rathbone, chief curator at the Phillips Collection, and Ellen W. Lee, the Wood-Pulliam Senior Curator at the Indianapolis Museum of Art, our institutions have overcome the very considerable challenges of a complex international loan exhibition project involving multiple artists, myriad far-flung loans, and a team of scholars.

This achievement is largely attributable to the determination of guest curator Elizabeth W. Easton, who discovered the rich trove of photographs in the Vuillard archive while researching her doctoral dissertation on that artist in the 1980s. This exhibition is a result of her resolute desire to reveal fully the integral importance of snapshot photography to the aesthetic and working methods of the post-Impressionist artists of the last decade of the nineteenth century.

Her enthusiasm and scholarship in this area were matched by that of Françoise Heilbrun, head curator of photography at the Musée d'Orsay, whose work with the late Philippe Néagu revealed the importance of Bonnard's photographic production. Madame Heilbrun's sustained collaboration has very substantially helped to shape this project and bring it to fruition. We are of course very thankful to all of the lenders to this exhibition, and are keenly aware of the exceptional generosity and collegial engagement of Guy Cogeval, president of the Musée d'Orsay, who has made available nearly one hundred photographs and paintings for the exhibition.

This project makes important new contributions to the field, adding to our understanding of how artists use a variety of media and creatively respond to new technologies. Several earlier exhibition projects have treated individual artists. An ambitiously broad project was curated by Erika Billeter in 1977 for the Kunsthaus in Zurich. *Malerei und Photographie*, which included artists from the advent of photography to contemporary art, allowed Pierre Bonnard, George Hendrik Breitner, Félix Vallotton, and Edouard Vuillard only cameo roles. The 1999 exhibition project *Degas to Picasso* organized by the Dallas Museum of Art focused more sharply on the late nineteenth and twentieth century. Though that exhibition did include the Nabis, it also embraced an international array of painters and sculptors.

Our project focuses much more precisely on the love affair with the handheld automatic camera introduced by Kodak in 1888. It examines in great depth the singular importance of this innovation to the Nabis, revealing the photographic practice of Bonnard, Maurice Denis, Vallotton, and Vuillard, as well as of Henri Rivière, a key member of the era's great printmaking revival. The exhibition includes two artists virtually unknown in the United States: the Belgian Henri Evenepoel and the Dutchman Breitner. The sheer volume of photographic material—over ten thousand photographs, most of which have never been publicly exhibited—amply demonstrates the artists' delight in experimenting with their new cameras. It is notable, too, that this project is distinguished by intensive collaboration between curators and historians of photography and of painting, insuring the technical accuracy of their scholarly interpretation.

We are pleased to acknowledge the many scholars who came together to investigate the subject of the exhibition and who contributed to this catalogue. Scholars in France, the Netherlands, Belgium, Switzerland, and the United States collaborated in this inquiry and have made insightful contributions: Clément Chéroux, curator of the photographic collection, Centre Pompidou, Paris; Michel Frizot, research director of the Centre National de la Recherche Scientifique, Paris; Todd Gustavson, curator of technology, George Eastman House, Rochester, New York; Françoise Heilbrun, head curator of photography, Musée d'Orsay, Paris; Anne McCauley, David Hunter McAlpin Professor of the History of Photography and Modern Art, Princeton University; Saskia Ooms, Netwerk, Belgium; Katia Poletti, curator, Fondation Félix Vallotton; Hans Rooseboom, curator of photography, Rijksmuseum, Amsterdam; and Elizabeth Easton, Eliza Rathbone, and Ellen Lee.

It is our hope that the research undertaken for this exhibition will shed light on a critical moment in art history, and will equip readers and museum goers alike with a newfound understanding of the prefiguration of our digital culture.

We are grateful to the Florence Gould Foundation and its president, John R. Young, for recognizing the merits of this project and for supporting our colleagues' efforts in researching and planning the exhibition.

Maxwell L. Anderson *Dorothy Kosinski* *Axel Rüger*

Acknowledgments

This exhibition and its accompanying catalogue are the result of many decades of research, during which rich troves of photographs by painters and printmakers working in the 1880s and 1890s were discovered. Never exhibited during the lives of these artists, the photographs that emerged opened up new avenues to understanding the artists' working methods and the scope of their visual innovation. The exhibition has also offered the possibility for curators from the fields of painting and photography to work together. Although this might not seem unusual, it is often not the case. The resulting collaboration produced a list of seven artists who would not otherwise be associated, and presents a new perspective on the first generation of artists who experimented with the *instantané photographique*, now known as the snapshot.

The organizers of *Snapshot: Painters and Photography, Bonnard to Vuillard* wish to thank Guy Cogeval, president of the Musée d'Orsay, for allowing the loan of almost one hundred photographs and paintings from the collection. The exhibition would not have been possible without the museum's participation, and we are very grateful for the generous assistance of the staff at the Musée d'Orsay.

Among the many people who have worked on this exhibition over the years, thanks are due first to Françoise Heilbrun, head curator of photography at the Musée d'Orsay. In 1984 Françoise Heilbrun and Philippe Néagu curated an exhibition at the Musée d'Orsay of the photographs of Pierre Bonnard, introducing the subject of painters' photographs and revealing it as worthy of further exploration. In 1988 they provided pioneering scholarship on Henri Rivière through their exhibition and catalogue of his little known photographs at the Musée d'Orsay. Françoise later embraced the idea of working with Elizabeth Easton on this exhibition, and the selection of artists is the result of their collaboration. Françoise's insights about the *instantané photographique* have informed the choice of works and their context in this exhibition. Over the years, several curators have worked with her, namely Quentin Bajac, now chief curator of photography at the Centre Pompidou, and Saskia Ooms, whose essay on Maurice Denis grew out of the dissertation she was writing while working at the Musée d'Orsay with Françoise. Both Quentin and Saskia traveled to various archives with the exhibition organizers, and their knowledge helped form the core of the show's thesis.

The first artist to have his photographs exhibited was Edouard Vuillard, in a landmark exhibition of twelve images at the L'Oeil Gallery in 1963. Following up on that initial presentation, thirty years ago, Elizabeth Easton, a young graduate student at the time, asked to see a variety of works during her first visit to the Vuillard family archive, then under the administration of the artist's great-nephew, Antoine Salomon. Among sketchbooks and ephemera were two manila envelopes, packed with photographs. A whole world — unorganized and undocumented — emerged from those Kodaks and planted the seed for further inquiry of this unexplored terrain. This exhibition and catalogue represent the fruit of that initial research. The archive is now known to contain almost two thousand photographs, and the exhibition curators are extremely grateful to Madame Colette Salomon and Mathias Chivot for granting access to it and for the loan of more than forty original prints.

Henri Evenepoel is almost unknown in America, and this catalogue publishes one of the few essays on his work in English. The artist died at the age of twenty-seven, and the majority of his oeuvre resides in his native Belgium. For their generous assistance in locating works for the exhibition, we acknowledge Véronique Cardon, Virginie Devillez, Francisca Vandepitte, Pieter Muys, Dominique Maréchal, and Anne Adriaens-Pannier of the Musées royaux des Beaux-Arts de Belgique; Gilles Marquenie of Galerie Patrick Derom, Brussels; Léonard Gianadda of the Fondation Gianadda in Martigny, Switzerland; Jane Block of the University of Illinois; and Danielle Derrey-Capon for her groundbreaking work on the artist.

The curators of the exhibition extend sincere thanks to Hans Rooseboom of the Rijksmuseum, Amsterdam, for his essay on George Breitner and his research on the three thousand photographs at the Rijksbureau voor Kunsthistorische Documentatie in The Hague, with special thanks to Mayken Jonkman. We are delighted that the exhibition's opening venue is the Van Gogh Museum, where Breitner's countrymen can see his art in the context of his contemporaries working elsewhere on the continent. For many American audiences, this will be the first opportunity to see his work.

Scholars of Maurice Denis have the good fortune to work with Claire Denis, who has labored tirelessly for decades on the catalogue raisonné of the artist's work. Claire's generosity and understanding of this exhibition brought key loans and critical help in contacting Denis collectors. We are especially pleased to have worked so closely with Claire and her colleague Fabienne Stahl.

Katia Poletti contributed the Félix Vallotton essay and was very helpful in her capacity as organizer of the artist's catalogue raisonné. We are also grateful to essayists Michel Frizot, Todd Gustavson, and Anne McCauley for their expertise on the context of Kodak experimentation in its earliest years.

Kate Zanzucchi, Patricia Fidler, and Mary Mayer of Yale University Press worked tirelessly to coordinate the production of the catalogue, a very complex undertaking. So many unpublished images from archives around Europe created a challenge that they met with good humor and dedication. We were fortunate to have Fronia Simpson as content editor; her piercing intelligence and tough questions helped to make this a better book. We also thank copyeditor Phil Freshman (assisted by Susan C. Jones), proofreader Laurie Burton, and indexer Susan Burke. We are also grateful to Rita Jules, Miko McGinty Inc., for the sensitive design of the catalogue.

Suzanne Bogman of the Van Gogh Museum was critical to production of the catalogue, and we thank her for her determination, patience, and heroic efforts organizing images and checklists. Her colleagues Geri Klazema and Anja Wisseborn worked diligently, and registrars Fouad Kanaan and Adrie Kok tracked many loans and orchestrated the shipment of a very complicated checklist.

At the Phillips Collection, the assistance of the following individuals was indispensable: Sarah Anderson, Trish Waters, and Joseph Holbach in the registrar's office, and Alexandra Morrison, Genevieve Hulley, and especially Catherine Ross, all curatorial interns. We are grateful to the installations team for their invaluable insight and attention to detail and to Val Lewton for his inspired design.

Several staff members at the Indianapolis Museum of Art deserve our thanks for their efforts and expertise in the organization of the project. Curatorial associate Petra Slinkard played a critical role in handling the large volume of loan correspondence and maintaining the checklist in its detail and complexity. Registrar Brittany Minton applied her organizational acumen to exhibition contracts, loan agreements, and shipping and courier arrangements. Senior exhibition designer Phil Lynam and lighting designer Carol Cody brought their imagination and taste to an exhibition with intriguing challenges of light levels and scale. Special thanks go also to curatorial assistant Rebecca Long for her steadfast support of all aspects of the exhibition.

Judith Dolkart, Chief Curator at the Barnes Foundation, spent years as part of the exhibition team. Her organizational and interpretive skills contributed to the formative stages of the exhibition, and the project benefited greatly from her insights. Along the way, research assistants Karen Hellman, Alison Chang, and Natasha Ruiz-Gomez also compiled information and helped with archival organization. More recently, Hannah Howe has served as curatorial assistant extraordinaire, compiling and organizing checklists, editorial information, and archival images. The exhibition's final realization would have been impossible without her help and critical eye.

Early in the genesis of the exhibition, the organizers realized that the presentation of these unknown, small-scale snapshots in a respectful fashion would require a framer who had a particular understanding of nineteenth-century photography. The best framer in the world for this material, Jared Bark, developed a body of mouldings for this exhibition that allowed each work to have individual dignity and yet be seen as part of a cohesive group. Jed Bark and his team at Bark Frameworks (Long Island City, New York), especially Chad MacDermid, worked for almost two years on the exhibition, and the organizers are particularly grateful for his patient attention and creative solution to the framing challenges. Thanks are due as well to Philippe Laumont and Tyko Lewis at Laumont Photographics for the careful printing of the photographs by Evenepoel and Breitner for the exhibition.

John R. Young, President of The Florence Gould Foundation, was an early and generous supporter of the exhibition. The planning grant from the Gould Foundation allowed the organizers to stage an international colloquium in preparation for the show, travel to the archives of so many unpublished photographs, and refine the exhibition's concept. We are extremely grateful for his confidence in the exhibition during a critical point of its development. In addition to several of our essayists, Geoffrey Batchen, Judith Dolkart, Mia Fineman, Dorothy Kosinski, Nancy Mathews, Rebecca Rabinow, Shelly Rice, and Liz Seigel participated. They helped refine the parameters of the exhibition and enrich the curators' understanding of that moment in the history of photography.

The curators are grateful to the friends and colleagues who have helped along the long road of loan negotiations, searches for pictures in private collections, and careful reading of the manuscript: Hilary Ballon, Jed Bark, Andrea Bayer, Emily Braun, Joan Easton, James Ganz, Christine Giviskos, Anne Goldrach, Paul and Ellen Josefowitz, Charlotte Lacour, Lionel Pissarro, Shelly Rice, Amy Stursberg, Valérie Sueur-Hermel, Alexander Traub, and James Traub.

This exhibition could never have taken place without the enthusiasm and support of the directors of the three institutions involved: Axel Rüger at the Van Gogh Museum, Dorothy Kosinski at the Phillips Collection, and Maxwell Anderson of the Indianapolis Museum of Art. They energetically supported the exhibition from the beginning, and set the stage for a great spirit of collegiality among the three collaborators.

And, finally, we extend heartfelt thanks to all the lenders — public institutions as well as private collectors — who have made this exhibition possible by entrusting their works of art to the realization of this project. We are grateful for your sacrifice and hope that this catalogue will be an enduring sign of your generosity.

—*Elizabeth W. Easton, Ellen W. Lee, Eliza Rathbone, and Edwin Becker*

Lenders to the Exhibition

The Art Institute of Chicago
Isabelle de la Brunière
Dumbarton Oaks, Washington, D.C.
Fine Arts Museums of San Francisco, Legion of Honor, Achenbach Foundation for Graphic Arts
Indianapolis Museum of Art
Collection KBL, European Private Bankers S.A., Luxembourg
Fondation Roi Baudouin, Brussels
Kunsthandel A.H. Bies, Eindhoven
Kunsthaus Zürich
Kunstmuseum Winterthur
The Metropolitan Museum of Art, The Lehman Collection, New York
Musée Carnavalet, Paris
Musée d'Ixelles, Brussels
Musée d'Orsay, Paris
Musée Maurice Denis, le Prieuré, Saint-Germain-en-Laye
The Museum of Modern Art, New York
National Gallery of Art, Washington, D.C.
Noortman Master Paintings, Amsterdam
Petit Palais, Musée des Beaux-Arts de la Ville de Paris
The Phillips Collection, Washington, D.C.
Rijksmuseum, Amsterdam
Collection RKD, The Hague
Royal Museums of Fine Arts of Belgium, Brussels
Collection of Kelly Simpson, Katonah, N.Y.
Stedelijk Museum, Amsterdam
Stedelijk Museum, Sint Niklaas
The Toledo Museum of Art
Van Gogh Museum, Amsterdam
Vincent van Gogh Foundation
Collection Malcolm Wiener, New York
Yale University Art Gallery, New Haven, Connecticut
Zimmerli Art Museum at Rutgers University

Private collections

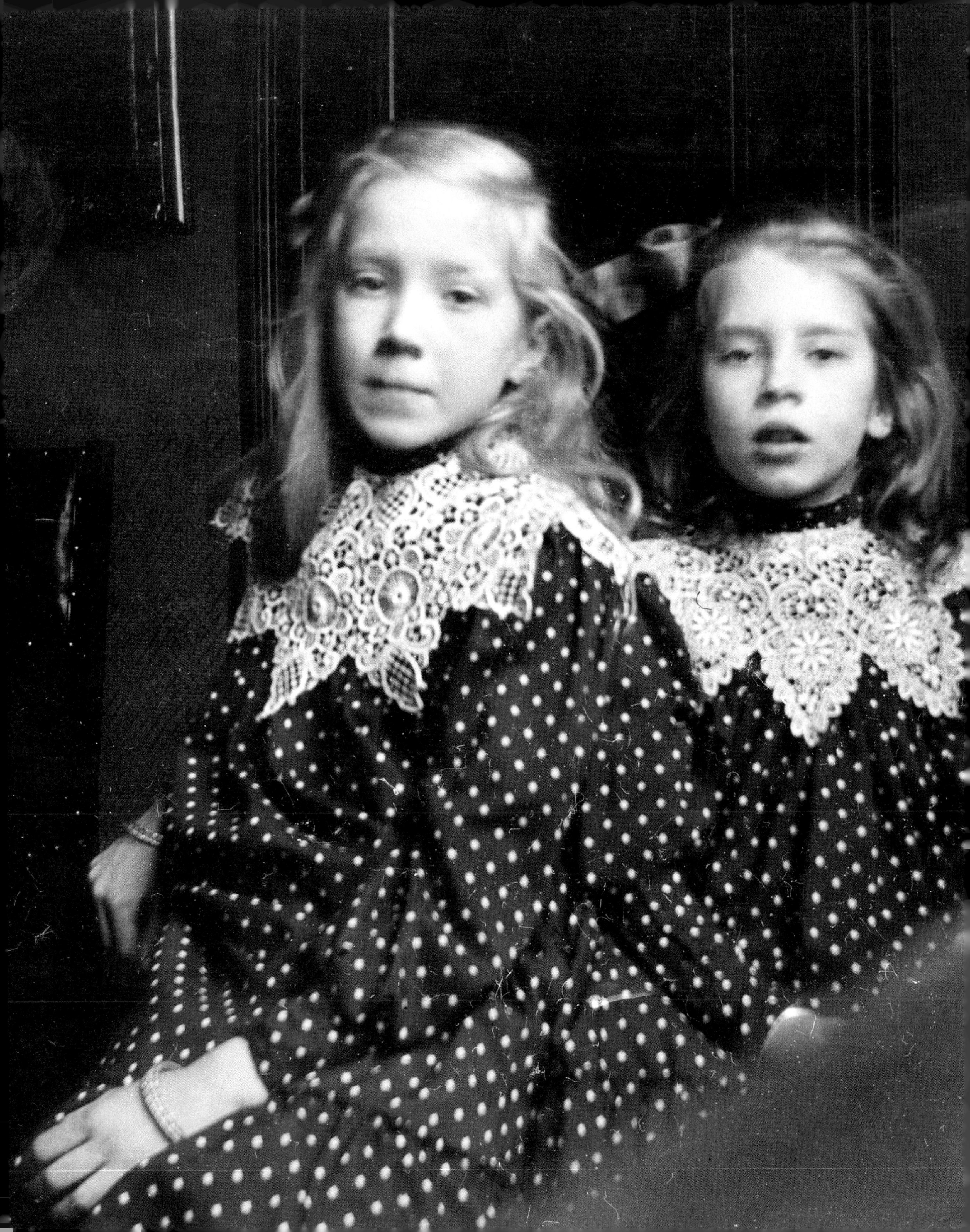

Introduction

Elizabeth W. Easton

This exhibition and its accompanying catalogue examine the experiments in photography made from the 1880s through the early 1900s by seven post-Impressionist artists. Pierre Bonnard, Maurice Denis, Félix Vallotton, and Edouard Vuillard, all members of the Nabis group, were well-known figures in the Parisian avant-garde of that time.[1] Although their paintings are familiar to museumgoers today, the same cannot be said about their photography. This exhibition suggests that use of the Kodak camera was widespread among artists working at the time it was introduced in 1888, and that the photographs taken by the artists whose imagery is gathered here comprise only a representative sample of those made by many of their contemporaries who also experimented with this new device. Three other artists working in Europe during that period and profiled on these pages—George Hendrik Breitner, Henri Evenepoel, and Henri Rivière—responded to the camera with equal enthusiasm and in similar ways.

While many painters used photography in one way or another around this time, these seven artists displayed common approaches and interests.[2] All except for Rivière, who was primarily a printmaker, worked in oil on canvas. Photographs by Evenepoel evoke lithographs of Bonnard, nudes by Bonnard and Breitner capture the directness and awkwardness often concealed by their paintings, and Vuillard's dark, tightly knit interiors correspond to a similar moodiness in Breitner's compositions. These artists kept their photographs private: although several of them photographed together, snapped pictures of one another on group trips, and shared the results afterward, none of them ever exhibited a photograph.

The advent of the Kodak camera—easily held in two hands and much more compact than the unwieldy tripod cameras it replaced—made photography accessible to both the general public and professionals. At about that time, artists working in all media began using the camera as an intriguing toy, as a means of providing images to be used as studies for final works, and as another way of observing the world. This exhibition and book feature some of these photographs, largely unknown, alongside paintings for which each artist is best known.

DETAIL OF CAT. 36

The Kodak's ability to seize an instant captured the spirit of technological innovation that dominated the late nineteenth century. But objective reproduction of reality would seem to be at odds with these artists' sensibility. Inspired by the work of Paul Gauguin, artists of the post-Impressionist generation championed the imagination over observed reality. They subscribed to the credo of the Symbolist poet and art critic Gustave Kahn, who declared, "The essential goal of our art is to objectify the subjective (the exteriorization of an idea) rather than to subjectify the objective (nature viewed through a temperament)."[3] Maurice Denis, the Nabis painters' scribe, wrote that they "realized that every work of art was a transposition, a caricature, the impassioned equivalent of a sensation experienced."[4] What's more, the rapid embrace of life seized in a photograph, while perhaps resembling the cropping and unexpected angles of a post-Impressionist painting, nonetheless reflects a completely different execution. The paintings of the Nabis, for example, are expertly crafted products of laborious layering of pigment, brushstroke, and *disegno*. Yet the artists whose work is shown here adapted the medium of photography to their own aesthetic ambitions. The way they composed their canvases, with figures looming large in the foreground, radically foreshortened in the background, and cropped unexpectedly with skilled manipulation of light and dark, naturally disposed them, in their photographs, to play with, exploit, and master the accident that was fundamental to the use of this new tool.

Before the Kodak was introduced, photography had been the domain of professionals, who used tripods and glass plates to register studied compositions. The drive in the 1880s and 1890s for an "instant" image was fueled by public clamor for a device that could record the events of everyday family life as they occurred. The essence of this new form of representation resided more in the emotions it prompted than in the formal qualities of its composition. Marcel Proust, an ardent enthusiast of photography, evokes the power of the medium to stir feelings when his narrator contemplates a photograph of the Duchess of Guermantes:

> This photograph was like a further encounter added to those I had already had with Madame de Guermantes; better still, an encounter *extended*, as if, by a sudden progress in our relations, she had stopped beside me, in her garden hat, and had let me examine at my leisure, for the first time, that full cheek, that turn of the neck, that corner of the eyebrows (hitherto concealed from me by the rapidity of her passing, the confusion of my impressions, the unreliability of memory); and their contemplation, like that of the throat and arms of a woman I had never seen except in a high-necked, long-sleeved gown, was for me a voluptuous discovery, a mark of favor. Those lines it had once seemed almost forbidden to look at I could now study as in a treatise of the only geometry which had any value for me.[5]

Here, Proust clarifies the function and enduring value of the snapshot: that looking at the photograph prolongs the pleasure of the actual moment when it was consigned to film, that fleeting moments of reality are extended for private delectation, and that things unrecognized by direct experience are revealed by the camera lens as it records without editing or interpreting the reality in its visual field. Proust was not alone in feeling this way. In his landmark essay "Camera Lucida," Roland Barthes observed that the snapshot is, by its very nature, a sentimental object.[6] It is not the making of the snapshot that distinguishes it but the intentionality: these photographs are made to be private records of a particular moment, without artistic pretense or commercial aspirations.

The Nabis were not the first artists to experiment with photography. Eugène Delacroix did so in the earliest years of its existence.[7] And Edgar Degas, the polymath who over the course of his career made sculpture and prints and designed picture frames, took up photography in the 1890s, using an apparatus more typically employed by professionals, with a tripod and glass plates. In a notable photograph of Pierre Auguste Renoir and Stéphane Mallarmé, Degas's reflection is seen in the mirror standing by this camera (fig. 1). The lighting for that photograph was carefully arranged and described by Paul Valéry in an account of this photo session (inscribed in the margin of the photograph), along with the fact that Mallarmé and Renoir had to maintain their pose for fifteen minutes. Apparently, Mallarmé was nearly burned by staying so close to the fireplace and not moving. The younger generation of artists in this exhibition generally employed the modern, handheld Kodak in the casual, incidental ways for which it was best suited. Their adoption and mastery of a simplified camera in part explains the significant differences in both approach and control between the Degas photographs and those made by the artists featured here.

In a view camera of the kind Degas used, the photographer focused through the lens. This method made possible precise imaging and framing, so the artist's selective attention in his compositions was not accidental. Because a Kodak could *not* produce a precise image, an artist could not frame the picture by looking through the lens. Instead, the photographer held the camera at waist height and looked at an arrow near the top of the device that helped direct the lens toward the desired object. Although it was impossible to focus with a late-nineteenth-century model Kodak, a circular reflecting viewfinder in those produced after 1895 provided a vague image of the scene being shot. And while cropping the scene and its focal point were difficult to do with this viewfinder, the artists highlighted here would no doubt have quickly determined the camera's parameters for capturing a scene in front of them. Although they might have mastered fairly quickly the area of the camera's visual field, these artists nonetheless explored deliberate distortions by, for example, putting themselves and the camera exceptionally close to their subjects and creating entire series of out-of-focus pictures (cats. 64, 207). The experiments of

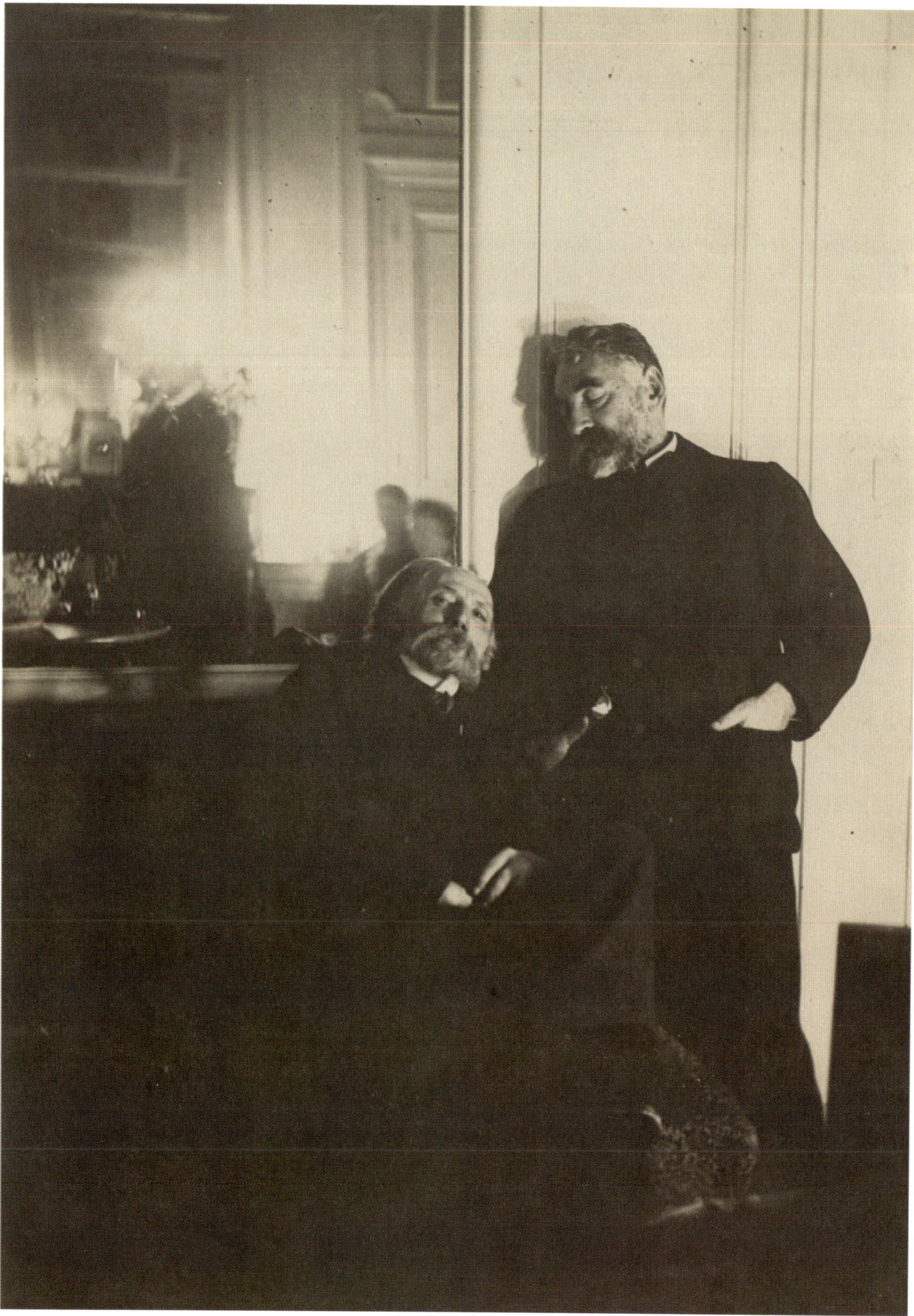

OPPOSITE: FIG. 1. Edgar Degas, Pierre Auguste Renoir and Stéphane Mallarmé, 1895. Gelatin silver print, 15³/₈ x 11³/₁₆ in. (39.1 x 28.4 cm). The Museum of Modern Art, New York. Gift of Paul F. Walter

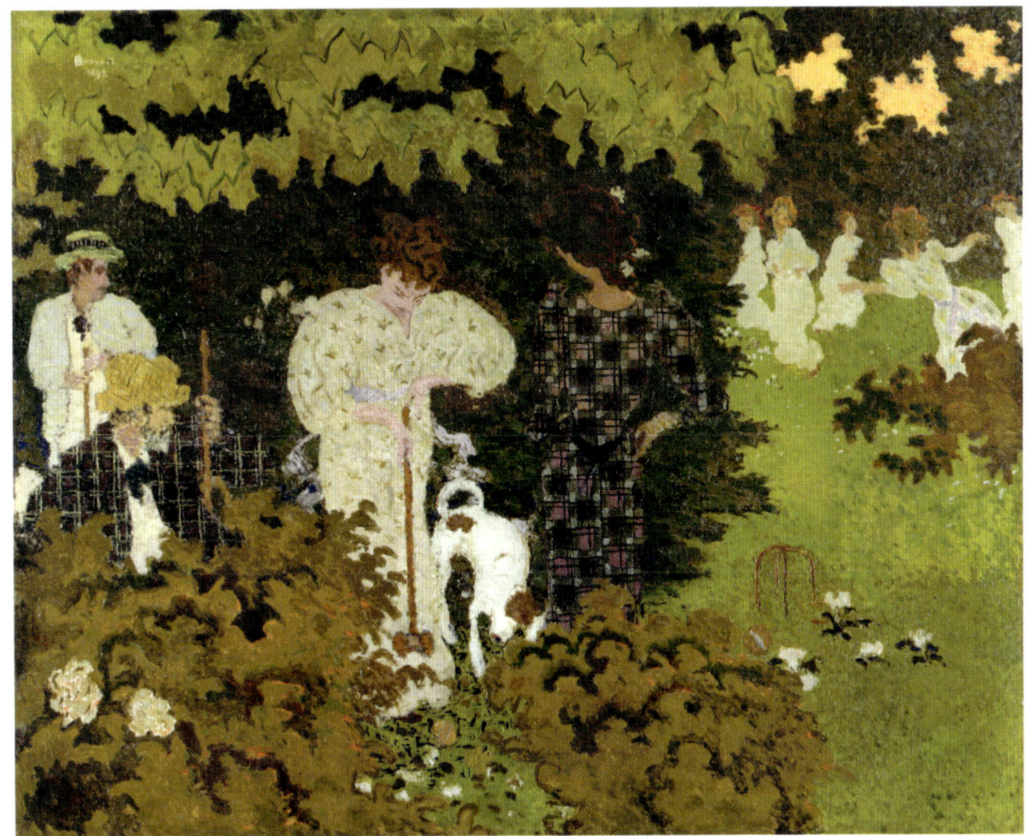

FIG. 2. Pierre Bonnard, *Crépuscule, ou La partie de croquet* (Twilight, or The Croquet Party), 1892. Oil on canvas, 51³/₈ x 63⁷/₈ in. (130.5 x 162.2 cm). Musée d'Orsay, Paris

Eadweard Muybridge and Etienne-Jules Marey had proved that the camera captured objective reality in a way the eye could not. By contrast, the wide-angle nature of the Kodak produced spatial distortions that were not experienced in visual reality.

Although the artists under consideration here may reveal a similar subject matter, composition, and even pictorial conception in their photographs and painted works, photography, as the art historian Meyer Schapiro noted, was more casual than painting, was limited to black and white, and lacked the texture and impasto of paint.[8] The casualness is evident in the way these artists tended to employ their cameras just as nonprofessionals have ever since the Kodak first appeared—that is, to record meaningful, often sentimental moments and events. A holiday trip, the birth of a baby, a special outing in the city or countryside: all these provided ample reason to use a camera. But beyond the mere anecdotal, the artists also used it in ways that paralleled the compositional choices evident in their paintings and works on paper. The camera did not supplant the sketch but rather added a different dimension to a wealth of visual information that could be drawn upon. Sometimes, photographs were taken deliberately as study material for paintings, because a snapshot obviously could be executed more quickly than a sketch. Bonnard crafted a studio photo session focused on his lover Marthe de Méligny, with poses surprisingly unidealized, and these, too, inspired lithographs (cats. 26, 27). At other times, however, the process was reversed, and a photograph recalled a painted composition from as much as a decade earlier (cat. 5 and fig. 2).

By the 1890s, the camera had become such an integral, if sometimes controversial, part of the painter's equipment that the English artist Walter Sickert petulantly demanded that works of art based on photographs be designated as such in exhibitions and catalogues.[9] By that time, photographs produced for use by academic artists and sculptors could be easily distinguished from those generated by the avant-garde. The "artistic" academic photographs of nudes, for example, embellished the figures with attributes of crowns, bouquets, or decorative accessories as a way of distancing them from erotica, whereas the nudes in Bonnard's or Breitner's pictures are not idealized but are highly charged, partly because of their private, intimate nature.

Early in the history of the medium, the merits of work done by nonprofessionals were recognized. "The Amateur Photographer," an article published in 1887, notes these virtues: "Working only for pleasure and attainment, the amateur thinks nothing of a risk. He indulges in most unorthodox measures, violating recognized rules of procedure, and with bewildering impunity."[10] The artists who experimented with their Kodaks would certainly fall into this category. Using their cameras to achieve a variety of visual effects, they avoided the aesthetic conventions of professional photography and instead captured their own views in images that at times resemble those of snapshot and amateur photographers. The artist-photographers documented such private realms as the studio, the apartment, their circles of relatives and friends, leisure activities, and travel. According to the art historian Ulrich Pohlmann, "[T]he instantaneous photograph taken in the private sphere brought with it a whole new iconography: incidental views, unsettled images, in other words, the iconography of the everyday, which at the same time was an expression of a modern awareness of life."[11]

The seven artists profiled in this exhibition and book captured in photographs spontaneous scenes of everyday life that also figured in their paintings and prints, where they conveyed a sensibility beneath the surface of quotidian life. Thus, while Vuillard depicted in his painted interiors the mundane activities of his sister and seamstress mother or the family eating dinner, these works were rife with psychological drama, conveyed through distortions of pictorial space. For example, his mother loomed large and his sister crouched to fit into the composition, or she seemingly faded into the wallpaper, or figures stared at each other across the vast expanse of a dining-room table. Evenepoel's snapshots of the Place de la Concorde refer back to the canvases of Degas and the Impressionist embrace of modern life, but they are also layered with an 1890s sensibility of decoration and silhouette derived from the shadow theater at the Chat Noir cabaret in Montmartre. Similarly, Rivière captured startling views and angles from a high perch in the Eiffel Tower during construction, but his vision was informed by Hokusai's print series of Mount Fuji. In these ways, the artists exploited the ability of the Kodak to seize the moment and, simultaneously, allowed it to inform their vision of the art they were making.

The Nabis painters, including Bonnard, Denis, Vallotton, and Vuillard, were the most cohesive post-Impressionist group, even devising a secret language and names for their members. Although they shared common values as well as membership in the Nabis brotherhood, each one used photography in quite different ways. Photographs from the Bonnard archive document summer days in the country, when friends came to visit and children frolicked. The artist also utilized photography to create a body of images to which he could refer for two large book-illustration commissions he received from the publisher Ambroise Vollard. Images of his companion Marthe, nude in the garden and in the studio, figure into his lithographic work for Vollard's editions of *Parallèlement* (1901), a posthumous collection of erotic poems by Paul Verlaine, and *Daphnis et Chloé* (1902), by the ancient Greek writer Longus, but they are also part of his persistent exploration of the female form (cats. 14–31). Photography did not stop him from sketching; indeed, he seemed to work in both media at the same time. Also, just as most tourists do, Bonnard took his camera along on trips and recorded what he saw.

Maurice Denis, too, used the camera the way many people do to this day. For instance, he proudly photographed his children from their earliest days (cats. 69, 70). He then had the pictures professionally enlarged and put into albums commemorating each child's infancy and childhood. He also took pictures on summer trips to the Brittany coast and on holidays in Italy (cat. 84). Denis was captivated by the Italian "primitives" and caught on film those family groupings that most resembled Quattrocento compositions. He clearly played with the camera, taking numerous close-ups of his wife nursing, for example, in which everything is seen so enlarged that the whole composition becomes a blur. These photos, in which physical details are obscure, do not so much capture a particular scene as evoke one; in this way, they recall the paintings of Eugène Carrière, in which minute particulars are sacrificed for the sentiment conveyed (cat. 79).

Denis was one of the few artists of the time to discuss, even if briefly, the relation of the camera to artistic production. In his 1909 article "From Gauguin and Van Gogh to Classicism," he wrote:

> We demonstrated that any emotion or state of mind aroused by a particular sight gave rise in the artist's imagination to symbols or concrete equivalents which were able to excite identical emotions or states of mind without the need to create a copy of the original sight; and that for each nuance of our emotional make-up there was a corresponding object in tune with it and able to represent it fully. Art is not simply a visual sensation that we receive, a photograph, however

sophisticated, of nature. No, it is a creation of the mind, for which nature is the springboard.[12]

Denis had been assiduously taking photographs for almost fifteen years when he wrote these words. His art, inspired by the classicism of the Renaissance and French seventeenth- and eighteenth-century painting, reconfigured observed reality into a monumental tribute to the history of art. Using a handheld Kodak to capture fleeting moments certainly was at odds with the eternal truths he sought for his painted works. And yet, although many of Denis's photographs were similar to the anecdotal, sentimental snapshots of amateurs of that time, a number of them captured a profile against a horizon (cat. 75) or figures with sunlit rectangles of a shadowy cloister (cat. 83) that evoked the classical painting he so admired and that influenced much of his own work.

From the few surviving photographs by Félix Vallotton, it appears that he quoted motifs caught on film and transposed them to canvas, adding elements here and there to alter the compositions. Sometimes, the photographs are more compositionally complex than the paintings, expanding the space and reflecting elements outside the picture (cats. 158, 157). Vallotton clearly shared and exchanged photographs with his fellow Nabis painters; photographs by Vuillard appear in the Vallotton family archive and even may have inspired some of Vallotton's compositions (cats. 203, 164).

Unlike Vallotton's scant photographic legacy, Edouard Vuillard's archive contains almost two thousand images, spanning decades of his career. The range of his photographic production is also vast. Some pictures, like Bonnard's and Vallotton's, were used as studies for paintings. Vuillard also combined photographic images taken over a period of years into a single picture, much as he combined sketches from his journal into paintings.[13] But this was the exception; mostly Vuillard, like the other artists, recorded trips, holiday outings, and weekends in the country with his close friends (cats. 184–86). The pictorial language of these images reflects his painted compositions. He continued photographing his family after they stopped appearing in his paintings. Most interesting of all, perhaps, are the photographs Vuillard took that bear no resemblance to his painted work; he explored the same subject matter—his intimate circle—in photography in ways that give no hint of his artistic output (cats. 187–90).

Another artist close to the Nabis, Henri Rivière, produced a body of photographs arguably more compelling than the lithographs for which he is renowned. His views of the Eiffel Tower, taken from high up inside the structure not long before its completion in 1889, presage in their stark modernity the work of Lewis Hine and Aleksandr Rodchenko (cats. 124, 127, 131). Rivière also took dramatic backstage photographs of the shadow theater at the Chat Noir (cats. 120–23). Some show the frenzied shifting of the zinc plates projected on a scrim to create shadows thrown on a screen. The black-and-white realm of the shadow theater obviously appealed to an artist whose photography could be unequivocal and sharply defined.

The works of Henri Evenepoel, virtually unknown in part because of the artist's untimely death at age twenty-seven in 1899, converge thematically and stylistically with those of the other artists in this exhibition. The young Belgian came to Paris to study and paint. Photographs of his family, silhouetted against the Place de la Concorde, recall both the graphic energy of the shadow theater and the early lithographic work of Pierre Bonnard. They also legitimize his position in the circle of the artists focused upon here (cat. 105).

George Hendrik Breitner, a Dutch contemporary of the rest of the group, photographed and painted in Amsterdam toward the end of the nineteenth century. In both media, he conveyed the isolation of the modern city and portrayed the compelling decorative aesthetic of the interior. While his silhouetted images may recall the work of other artists in the exhibition (cat. 48), his numerous pictures of nudes address a different tradition in the photographic medium (cat. 56). And his photographs of vast construction projects under way in Amsterdam hint at modern compositions that border on the abstract.

Painters have used photography ever since its discovery, and they continue to do so today. Andy Warhol, for example, based his silkscreen paintings on photographs. His Polaroid cameras served some of the same functions for him as the Kodaks did for the artists highlighted here: they allowed him to seize moments in time that he ultimately could render in paint. While Warhol's paintings based on photographs are iconic images of the Pop-art era, his Polaroid shots reveal a more private, personal universe. Similarly, although Chuck Close uses photography as a basis for his paintings, his work in daguerreotype signals a specific interest in early photography. David Hockney has hovered between the realms of painting and photography for decades, first using photographs for his paintings and then concentrating on photographs as art forms themselves. When he returned to England to paint out-of-doors in his native Yorkshire, he attempted to capture the changing landscape one brushstroke at a time. Hockney could not escape the allure of the camera, however, and through photographing the paintings and then working in paint on top of the photographs, he continued to explore the parallel realms of painting and photography.

This exhibition and catalogue focus on the first generation of painters to adopt the Kodak camera, a device that was easy to use and met their needs. And now the Kodak era is over, the focus having switched from roll film to digital cameras and accessories. The contemporary artist Tacita Dean, who explores themes of obsolescence in her work, was prompted by her own frustrations in obtaining black-and-white 16mm film to produce *Kodak* and *Noir et blanc* (both 2006), two documentaries that address the approaching obsolescence of celluloid film. As the Kodak factory in Chalon-sur-Saône, France, was about to close its film-production facility, Dean detailed the fabrication of the last roll. Both her films follow the production of celluloid as it runs through several miles of machinery, and they serve as elegies for the end of an era.

The present exhibition, however, marks the *dawn* of that era, when artists used their Kodaks to explore new realms that would inform their creative output. What they chose to portray was not significantly different from what people snap and click today with digital cameras and iPhones. But artistic experimentation with photography in the late nineteenth century was private, as opposed to the digital universe, where the click of a shutter produces an image that can quickly become available to the world at large. Artists continue to employ photography as an adjunct to their work, but that sense of capturing a private world, in terms of both subject matter and material, is but a distant historical memory.

Scholars have investigated the work of professional photographers from the invention of the medium in the late 1830s to the present day. Until recently, however, little has been known about the photographic experiments of artists whose work was primarily in other media. For artists whose painted subject matter comprised images of everyday life imbued with secret meaning, their photography reveals a more human element. The immediate connection viewers can feel with moments captured on film—the unguarded expressions of subjects, the playful interludes, the intimacy of family life, the image of a loved one—invites a singular kind of entry into the artist's realm. Where the paintings and prints of the seven artists featured here are sometimes mystifying, the photographs are compelling in part because of their artlessness. The human connection we experience in looking at the photographs opens a beguiling path toward a better understanding of the rest of their work.

NOTES

1. These artists called themselves the "Nabis brotherhood," using the Hebrew word for prophet in order to evoke their own desire to create a new, forward-looking kind of art.
2. Two previous exhibitions have covered the subject of artists' use of photography: Erika Billeter, *Malerei und Photographie im Dialog: Von 1840 bis heute*, exh. cat. (Bern: Benteli, 1977), which was a broad survey; and Dorothy Kosinski et al., *The Artist and the Camera: Degas to Picasso*, exh. cat. (Dallas: Dallas Museum of Art, 1999).
3. Gustave Kahn, "Réponse des symbolistes," *L'événement*, September 28, 1886.
4. Maurice Denis, *Théories* (Paris: L. Rouart et J. Watlin, 1920), p. 167.
5. Marcel Proust, *The Guermantes Way*, as quoted in Brassaï, *Proust in the Power of Photography*, trans. Richard Howard (Chicago and London: University of Chicago Press, 2001), pp. 84–85.
6. Roland Barthes, *Camera Lucida: Reflections on Photography* (New York: Hill and Wang, 1981). So much has been written about Barthes's essay that I refer to it only in passing here. But an extensive critique can be found in Geoffrey Batchen, *Photography Degree Zero: Reflections on Roland Barthes's "Camera Lucida"* (Cambridge: MIT Press, 2009).
7. Christophe Leribault, *Delacroix et la photographie* (Paris: Louvre Editions, 2008), examines the artist's use of photographs. Delacroix himself wrote: "As far as I am concerned, I can only say how much I regret such an admirable discovery should have come so late! The possibility of studying such images would have had an influence on me that I can only guess at from the usefulness which they have now, even in the little time left me for more intensive study. It is the tangible proof of nature's own design, which we otherwise see only very feebly." As quoted in *"From today painting is dead": The Beginnings of Photography*, exh. cat. (London: Victoria and Albert Museum, 1972), p. 48.
8. Meyer Schapiro, "Portraiture and Photography," *Impressionism: Reflections and Perceptions* (New York: Braziller, 1997), pp. 153–78.
9. Walter Sickert, as cited in Ulrich Pohlmann, "Another Nature; or, Arsenals of Memory: Photography as Study Aid, 1850–1900," in Kosinski et al., *The Artist and the Camera*, p. 43.
10. Alexander Black, "The Amateur Photographer," *Century Magazine* 34 (September 1887): pp. 722–29, excerpted in Beaumont Newhall, ed., *Photography: Essays and Images* (New York: Museum of Modern Art, 1980), pp. 149–53.
11. Pohlmann, "Another Nature; or, Arsenals of Memory," in *The Artist and the Camera*, p. 55.
12. Maurice Denis, "De Gauguin et de Van Gogh au classicisme," *L'Occident*, no. 90 (May 1909), included in *Théories*, pp. 262–78; cited in Gilles Genty, "Maurice Denis after 1900: 'The Joys of Classicism,'" in *Maurice Denis* (Ghent: Snoeck-Ducaju & Joon, 1994), p. 52.
13. Juliet Wilson Bareau has established that Vuillard used photographs taken at two different moments as studies for the figures. See Bareau, "Edouard Vuillard et les princes Bibesco," *Revue de l'Art*, no. 64 (1986): pp. 37–46.

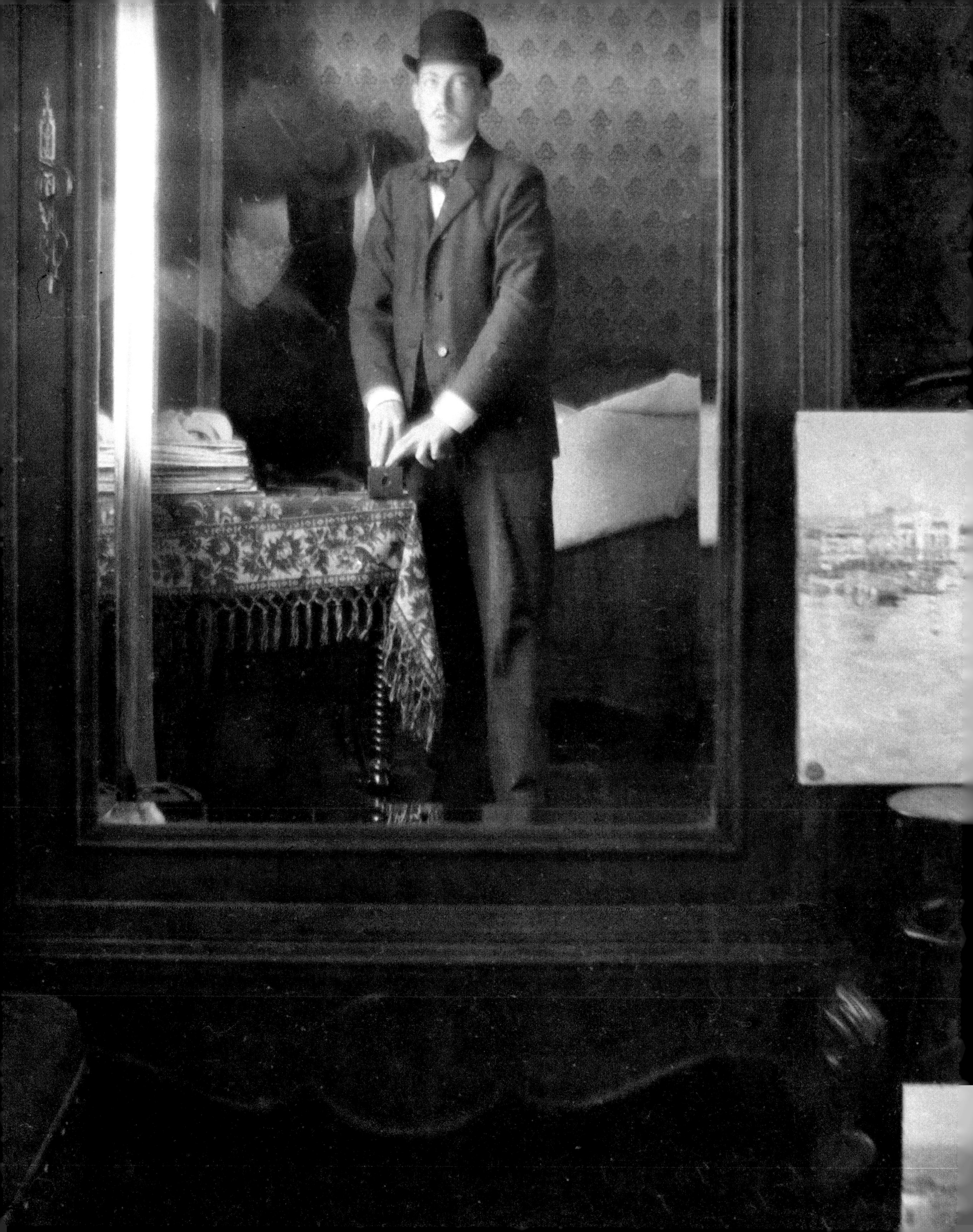

Innovative Devices

George Eastman and the Handheld Camera

Todd Gustavson

In the digital age, making photographic images is so very simple—requiring about the same effort as throwing a light switch—that we do so almost without thinking about it. It's easy to take for granted a process that seems to involve nothing more than pressing the button and instantaneously viewing the picture. But photography has not always been a simple practice. For nearly a half century after its invention, the medium was almost exclusively the domain of professionals. Not until the 1880s, when George Eastman's Kodak camera and other instruments intended for the consumer-photography market set the cornerstones of amateur snapshot photography, did the camera begin to become a ubiquitous device.

The photographic process, announced in 1839 by the Frenchman Louis Jacques Mandé Daguerre, captured and fixed the images that were viewed through a camera obscura. This was accomplished through a combination of mechanics (the camera), optics (to improve the image), and chemistry (to sensitize and process the image). Over the next forty years, improvements made to all aspects of the process—cameras, shutters, lenses, and chemistry—led to cheaper and simpler image-making, generating a growing interest for the nonprofessional photographer.

The technicalities of early photography required the photographer, first, to sensitize the media and then to process the image immediately after exposure.[1] Although this system was fine for the professional, it was generally too cumbersome and time-consuming for most amateurs. On April 13, 1880, George Eastman, of Rochester, New York, was issued U.S. Patent No. 226,503 for his machine to coat gelatin dry plates. The following January, with the financial backing of Rochester businessman Henry Strong, he formed the Eastman Dry Plate Company, becoming one of the first commercial producers of light-sensitive photographic emulsions. With reliable plates now available, companies worldwide began manufacturing cameras designed specifically to use them.

Although they were convenient, dry plates had several drawbacks: they were both fragile and heavy to transport. Lightweight, flexible support for photographic emulsion

DETAIL OF CAT. 100

had been investigated starting in the mid-1860s, but without much success. George Eastman aimed his emulsion-making skills at this target and, late in 1884, introduced Eastman's American Film, which used Rives paper—both flexible and lightweight—as support for its emulsion. Yet because this material was not transparent, during processing the images had to be stripped from the paper support, adhered temporarily to glass for printing, and finally, stored on a "skin" made of a semitransparent plastic. To complement his American Film, Eastman and a partner, William H. Walker (a pioneer builder of cameras with standardized parts), designed and patented the Eastman-Walker Roll Holder, which attached to most existing cameras to allow the use of roll film (fig. 1). To reflect its new product line, the firm changed its name to the Eastman Dry Plate and Film Company. Around this time, Eastman built an emulsions-manufacturing plant in London to avoid spoilage problems he had experienced a few years earlier with film that had been shipped across the Atlantic. From early on, he planned to produce and sell his products worldwide; the London plant was the first of many to be located in major European cities.

All seemed to be going well for Mr. Eastman's young enterprise, though in reality not many professional photographers were making the switch from dry plates to the new flexible film, as it was difficult to process. To compound the situation, it was found that the indexing spool of the roll holder might infringe upon an earlier patent, issued to David H. Houston, of Cambria, Wisconsin.[2] Only an agreement to pay Houston an annual fee of $700, negotiated by William H. Walker, averted legal action.

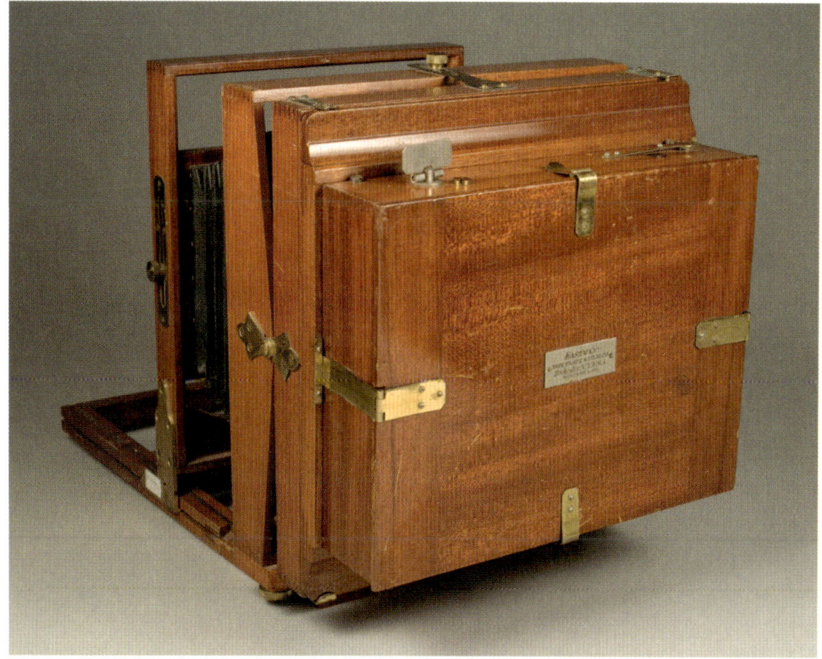

FIG. 1. Empire State View fitted with Eastman-Walker Roll Holder, ca. 1885, Rochester Optical Company, Rochester, N.Y. George Eastman House, International Museum of Photography and Film, Rochester, N.Y. (1993.1373.0001)

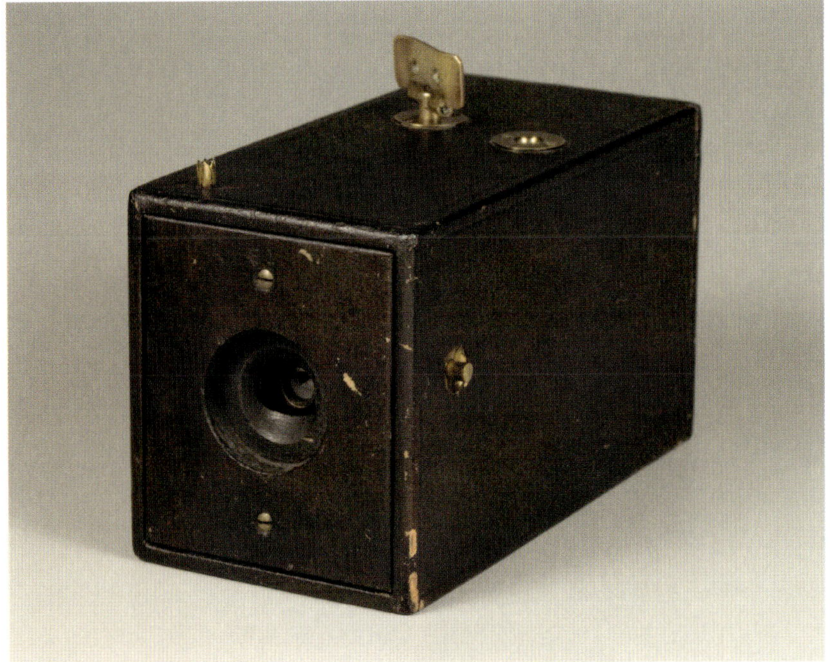

FIG. 2. Kodak camera, 1888, Eastman Dry Plate and Film Company, Rochester, N.Y. George Eastman House, International Museum of Photography and Film, Rochester, N.Y. Gift of Margaret Church Weston (1974.0028.3231)

All things considered, Eastman clearly needed a new product; he looked to the so-called detective camera to use as a model.[3] The first detective camera was introduced by Thomas Bolas in 1881, but the moniker was applied to just about any camera that could be operated without the knowledge of the person being photographed. Such devices were fairly popular with amateur photographers but were usually designed for dry plates. In 1886, Eastman and one of his technicians, Frank Cossitt, began designing their own version of the detective camera, a boxlike instrument with a built-in roll-film holder. This was Eastman's first camera for amateurs, but it had so many problems that only a few were actually produced. The experience he gained from this abortive project, however, soon led him to develop the Kodak.

Introduced to the public in the September 15, 1888, issue of *Scientific American*, the Kodak was Eastman's first successful amateur camera (fig. 2). Frank Brownell, a cabinet-maker whose shop was near Eastman's State Street establishment, had been hired to assist with design and production of the new device. The Brownell Manufacturing Company would fill those roles on all Eastman cameras until 1902, when Eastman Kodak purchased it outright and it became the company's Camera Works Division. Brownell was put in charge of camera design, a job he held until leaving in 1906 to pursue nonphotographic projects.

The first Kodak was a small (3¼ x 3½ x 6¾–inch) box-style device fitted with a built-in, yet removable, holder for a 100-exposure roll of Eastman's American Film. It was made of eastern hardwood (usually cherry or maple) with box-joint corners and covered in dark brown, fine-grained Moroccan leather.[4] The camera was not equipped with a reflecting viewfinder—a cost-saving move; only the "V" sighting lines inscribed atop the device guided the composition of images. Nor was there an exposure counter. Instead, the customer was provided with a small card printed with numbers (1–100) that were to be crossed off as pictures were shot. The camera's slightly wide-angle 57mm *f*/9 periscopic lens was mounted in a barrel shutter, designed by Eastman himself, and had a single speed of 1⁄25 second. The lens was actuated by a common pocket-watch spring, wound by raising the "tulip-tied" string at the right front of the camera. Covering the lens was a pluglike green-felt cap, which, besides providing protection when the camera wasn't in use, could be used for time exposures. The Kodak's 2½-inch images were circular, formed by a mask located in front of the film plane that made use of only the sharpest part of the lens, sometimes called its "sweet spot."

Eastman knew that marketing would be the key to his little camera's success and that a memorable name would be essential to its reception. In coining the name, he is said to have favored the letter K because it was not only "strong and incisive" but also the first letter of his mother's maiden name, Kilbourn. Additionally, he thought the name pronounceable in many languages, an important factor in overseas advertising. His cousin Kilbourn Tompkins, a New York City advertising writer, was hired to write the instruction manual and accompanying primer for the Kodak camera. The dissatisfying result led Eastman to refer to Tompkins as a "camera-ignoramus" and, eventually, to write the manual himself—in the process coming up with the famed ad slogan, "You press the button, we do the rest." Avoiding the flowery language typical of the day, the manual employed short, simple phrases and illustrations to show new owners how to use the camera. The headers for the five steps: "Pull the cord gently; Hold it Firmly; Point the Kodak; Press the Button; Turn the Key." Also included in the manual was what might be considered the forerunner of the long-running company publication *How to Take Good Pictures*, which would debut in 1913.

The Kodak sold for $25 (about $600 in today's money), a price that included a hand-tooled leather carrying case with shoulder strap and a roll of film (fig. 3). It came in a crate-wood shipping box with a slide-off top. After shooting a full roll, and with the film still inside the camera, the photographer-owner used the box to send the camera back to Eastman's Rochester factory, where the film would be processed. Ten dollars paid for development and printing, with finished images adhered to decorated Kodak mounts, plus a fresh roll of film loaded into the camera before it and the prints were returned to the customer. This creative arrangement solved the problem of messy home processing, and it also marked the beginning of the professional photofinishing industry. For the more advanced amateur photographer, Eastman provided detailed developing instructions with each camera model; he also sold darkroom equipment and processing chemicals through his international network of dealers.

Despite being fairly expensive for its day, the Kodak and its 100-exposure load made an ideal tourist camera. For example, it was a popular foreign-travel accessory, with views of the gardens at Versailles, the Colosseum, and the Parthenon being typical subject matter (figs. 4–6). Because the film was rather slow by today's standards, roughly ASA 5, most imagery made by these cameras was shot outdoors. Indoor photography was possible, with the subjects being illuminated by window light.

About five thousand Kodak cameras were manufactured during the first year of production. Late in 1889, a larger model, one producing a 3½-inch diameter image and fitted with a reflecting viewfinder, was introduced. It was called the No. 2 Kodak (fig. 7). At the same time, the earlier model was renamed the No. 1 Kodak. The new models came loaded with the new Eastman's Transparent Film, using a nitro-cellulose (nitrate) support base that made processing much easier. Though Eastman's American Film would remain on the market until 1900, Transparent Film became the medium of choice for the next generation of cameras.

These earliest Kodaks and the models developed over the next decade or so represent the beginning of snapshot photography.[5] The snapshot, a term borrowed from hunting, is one taken quickly and without careful aim. Amateur photographers of the time met with derision for this type of shooting; nevertheless, the snapshot meant lots of exposed film and big business for photographic suppliers. Soon, the many new products made for the amateur market eclipsed those made for the professional, revolutionizing the

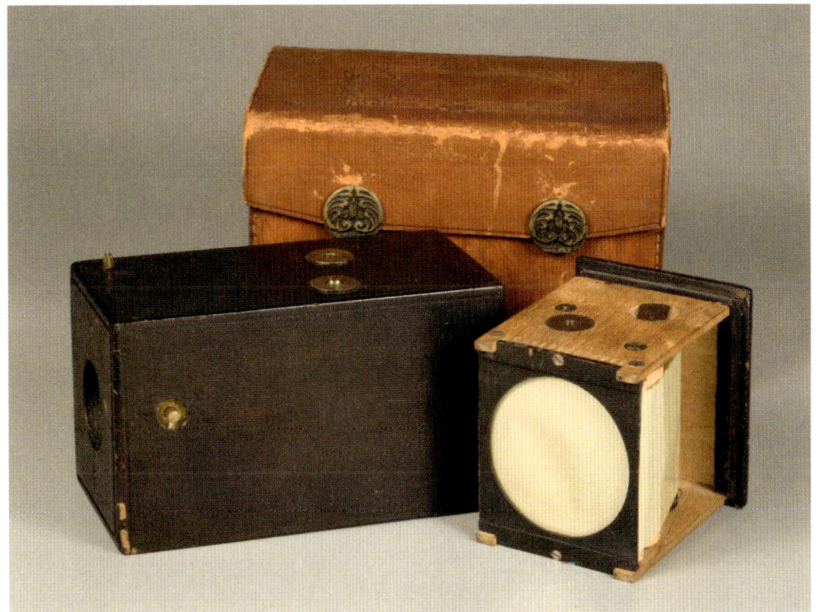

FIG. 3. Kodak camera with case and roll-film holder, 1888, Eastman Dry Plate and Film Company, Rochester, N.Y. George Eastman House, International Museum of Photography and Film, Rochester, N.Y. Gift of Margaret Church Weston (1974.0028.3231)

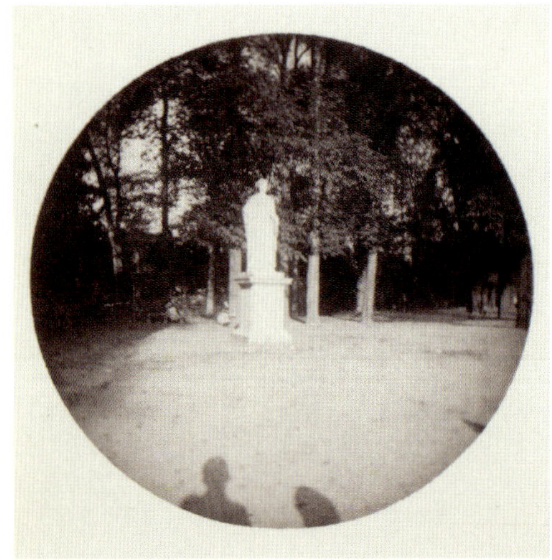

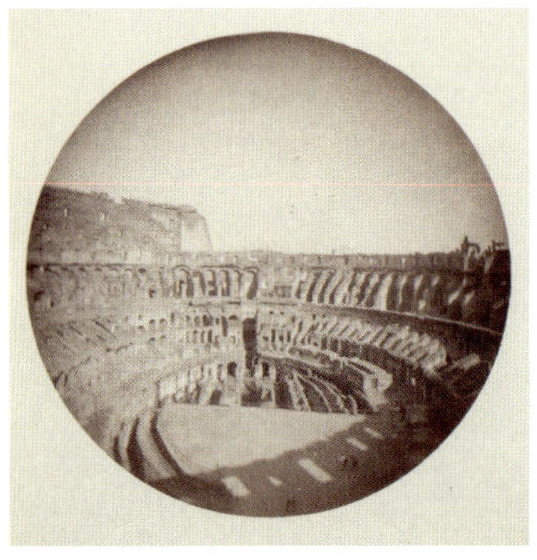

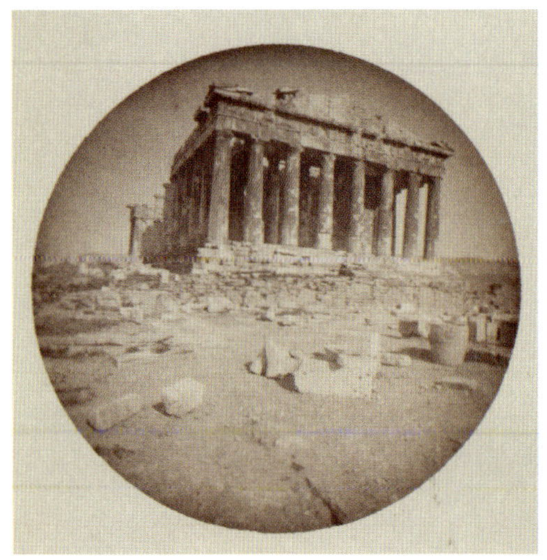

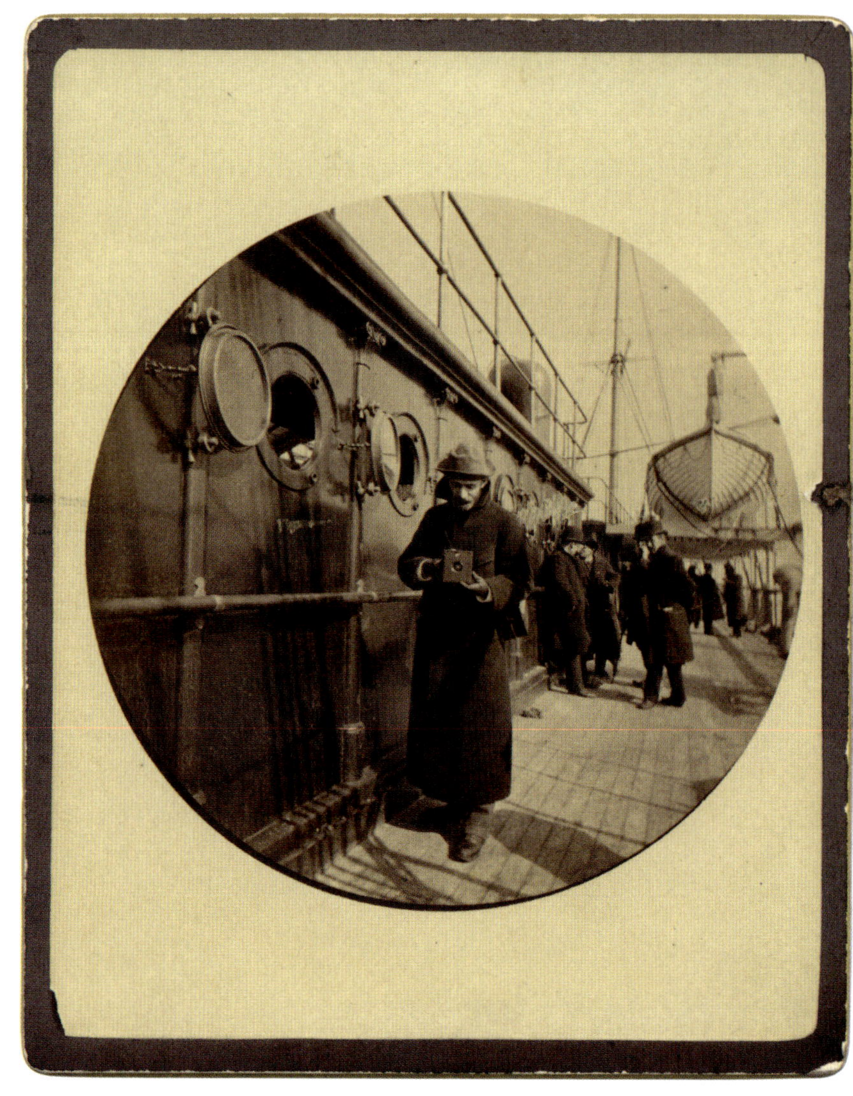

LEFT, TOP TO BOTTOM:

FIG. 4. Raymond K. Albright, Statue at Neptune Fountain, Versailles, ca. 1892. Albumen print (No. 1 Kodak snapshot). George Eastman House, International Museum of Photography and Film, Rochester, N.Y. Gift of Mrs. Raymond Albright (1974.0251.0008)

FIG. 5. Raymond K. Albright, Colosseum, Rome, ca. 1892. Albumen print (No. 1 Kodak snapshot). George Eastman House, International Museum of Photography and Film, Rochester, N.Y. Gift of Mrs. Raymond Albright (1974.0250.0052)

FIG. 6. Raymond K. Albright, Parthenon, Athens, ca. 1892. Albumen print (No. 1 Kodak snapshot). George Eastman House, International Museum of Photography and Film, Rochester, N.Y. Gift of Mrs. Raymond Albright (1974.0250.0009)

ABOVE:

FIG. 7. Frederick F. Church, George Eastman holding a No. 2 Kodak camera on board the U.S.S. *Gallia*, February 1890. Albumen print (No. 2 Kodak snapshot). George Eastman House, International Museum of Photography and Film, Rochester, N.Y. Gift of Margaret Church Weston (1981.1159.0026)

industry. In 1892, to better connect the success of its cameras to their manufacturer, the Rochester firm changed its name to the Eastman Kodak Company.

Early Kodaks all suffered the same drawback: as noted, the entire device had to be shipped to an Eastman lab for processing, leaving its owner cameraless in the meantime. A photographer without a camera uses no film, which clearly was not good for business. Eastman assigned Brownell to remedy this problem, with the first solution being the Daylight Kodaks — Models A, B, and C — introduced in 1891. These used a special version of Eastman's Transparent Film, which was mounted in a cardboard container with the film between a cloth leader and trailer, not unlike today's 220 roll film. This arrangement meant the camera could be loaded in subdued daylight. More important, only the cardboard film container had to be sent to the lab for processing. The photographer could now use the camera continuously. In 1892, Samuel Turner, of the Boston Camera Manufacturing Company, introduced a further improvement to the daylight-loading camera: paper-backed roll film mounted on a wooden spool. Always alert to the competition, Eastman negotiated sole rights to Turner's so-called cartridge film as well as to his small, translucent red window, which let the photographer see exposure numbers printed on the film's backing. In 1895, Eastman purchased Boston Camera outright. The "little red window" would be part of most roll-film cameras for the next sixty years or so.[6] It was a simple yet elegant means of counting exposures that, along with the removable indexing idle spool, led to cameras with fewer parts — in other words, ones that could be made more cheaply and sold more affordably. The first Eastman models to take advantage of the red window/cartridge-film technology were the No. 2 Bullet and Pocket Kodak cameras.

Introduced in 1895, the Pocket Kodak, with its five-dollar list price, became one of the best-selling cameras of its time (fig. 8). Like all Eastman cameras from this period, it

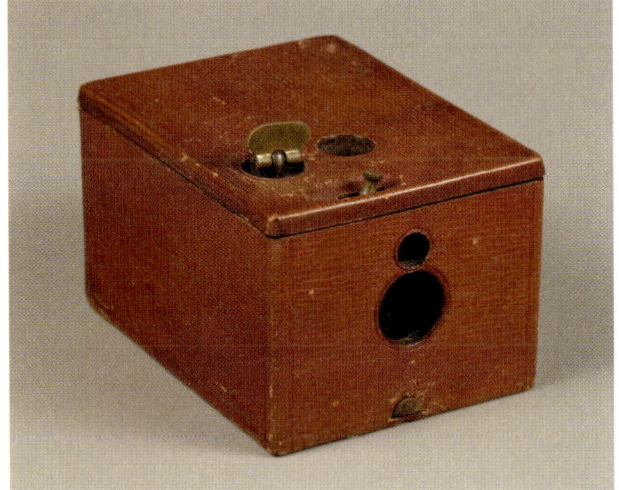

FIG. 8. Pocket Kodak Model '95, 1895, Eastman Kodak Company, Rochester, N.Y. George Eastman House, International Museum of Photography and Film, Rochester, N.Y. Gift of Per A. Gyzander (1978.1278.0001)

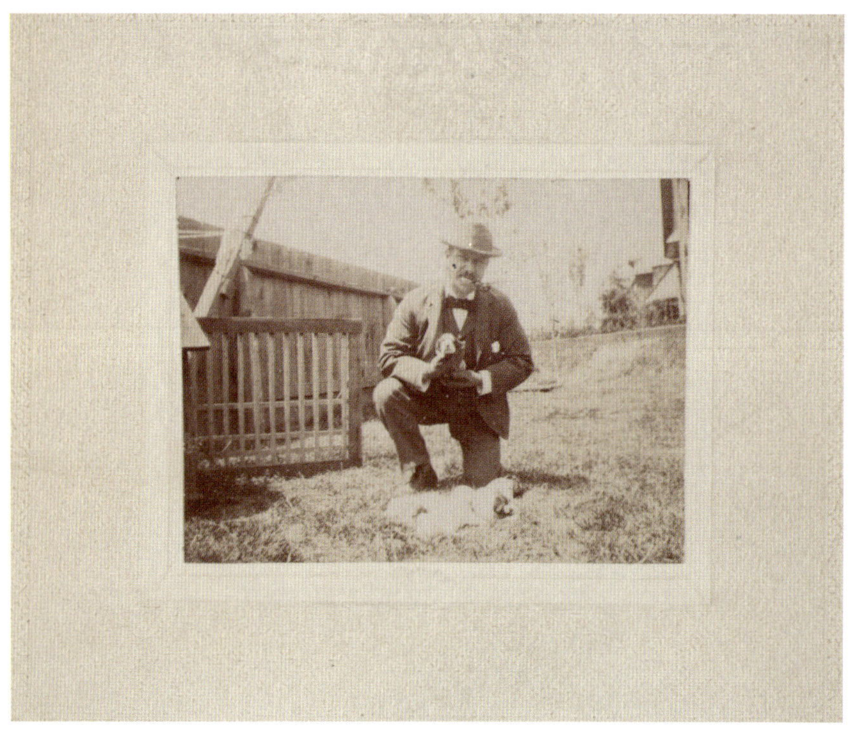

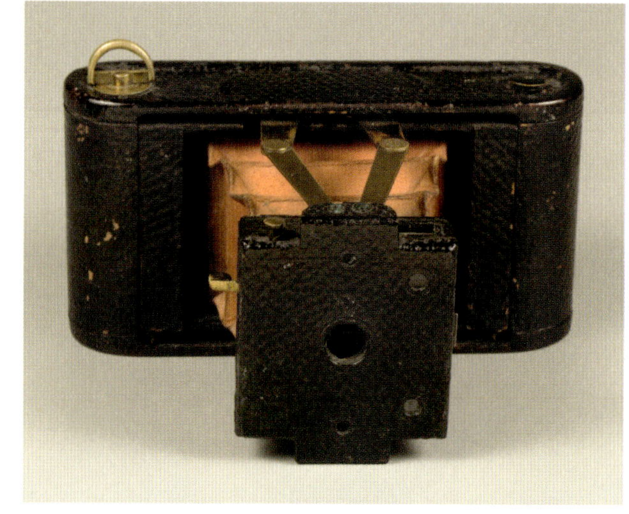

FIG. 9. Unidentified photographer, Man with two dogs, ca. 1895, Pocket Kodak snapshot. George Eastman House, International Museum of Photography and Film, Rochester, N.Y. Gift of 3M; ex-collection Louis Walton Sipley (1988.0284.0005)

FIG. 10. Folding Pocket Kodak, 1897, Eastman Kodak Company, Rochester, N.Y. George Eastman House, International Museum of Photography and Film, Rochester, N.Y. Gift of Eastman Kodak Company (1974.0037.0026)

was well made, with a body assembled from box-jointed wood, usually poplar, that was covered with black pebble-grained leather. The first year's production, called the Model '95, used a circular reflecting viewfinder, while the subsequent issues—models '96, '98, '99, and Model D (from 1900)—had rectangular finders.[7] Some versions of the Model '95 employed pebbled red leather, and at least one had dark brown leather covering, like that used on the 1888 Kodak. These variations are attributed to a demand for the camera that outpaced the supply of raw material. The palm-sized Pocket Kodak produced 1 x 1½–inch images on No. 102 film.[8] As with the original Kodak, its prints were returned to the customer on mounts unique to that model, making factory-processed images from the camera easy to identify (fig. 9).

Among the most popular cameras Eastman Kodak ever made were those in the Folding Pocket Kodak series, which debuted in 1897 (fig. 10). Designed and built by Brownell, this style remained in production until well after World War II; the last of the line, the Kodak Tourist II, was not discontinued until 1958. Like the ubiquitous box camera, the FPK (as it usually was called) was copied by just about every camera manufacturer. The first model in the series produced a 2¼ x 3¼–inch image, fairly large for a camera whose lazy-tongs folding mechanism collapsed it to a mere 1½-inch thickness, so it could easily be carried in a coat pocket. Eventually, the FPK was available for numerous image sizes, ranging from 1⅝ x 2½ inches to 4¼ x 6½ inches.

The handheld camera loaded with roll film was a collector of moments, facilitating the preservation of visual impressions. Many artists, including those featured in this exhibition and catalogue, frequently used the camera as a sketchbook, a tool for quickly transcribing a likeness that could later be "developed" into a more finished work. They were drawn to its potential for capturing the fast-paced, ever-changing nature of modern life and culture. An early "mobile device," the handheld camera advanced a fresh way of seeing based on a new way of measuring time. Although the snapshot was not exactly an instantaneously produced image, it represented shorter pieces of time than previous photographic technology had allowed. And the camera's waist-level perspective — differing greatly from that of the human eye — is readily apparent in many works of art. Frequently, the results were unconventional images that reflected the poet Charles Baudelaire's influential characterization of modernity as "the transitory, the fugitive, the contingent."[9]

NOTES

1. The daguerreotype was made with a copper plate coated with a thin veneer of metallic silver sensitized with iodine. The latent image was then processed with mercury vapor and was made permanent with a bath of sodium hyposulfite. An image made through the wet-plate process had a glass support coated with collodion, which served as the binder to adhere the light-sensitive silver nitrate. The glass plate was then exposed and processed while wet.
2. When film is advanced from the supply spool to the take-up spool, the distance required to rotate each shaft for each exposure changes relative to the amount of film on the given shaft. Eastman used an idler shaft fitted with marking pins to identify the space between images. The top of the indexing spool is visible atop of the camera, with one rotation required between exposures.
3. On November 3, 1881, Bolas was granted a provisional British patent for a small box camera, which he called the detective camera. Shortly after the introduction of his device, the term began to be loosely applied to a range of handheld box-form cameras.
4. Box joints (also called finger joints due to their use of alternating rectangular cuts resembling interlaced fingers) were commonly employed in assembling wooden drawers and boxes, objects with 90-degree angles. They have been used for centuries as a simple yet strong means of forming joins.
5. Several models were included in the first series: the No. 3 Kodak and No. 3 Kodak Junior, which produced 3¼ x 4¼–inch images; and the No. 4 Kodak and No. 4 Kodak Junior, which produced 4 x 5 inch–images.
6. Film manufactured between about 1890 and 1915 was sensitive only to blue light. Thus, light passing through the small red window would not expose or fog the film.
7. The company production records list the Model '97, but no examples are known to exist.
8. Originally, Eastman designated film sizes according to the cameras they fit. Beginning in 1913, a new system of consecutive film numbering was established, with No. 101 film, used in the 1895 No. 2 Bullet camera, being the first. Each new film size corresponded to the release of a given model. No. 102, the second film manufactured under this system, was in use until September 1933.
9. Charles Baudelaire, *The Painter of Modern Life and Other Essays* (1964; repr. London: Phaidon, 1995), p. 13.

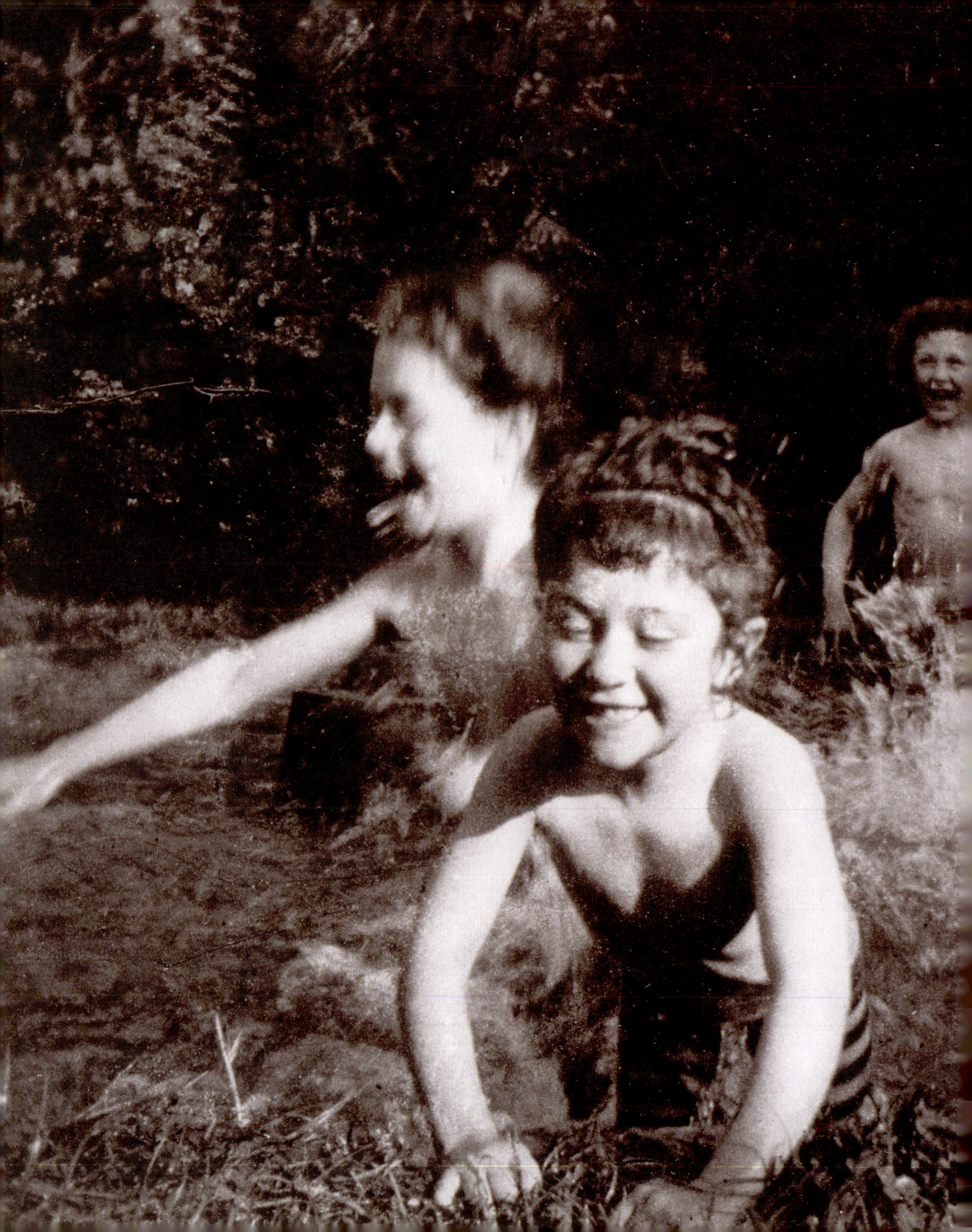

The New Truths of the Snapshot

Michel Frizot

The term *instantané* (literally instantaneous or instant, also used to mean snapshot) pervades the history of photographic practices in France and is descriptive of the late-nineteenth-century "revolution" that linked the new ease and speed of taking a photograph with a vogue for amateur photography. *Instantané* can be either a noun or an adjective, and it is not limited to photography or the description of photographic operations. For example, in 1863 one could buy an *indicateur instantané* (instantaneous indicator) with a "Pocket Paris" plan, while in 1867 there is mention of a handy city map known as *Paris instantané* (Instant Paris) and of a *diviseur instantané* (instant divider). Returning to photography, in 1853, André Adolphe Disdéri published his *Manuel d'opératoire de photographie sur collodion instantané* (Practical Manual of Photography on Instantaneous Collodion), and ten years later, Alphonse de Brébisson marketed a *collodion sec instantané* (instantaneous dry collodion), meaning it was quick to prepare, not that the process of taking the photograph itself was instantaneous.[1]

Because *instantaneous* means "lasting only an instant, a very short space of time," the definition is necessarily imprecise: it depends on a subjective conception of what, exactly, an instant measures. This is as true in French as for the English term *instantaneous photography*. On this point, Josef Maria Eder, in his *History of Photography* (1905) cites Th. Skaife, inventor in 1860 of the Pistolgraph (or pistol camera), who wrote, "Speaking in general, instantaneous photography is as elastic a term as the expression 'long and short.' "[2] This example shows that the question of the instantaneous nature of instantaneous photography dates back to the origins of the process itself, that is, to the early days of photography. The procedure in which an image is produced by exposing a sensitive surface to the effects of light for a certain length of time was contrary to all preceding manual practices—the time it took to paint a picture or draw a sketch, for instance. In 1839 and 1840, limited "exposure time" to make a photograph was a matter of minutes; soon afterward, it was reduced to seconds.[3] This technology-dependent exposure time

DETAIL OF CAT. 13

was accepted as a constituent part of the invention and its demands, especially when the resulting images were remarkably clear and detailed. Attempts to reduce exposure time to about one second were motivated by the desire to create photographic portraits; these would be blurred if more than a few seconds were required, as it was hard for their subjects to remain absolutely still for longer.

From the early days of photography, the question of reducing exposure times was determined by the nature of the subject to be photographed, be it a person posing, seated or standing, or moving—for example, walking or engaged in some other activity. The first photographers wanted to go beyond the posed portrait to produce a less stilted, more lifelike representation of an active subject without blurring and even obscuring some elements of the image.[4] In photography as in painting, the problem was how to represent movement using an apparently still figure. The painter's model in the studio is a living subject who mimes movement while remaining fixed in a position that is intended to suggest actual motion. In photography, the issue of the instantaneous image is never purely technical; it is based on the challenge of both representing the subject and capturing the truth.

Charles Nègre confronted this challenge when, in 1851 and 1852, he produced and made known his series of photographs of three young chimney sweeps at rest or walking on the banks of the Seine in Paris (fig. 1). The two options, rest and walking, prove that these studies of living subjects were made in the context of discovering the fastest possible photographic capture. For that purpose, Nègre explained that he had developed a special lens that concentrated the light on a small surface: "I think it worth noting a combination of glasses which, in the spring of 1851, gave me instantaneous prints on paper."[5]

The term *instantanée* was often used at this time, in its feminine form, to refer to a photograph taken in a brief instant, on the spur of the moment, in order to respect the autonomy of the subject. In terms of actual exposure time, only imprecise indications exist. One of these is the art critic Henri de Lacretelle's comment in 1852 about a Paris market scene by Nègre that includes several very blurry figures: "It's life itself, and M. Nègre has achieved the feat of stilling it in a hundredth of a second."[6] (The term "hundredth of a second" was simply a figure of speech, not a precise measure of time.) Elsewhere Ernest Lacan, the renowned early commentator on photography, described Nègre's stonecutter (1853) as "full of movement and life," and his special (collodion) technique as having "such speed that in three seconds a portrait is burned. So it operates almost instantaneously."[7] The suggested three-second time seems perfectly plausible, but the speed claimed is insufficient for the subject really to be moving (so he must be still).

Indeed, the same was true of Nègre's famous chimney sweeps, shown walking along the Seine in profile, in two different versions. In the mid-nineteenth century, these

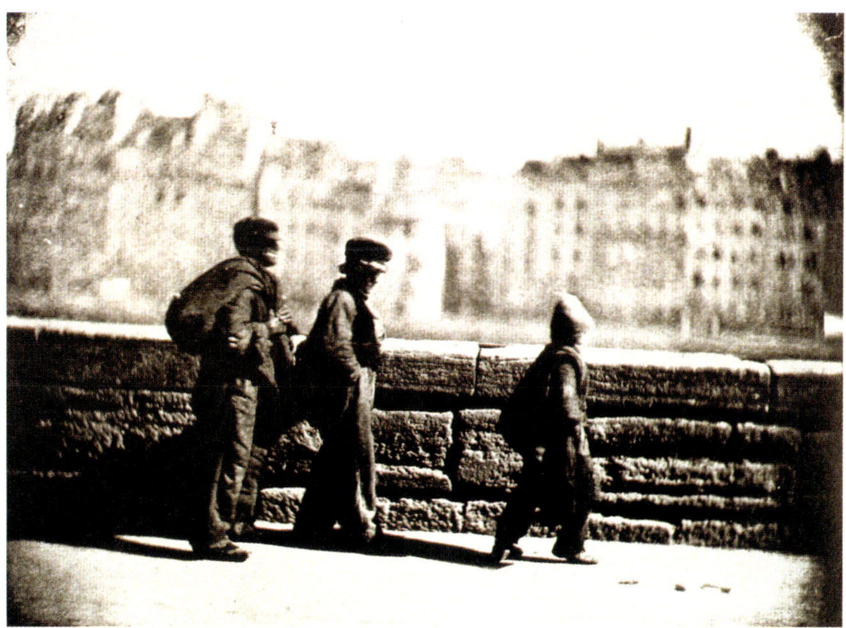

FIG. 1. Charles Nègre, Chimney sweeps walking, 1851–52. Private collection

images were considered the ultimate in realistic representation, comparable to imagery by Rembrandt and Murillo.[8] Upon careful observation of these images—particularly, the position of the subjects' feet—and comparison with those that appeared in late-nineteenth-century scientific snapshots, it is evident that their positions are "anti-physiological," that is, impossible to maintain as part of continuous walking.[9] These are stationary, posed positions, devised to offer the best possible illusion of walking, but with nothing of the physiological reality of movement. These photographs do not demonstrate the instantaneous capture of ongoing movement. Instead, the technology imposed certain conditions, and the photographer, seeking to represent reality, had to work within those bounds.

Everything changed with the arrival of dry, ultrasensitive gelatin silver-bromide negative plates, which became widespread, at least in France, by 1881. Because they were dry, it was possible to prepare them industrially, making the technical processes easier, while their sensitivity permitted very short exposure times, on the order of one-hundredth of a second. They continued to be described as "instantaneous" but with different characteristics. According to Josef Maria Eder, "The name instantaneous prints generally applies to those that are obtained by an exposure of between ⅒th–⅕0th of a second. If the subject to be photographed is at rest, the exposure time may be as much as ½ a second; if, on the other hand, it is moving fast, this time must be reduced to ⅟100th or ⅟200th of a second and, in some cases, even further."[10] Eder went on to mention "jumpers, racing horses and breaking waves" as extra-fast movements that instantaneous photography could capture.

Eventually, the portable handheld camera supplanted the camera obscura on a tripod. In practice, it was manually impossible to implement the potential exposure time of $1/100$ second. The shutter is a tool that normally blocks the lens and then unblocks it, allowing light to enter for an instant and a photograph to be made. In the early days of photography, there was a simple cap in front of the lens. Once exposure times had been reduced to less than one second, photographers sought a camera that could allow light to pass only for that precise length of time. The invention of the instant shutter, a feature of the handheld camera, made that possible. A precision mechanism activated by means of a button or pneumatic bulb caused the pivoting of blades or a pierced disc that moved in front of the lens (fig. 2). The gradual integration of this device into the lens became widespread in the late 1880s, so that all cameras thus equipped could take instantaneous photographs. For instance, the Kodak version boasted a simple instantaneous shutter consisting of a cylinder with a transverse perforation that spun on its axis.[11] An American manual published in 1883 promoted the shutter innovation this way: "It seems proper to introduce the consideration of *instantaneous pictures*, the taking of which will be found by the amateur to have a peculiar charm. To make these effectually, it is necessary to have a Dallmeyer Rapid Rectilinear Lens, a drop shutter for giving very short exposures, and the very quickest of plates (Eastman's Special)."[12]

Historically, scientific applications of photography gave rise to developments in instantaneous photography using gelatin silver-bromide emulsion. In France, the physiologist Etienne-Jules Marey was among the first to use this emulsion (no doubt supplied by his friend the Belgian scientist Desiré von Monckhoven), in 1881, and to develop cameras with exposure times that facilitated his research into rapid movement, notably that of birds (fig. 3). The photographic gun of 1881 and chronophotograph of 1882 had shutter systems that permitted ultrafast exposure times; Marey believed he had attained $1/500$ second with the photographic gun and $1/1000$ second with the chronophotograph.[13] The

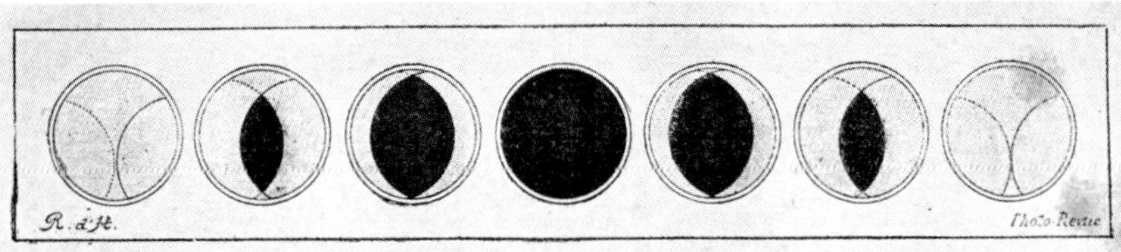

FIG. 2. Different stages of blade shutter opening, after Georges Brunel and Paul Chaux, *La photographie en plein air, excursionniste et instantanée* (Paris: Bernard Tignol, 1897–99), p. 17

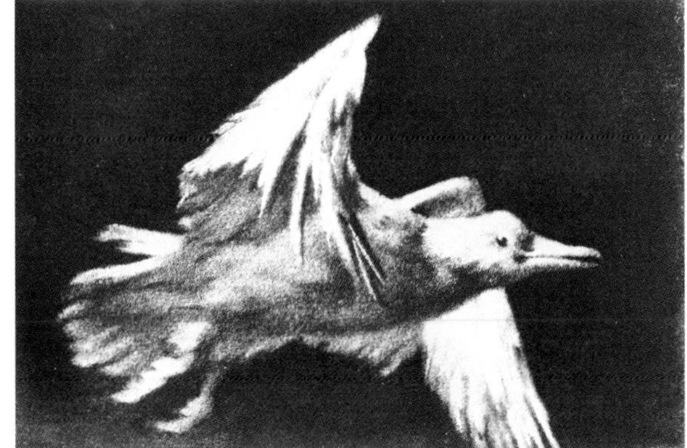

FIG. 3. Etienne-Jules Marey, Snapshot of a seagull in flight, extract from a chronophotograph, 1886

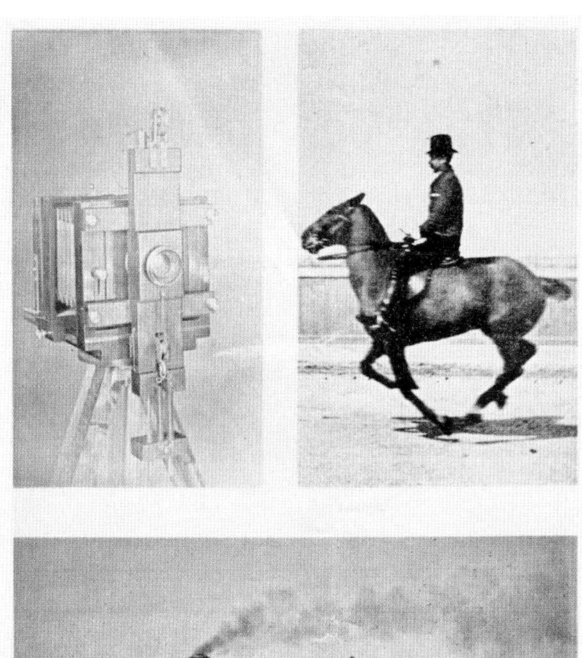

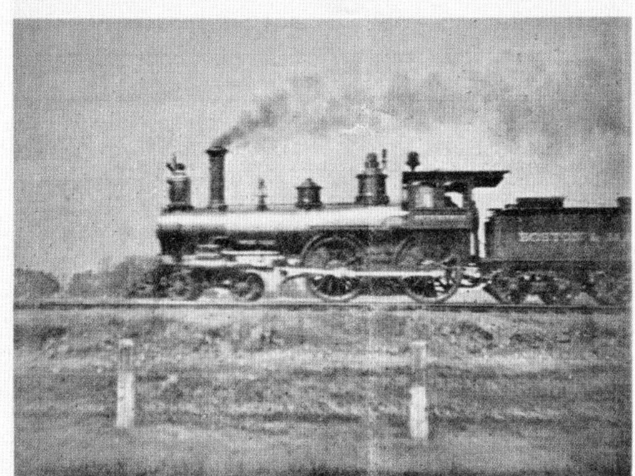

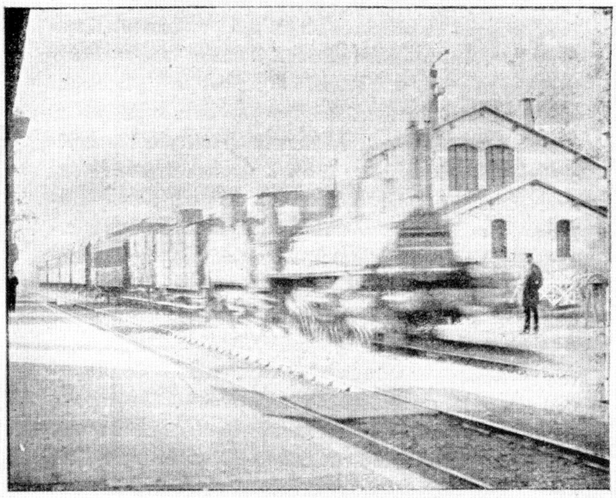

Fig. 21. Mauvaise épreuve d'un train en marche.

FIG. 4. Camera and exposer, Horse at full gallop, and Express train passing through Medford (over 50 miles per hour), plate from William H. Pickering, *Methods of Determining the Speed of Photographic Exposers* (Cambridge, Mass.: J. Wilson, 1885)

FIG. 5. Poor proof of a moving train, after Georges Brunel and Paul Chaux, *La photographie en plein air, excursionniste et instantanée* (Paris: Bernard Tignol, 1897–99), fig. 21

disc of the chronophotograph, with its radial perforations spinning in front of the sensitive plate, was simply a repeating instantaneous shutter, producing several instantaneous images per second. Marey was not only a pioneer of the uses of instantaneous photography; he also aptly described the instantaneous shutter as providing "an exposure time short enough for moving objects to be shown in the print with outlines as clear as if they had been motionless."[14] This description is based not on a preconceived notion of the instantaneous image but on the fact that it is a relative notion dependent on many parameters. It emphasizes that the image obtained (the print) is a representation of a moving object, captured as if it were motionless; the objective criterion of this immobility is the clarity of outline in the image, with no blurring.[15] Thus, the instantaneous image is something of a visual paradox: an object (or subject) known to be in motion (bird, horse, train) is shown in the image with no appearance of movement. The best instantaneous photograph of a train moving at full speed shows it stationary (figs. 4, 5).

Where horses are concerned, the still image of the animal's moving legs had scientific consequences. For example, in 1878 Eadweard Muybridge was able to confirm Marey's assertion that, at a particular moment, none of the horse's hooves was touching the ground. In this respect, instantaneous photography was primarily a means of verification and experimentation, answering specific questions that unaided human senses could not resolve.

The results obtained by instantaneous photography (starting with Marey in 1882), in carefully regulated study conditions, of exactly how human beings walk—a motion often represented in the history of art—provoked astonishment and sometimes even arguments. In "Man in Movement," a chapter of his treatise on instantaneous photography, Eder noted the seemingly unlikely position of the feet of a walking man as captured by photography: "On examining a street snapshot, even superficially, one is very surprised by the strange positions of the figures; looking closely one finds the strangest lines, which do not correspond in any way to what art conventionally shows us. . . . What is most striking in these snapshots is the position of the leading foot. Contrary to all accepted ideas, it is the heel that first touches the ground; at the same time the end of the foot is raised firmly into the air." He goes on, bemusedly, "Would a painter dare to draw [these] figures?"[16] (fig. 6).

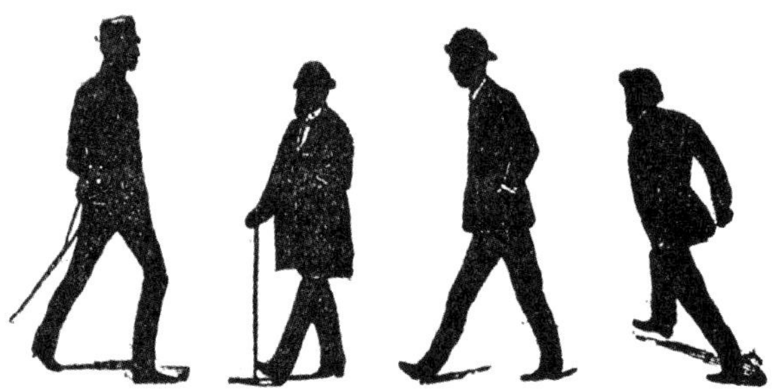

FIG. 6. People out walking, in Josef Maria Eder, *La photographie instantanée: Son application aux arts et aux sciences* (Paris: Gauthier-Villars, 1888), p. 201

Here is further proof that Nègre's pictures of the walking chimney sweeps were faked: the observer, who never sees any of the still forms conveyed by a photograph, is more satisfied with a depiction that is false overall than with an instantaneous representation that is necessarily "correct" in relation to the moment in question. In other words, the instantaneous photographic image of the walker does not reconstruct a visual impression of walking for the viewer. In 1888, it merely reflected a scientific concept, which we have since adopted because we have seen countless snapshots, regarded as credible for more than a century.

The introduction of and developments in instantaneous photography during the late nineteenth century stimulated considerable artistic creativity based on growing trust in the medium. To understand why many painters who previously had ignored photography decided to embrace it, it is necessary to appreciate the visual novelty of instantaneous photographic images and their pictorial characteristics. Consider, for instance, Eder's description of a snapshot of a pole-vaulter (fig. 7): "A man leaps, with a pole, over a rope and then a ditch; at the moment when his leap is at its peak, he lets go of the pole and falls back on the other side. Inspection of the snapshot taken with the Thury and Amey shutter shows us a strangely broken equilibrium: it seems the man must fall very badly, instead of continuing the translational movement acquired by his leap."[17] So it is the incongruity of the result that strikes the observer and makes it difficult to understand. In other words, a viewer from that time did not restore the entire movement to a snapshot: he could not imagine a "before" and an "after" to the instant that is part of that movement. The "reading" of a snapshot in 1888 frequently inspired either incredulity or bewilderment; it did not restore the mental image of movement. There remained an apparent contradiction — in the man's walk, in the positions of animals' legs, and in the pole vault as well as in Bonnard's children bathing and his dog — between what was seen with the naked eye and the images of an instantaneous photographic print, obtained using

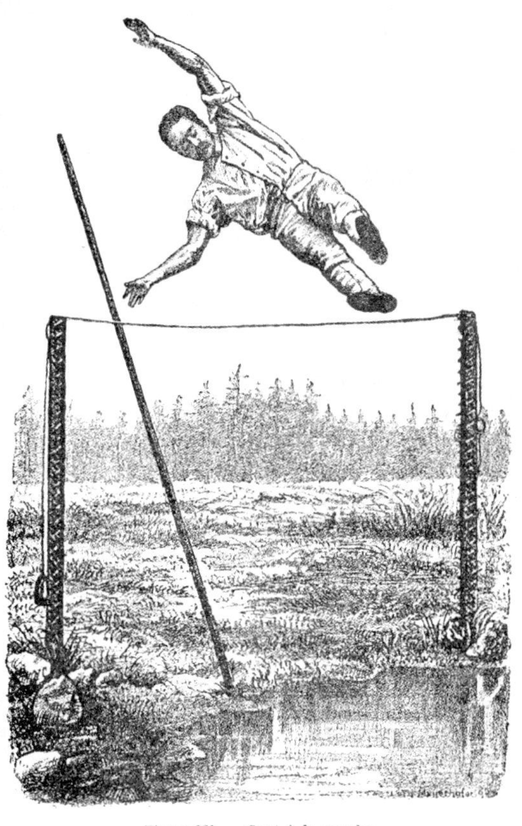

FIG. 7. Pole vault, in Josef Maria Eder, *La photographie instantanée: Son application aux arts et aux sciences* (Paris: Gauthier-Villars, 1888), fig. 181

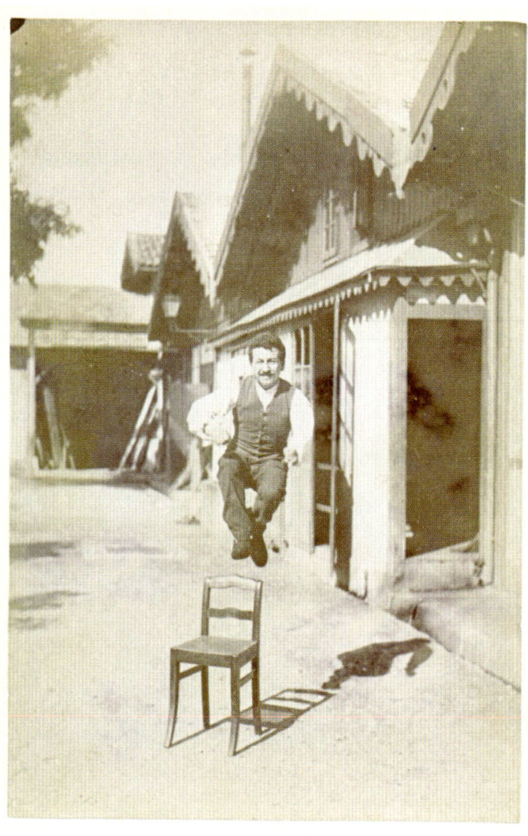

FIG. 8. Snapshot proof of M. Lumière of Lyon, in *L'amateur photographe* 4, no. 3 (February 1, 1888): pp. 62–63

"technological" equipment and operating on scientific principles (fig. 8). In other words, photographs belong to the world of physics, the principles of which are foreign to the human senses. Although it may be possible to comprehend a hundredth or thousandth of a second, this is not a length of time that can be measured or used physiologically. The relevance of photography in the late nineteenth century, the evaluation of its objectivity, thus depended upon people believing in its scientific validity, just as they believed in other scientific advances of the time that they could not "understand," such as electricity, engines, and artificial light.

Commenting on his own *Saint Jean Baptiste* (1878), shown walking, with both feet firmly on the ground, Auguste Rodin noted the contrast between two modes of representation: one drawing on "photographic belief" and the other on "visual trust." The position of the subject's feet is physiologically unrealistic according to instantaneous photography, but Rodin contended, "It is the artist who is true and photography that lies; for in reality time does not stop."[18] The sculptor thus contrasted mechanical instantaneousness (which is not related to sight) with visual and mental impressions (the continuity of ocular vision at the time), which he arbitrarily restored by combining instants: "[I]f the artist succeeds in giving the impression of a movement made in several instants, his work is certainly far less conventional than the scientific image in which time is suddenly suspended."[19] What mattered to Rodin was the visual "impression," not mechanical truth.

For late-nineteenth-century artists, the appeal of instantaneous photography, now within the grasp of the amateur, was undoubtedly linked with a desire for new knowledge and a rejection of "conventional" representations of movement, particularly those simulated by models in the studio.[20] Artists were interested in what was happening outside, in the street, and were torn between relying upon direct observation and scientifically accurate representation, which partakes of modernity. As a technological process, with an apparatus based on physics, photography played the role of intermediary and support for representation, even if it was not fully "copied." It at least could be trusted, more than one's own eyes, which were now known not to be adequate for capturing color, forms, or movement. Instantaneous photography opened up possibilities; it opened the eyes to an "invisible" form of reality and gave a fixed shape to things that changed shape constantly. By doing so, it provoked astonishment, and this astonishment at the "photographic" transposed back into painting was surely the bust spur to creativity.

Painters were less interested in making spectacular or sensational snapshots than they were in using handheld cameras to capture everyday, ordinary actions as they occurred. They fall into the category of "excursionists" (the bicycle was in fashion!) and sought picturesque subjects wherever they went (fig. 9). "The excursionist will not so

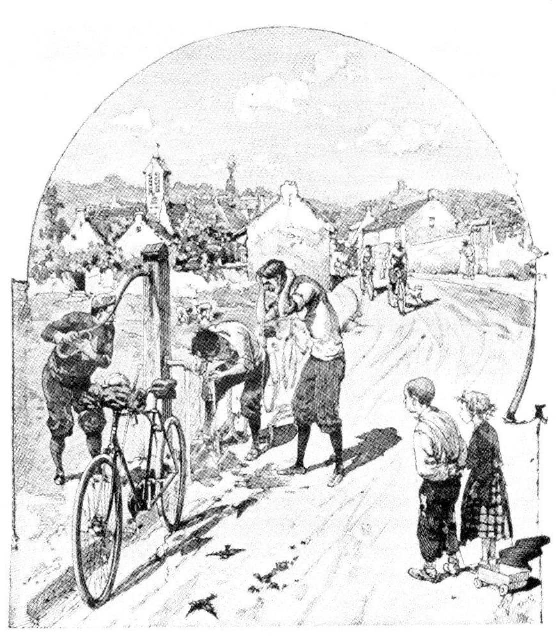
Fig. 17. La halte de l'amateur photo-cycliste.

FIG. 9. The amateur cyclist-photographer makes a stop, after Georges Brunel and Paul Chaux, *La photographie en plein air, excursionniste et instantanée* (Paris: Bernard Tignol, 1897–99), fig. 17

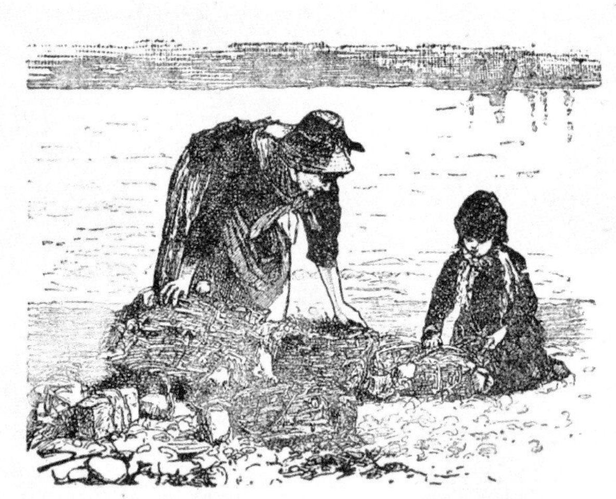

FIG. 10. Photographic composition (Seaside snapshots), after Josef Maria Eder, *La photographie instantanée: Son application aux arts et aux sciences* (Paris: Gauthier-Villars, 1888), fig. 50

much take instantaneous photographs — true studies of movement — as animated scenes, animated by calm figures, outdoor scenes — ploughing oxen, grazing sheep, boats in full sail and so on. Indeed he will often photograph only completely inanimate objects, landscapes or historic buildings. Instantaneousness is thus reduced to the speed strictly necessary to allow one to hold the camera in one's hand and do without the stability of a tripod."[21]

These amateur photographers were looking for "true poses, scenes taken as they happen and to preserve the impression of truth, they preferred to work incognito, unseen by their subjects"[22] (fig. 10). "[F]or as soon as [the photographer] has been discovered, the most graceful or picturesque scenes disappear as though by magic, most frequently leaving him looking at surprised figures that are no longer of any interest." New cameras were discreet black boxes that could be put to such surreptitious use. "[I]t is here above all that the small hand-held cameras will provide many favours, for their small size makes it possible to get close to groups without their being aware of the presence of an inquisitive photographer."[23]

During the final decade of the nineteenth century, the development of halftone engraving made it possible to print photographs in newspapers, magazines, and books. This sparked an enormous demand for photographs, mostly those taken with handheld cameras. For example, *L'instantané: Album photographique de l'actualité* (The Snapshot: A Photographic Album of Topical Subjects), a weekly newspaper supplement that first appeared in December 1897, offered sixteen pages of photographs of "topical subjects" that included portraits, travelers' photographs, and impromptu shots of interesting situations.[24]

Representations of a kind never seen before suddenly emerged — spontaneous, unexpected, and caught by photography as they took place, including preparations for

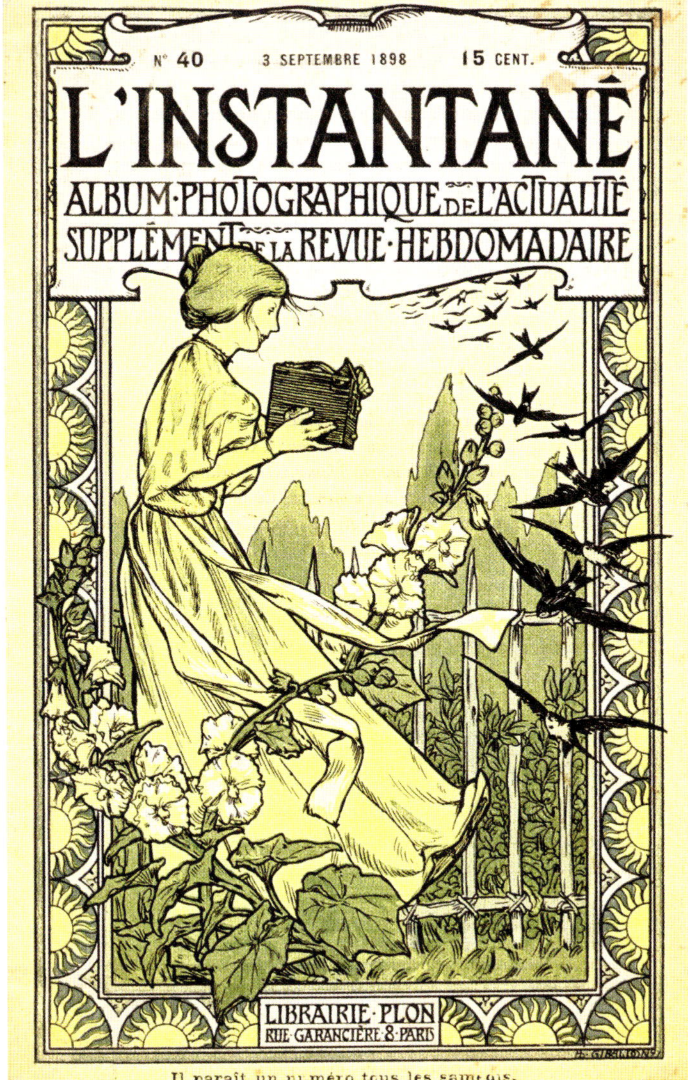

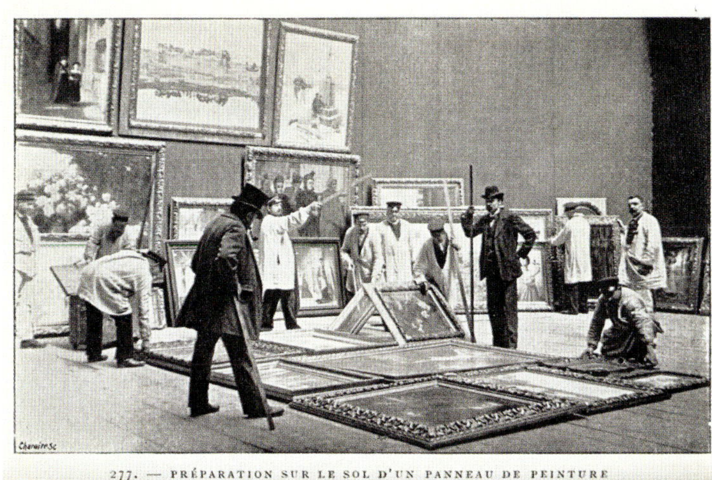

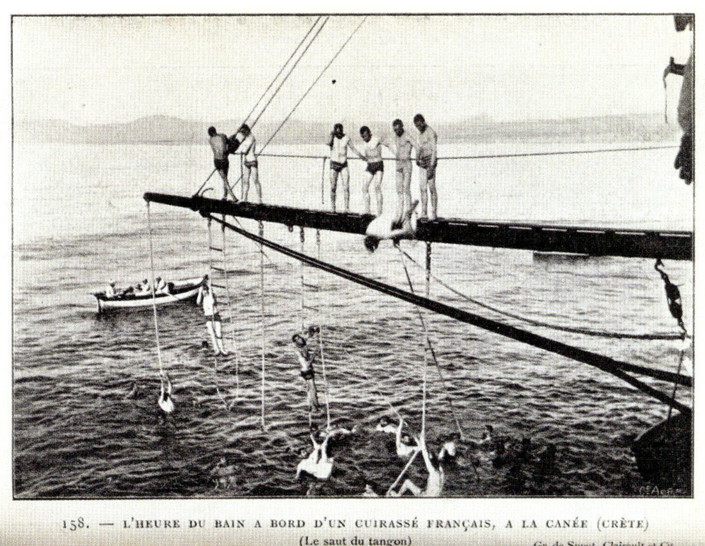

FIG. 11. Cover of *L'instantané*, no. 40 (September 3, 1898)

FIG. 12. Fine art exhibition, 1898: Preparing on the floor the hanging of a panel painting, *L'instantané*, no. 23 (May 7, 1898)

FIG. 13. Bath time on a French battleship, *L'instantané*, no. 38 (August 20, 1898)

the hanging of the Salon des Beaux-Arts exhibition in 1898 and bathing time on a French battleship (figs. 11–13). Magazines such as *Illustrated American* would gather, on a single page, images related to a given theme (sailing, the beach, pedestrians) in order to offer a composite "commentary" on the variety and popularity of that theme (fig. 14). The many popular publications featuring images of this kind were a source of inspiration for painters, as were their own photographs.

The snapshot, sometimes merely the product of a handheld camera, was a representation of the activities of living beings. As such, the production of a mechanical device superseded or, at least, enhanced the visual acuity of painters. In some cases, snapshots also provided additional detailed information and even ideas for artistic endeavor.

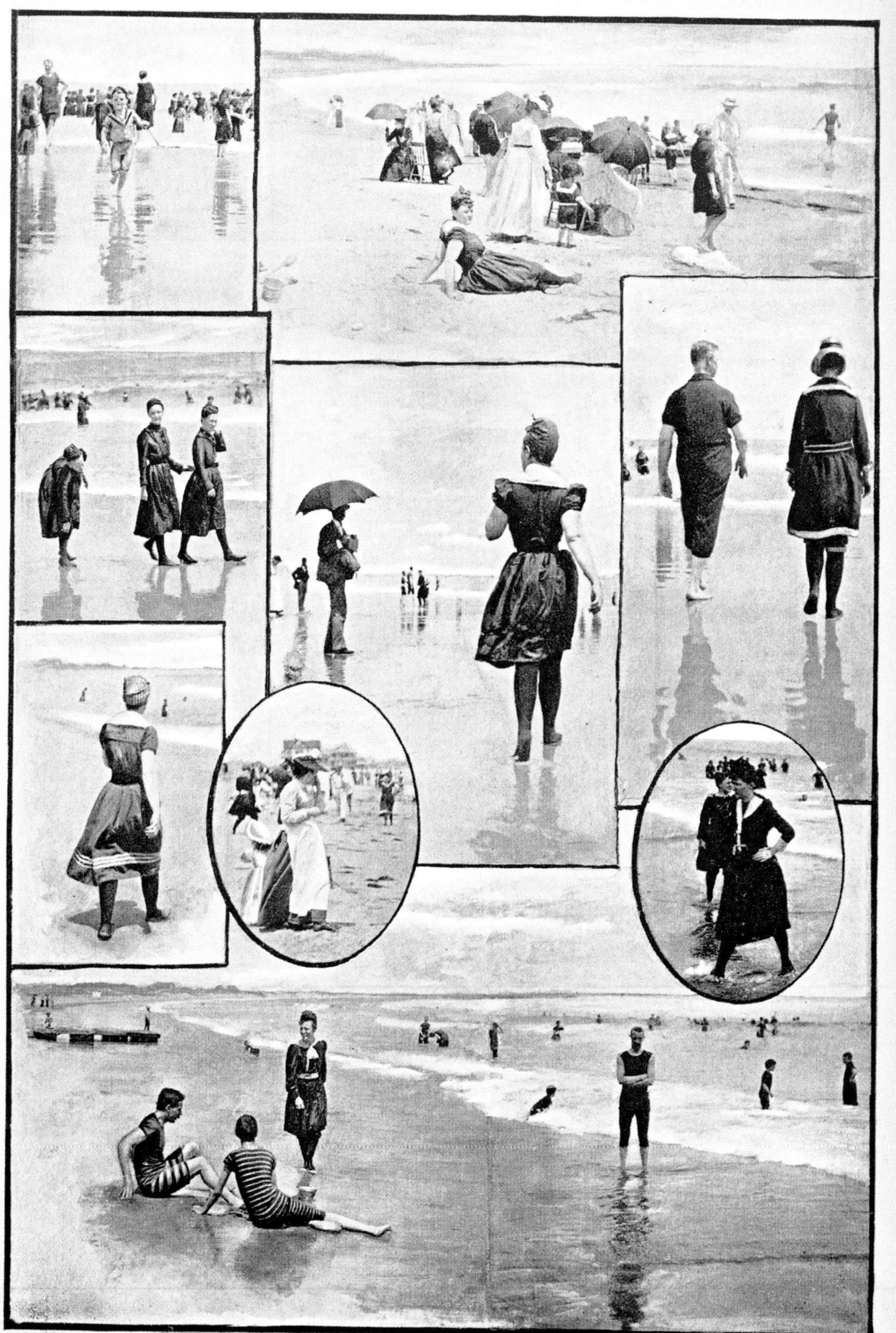
260 THE ILLUSTRATED AMERICAN. SEPTEMBER 2, 1893.

NARRAGANSETT PIER, RHODE ISLAND—STRAY SHOTS ON THE GREAT BATHING BEACH.

FIG. 14. Narragansett Pier, Rhode Island: Stray shots on the great bathing beach, *Illustrated American*, September 2, 1893, p. 260

NOTES

1. Even today, any "instant drink" is prepared with a ready-to-use powder.
2. Josef Maria Eder, *History of Photography* (1945; repr. New York: Dover, 1978), p. 358. This is an English translation of the original 1905 German edition.
3. For example, in October 1840 William Henry Fox Talbot made a negative calotype (his most recently perfected invention) in just one minute.
4. One such image is Fox Talbot's *Carpenters, Woodworkers* (1841–43). See H. von Amelunxen, *Die aufgehobene Zeit* (Berlin: Nishen Verlag, 1988), pp. 86, 87, 90.
5. Charles Nègre, *La lumière*, December 23, 1854, pp. 201–2, as cited by F. Heilbrun, *Charles Nègre*, exh. cat. (Paris: Editions des musées nationaux, 1980), pp. 64, 307 n47.
6. Henri de Lacretelle, *La lumière*, February 28, 1852, p. 37.
7. Ernest Lacan, *La lumière*, September 10, 1853, pp. 146–47.
8. Charles Bauchal, *La lumière*, May 29, 1852, pp. 90–91.
9. Michel Frizot, "Comment on marche: De l'exactitude dans l'instant," *48/14, La revue du musée d'Orsay*, no. 4 (Spring 1997): pp. 74–83.
10. Josef Maria Eder, *La photographie instantanée: Son application aux arts et aux sciences*, trans. O. Campo of 2nd German edition (Paris: Gauthier-Villars, 1888), p. 13.
11. "For exposure times of no more than 1/5–1/10 of a second, it is possible to use a simple guillotine of wood or card or a spinning disc moved by a weak spring. But once exposure times must be further reduced, it is necessary to use more powerful springs or, better still, precise mechanisms in which two holes are quickly and regularly opened and closed by moving them backwards. The shutters of Thury and Amey, Hunter and Sands, and so on are of this kind, enabling them to vary exposure from 1 to 1/400 of a second." Eder, *La photographie instantanée*, p. 17.
12. T. C. Roche, *How to Make Photographs: A Manual for Amateurs*, ed. H. T. Anthony (New York: E. and H. T. Anthony, 1883), p. 77.
13. For Marey's work, see Michel Frizot, *E. J. Marey: Chronophotographe* (Paris: Delpire éditeur, 2001).
14. E. J. Marey, *Le mouvement* (Paris: Masson, 1893), p. 14.
15. What matters here is the nature of the outline in the image and hence its movement over the sensitive surface during a short period of time. The farther off the subject, the smaller its image and the lesser its movement. But if the negative is to be enlarged to obtain a print, the blur caused by the movement becomes more visible.
16. Eder, *La photographie instantanée*, p. 201.
17. Ibid., pp. 203–4.
18. Auguste Rodin, *L'art: Entretiens réunis par Paul Gsell* (Paris: Grasset, 1911), p. 63.
19. Ibid. Rodin then produced *L'homme qui marche* (Man Walking) (1900), without head or arms and with the legs and torso of John the Baptist. This "abstract" vision of walking, false from the physiological point of view, epitomizes Rodin's confidence in "his own" form of representation.
20. Rodin's use of the word *conventional* is the direct opposite of Eder's. For Rodin photography was conventional, whereas for Eder the representations of painting before photography were conventional.
21. Georges Brunel and Paul Chaux, *La photographie en plein air, excursionniste et instantanée* (Paris: Bernard Tignol, 1897–99), p. 75.
22. Jacques Ducom, *Les débuts d'un photographe amateur* (2nd ed., Paris: Georges Carré and G. Naud, 1898), p. 91.
23. Ibid.
24. *L'instantané*, a small supplement to the *Revue hebdomadaire*, was published from 1897 to 1920.

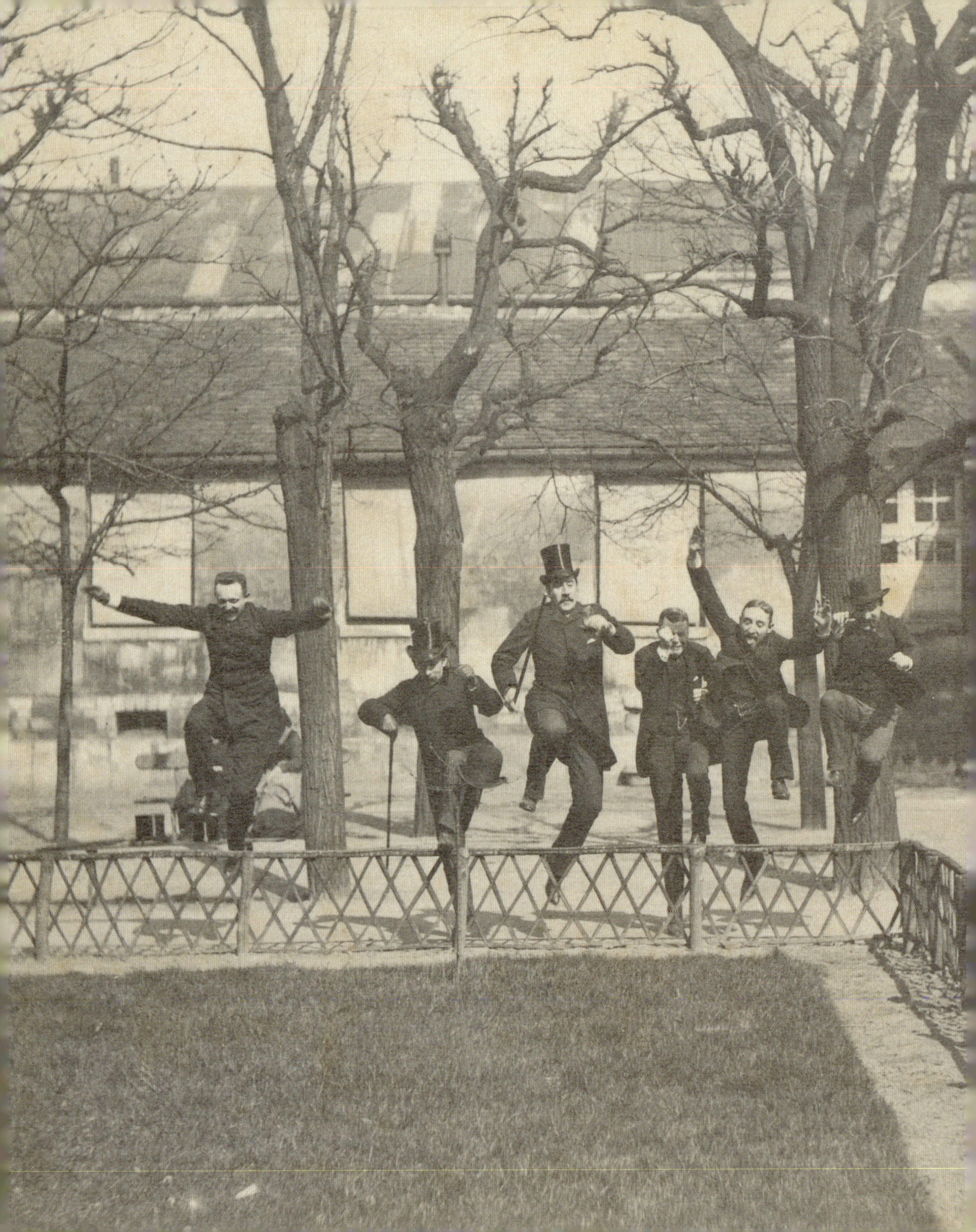

A Sense of Context: Amateur Photography in the Late Nineteenth Century

Clément Chéroux

Over the course of the nineteenth century, the meaning of the French word *amateur* changed. When the century began, the amateur was a connoisseur, a man who cultivated a passion for the arts and sciences with a noble high-mindedness. His expertise was almost equivalent, if not superior, to that of a professional. By the century's end, with the democratization of sport, science, and technology, the word had become more widely applicable. *Amateur* and its derivative *amateurisme*, which, according to the *Dictionnaire historique de la langue française*, was first used by bicyclists in 1892 to mean a "lack of professionalism," had begun acquiring derogatory connotations.[1] The amateur had now become the antithesis of the professional, with all that implied in terms of lack of knowledge and rigor; he had become a mere dilettante.

The development of amateur photography in the nineteenth century mirrors the semantic evolution of the term. The early generations of amateurs in the 1840s were proficient technicians. Generally members of the aristocracy or bourgeoisie, they were experienced practitioners with an extensive knowledge of chemistry, physics, and photographic optics. They would own several cameras of different formats and a well-equipped laboratory. They would meet in societies and clubs and be informed about the most recent inventions—when they were not themselves the inventors. Their images bear the traces of this interest in photographic technology and laboratory manipulation, often being the results of experiments with a new lens or emulsion. This passion for the technical aspect drove them to feats of camerawork involving subjects that were rare or hard to photograph (too fast, poorly lit, against the light), awkward situations in which to take photographs (from a moving position, in low light), and experimentation in the darkroom (superimposition, montage, toning). With the arrival of gelatin silver-bromide emulsion in the early 1880s, they concentrated on the capacity of the new process to capture movement. For a while, their world seemed to consist entirely of leaping acrobats, galloping horses, and speeding trains (figs. 1–3).[2]

DETAIL OF FIG. 1

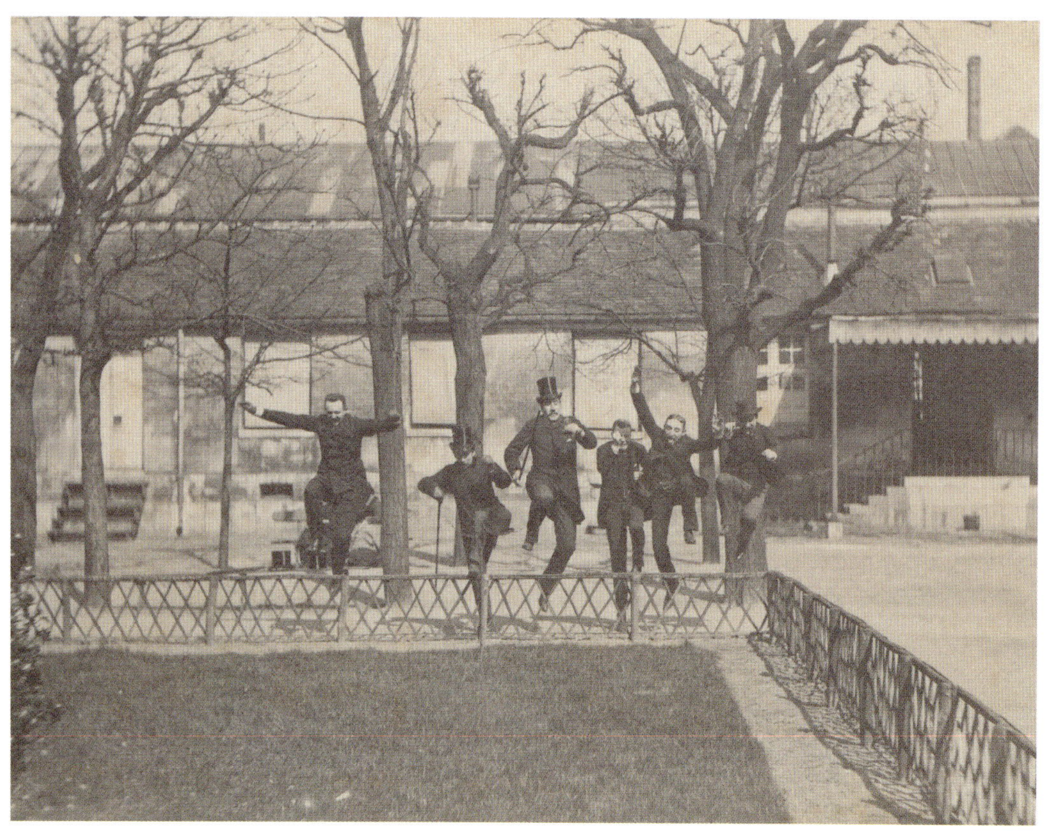

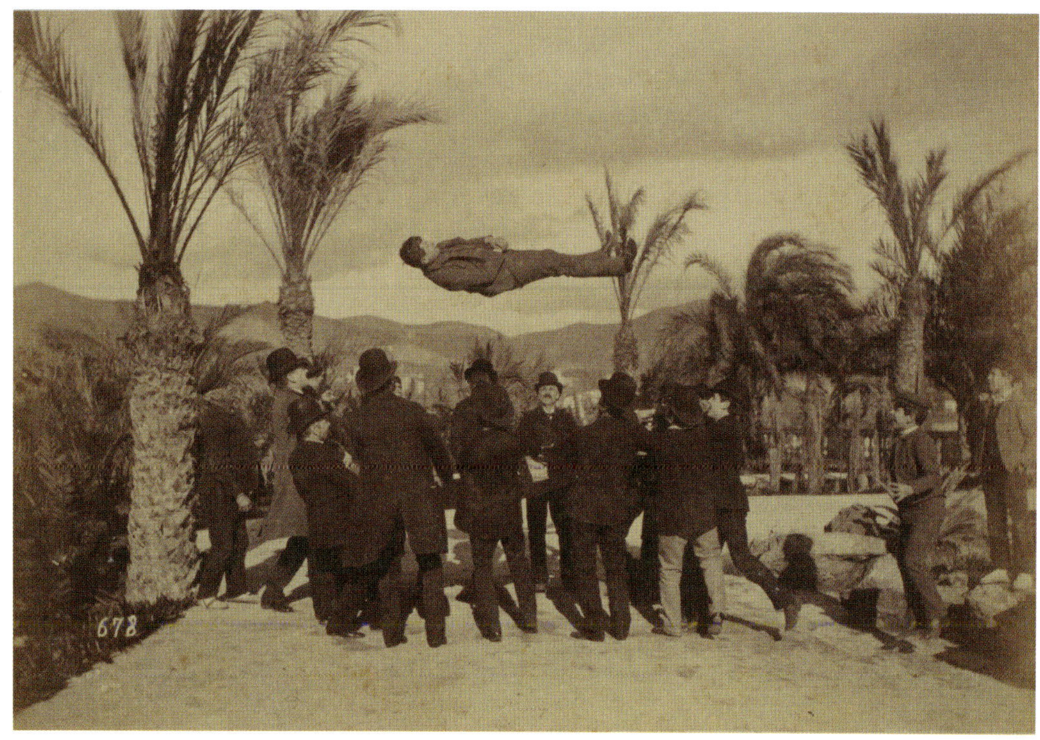

FIG. 1. Albert Londe, Jumping the barrier, Salpêtrière gardens, ca. 1888. Platinotype, 4⅝ x 6⅛ in. (11.7 x 15.7 cm). ASOAL/ Société française de photographie, Paris

FIG. 2. Kimm, *A la couverte* (On the Blanket), 1888. Photograph published in *L'amateur photographe* (March 1889). Albumen print, 4¾ x 6⅞ in. (12 x 17.5 cm). Société française de photographie, Paris

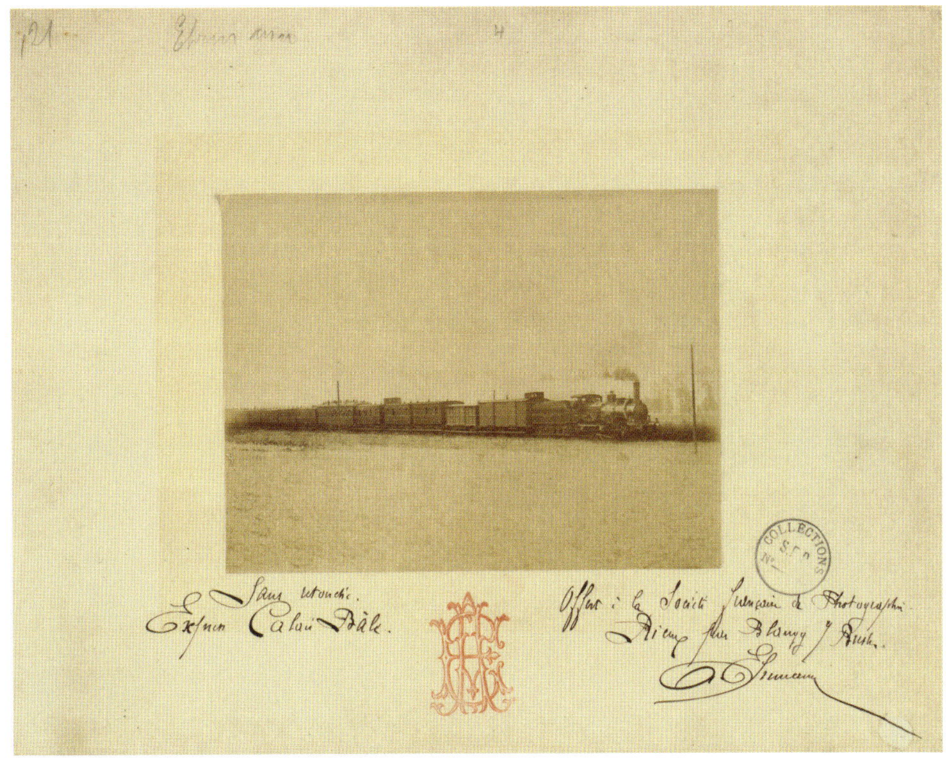

FIG. 3. Alfred Ehrmann, *Express Calais-Bâle*, 1888. Albumen print, 4³/₄ x 6³/₈ in. (12 x 16.3 cm). Société française de photographie, Paris

In addition to its greater speed, gelatin silver-bromide emulsion had the advantage of being a dry process. Previously, in the days of wet collodion, the photographer had been obliged to prepare the plates, take the photograph, and develop the image in quick succession. But because gelatin silver-bromide emulsion was a dry process with greater stability, it became possible to separate the different stages of the photographic process and, crucially, to relieve the photographer of the need to undertake the more difficult among them. George Eastman clearly understood this when he introduced the Kodak in 1888.[3] His cameras were sold already loaded with 100-exposure rolls of film. The focus, aperture, and shutter speed were preset, so the process of taking a photograph was quite simple, involving no more than pointing the camera at the subject and pressing the button. Eastman's company also developed and printed the resulting images: "You press the button, we do the rest," as its advertising slogan aptly put it (fig. 4). Released from the need to perform difficult, meticulous tasks in a dark, hot, and stuffy laboratory, amateurs now could concentrate on the pleasure of capturing the image. The number of amateur photographers rose dramatically as photography became more attractive and garnered new enthusiasts. In 1900, in France, they numbered between two hundred fifty thousand and three hundred thousand, according to figures from the Ministry of Trade and Industry—in other words, around 1 percent of the nation's population.[4]

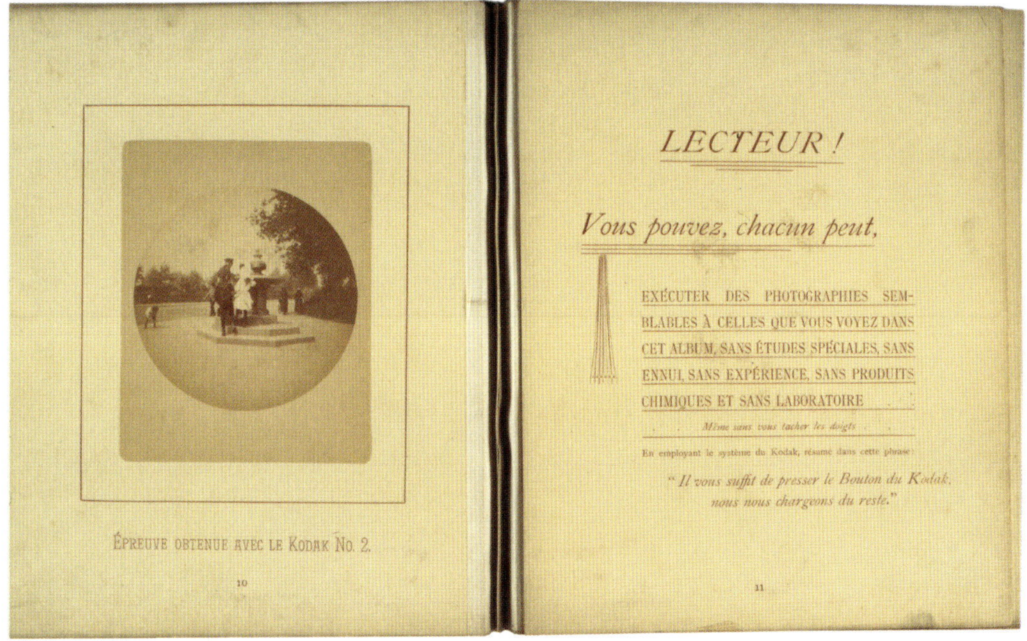

FIG. 4. Kodak publicity album, ca. 1900, pp. 10–11. Société française de photographie, Paris

The same source, however, reveals that only one amateur photographer in forty belonged to a photography club. This indicates that the arrival of gelatin silver-bromide emulsion and subsequent development of ready-to-use cameras had triggered the emergence of a fresh form of amateurism. The new amateurs differed from the earlier experts in that they tended to take photographs in a family context rather than as members of a club. This gave rise to the popularity of family photographs, which everybody involved, including women and children, could take. Furthermore, almost all the subjects photographed related to family life, from wedding ceremonies to holiday memories to baby's first steps (figs. 5–7). These new amateurs were notably uninterested in technical matters. They used simple cameras and seldom developed or printed their own pictures. They were not so much interested in photography itself as in its capacity to record and preserve moments of domestic life, and they spent more time looking at their photographs than they did making them. Their images — often badly framed and out of focus (fig. 8) — have nothing in common with those of the experts, whose collections resemble catalogues of technical feats. The era of the snapshot had arrived.[5] So the difference between expert amateurism and dilettante use lay not just in the context or manner in which photography was practiced but also in the aesthetics of the images. Although both practices are described as "amateur," they are profoundly different. The difficulties historians confront in considering amateur photography lie both in the evolution of the general meaning of the word *amateur* during the nineteenth century and in the coexistence, from the late 1880s on, of these two distinct approaches to the medium.

To gain a better understanding of the photographs taken by Pierre Bonnard, George Hendrik Breitner, Maurice Denis, Henri Evenepoel, Henri Rivière, Félix Vallotton, and Edouard Vuillard around the turn of the century, it is important to consider this distinction.[6] Where photography was concerned, these painters were undoubtedly amateurs, but in which category? None of them seems to have belonged to a photography club, and they all took pictures in family settings, often passing the camera around. With a few exceptions in the case of Breitner and Rivière, most of their subjects are aspects of domestic life — children's games, sightseeing trips, holidays in the country or by the sea, shared moments of happiness, portraits of friends and family, and so on. The few accounts we have suggest that they had little interest in the technical side. Typically, they used a Kodak or similar camera and only rarely developed or printed their own pictures. In the Vuillard household, rolls of film were either taken to the nearest photography shop or printed by the artist's mother. In his journal, Vuillard noted, "Take photos to be developed so as not to lose time."[7] Four days earlier, he mentioned having spent part of the day looking at family photographs with his friends Arthur Fontaine and Ker-Xavier Roussel. As often for these amateurs, time was spent looking at the images rather than making them; as a result, they typically were taken in a hurry, badly exposed, and as unremarkable as most others collected in family albums of the day.

Apparently then, these artists approached photography not just as amateurs but also as complete dilettantes. This distinction enables us to define the reasons for their interest in the medium more precisely, evaluate the formal qualities of their images more successfully, and dispassionately assess the possible effects of their photographic images on their paintings and other work. Primarily motivated by the impulse to record family

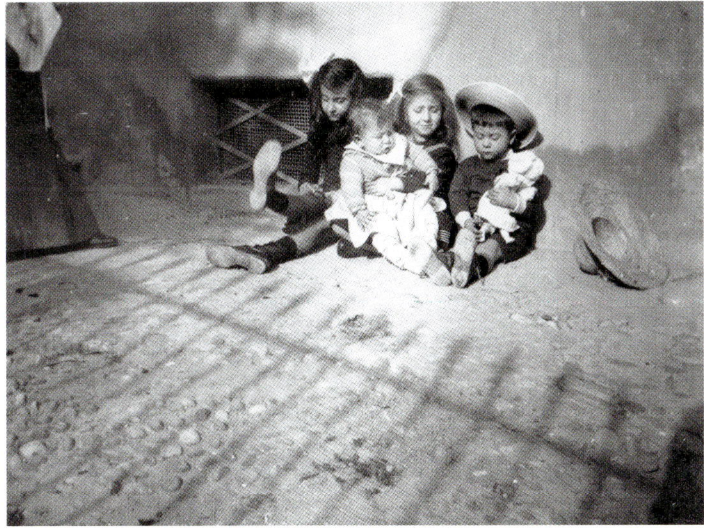

FIG. 5. Anonymous amateur, Children playing on the ground, ca. 1900. Gelatin silver print, 2⅞ x 4 in. (7.4 x 10.2 cm). Private collection

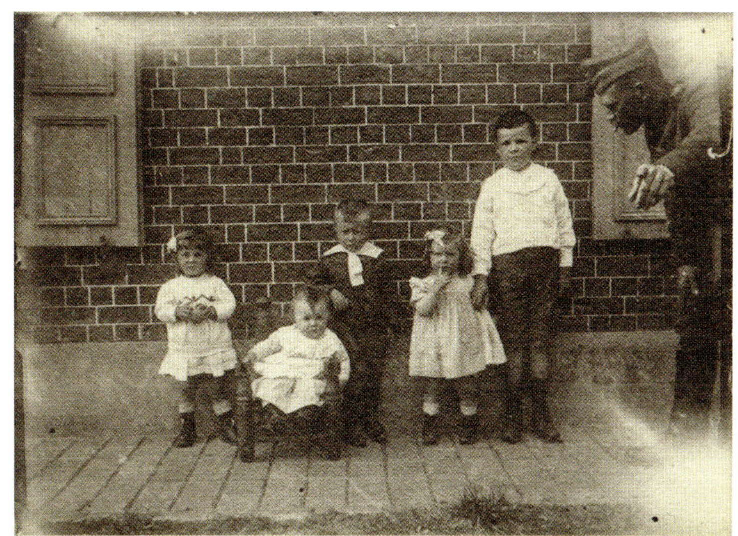

FIG. 6. Anonymous amateur, Five children and an adult pointing at the photographer, ca. 1900. Gelatin silver print, 2½ x 3½ in. (6.4 x 8.9 cm). Private collection

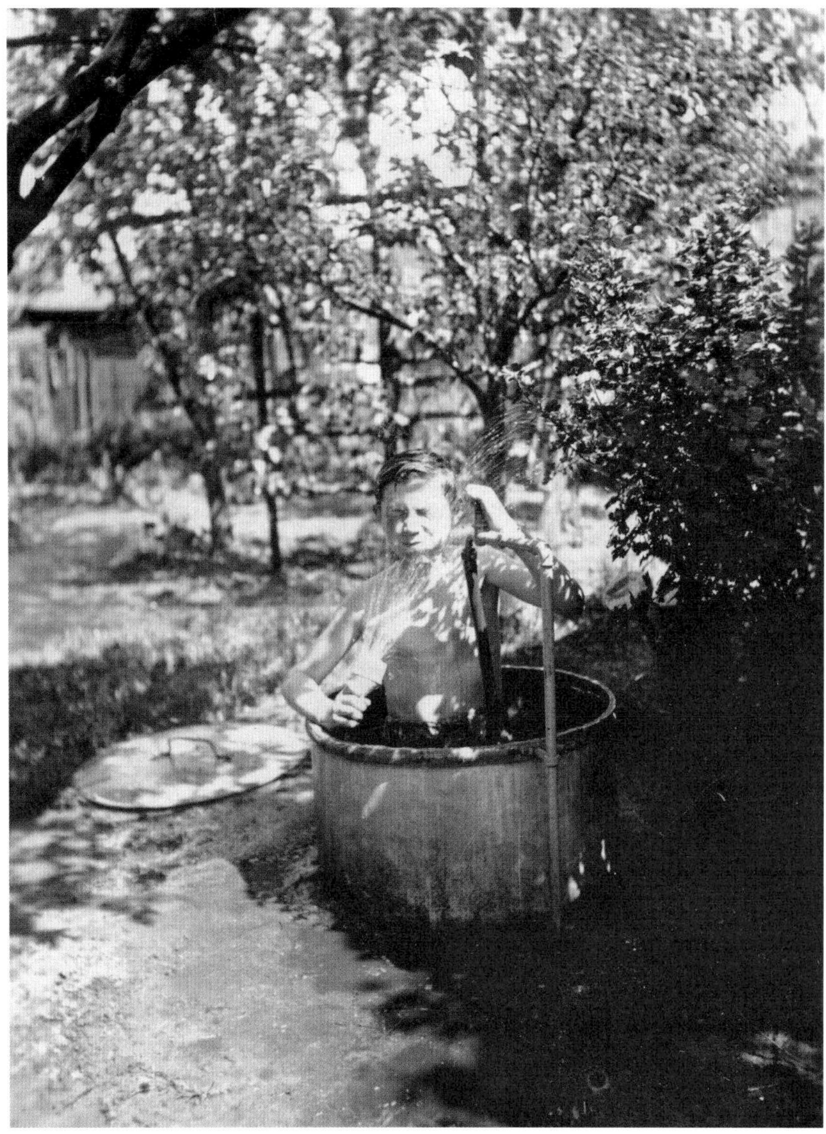

FIG. 7. Anonymous amateur, Child playing with water in a garden, ca. 1910. Gelatin silver print, 4³/₈ x 3¹/₄ in. (11 x 8.2 cm). Private collection

memories, Bonnard, Breitner, Denis, Evenepoel, Rivière, Vallotton, and Vuillard rarely meant their photographs to serve as models or preparatory studies for paintings and prints, unlike those of, say, Edgar Degas, Thomas Eakins, and José-Maria Sert. They were taken on the spur of the moment, not staged in any kind of premeditated or systematic way or intended as elements of a series. Nor do they meet the usual criteria of visual investigation or experimentation. These are photographs shot by and for the family, with no artistic intention — or *Kunstwollen* (artistic will), as defined by the Austrian art historian Aloïs Riegl during the same period. Yet the fact that they were produced without deliberate aesthetic aim does not mean they lack visual interest. As Susan Sontag noted in her

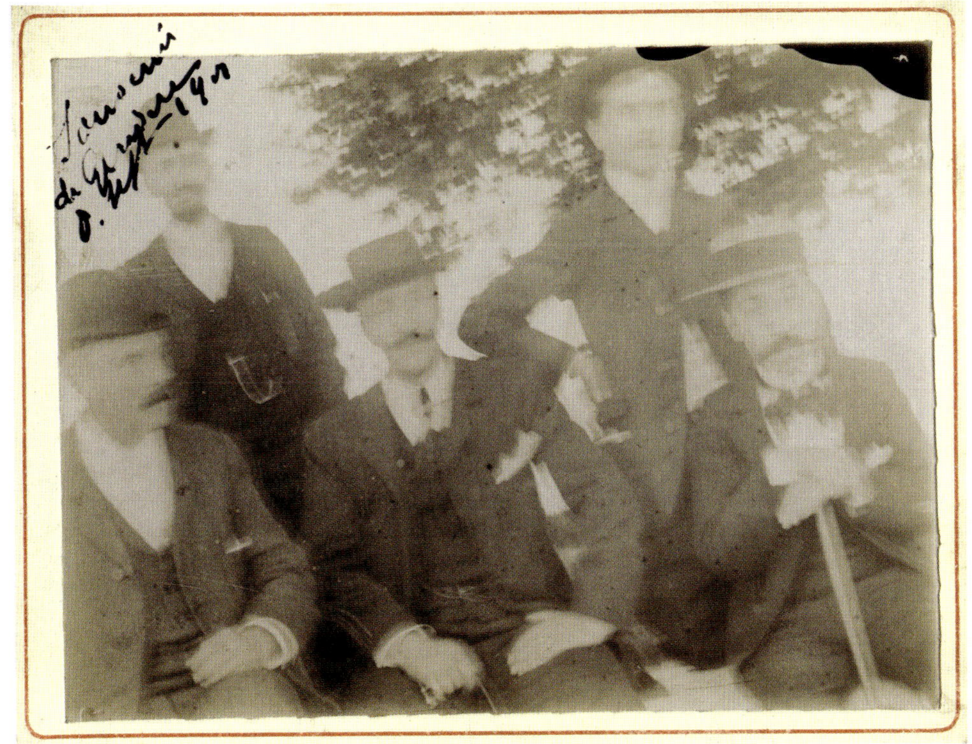

FIG. 8. Anonymous amateur, Souvenirs, 1901. Gelatin silver print, 3¹/₈ x 4³/₈ in. (8 x 11.1 cm). Private collection

seminal work *On Photography*, a simple snapshot with no artistic pretensions can be "as visually interesting, as eloquent, as beautiful as the most acclaimed fine-art photographs."[8]

Although made by dilettante amateurs, the images gathered for this exhibition and catalogue have undeniable aesthetic qualities, which are less the expression of artistic intent as the result of many other factors. Where amateur photographs are concerned, the shooting of an image is motivated above all by the desire to preserve the trace of a subject; this is primarily what dictates the form of the images produced. If Rivière's photographs are noticeably different from the others, it is because he stepped outside the family context more often, turning his attention to other motifs. The aesthetics of these images are also largely dependent on technical aspects: the focal length of the lens, the presence or absence of a viewfinder, whether the camera was held at stomach height or in front of the face, and so on. If, for example, Denis's pictures are similar to Breitner's, it is less a matter of eye or style than of camera. But above and beyond the characteristics of their cameras, it is perhaps the lack of technical knowledge that most determined the appearance of their photographs. The inexperience of these amateurs led to many small errors—blurring, inelegant positions caught as they happened, bodies that look strangely fragmented, shots taken against the light, and optical distortions—that ultimately gave their work a visual quality by default, an unintended artistry.[9]

The distinction between the two categories of amateur suggests that perhaps for the dilettantes, looking at their photographic images was more meaningful than making them; this is particularly apparent for the seven artists under consideration here. It is mainly during the moment of looking when artistic reinvestment of the images takes place and when the artist might decide to transform the photographic material into an idea for a painting or other work. (Likewise, it is a moment when Riegl's concept of *Kunstwollen* comes into play.) So, while the pictures themselves reflect an uncalculated aesthetics, the eye looking at them might discern artistic potential. Caution is required in this regard, however, as is a meticulous, case-by-case approach. Art history has often reduced the relationship between painting and photography to being merely the reproduction of a photograph on a canvas. But for the artists discussed here, such an analogical approach is misguided. Of some two thousand family photographs Vuillard took, he drew upon very few while painting. Rather than transferring photographic motifs onto canvas, these amateurs seemed to consider certain formal characteristics that are specifically photographic: optical distortion, the flattening of the image, fragmentation, effects of lighting and contrast, and high and low angles. Seldom are the effects of photography on painting direct and complete; rather, they tend to be diffuse and multifaceted.

The artists with whom we are concerned here did not require photography to serve their art — that is, to be the basis for their paintings or prints. They took photographs without preconceptions and only later realized they could use them as visual sources. This introduces a fundamental distinction into assumptions about the history of the relationship between photography and painting. Consider, for instance, that the models in the photographs of Julien Vallou de Villeuneuve and Eugène Durieu, used by Gustave Courbet and Eugène Delacroix, respectively, adopted poses dictated by the canons of academic painting. Eadweard Muybridge's views of the moving bodies he documented are also determined by the use his clients, mostly painters and sculptors, intended to make of them. Yet because the photographs in this exhibition and book were made without artistic intent, they more clearly display their photographic nature, which has not been entirely effaced by *Kunstwollen*. Their characteristic faults (poor framing, distortions, blurring, and so on), which are absent from the professional work of Vallou de Villeuneuve, Durieu, and Muybridge, make their photographic nature — and that of the photographic process — more apparent. Because they generally took pictures unbound by aesthetic considerations, and also because they were true amateurs, Bonnard, Breitner, Denis, Evenepoel, Rivière, Vallotton, and Vuillard produced images that seem refreshingly liberated. And it is precisely the freedom afforded by new, alternative forms that led them to look with fresh eyes at their simple family photographs.

The artists represented in the present study belonged to the first generation to use cameras as dilettantes. They were also among the first to recognize a specifically photographic aesthetic in this practice, before introducing some of its characteristics into their art. In this way, they were decades ahead of many artists working in the second half of the twentieth century in the currents of Pop, hyperrealism, new realism, narrative figuration, and capitalist realism who painted after family photographs. Robert Bechtle, Franz Gertsch, Richard Hamilton, Malcolm Morley, and Gerhard Richter, to mention only a few, undoubtedly shared with Vuillard the idea that, in comparison to photography, painting always had "the advantage of being hand-made."[10] It is surely no coincidence that historians' interest in the photographs of Bonnard, Breitner, Vallotton, and Vuillard came late, at the very time these artists of the 1960s and 1970s were gaining institutional recognition.

NOTES

1. Alain Rey, ed., *Dictionnaire historique de la langue française* (Paris: Le Robert, 1998), pp. 103–4.
2. See Denis Bernard and André Gunthert, *L'instant rêvé: Albert Londe* (Nîmes: Jacqueline Chambon; Laval: Trois, 1993).
3. See Douglas Collins, *The Story of Kodak* (New York: Harry N. Abrams, 1990); and François Brunet, "Refondations: Le moment Kodak," in *La naissance de l'idée de photographie* (Paris: Presses universitaires de France, 2000), pp. 213–329.
4. Louis Gastine, "L'oeuvre des sociétés photographiques françaises," *La photographie française* (1902): pp. 231–32.
5. See Timm Starl, *Knipser: Die Bildgeschichte der privaten Fotografie* (Munich: Fotomuseum im Münchner Stadtmuseum, 1995); Sarah Greenough and Diane Waggoner, eds., *The Art of American Snapshot, 1888–1978* (Washington, D.C.: National Gallery of Art; Princeton, N.J.: Princeton University Press, 2007); and Barbara Levine and Stephane Snyder, eds., *Snapshot Chronicles: Inventing the American Photo Album* (New York: Princeton Architectural Press, 2006).
6. Françoise Heilbrun and Philippe Néagu, *Pierre Bonnard, photographe* (Paris: Philippe Sers and Réunion des Musées nationaux, 1987); Jean-François Chevrier, "Bonnard et la photographie," in *Bonnard* (Paris: Centre Pompidou, 1984), pp. 219–39; Michel Frizot, "Pierre l'éberlué: L'ouvert de la photographie," in *Bonnard: L'oeuvre d'art, un arrêt du temps* (Paris: Paris Musée; Ludion, 2006), pp. 262–67; Françoise Heilbrun and Saskia Ooms, *Maurice Denis* (Paris: Musée d'Orsay; Milan: 5 Continents, 2006); François Fossier, Françoise Heilbrun, and Philippe Néagu, *Henri Rivière, graveur et photographe* (Paris: Réunion des musées nationaux, 1988); Elizabeth W. Easton, "Vuillard's Photography," *Apollo* (June 1994): pp. 9–17; Isabelle de la Brunière and Philippe Grapeloup, "Valloton and the Camera," *Apollo* (June 1994): pp. 18–23; and Dorothy Kosinski, ed., *The Artist and the Camera* (New Haven, Conn.: Yale University Press, 2000).
7. "Porte photos à développer pour ne pas y perdre mon temps." Edouard Vuillard as quoted in Emilie Daniel, "L'objectif du subjectif: Vuillard Photographe," *Cahiers du Musée national d'art moderne*, no. 23 (Spring 1988): p. 83.
8. Susan Sontag, *On Photography* (London: Penguin, 1979), p. 103.
9. See Clément Chéroux, *Fautographie: Petite histoire de l'erreur photographique* (Belgium: Crisnée; Paris: Yellow Now, 2003).
10. "L'avantage d'être faite à la main." Edouard Vuillard as quoted in Jacques Salomon, "Vuillard et son Kodak," *L'oeil*, no. 100 (April 1963): p. 19.

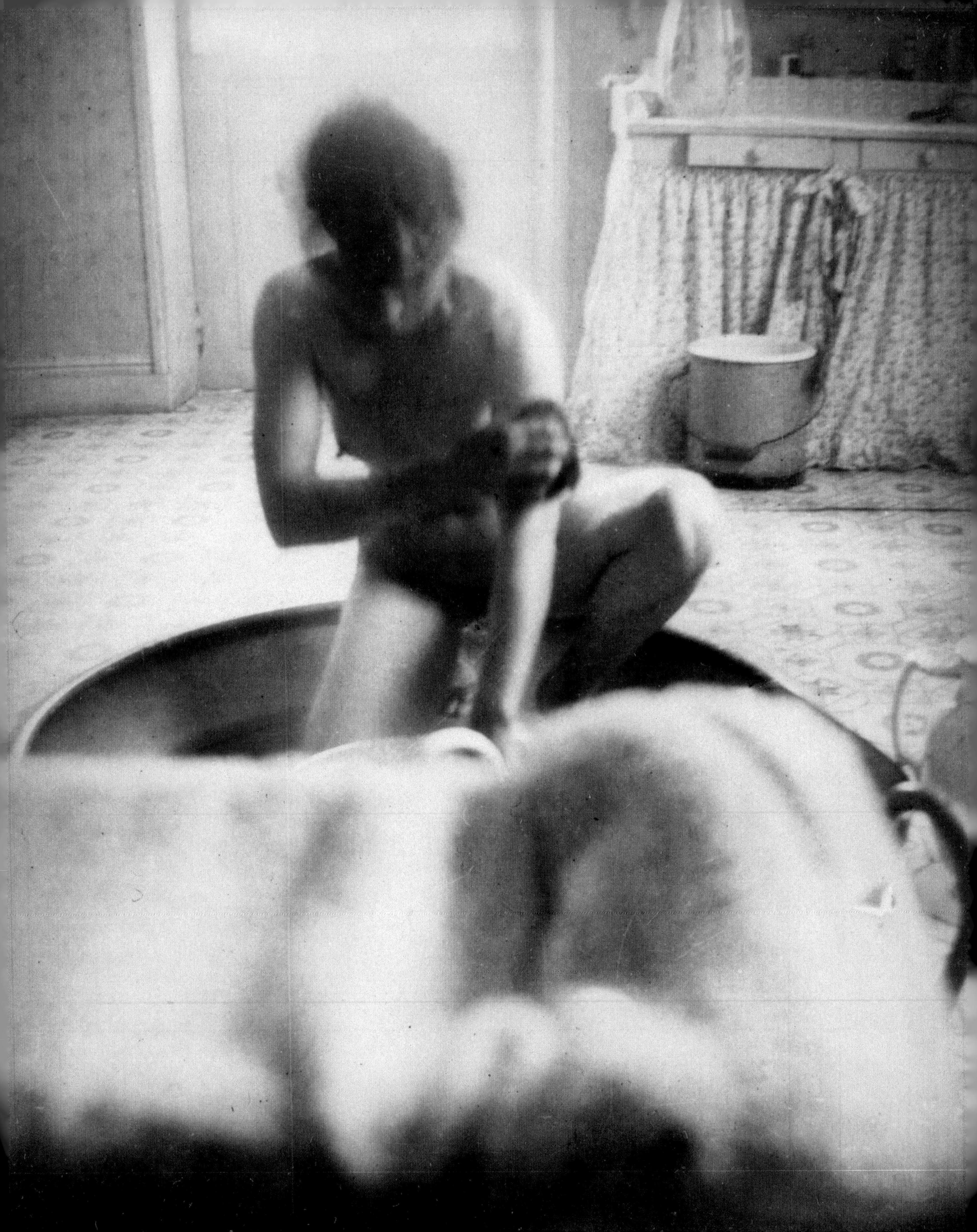

Sneak Previews: Nude Photographs by Pierre Bonnard and George Hendrik Breitner

Anne McCauley

In 1885, an enthusiastic Wall Street broker noted all the remarkable things that could be captured with the new, handheld detective camera—"street scenes about New York and other cities, scenes about the river front and on the harbor, scenes pathetic, scenes comical, scenes picturesque, and scenes that no adjective will describe."[1] Significantly, what he didn't mention were nudes. How to take pictures of naked men and women, whether in prudish America or carefree Paris, did not figure in the manuals and publicity campaigns directed at amateurs who avidly snapped up the easy-to-use box cameras. Although the prospect of being a sleuth, hiding cameras in vests and picnic baskets, may have excited consumers eager to nab thieves or sneak pictures of bathing beauties at Narragansett Beach, the official photographic establishment asserted that "most of the young picture takers are gentlemen and do not attempt to steal likenesses of strangers by snap shots."[2]

Gentlemen were, nonetheless, taking advantage of unobtrusive, small cameras to invade the privacy of people in the public sphere and, at the same time, recognizing they now were equipped to craft much less spontaneous scenarios with loved ones or paid models in their bedrooms. Some of those gentlemen were artists, such as the Frenchman Pierre Bonnard and the Dutch painter George Hendrik Breitner, both of whom began using cameras when they were around thirty years old, with their careers on the ascent. Their photographs of undressed young women were only a small part of larger campaigns to preserve family outings and foreign travel (for Bonnard) or the working people, street life, and architecture of Amsterdam (for Breitner). But unlike their more public snapshots—public in the sense of where they were shot and to whom they could be shown—the nude studies were secret, incriminating treasures within the bigger secret of artists taking photographs at all.

Just as Bonnard and Breitner's styles as painters differed, so too did their infrequent photographs of nudes, which bear the signs of their individual visual sensibilities and sexual tastes. Bonnard painted and drew the nude hundreds of times over the course of

DETAIL OF CAT. 30

his long career, but, according to surviving evidence (which may be deceptive), he only photographed them during four sessions and rarely based a painting exactly on a photograph. By contrast, Breitner painted nudes only during the late 1880s and 1890s but promiscuously photographed many models during that period in poses ranging from disinterested to overtly erotic. Emulating French naturalist literature and the studio novels of Emile Zola and the brothers Edmond and Jules Goncourt, Breitner appreciated non-idealized details in both his photographs and his oils, whereas Bonnard made a cult of avoiding careful modeling in favor of hesitant, broken contours and flat areas of tone.

Bonnard launched his photographic figure studies when two factors coincided: he had a mistress who agreed to pose for him, and he was faced with book-illustration projects that forced him to generate drawings in short order. In 1893 he had met Maria Boursin (née Marthe de Méligny), who hid her modest origins and real name but eagerly uncovered her black stockings and chemise for Bonnard's drawings and lithographs. In what may be his earliest photographs of her, made around 1897 to 1899, she sits or reclines on the near side of an unkempt, narrow bed strewn with her clothes, umbrella, and castoff boots, in front of an elaborate porcelain heater and exotic Indian textiles (cats. 26, 28). Either propping the camera on a table or resting it on his lap (it is only slightly above the level of the low mattress), Bonnard kept the vantage point and framing remarkably constant as he directed Marthe through ten poses that seem like distorted dreams of the history of art. She awkwardly rests her left leg on the floor with her right calf tucked under her body while her hands extend behind her to keep her torso erect; pulls her knees up and clasps her hands to approximate the famous profile of Hippolyte Flandrin's *Young Man by the Sea* (1837; Musée du Louvre, Paris); balances on the edge of the bed facing frontally with her feet on the floor, while shifting her arms to the left and then behind her; radically turns her back to the camera like a legless version of Ingres's *Valpinçon Bather* (1808; Musée du Louvre); and, in the majority of views, plays on conventional imagery of reclining odalisques from Ingres to Manet. The camera frames a tight, horizontal swath that excludes the entire length of the bed or any clear markers of the three-dimensional space of the room. Marthe's body is the center of attention here, even though her face is largely hidden and her eyes diverted.

What is striking about these tiny (1½ x 2 inch) contact prints, admittedly amateur efforts, is how bad they are. Bonnard did not bother to clean up the objects on the bed or arrange the background, because he knew in advance that he was only interested in the figure. More problematic was the lighting. Most early, handheld cameras were designed for outdoor shooting, but the Pocket Kodak Model '96 that Bonnard used had three stops, which allowed greater flexibility. Given that Marthe's face is blurred in several of the images and her body bleached out, we can speculate that he found the 1/20-second exposure too fast even with the most open stop (*f*/10), and thus tried the bulb setting, which let him keep the shutter open longer. Or else he tried to direct artificial light onto the foreground; some strong cast shadows behind her arm suggest this. He may even have placed a lighted candle on the heater.

It is generally recognized that these photographs are similar in subject to Bonnard's contemporaneous paintings, which updated the nudes of the Impressionist generation by introducing more radical vantage points, harsh flat lighting, and scandalous exposés of the psychological tension between a nude artist and his infantilized, self-absorbed nude model (cat. 18). In their play of poses on a bed, they are close in spirit to a shockingly frank confessional novel by the Danish writer Peter Nansen that the staff of *La revue blanche* commissioned Bonnard to illustrate in 1896. *Marie*, serialized in the magazine with the artist's drawings in 1897 and essentially set in the bedroom of the first-person narrator, could have been an autobiography of Bonnard, so close was its heroine to Marthe, with her pink-and-white flesh, flower-printed blouse, childlike innocence, and ingenuous willingness to succumb to her lover. Bonnard's earlier paintings of a mop-haired girl putting on black stockings (see cat. 18) were seamlessly recast as illustrations to the story, in which the narrator helps Marie take off her stockings (white, rather than black; fig. 1) and describes his delight in watching her undress, changing personality with each layer of

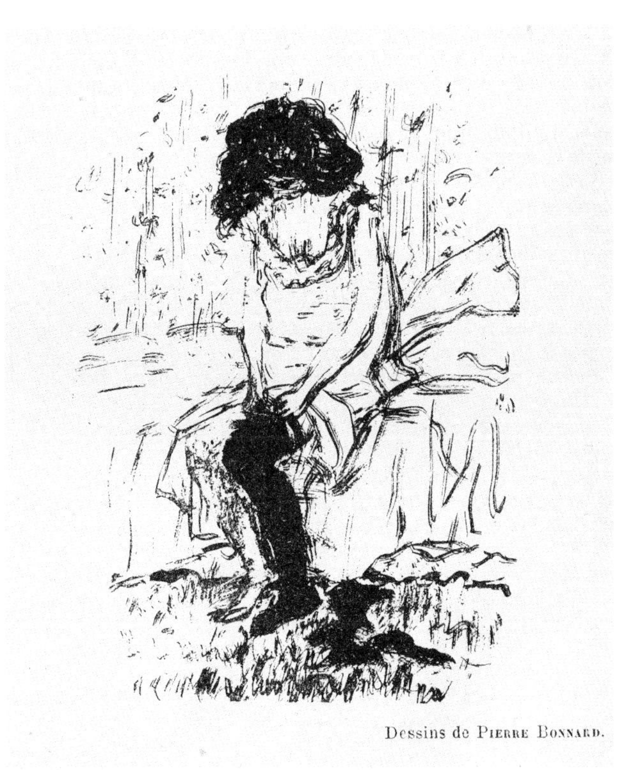

FIG. 1. Pierre Bonnard, illustration for *Marie*, *La revue blanche*, 1897, p. 700

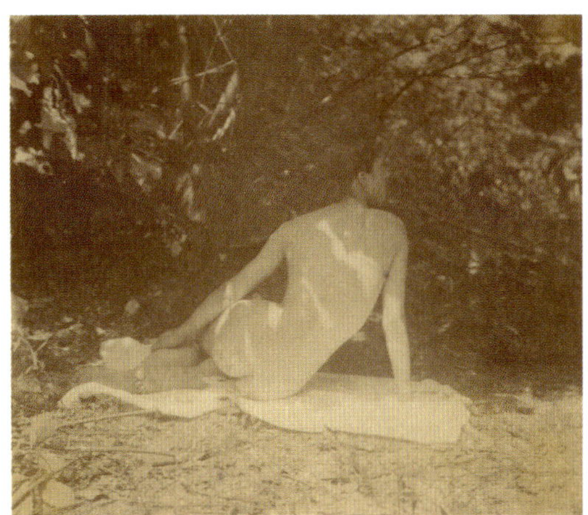

FIG. 2. Thomas Eakins, Susan Macdowell Eakins, nude, sitting on a blanket, looking over her right shoulder, outdoors, ca. 1883. Cyanotype, 3¼ x 3¾ in. (8.3 x 9.5 cm). Pennsylvania Academy of the Fine Arts, Philadelphia. Charles Bregler's Thomas Eakins Collection, purchased with the partial support of the Pew Memorial Trust

clothes until, in her nightgown, she is "only a little girl, a little girl who extends her arms to ask to be put to bed."[3] The proximity in time of the four drawings for Nansen's novel that feature nude or partially undressed views of Marie/Marthe (among other illustrations) and the purchase of a camera (only available after 1896) suggests a connection between the two.

Bonnard's new commission from the art dealer and publisher Ambroise Vollard around 1898 to illustrate the late Paul Verlaine's book of erotic poems, *Parallèlement*, yielded 109 published lithographs.[4] It also pressured the artist to depict numerous views of lesbian lovers in bed (for the first section, "Les amies") and adored mistresses (for "Filles"). As Antoine Terrasse and Philippe Néagu were the first to note, the bedroom photographs formed the basis for the hesitant contour drawings that appear at the end of two poems, "Eté" (Summer) in the section inspired by lesbian love, and "Limbes" (Limbo), an allegorized evocation of the play between imagination and thought (cat. 27).[5] In neither case, however, does Bonnard's lithograph illustrate its adjacent poem; the nudes are minimal signifiers of anonymous femininity, detached memories of bodies that have lost their corporeality. The lack of visual specificity in the photographic contact prints is even more pronounced in the lithographs' vaporous line work, where a hand or leg disappears into the white of the paper, and the greatest graphic attention is given to areas such as the scrawl of hair or shadows behind the decapitated body that are unrelated to the narrative.

Bonnard's interest in stories of sexual awakening inspired him to negotiate with Vollard to illustrate a second book, Longus's *Daphnis et Chloé*. Apparently, Vollard had been considering giving the commission to Maurice Denis, but Bonnard rapidly completed a number of drawings, and 151 of his lithographs were included in the deluxe edition published in 1902.[6] The need for haste may be why he undertook a second photographic session with Marthe—this time, outdoors at the country house in Montval that he rented in 1900 (cats. 14–17, 19, 22). Even though he could more easily have posed Marthe inside, Longus's story gained its charm by showing the young shepherd and shepherdess discovering each other's bodies and love outside, where they kissed, bathed, and worked in total harmony with nature.

By disrobing in the garden, sheltered by dense summer foliage, Bonnard and Marthe could in a sense experience the spirit of the narrative and simultaneously study the effects of sunlight on flesh. Bonnard took most of the pictures (he appears naked in four that, presumably, she shot; cat. 25), and he choreographed Marthe through a range of poses that could serve as visual notes for the illustrations as well as for other works. With only a chair, a towel, a watering can, and her nightgown as props, she pretends to wash and dry herself, stoop down, take off her chemise, and asymmetrically touch one hand to her neck, breast, diaphragm, hip, and the ground, as he moves up toward the house or closer to include a tree trunk, always keeping her centered in the viewfinder and spotlighted in sun. Tellingly, the deep shadows blotting out Marthe's head or dappling Bonnard's own white back never entered into the Longus lithographs, which generally give no signs of a light source.[7]

In their lighting, setting, and poses, these two rolls of film, with twelve shots per roll, find few precedents in amateur or professional photography. They are perhaps closest to the mutual nude studies of Thomas Eakins and his bride, Susan, standing with a horse in a sunlit field in 1890, or to the less discreet studies Eakins made of Susan seated in shadow on a blanket around 1883, before they were married (fig. 2). But unlike Eakins's work with a larger-format camera, Bonnard in a few cases arrested Marthe in mid-gesture (fig. 3). Attempting this with a nude was controversial, since such poses were still deemed unattractive and unlike normal vision. Eadweard Muybridge's studies of galloping horses

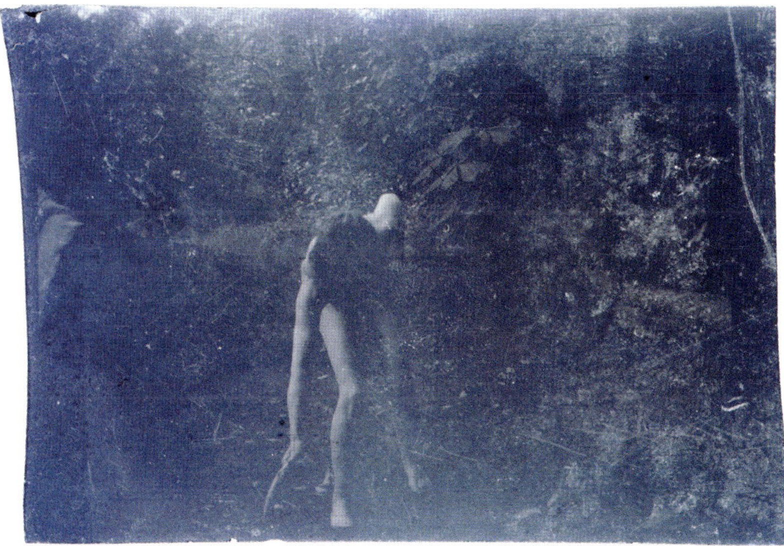

FIG. 3. Pierre Bonnard, Marthe stooping to pick up a watering can, 1900–1901. Gelatin silver print, 1½ x 2⅛ in. (3.8 x 5.3 cm). Musée d'Orsay, Paris (PHO 1987-27-26)

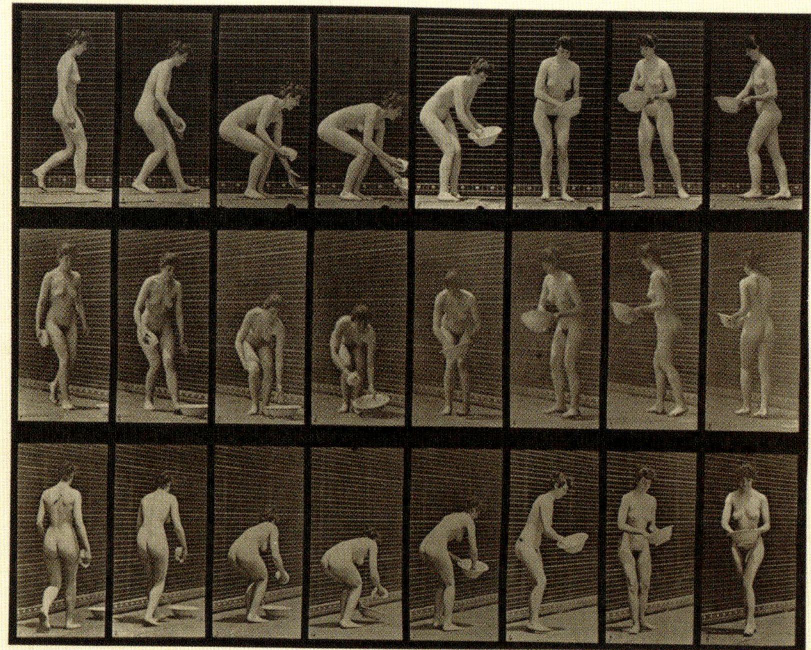

FIG. 4. Eadweard Muybridge, *Animal Locomotion: An Electric-Photographic Investigation of Consecutive Phases of Animal Movement* (Philadelphia: J. B. Lippincott, 1887), v. IV, plate 223. Collotype. Rare Books and Manuscripts, Boston Public Library

had prompted a writer in the *Gazette des beaux-arts* in 1882 to claim that such views might be acceptable to "great realists" like the Americans, but true artists "must respect the syntax governed by the elementary rules of vision."[8] Muybridge's massive compendium of 781 plates, *Animal Locomotion* (1887), volumes three and four of which were devoted to nude females, showed, for the first time, intermediary movements of women engaging in activities Muybridge and his colleagues at the University of Pennsylvania thought were appealing to painters: drinking tea, bathing (fig. 4), smoking cigarettes, lounging on the ground, and occasionally jumping or trying to throw a baseball. In direct contrast to these "scientific" motion studies, Bonnard was less interested in interrupting motion than in suggesting that the sitter was unaware of the photographer's presence. He also rejected Muybridge's preference for shooting in full sunlight in order to see as clearly as possible (and with a maximally short exposure) the subtle signs of the body's underlying skeletal and muscular structure. Even though Bonnard would have seen much more detail in the shadows than what his film recorded, he surrounded Marthe with protective greenery and kept his camera far enough away to reveal few details of her body.

The lack of visual information and subtle halftones in all of Bonnard's photographs, as well as the pointedly clumsy poses measured against contemporary professional photographic *académies* by Igout, Marconi, and Giraudon, becomes especially apparent when they are compared with Breitner's carefully staged scenarios. In some cases, Breitner knew in advance exactly what pose he wanted to photograph. A back view of a girl with both hands raised to adjust her coiffure recurs in three prints (fig. 5) and is translated, with simplifications of the background and musculature of the back, into his painting *Standing Nude before Mirror* (1893; fig. 6). This pose, staged in his studio with and without the addition of the mirror in front of the model's face and from different angles, had an astonishing resonance in the late nineteenth century. It recurs in prints by Eakins around 1898 (fig. 7) and by Pierre Louÿs, a celebrated poet, collector of erotica, and amateur photographer in the Bonnard circle, who obsessively photographed his mistress, Marie de Régnier, in various stages of undress during the 1890s. Using girls off the streets (including

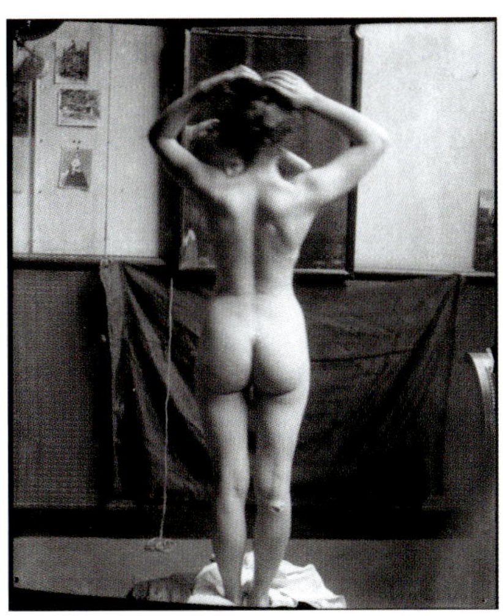

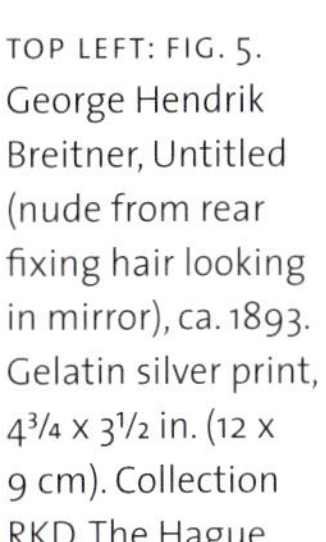

TOP LEFT: FIG. 5. George Hendrik Breitner, Untitled (nude from rear fixing hair looking in mirror), ca. 1893. Gelatin silver print, 4¾ x 3½ in. (12 x 9 cm). Collection RKD, The Hague

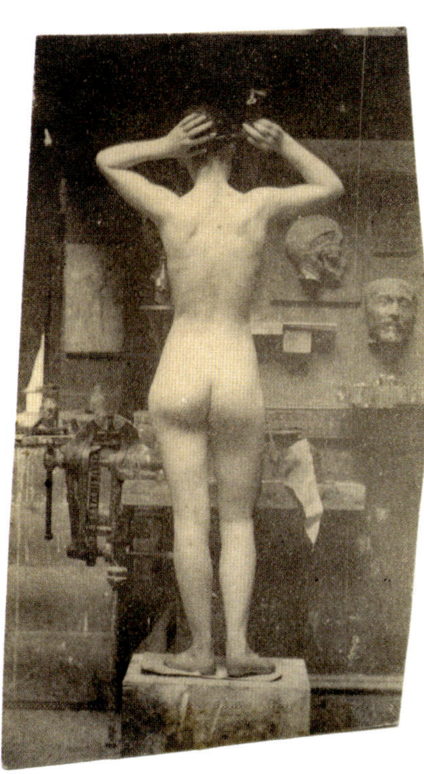

BOTTOM LEFT: FIG. 7. Thomas Eakins, Female nude standing on wooden block, arms raised, from rear, ca. 1898. Platinum print, 2¾ x 1⅛ in. (7 x 2.9 cm). Pennsylvania Academy of the Fine Arts, Philadelphia. Charles Bregler's Thomas Eakins Collection, purchased with the partial support of the Pew Memorial Trust

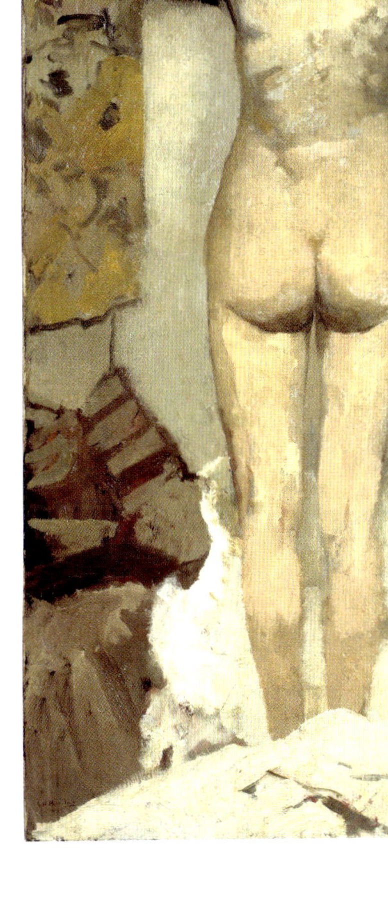

FIG. 6. George Hendrik Breitner, *Standing Nude before Mirror*, 1893. Oil on canvas, 63¾ x 29½ in. (162 x 75 cm). Museum of Fine Arts, Antwerp

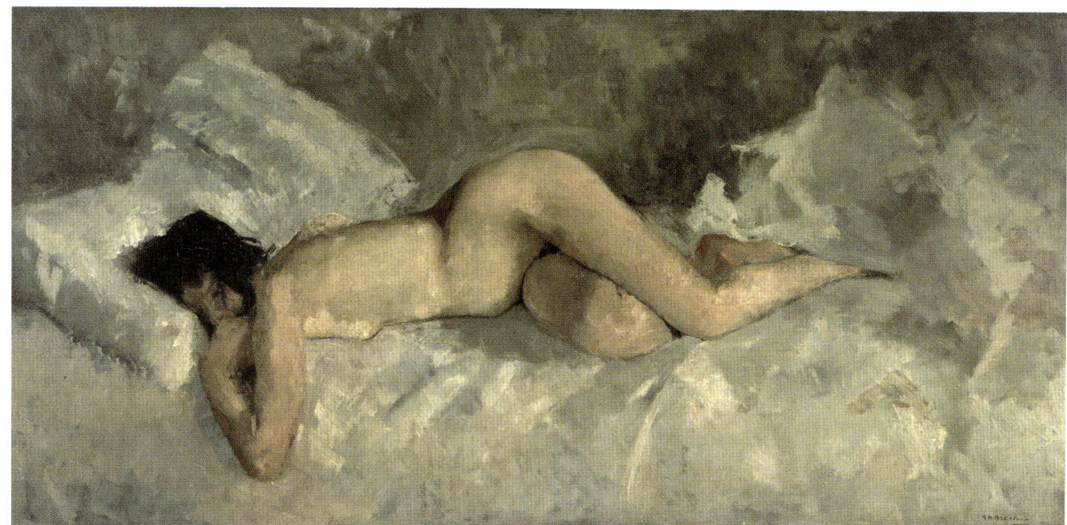

FIG. 8. George Hendrik Breitner, *Nude*, ca. 1887. Oil on canvas, 38 3/8 x 79 3/4 in. (97.5 x 202.5 cm). Collection Centraal Museum, Utrecht

a young black woman), who, as he observed in an 1893 letter, were remarkably willing to pose for him, Breitner stayed close to popular erotic stereotypes most identified with France, where he had lived in 1884 and visited in 1889.[9] For another series of photographs, he placed the models on their stomachs with an uncomfortable twist of the pelvis toward the viewer to expose their genitals (cats. 57, 58). Even though he had painted a more frontal variation of this pose in 1887–88 (now in the Stedelijk Museum, Amsterdam), he transferred from the photograph the shapes of the figure, ruffled pillow, and pile of sheets around the feet onto a rapidly brushed, pastel-hued oil painting (fig. 8).[10]

Breitner treated his reclining views as if these nude studies were ends in themselves instead of merely aides-mémoire. Never snapshots, they are carefully composed and subtly lit by indirect daylight filtered through unseen windows. In fact, as the image caught in a mirror of the photographer who stood and then bent over the viewfinder reveals, he relied on a tripod and a multiple-second exposure. In this and a second beautiful picture where a mirror doubles the image of a standing model (cat. 60), a motif popularized in erotic photographs of the 1850s, Breitner created compositions that he didn't pursue in oils; ironically, it was Bonnard who played with this mode of indirect seeing in many later paintings and drawings (see cat. 21). Breitner also made images that were overtly pornographic, encouraging two girls in black stockings to stage a lesbian romance (cat. 59) and asking undressed midinettes to spread their legs and smile at the camera or imitate Manet's *Olympia* (1863; Musée d'Orsay, Paris) (cat. 56).

Only in Breitner's least technically successful pictures does he approach the blurs and overexposures that characterize Bonnard's style. Two unusual enlargements of a bather twisting to wipe her hip and bending over a tub (fig. 9) approximate the seeming spontaneity of an atypical Bonnard negative of a squatting bather that has been dated to 1907, based on its resemblance to a painting.[11] Both photographers pay homage to Manet, who introduced a stooping bather standing in a round tub in a pastel of 1878–79, and Degas, who tilted up the vantage point and crushed the scrawny model's back onto her legs in *Le tub* (1886; Musée d'Orsay), displayed in the last Impressionist exhibition, in 1886.[12] To shoot such a scene in an often dimly lit bathroom (or studio corner, in Breitner's case) posed problems. Bonnard seems not to have looked through the viewfinder but placed the camera on a piece of furniture without removing piles of fabric that rose in front of the lens, shot toward the light, and accepted the fixed focus on the plane of the dressing table rather than on Marthe. The obstructed foreground — for all its modernist appeal to us today — was eliminated in the subsequent paintings and drawings he made of the motif, which suggests that it wasn't an acceptable distraction (cat. 31). Breitner similarly tried to fight the low light by pushing the tub next to the window, but the model still quivered, with her hand vanishing into shadow in one image.

It is tempting to regard the distortions of forms, high contrast, and signs of the specific location of the camera eye (and the viewer) as revolutions in seeing that these two artists subsequently incorporated into their paintings. For Breitner's painted nudes,

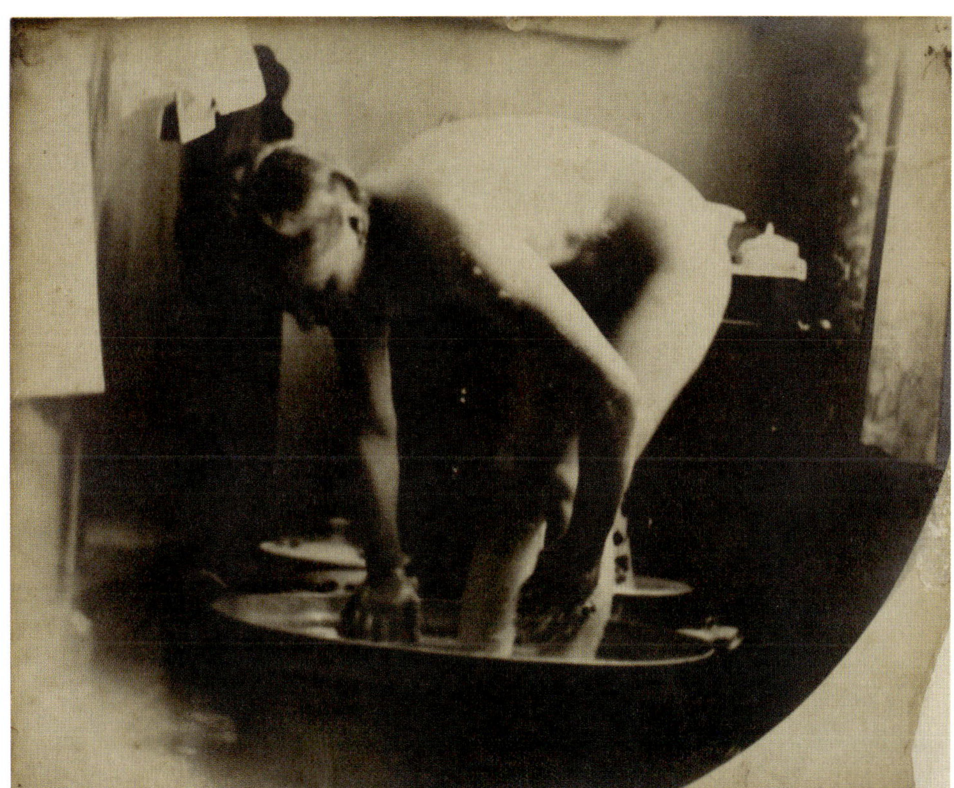

FIG. 9. George Hendrik Breitner, Bather, ca. 1890–1900. Gelatin silver print, 12 3/8 x 15 1/2 in. (31.5 x 39.4 cm). Leiden University (PK-F-GHB 078)

however, this is certainly not the case. The large bathers and the girl with her image reflected in a mirror did not make their way into compositions, and the erotic scenes in which the sitters stared at the camera remained amusing records or fantasies of flirtations and conquests in the studio.

For Bonnard, the story is more complicated, because he took as the very subject of his work the simulation of furtiveness and avoidance, double blinds in which the viewer can't quite discern the forms and the represented subjects show no signs of seeing the viewer. Gazing at his painted nudes, one can make out a triangle of pubic hair, a touch of mauve to suggest a nipple, and cartoonlike stringy contour lines representing boneless arms and legs but little to indicate the differences in texture between flesh and fabric. The faces, on the rare occasions when they are visible, are similarly doll-like — pug-nosed and pleasant but lacking personhood. Despite their desexualized bodies and cuteness, these ingénues are drawn so that their buttocks or pudenda are front and center. Thus, an uneasy tension is established as the viewer registers the stereotypical visual triggers of sexual arousal, the clueless youthfulness of the girls, and the obscuring unblended brushstrokes, which leave much to the imagination. Bonnard creates in the viewer a sensation of peering around corners, in mirrors, or staring from a close vantage point seated at a foreground table. Yet what we are allowed to see is pointedly chaste. Whereas Bonnard was forced for many years to keep his relationship with the socially unacceptable, lower-class Marthe away from the disapproving eyes of his wealthy family, he crafted in his paintings images of unguarded naked girls whose desirability could not be acknowledged.

Where does the camera fit in? As an intermediary between artist and world, the box camera redirects vision through a tiny peephole, the viewfinder, and cuts its operator out of what is going on peripherally. It is an ideal medium for people who want to distill all sensory experience instantaneously and exactly but who do not want to touch or interfere. For a culture that, increasingly, made the detective one of its heroes — the man of pure ratiocination and keen observation who could assemble fragmentary details into a meaningful narrative — the camera became the epistemological tool of choice. That same culture diagnosed a new psychopathology of sexual arousal triggered by watching others have sex. It was dubbed mixoscopia by the German doctor Albert Moll in 1891 and voyeurism by Richard Krafft-Ebbing in 1894, based on an 1888 account using this term to describe clients in Parisian brothels who gazed through small orifices at sexual action in the next room.[13] The withdrawal from physical ungainliness and potential discomfort into mental pleasures, the recognition that this was, increasingly, the condition of modernity — these were the feelings linking Bonnard's timid turn to the camera and his numerous iterations in paint of an always young, and always unknowable, female body.

NOTES

1. "Photographs on the Wing: What Can Be Done with the Detective Camera," *New York Times*, August 18, 1885.
2. The availability for sale of photos of bathing beauties taken by two or three gentlemen traveling to beach resorts was announced in a newspaper column in 1886 as a warning to girls. "Society Topics of the Week," *New York Times*, September 5, 1886. Another account describing darkrooms for use by guests in some Virginia and North Carolina resort hotels reported that there had already been complaints by young women "who happened to be caught in the detective camera." "With the Picture Takers—Camera Amateurs Take Advantage of the Fine Weather," *New York Times*, December 30, 1889.
3. Peter Nansen, *Marie*, trans. Gaudard de Vinci, 2nd ed. (Paris: Editions de la Revue Blanche, 1898), pp. 39–40.
4. Vollard wrote Lucien Pissarro in 1896 about doing an illustrated edition of Verlaine's poems but then hired Gustave Leheutre to begin work on drawings for *Parallèlement*. Rebecca Rabinow noted that Vollard's account books indicated payments to Leheutre between March and September 1897. Rebecca A. Rabinow, "Vollard's *Livres d'Artiste*," in *Cézanne to Picasso: Ambroise Vollard, Patron of the Avant-Garde*, ed. Rebecca A. Rabinow (New Haven, Conn.: Yale University Press, 2006), p. 197. Sasha Newman suggested that Bonnard made the drawings only after the page proofs had been printed (so that they complemented the layout of the poems). Sasha M. Newman, "Nudes and Landscapes," in Colta Ives, Helen Giambrun, and Sasha M. Newman, *Pierre Bonnard: The Graphic Art*, exh. cat. (New York: Metropolitan Museum of Art, 1989), p. 163. Therefore, I would posit that Bonnard's involvement was compressed between 1898 and 1899. In fact, Bonnard wrote his mother in the fall of 1899 that he was hard at work on the Verlaine lithographs. Letter cited in Antoine Terrasse, "Chronology," in *Bonnard: The Late Paintings*, exh. cat., ed. Sasha M. Newman (Paris: Musée National d'Art Moderne, 1984), p. 248.
5. Jean-François Chevrier, "Bonnard and Photography," in *Bonnard: The Late Paintings*, p. 88, credits Terrasse and Néagu as having been the first to pair the photographs with the Verlaine illustrations. Néagu published this information with Françoise Heilbrun in their *Pierre Bonnard: Photographs and Paintings*, exh. cat. (New York: Aperture Foundation, 1988; orig. French edition, 1987).
6. Rabinow cites letters from Vollard to Denis in 1896 and 1897 discussing an album of twelve illustrations to Longus's work that they were contemplating. Payment for printing the text was made to the Imprimerie Nationale in 1900, and the book appeared in 1902. Rabinow, *Cézanne to Picasso*, p. 332. Thus, Bonnard's drawings were produced presumably soon after he completed the Verlaine project. One finds echoes of the same poses, but the Longus drawings are contained within clear squares or frames separated from the text and show greater definition of the contours and interior modeling than do the Verlaine illustrations.
7. Bonnard's paintings of outdoor scenes rarely explore the effects of high contrast, broken sunlight on human forms. The only oil that approximates the spotting effects seen in these photographs is *Nude against a Background of Foliage*, reproduced in Heilbrun and Néagu, *Pierre Bonnard*, p. 145; the work is dated 1894, that is, earlier than the photographs.
8. George Guéroult, "Formes, Couleurs et Mouvements," *Gazette des beaux-arts* (1882): p. 179.
9. Breitner to H. J. Van der Weele, June 14, 1893, cited in P. H. Hefting, "Brieven van G. H. Breitner aan H. J. van der Weele," in *Nederlands Kunsthistorisch Jaarboek, 1976* (Haarlem, 1977), p. 152.
10. The dating of Breitner's photographic and painted nudes is open to question. The oils that are closest to the photographs have been dated 1887–89. I would posit that the photographs were taken very close in time, but the hairstyles of the women seem to place them closer to about 1895.
11. Bonnard did dozens of drawn and painted versions of bathers in round tubs, the first of which was a lithograph from the catalogue for the May 1894 exhibition sponsored by the newspaper *La dépêche de Toulouse*. He took up the subject again in 1903 and also, frequently, between 1912 and 1917. Michel Terrasse, who argued against Bonnard's reliance on photographs, reproduced a series of these tub paintings and drawings in *Bonnard: Du dessin au tableau* (Paris: Imprimerie Nationale, 1996), pp. 118–23, 126. The surviving negative is $3\frac{1}{16} \times 2\frac{3}{16}$ in., thus from a different camera than the earlier nudes. The two Breitner prints are also unusual in his photographic oeuvre in that they are huge (possibly later) enlargements ($15\frac{9}{16} \times 12\frac{7}{16}$ in. and $12\frac{7}{16} \times 15\frac{1}{2}$ in.).
12. Degas had first shown round tubs in his private brothel monotypes in 1878 and 1879, and they reappeared in works by Forain, Zorn, and many caricaturists and painters of Montmartre life in the 1890s. Serge Nazarieff, in *Der Akt in der Photographie: The Stereoscopic Nude* (Berlin: Benedikt Taschen, 1990), fig. 181, reproduces a stereoscopic view of a bather squatting in a tub with her back to the camera and facing a window, which indicates that the subject had made its way into commercialized erotic photography by the turn of the century. The stereoscopic photograph includes a small bowl of water sitting inside the tub that one can also see in Bonnard's drawings of this scene, but not the photograph. One did not fill the tub but used it to catch water that was poured from a pitcher or dropped from a washcloth dipped into the small bowl.
13. Moll's definition of mixoscopia from *Die Conträre Sexualempfindung* (1891) is cited in the 1892 edition of Krafft-Ebbing's *Psychopathia Sexualis* under a section added on "so-called voyeurs." Krafft-Ebbing got his term from descriptions of brothels with peepholes and tales of men on the Champs-Elysées who hid in bushes to look at other people's sexual trysts that were published in Ali Coffignon, *La Corruption à Paris* (Paris: Librairie Illustrée, 1888), pp. 318–21. Coffignon, in a chapter on sadism, recounts stories of what he calls "les trous-voyeurs," a term apparently already known within the Parisian demimonde. Originally, the French word *voyeur* was used to refer merely to a person looking, without a sexual connotation necessarily attached. In 1910 Freud used the term *Schaulust* (literally, "pleasure in looking") to describe the related activities of exhibitionism (passive pleasure in showing) and voyeurism (active pleasure in looking).

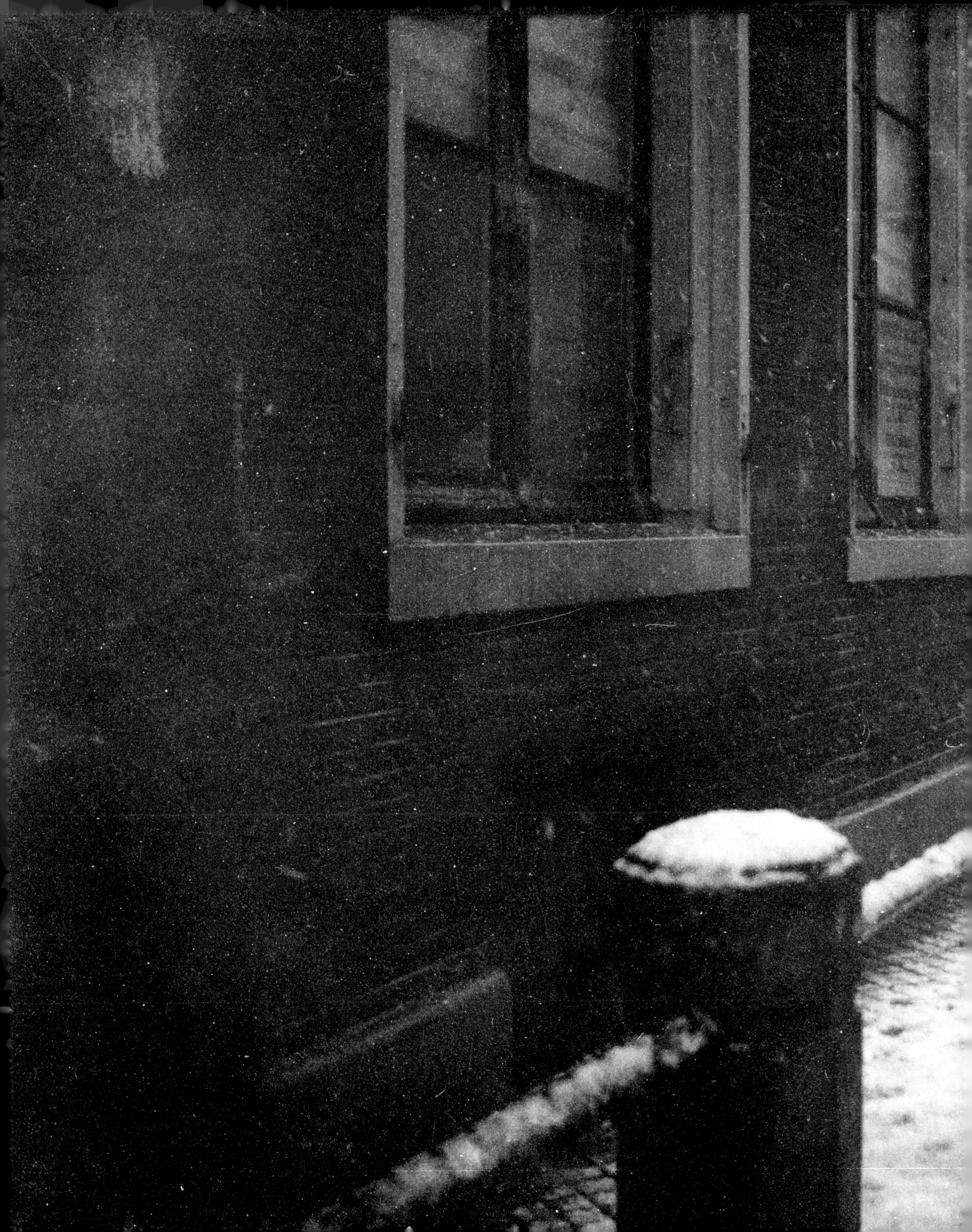

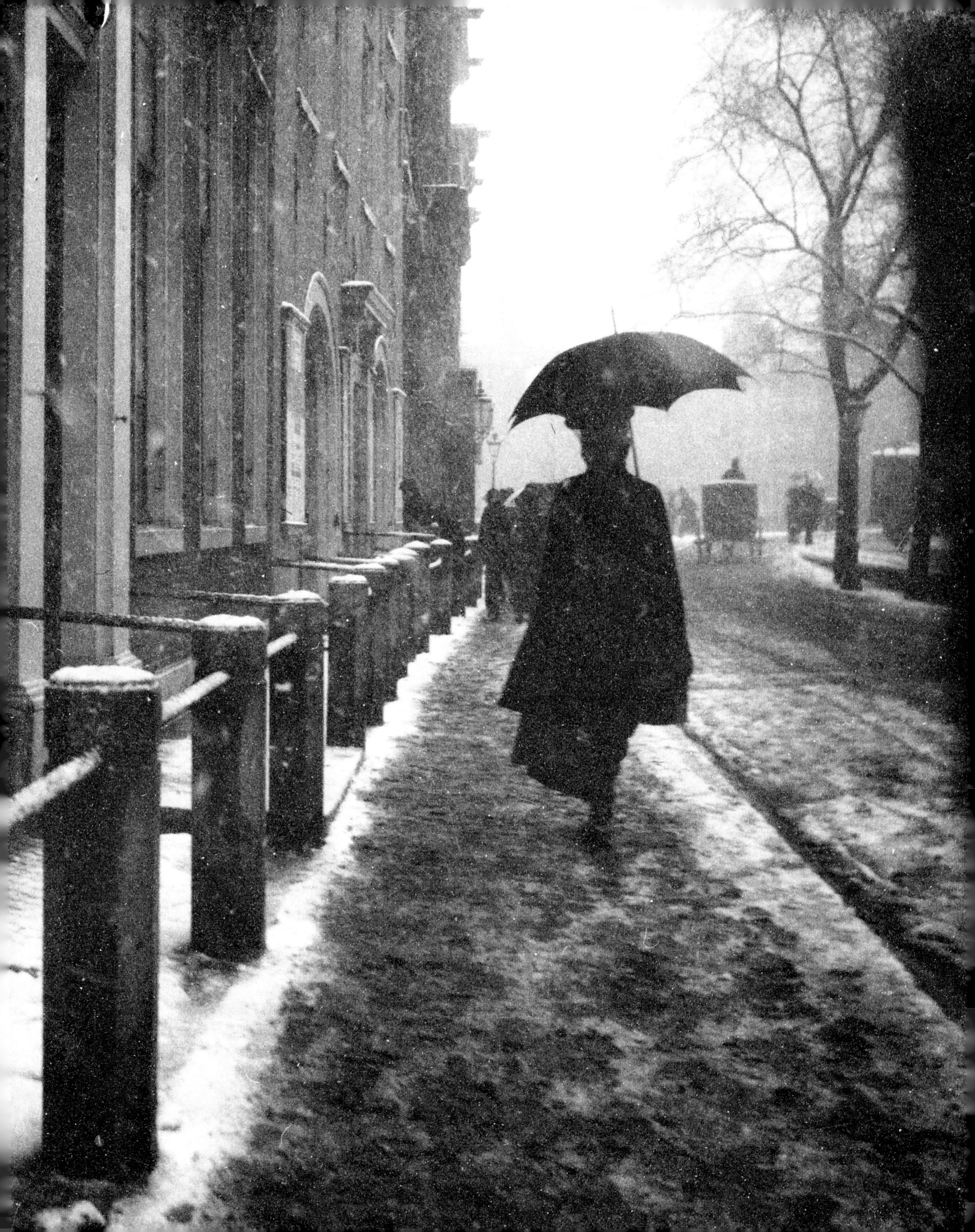

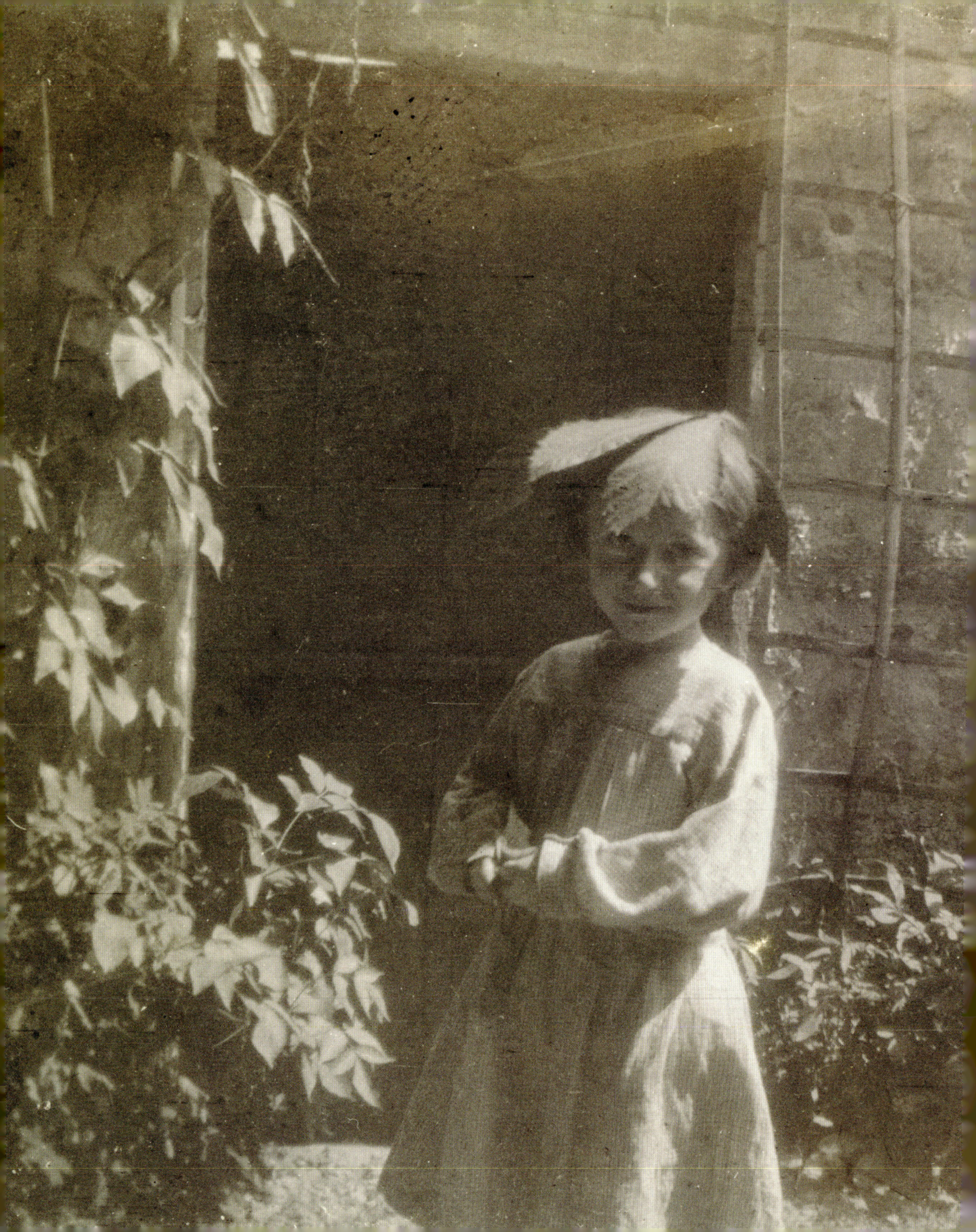

Pierre Bonnard's Amateur Photographs
A Poetic, Dancing World

Françoise Heilbrun

Historians have long considered the impact of amateur photography, a social phenomenon sparked by the burgeoning photographic industry at the turn of the twentieth century. Although initially it was without artistic pretensions, photography was nevertheless inseparable from the work of many artists, particularly the Nabis painters Pierre Bonnard, Maurice Denis, and Edouard Vuillard. Studies in this area have advanced significantly since 1977, when Erika Billeter included a few amateur prints taken by the Nabis in an exhibition of photographs and paintings in Zurich.[1]

For example, the catalogue accompanying the major retrospective of Bonnard's work mounted by the Musée national d'art moderne, Centre Georges Pompidou, in 1984 included an essay by Jean Clair about how photographic optics were evident in the exhibited paintings.[2] And Jean-François Chevrier wrote a notable article about Bonnard's photographs. These had just been found in the home of the artist's nephew Charles Terrasse, whose children donated them to the Musée d'Orsay in 1987. That same year, the museum staged the first exhibition devoted to this aspect of Bonnard's activity, accompanied by a catalogue identifying all of his approximately two hundred photographic prints and linking them to his art.[3] The Edouard Vuillard retrospective at the Grand Palais followed in 2004, displaying that artist's snapshots in the same rooms as his paintings. The accompanying catalogue featured an essay by Elizabeth Easton on Vuillard's vision as an amateur photographer and another, by Guy Cogeval, on the contribution of the artist's photographic work to his painting. Finally, in 2006 Maurice Denis was the subject of a retrospective at the Musée d'Orsay. Although the artist's personal photographs—some of which had just been donated to the museum by his granddaughter Claire Denis—were shown in a room some distance from his canvases, it was nevertheless clear that many of them were closely related to the paintings and sometimes showed similar, if not identical, motifs. I single out the photographs of the Nabis because, unlike those of most amateurs—with the exception of Jacques Henri Lartigue and a few others—they show a consistency of vision and an understanding of the possibilities of the snapshot, both undoubtedly acquired from their experience of painting, their familiarity with Japanese prints, and the impact of the cinematograph on all artists of their generation and those who followed.

In developing Kodak cameras, George Eastman was seeking to reach a rapidly growing number of amateur customers. Cheap, light, and easy to handle, the

DETAIL OF CAT. 12

Pocket Kodak, which Bonnard initially used and which was readily available in 1895, was a simple square case loaded with a roll of film. It could capture a snapshot in 1/25 second, eliminating the need to make subjects pose and guaranteeing the spontaneity of the scene. Better yet, there was no need to alter settings for distance or light: "You press the button, we do the rest" was the company's slogan. There was an inch-wide viewfinder atop the box. Several photographs Bonnard took in which Vuillard is seen framing a shot (cats. 1, 2) reveal how the camera was held: in both hands and at waist level.[4] To make things as easy as possible for users, the film could be developed and the photographs printed at home or at a Kodak service outlet. In other words, the new amateurs were barely involved in the technical process, unlike their predecessors in earlier decades who had to devote considerable time, craft, and care to their photography.

With a Kodak, it was the quality of the photographer's eye that mattered. Although Bonnard's minuscule prints are not very polished, they reveal that he had an instinct for framing off-center images and figures abruptly truncated or out of focus with his lightweight, easily manageable Kodak.[5] It is therefore evident that he used photography as another way to "sketch" the motifs for paintings yet to be. This parallel between pencil and camera is all the more obvious because in Bonnard's art, as in that of the other Nabis, there is no separation between work and private life, the latter providing the very stuff of their paintings. Several times, Bonnard used photographs as motifs for his lithographs, and more generally, snapshots were for some years a part of his working method.

Bonnard took most of his photographs while visiting the countryside. Specifically, he used his camera in Noisy-le-Grand, where he stayed in 1898 and 1899 in a house briefly rented by the composer Claude Terrasse, husband of his sister Andrée; in Le Grand-Lemps (in the Dauphiné), at the home of his mother, Madame Eugène Bonnard, where he would see the Terrasse family every summer, sometimes his brother Charles, and the painters Vuillard and Ker-Xavier Roussel, and where, from 1897 to 1900, he shot numerous pictures of children playing; in Montval (near Marly-le-Roi), where, in 1900 and 1901, he took a series of nude photographs of his muse, Marthe de Méligny; in Vernouillet, where, around 1908, he produced one of his strongest images, showing Marthe in the bathtub (cat. 30); and in Vernon. Bonnard's Paris photographs are confined to a few nudes of Marthe made in 1899 and 1900 in the apartment next to his studio at 65 rue de Douai (cats. 26, 28) and a few family scenes shot in the same dwelling. Apparently, Bonnard took no pictures in the street that inspired so many of his Nabis paintings and prints, but he did travel with his camera—to Venice, where he stayed with the painter Theodore Roussel and with Vuillard in 1899 (cat. 1), and to Spain, where he went in early 1901 with Vuillard and Prince Emmanuel Bibesco.[6] Finally, in addition to all these images, mainly of family and friends, are two short series of photographs of models in the studio, the most remarkable of which date to around 1916 (cat. 32).

There is a marked subject-matter similarity between the paintings and photographs of Bonnard's Nabis period, notably in relation to the time spent with the Terrasse family in Le Grand-Lemps, with children bathing (cat. 13), women hanging out the wash, picking fruit (cats. 5, 6), and having meals outdoors. Interestingly, however, none of these paintings is based on motifs from the snapshots. The same is true of the Paris subjects. While the painting *La sieste* (Siesta) (1900; National Gallery of Victoria, Melbourne, Australia) shows a nude Marthe lying on the bed in the rue de Douai apartment, Bonnard imbues her with considerably more sensuality than is apparent in the photographs, which are quite restrained. He transposed two of these, which are clearly recognizable in his lithographs for Paul Verlaine's posthumously published book of erotic poems, *Parallèlement*, published by Ambroise Vollard in 1901 (cats. 27, 29); here again, the pink pencil outline lends the female body a kind of feverish sensuality that is in keeping with the poems.

In making the series of Marthe and himself naked in the garden at Montval, Bonnard undoubtedly was thinking of Vollard's second commission for Longus's *Daphnis et Chloé* (cats. 23, 24), a work completed in 1902 for which the artist also drew upon several photographs, notably the chaste images of a nude Marthe squatting and standing in the sun (cats. 19, 22). For the cover of a book by René Boylesve, Bonnard again used the motif from a snapshot of his nephew Charles Terrasse after a bath (Musée d'Orsay, PHO 1987-28-12).[7] The artist, however, did not take photographs in order to interpret them using other techniques. Instead, he regarded them as research outcomes that would help him formulate the content of his paintings and drawings more precisely. Thus, the juxtaposition in one room of the photographs from the Musée d'Orsay and the books of sketches of Marthe dressing, as part of the 2006 Bonnard retrospective at the Musée d'art moderne de la ville de Paris, revealed the painter's quest to capture the private moments of his partner and favorite model in as much detail as possible, using both techniques.[8] Notably, a few pencil studies and one photograph on the theme of Marthe in the tub — which would eventually inspire Bonnard to execute several monumental paintings — were also on display in the neighboring exhibition rooms.

In his photographs and paintings alike, Bonnard was gifted at transforming the everyday into something poetic and wondrous. Usually, he captured his subject at a distance, accentuating the effect of mystery. Marthe's luminous silhouette, outlined against the dark vegetation of the garden in Montval (cats. 14–17), conjures up a heroine of the ancient Greek romanticist Longus. Bonnard infused even his most trivial family photographs with a sense of grace — the three Terrasse children dancing near their mother in Noisy-le-Grand (Musée d'Orsay, PHO 1987-31-3), for example, and a cat jumping at the nightgown of Andrée Terrasse while shadows playing at her feet reveal a cat and dog (Musée d'Orsay, PHO 1987-30-2).[9] By comparison, photographs by Vuillard, who was a better photographer than Bonnard technically and also a fine interpreter of moments, show us a very different world, one more concerned with portraying aspects of modern life. Be that as it may, Bonnard and Vuillard were equally adept at capturing what Henri Cartier-Bresson called "the decisive moment." (Incidentally, Cartier-Bresson greatly admired both artists, an admiration he expressed in print on at least one notable occasion.[10])

In his paintings, Bonnard made no systematic attempt to exploit the formal innovations facilitated by his Kodak. I am thinking, for example, of the dynamic arrangement of the Terrasse children bathing (cat. 13),[11] and of their silhouettes rising up in the foreground where an avenue turns a corner (Musée d'Orsay, PHO 1987-30-16). Subtle manifestations appear in his paintings from 1907, however, notably in a new stretched, distorted space of the kind he might see through the lens.[12]

Bonnard's paintings from around 1907 and 1908 demonstrate a shift from the essentially graphic and decorative Nabis style to one that is more monumentally visual. Significantly, the artist changed cameras at the same time, turning to his Folding Pocket Kodak, introduced by Eastman in 1897. Few images taken with the new camera are known, but the one of Marthe in the bathtub marks a turning point (cat. 30).[13] Whereas in the Montval series of nudes, he shows Marthe as delicate and fragile, in this picture, shot from closer in and no doubt at floor level, she has a sculptural presence. In the photographs Bonnard took of a model around 1916 in his rue Tourlaque studio, as in the paintings he did of Marthe at the same time, he exhibited a new interest in vertical lines and geometric compositions, particularly in the remarkable image of the model taking off her blouse before a mirror (cat. 32).[14] At this time, the tenets of Cubism were prompting him to question the supremacy of color over construction.

Bonnard lost interest in photography around 1916, when he was returning to color. Being primarily a painter, he did not experiment further with a technique that, had he pursued it other than as an amateur, would have become too exclusive. He was, however, among those painters who best grasped the expressive possibilities of photography, thereby showing that, even as an amateur, he recognized how originality of vision was more important than technical expertise.

NOTES

The title *Bonnard photographe*, adopted by Philippe Néagu, Antoine Terrasse, and myself for the catalogue accompanying the exhibition of photographic proofs, paintings, and engravings at the Musée d'Orsay in 1987 (Françoise Heilbrun and Philippe Néagu, *Bonnard photographe* [Paris: RMN and Philippe Sers, 1987]), was a title chosen out of convenience; it does not properly reflect reality, as Michel Frizot rightly noted (Frizot, "Pierre l'éberlué: L'ouvert de la photographie," in *Bonnard: L'oeuvre d'art, un arrêt du temps*, exh. cat. [Paris: Musée d'art moderne de la ville de Paris, 2006], p. 262, note 1). See note 5 below.

1. Erika Billeter and J. A. Schmoll Eisenwerth, *Malerei und Photografie im Dialog von 1840 bis Heute* (Zurich: KunstHaus; Bern: Benteli, 1977), nos. 183–92, pp. 81–83 for Bonnard and nos. 193–212 for Vuillard, ill. pp. 84, 85.
2. Jean Clair, "Les aventures du nerf optique," in *Bonnard*, exh. cat. (Paris: Centre Georges Pompidou, 1984), pp. 1–37.
3. Heilbrun and Néagu, *Bonnard photographe*.
4. Ibid., cat. nos. 72, 73, 100, 101, ill. pls. 36, 37, 38, 42, 81. Bonnard's Pocket Kodak was even smaller than Vuillard's, as can be seen in an anonymous portrait reproduced in Heilbrun and Néagu, *Bonnard photographe*, p. 148.
5. The 1³/₈ x 2–inch format of Bonnard's negatives and contact prints provides clear evidence that he used a Pocket Kodak. Frizot ("Pierre l'éberlué," p. 263) was the first to provide a clear technical explanation of the use of the Pocket Kodak. In framing, the photographer had to "keep glancing back and forth, maintaining a link between the scene he was after and the uncertain gauge of the viewfinder." In Frizot's view, the images were formed, to some extent, independently of the photographer. I believe, however, that as a painter used to the art of composition, Bonnard was able to make chance do his bidding. For a Bonnard image taken in close-up, see ibid., p. 265.
6. These photographs were anonymously donated to the Musée d'Orsay; published in Françoise Heilbrun, *Mélanges en l'honneur de Françoise Cachin* (Paris: Gallimard and RMN, 2002). The attribution of snapshots to Bonnard, Vuillard, and perhaps Bibesco still poses problems.
7. Heilbrun and Néagu, *Bonnard photographe*, no. 55 and book cover, ill. p. 98.
8. In *Bonnard*, 2006, the notebooks are reproduced on pp. 257–61 and the photographs appear on pp. 115–17.
9. Heilbrun and Néagu, *Bonnard photographe*, no. 4.
10. Henri-Cartier Bresson, preface to Jeanne Bucher, *Bonnard, Degas, Vuillard photographes*, exh. cat. (Paris: Centre d'art, 2003).
11. Heilbrun and Néagu, *Bonnard photographe*, pp. 186, 187, and nos. 23, 18, 36.
12. On this subject, see Clair, "Les aventures du nerf optique," pp. 24–25.
13. Heilbrun and Néagu, *Bonnard photographe*, no. 214.
14. For the model in the rue Tourlaque studio, see ibid., nos. 219–22.

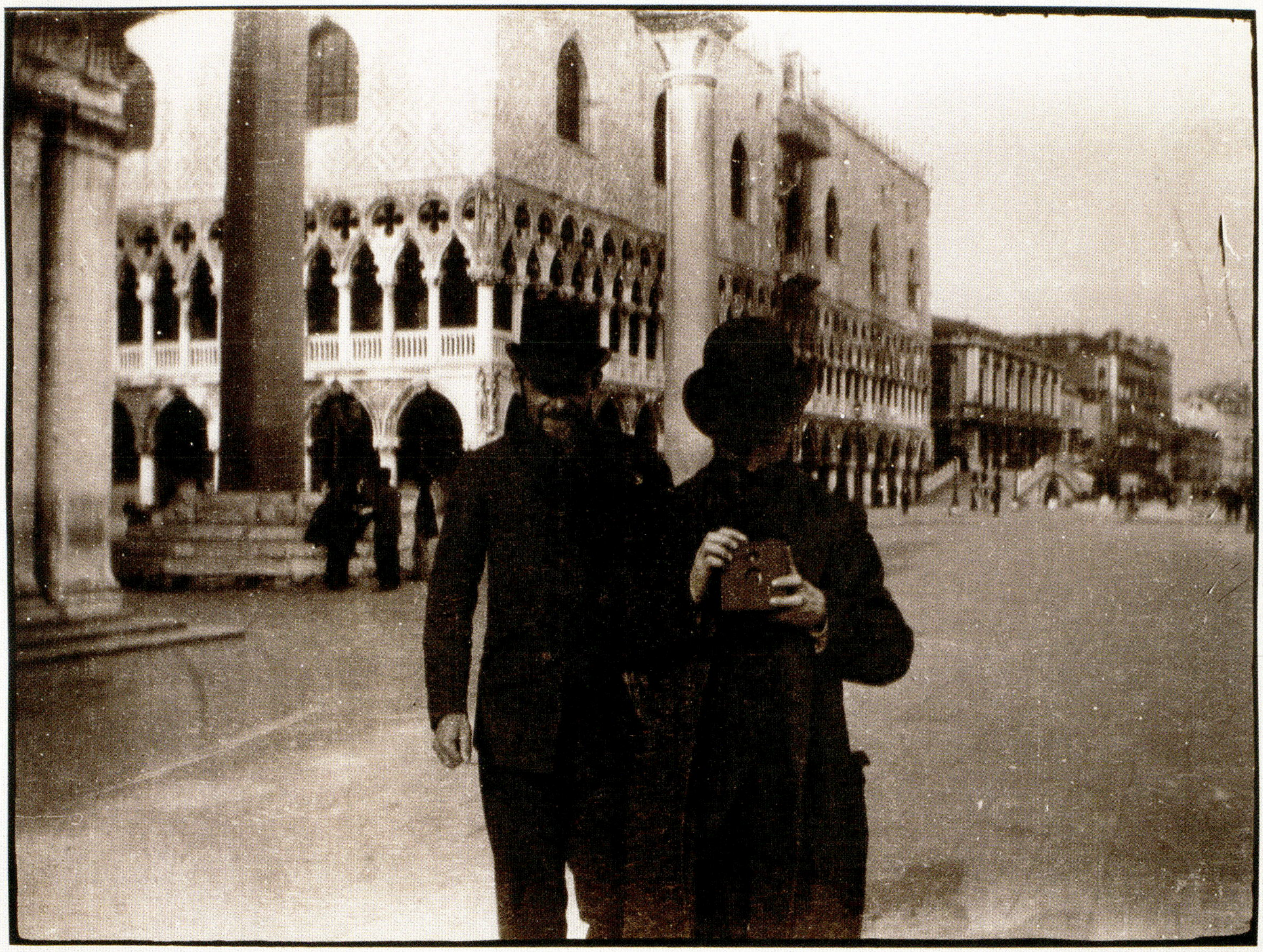

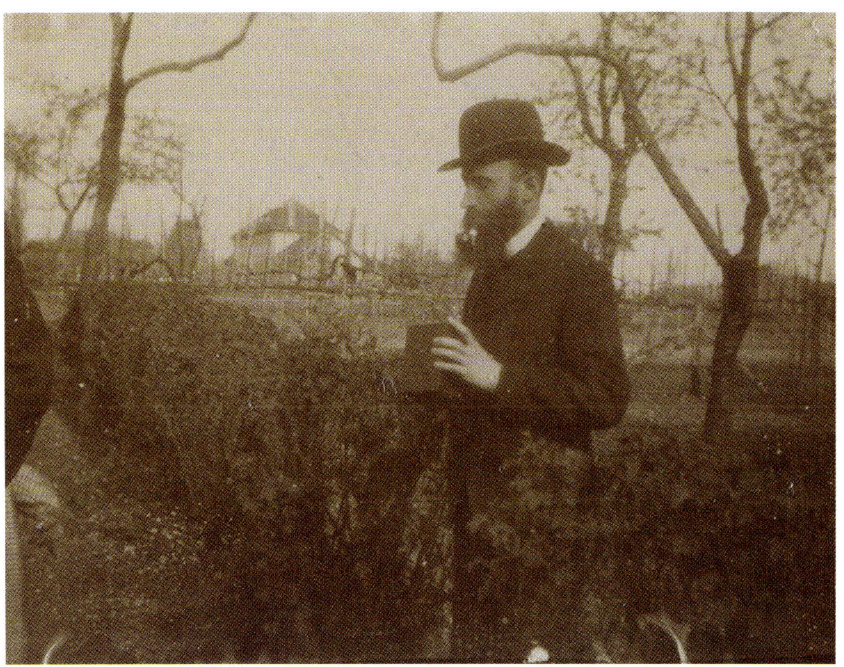

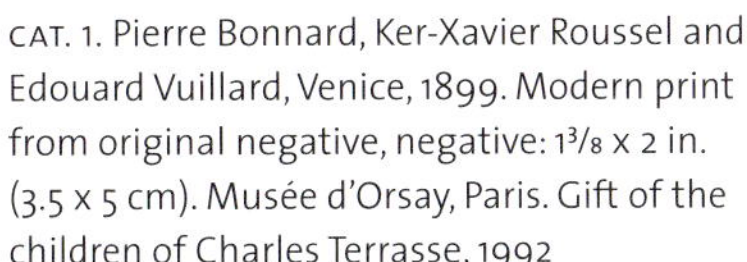

CAT. 1. Pierre Bonnard, Ker-Xavier Roussel and Edouard Vuillard, Venice, 1899. Modern print from original negative, negative: $1\frac{3}{8}$ x 2 in. (3.5 x 5 cm). Musée d'Orsay, Paris. Gift of the children of Charles Terrasse, 1992

CAT. 2. Pierre Bonnard, Vuillard holding his Kodak camera, spring 1900. Modern print from original negative, negative: $1\frac{1}{2}$ x $2\frac{1}{8}$ in. (3.8 x 5.5 cm). Musée d'Orsay, Paris. Gift of the children of Charles Terrasse, 1992

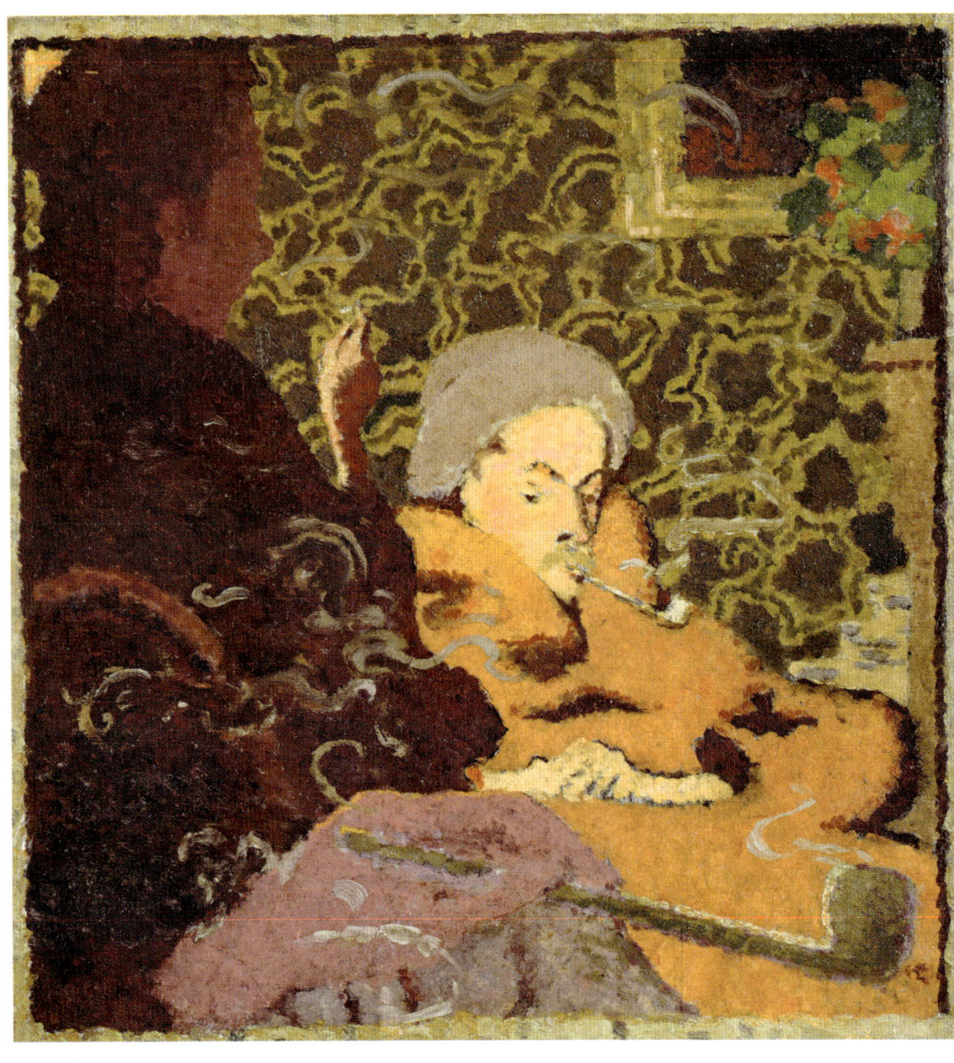

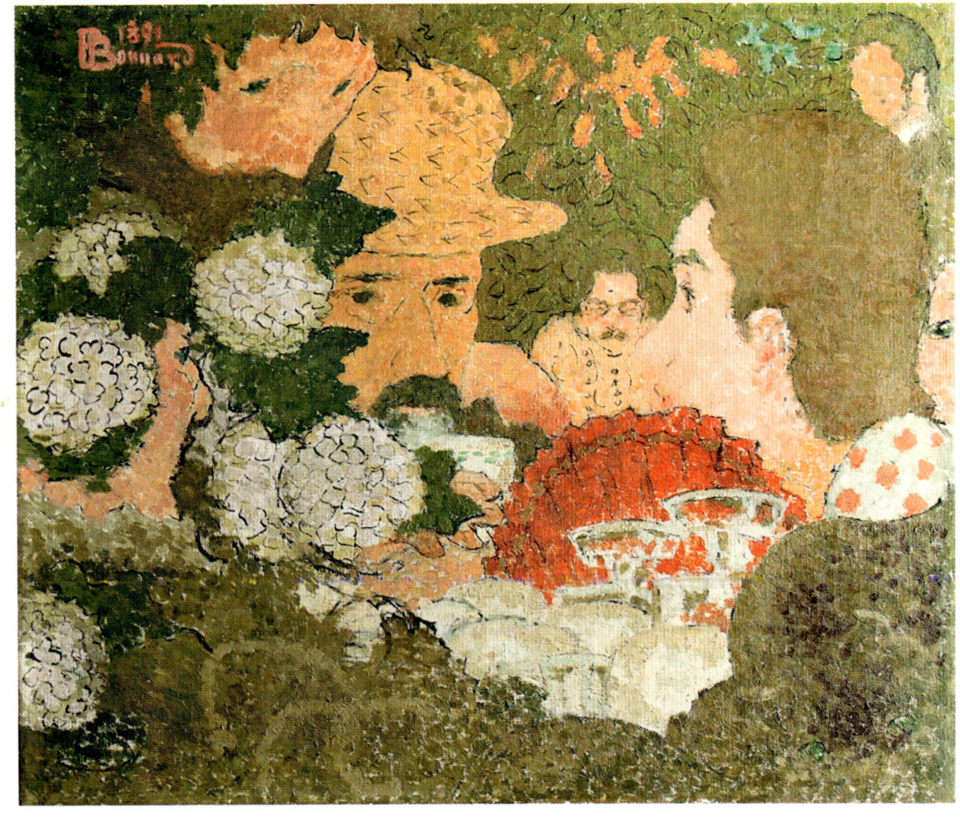

CAT. 3. Pierre Bonnard, *Intimité (Portrait de Monsieur et Madame Claude Terrasse)* (Intimacy [Portrait of Monsieur and Madame Claude Terrasse]), 1891. Oil on canvas, 15 x $14\frac{1}{8}$ in. (38 x 36 cm). Musée d'Orsay, Paris, acquired with the assistance of Philippe Meyer through the Foundation for French Museums, 1992

CAT. 4. Pierre Bonnard, *Afternoon in the Garden*, 1891. Oil and pen and black ink over pencil on canvas, $14\frac{3}{4}$ x $17\frac{3}{4}$ in. (37.5 x 45.1 cm). Private collection

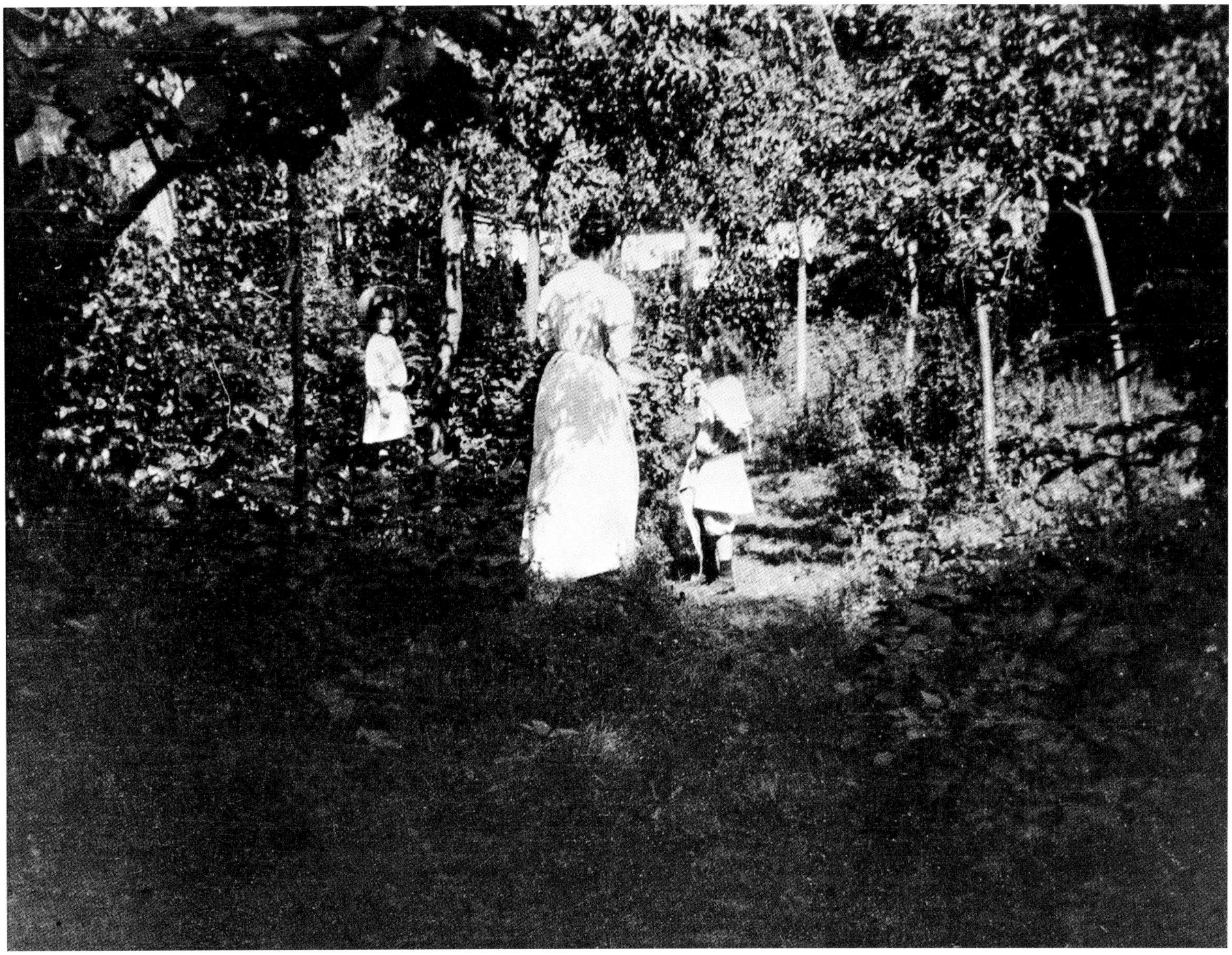

CAT. 5. Pierre Bonnard, Andrée Terrasse, a child by her side, and, in the background, Renée, 1899–1900. Modern print from original negative, negative: $1\frac{1}{2} \times 2\frac{1}{8}$ in. (3.8 x 5.5 cm). Musée d'Orsay, Paris. Gift of the children of Charles Terrasse, 1992

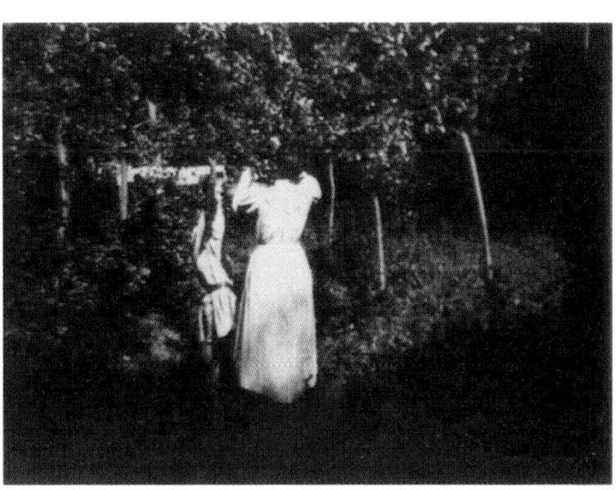

CAT. 6. Pierre Bonnard, Andrée Terrasse and Renée picking fruit in Le Grand-Lemps, 1899–1900. Modern print from original negative, negative: $1\frac{3}{8} \times 2$ in. (3.5 x 5 cm). Musée d'Orsay, Paris. Gift of the children of Charles Terrasse, 1992

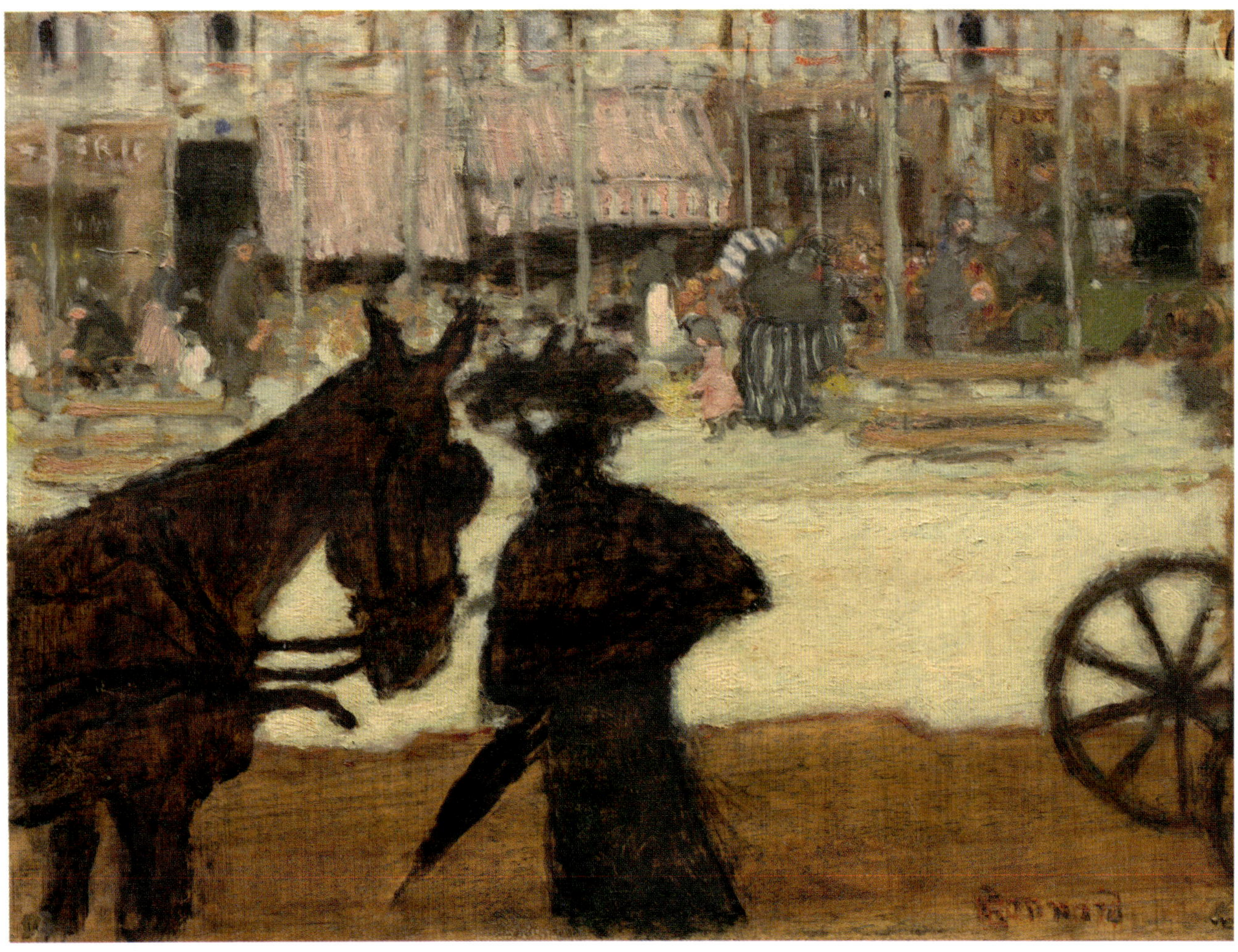

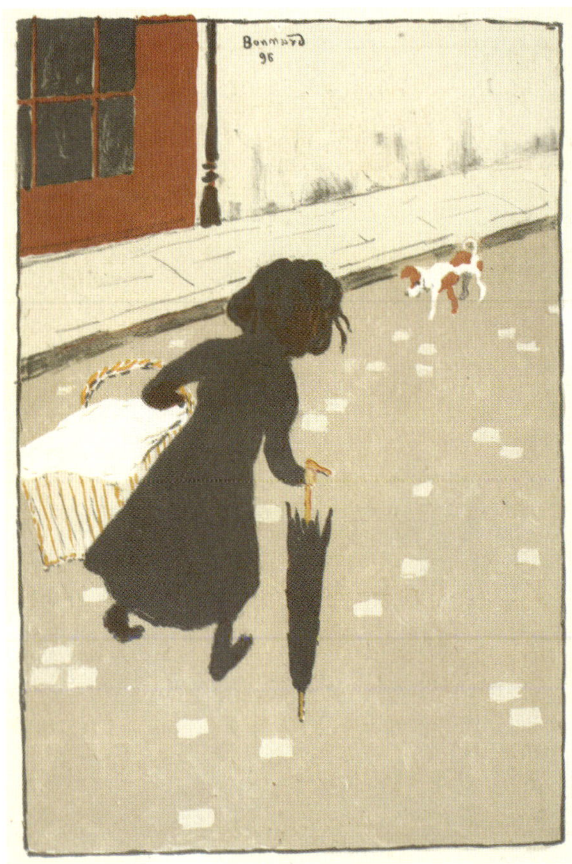

CAT. 7. Pierre Bonnard, *The Cab Horse*, ca. 1895. Oil on wood, 11¾ x 15¾ in. (29.7 x 40 cm). National Gallery of Art, Washington, D.C. Ailsa Mellon Bruce Collection

CAT. 8. Pierre Bonnard, *The Little Laundress*, 1896. Color lithograph, 11¾ x 7½ in. (30 x 19 cm). Van Gogh Museum, Amsterdam (Vincent van Gogh Foundation)

BELOW: CAT. 9. Pierre Bonnard, *Jeune femme et enfant* (Young Girl and Child, study for a lithograph), 1892. Pencil, $7^{7}/_{8}$ x $4^{3}/_{16}$ in. (20 x 10.6 cm). Private collection

RIGHT: CAT. 10. Pierre Bonnard, *Narrow Street in Paris*, ca. 1897. Oil on cardboard, $14^{5}/_{8}$ x $7^{3}/_{4}$ in. (37.1 x 19.6 cm). The Phillips Collection, Washington, D.C.

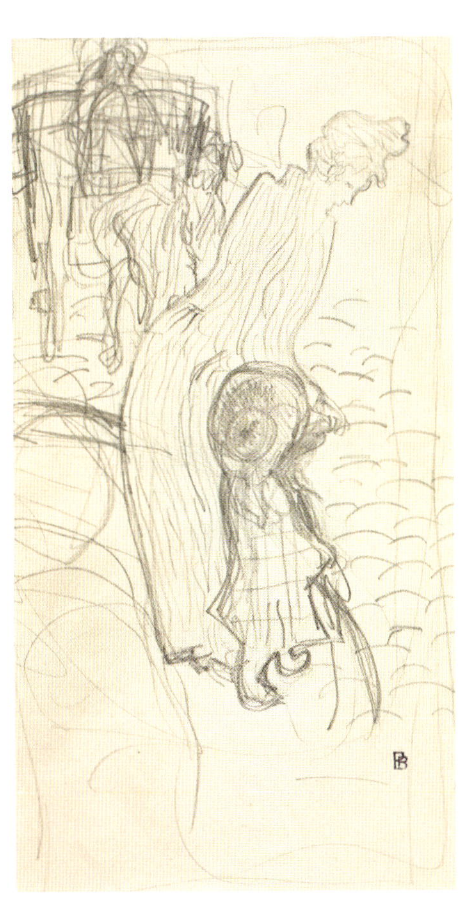

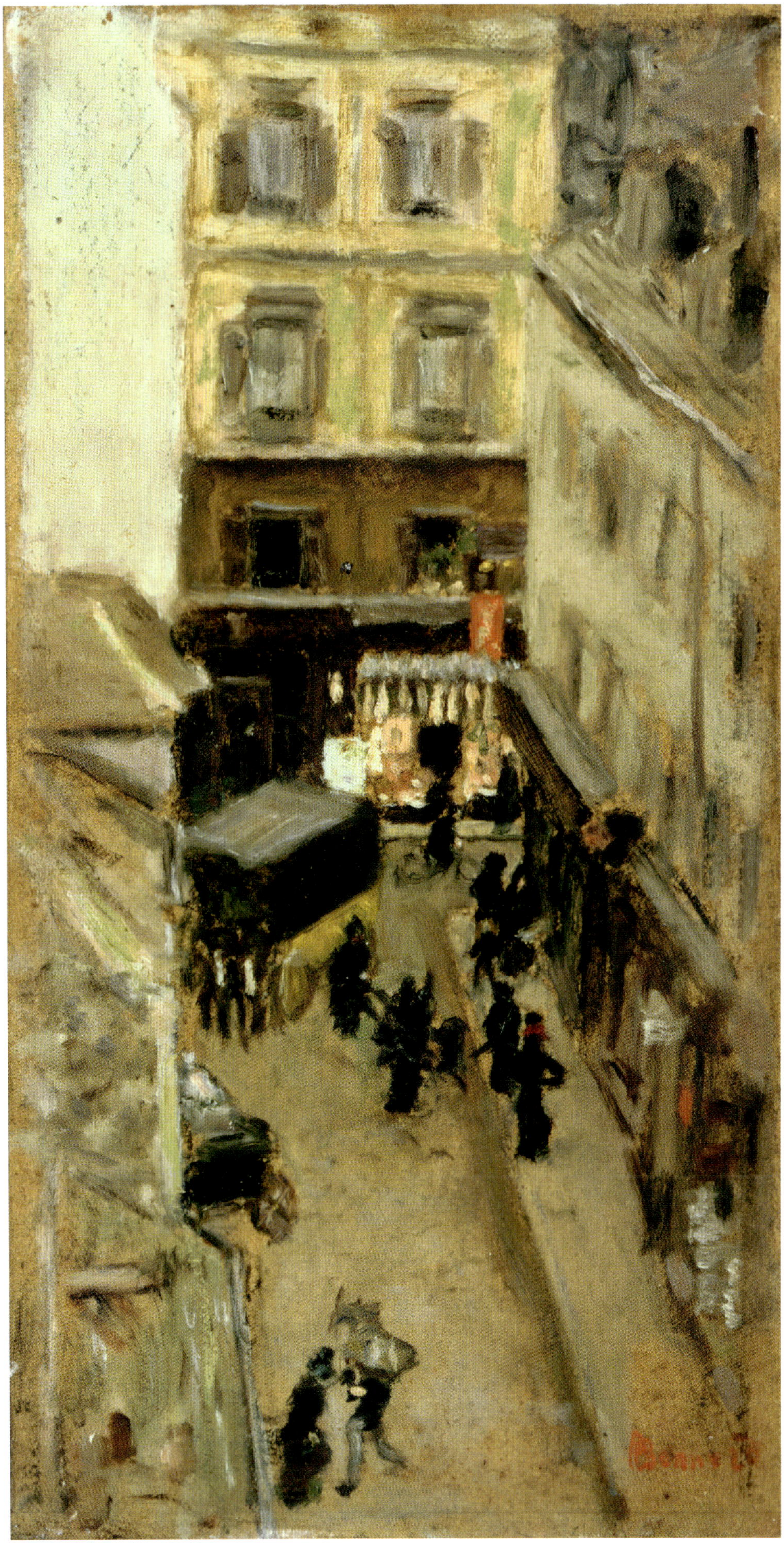

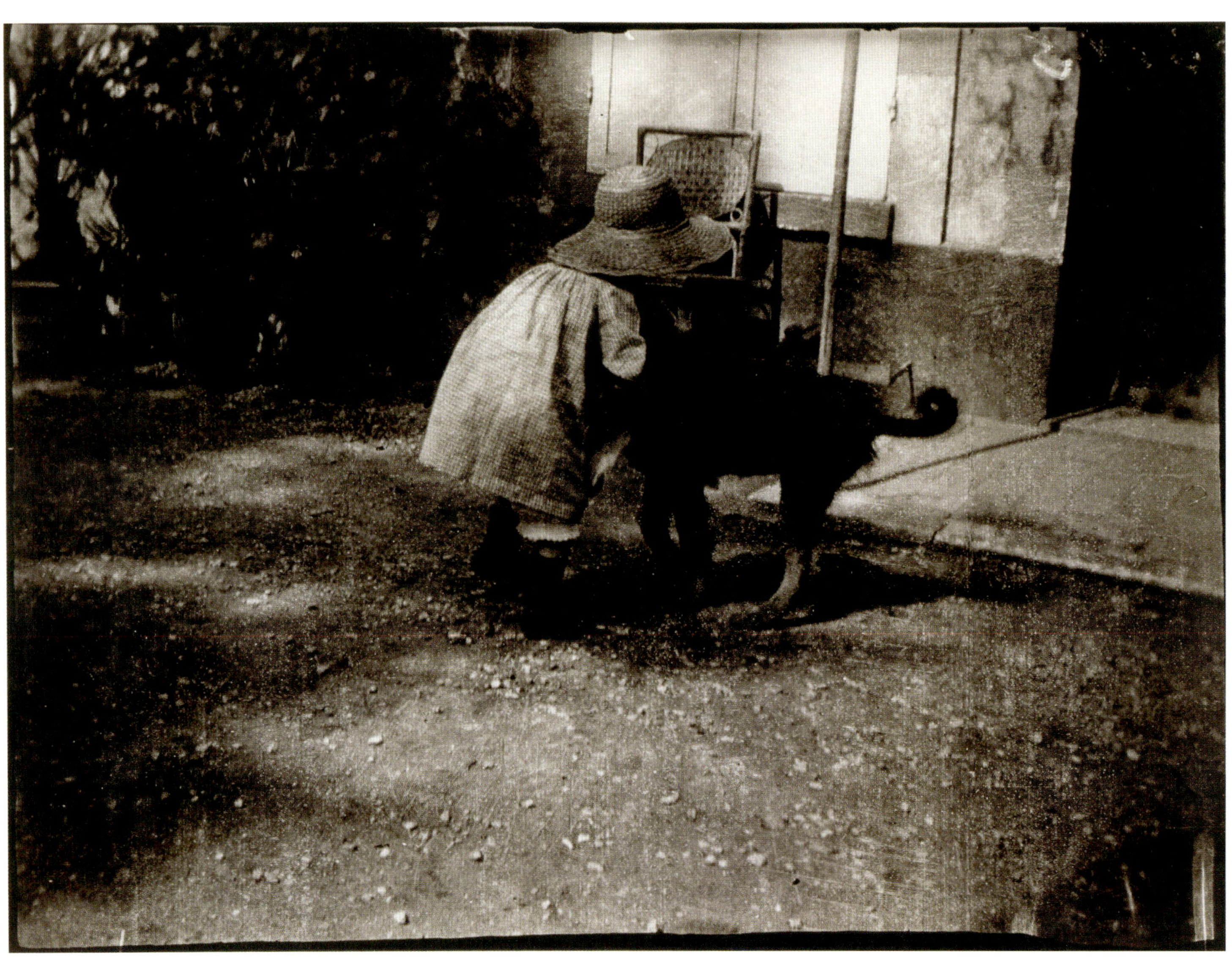

CAT. 11. Pierre Bonnard, Renée embracing a dog, 1898–99. Gelatin silver print, 1½ x 2⅛ in. (3.8 x 5.5 cm). Musée d'Orsay, Paris. Gift of the children of Charles Terrasse, 1992

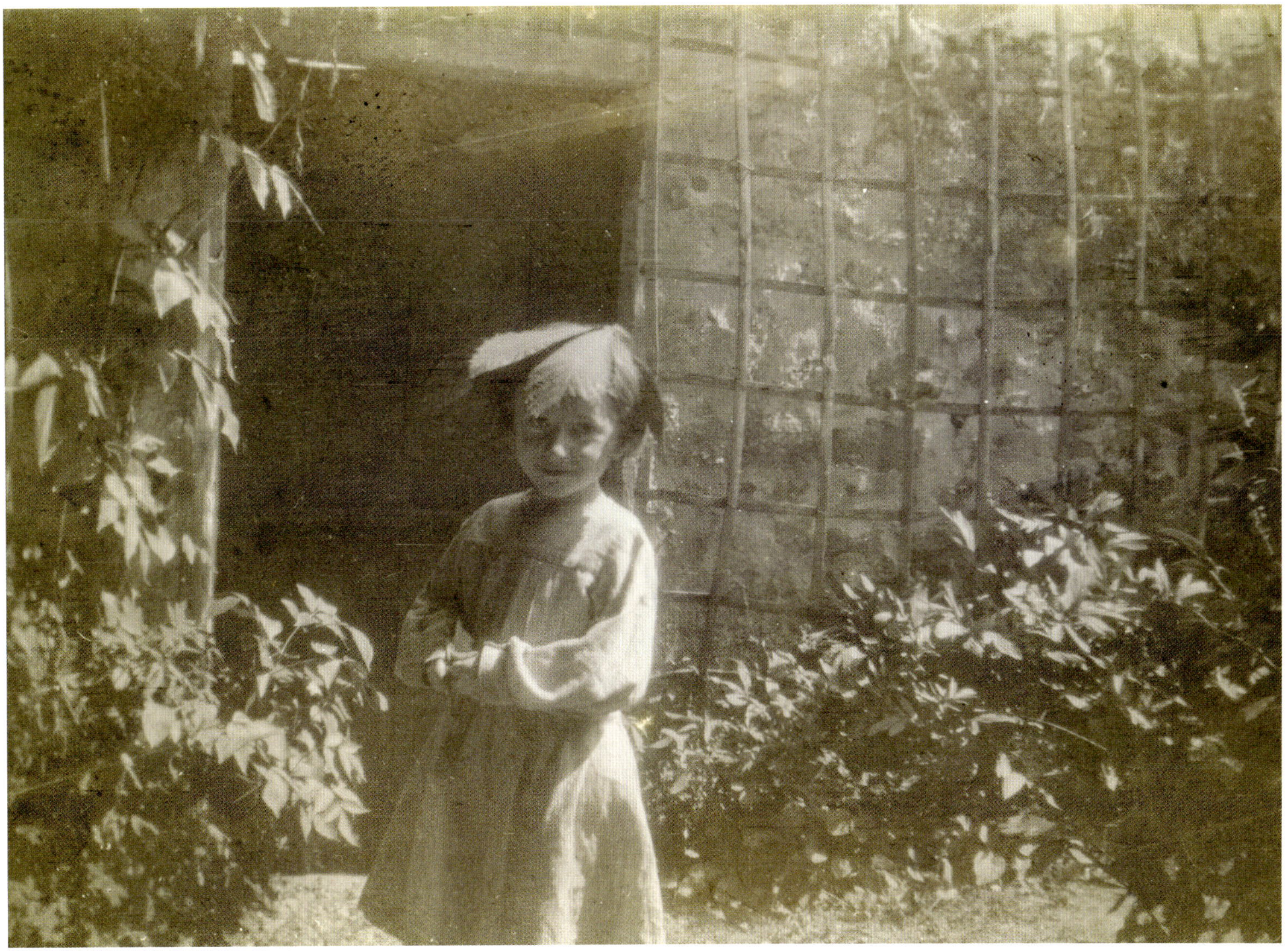

CAT. 12. Pierre Bonnard, Little girl wearing a crown of leaves, ca. 1902. Modern print from original negative, negative: 1½ x 2⅛ in. (3.8 x 5.5 cm). Musée d'Orsay. Gift of M. Antoine Terrasse, 1992

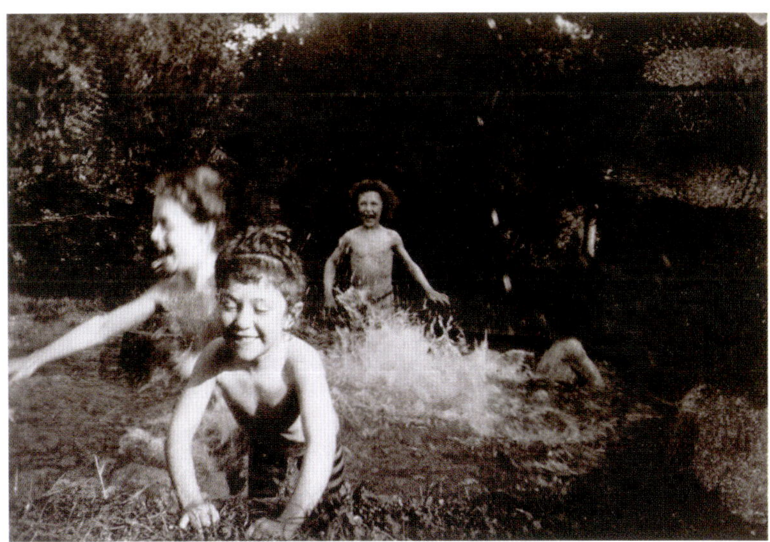

CAT. 13. Pierre Bonnard, Bathing: Vivette in the foreground, Robert in the background, and two other children, 1903–5. Modern print from original negative, negative: 1½ x 2⅛ in. (3.8 x 5.5 cm). Musée d'Orsay, Paris. Gift of M. Antoine Terrasse, 1992

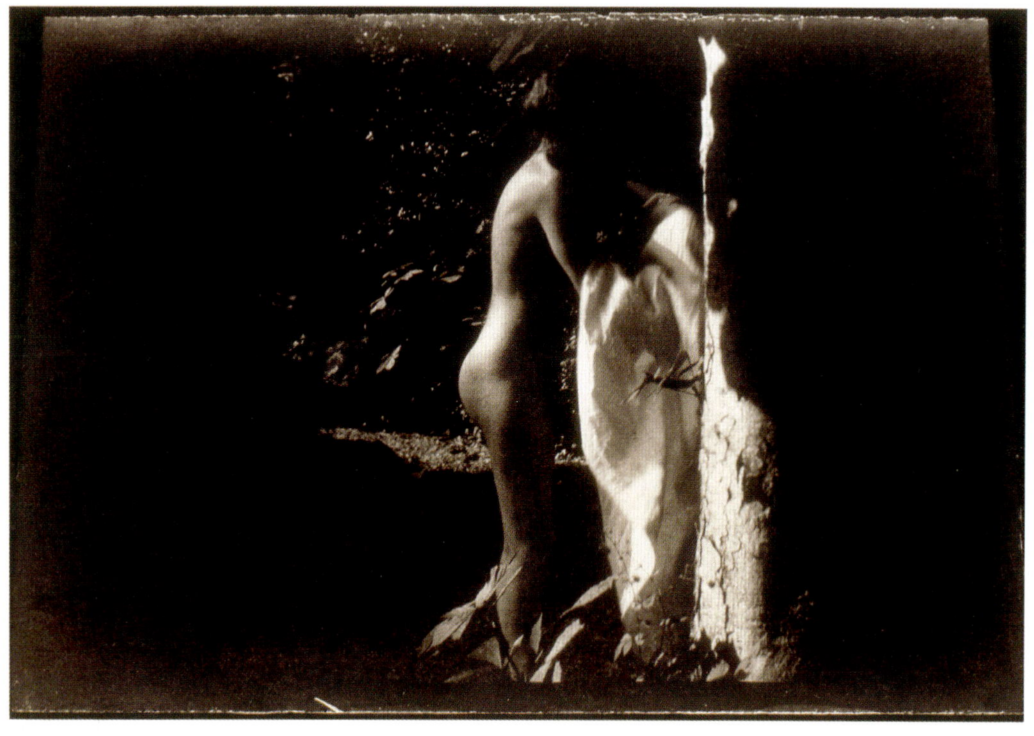

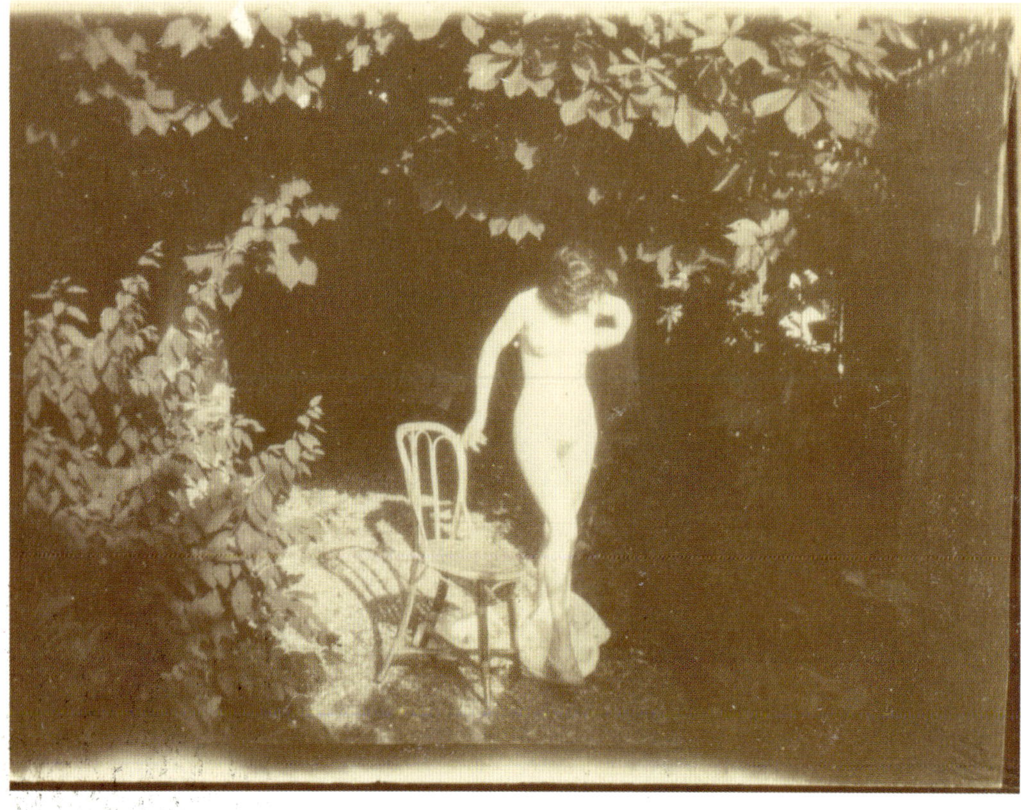

CAT. 14. Pierre Bonnard, Marthe in Montval, in profile, taking off her nightdress, 1900–1901. Modern print from original negative, negative: 1³/₈ x 2¹/₈ in. (3.5 x 5.5 cm). Musée d'Orsay, Paris. Gift of the children of Charles Terrasse, 1992

CAT. 15. Pierre Bonnard, Marthe in Montval, standing by a chair, 1900–1901. Modern print from original negative, negative: 1¹/₂ x 2¹/₈ in. (3.8 x 5.5 cm). Musée d'Orsay, Paris. Gift of the children of Charles Terrasse, 1992

CAT. 16. Pierre Bonnard, Marthe in Montval, seated, one hand on the back of her neck, 1900–1901. Modern print from original negative, negative: 1½ x 2⅛ in. (3.8 x 5.5 cm). Musée d'Orsay, Paris. Gift of the children of Charles Terrasse, 1992

CAT. 17. Pierre Bonnard, Marthe in Montval, seated, her left hand on her right breast, 1900–1901. Sepia-toned gelatin silver print, 1½ x 2 in. (3.9 x 5.1 cm). Musée d'Orsay, Paris. Gift of M. Antoine Terrasse, 1992

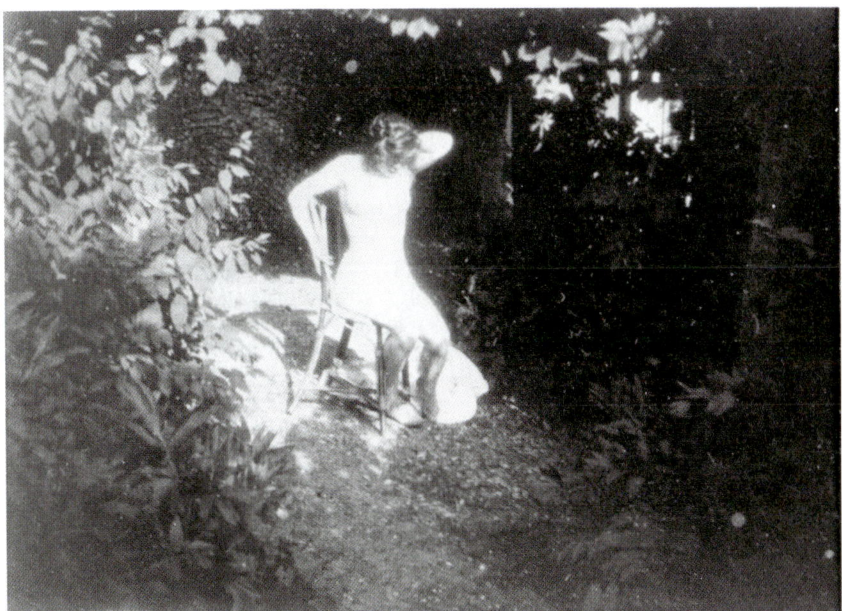

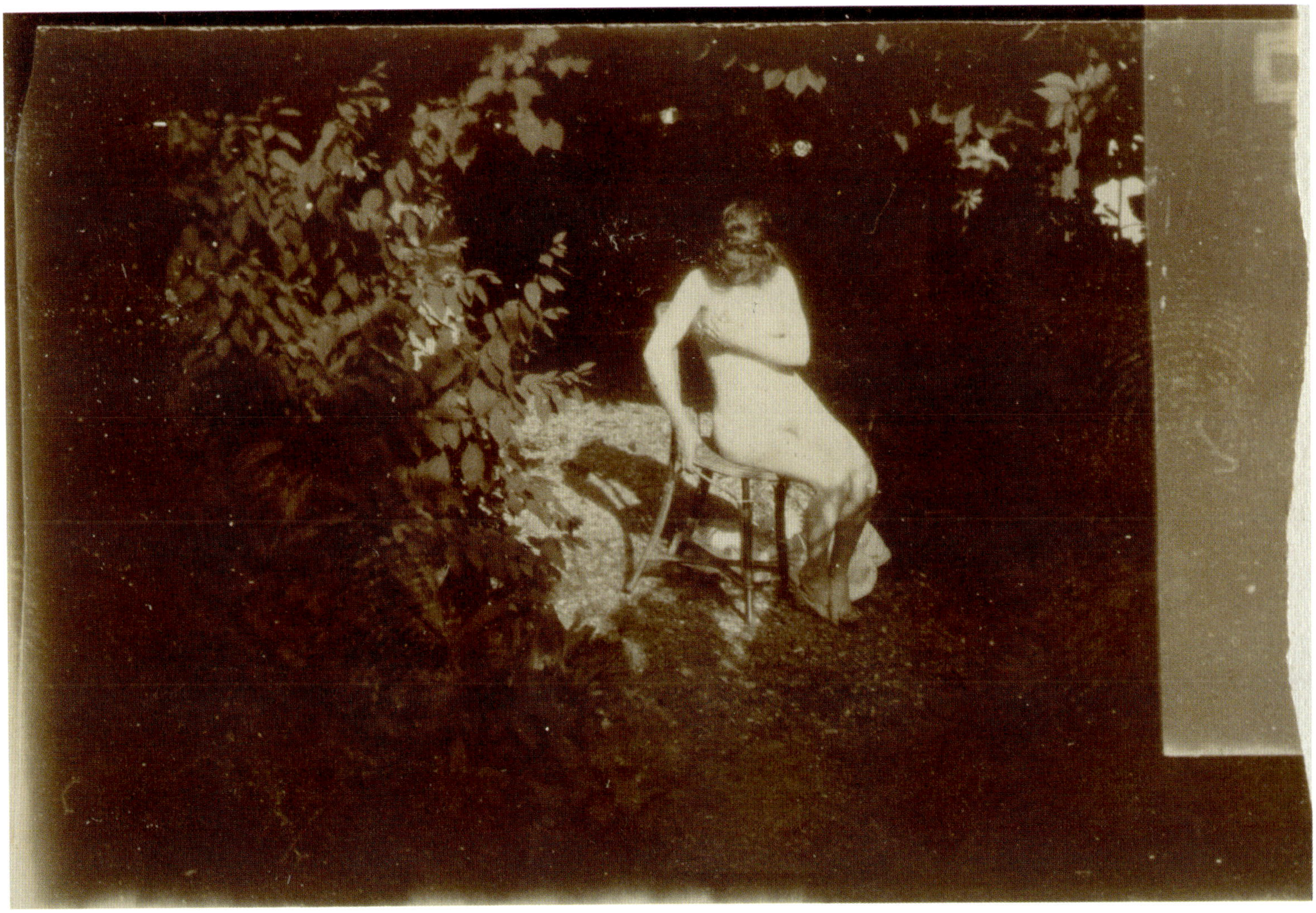

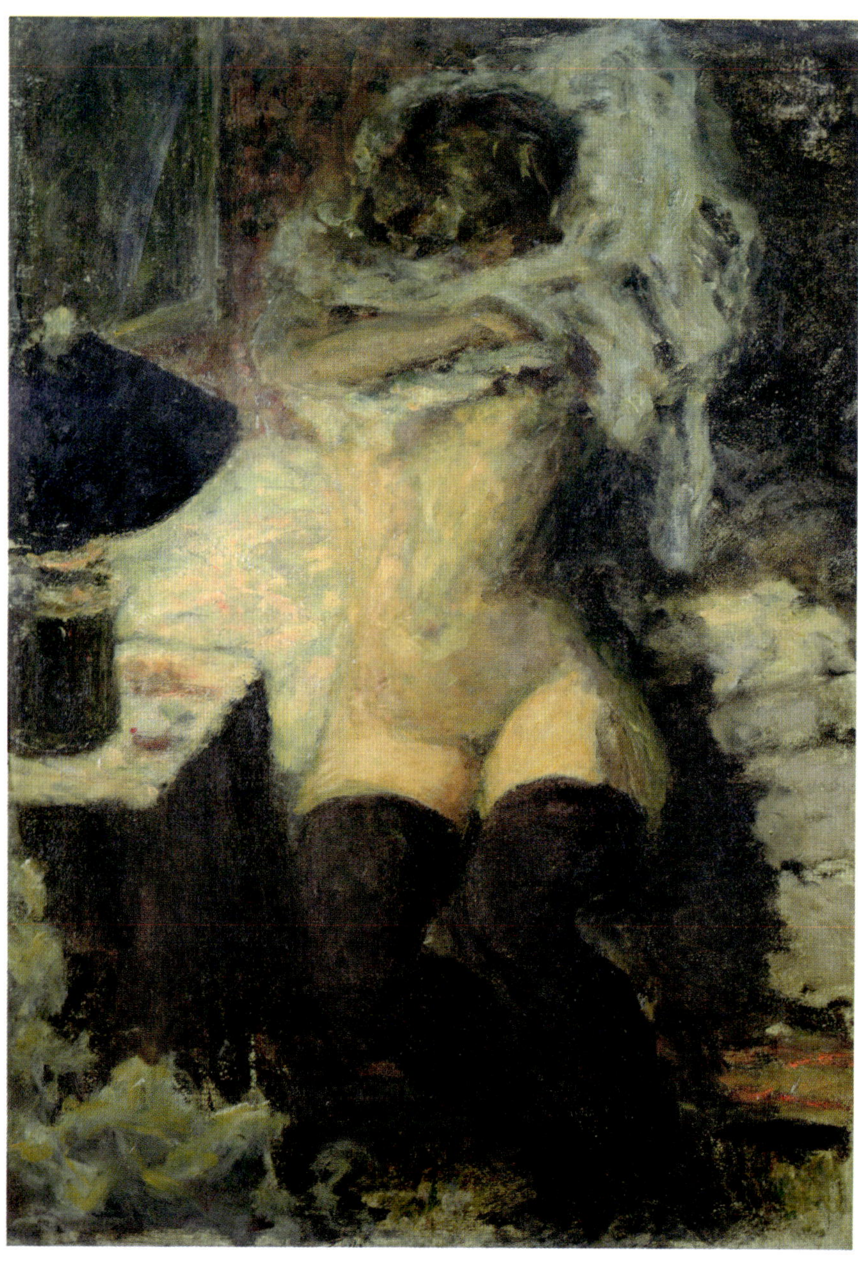

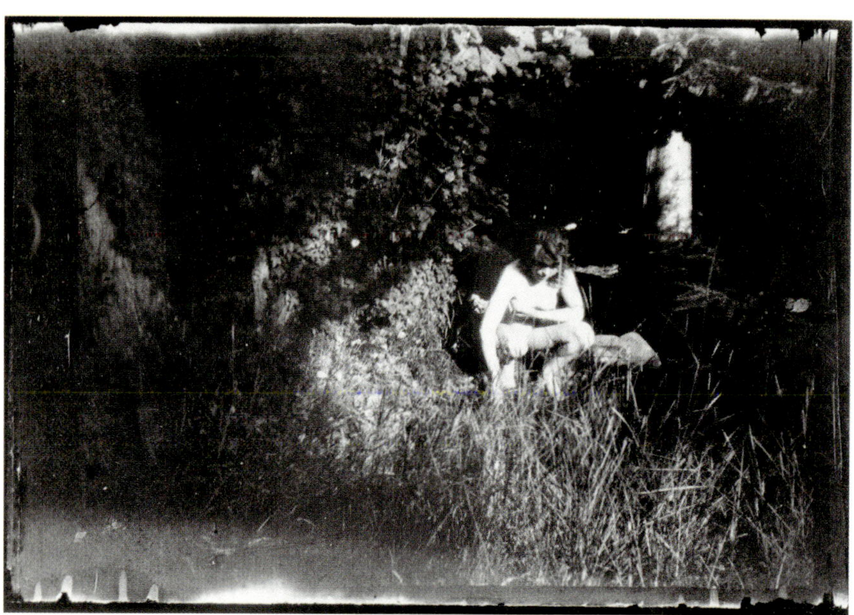

CAT. 18. Pierre Bonnard, *Nude in Black Stockings*, ca. 1900. Oil on canvas, 23¼ x 16⅞ in. (59 x 43 cm). Private collection, on deposit at Sheffield Galleries and Museums

CAT. 19. Pierre Bonnard, Marthe nude squatting, 1900–1901. Modern print from original negative, negative: 1½ x 2 in. (3.7 x 5.2 cm). Musée d'Orsay, Paris. Gift of M. Antoine Terrasse, 1992

CAT. 20. Pierre Bonnard, *The Model and the Artist Reflected in a Mirror (Study for "La Cheminée")*, 1916. Pencil and black chalk, 12¼ x 9¾ in. (31.1 x 24.8 cm). Private collection

CAT. 21. Pierre Bonnard, *The Mirror in the Green Room (La Glace de la chambre verte)*, 1908. Oil on paper, 19¾ x 25¾ in. (50.2 x 65.4 cm). Indianapolis Museum of Art. James E. Roberts Fund

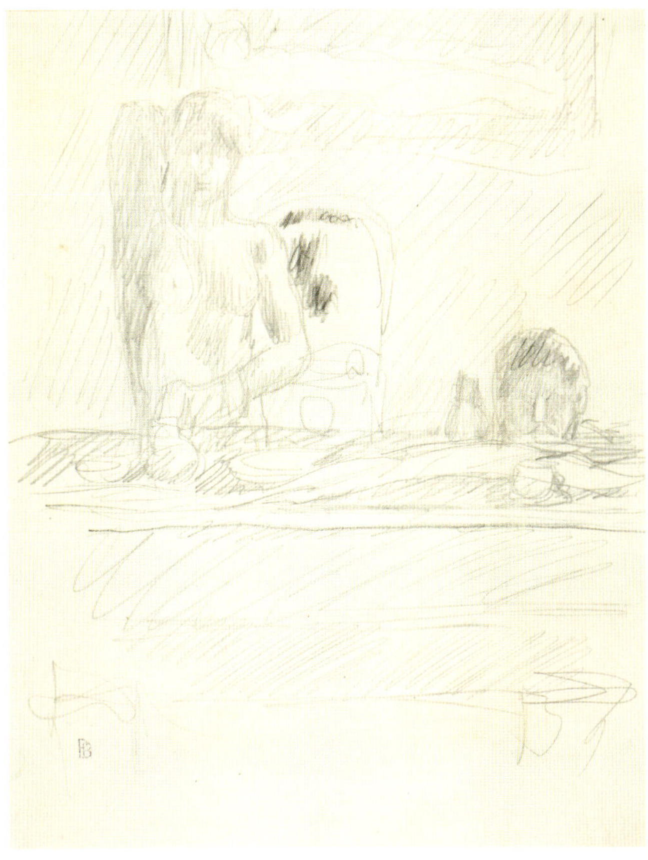

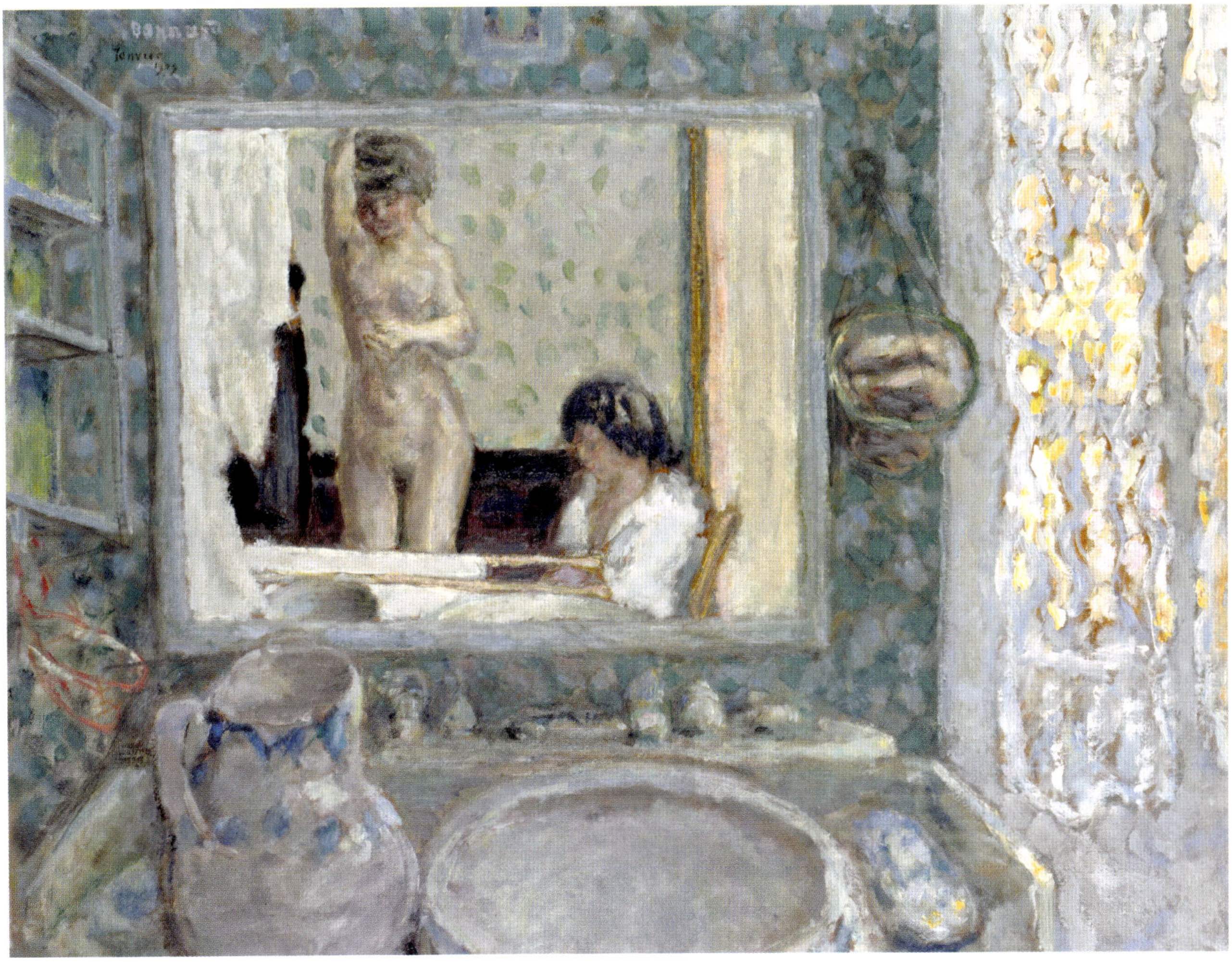

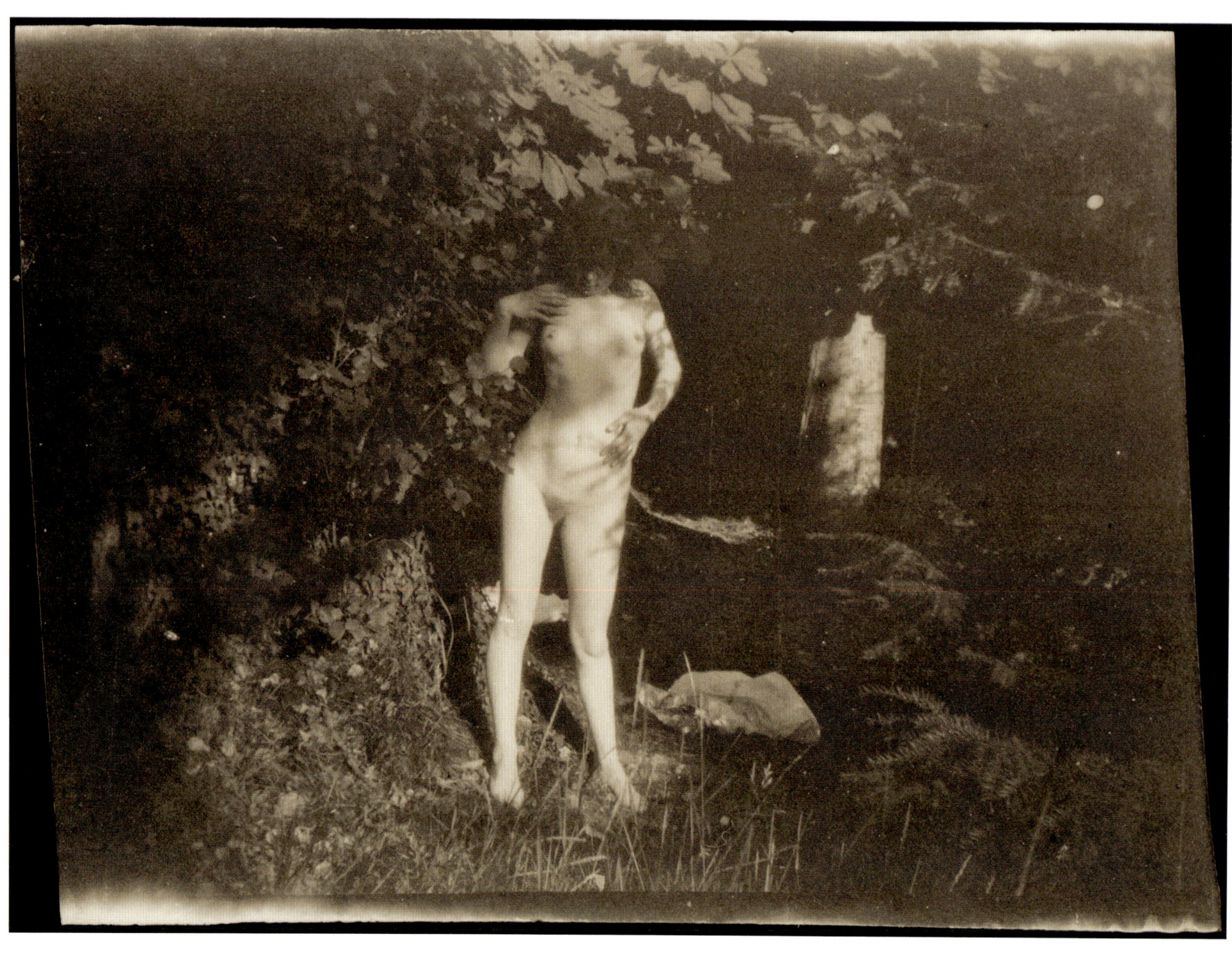

CAT. 22. Pierre Bonnard, Marthe standing in the sun, in Montval, 1900–1901. Modern print from original negative, negative: 1½ x 2⅛ in. (3.8 x 5.5 cm). Musée d'Orsay, Paris. Gift of M. Antoine Terrasse, 1992

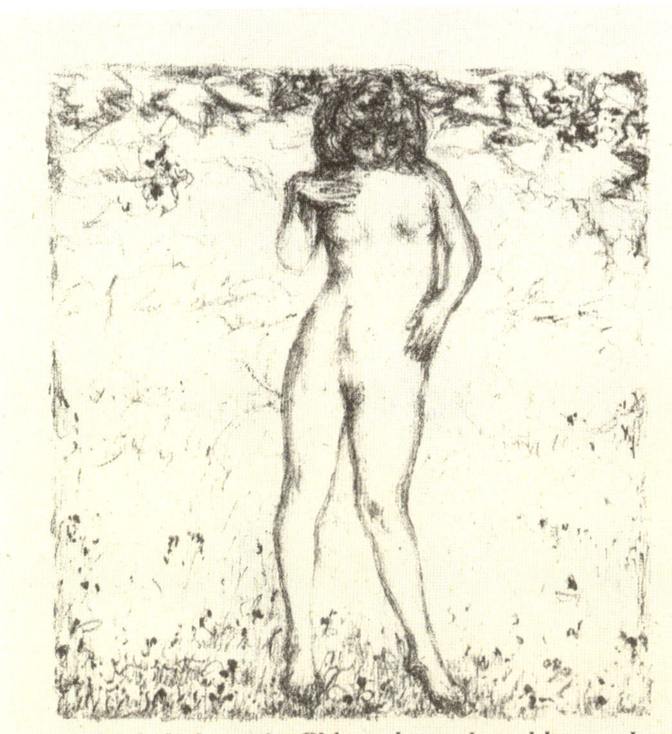
sembloit le bain de Chloé plus redoutable que la mer dont il étoit échappé. Bref, il lui étoit avis que son âme fût toujours entre les brigands, tant il avoit de peine, jeune garçon nourri aux champs, qui ne savoit encore que c'est du brigandage d'amour.

69

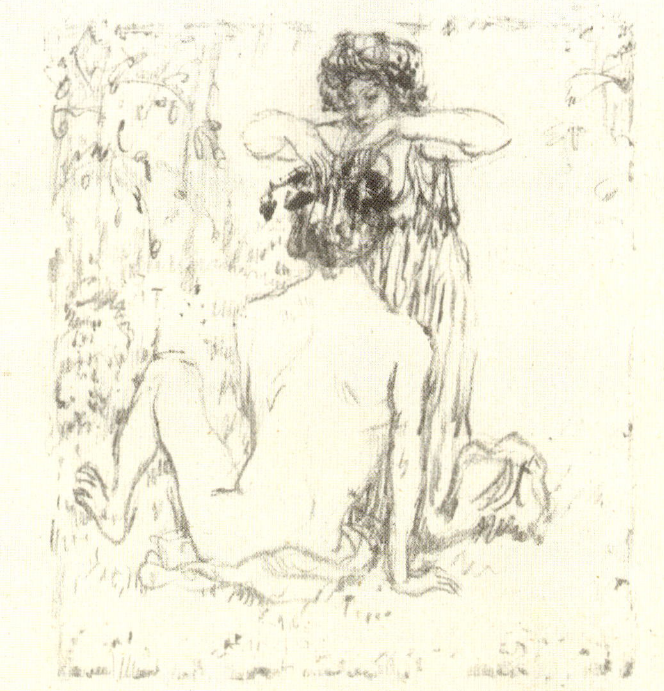
autres, de même qu'en un chœur de musique, unissoient par intervalles leur voix à celle du chanteur. Or, tant qu'ils voguèrent en pleine mer, le son dans cette étendue se perdoit et la voix s'évanouissoit en l'air; mais quand ils vinrent à

185 24

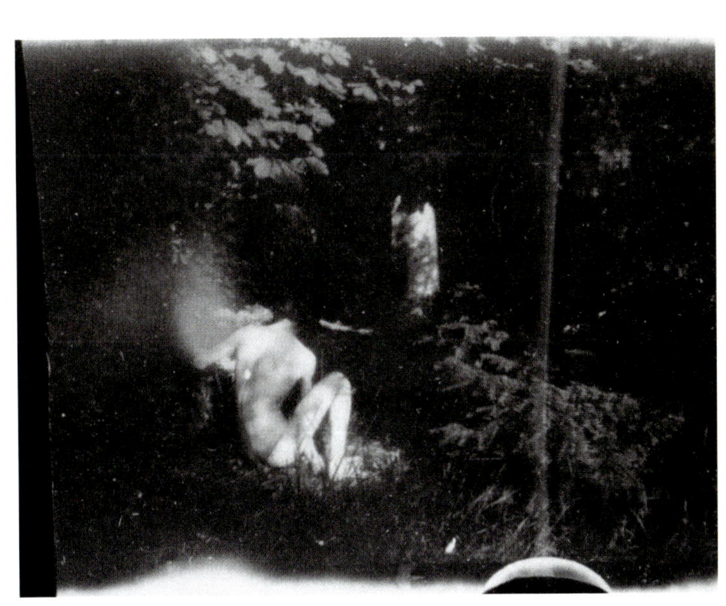

CAT. 23. Pierre Bonnard, "Daphnis et Chloé" (Daphnis and Chloé), illustration for *La pastorale de Longus*, p. 69, 1902. Lithograph, 12 x $9\frac{7}{8}$ in. (30.5 x 25 cm) page. Private collection

CAT. 24. Pierre Bonnard, "Daphnis et Chloé" (Daphnis and Chloé), illustration for *La pastorale de Longus*, p. 185, 1902. Lithograph, 12 x $9\frac{7}{8}$ in. (30.5 x 25 cm) page. Private collection

CAT. 25. Marthe Bonnard, Pierre Bonnard seated in the grass, 1900–1901. Modern print from original negative, negative: $1\frac{1}{2}$ x $2\frac{1}{8}$ in. (3.8 x 5.5 cm). Musée d'Orsay, Paris. Gift of the children of Charles Terrasse

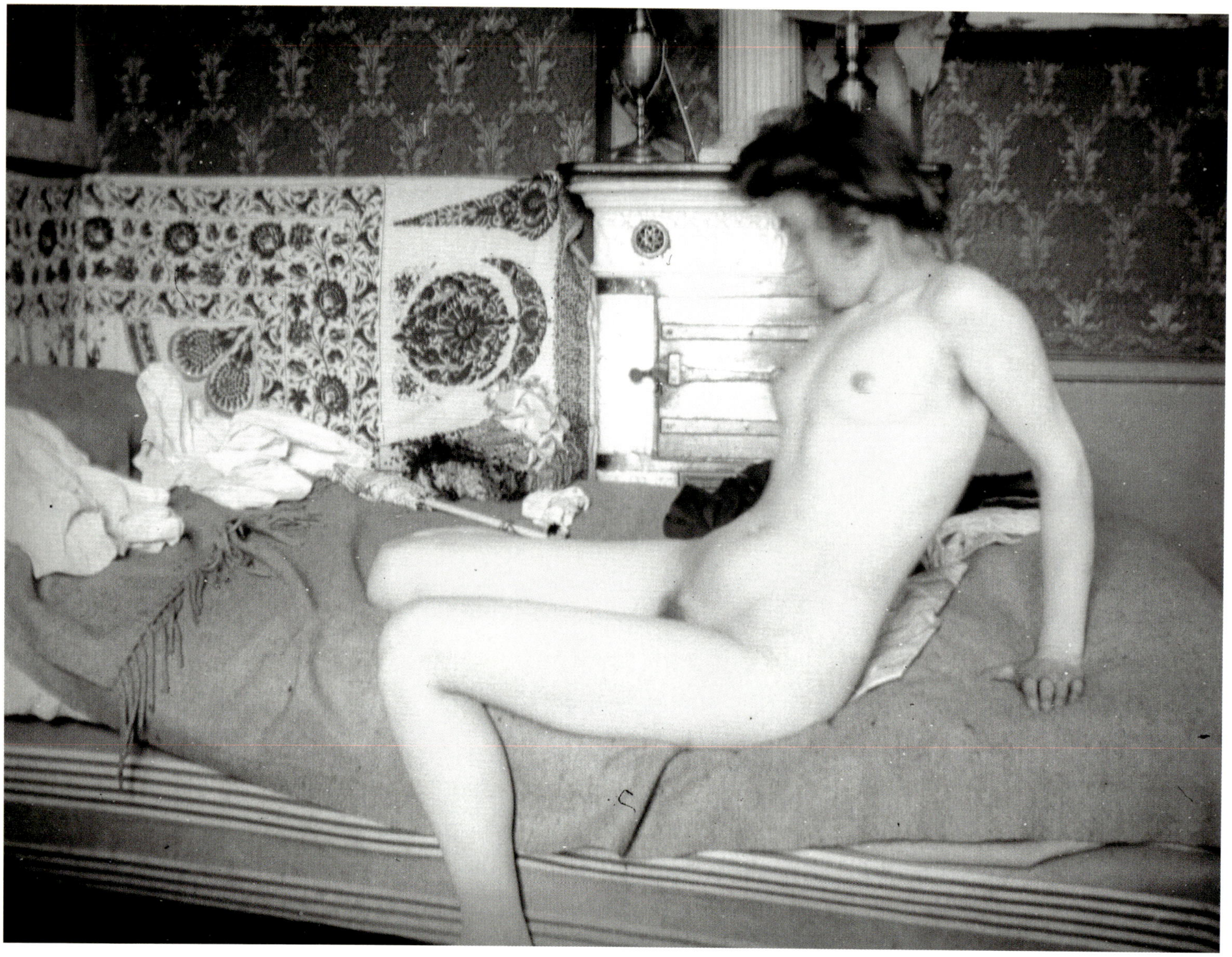

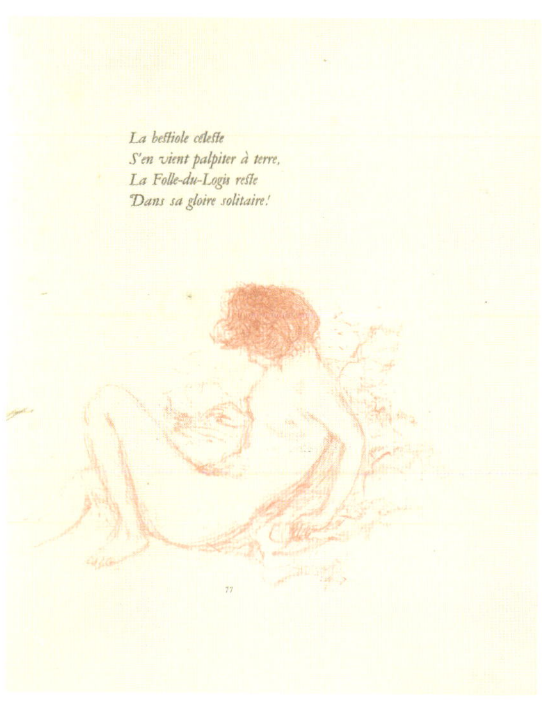

La bestiole céleste
S'en vient palpiter à terre,
La Folle-du-Logis reste
Dans sa gloire solitaire!

77

CAT. 26. Pierre Bonnard, Marthe seated in profile on the bed, her left leg hanging down, 1899–1900. Modern print from original negative, negative: 1⅝ x 2 in. (4 x 5.1 cm). Musée d'Orsay, Paris. Gift of M. Antoine Terrasse, 1992

CAT. 27. Pierre Bonnard, "Limbes" (Limbo), illustration from *Parallèlement* by Verlaine, 1900. Lithograph with rose-sanguine ink, 11⅝ x 9⅝ in. (29.6 x 24.6 cm). Van Gogh Museum, Amsterdam (Vincent van Gogh Foundation)

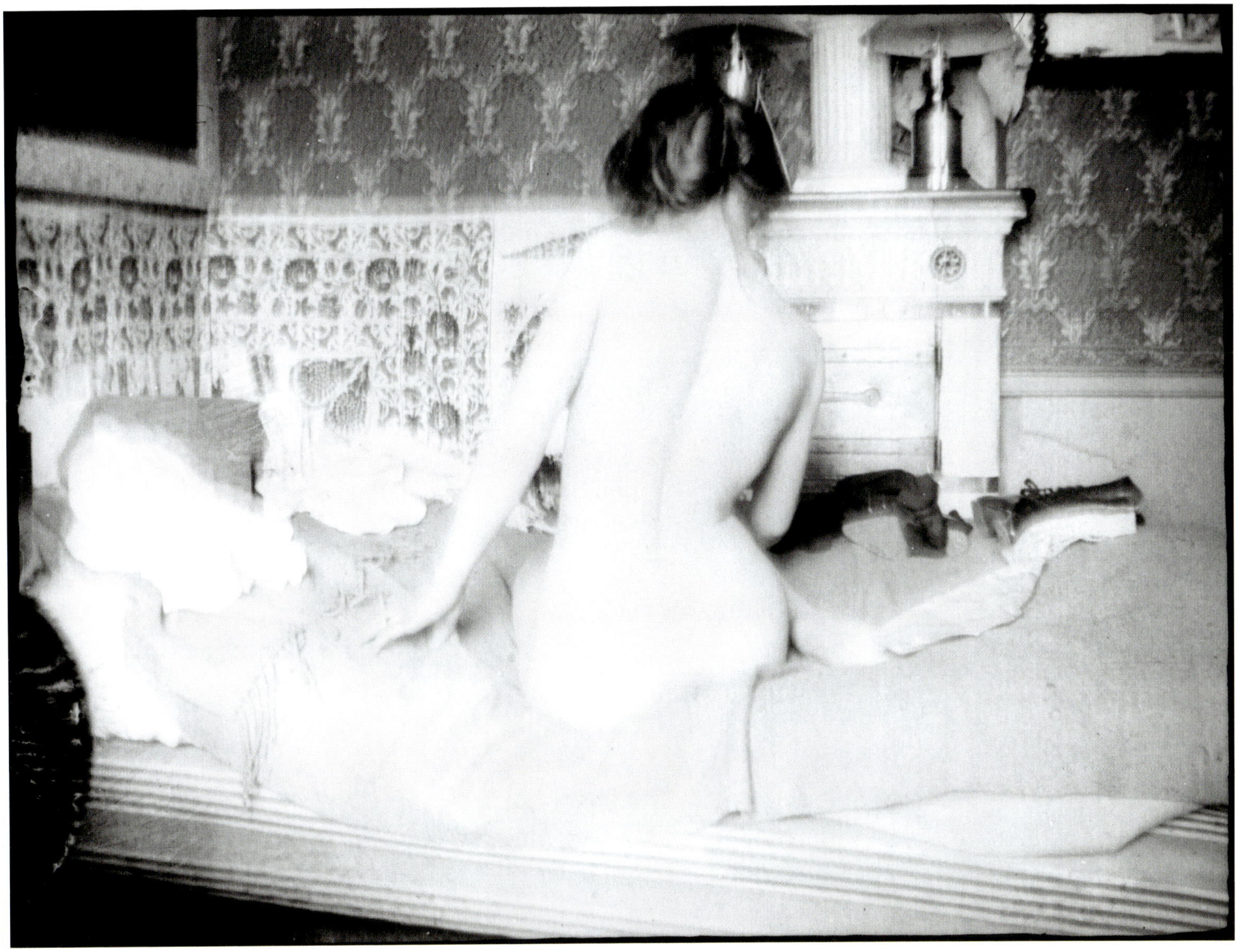

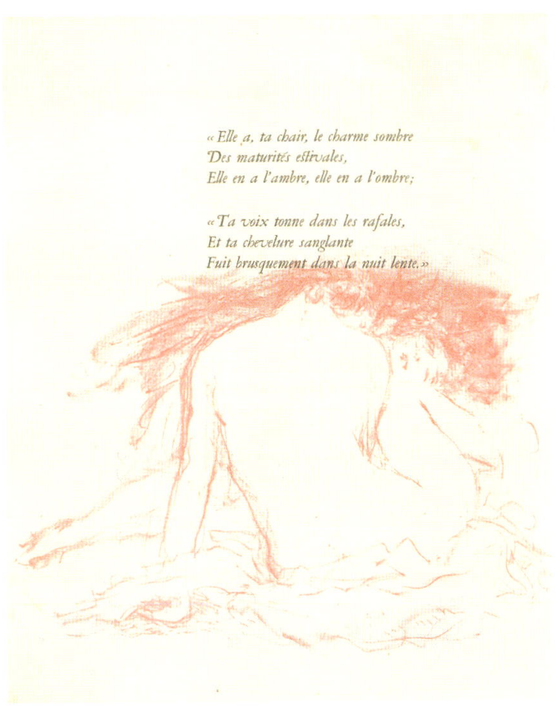

CAT. 28. Pierre Bonnard, Marthe nude, seated on the bed with her back turned, 1899–1900. Sepia-toned gelatin silver print, 1½ x 2 in. (3.8 x 5 cm). Musée d'Orsay, Paris. Gift of the children of Charles Terrasse, 1992

CAT. 29. Pierre Bonnard, "Eté" (Summer), illustration from *Parallèlement* by Verlaine, 1900. Lithograph with rose-sanguine ink, 11⅝ x 9⅝ in. (29.6 x 24.6 cm). Van Gogh Museum, Amsterdam (Vincent van Gogh Foundation)

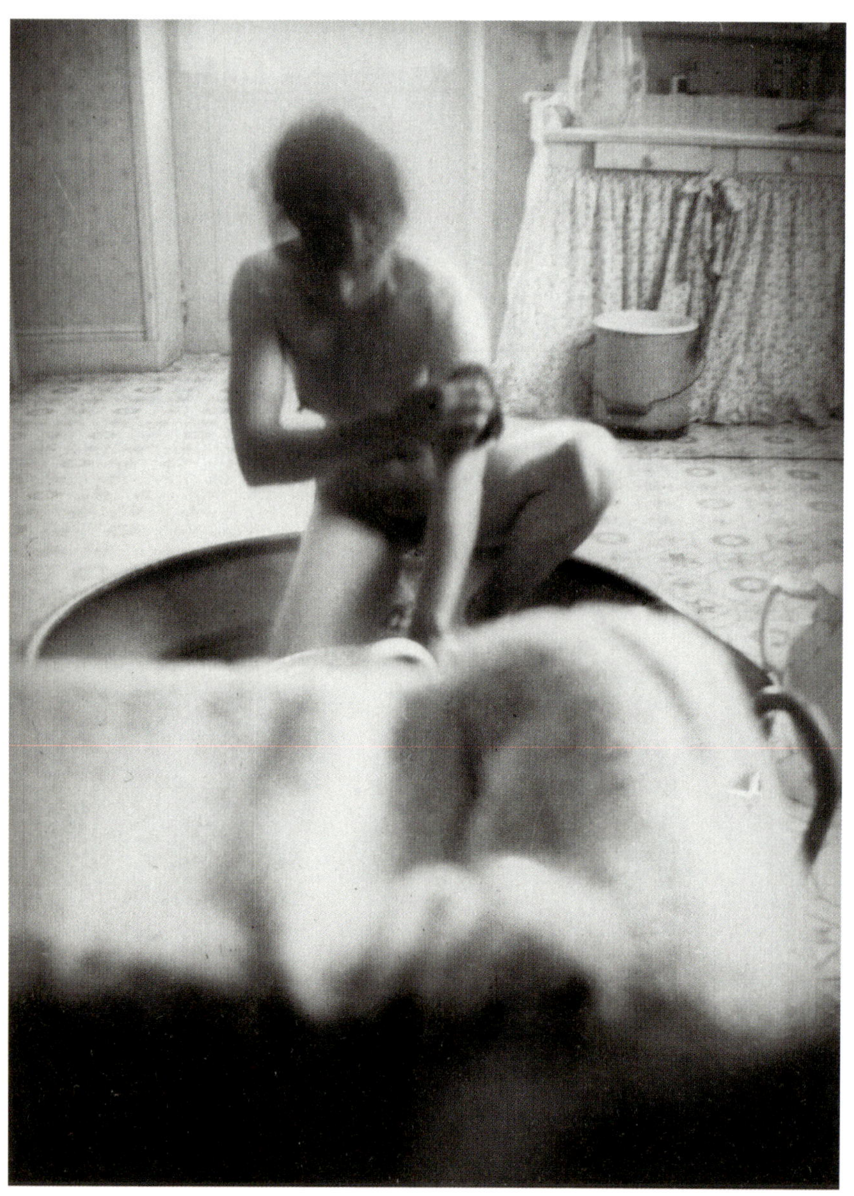

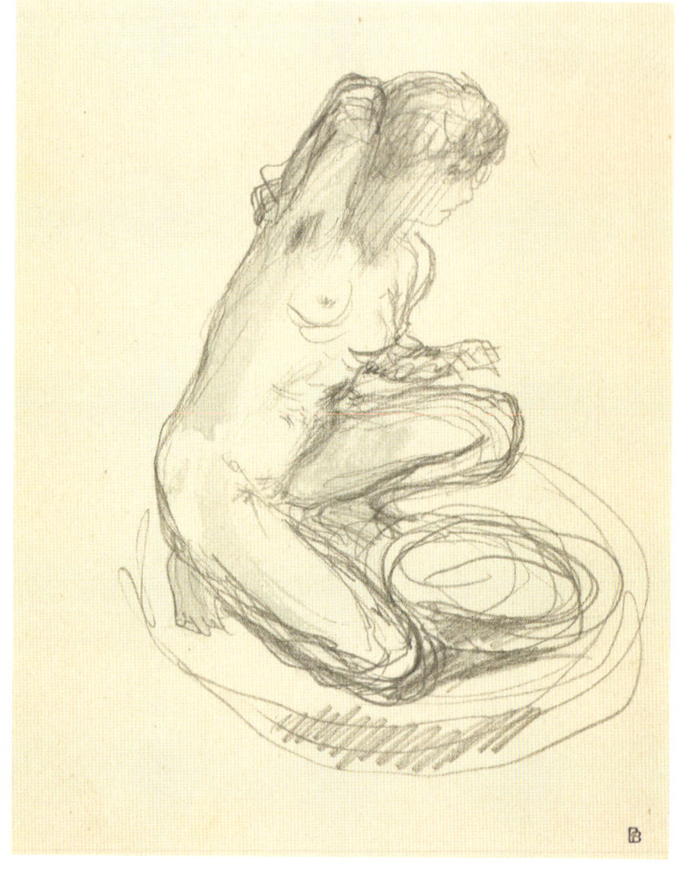

CAT. 30. Pierre Bonnard, Marthe in the bathtub, Vernouillet, ca. 1908–10. Modern print from original negative, negative: 3 1/8 x 2 1/8 in. (7.8 x 5.5 cm). Musée d'Orsay, Paris. Gift of the children of Charles Terrasse, 1992

CAT. 31. Pierre Bonnard, *Crouching Nude in a Tub*, 1925. Pencil and gray wash, 8 5/16 x 6 13/16 in. (21.7 x 17. 4 cm). Private collection

OPPOSITE: CAT. 32. Pierre Bonnard, Model taking off her blouse in Bonnard's Paris studio, ca. 1916. Original untinted print, 3 1/4 x 2 1/4 in. (8.2 x 5.8 cm). Musée d'Orsay, Paris

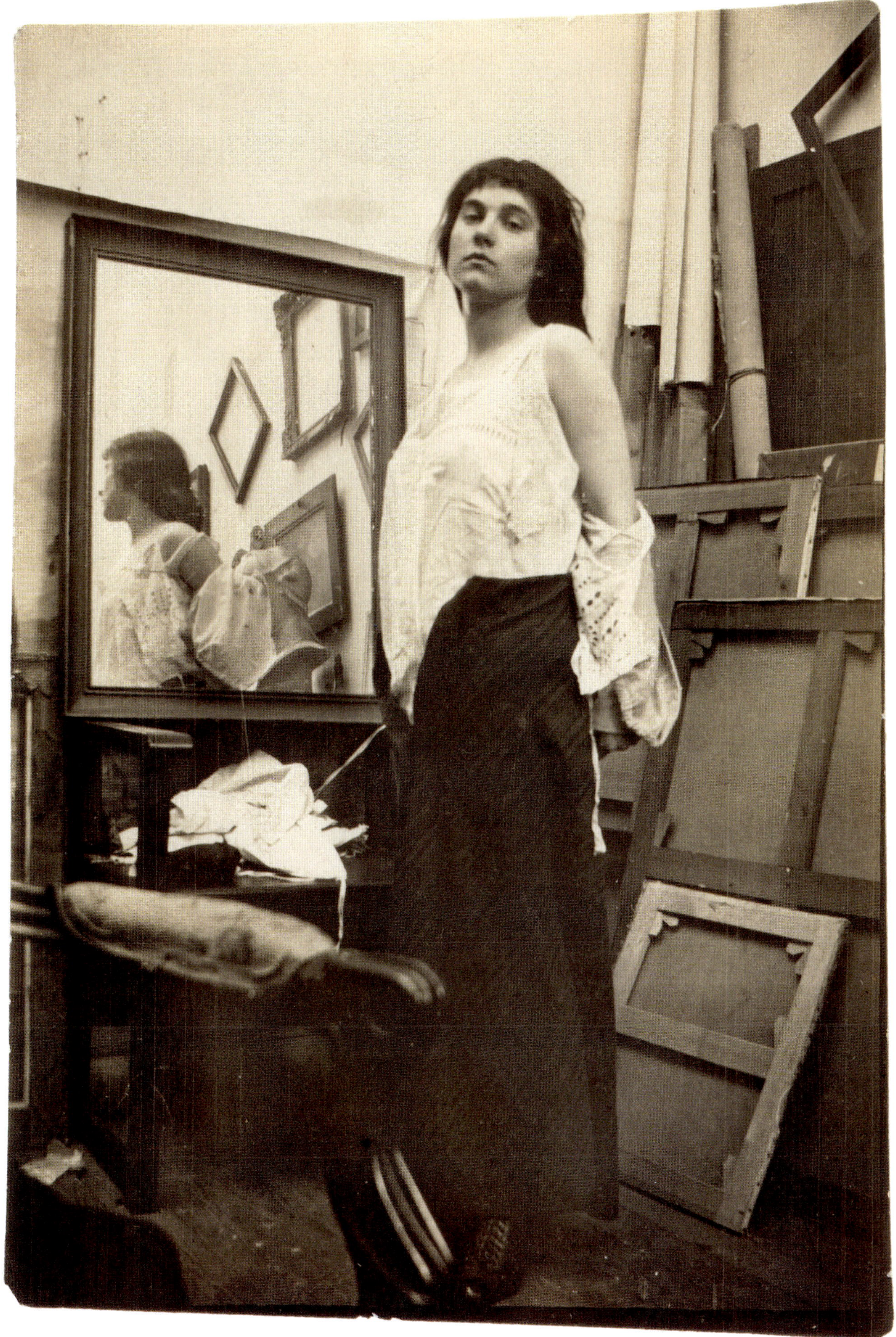

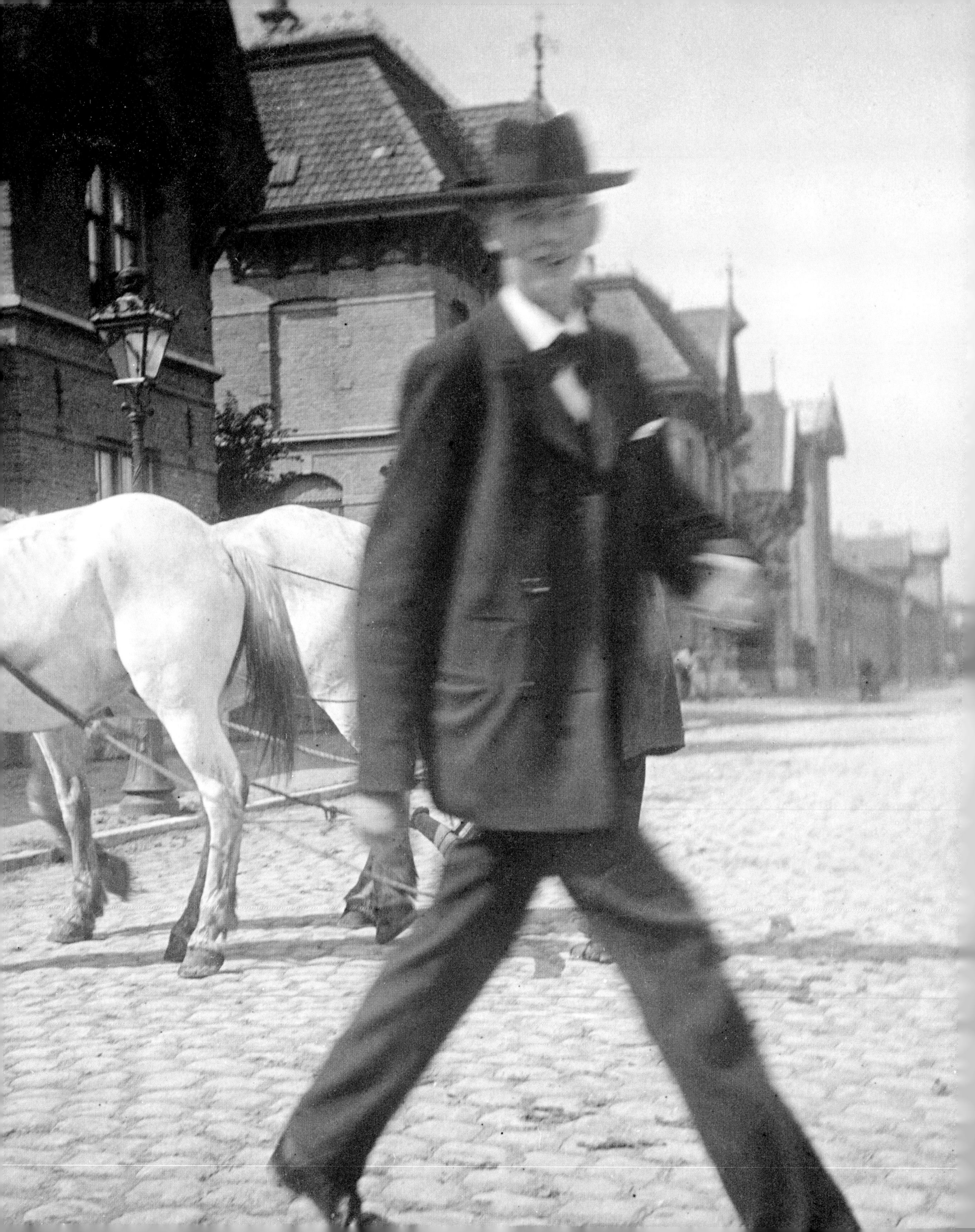

Movement Studies in an Urban Setting
The Photographs of George Hendrik Breitner

Hans Rooseboom

DETAIL OF CAT. 46

George Hendrik Breitner must have walked thousands of kilometers in Amsterdam, the city where he lived most of his life. He probably seldom left his house or studio without a sketchbook, paintbox, or camera. On one of his many walks, he went to the Oudezijds Achterburgwal, where—at some time between 1894 and 1898—he took a photograph in which a man can be seen urinating against a wall (fig. 1). That is, his pose permits almost no other conclusion. It seems very much as if the man saw there was a camera pointed at him; his head is turned to one side, and he looks straight at it. Admittedly, the 3½ x 4¾–inch camera Breitner used for this picture could be operated simply and quickly, but it was not very small (around 7½ inches high, 9 inches long, and 4⁵⁄₁₆ inches wide). So it is not surprising that the urinating man figured out he had been caught in the act. It is equally unsurprising that he did not expect to have his photograph taken just then. After all, at that time it was unusual to encounter someone with a camera in Amsterdam, where few private citizens owned such devices.

When Breitner started taking photographs, the No. 1 Kodak had recently been introduced, so the revolution in photography created by this camera was just beginning. Like the No. 1 Kodak, the camera Breitner used to photograph the urinating man was a box model, which did not have to be set on a tripod. It was somewhat larger, however, and instead of roll film, it had a magazine for twelve glass plates with which that number of pictures could be shot in sequence.[1]

Breitner took photographs for about twenty-five years, probably starting in 1889 and continuing until at least 1915, and he mainly shot Amsterdam street scenes. Quite a few of them are devoid of human figures, or nearly so, and consequently have a tranquil feel, but a considerable number of the nearly three thousand surviving negatives and prints have passersby as their main subjects. Breitner was one of the first photographers anywhere to capture bustling city life. Whereas the majority of his colleagues in Amsterdam, professional and amateur alike, preferred to photograph empty streets in which one's attention was not distracted by passersby, Breitner applied himself to making movement studies in an urban setting. He was not bothered by the fact that people often walked straight through the picture, were depicted out of focus, or were only partially visible. This approach was highly unusual in his day.

Breitner was first and foremost a painter. He had been trained in that profession, made his living from it, and owed his considerable reputation to it. Not until 1961, almost forty years after his death, did the

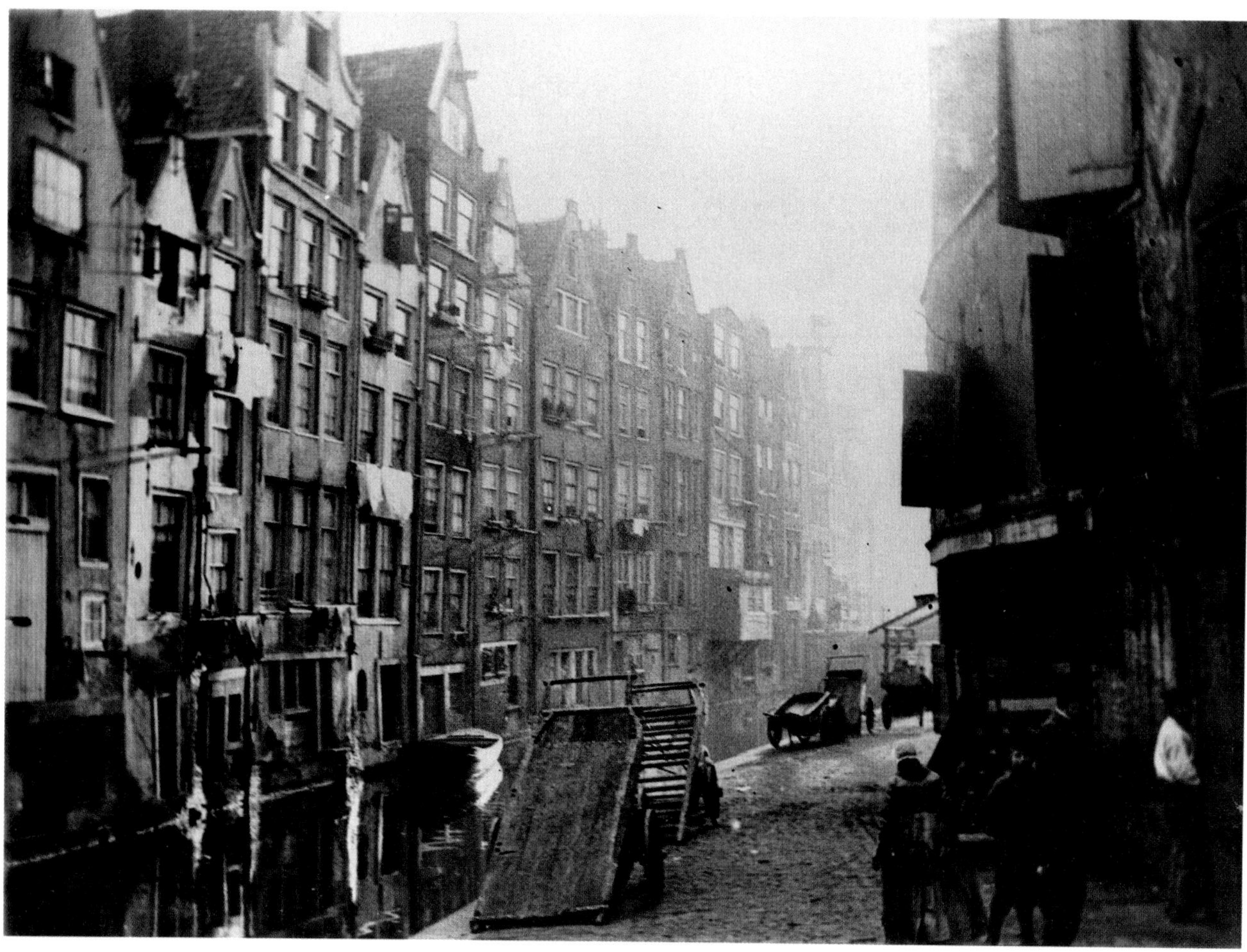

FIG. 1. George Hendrik Breitner, Oudezijds Achterburgwal, 1894–98. Gelatin silver print, 11¾ x 14½ in. (29.9 x 36.2 cm). Rijksmuseum, Amsterdam (RP-F-00-621)

photographic work come to light. Few people knew about it while he was alive, but now he is recognized as a photographer in his own right.

The discovery that Breitner had taken several thousand photographs over a quarter century naturally raised questions about the relation of those pictures to his painting. Why, for instance, did he take pictures, and what purpose did they serve? These questions have never been answered with complete certainty. Among all the surviving negatives and prints, only a few can be directly related to a drawing, a painting, or a watercolor. This leaves open the possibility that he also shot them for his own pleasure, like any other amateur photographer—albeit an exceptionally talented one who dismissed the conventions. The literature on Breitner is unclear in its findings on that point, but we do have clues as to how he made his photographs and what he intended them for. Recent investigation reveals that he occasionally set out with more than one camera.[2] This can only mean that he deliberately used different cameras for specific reasons. Presumably, Breitner was aware of the pictorial opportunities inherent in photography, however imperfect his technique may have been. Written on the envelopes in which he kept his negatives are such notations as "horses against the light."[3] The fact that he wanted to keep a number of negatives together in that envelope shows he was particularly interested

FIG. 2. George Hendrik Breitner, Military maneuvers, n.d. Printing-out paper, 3 x 3⅞ in. (7.7 x 10 cm). Collection RKD, The Hague (BR2173)

in the effect of backlighting. In addition to horses, he shot many cityscapes against the light. The contrast created by backlighting was heightened in rainy weather, when the sunlight reflected by cobblestones made them stand out against the shady areas of the image (cat. 34).

Two prints of military maneuvers from one and the same negative suggest that Breitner was aware of the effect of backlighting and of the contrast of silhouettes that stood out against a light sky and against walls bathed in sunlight. In one of them, everything is clearly visible—if somewhat pale and lacking in contrast—whereas the other contact print is underexposed, with barely defined dark areas. In many shots of military maneuvers, he captured the riders, horses, carts, and cannons in silhouette (fig. 2). From a technical standpoint, these prints were unsuccessful. Yet technical perfection meant little to Breitner. Underexposure and backlighting created a powerful chiaroscuro effect, and they lent the images in which he used this stylistic device a certain drama that is lacking in the work of other photographers.[4] A view of Prinsengracht, for example, is also underexposed, resulting in a magnificent silhouette of a ship's mast, the tower of the Westerkerk, and a lamppost (fig. 3). In the same way a maker of stereo photographs used *repoussoirs* to reinforce the suggestion of depth, Breitner used backlit objects to enhance the silhouette effect.

The way Breitner exposed and printed his negatives indicates that he played with technical possibilities in ways unknown to his contemporaries, who might have mocked him had they been aware of his approach. The silhouette effect makes his work appear undeniably modern (cat. 35). We only know of original prints from a small number of negatives—around 20 percent—whereas many an enlargement was printed with poor contrast (grayish), and many of Breitner's negatives are "soft" or "thin" and also with poor contrast, which was why they were sometimes chemically intensified.[5] On the other hand, the images from which only a negative has survived are occasionally reproduced in books on Breitner's photographs with excessive contrast, reflecting the modern preference for prints with marked contrast.[6]

Breitner's photographs also look modern because of their snapshotlike nature and because of the fragmented view they give of life in cities such as

FIG. 3. George Hendrik Breitner, View of Prinsengracht, with the Westerkerk in the background, n.d. Printing-out paper, 3¼ x 3¾ in. (8.2 x 9.4 cm). Collection RKD, The Hague (BR2185)

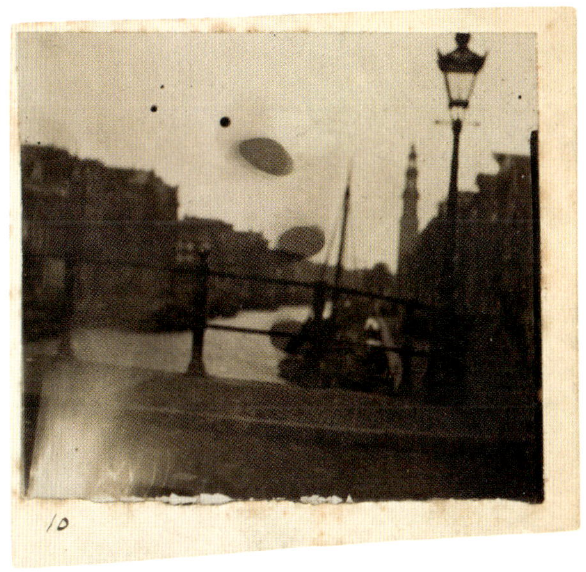

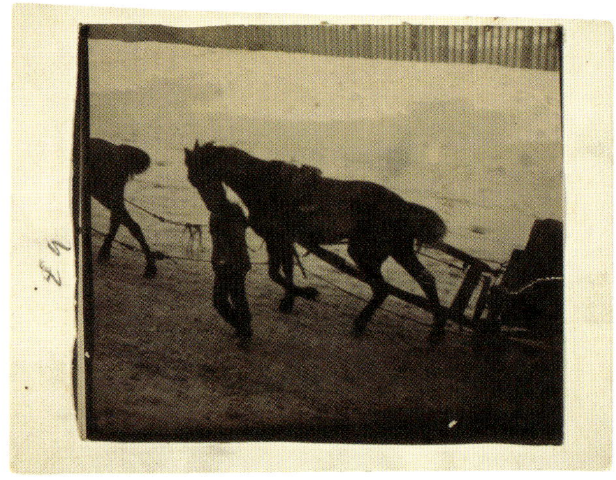

FIG. 4. George Hendrik Breitner, Horses seen from above, n.d. Printing-out paper, 3¹/₈ x 3³/₄ in. (8.1 x 9.6 cm). Collection RKD, The Hague (BR2194)

Amsterdam, Rotterdam, Paris, and London. Consider, for example, the many people walking across the picture, the juxtaposition of mutually unconnected elements in one image (cat. 46), and the radical cropping, blurred movement, and unconventional high and low viewpoints in other images (e.g., fig. 4). On the other hand, Breitner also photographed numerous serene cityscapes and even made intimate portraits (cat. 36). He used different cameras, including a large model for 5⅛ x 7–inch shots and the small Folding Pocket Kodak, introduced in 1897; these made different working methods alternately possible and necessary.

As a photographer, Breitner showed two faces. Alongside the many gritty snapshots that tellingly depict busy city life there are muted, thoughtful shots showing the city as it might look on a quiet Sunday morning. There is also a disparity between his technique and his choice of subject. On the one hand, Breitner's photographs are modern in that they are early examples of the snapshot aesthetics that only became "socially acceptable" decades after his death. On the other hand, however, their subject matter is conservative. His camerawork records few of the radical changes to the face of Amsterdam that occurred after he moved there in 1886. Large, new, eye-catching buildings such as the Central Station (finished in 1889) or the Berlage Stock Exchange (1903) are seldom shown—and then only in the background. Instead, Breitner focused on the intimate "old city." Certainly, he enjoyed taking pictures of building excavations and frequently did so, but only so long as pilings were being driven and laborers and horses were working in the sand and the mud (fig. 5). Once such preparatory work was completed and the actual construction started, his interest waned. He was intrigued by horses and horse trams but would have nothing to do with electric trams, which appeared in 1900; he called them "nasty, soulless boxes."[7] Breitner did not take an interest in how his hometown of Rotterdam was being changed and modernized even faster than Amsterdam. He only depicted the Rotterdam of his youth, and then only the old center, as if there were no large, new, and rapidly expanding docks. "Yesterday I was in Rotterdam," he wrote in 1882, half a dozen years before starting to take photographs. "It's still a fine city, always bustling, dirty and picturesque. . . . I wouldn't give you a penny for the new part."[8]

The notes on the negative envelopes tell us not only something about Breitner's interest in backlighting but also about his intentions. In some cases, the references are simply topographic—"Overtoom," "Kalverstraat," "Spui," and so forth—but other references suggest a motif. For example, he classified the many negatives of horses as "horses against the light," "horses seen from the side" (fig. 6), and "horse and cart." That Breitner grouped his negatives this way indicates that he regarded them as a sample collection.[9] An ordinary amateur photographer would be highly unlikely to arrange them in such a manner. Other notes also reveal that he apparently organized negatives by motif, such as "children in the street" and "road menders"—subjects that also appear in his paintings.

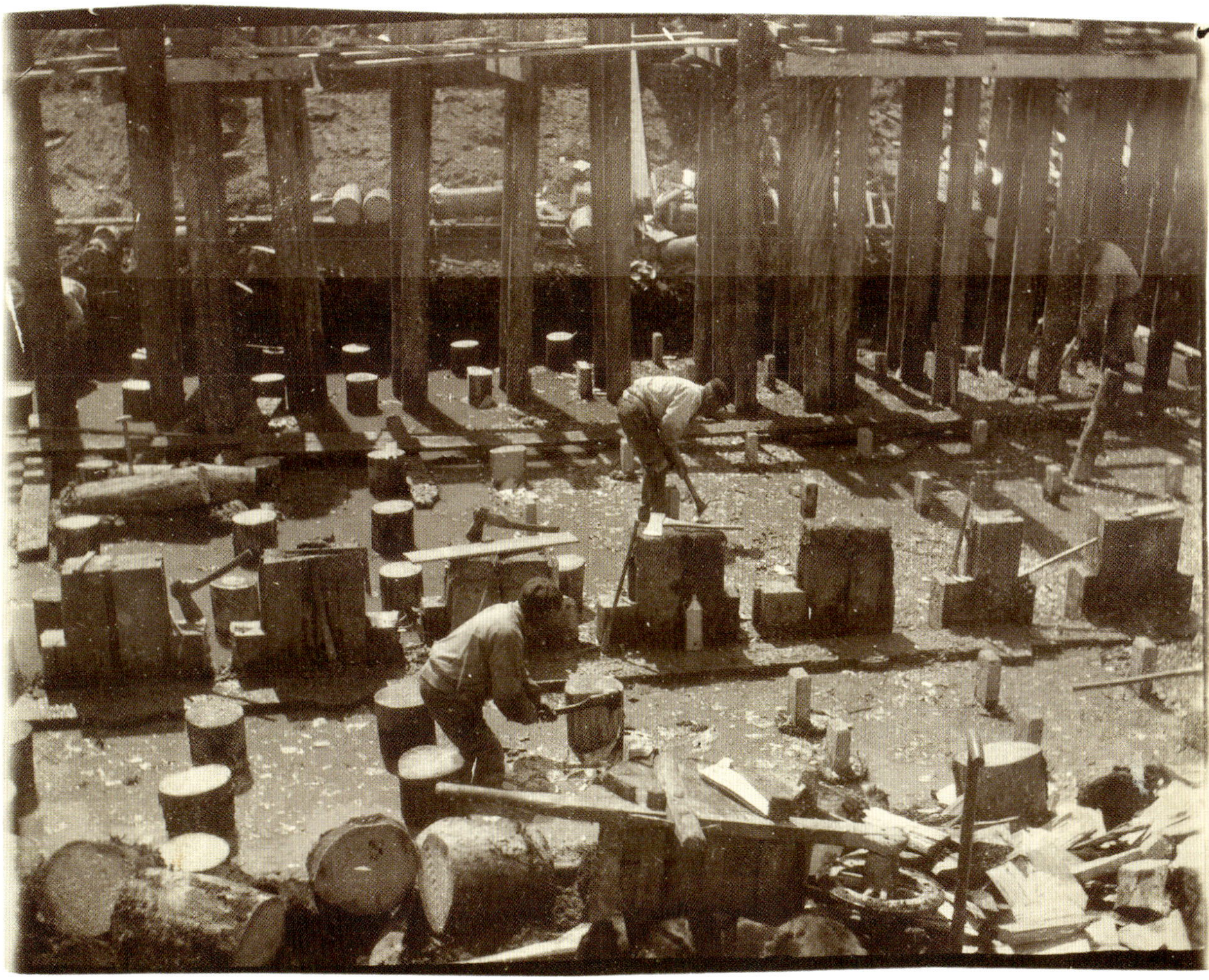

FIG. 5. George Hendrik Breitner, Excavation near Van Diemenstraat, 1897. Printing-out paper, 3 1/8 x 4 1/8 in. (7.9 x 10.4 cm). Collection RKD, The Hague (BR2223)

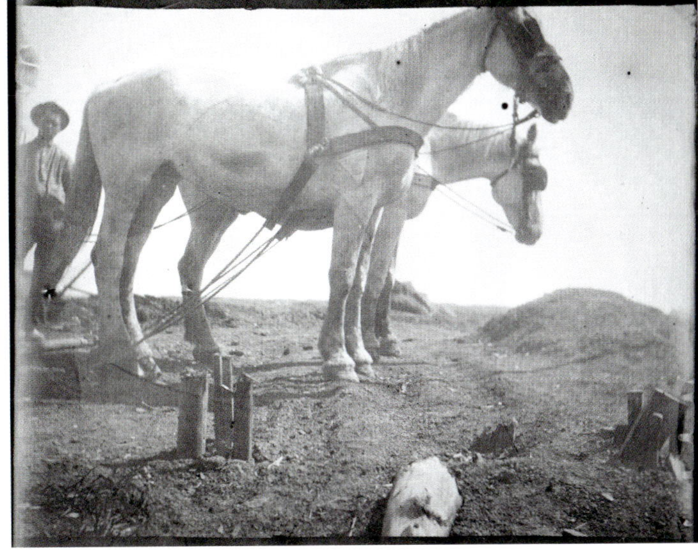

FIG. 6. George Hendrik Breitner, Two horses on the building site in Cruquiusweg, n.d. Modern scan from original negative. Collection RKD, The Hague (BR2271)

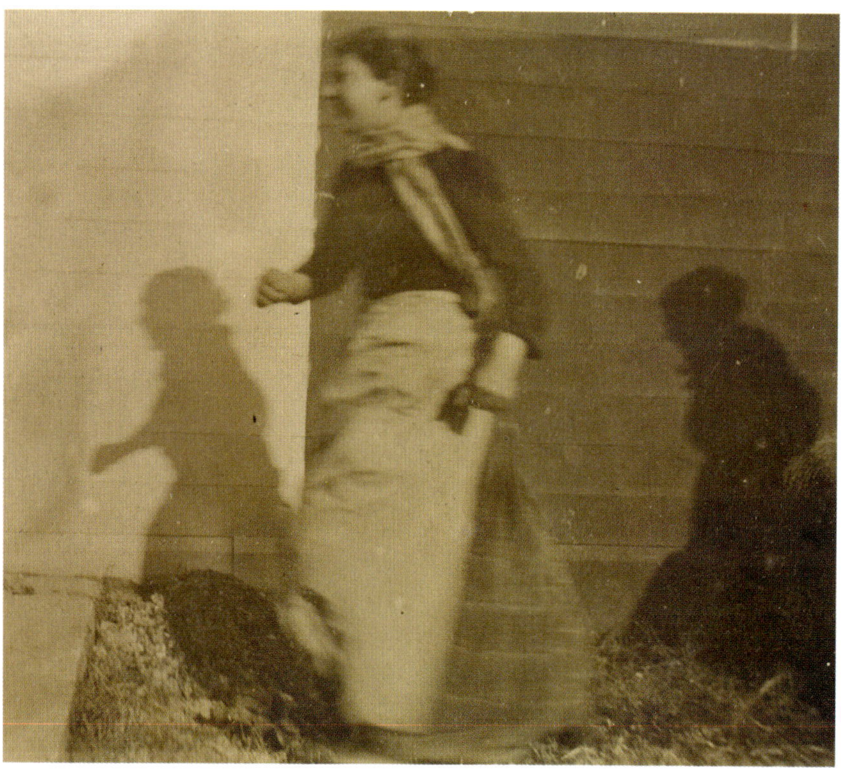

FIG. 7. George Hendrik Breitner, Woman running, n.d. Printing-out paper, 3 x 3³/₈ in. (7.5 x 8.6 cm). Collection RKD, The Hague (BR2021)

The strongest clue that Breitner took his photographs, at least in part, as a basis for his paintings may be the envelope on which he jotted "Damrak as a study/ corner of Oude Brugsteeg."

The surviving negatives and prints show that Breitner photographed passersby on the street both "on the move" and at a standstill, posing for him; some of these people posed as if they were walking. In addition, there are various shots of his models posing in a back garden, allowing him to make what were undeniably movement studies (fig. 7). These also indicate that Breitner wanted to use photographs as study material. Obviously, he sometimes waited at certain spots in the city until a passerby walked across the scene in a way he wanted. This is evident, for example, in two shots taken at the corner of Prinsengracht and Rozengracht, where a servant girl is visible in the picture on the right in front of the otherwise nearly empty Westermarkt (fig. 8).[10] Occasionally, he even followed pedestrians for some distance, prompting them to notice him and look around (fig. 9).

Because there is as yet no catalogue raisonné of Breitner's paintings, watercolors, drawings, and photographs, it is not clear if he regarded his photographs primarily as study material or if he also took pictures for pleasure. The technical imperfection of many shots cannot be attributed solely to carelessness or incompetence. It is apparent, rather, that he sought to capture the pictorial or atmospheric effect, not a technically exact image. In so doing, Breitner demonstrated that he was the painter-turned-photographer par excellence.

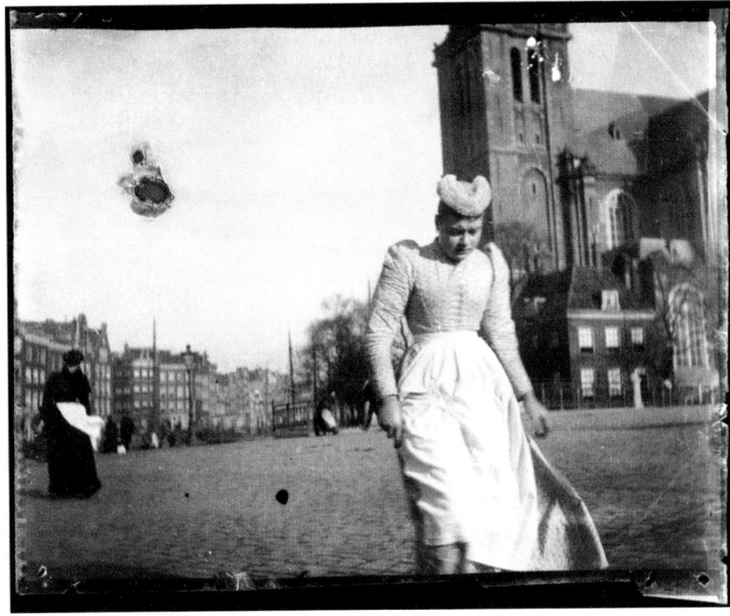

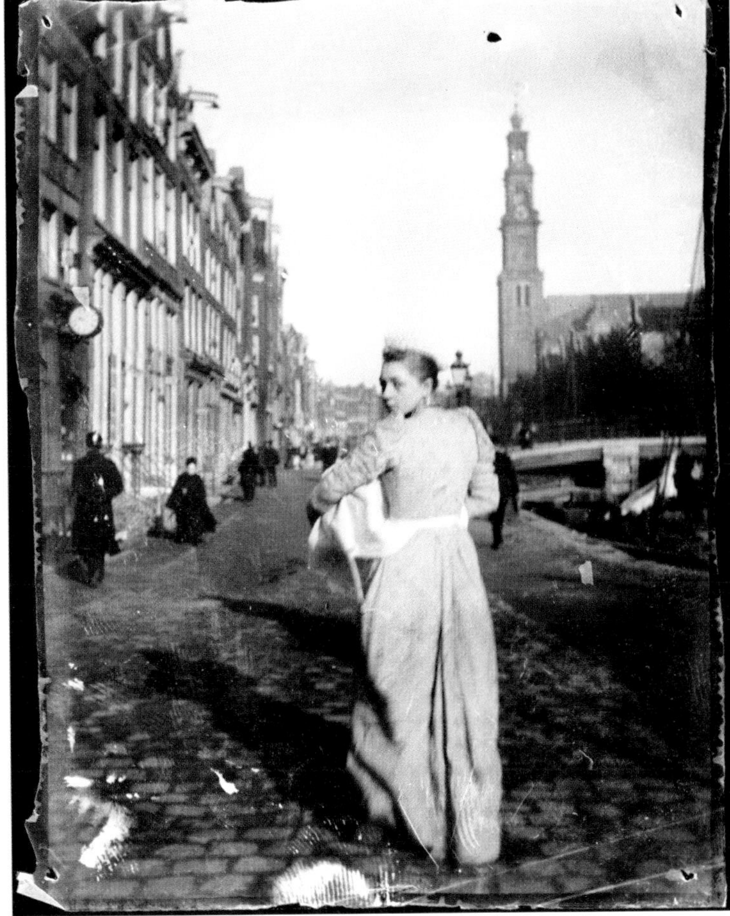

NOTES

1. For this camera, see for example Paul Hefting, "Notities over G. H. Breitner," *Bulletin van het Rijksmuseum* 16, no. 4 (1968): pp. 170, 172.
2. Anneke van Veen, ed., *G. H. Breitner: Fotograaf van het Amsterdamse stadsgezicht* (Bussum: Thoth, 1997), p. 124, cat. nos. 245–48. Cf. also pp. 113, 144.
3. "Paarden tegen het licht in." These envelopes—probably incomplete—are in the collection of the Rijksbureau voor Kunsthistorische Documentatie (RKD, Netherlands Institute for Art History), The Hague.
4. Cf. Tineke de Ruiter, "Breitner en het fotografisch ambacht," in Van Veen, *G. H. Breitner*, pp. 114–15.
5. See Van Veen, *G. H. Breitner*, pp. 114, 125, 152, 171, where mention is made of the artist's methods for heightening contrast or improving definition. Cf. also p. 45.
6. See, for example, Rieta Bergsma and Paul Hefting, eds., *George Hendrik Breitner, 1857–1923: Schilderijen, tekeningen, foto's* (Bussum: Thoth, 1994), p. 223.
7. "Leelijke, ziellooze doozen," ibid., p. 182.
8. "Gisteren was ik nog even in Rotterdam . . . 't Is toch een mooi[e] stad. altijd woelig, smerig en schilderachtig. . . . voor 't nieuwe gedeelte geef ik geen duit." Paul Hefting, *G. H. Breitner: Brieven aan A. P. van Stolk* (Utrecht: Haentjens Dekker and Gumbert, 1970), p. 28.
9. Cf. de Ruiter, "Breitner en het fotografisch ambacht," in Van Veen, *G. H. Breitner*, pp. 109–11.
10. Cf. Tineke de Ruiter, "Tussen dynamiek en verstilling: Breitners glazen foto's van Amsterdam," in Van Veen, *G. H. Breitner*, pp. 14–15, figs. 4–6.

FIG. 8. George Hendrik Breitner, Corner of Prinsengracht and Rozengracht, with the Westerkerk in the background, n.d. Modern scan from original negative. Collection RKD, The Hague (BR126)

FIG. 9. George Hendrik Breitner, Servant girl on Prinsengracht, with the Westerkerk in the background, n.d. Modern scan from original negative. Collection RKD, The Hague (BR116)

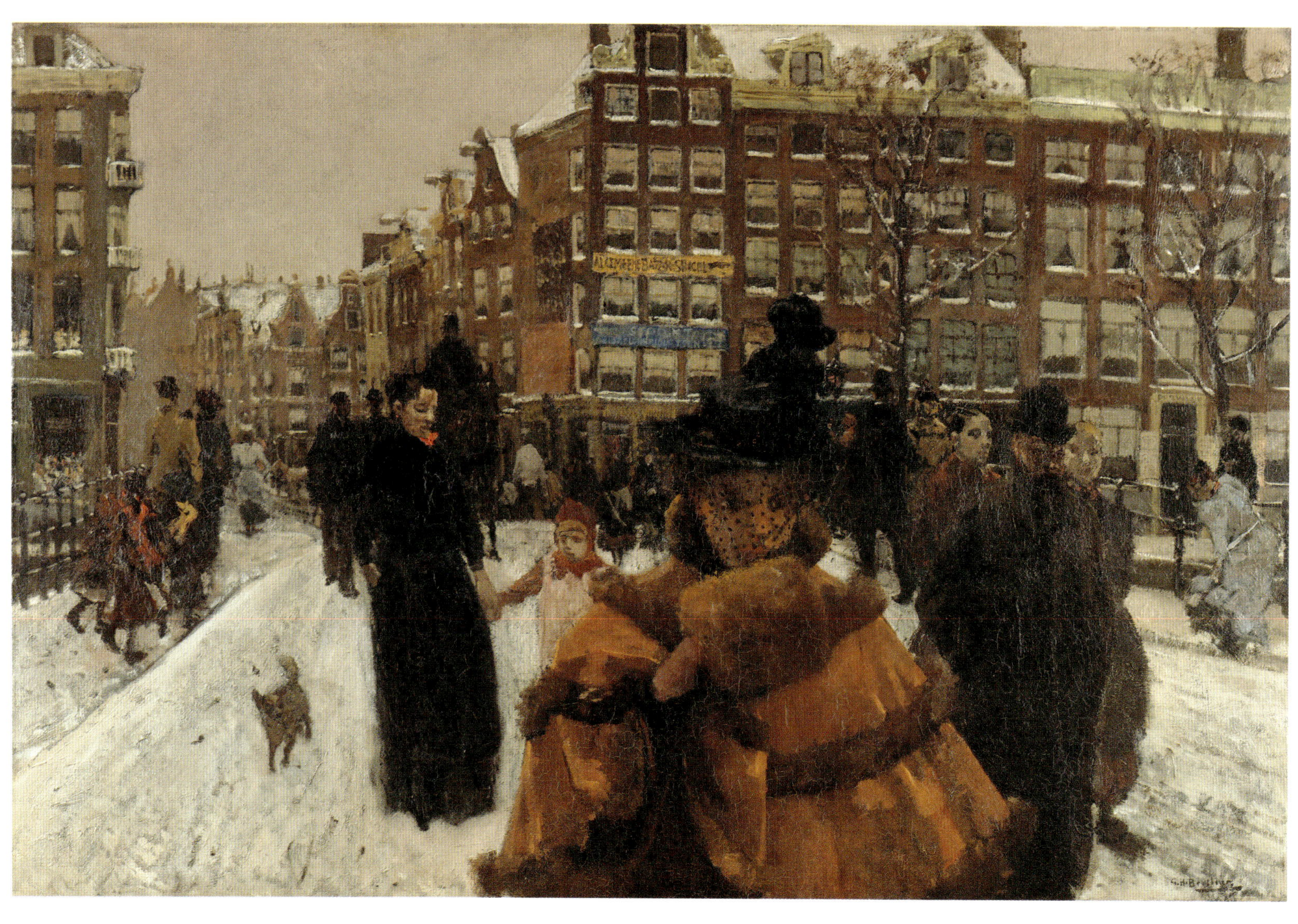

CAT. 33. George Hendrik Breitner, *Bridge over the Singel near Paleisstraat in Amsterdam*, ca. 1897. Oil on canvas, 39 3/8 x 59 7/8 in. (100 x 152 cm). Rijksmuseum, Amsterdam. Bequest of Mr. and Mrs. Drucker-Fraser

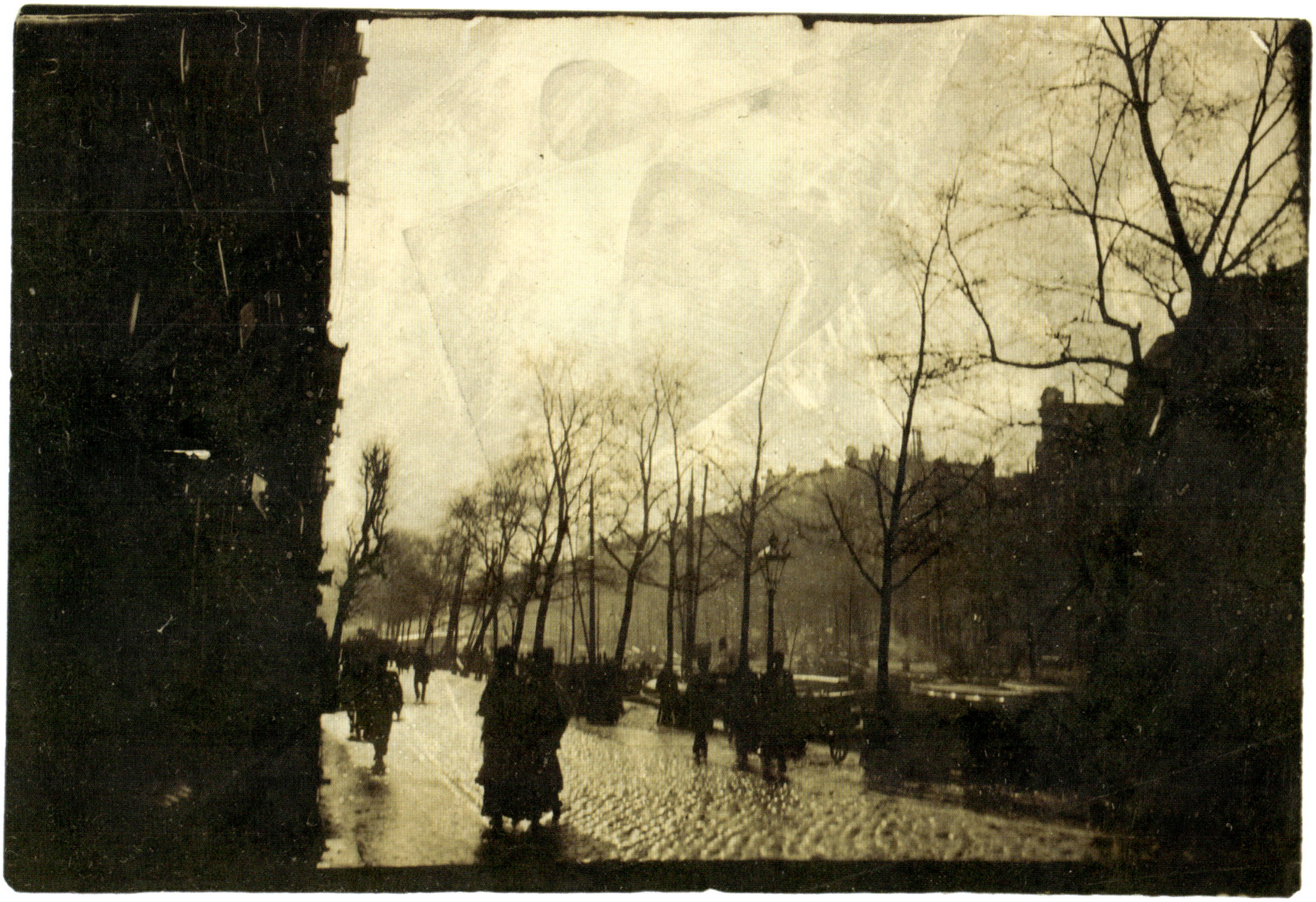

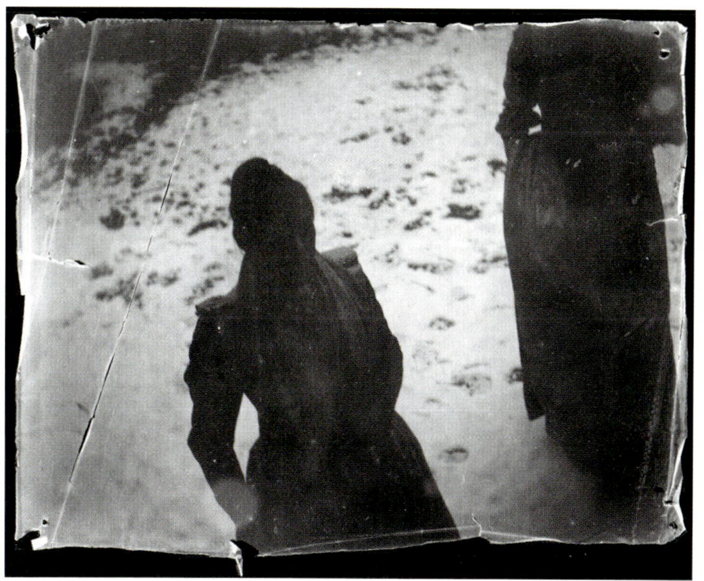

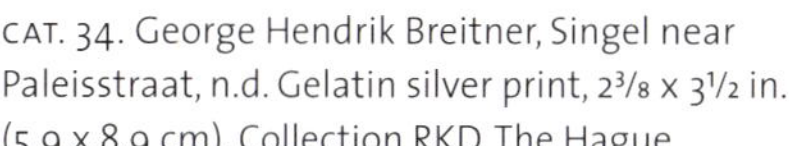

CAT. 34. George Hendrik Breitner, Singel near Paleisstraat, n.d. Gelatin silver print, 2³/₈ x 3¹/₂ in. (5.9 x 8.9 cm). Collection RKD, The Hague

CAT. 35. George Hendrik Breitner, Two girls in a snowy garden, n.d. Modern scan from original negative. Collection RKD, The Hague

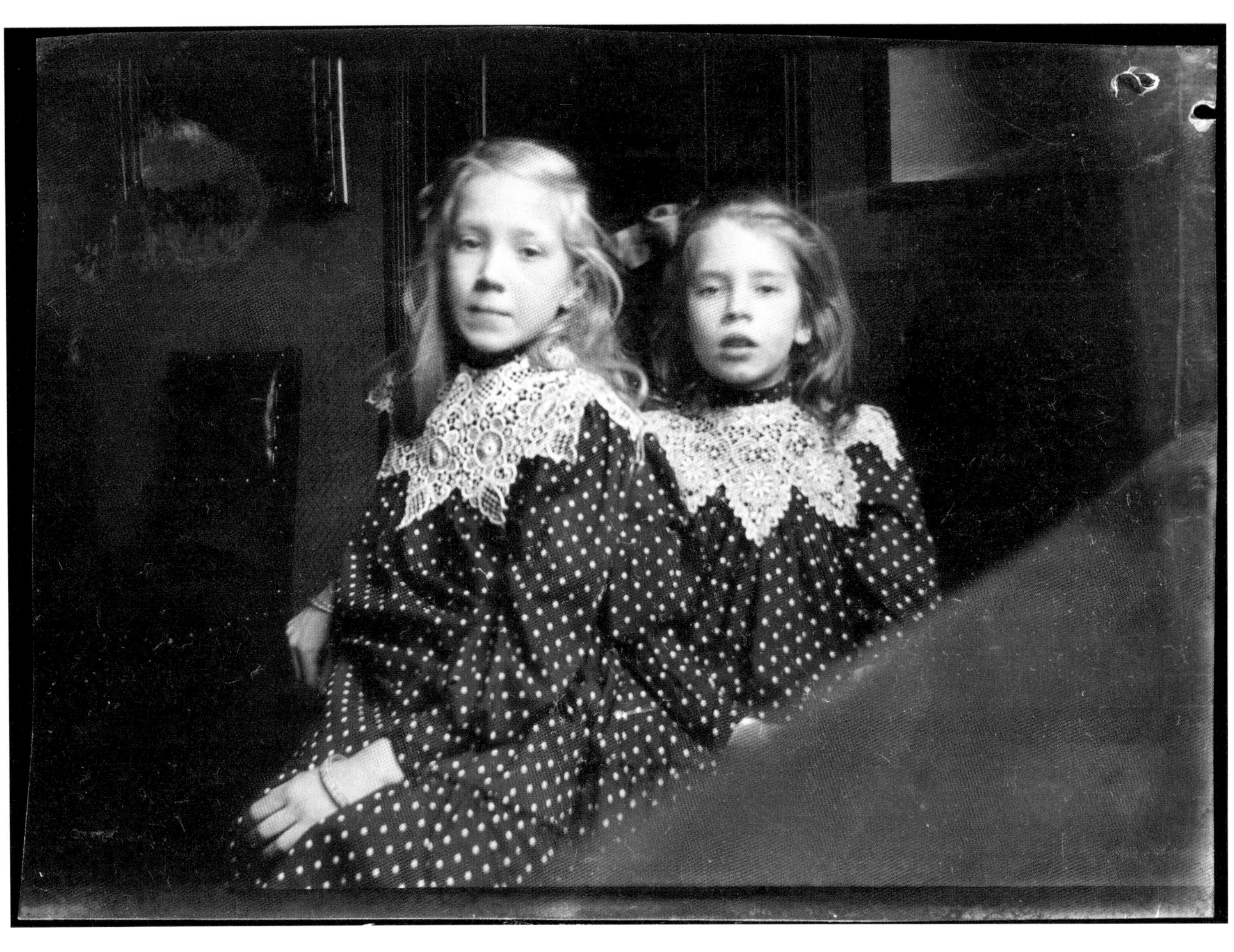

CAT. 36. George Hendrik Breitner, Portrait of Emma and Bé Hermsen, ca. 1905. Modern scan from original negative. Collection RKD, The Hague

CAT. 37. George Hendrik Breitner, Women dancing, n.d. Gelatin silver, printing-out paper. Collection RKD, The Hague

CAT. 38. George Hendrik Breitner, Girls holding hands on "Hartjesdag" in Amsterdam, n.d. Modern print/scan from original negative. Collection RKD, The Hague

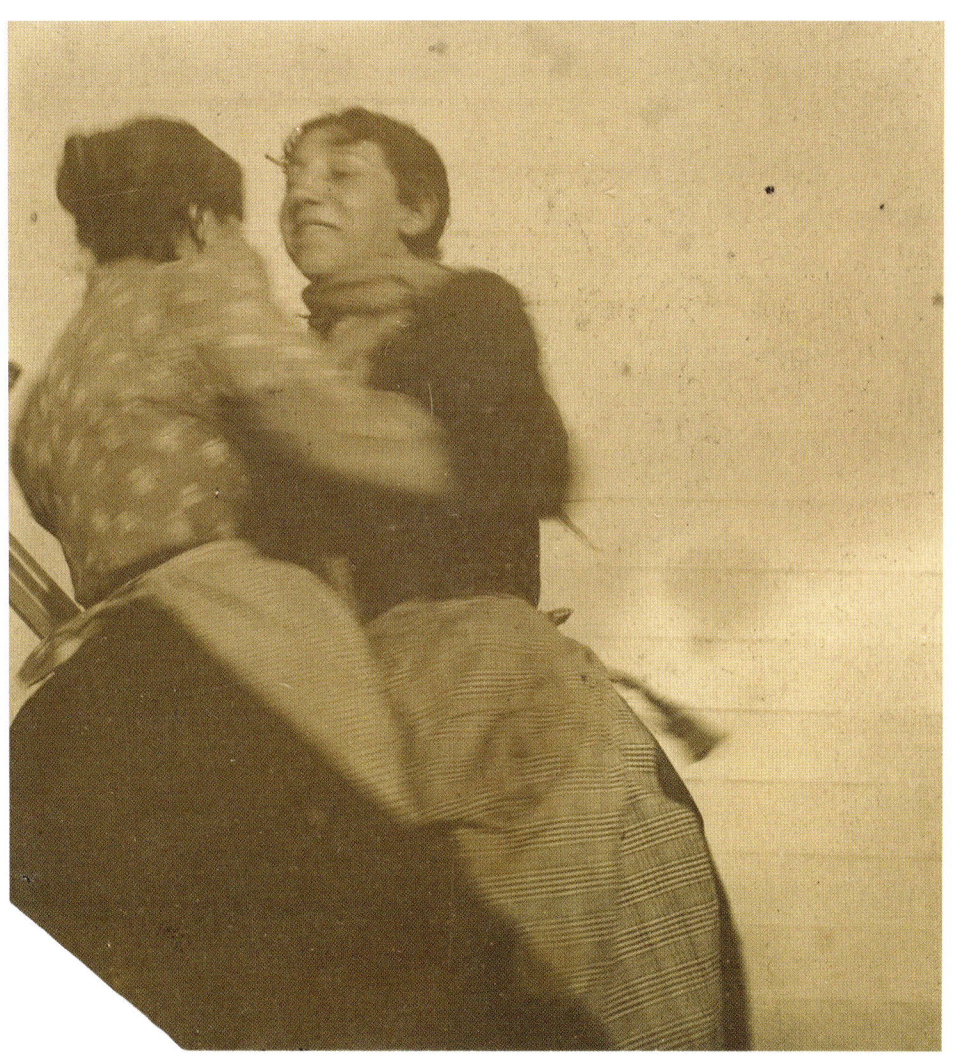

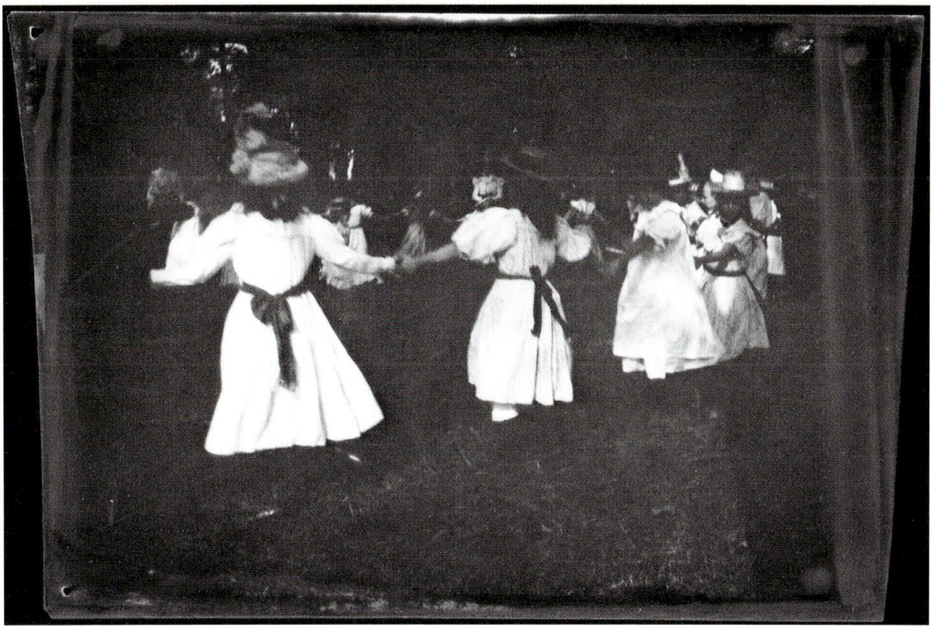

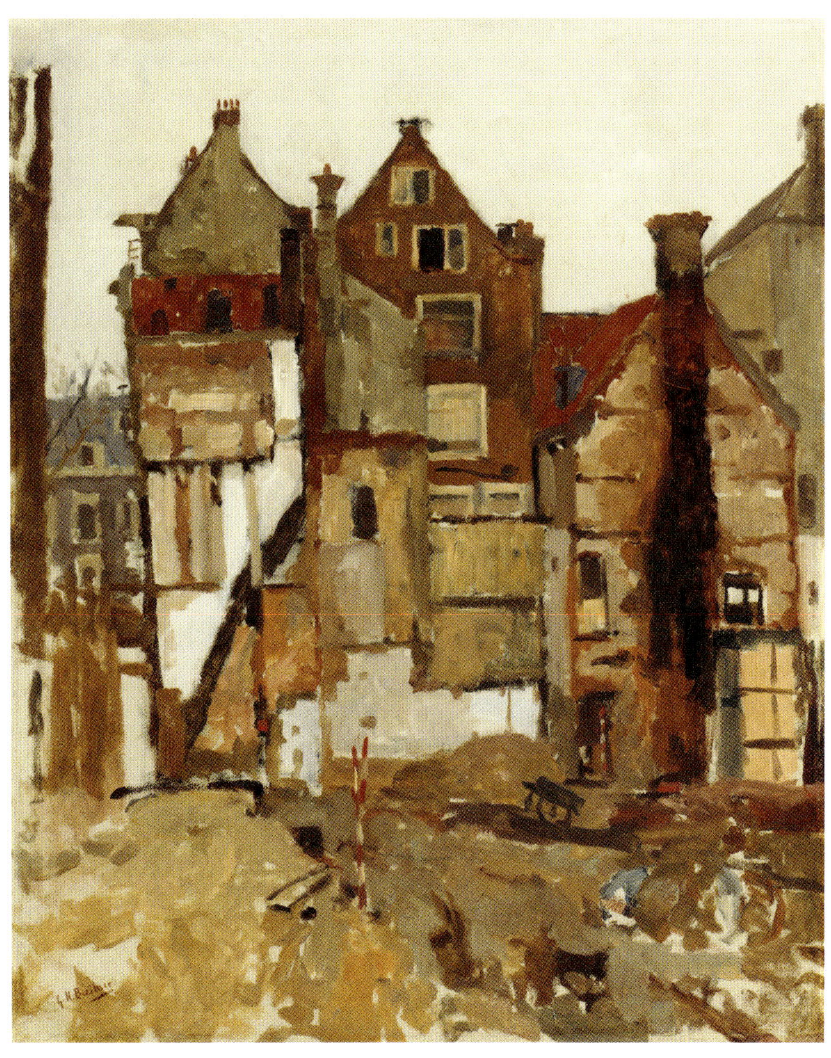

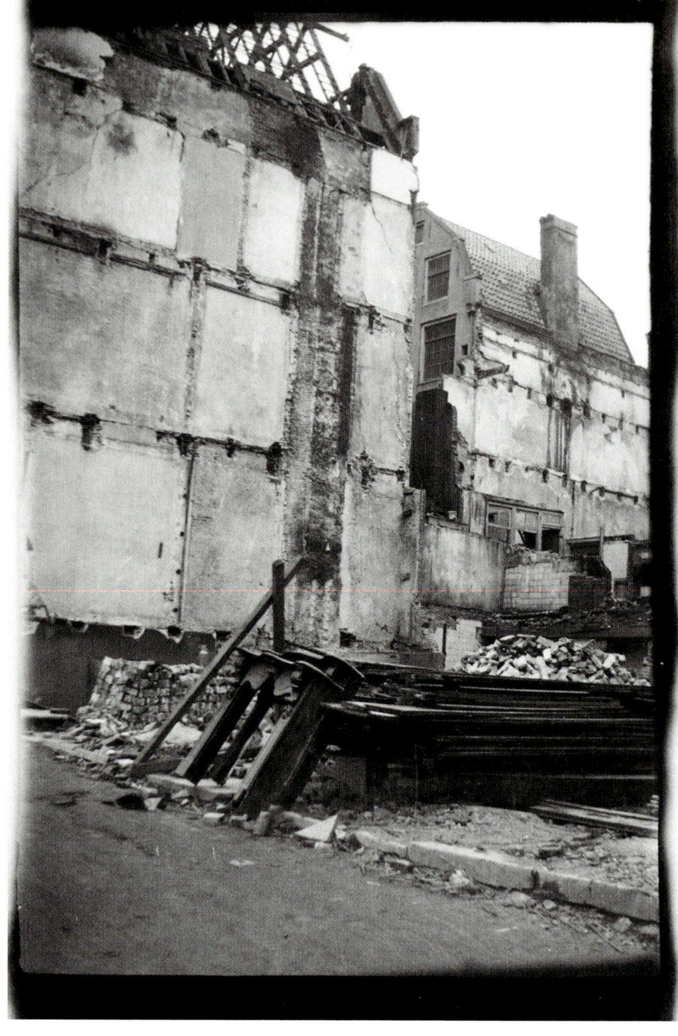

CAT. 39. George Hendrik Breitner, *Demolition of Oudezijds Achterburgwal*, 1903–4. Oil on board on panel, 30½ x 25 in. (77.5 x 63.5 cm). Kunsthandel A.H. Bies, Eindhoven

CAT. 40. George Hendrik Breitner, Demolition, n.d. Gelatin silver print. Collection RKD, The Hague

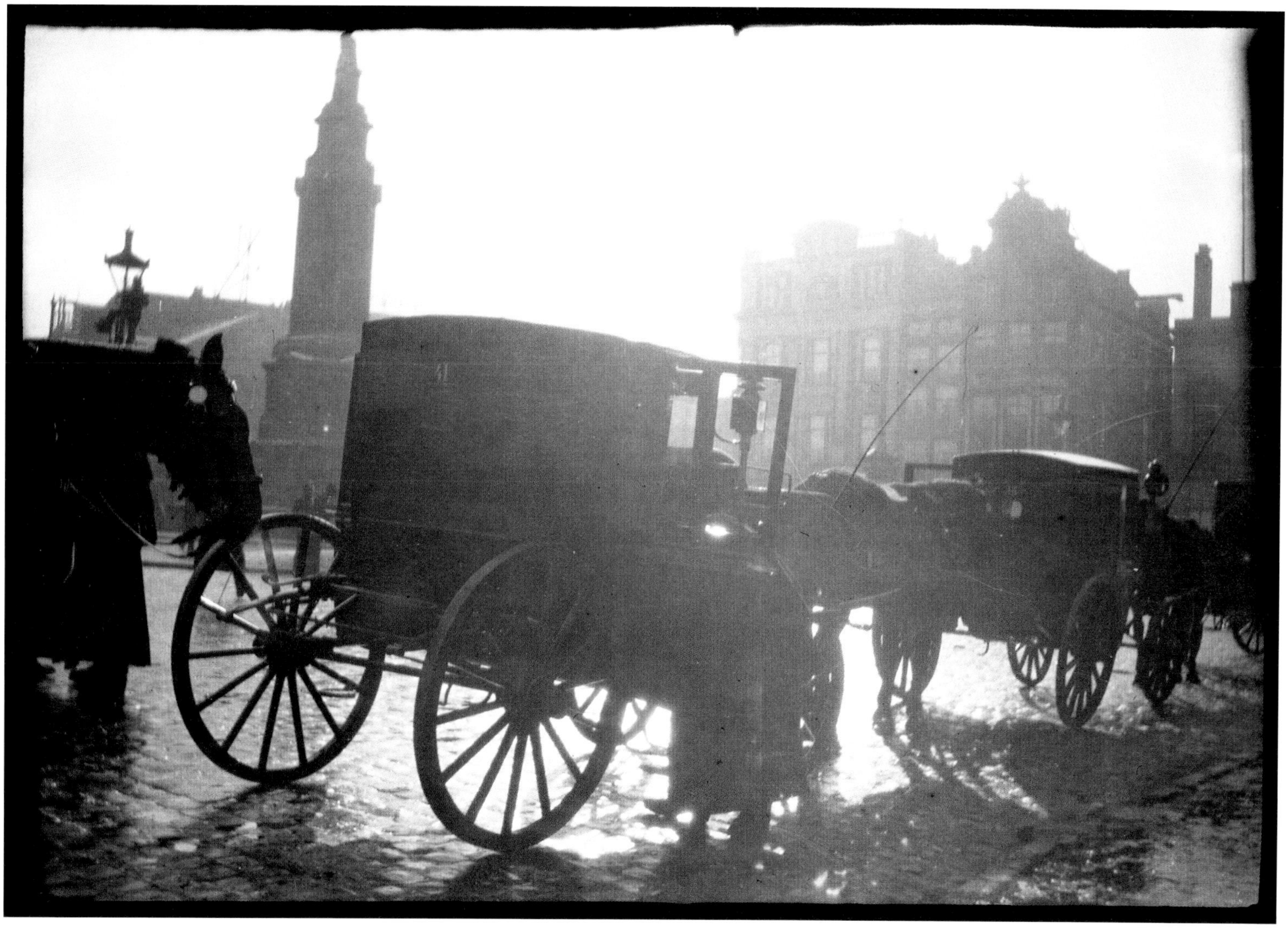

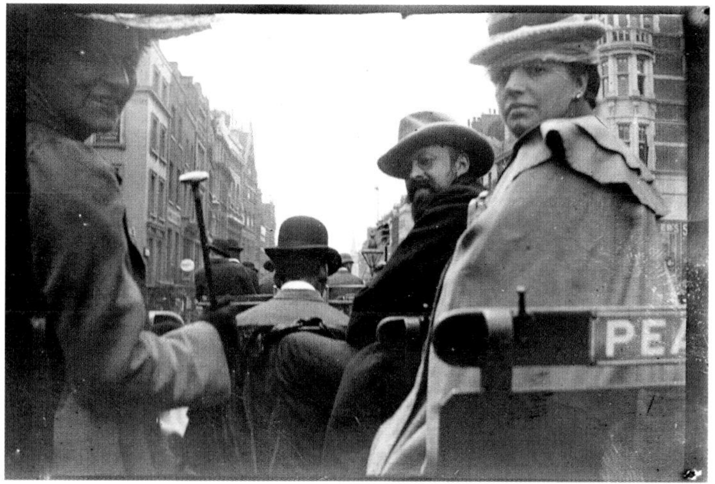

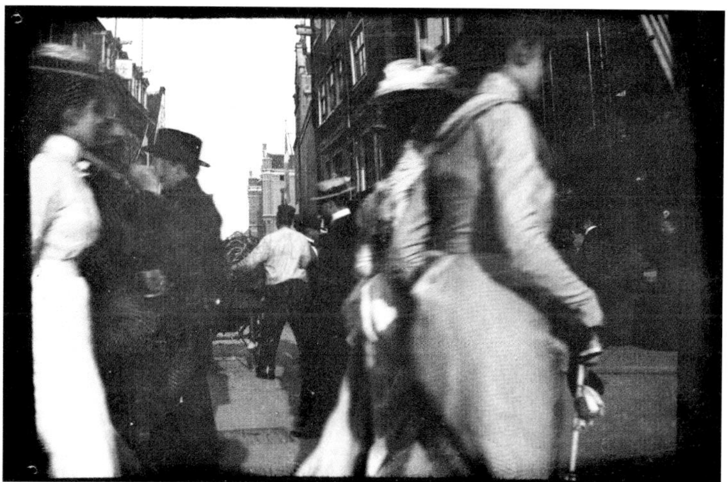

TOP: CAT. 41. George Hendrik Breitner, The Dam, n.d. Gelatin silver print. Collection RKD, The Hague

BOTTOM LEFT: CAT. 42. George Hendrik Breitner, In London with Marius Bauer, n.d. Gelatin silver print. Collection RKD, The Hague

BOTTOM RIGHT: CAT. 43. George Hendrik Breitner, Spui and walkers in the Kalverstraat, n.d. Gelatin silver print. Collection RKD, The Hague

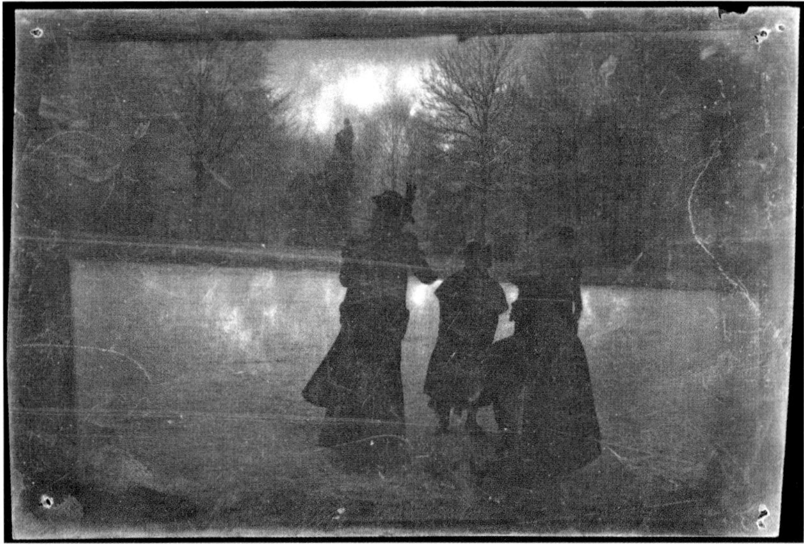

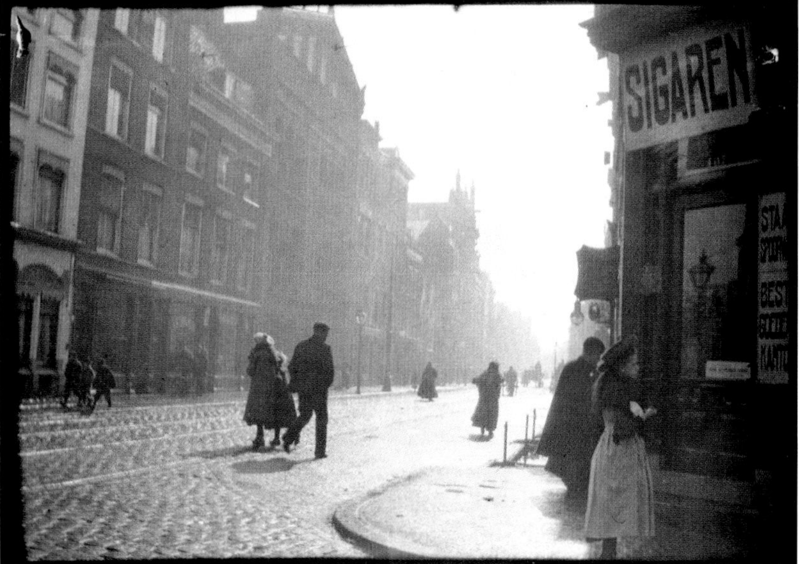

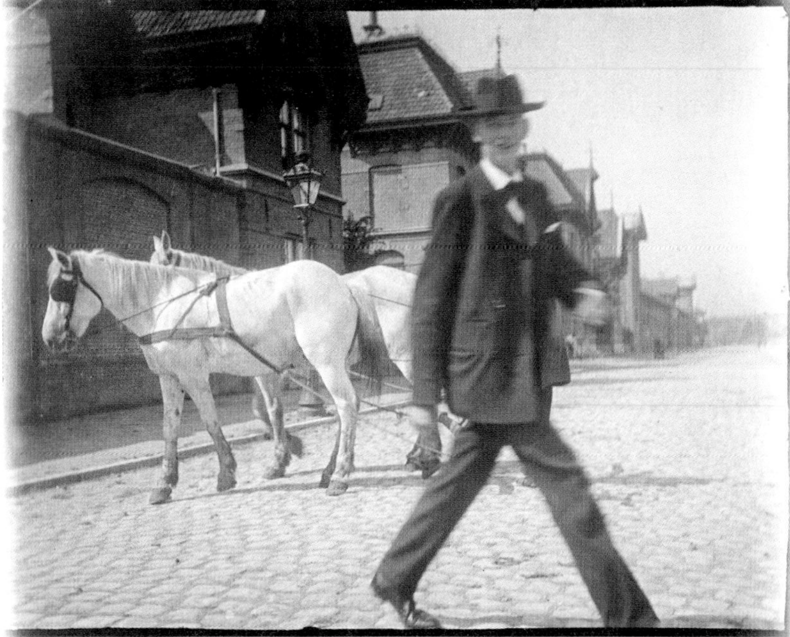

CAT. 44. George Hendrik Breitner, Figures walking in snowy landscape, n.d. Gelatin silver print. Collection RKD, The Hague

CAT. 45. George Hendrik Breitner, Street scene, n.d. Gelatin silver print. Collection RKD, The Hague

CAT. 46. George Hendrik Breitner, Horses and a passerby on Cruquiusweg, n.d. Modern scan from original negative. Collection RKD, The Hague

OPPOSITE:
CAT. 47. George Hendrik Breitner, Prinsengracht, n.d. Gelatin silver print. Collection RKD, The Hague

CAT. 48. George Hendrik Breitner, Singel, n.d. Gelatin silver print. Collection RKD, The Hague

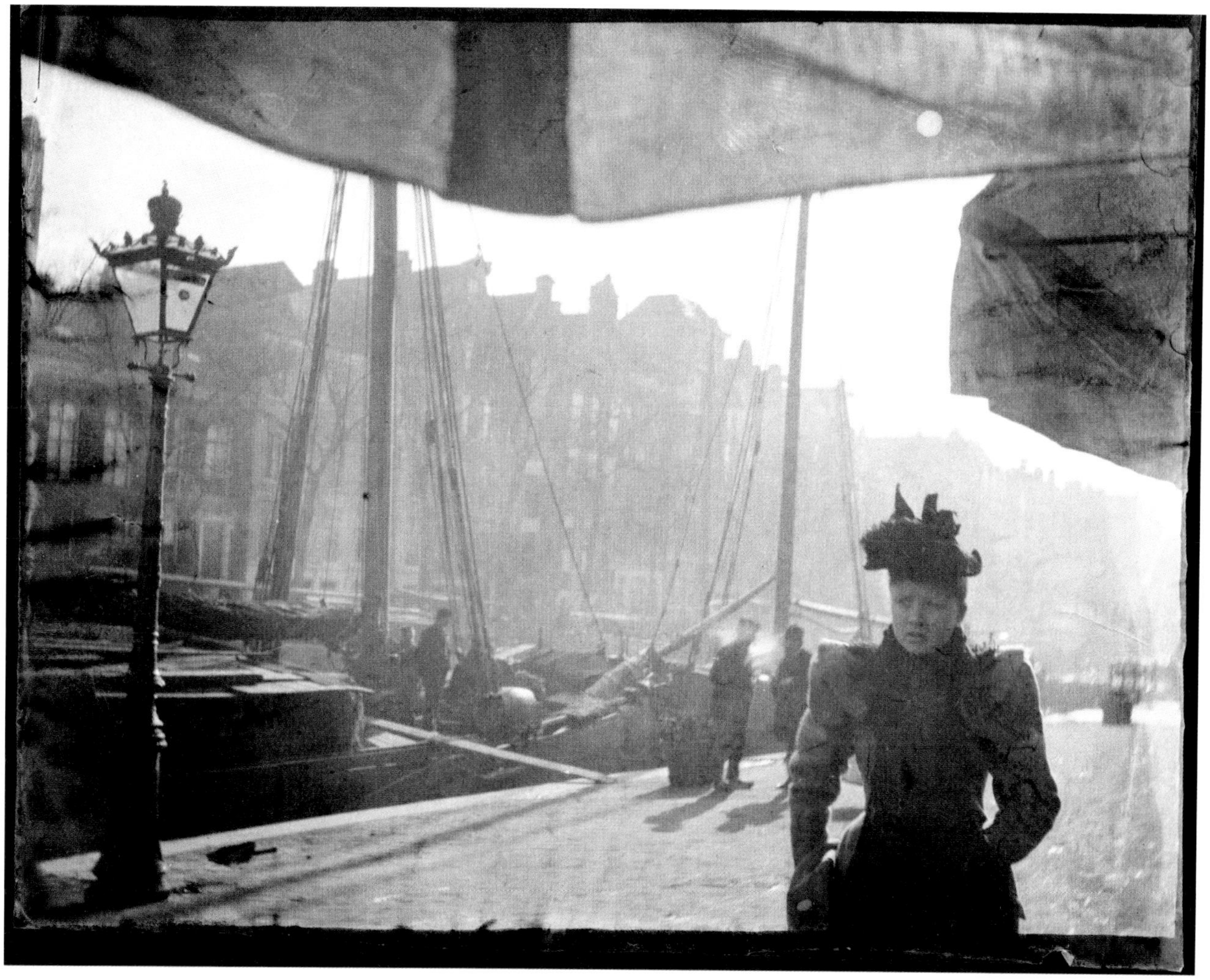

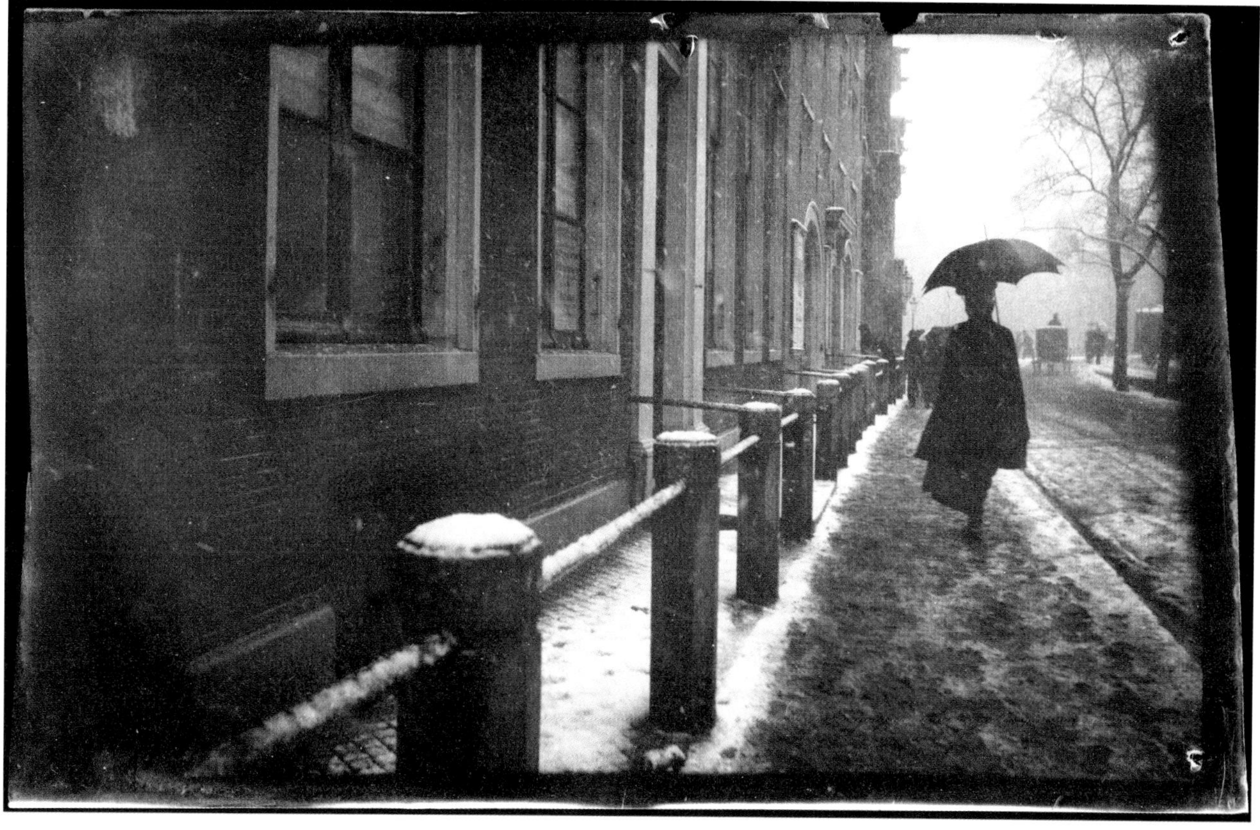

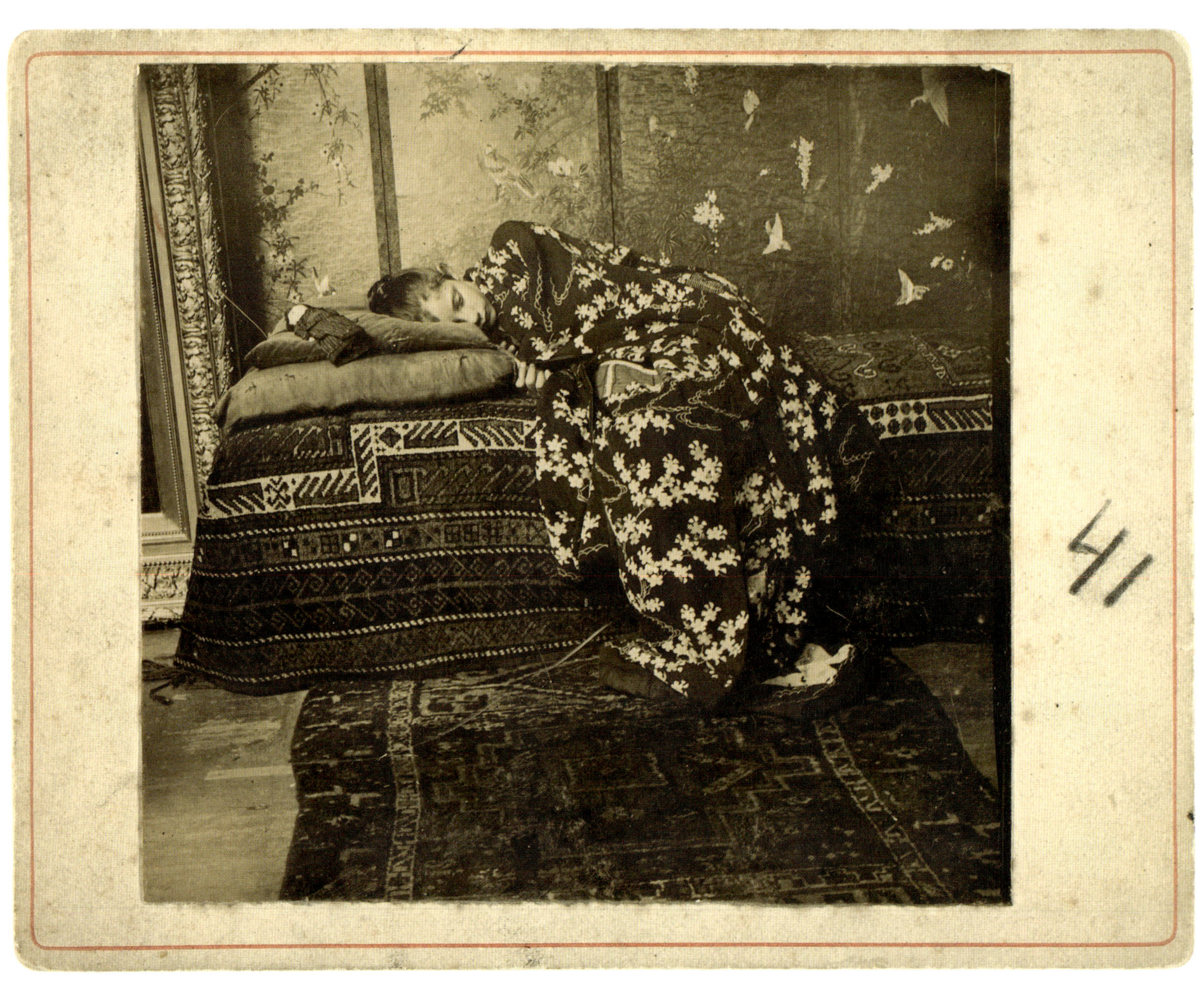

CAT. 49. George Hendrik Breitner, Girl in a kimono (Geesje Kwak) at Breitner's studio on Lauriersgracht, n.d. Gelatin silver print. Collection RKD, The Hague

CAT. 50. George Hendrik Breitner, *Girl in Red Kimono, Geesje Kwak*, 1893–95. Oil on canvas, 24 x 19½ in. (61 x 49.5 cm). Noortman Master Paintings, Amsterdam, on behalf of private collection, Netherlands

CAT. 51. George Hendrik Breitner, Girl in a kimono (Geesje Kwak) at Breitner's studio on Lauriersgracht, n.d. Gelatin silver print. Collection RKD, The Hague

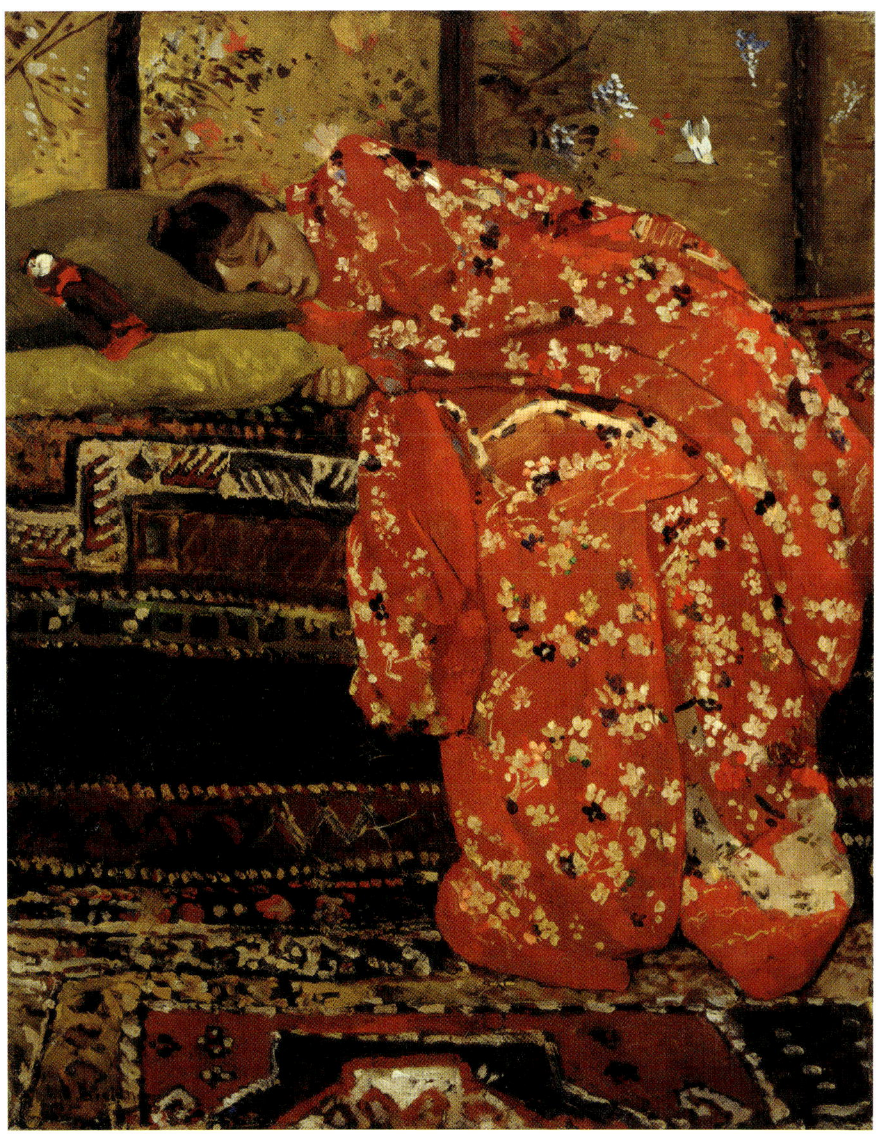

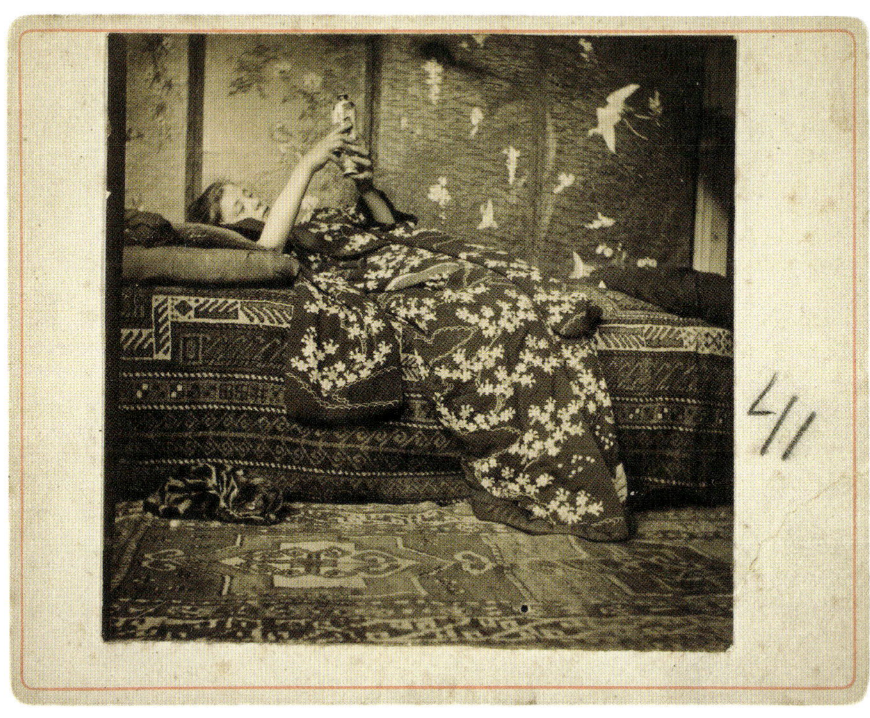

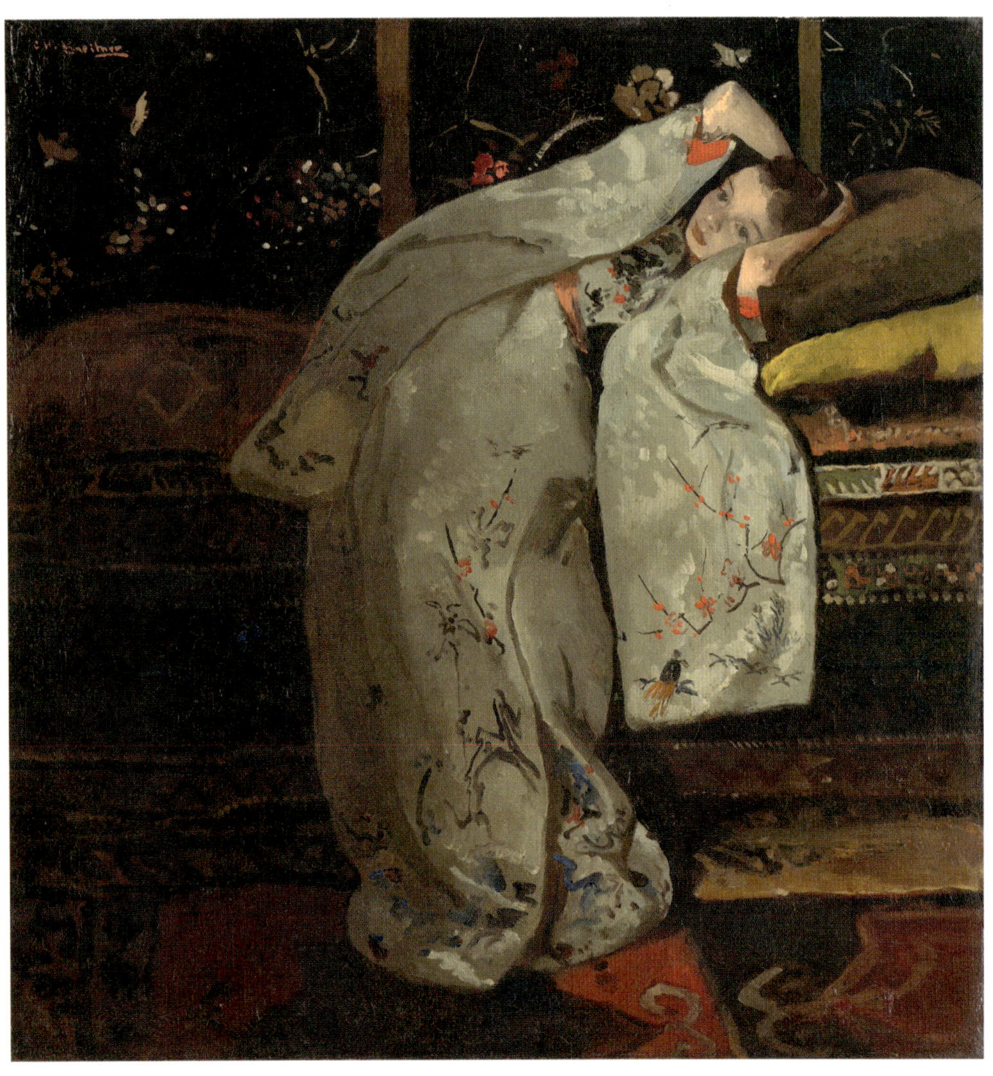

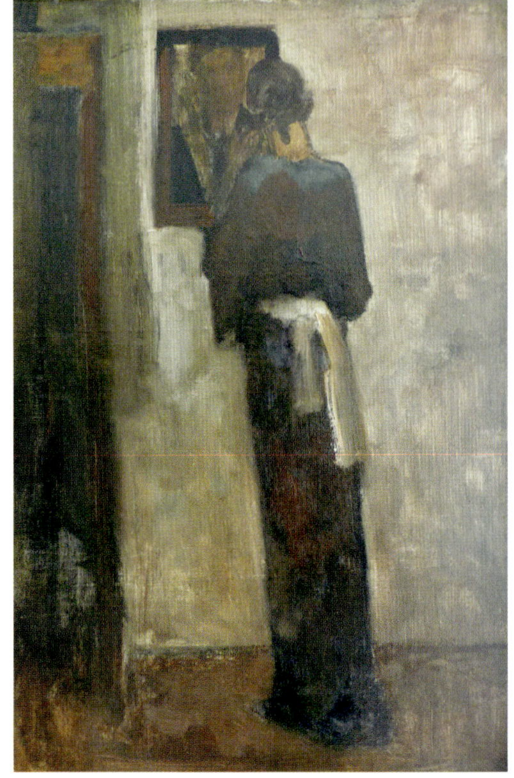

CAT. 52. George Hendrik Breitner, *Girl in a White Kimono (Geesje Kwak)*, 1894. Oil on canvas, 23¼ x 22⅜ in. (59 x 57 cm). Rijksmuseum, Amsterdam (SK-A-3584)

CAT. 53. George Hendrik Breitner, *Het Oorringetje* (The Earring), 1893. Oil on canvas, 26⅜ x 17¾ in. (67 x 45 cm). Private collection

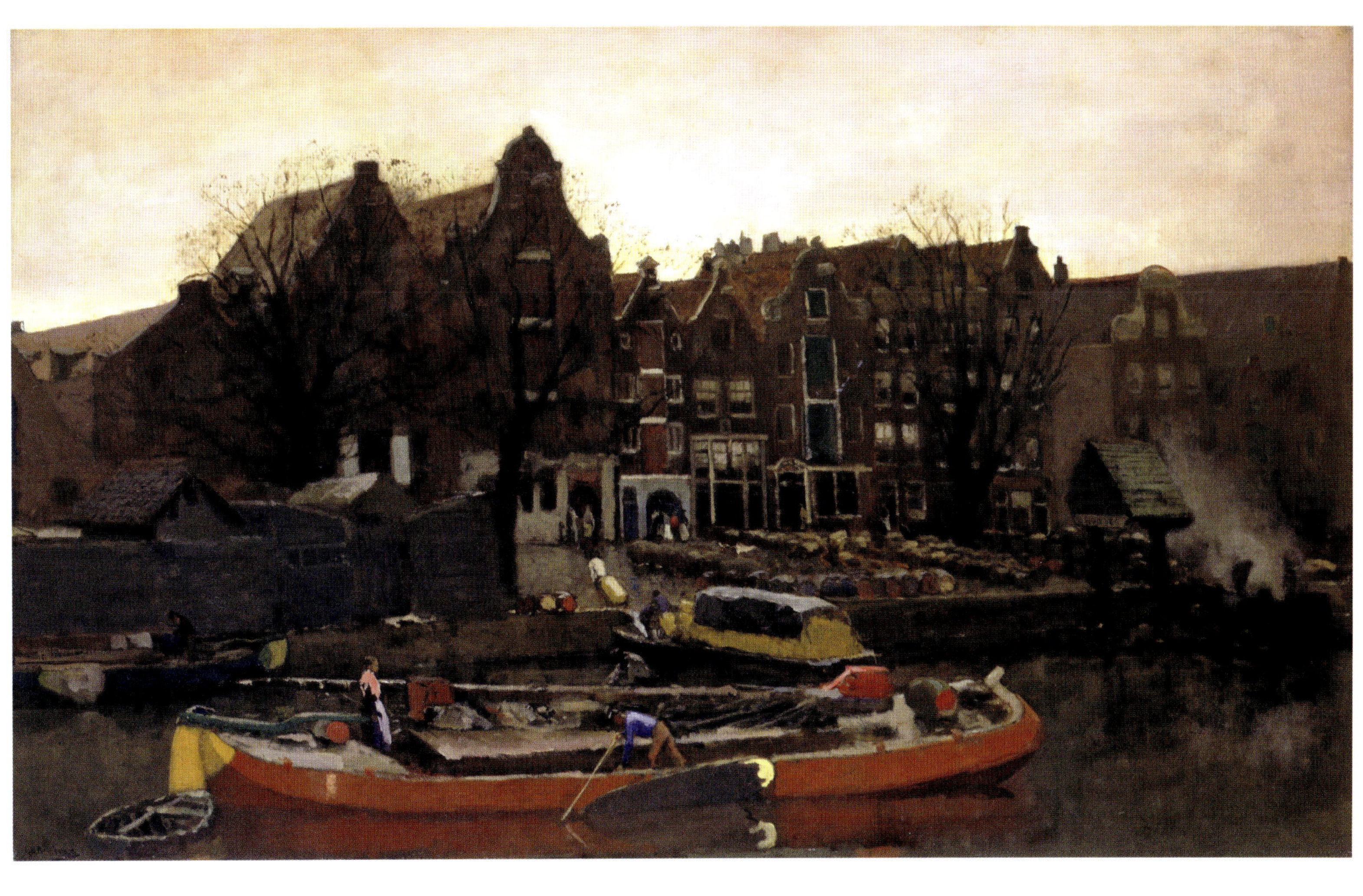

CAT. 54. George Hendrik Breitner, *Warehouses, Amsterdam*, 1901. Oil on canvas, 32⅛ x 51⅛ in. (81.5 x 130 cm). The Toledo Museum of Art

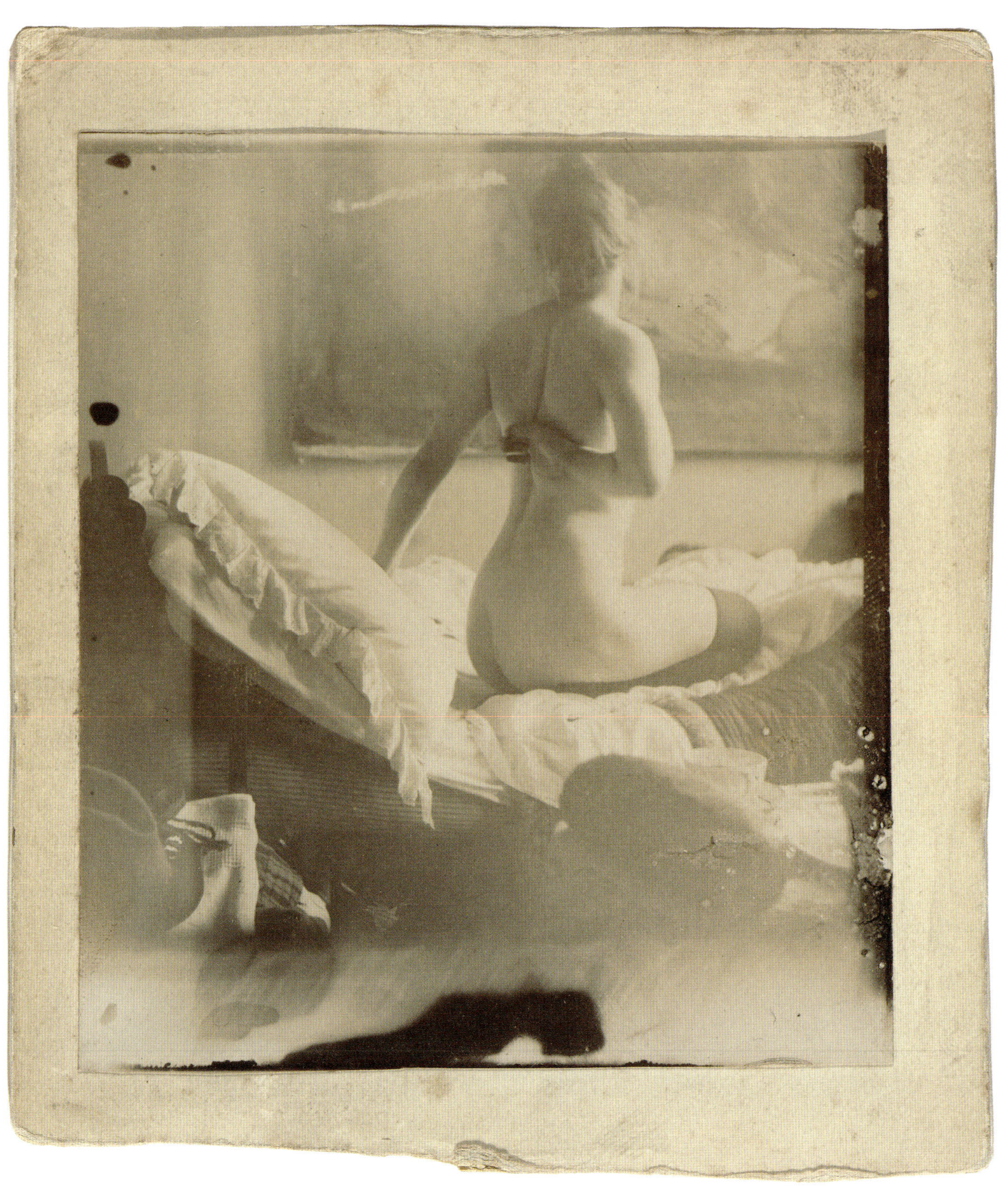

CAT. 55. George Hendrik Breitner, Seated nude, n.d. Printing-out paper, 3⅞ x 3½ in. (9.9 x 8.9 cm). Rijksmuseum, Amsterdam

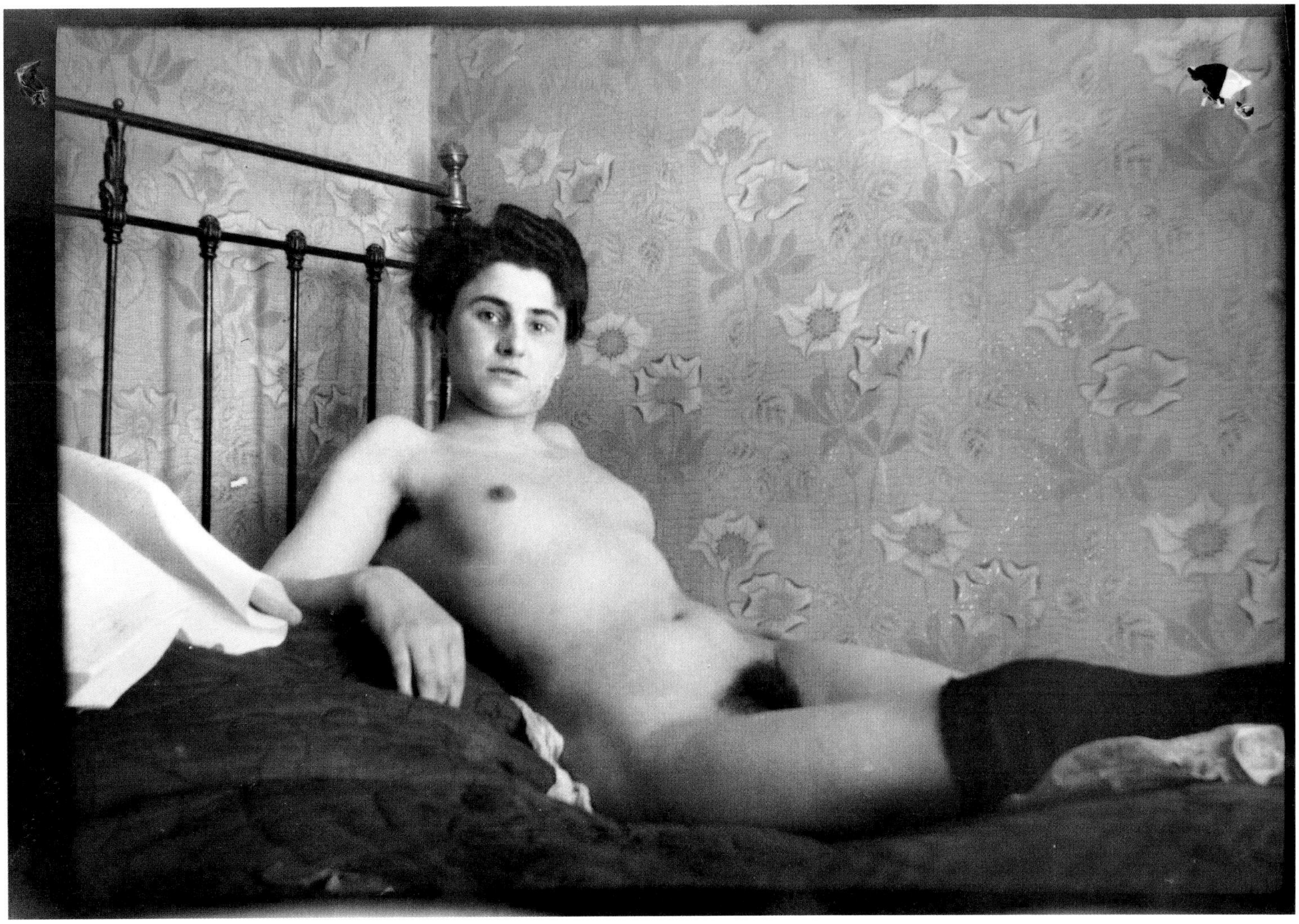

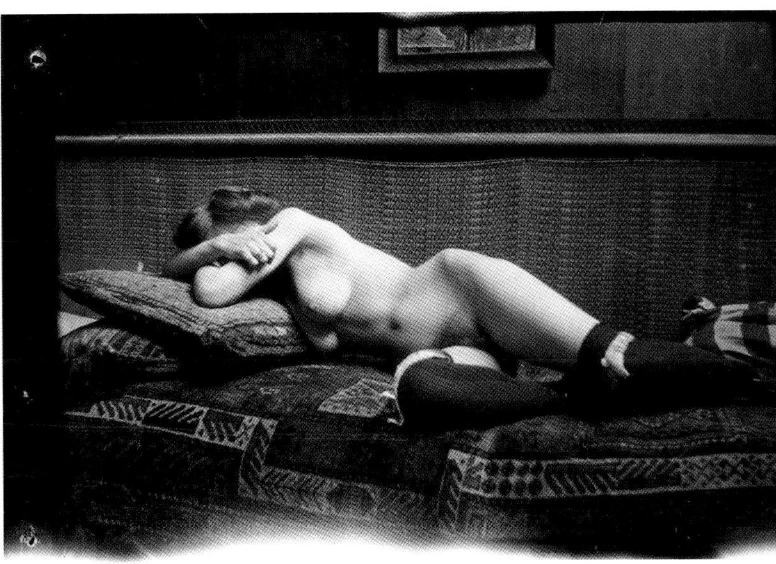

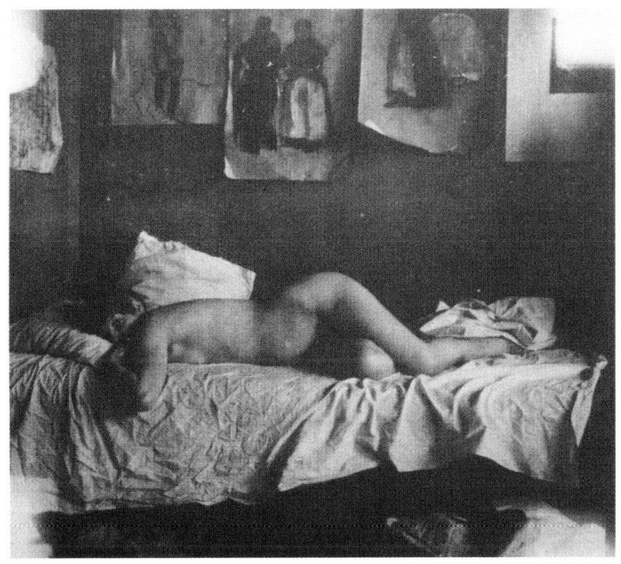

TOP: CAT. 56. George Hendrik Breitner, Reclining nude, n.d. Gelatin silver print. Collection RKD, The Hague

BOTTOM LEFT: CAT. 57. George Hendrik Breitner, Reclining nude, n.d. Gelatin silver print. Collection RKD, The Hague

BOTTOM RIGHT: CAT. 58. George Hendrik Breitner, Reclining nude, n.d. Printing-out paper, $3\frac{1}{2}$ x $3\frac{7}{8}$ in. (9 x 9.9 cm). Rijksmuseum, Amsterdam

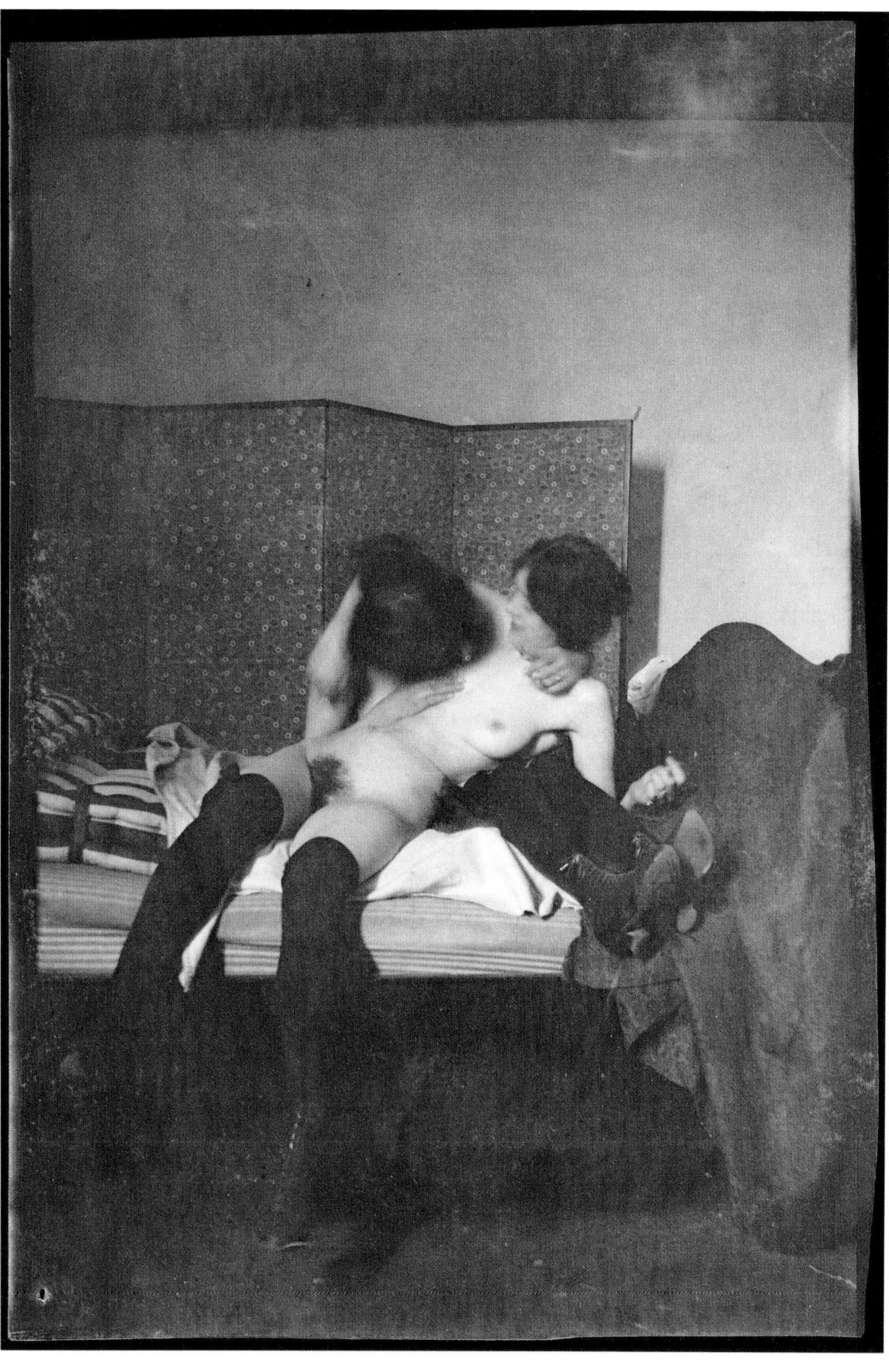

CAT. 59. George Hendrik Breitner, Two women on bed, n.d. Gelatin silver print. Collection RKD, The Hague

OPPOSITE: CAT. 60. George Hendrik Breitner, Nude before a mirror (Mina Otten?), n.d. Gelatin silver print. Collection RKD, The Hague

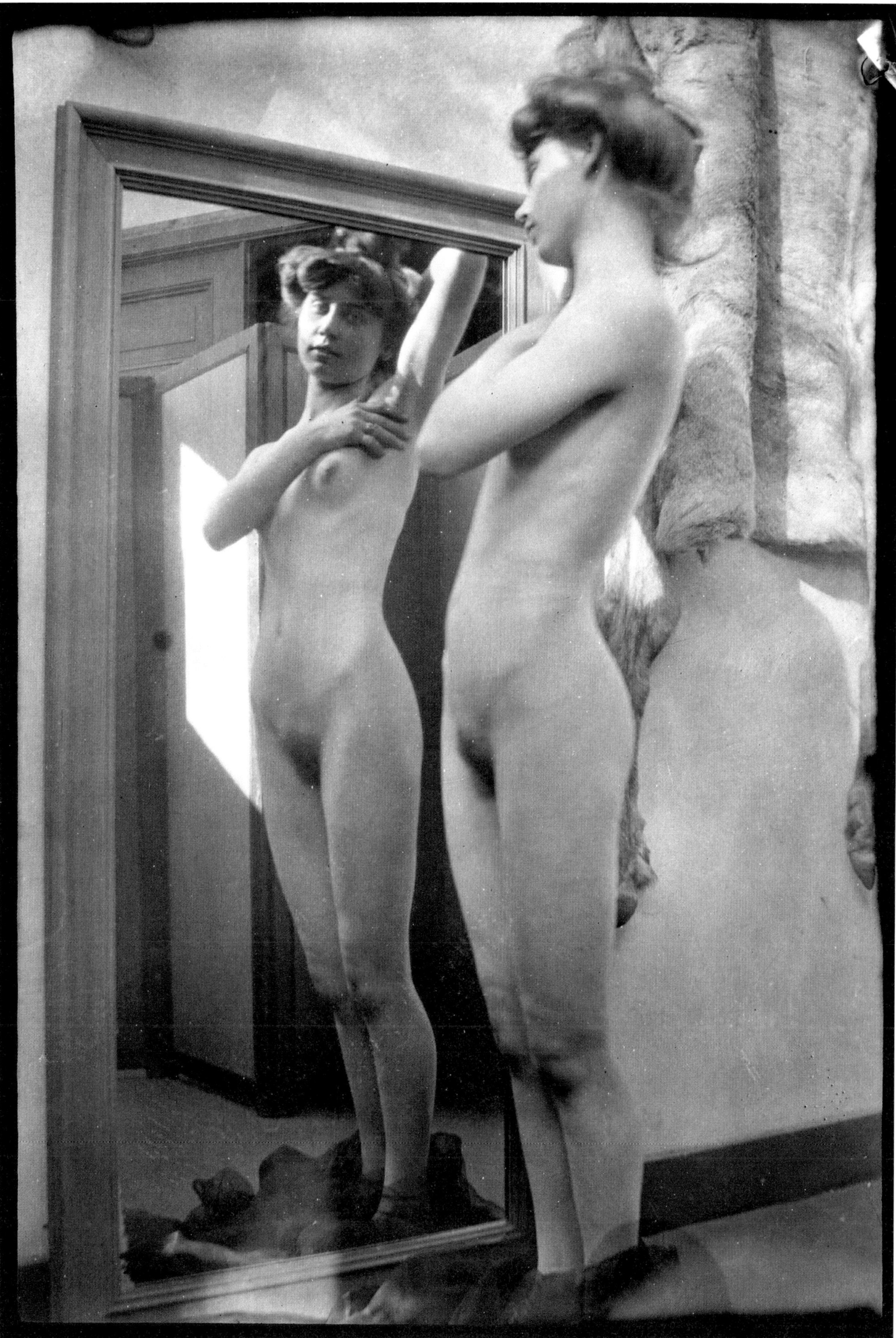

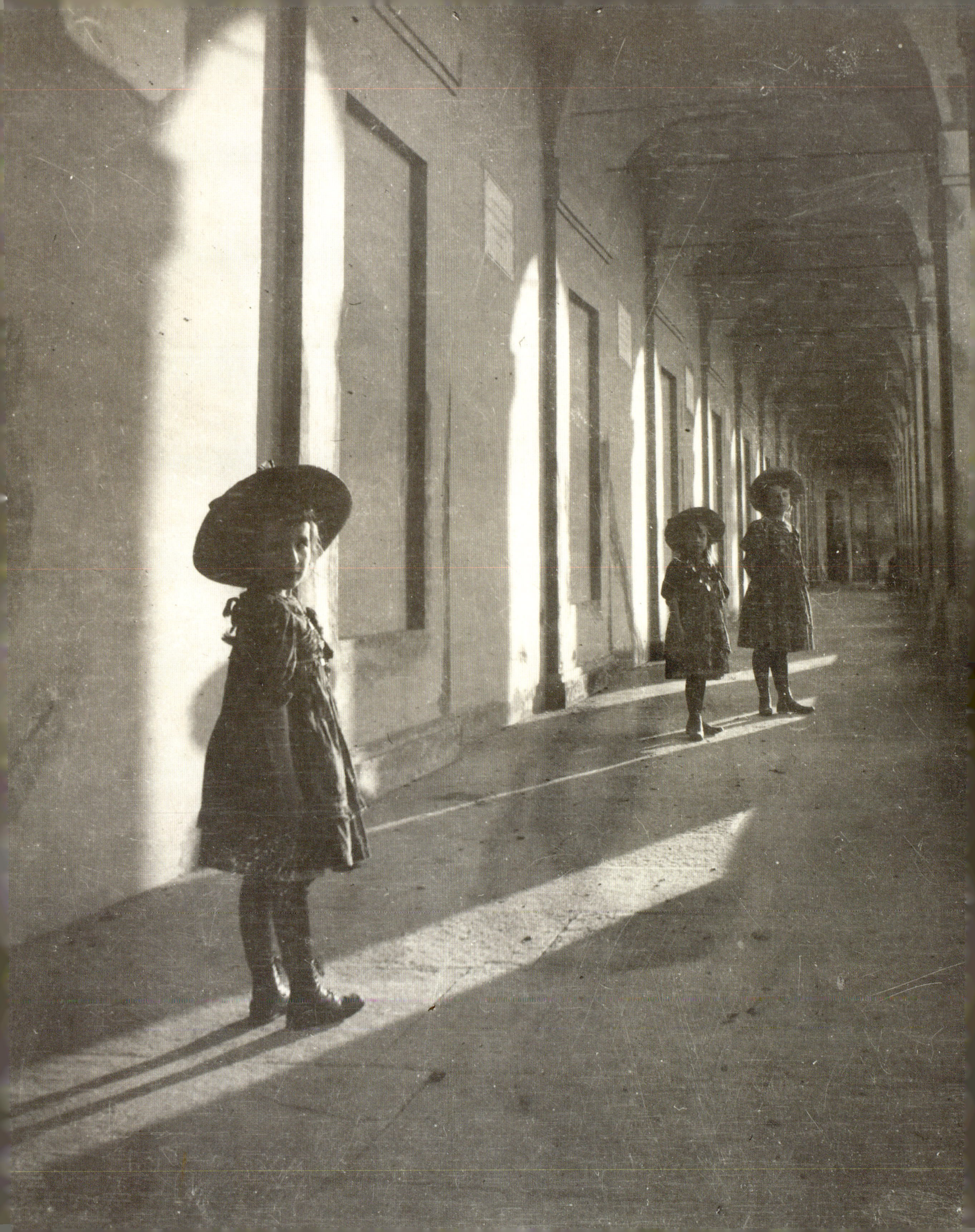

Pushing the Boundaries of the Kodak

Maurice Denis's Innovative Snapshots

Saskia Ooms

Maurice Denis's painting *Sur la plage (fillettes à contre-jour)* (On the Beach [Two Girls against the Light]; cat. 68) presents its subjects with their backs to the light. The work depicts only outlines of the large figures, and is suggestive of a snapshot, though the artist made it in 1892, four years before he began taking photographs. A cofounder of the Nabis, Denis was active not only as a painter but also as a lithographer, set designer, and book illustrator. He revisited the same compositions in all his art—and not just as studies but as variations on a theme.

The public first saw Maurice Denis's photographs in 2006, when they were exhibited at the Musée d'Orsay, Paris, the Musée des Beaux-Arts de Montreal, and the Museo d'Arte Moderna e Contemporanea di Trento e Rovereto.[1] His photographic oeuvre stretching from 1896, when he took his first photograph, to 1919, the year his first wife, Marthe, died, is the focus of a catalogue raisonné published in 2009.[2] There are 2,689 prints and 1,250 negatives dating from this period; most of the negatives are on nitrocellulose film, but a few are glass negatives dating from 1897. Denis's Kodak cameras have not survived, but the sizes of the negatives indicate that he used at least three different models: first, a Pocket Kodak, as did Pierre Bonnard; then—for most of the photographs—a No. 2 Bullet, similar to Edouard Vuillard's; and finally, a Folding Pocket Kodak.[3]

DETAIL OF CAT. 83

There are two large groups of albums of Denis's photographs: Marthe assembled twelve family albums, and Eugène Druet also put together twelve looseleaf albums of prints.[4] The former contain a combined total of 1,945 photographs: Marthe compiled nine albums of pictures of the couple's seven children and three albums largely devoted to photographs of Denis's friends and of his travels. She made the prints at home.[5] In 1914, Denis commissioned Druet's photographic studio to make enlargements of his negatives; the handwritten date on an envelope containing several negatives printed by Druet confirms this arrangement.[6] The dozen Druet albums, holding 744 prints, have survived in good condition.[7] The negatives and the original prints are in the family archives, the Musée d'Orsay, the Musée des Beaux-Arts de Montréal, the Maurice Denis Museum in Saint-Germain-en-Laye, and in private collections.[8]

The discovery of the photographs in the family archives prompted a question about the enlargements made by the Druet studio: Did Denis pick and choose which images would be enlarged, or were all the negatives made before 1914 printed by Druet as a matter of course? The research and dating of the negatives

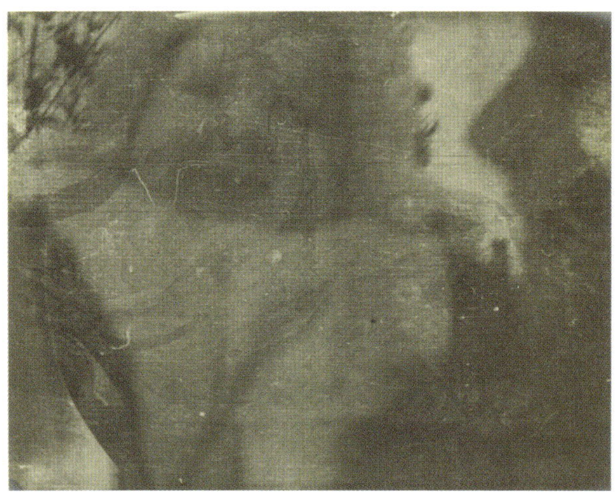

FIG. 1. Maurice Denis, Noële in Marthe's arms, November 30, 1896. Gelatin silver print, 4¾ x 6¼ in. (12 x 16 cm). Musée Maurice Denis, le Prieuré, Saint-Germain-en-Laye, Druet Album 11.38

prior to publication of the catalogue raisonné showed that Denis himself had selected which of his negatives (57 percent of the total) should go to the studio. He wanted to present them to Marthe and his children so they could recall happy moments from their family life.

The inventory of the photographs provides telling information about certain Denis paintings. For example, the composition of the photograph of Noële in Marthe's arms (fig. 1) is copied almost exactly in the painting previously known as *Bernadette et sa mere* (Bernadette and Her Mother; cat. 61). The painting's title was changed because the child actually is another of their daughters, Noële; a small print of this photograph in the Noële 1 album (Musée d'Orsay, PHO 2007-9-1-8) bears a handwritten date and identification by Marthe. There is also a Druet print of this photograph.

Denis never referred to his photography in his diary and rarely mentioned it in the art reviews he wrote, although he did criticize academic painters who literally copied from photographs without making a new composition.[9] The Nabis painters were for the most part reticent about their photographic work, probably in part because art critics of the time were skeptical about this practice. Denis certainly did not use photography to reproduce realistic details in his paintings or to make formal portraits. Naturally, though, he appreciated how the Kodak camera made it easy to take spontaneous snapshots quickly (cat. 62), and he often carried the device with him, especially during holidays in Brittany and Italy. Denis was excited by the visual possibilities inherent in photography—for instance, the ability to capture movement, backlighting, and chiaroscuro (as in cat. 85). He enjoyed experimenting with his Kodak, concentrating especially on close-ups, some of which are tightly framed (cat. 63). Occasionally, faces in these snapshots are slightly blurred (cat. 64). His intimate circle provided ample subject matter—Marthe with their children, children's portraits, beach scenes, images from the artist's travels, and pictures of his friends. His obvious desire to capture and preserve memories of experiences and individuals indicates a response (shared among many consumers) to the Kodak company's advertising campaign, which promoted use of the camera for that purpose.[10]

There are three categories among Denis's photographs that relate to his painting. One small group consists of preliminary studies. Another comprises "photographic sketches"—that is, photographs of subjects he eventually drew upon for his paintings. And finally, there are the artist's snapshots that evoke the atmosphere and style of his painted works.

One photograph (1900; Brigitte and Marc Pagneux Collection, Saint-Germain-le-Vasson) belongs to a set of studies of fabric folds taken to help prepare the figure of Christ for the 1900 painting *Laissez venir à moi les petits enfants* (Suffer the Little Children to Come unto Me; fig. 2). In another of these studies, Marthe posed and Denis took the photograph; and in still another, the artist himself posed. In Brittany, he took pictures that functioned as sketches. One example is the snapshot of the Regatta ball in Perros-Guirec, Brittany, that captures two Denis daughters dancing (cat. 65). He also made a sketch of the two girls, wearing little round hats (n.d.; private collection), in preparation for the painting *Régates au port de Perros-Guirec* (Regatta at the Port of Perros-Guirec) (1906; private collection). Because the Pocket Kodak's shutter speed was no faster than 1/30 second, the resolution in this photograph lacks clear definition. *La plage au petit garçon* (Little Boy on the Beach) (Clemens-Sels-Museum, Neuss) is another instance of Denis referring to a photographic sketch; here, he transferred the detail of cavorting little Madeleine into the background of the painting (cat. 67). And there is an echo of Noële with her walker on the balcony of the Villa Montrouge (cat. 70) in the drawing *Jeux d'enfants* (Children's Games) (1902; private collection, Saint-Germain-en-Laye), which probably was a study for ceramic tiles.

The great majority of Denis's photographs — the third group — reflect the aesthetic, in terms of stylistic features and themes, embodied in his paintings. He frequently painted and photographed Marthe, who was both wife and muse, in profile. *La dormeuse* (The Sleeper) (1892; Musée Bonnat, Bayonne) and a photograph of Marthe in profile on the Capri boat (March

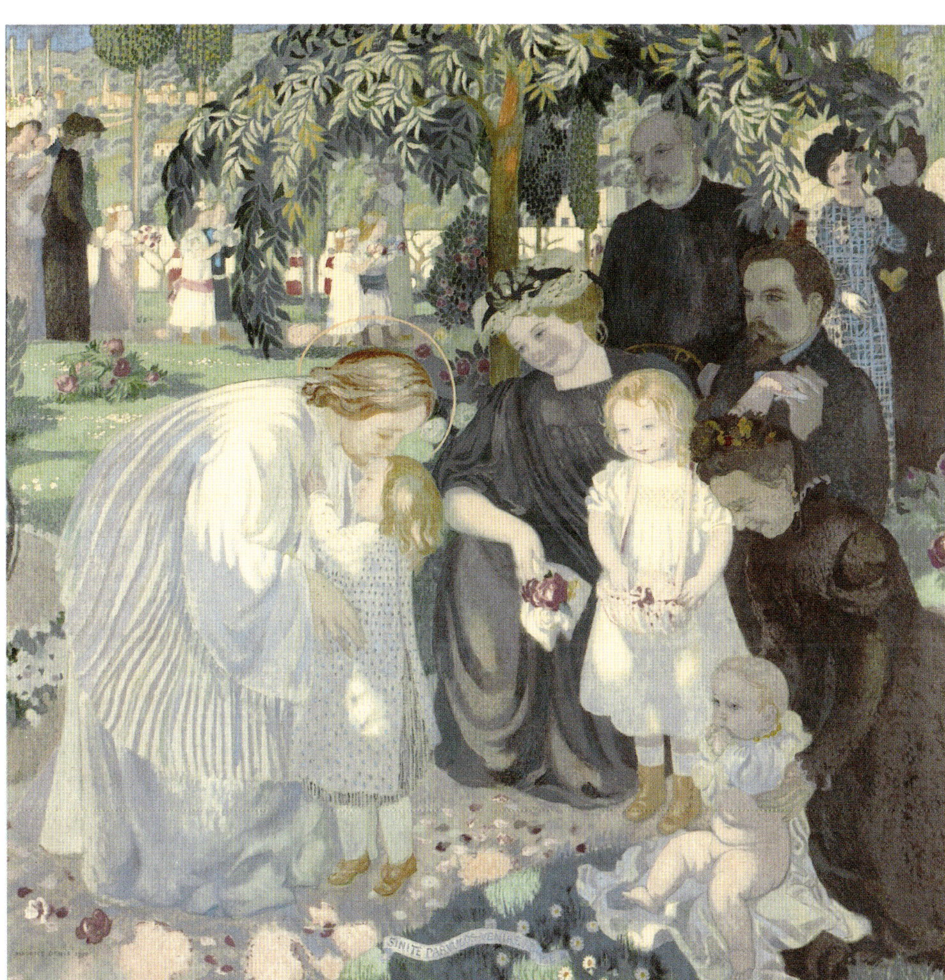

FIG. 2. Maurice Denis, *Laissez venir à moi les petits enfants* (Suffer the Little Children to Come unto Me), 1900. Oil on canvas, 72 7/8 x 72 7/8 in. (185 x 185 cm). Clemens-Sels-Museum, Neuss (1961/Ma 50)

FIG. 3. Maurice Denis, *La forêt victorieuse* (The Victorious Forest), 1897. Lithograph, 7 x 3³/₈ in. (17.8 x 8.5 cm). Private collection

1904; Musée d'Orsay, PHO 2006-4-37) typify these images. The painting *Maternité à la fenêtre (au Le Pouldu)* (Motherhood at the Window [in Le Pouldu]; cat. 77) conveys the intimacy of a mother and child's kiss, as do the photographs of Bernadette, three months old, in Marthe's arms, Saint-Germain-en-Laye (cat. 63), and Noële undressed on her mother's lap (March 1896; Musée d'Orsay, PHO 2006-4-14).

The photograph of Marthe offering Bernadette grapes, Le Pouldu (cat. 72), shows his wife and their second daughter. The diagonal line of the arm in the foreground frames the child and the grapes. We can link this image to *La dormeuse* because of the cropping, tight framing, and blurred perspective. The emphasis is on the abstraction of the shapes and the decorative aspects. All these Nabis stylistic features reveal the influence of Japanese Ukiyo-e woodcuts, in which figures were cropped at the edge of the paper.

Some photographs Denis took are the equals of his best paintings. For example, the way he depicted Noële's silhouette amid tangled foliage in the photograph of Noële in the little woods at Silencio, Perros-Guirec (n.d.; Brigitte and Marc Pagneux Collection, Saint-Germain-le-Vasson) and the attention he obviously paid to chiaroscuro betray his painter's eye. The art historian Françoise Heilbrun pointed to the Symbolist influence of the forest scene in Maurice Maeterlinck's *La princesse Maleine* (1889), a play of which Marthe Denis was particularly fond.[11] The forest was one of Denis's favorite themes as a painter, as evidenced by *Les muses* (1893; Musée d'Orsay) and *La procession dans les arbres (Les arbres verts)* (The Procession in the Trees [The Green Trees]) (1893; Musée d'Orsay), the lithograph that served as an illustration for André Gide's book *Le voyage d'Urien* (1893; Bibliothèque Nationale de France, Paris), and the 1897 lithograph *La forêt victorieuse* (The Victorious Forest; fig. 3), where a

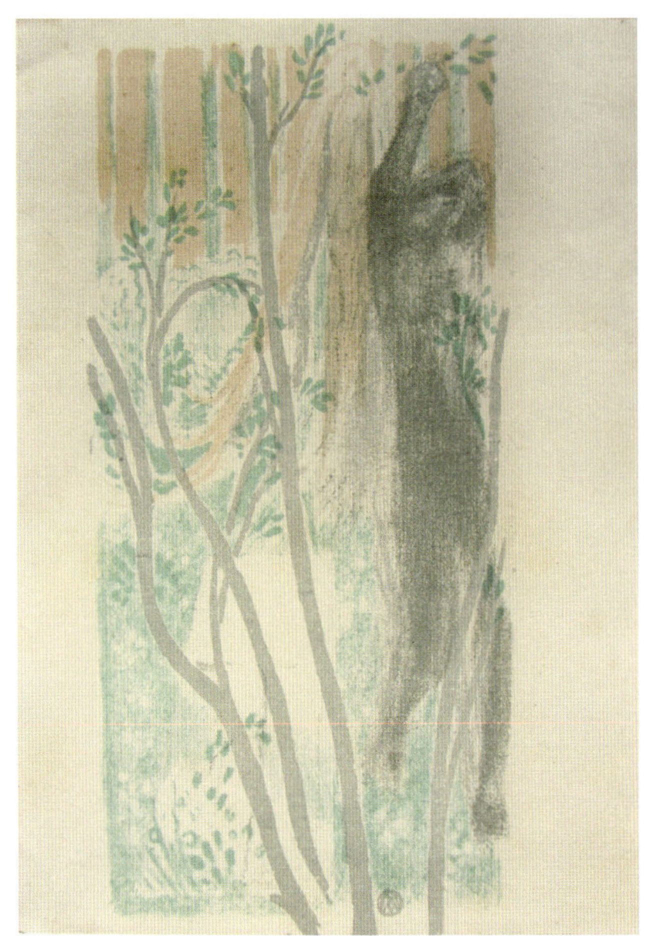

Symbolist silhouette is visible among the tree branches.[12]

As both a painter and a photographer Denis experimented with perspective and with unusual spatial compositions. The 1907 photograph of Anne-Marie, Bernadette, and Noële under an arcade, Bologna (cat. 83), aptly illustrates his aesthetic explorations. The diagonal line in which the little girls pose and the play of light through the arcades reinforce the sense of perspective. With his daring compositions, off-center framing, close-ups, radical cropping, and inventive perspective, Maurice Denis pushed the boundaries of amateur photography and therefore can be considered a forerunner of the avant-garde photographers of the 1920s and 1930s.

NOTES

1. Françoise Heilbrun and Saskia Ooms, *Maurice Denis: Photography at the Musée d'Orsay* (Milan: 5 Continents, 2006); Nathalie Bondil, *L'oeil mange la tête*, in Serge Lemoine et al., *Maurice Denis*, exh. cat. (Paris: Réunion des Musées nationaux, Musée d'Orsay; Montreal: Musée de Beaux-Arts de Montreal, 2006).
2. Saskia Ooms, "Catalogue raisonné de l'oeuvre photographique de Maurice Denis (1896–1919)" (Ph.D. diss., Paris 4, Sorbonne/University of Louvain, 2009), under the guidance of professors S. Lemoine and J. Baetens. Thanks to the assistance of Claire Denis, Maurice Denis's granddaughter, the dissertation includes an inventory of the photographic archives, with precise dates and identification of the photographs. Index cards containing iconographic description, date, technique, dimensions, and provenance have been created for each photograph.
3. The first camera Denis used was the Pocket Kodak, which corresponds with the 102 size (1½ x 2 in.); 25 percent of the negatives are this size. The majority of the negatives (69 percent) are size 101 (3½ x 3½ in.). They were probably taken with an 1896 No. 2 Bullet. In addition, 6 percent of the negatives are size 105 (2³⁄₁₆ x 3⅛ in.). Denis also took photographs with a No. 1 Folding Pocket Kodak.
4. The photographer and gallery owner Eugène Druet mounted the first monographic exhibition of Maurice Denis's work in 1904. The Druet studio, which operated from 1903 to 1916, was primarily renowned for its reproductions of works by painters and sculptors such as Denis, Gauguin, and Rodin. Rodin, in particular, urged Druet to take photographs of the works. Druet showed the works in the gallery, sold the reproductions, and gave a copy to the artists in exchange.
5. In a 1906 letter to his friend Madame de la Laurencie (private collection), he wrote, "Mrs. Denis has unfortunately not yet printed the photographs from my Kodak." Marthe's prints are different sizes: 1⅛ x 2 in. and, more often, 3½ x 3½ in.
6. The envelope also contains a negative showing Denis while on duty during World War I, guarding Evreux railway station (E33. 05, Maurice Denis with rifle, 1914 [private collection]).
7. The gelatin silver prints from the Druet studio were obtained by a unique process and are all the same size, 5⅞ x 6⁵⁄₁₆ in.
8. There are three Druet albums in the Musée Départemental Maurice Denis, le Prieuré in Saint-Germain-en-Laye; they were donated by the Denis family when the museum was established in 1976. In 2006, the Musée d'Orsay received a donation of fifty-eight Druet prints, one glass negative, and three negatives on nitrocellulose film, and the Musée des Beaux-Arts de Montreal received a donation of twenty-five Druet prints. The following year, the Denis family gave the Musée d'Orsay two family photo albums. See Saskia Ooms, "Acquisitions, Maurice Denis, Album de photographies de Noële 1, Album de photographies de Noële 2," *4814, La revue du Musée d'Orsay* 15 (Autumn 2007): pp. 76–77. One Druet album is in the Marc and Brigitte Pagneux Collection. The other albums are in the family archives (private collection).
9. "Ceux qui fréquentent l'atelier Bouguereau [(1825–1905), prix de Rome et couvert de distinctions académiques, surtout célèbre pour le réalisme 'léché' de ses nus féminins] n'ont point reçu d'autre enseignement, comme ce jour où le maître prononça, 'Le dessin, c'est les emmanchements.' Les braves gens qui trouvent que ça ressemble à Ingres! Je ne m'étonnerais pas de cette arrière-pensée qu'il est en progrès sur Ingres. En naturalisme, certes oui! Il photographie. Ils en sont tous là, les très petits peintres qui sont les maîtres d'aujourd'hui." (Those who go to the studio of Bouguereau [(1825–1905), winner of the Prix de Rome and many academic awards, particularly famous for the "lip-smacking" realism of his female nudes] have had hardly any other instruction, like the day when the master said "Drawing is just putting things together." Those splendid folk who think that it is like Ingres! I wouldn't be at all surprised about these current reservations about Ingres. In naturalism, that's certainly true! He [does] photographs. They are all there, the very minor painters who are the masters today.) Maurice Denis, "Du symbolisme au classicisme: Théories," in *Miroirs de l'art: Textes de critique et d'histoire de l'art*, ed. Olivier Revault d'Allonnes (Paris: Hermann, 1964), pp. 37–38.
10. François Brunet, *La naissance de l'idée de la photographie* (Paris: Presses Universitaires de France, 2000); Nancy Martha West, *Kodak and the Lens of Nostalgia* (Charlottesville: University Press of Virginia, 2000).
11. "Une forêt. MALEINE: Oh, qu'il fait noir ici! LA NOURRICE: Il fait noir! Il fait noir! Une forêt est-elle éclairée comme une salle de fête? J'en ai vu de plus que celle-ci; et où il y avait des loups et des sangliers. Je ne sais d'ailleurs s'il n'y en a pas ici; mais, grâce à Dieu, il passe au moins un peu de lune et d'étoiles entre les arbres." (A forest. MALEINE: Oh, how dark it is in here! THE NURSE: It's dark! It's dark! Would a forest be lit up like a village hall? I've seen darker ones than this; and where there were wolves and wild boar. I don't know if there are any here, by the way; but, thank God, at least a little light from the moon and the stars is filtering through the trees.) Maurice Maeterlinck, *La princesse Maleine* (1889), in *Maurice Maeterlinck: Oeuvres II, théâtre, tome 1*, intro. Paul Gorceix (Brussels: Editions complex, 1999), pp. 79–241.
12. Adrien Mithouard, *La forêt victorieuse* (lithograph, private collection), in *L'ermitage*, March 1897; Pierre Cailler, *Catalogue raisonné de l'oeuvre gravé et lithographié de Maurice Denis* (Geneva: Editions Pierre Cailler, 1968), p. 96.

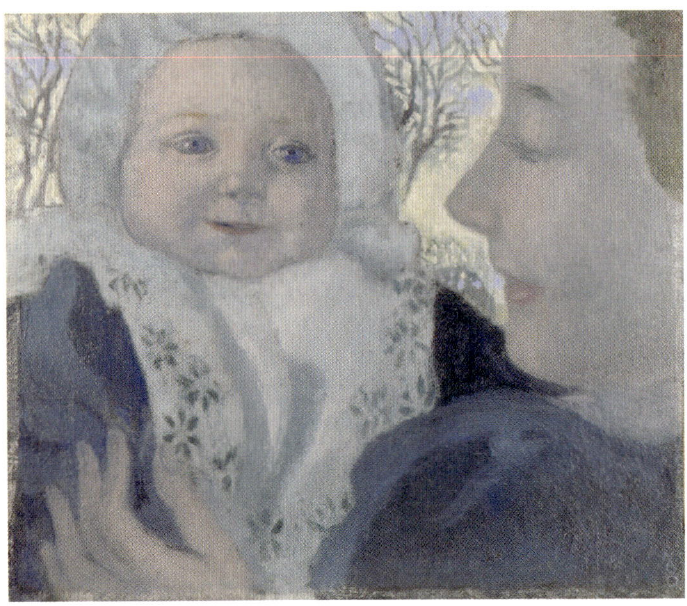

CAT. 61. Maurice Denis, *Noële et sa mère* (Noële and Her Mother), 1896. Oil on canvas, 13 1/8 x 15 1/2 in. (33.5 x 39.5 cm). Private collection

CAT. 62. Maurice Denis, Bernadette, Noële, and a boy playing with a skipping rope, September 1903. Gelatin silver print, 4 3/4 x 6 1/4 in. (12 x 16 cm). Musée d'Orsay, Paris. Gift of Mme Claire Denis, through the Société des Amis du Musée d'Orsay, 2006

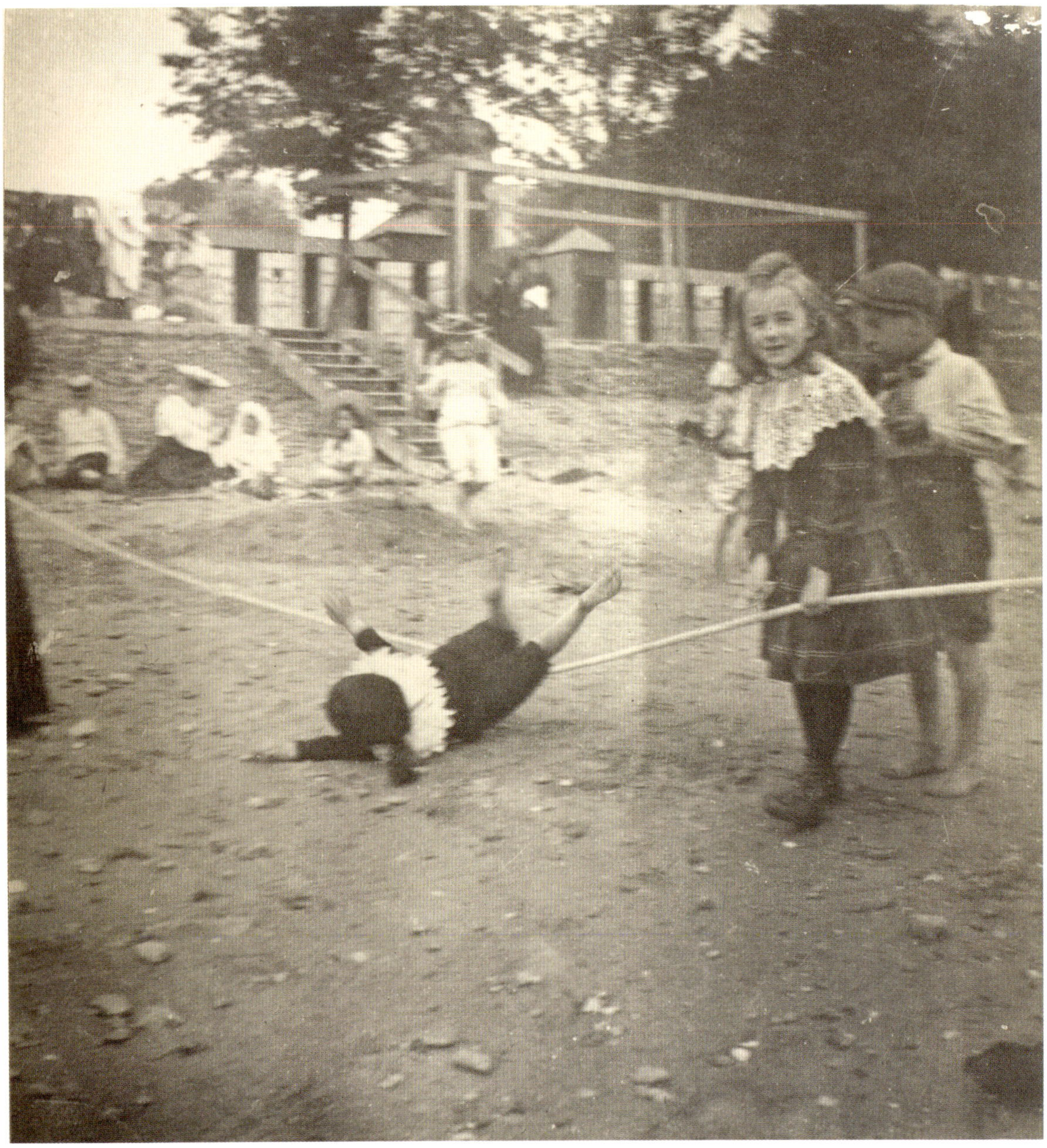

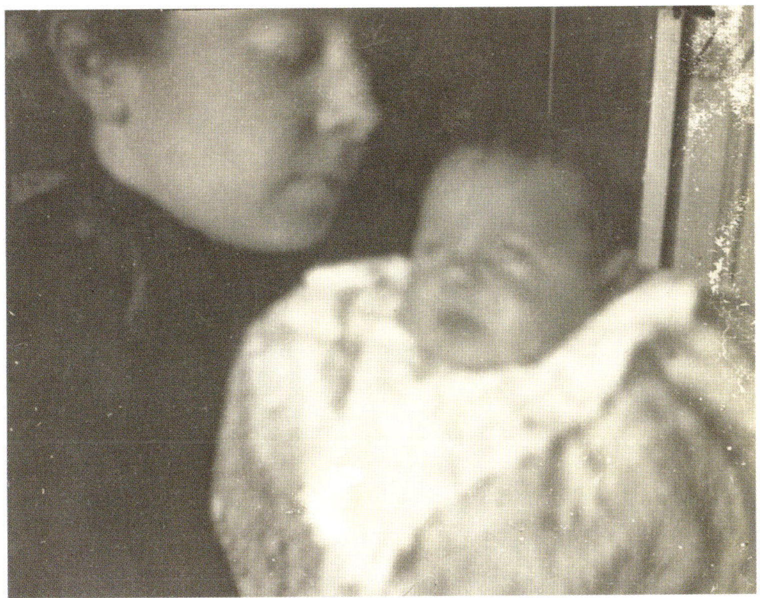

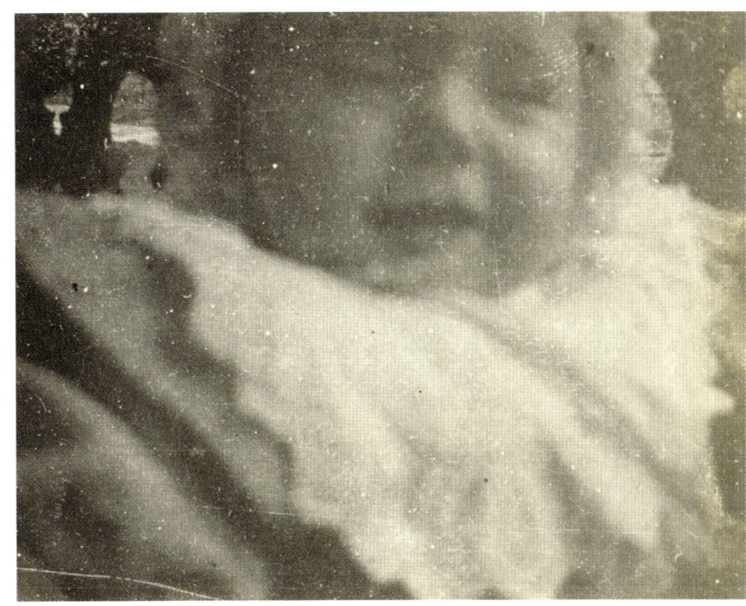

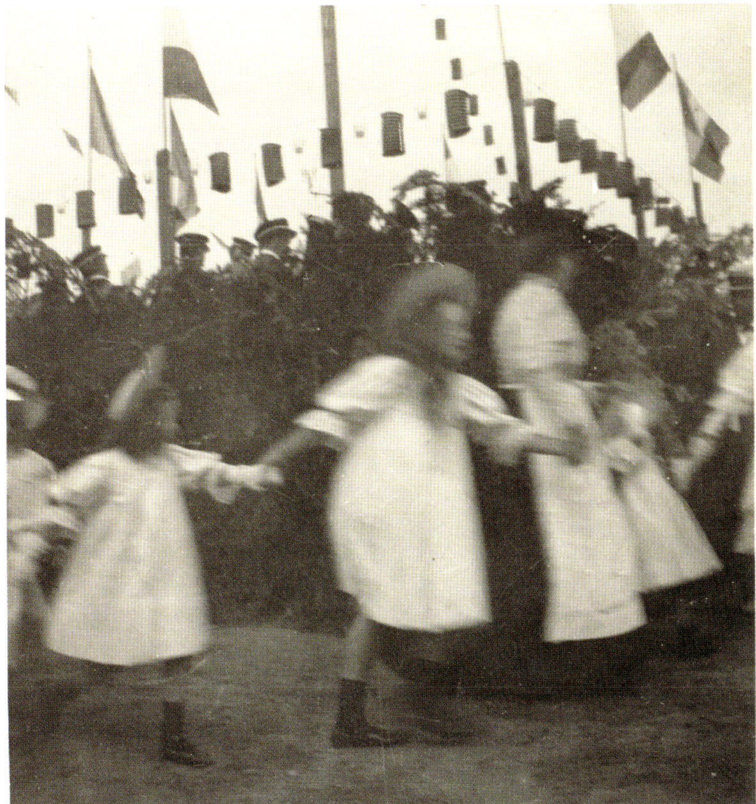

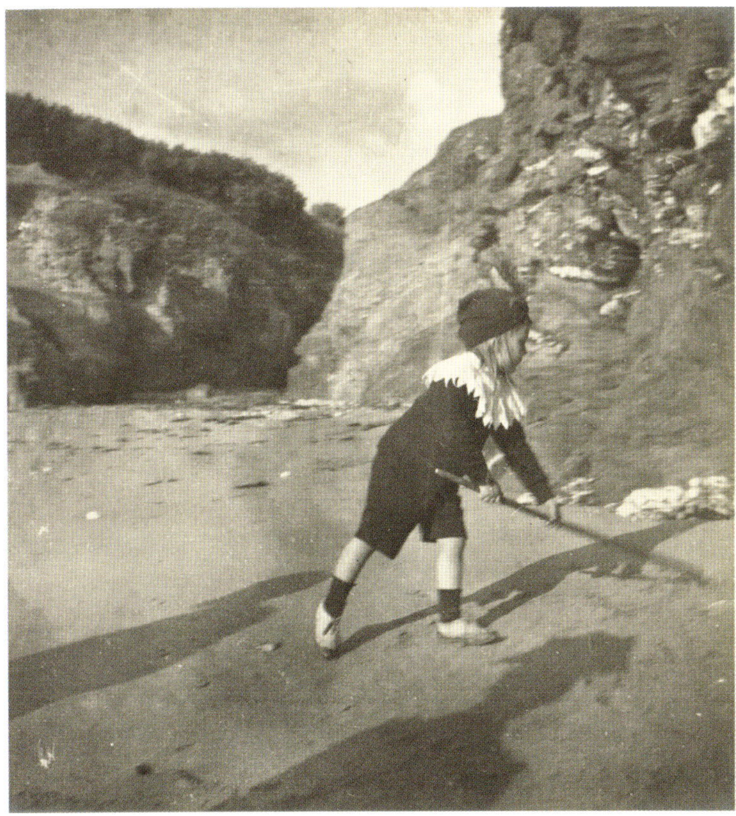

CAT. 63. Maurice Denis, Bernadette, three months old, in Marthe's arms, Saint-Germain-en-Laye, July 1899. Gelatin silver print, 4¾ x 6¼ in. (12 x 16 cm). Musée d'Orsay, Paris. Gift of Mme Claire Denis, through the Société des Amis du Musée d'Orsay, 2006

CAT. 64. Maurice Denis, Bernadette, close-up, Saint-Germain-en-Laye, Villa Montrouge, December 1899. Gelatin silver print, 4¾ x 6¼ in. (12 x 16 cm). Private collection, Saint-Germain-en-Laye

CAT. 65. Maurice Denis, Perros-Guirec, farandole at the Regatta ball, August 1906. Gelatin silver print, 4¾ x 6¼ in. (12 x 16 cm). Musée d'Orsay, Paris. Gift of Mme Claire Denis, through the Société des Amis du Musée d'Orsay, 2006

CAT. 66. Maurice Denis, Bernadette playing with a stick on the beach, near La Bernerie, 1903. Gelatin silver print, 4¾ x 6¼ in. (12 x 16 cm). Musée d'Orsay, Paris. Gift of Mme Claire Denis, through the Société des Amis du Musée d'Orsay, 2006

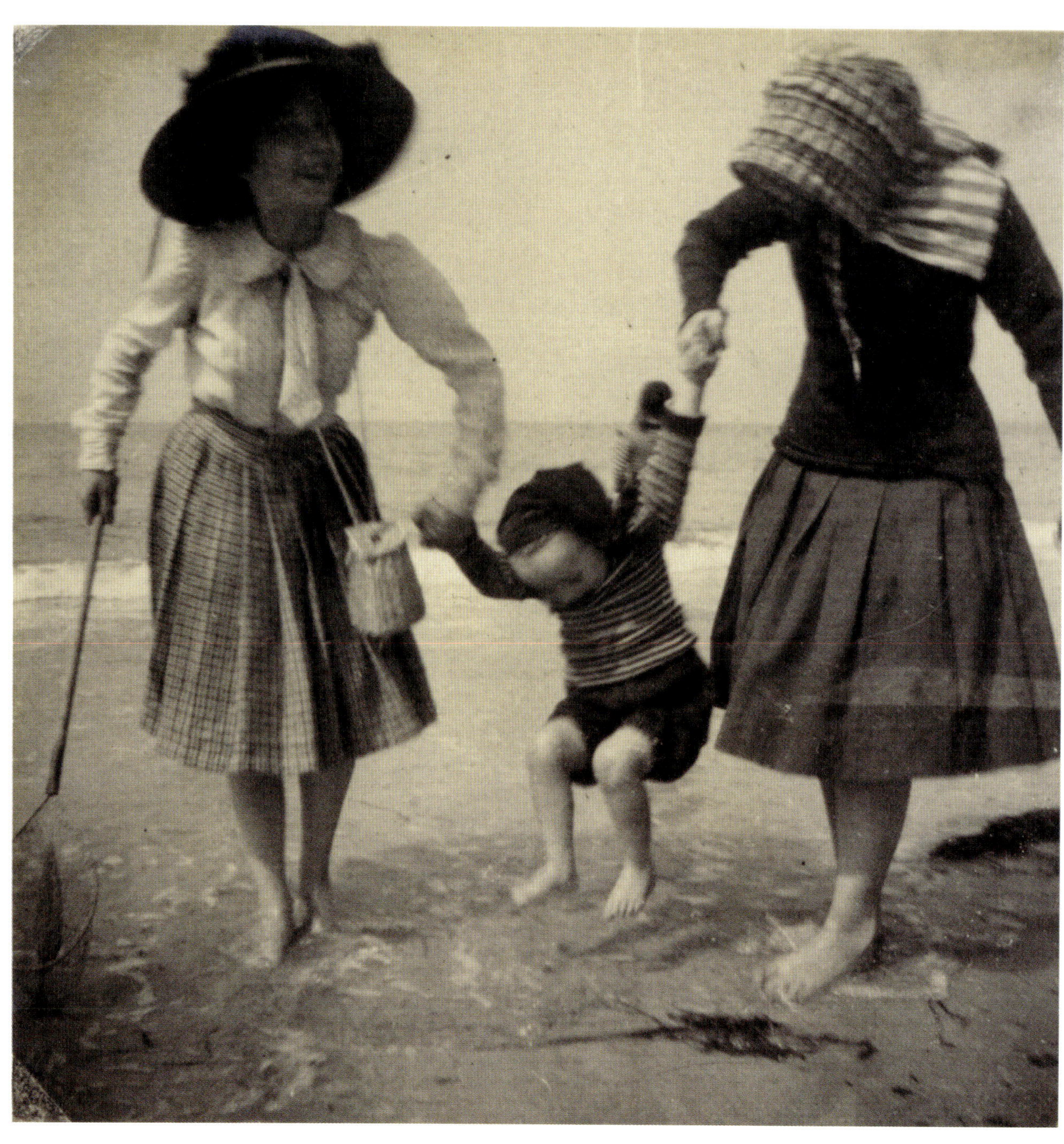

CAT. 67. Maurice Denis, Two girls, paddling in the sea, swinging little Madeleine, Perros-Guirec, 1909. Gelatin silver print, 5⅞ x 6½ in. (15 x 16.5 cm). Musée Maurice Denis, le Prieuré, Saint-Germain-en-Laye

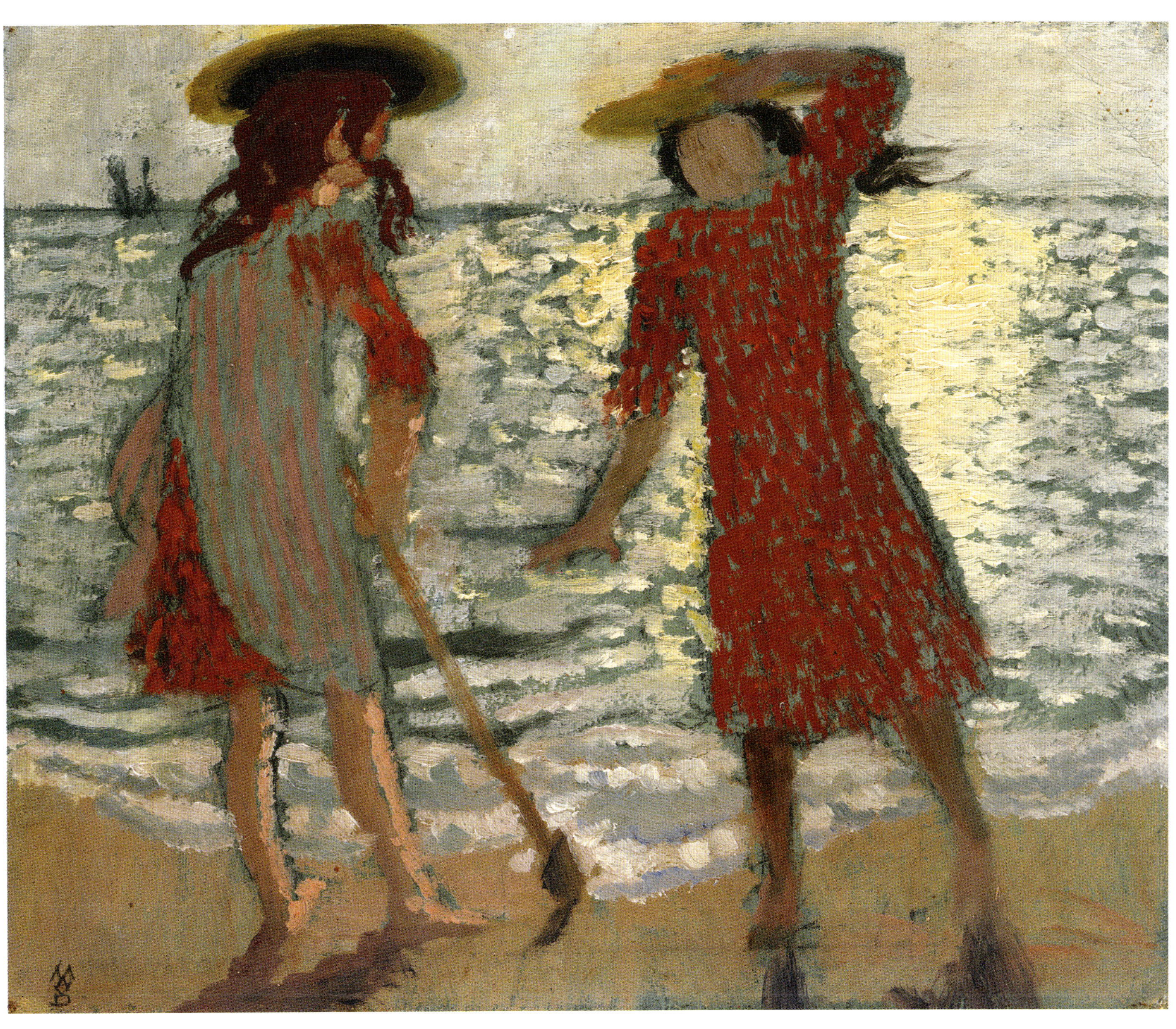

CAT. 68. Maurice Denis, *Sur la plage (fillettes à contre-jour)* (On the Beach [Two Girls against the Light]), 1892. Oil on board mounted on panel, 8⅛ x 9⅞ in. (20.5 x 25 cm). Private collection, Germany

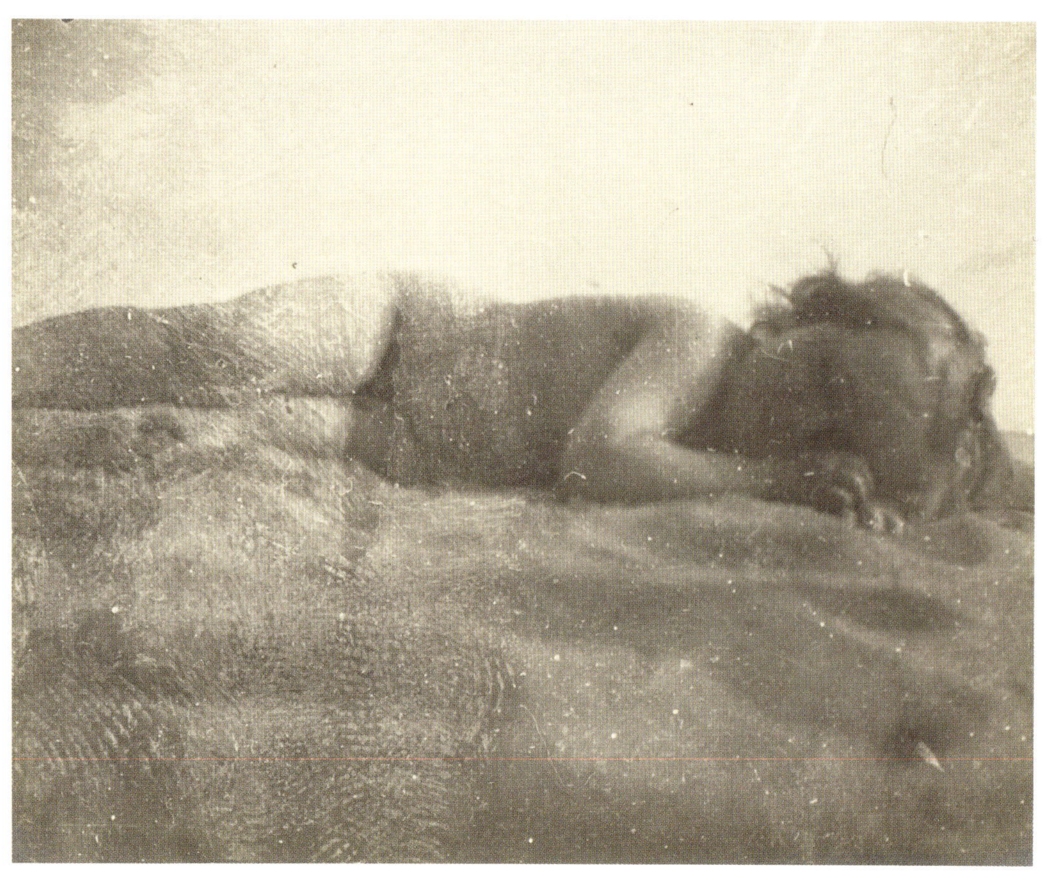

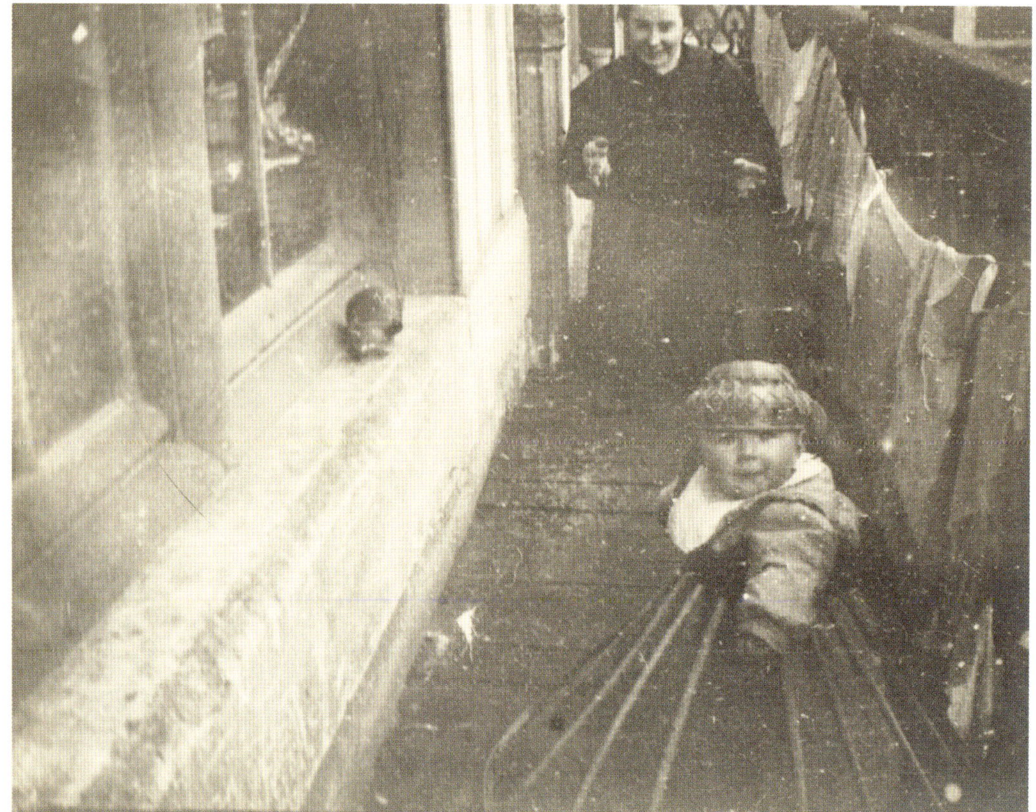

CAT. 69. Maurice Denis, Noële nude stretched out on the beach, Le Pouldu, summer 1899. Gelatin silver print, 4¾ x 6¼ in. (12 x16 cm). Musée d'Orsay, Paris. Gift of Mme Claire Denis, through the Société des Amis du Musée d'Orsay, 2006

CAT. 70. Maurice Denis, Noële with walker and her mother, hands outstretched, on the balcony of the Villa Montrouge, Saint-Germain-en-Laye, April 1897. Gelatin silver print, 4¾ x 6¼ in. (12 x 16 cm). Musée d'Orsay, Paris. Gift of Mme Claire Denis, through the Société des Amis du Musée d'Orsay, 2006

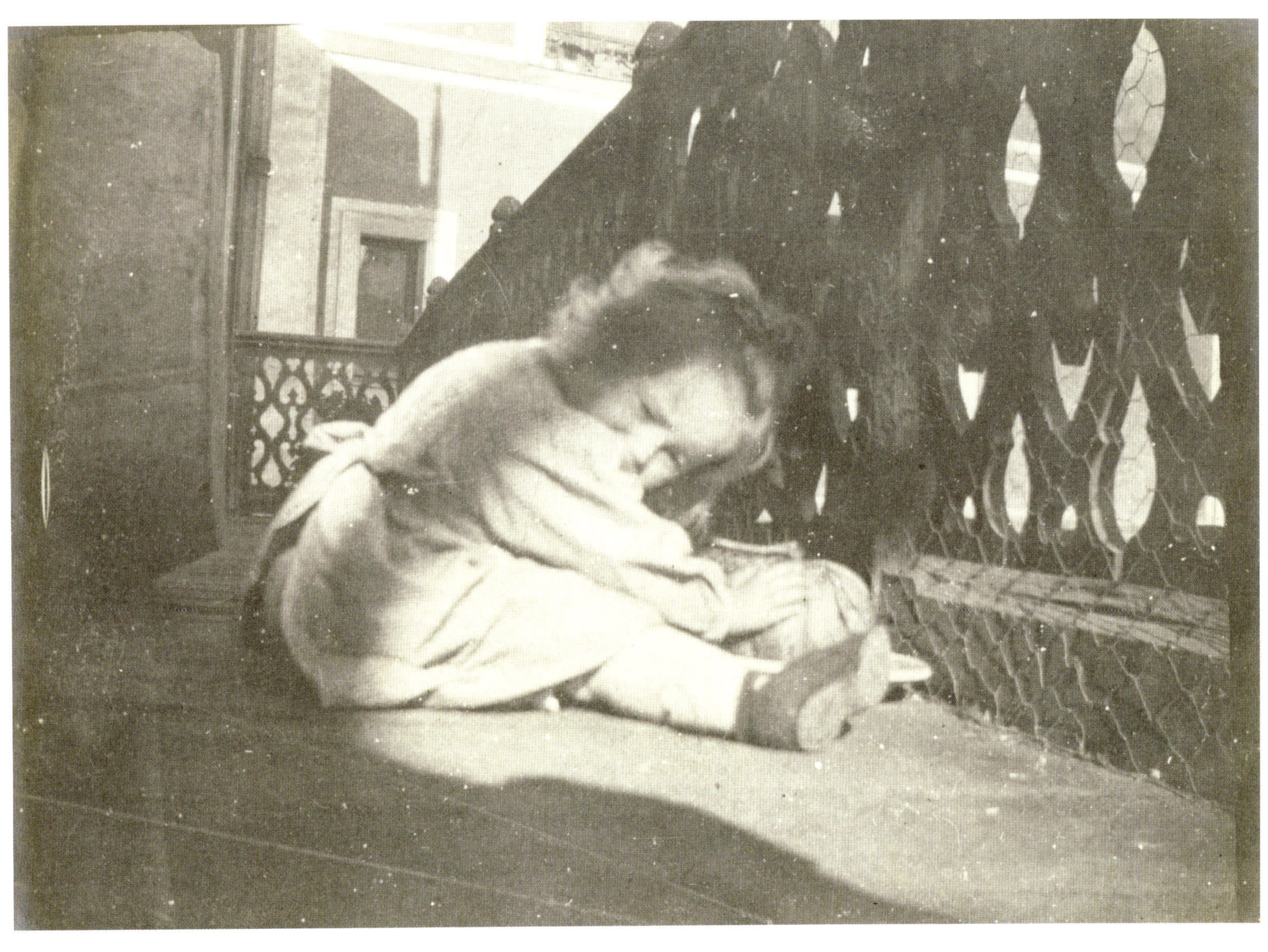

CAT. 71. Maurice Denis, Noële seated on a balcony, n.d. Gelatin silver print, 4½ x 6¼ in. (11.5 x 16 cm). Musée Maurice Denis, le Prieuré, Saint-Germain-en-Laye

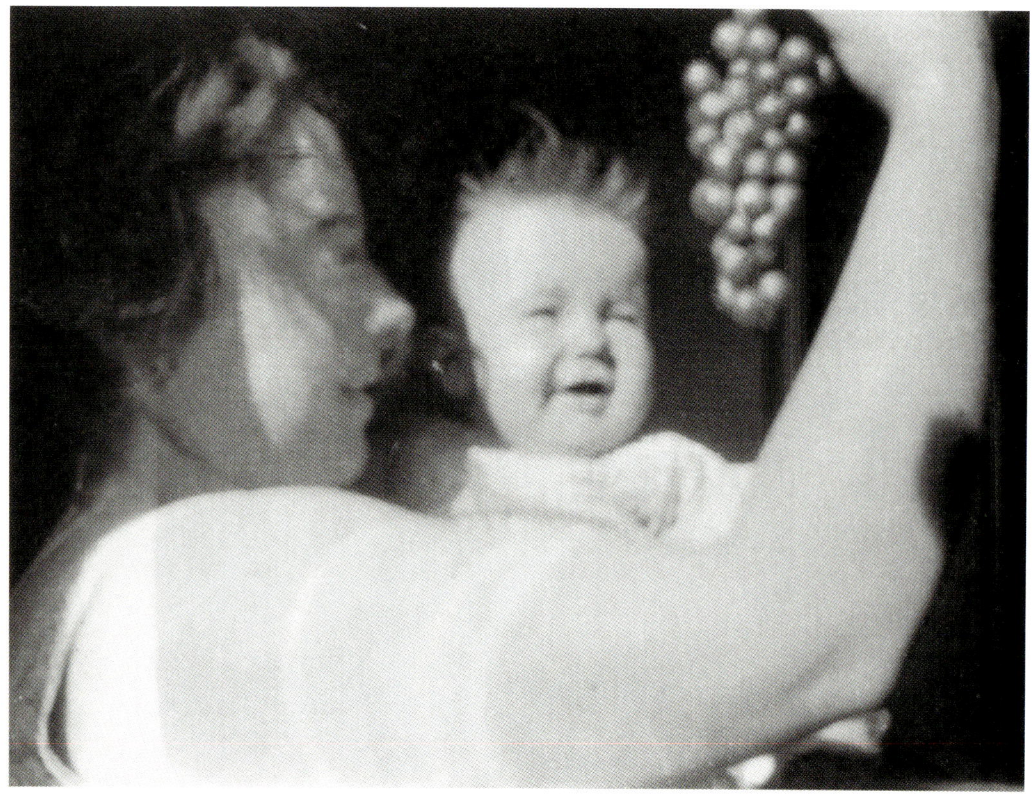

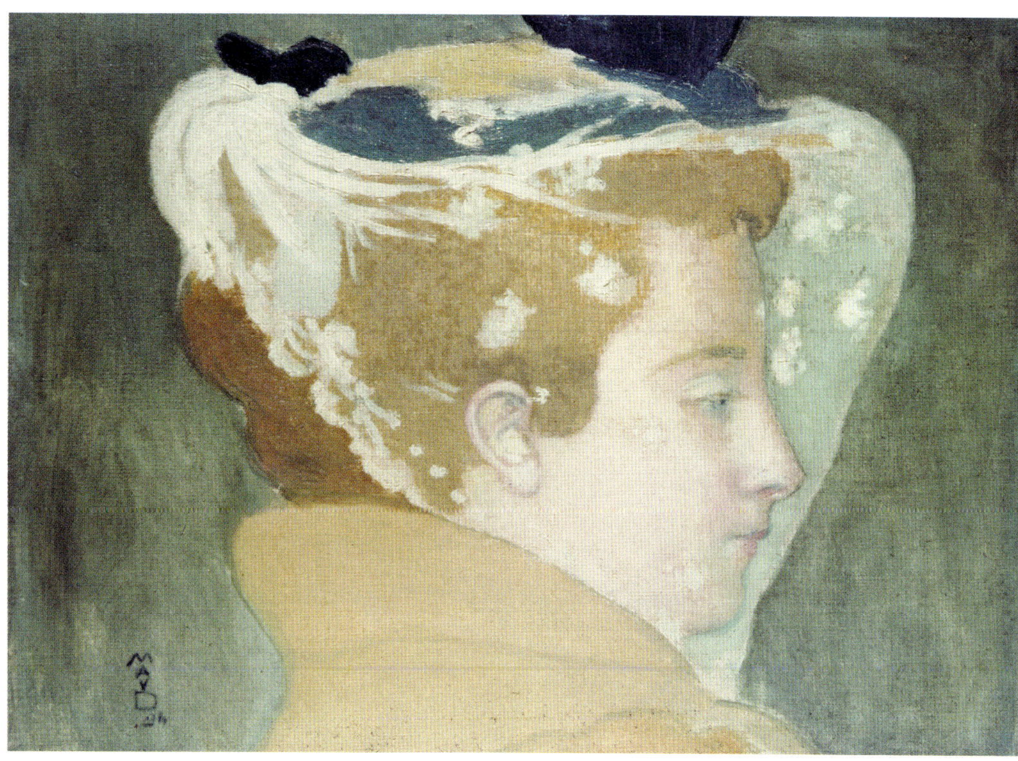

CAT. 72. Maurice Denis, Marthe offering Bernadette a bunch of grapes, Le Pouldu, September 15, 1890. Negative on nitrate cellulose film, 1½ x 2¼ in. (3.7 x 5.8 cm). Musée d'Orsay, Paris. Gift of Mme Claire Denis, through the Société des Amis du Musée d'Orsay, 2006

CAT. 73. Maurice Denis, *Portrait de Marthe à voilette blanche* (Portrait of Marthe in a White Veil), 1894. Oil on canvas, 12⅝ x 16⅛ in. (32 x 41 cm). Private collection

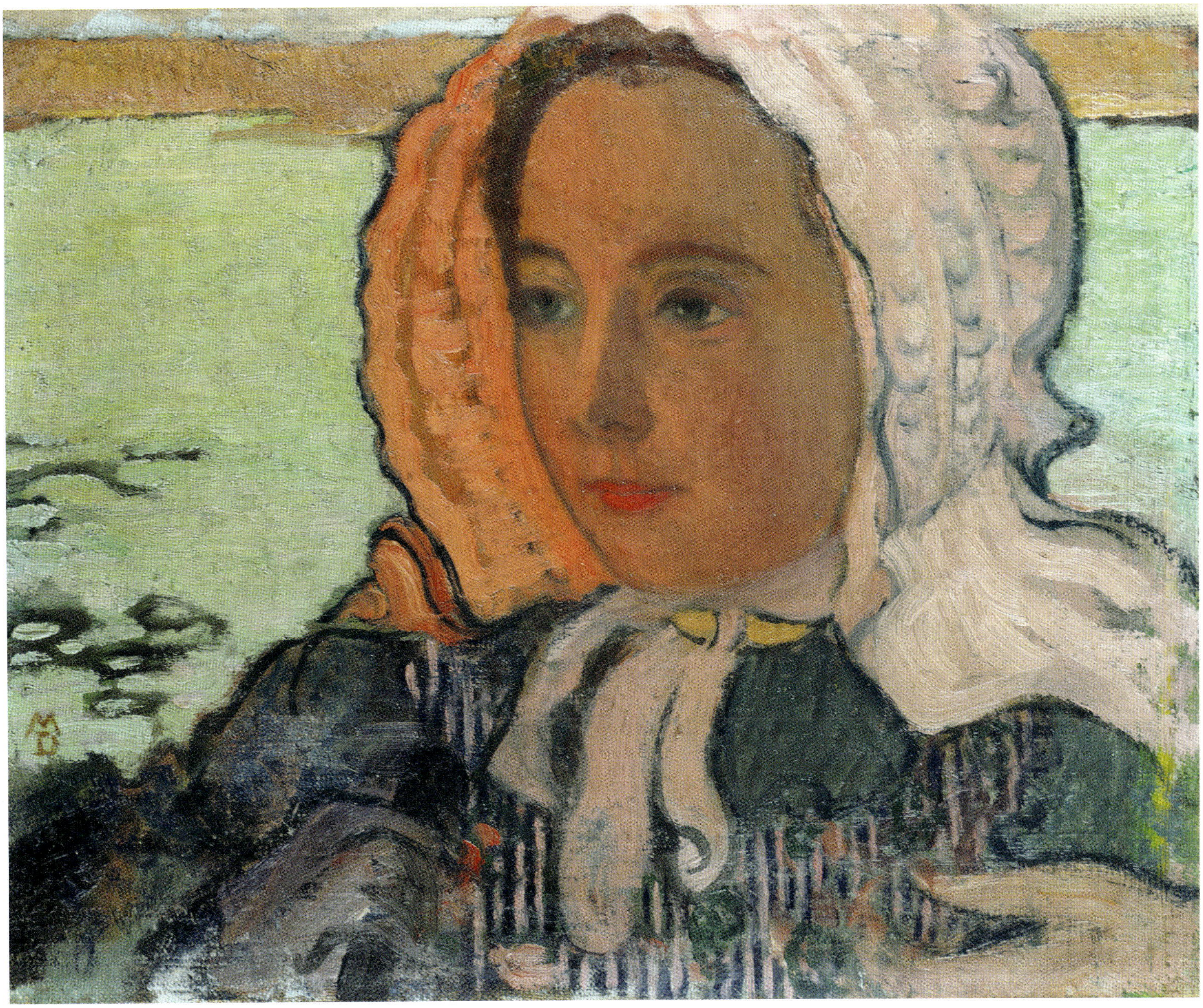

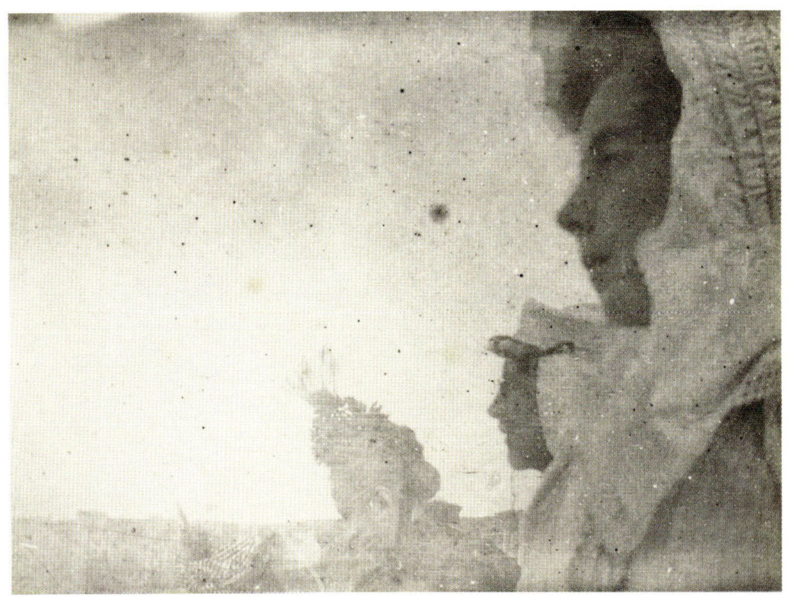

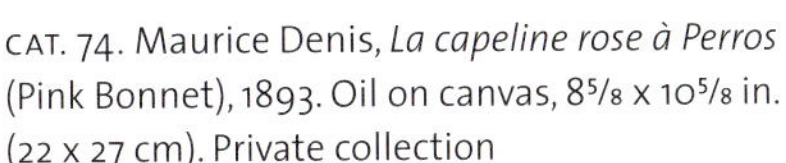

CAT. 74. Maurice Denis, *La capeline rose à Perros* (Pink Bonnet), 1893. Oil on canvas, $8\frac{5}{8}$ x $10\frac{5}{8}$ in. (22 x 27 cm). Private collection

CAT. 75. Maurice Denis, Marthe in a bonnet, M. and Mme Genêt?, n.d. Gelatin silver print, $4\frac{3}{4}$ x $6\frac{1}{4}$ in. (12 x 16 cm). Private collection, Saint-Germain en Laye

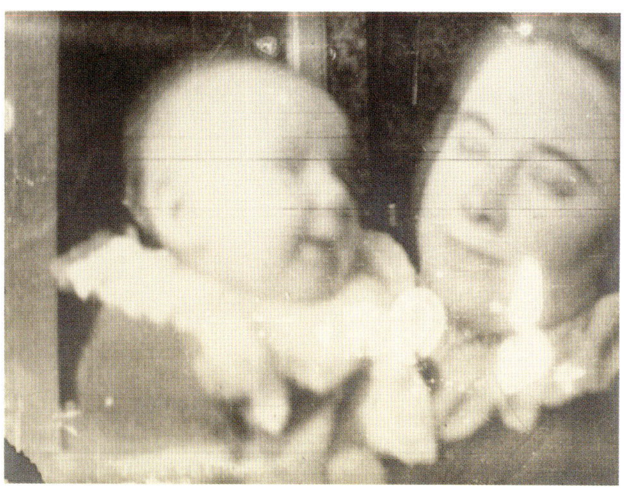

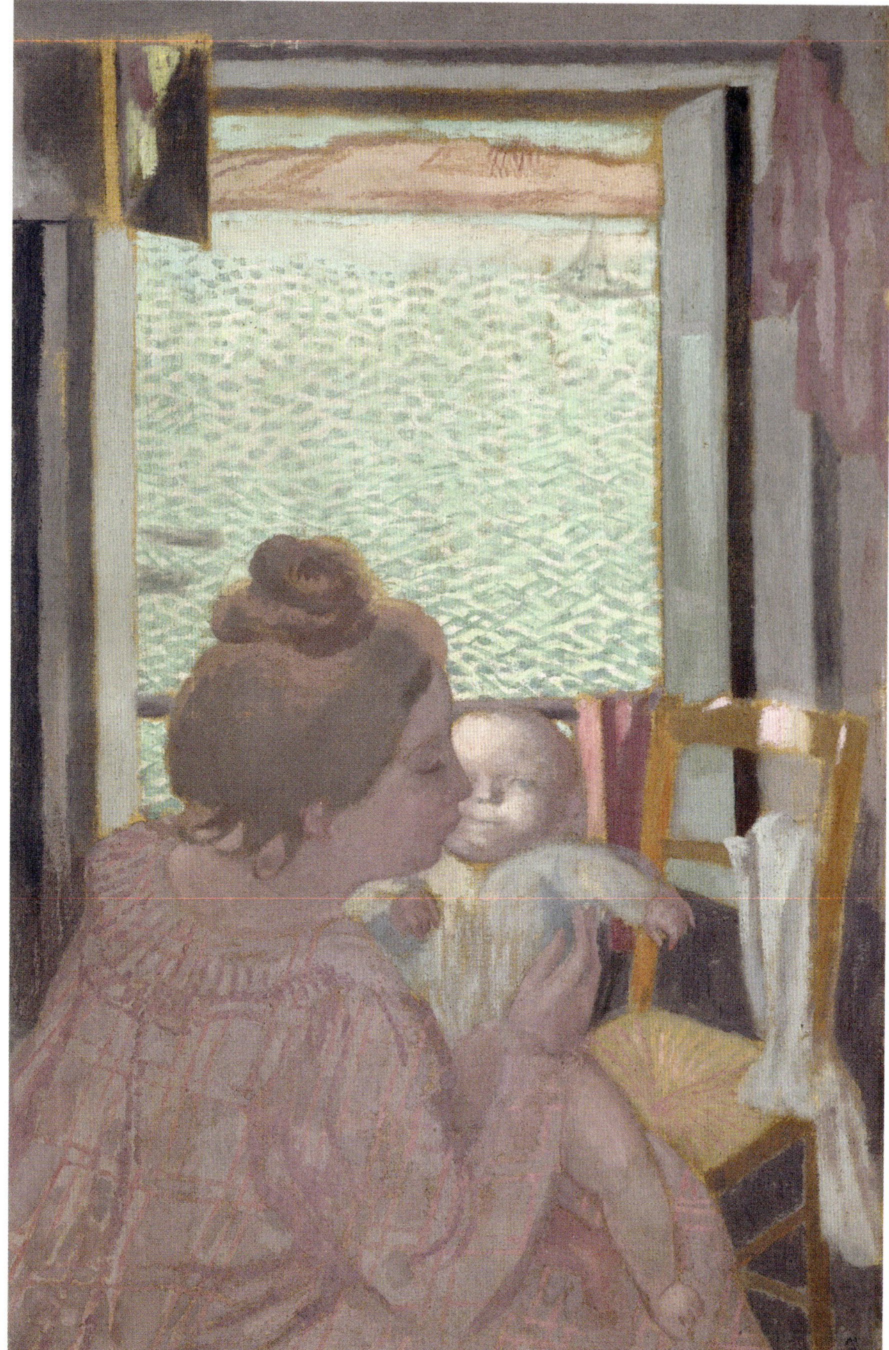

CAT. 76. Maurice Denis, Close-up of Noële in a white collar in her mother's arms at Mercin, Arthur Fontaine's home, November 1896. Gelatin silver print, 4¾ x 6¼ in. (12 x 16 cm). Musée d'Orsay, Paris. Gift of Mme Claire Denis, through the Société des Amis du Musée d'Orsay, 2006

CAT. 77. Maurice Denis, *Maternité à la fenêtre (au Le Pouldu)* (Motherhood at the Window [in Le Pouldu]), ca. 1899. Oil on canvas, 27½ x 18⅛ in. (70 x 46 cm). Musée d'Orsay, Paris. Paul Jamot bequest, 1941

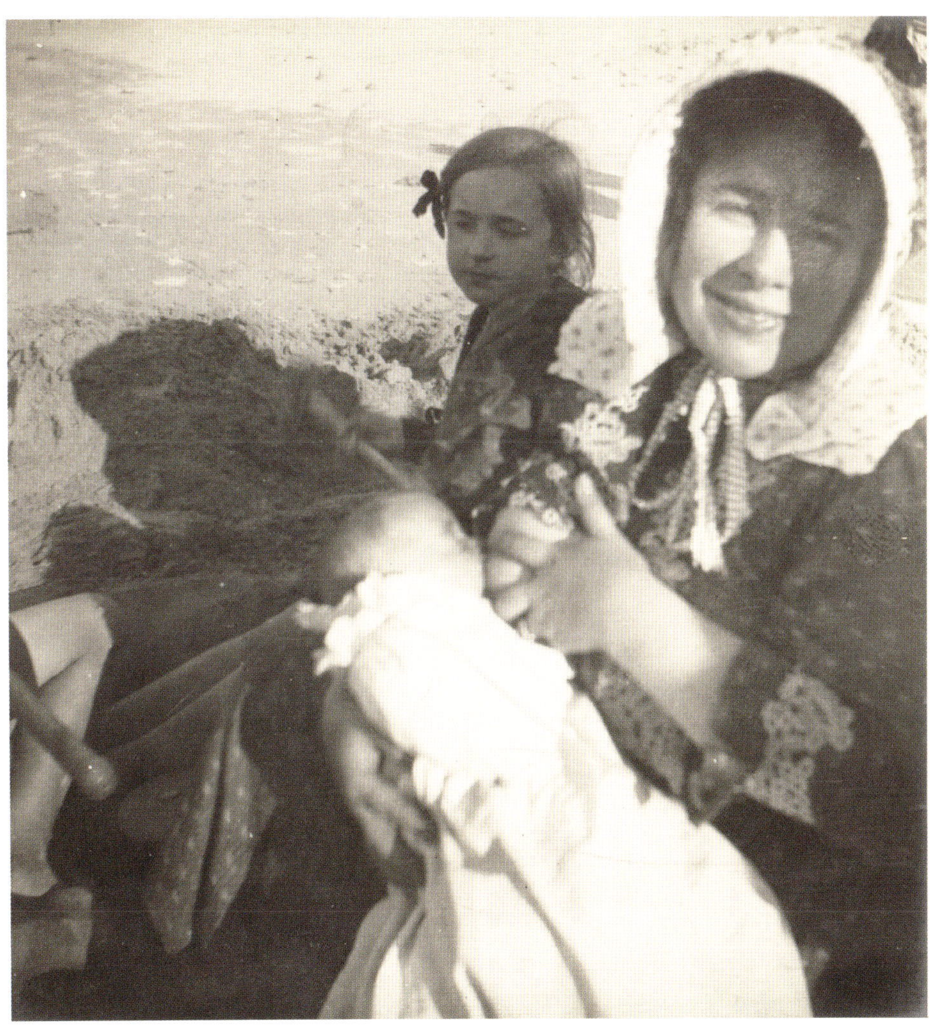

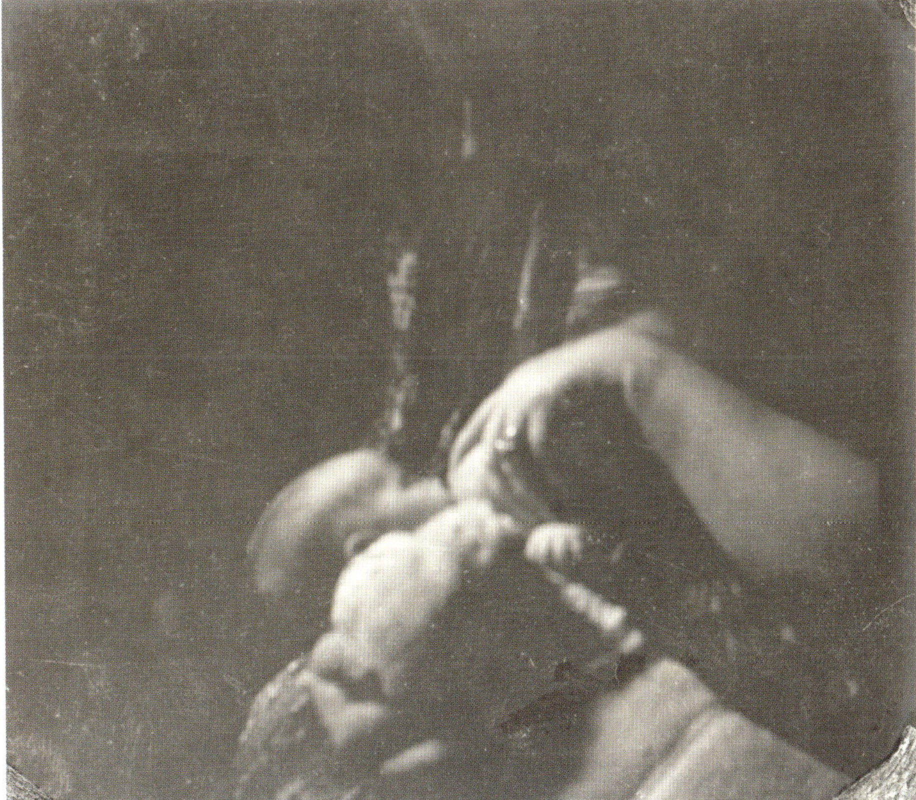

CAT. 78. Maurice Denis, Marthe nursing Madeleine in front of Noële on the beach, Perros-Guirec, October 1906. Gelatin silver print, 4¾ x 6¼ in. (12 x 16 cm). Musée d'Orsay, Paris. Gift of Mme Claire Denis, through the Société des Amis du Musée d'Orsay, 2006

CAT. 79. Maurice Denis, Marthe nursing Dominique, three weeks after the birth, September 1, 1909. Gelatin silver print, 4⅞ x 5⅞ in. (12.5 x 15 cm). Musée d'Orsay, Paris. Gift of Mme Claire Denis, through the Société des Amis du Musée d'Orsay, 2006

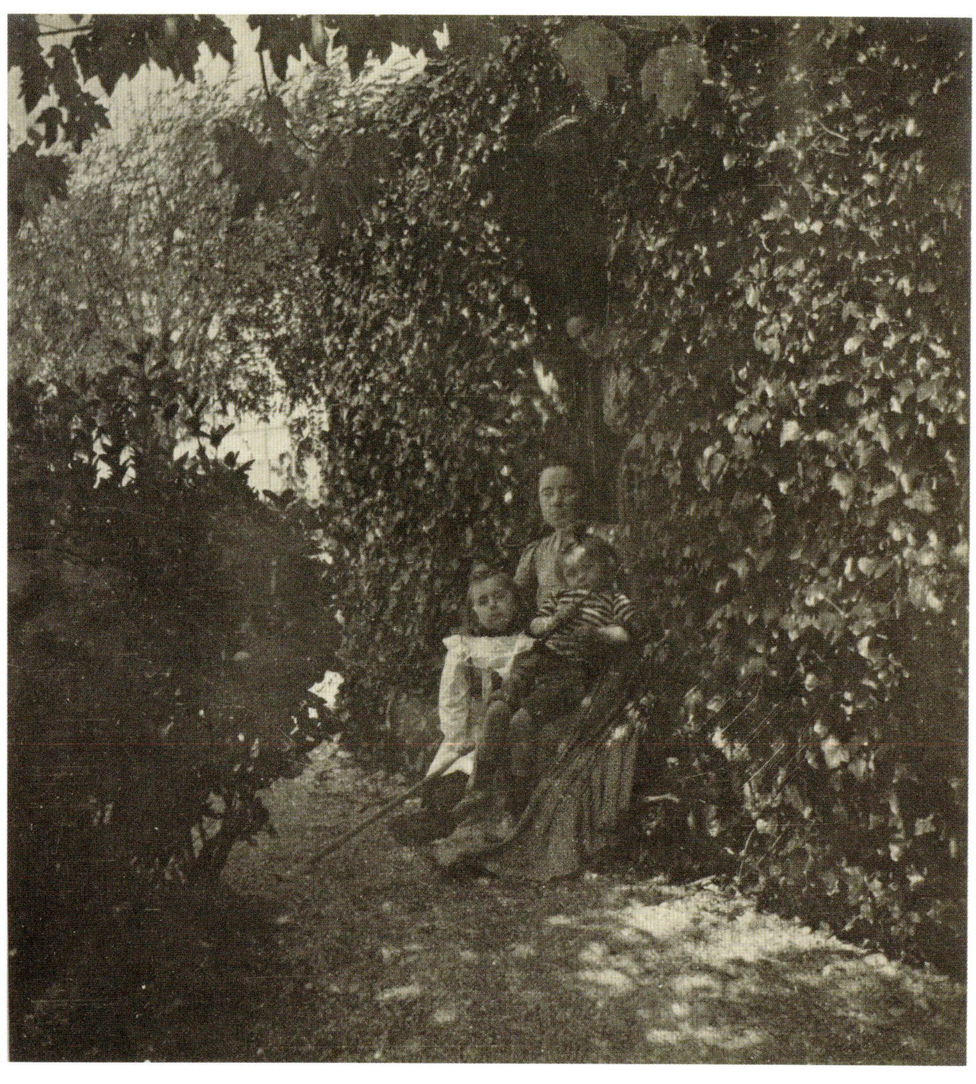

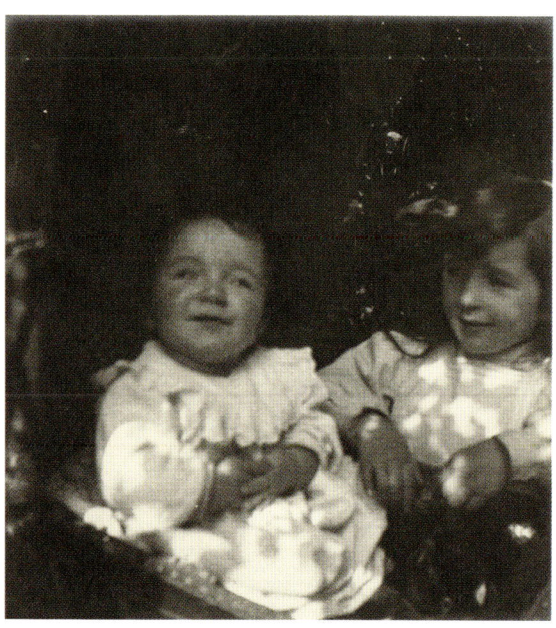

CAT. 80. Maurice Denis, Noële and Bernadette sitting on the doorstep, wall of greenery, 1903. Gelatin silver print, 6¼ x 5⅞ in. (16 x 15 cm). Private collection, Saint-Germain-en-Laye

CAT. 81. Maurice Denis, Anne-Marie standing behind the carriage of smiling Madeleine, May 1907. Gelatin silver print, 6¼ x 5⅞ in. (16 x 15 cm). Private collection, Saint-Germain-en-Laye

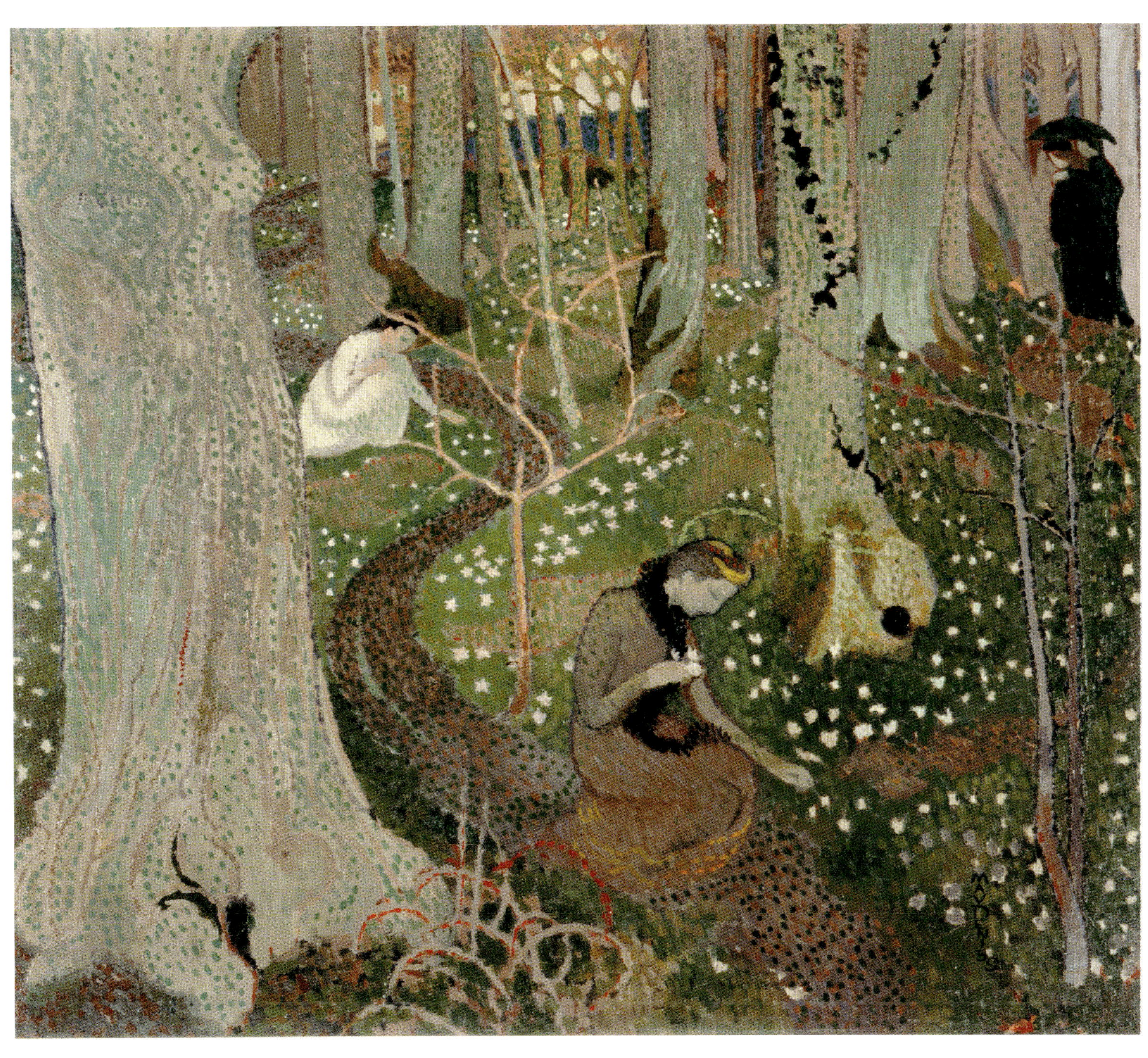

CAT. 82. Maurice Denis, *Avril (Anémones)* (April [Anemones]), 1891. Oil on canvas, $25^{5}/_{8}$ x $30^{3}/_{4}$ in. (65 x 78 cm). Private collection

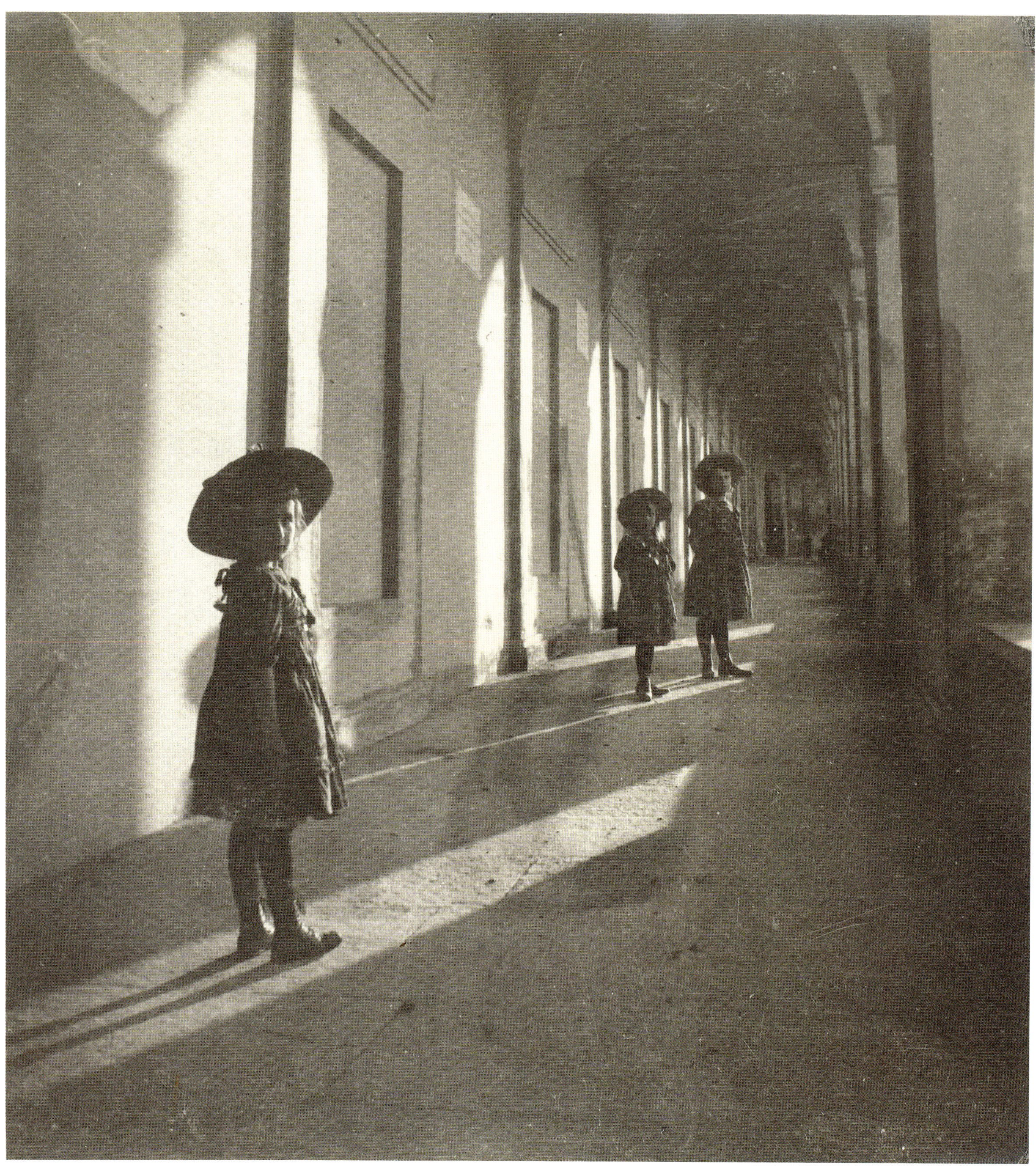

CAT. 83. Maurice Denis, Anne-Marie, Bernadette, and Noële under an arcade, Bologna, October–November 1907. Gelatin silver print, 5½ x 5¼ in. (14 x 13.5 cm). Musée d'Orsay, Paris. Gift of Mme Claire Denis, through the Société des Amis du Musée d'Orsay, 2006

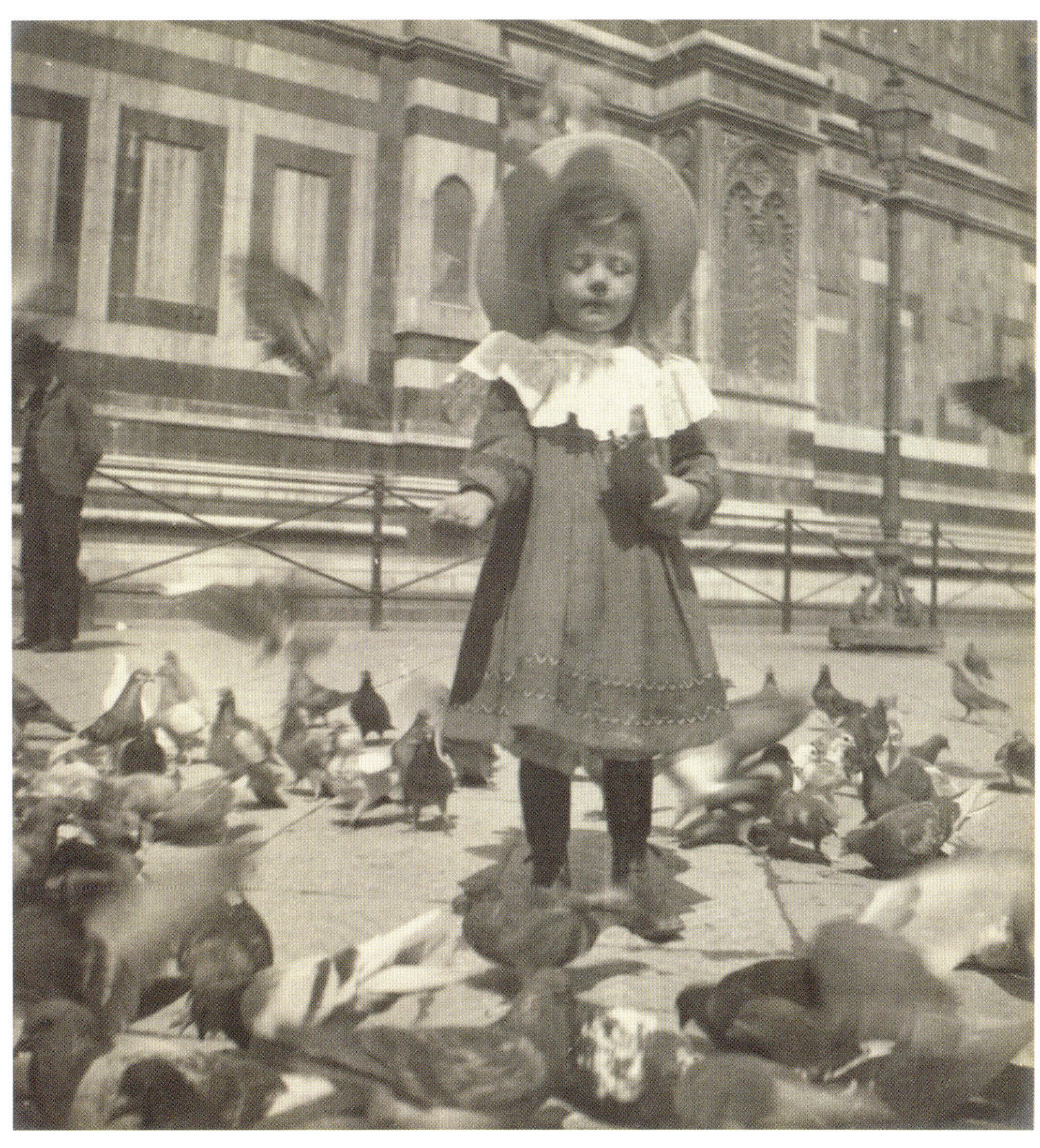

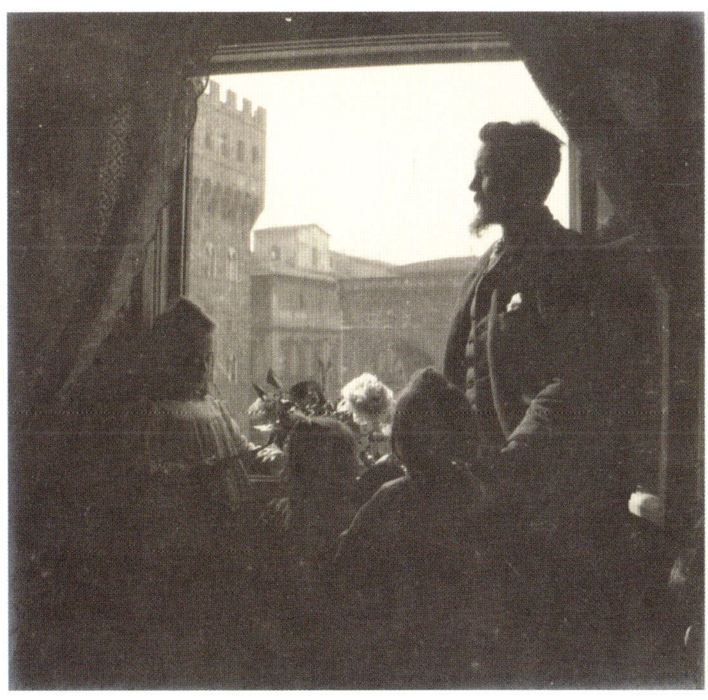

CAT. 84. Maurice Denis, Bernadette feeding pigeons in front of the Duomo, Florence, 1904. Gelatin silver print, 4¾ x 6¼ in. (12 x 16 cm). Musée d'Orsay, Paris. Gift of Mme Claire Denis, through the Société des Amis du Musée d'Orsay, 2006

CAT. 85. Marthe Denis, View of La Place de la Seigneurie, Noële, Anne-Marie, and Bernadette with Maurice Denis, Florence, April 1904. Gelatin silver print, 4¾ x 6¼ in. (12 x 16 cm). Musée d'Orsay, Paris. Gift of Mme Claire Denis, through the Société des Amis du Musée d'Orsay, 2006

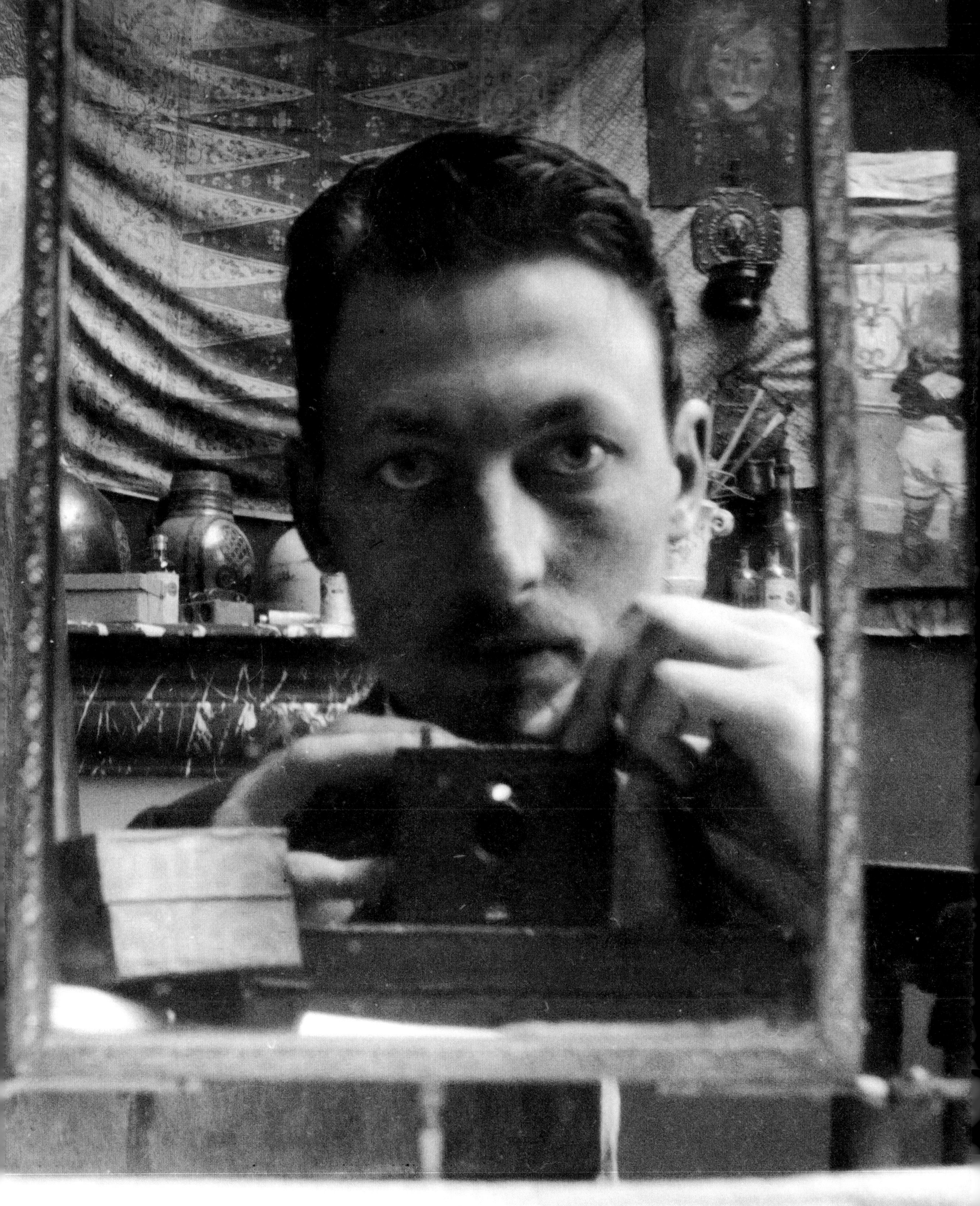

Henri Evenepoel: An Abundance of Gifts

Eliza Rathbone

With his omnivorous eye, passionate loving heart, and natural artistic gifts, Henri Evenepoel carved out for himself a place in history during the scant seven years he lived and worked in Paris in the 1890s. Given his talents and sensibility, he could not have been there at a more auspicious time. The year 1894 saw a notable exhibition at the Galerie Durand-Ruel of works by Edouard Manet; previously, Evenepoel had known the work of the acknowledged leader of modernist painting only through his *Olympia*, on view at the Musée du Luxembourg. To Evenepoel, the Durand-Ruel exhibition was a "revelation." The decade also saw the development and proliferation of the handheld Kodak (first introduced in 1888), with which Evenepoel made some 875 photographs in a mere two and a half years. Finally, Paris in the 1890s afforded him the opportunity to study with Gustave Moreau, one of the most esteemed and rigorous, yet open-minded, artists then teaching in the city.[1]

After Evenepoel died at the age of twenty-seven, critics extolled him especially for his "spontaneity" and for his innate gifts as a colorist—a "born painter in immediate possession of an intense means of expression." No less a critic than the brilliant champion of the avant-garde Roger Marx noted similar qualities, while adding that Evenepoel had a curiosity about new modes of expression.[2] Although Marx did not cite amateur photography among them (and may well not have known of Evenepoel's interest in this medium), he might as well have done so, because Evenepoel not only was curious and excited about the possibilities inherent in the handheld camera but also set about mastering how it worked. As he wrote to his father, "I've studied the mechanism very carefully: I now understand it completely"; he also called it "a real gem."[3]

But do the photographs Evenepoel made with his Kodak have artistic merit in and of themselves? Or is it because they document the artist's private life that they have value? The answer may be yes in both cases. Evenepoel's photographs offer insight into his private life and also into his engagement with a visual medium that opened up unexpected ways of seeing the world. On occasion, he used photography deliberately as a source for his painting, but more often he explored it as a device—with its own unique properties—for inventing new and resonant images. So how do Evenepoel's photographs, never intended for exhibition and largely unknown to the general public, affect our understanding of his achievement? How does his exploration of this black-and-white medium relate to his gifts as a painter and a colorist, and what

DETAIL OF CAT. 94

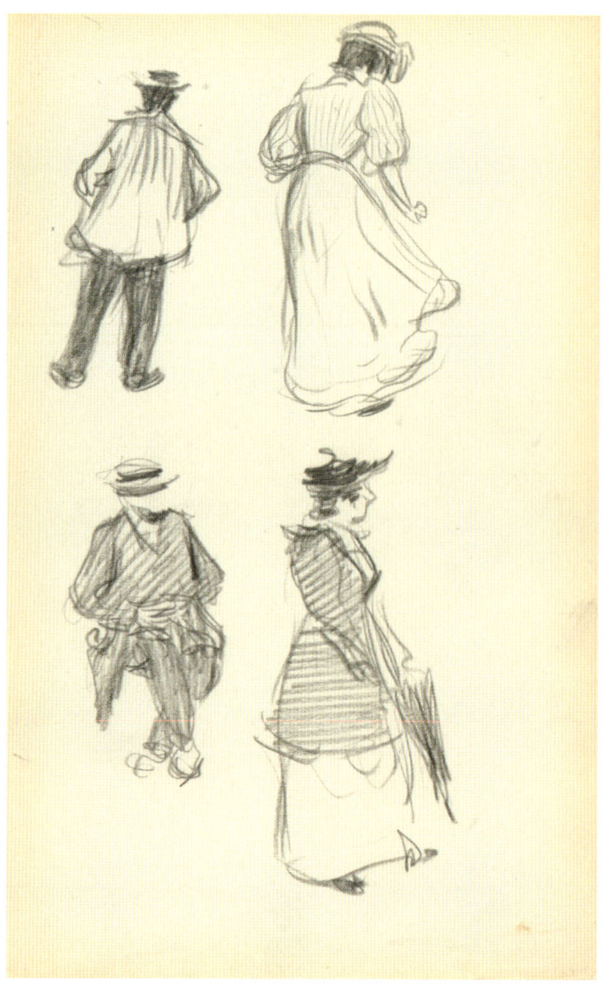

CAT. 86. Henri Evenepoel, Page from Evenepoel's sketchbook, 1893. Conté crayon on paper, 8¼ x 5¼ in. (21 x 13.2 cm). Royal Museums of Fine Arts of Belgium, Brussels

does it tell us about where he might have gone with this discovery had he lived longer?

Henri Jacques Edouard Evenepoel, son of bourgeois Belgian parents, was born in Nice and lived most of his brief life as an artist in Paris, arriving at age twenty in 1892 and dying there, of typhoid, in 1899. He adored his adopted city and felt frustrated at being unable to capture all its radiant beauty. Virtually every day, he saw new scenes he wanted to paint. As he walked down the avenue Rapp, along the quays, crossing the bridge to the Place de la Concorde, and through the Tuileries, he observed (and described in letters to his father) the morning mist, midday brilliance, and the chromatic intensity of the sunset.[4] By the time he acquired his camera, in 1897, he had already discovered his talent for drawing, a skill that had become for him "an obsession."[5] It was for his drawings that he was accepted into Moreau's studio and as a draftsman as well as a painter that he was recognized posthumously. The camera never displaced the role of drawing for Evenepoel, although his sketching may have diminished once he had the Kodak in hand. Both drawing and photography were achieved with handheld tools, and both relied on spontaneity for maximum effect. Although each related differently to his paintings, both took as their predominant subject the human figure.

In addition to some one thousand drawings and sketches that Evenepoel left behind, the artist often illustrated his voluminous correspondence, especially with his father but also with friends and teachers, sketching within the text or in the margins.[6] Entranced by the movement of people in the streets and parks of Paris, he captured with ease the swirl and ripple of a skirt in motion, the tilt of a headlong stride, the posture of a woman sewing or of a laborer carrying his burden. In his sketchbook, Evenepoel rapidly recorded these individuals as they went about their business (cat. 86).

Once in possession of a camera, he took some of his most memorable snapshots in outdoor urban settings. These, like most of his photographs (except for those he made during an extended stay in Algeria in 1897 and 1898), are focused on his relatives. For example, he photographed his cousin, Louise, her two girls, and his son, Charles de Mey, on the edge of the vast Place de la Concorde, his presence implied in the foreground shadow (cat. 105). Another picture of the children and their nanny skirting the edge of the Place de la Concorde recalls Edgar Degas's 1875

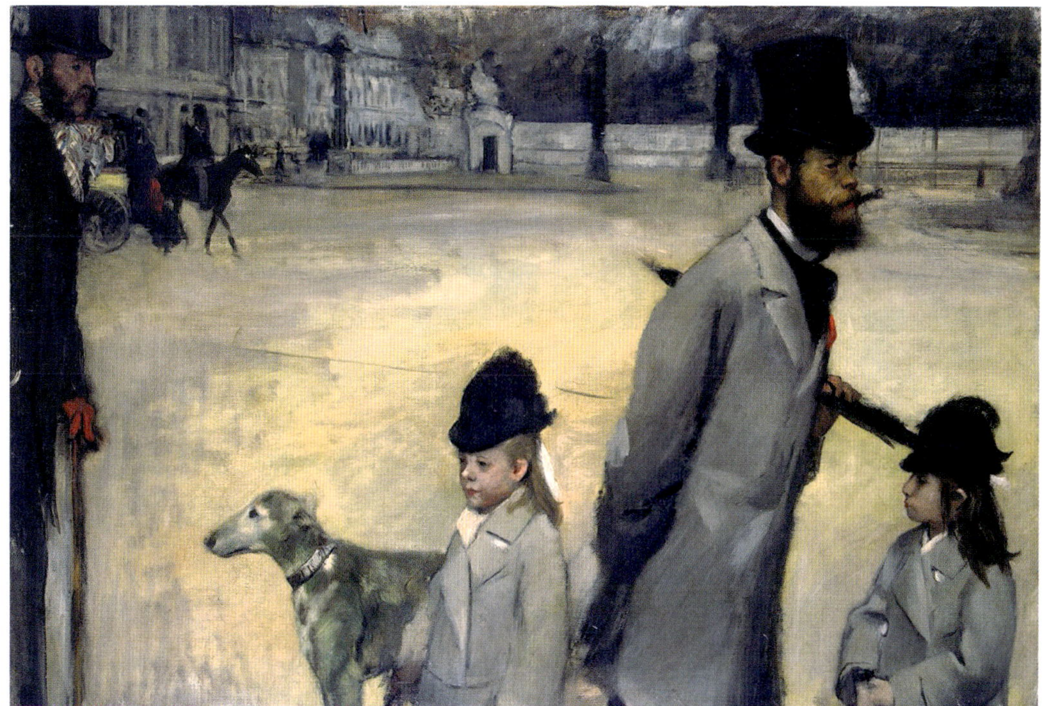

FIG. 1. Edgar Degas, *La Place de la Concorde (Vicomte Lepic and His Daughters)*, 1875. Oil on canvas, 30⅞ x 46¼ in. (78.4 x 117.5 cm). The Hermitage, St. Petersburg

portrait of the Vicomte Lepic with his daughters (fig. 1), an image that itself suggests the spontaneity and captured movement of a snapshot (cat. 103). While as a painter Evenepoel emulated the works of Degas and Manet, the camera liberated him from any constraints that a mentor or an intended audience might impose. His drawings, however, often prepared him for major projects, paintings such as *At Café d'Harcourt in the Quartier Latin* (1897; Städelsches Kunstinstitut, Frankfurt-am-Main) or *Le caveau du Soleil d'Or* (The Cave of the Golden Sun in the Latin Quarter) (1896; Musées royaux des Beaux-Arts de Bruxelles)—both multi-figure compositions of Parisian life of the sort depicted by Henri de Toulouse-Lautrec. In works such as these, Evenepoel's sketches translated readily into lively scenes of Paris nightlife. Distinguished by their sublimation of detail and attention to the properties of paint, these paintings reveal Evenepoel's ease with a medium that he applied with relish and panache. By contrast, he rarely tried to photograph the movement he succeeded in conveying so adroitly in his paintings and sketches.

As soon as he had his camera, Evenepoel looked forward to creating with it what he described as "tangible, eternal souvenirs."[7] He had especially in mind a summer holiday in Wépion, at a house (called Trieu Colin) beside a lake in the Belgian countryside where he would spend two months away from Paris with Louise, her two daughters, Henriette and Sophie, and Charles, his son born illegitimately to Louise. There, he made numerous photographs of family members, several of which became the basis of individual painted portraits. A snapshot of Louise looking radiantly happy (cat. 87), though not made as an intentional study, also inspired a subsequent painting—*Le chapeau blanc* (The White Hat; cat. 88).

His host in Wépion was his aunt, Sophie Fraiken-Devis, whose grandsons, Albert and André, posed for

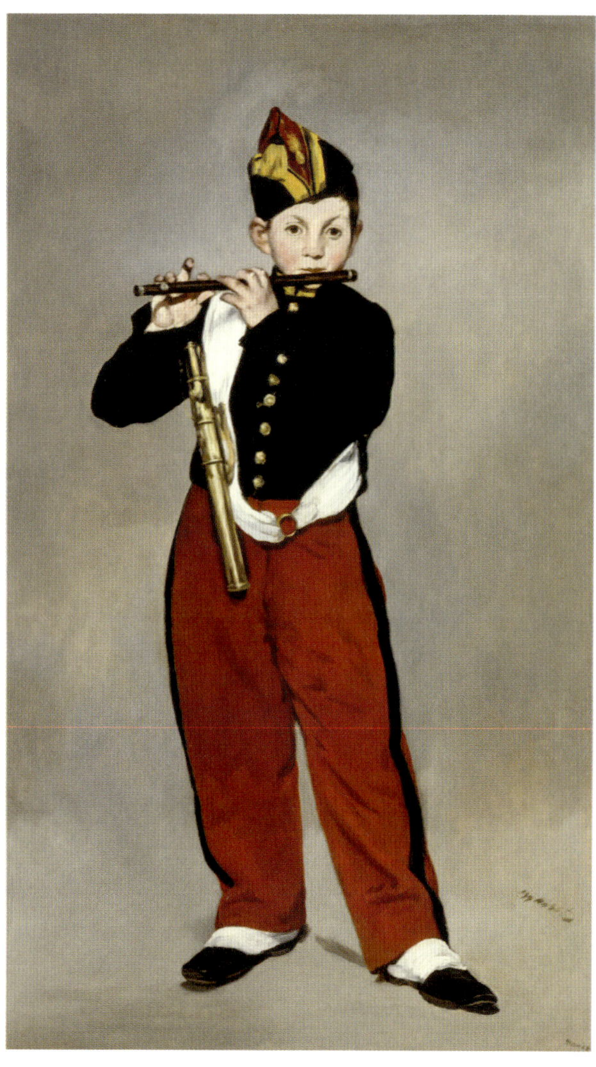

FIG. 2. Edouard Manet, *Le fifre* (The Fifer), 1866. Oil on canvas, 63³/₈ x 38¹/₈ in. (161 x 97 cm). Musée d'Orsay, Paris

the camera in their best clothes, providing the artist with a visual source for the painted portraits that would follow (cat. 89). Evenepoel photographed André with the child's left hand on his hip, thumb in pocket; his right hand awkwardly holds a walking stick; and his face wears a self-conscious expression. He stands on a small rug in a room with a door, a mirror, and a table with bouquets on it. In his painted portrait of André, Evenepoel clearly relied on the photograph, while also echoing Manet's *Le fifre* (The Fifer; fig. 2), which he had seen and admired at the Galerie Durand-Ruel in 1894. In his portrait of Albert Devis, as in that of André, the figure fills the field (cat. 90).[8] The elegantly dressed Albert wears black shoes, a jacket and vest over a white shirt, and a voluminous pink necktie—a brilliant dash of color invisible in a black-and-white photograph but quite striking in the painting. The subject looks straight at us, his right foot slightly forward, his right hand on his hip and his left at his side, holding a walking stick. Evenepoel executed the bamboo stick with a series of fluent brushstrokes in golden pigment that casually trail off toward the edge of the composition.

During this same holiday, Evenepoel also took many photographs of little Charles: in a huge armchair in the bedroom, outside playing with the other children, sitting on the potty (cat. 92), and walking through the fields. Often, these compositions reveal that he has joined his son on the floor to photograph him at eye level. In a few rare instances, Evenepoel experimented with capturing movement with the camera: in a photograph of Sophie de Mey dropping a ball that becomes a blur midair in front of her and in one of Charles running toward the camera (cats. 91, 115). What distinguishes these images is the degree to which they reflect the emotion of the photographer. In fact, for Evenepoel, this depth of feeling is as palpable in his photographs as in his paintings—or even more so. In October 1897, Evenepoel wrote to his father that he had been leafing through his "small photographs" from the time spent in Wépion: "I savor them with the slightly sad joy of reflecting that all this good time is past."[9] Is this the moment he immortalized in a photograph of himself poring over a selection of prints spread on a table (cat. 95)? Certainly, the very fact that he made the picture would seem to indicate pride in identifying himself as a photographer. He then added, "We must recognize they're gone." A poignant sense of the fragile evanescence of life imbues Evenepoel's photographs, a moment-in-time quality that further distinguishes them from his paintings.

Death and illness seemed to plague Evenepoel his entire life. At age two, he lost his mother, soon after that an uncle, and then the grandfather who helped raise him. His own health was delicate. Perhaps for these reasons, he photographed his children when they were sick — as if to create a "tangible, eternal" image before time erased it. These images reflect poignant parental anxiety as well as the charmed innocence of a bed-ridden child. In the photograph of Louise watching over Charles, an anxious mother looms in the foreground, while her son appears exaggeratedly small and vulnerable in his bed across the room (cat. 109). The father tenderly observes the sick Charles in bed from various angles. As if wishing to put his own face as close to his infant son as possible, Evenepoel created one of his most surprising and radical images in a photograph of Charles asleep in his crib, in which the boy is viewed through the curlicues of the bed's wrought-iron sides (cat. 108). His small limbs become volumes and contours lost within the folds of the blanket and bedding, seen through the rigid arabesques of the crib that frame the whole composition. Here again, prompted by his camera to take a novel vantage point, Evenepoel created an image of greater originality than he had attempted in painting.

Although his master, Gustave Moreau, made use of photographs as sources for his painting, he never pursued the medium as a means of exploring the world around him. And though Moreau didn't share his student's interest in Manet or in depicting modern life, he nonetheless took a keen interest in the younger man's work. An "old modern," Moreau called his student, whom he also hailed with satisfaction, declaring, "You are you!"[10] Moreau, under whom the young artist studied from 1893 to 1898, was devoted to his pupils and clearly enjoyed the charming, educated, and talented Henri Evenepoel. Described by the art historian Lawrence Gowing as "the most sensitive of masters, with a devotion to the mystery of talent," Moreau taught that the highest aim of art was self-expression.[11] Moreover, he believed that the artist must paint with his heart in order to produce praiseworthy work, and that every brushstroke must reflect the artist's sensibility. Neither technique nor virtuosity could equal the power of the spirit in which a work is achieved. In this respect, the subjects of Evenepoel's paintings often overlap those that are evident in his photographs. From the moment he fell in love with Louise, Evenepoel said he pursued his work with a passion that love inspired. Although he eschewed Moreau's subjects from mythology and the Bible, he derived from his teacher an appreciation for the medium of paint itself, a profound sense of the artist's connection to his subject, and the encouragement to use color to express feeling. Moreau advocated painting nature with an imaginative approach. "Color must be conceived, dreamed, imagined," he said.[12]

It was in Moreau's studio that Evenepoel met Georges Rouault and Henri Matisse, two artists who would become famous in the twentieth century, expanding and developing the scope and power of their art in ways he would never have the opportunity to do. The two Henris became close friends; they shared striking similarities. Both had fathers who doubted their sons' chosen profession, and both were keenly conscious of the need to prove themselves. Both experienced some official success with their painting while studying with Moreau, were well read, played musical instruments, fell in love, and fathered children. Evenepoel made a charming portrait of Matisse's daughter — captured in profile at eighteen months — *La petite Matisse* (The Little Matisse, or The Daughter of Matisse) (1896; Museum Mevrouw Jules Dhondt-Dhaenens, Deurle). The two painted together *en plein air* and visited each other's studios (cat. 111).

For both artists, the figure became a paramount subject; at the same time, each produced several studio interiors. A comparison highlights some ways in which Evenepoel's paintings prefigure aspects of work by Matisse, who avidly developed the subject of the artist's studio later in his career. As early as 1891, Evenepoel painted views of his own studio, which he also would eventually photograph. In his early interiors, Evenepoel, like Matisse, produced what Lawrence Gowing called "pictures of untidiness" and "domestic clutter clarified by light."[13] In 1897, he painted his most celebrated and beautiful studio interior, *La robe blanche* (The White Dress), for which he lined his easel up directly parallel to the wall, an approach that offered him an arrangement of elements on or in front of the wall itself so that design, color, texture, shape, and pattern seem to dominate (cat. 97). The painting anticipates a compositional approach that Matisse would develop in the future in more radical works, such as *L'atelier rouge* (The Red Studio) (1911; Museum of Modern Art, New York). Like Matisse, Evenepoel used colorful patterned materials as key elements in his composition, while adding, as a centerpiece, his mother's wedding dress. Likewise, in anticipation of a practice Matisse would later adopt, Evenepoel photographed works in progress in his studio — for example, his portrait *Henriette au grand chapeau* (Henriette in a Large Hat; cats. 113, 114). A photograph reveals that the pink feather, which adds a brilliant finishing touch to the painting, was the artist's invention, a late addition that provides a single Manet-like dash of color to an otherwise subdued palette. In a photograph of Henriette seated in his studio with the hat in her lap, Evenepoel included in the foreground a stool with his own palette and brushes poised on top of it, introducing a future Matissian pictorial trope (cat. 112). Later, according to Hilary Spurling, a biographer of Matisse, the artist recalled his friendship with Evenepoel "as one of the best things in his life."[14]

Although Evenepoel used his photographs as a specific source for some of his most successful works (for example, the image of Charles in his striped jersey; see cats. 116, 117), he understood the limits of their relationship to his paintings, always allowing each medium its own particular properties and engaged by its unique technical challenges. Furthermore, the photographs he made specifically to be the basis for paintings seem prosaic beside his more spontaneous ones. Unlike other painter-photographers, Evenepoel was intent on mastering the new medium. Soon after purchasing his camera, he was developing and printing his own pictures, and he even considered at one time becoming a professional photographer. In contrast to Matisse, who never took up photography and saw the camera as "devoid of feeling," a tool for "[ridding] us of previous imaginations," Evenepoel used photography to record subjects he loved and for which he only occasionally made a painted equivalent.[15]

Evenepoel made numerous self-portraits with his camera, including one of himself leaning forward and looking into a three-way mirror (cat. 94). Delighted with the result, he sent it to his father, exclaiming, "You can see me taking a picture of myself!"[16] The photograph reflects not only his own face but also objects in the studio behind him and on the dressing table before him. In this way he created an image later taken up in painting, for example by Pierre Bonnard, who similarly explored in self-portraits the psychological and visual potential of the mirror as overt framing device.[17] The inquiring expression on the face of Evenepoel, who picked up the camera only two and a half years before he died, will always haunt us. What his future may have held we will never know. Roger Marx, noting the artist's "abundance of gifts," believed that there were few others of his generation for whom the future looked more "superb."[18] Certainly what we do know of the man through his photography expands and deepens our sense of him as an artist and as a human being. Moreover, although the paintings he made can be considered conservatively modern, had he lived longer, he might have explored some of the more audacious avenues that only the camera led him to discover.

NOTES

1. Henri Evenepoel to Edmond Evenepoel, May 13, 1894, *Lettres a mon père, 1892–1899*, ed. Danielle Derrey-Capon, 2 vols. (Brussels: Musées royaux des Beaux-Arts de Belgique, 1984), 1: p. 320. In 1969 the Musées royaux des Beaux-Arts de Bruxelles began negotiations to acquire for its Archives de l'Art Contemporain en Belgique 394 letters and postcards from the artist to his father and 875 photographic negatives; they were acquired two years later. No original prints appear to have survived. See Gisele Ollinger-Zinque, "Fixer le souvenir: L'artiste et son 'Pocket-Kodak,'" in *Henri Evenepoel, 1872–1899* (Snoeck-Ducaju and Zoon, 1994), p. 183.
2. Roger Marx, *Revue encyclopédique* (February 1900), as quoted in Edouard Michel, "Henri Evenepoel, 1872–1899," *Gazette des Beaux-Arts* (Paris) 5 (January 1922): pp. 51–52. Roger Marx: "A un sens moderne tres spontane et tres vif, à une abondance de dons peu commune, Evenepoel unissait une curiosité des modes d'expression nouveaux." (Evenepoel combined a very spontaneous, very sharp modern sense and unusually abundant gifts with a curiosity about new modes of expression.) Michel: "Peu d'artistes du XIX siecle, nous semble-t-il . . . ont montré une pareille spontaneité, une si merveilleuse aptitude à faire sans effort, chanter la couleur . . . on sent le peintre-né, en possession immediate d'un intense moyen d'expression." (Few nineteenth-century artists, it seems . . . showed such spontaneity, such a wonderful capacity for doing things effortlessly, for making color sing . . . we sense the born painter taking immediate possession of an intense means of expression.)
3. "J'ai bien etudié son mechanisme: je le possède maintenant à fond" and "un veritable bijou." Henri Evenepoel to Edmond Evenepoel, July 8, 1897, *Lettres a mon père*, 2: p. 141.
4. Henri Evenepoel to Edmond Evenepoel, April 8, 1893, *Lettres a mon père*, 1: p. 158. After describing his daily walk through Paris, he wrote, "Je peins par les yeux constamment." (I paint with my eyes all the time.)
5. "Le croquis, cela devient une obsession chez moi. Il me serait impossible de passer un jour sans en faire." (Sketches are becoming an obsession with me. I couldn't go for a day without doing any.) Ibid., February 22, 1893, 1: p. 125.
6. Paul Haesaerts, *Les dessins d'Evenepoel* (Brussels: Les Editions Apollo, 1943), p. 9.
7. Henri Evenepoel to Edmond Evenepoel, July 8, 1897, *Lettres a mon père*, 2: p. 141.
8. Presumably, he made photographs of both Albert and André Devis, just as he painted a portrait of each of them, but the only photograph known to me is that of André.
9. "Je les savoure avec la joie un peu triste de me dire que tout ce bon temps est passé." He added, "Il faut en faire son deuil." Henri Evenepoel to Edmond Evenepoel, October 5, 1897, *Lettres a mon père*, 2: p. 150. In *Lettres a mon père*, this photograph is assigned a date of summer 1898.
10. Moreau, as quoted by Evenepoel in a July 8, 1896, letter to his father, *Lettres a mon père*, 2: p. 66.
11. Lawrence Gowing, *Matisse* (New York and Toronto: Oxford University Press, 1979), p. 12.
12. "La couleur doit etre pensée, revé, imaginée." Moreau, as quoted by Henri Evenepoel in Edouard Michel, "Gustave Moreau et Henri Evenepoel," *Mercure de France*, January 1, 1923, p. 51.
13. Gowing, *Matisse*, p. 14.
14. Hilary Spurling, *The Unknown Matisse: A Life of Henri Matisse, The Early Years, 1869–1908* (New York: Alfred A. Knopf, 1998), p. 107.
15. Matisse, as quoted in Dorothy Kosinski, Jay McKean Fisher, and Steven Nash, *Matisse: Painter as Sculptor* (New Haven, Conn.: Yale University Press, 2007), p. 36.
16. "On me voit me prenant moi-meme!" Henri Evenepoel to Edmond Evenepoel, October 11, 1897, *Lettres a mon père*, 2: p. 153.
17. For example, Bonnard's *Self-portrait* (ca. 1938–40), The Art Gallery of New South Wales; *Portrait of the Painter in a Red Dressing Gown* (1943), private collection; and *Self-portrait in the Bathroom Mirror* (1943–46), Centre Georges Pompidou, Paris.
18. Roger Marx, *Revue encyclopédique* (January 1922), as quoted in Michel, "Henri Evenepoel," p. 52.

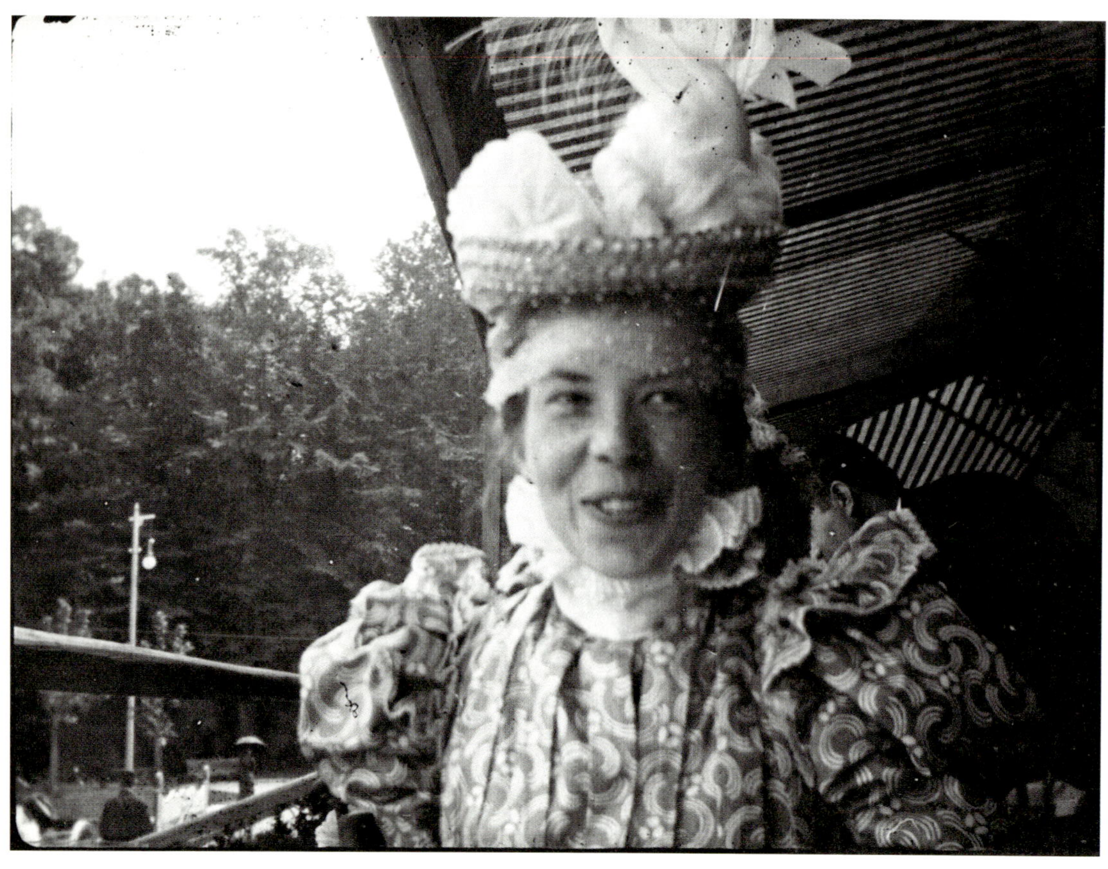

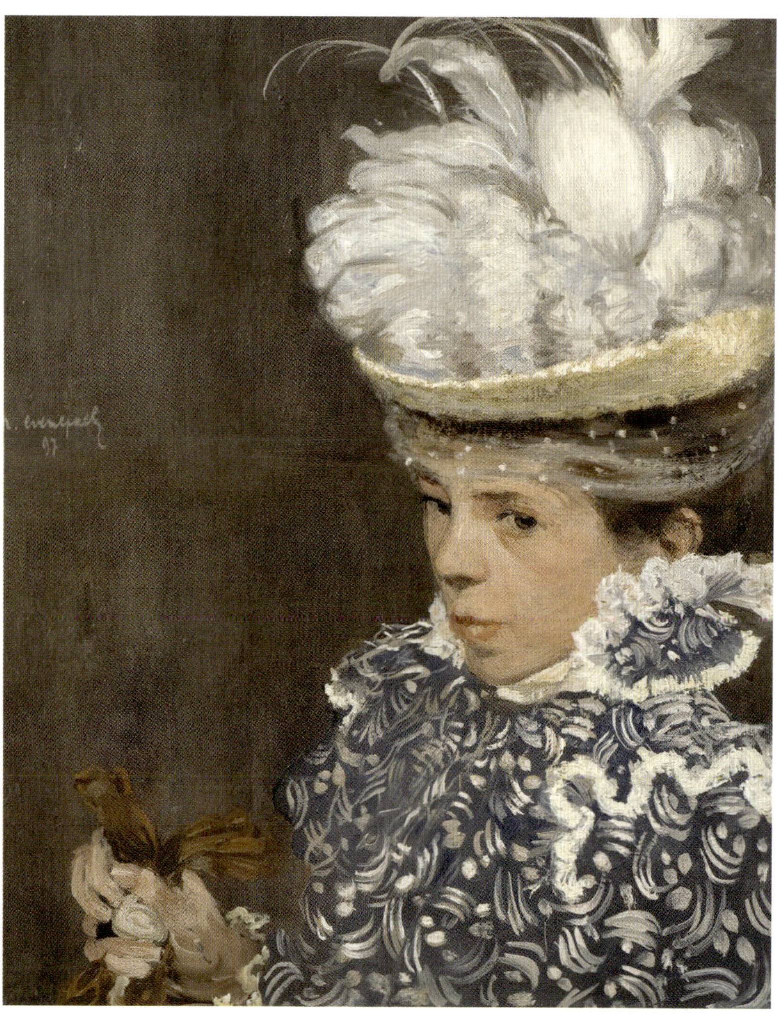

CAT. 87. Henri Evenepoel, Louise at Wépion, summer 1897. Modern gelatin silver print, 2011, from original negative, 1½ x 2 in. (3.8 x 5 cm). Royal Museums of Fine Arts of Belgium, Brussels, Archives of Contemporary Art in Belgium

CAT. 88. Henri Evenepoel, *Le chapeau blanc* (The White Hat), 1897. Oil on canvas, 22⅜ x 18⅛ in. (57 x 46 cm). Private collection

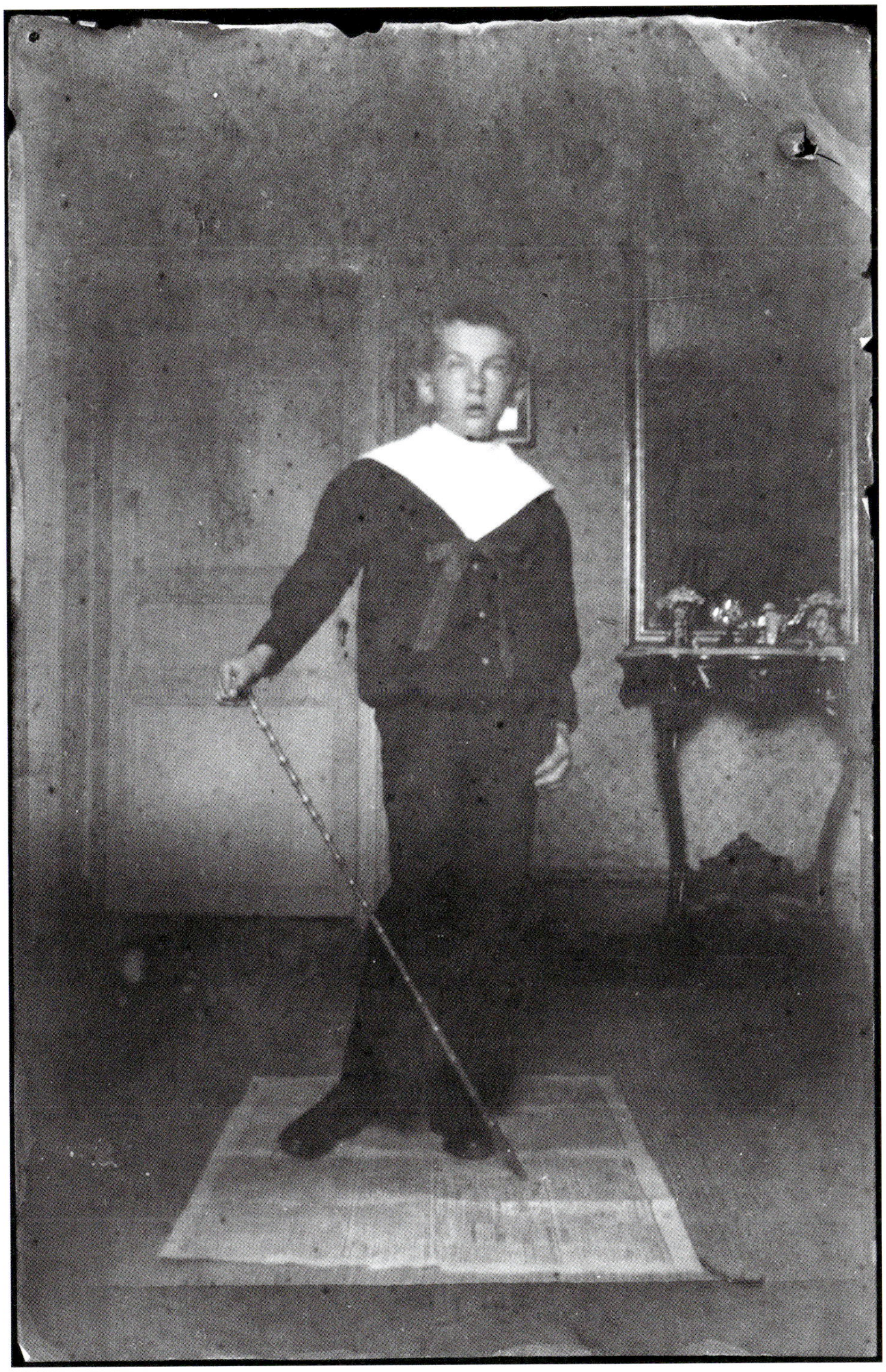

CAT. 89. Henri Evenepoel, André Devis, Wépion, summer 1897. Modern gelatin silver print, 2011, from original negative, 2 x $1\frac{1}{2}$ in. (5 x 3.8 cm). Royal Museums of Fine Arts of Belgium, Brussels, Archives of Contemporary Art in Belgium

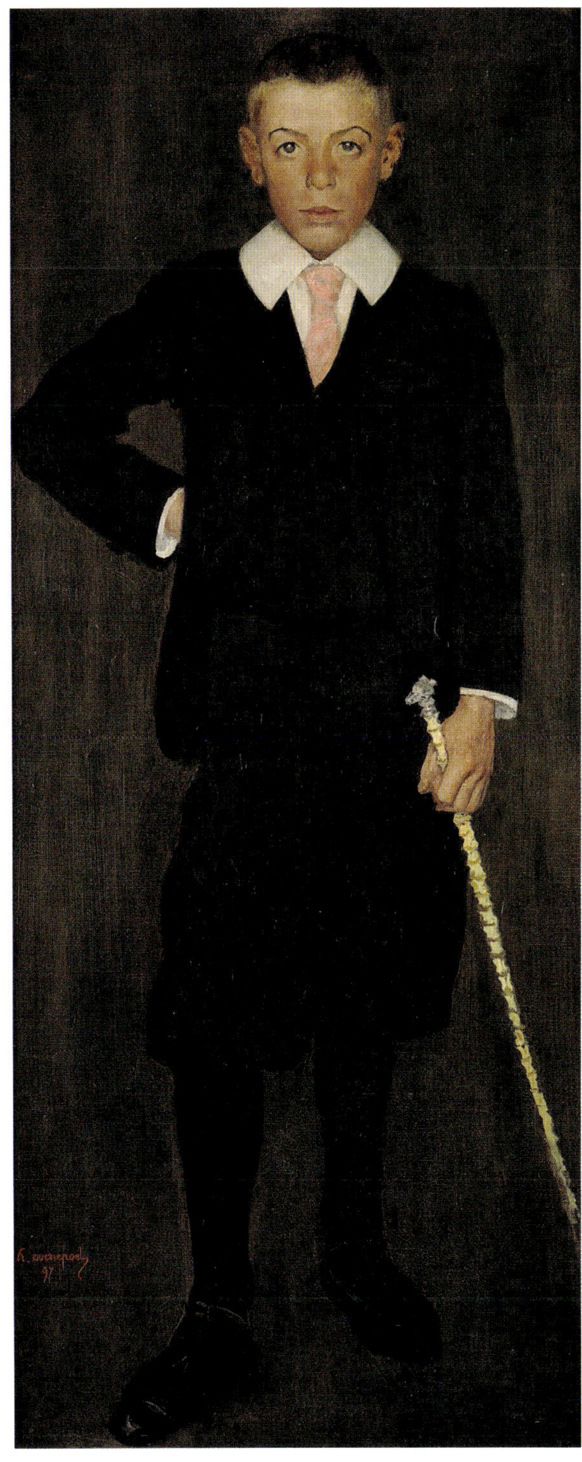

CAT. 90. Henri Evenepoel, *Albert Devis*, 1897. Oil on canvas, $47\frac{1}{4}$ x $19\frac{5}{8}$ in. (120 x 50 cm). Musée d'Ixelles, Brussels

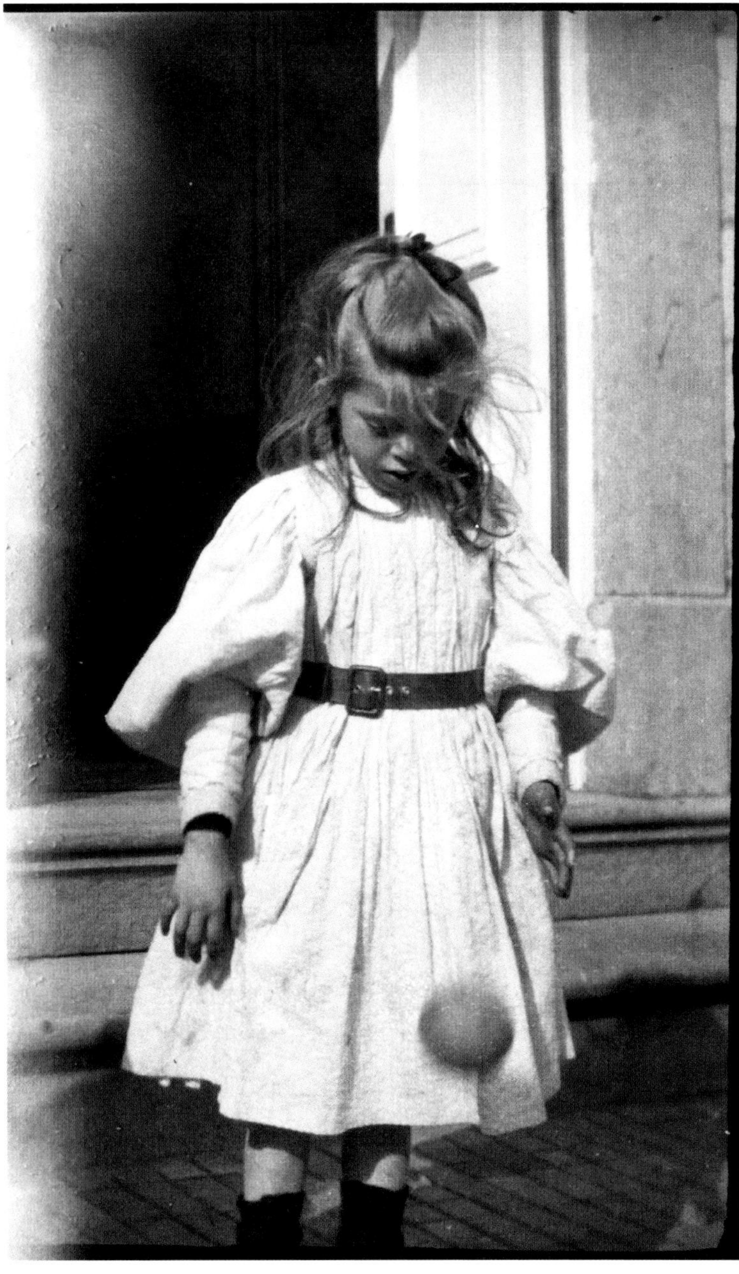

CAT. 91. Henri Evenepoel, Sophie de Mey, Fooz-Wépion (detail), summer 1897. Modern gelatin silver print, 2011, from original negative, 1½ x 2 in. (3.8 x 5 cm). Royal Museums of Fine Arts of Belgium, Brussels, Archives of Contemporary Art in Belgium

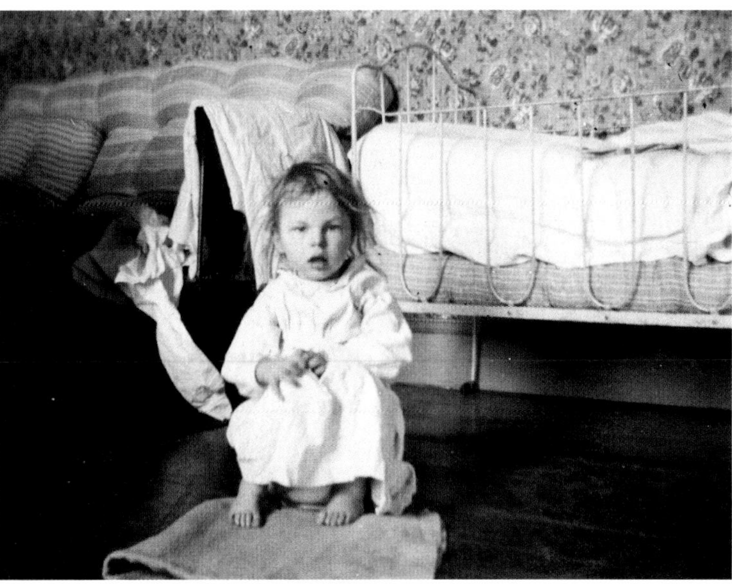

CAT. 92. Henri Evenepoel, Charles on the potty, 1897. Modern gelatin silver print, 2011, from original negative, 1½ x 2 in. (3.8 x 5 cm). Royal Museums of Fine Arts of Belgium, Brussels, Archives of Contemporary Art in Belgium

OPPOSITE:
CAT. 93. Henri Evenepoel, Self-portrait with pipe, n.d. Modern gelatin silver print, 2011, from original negative, 1½ x 2 in. (3.8 x 5 cm). Royal Museums of Fine Arts of Belgium, Brussels, Archives of Contemporary Art in Belgium

CAT. 94. Henri Evenepoel, Self-portrait in three-way mirror, 1898. Modern gelatin silver print, 2011, from original negative, 1½ x 2 in. (3.8 x 5 cm). Royal Museums of Fine Arts of Belgium, Brussels, Archives of Contemporary Art in Belgium

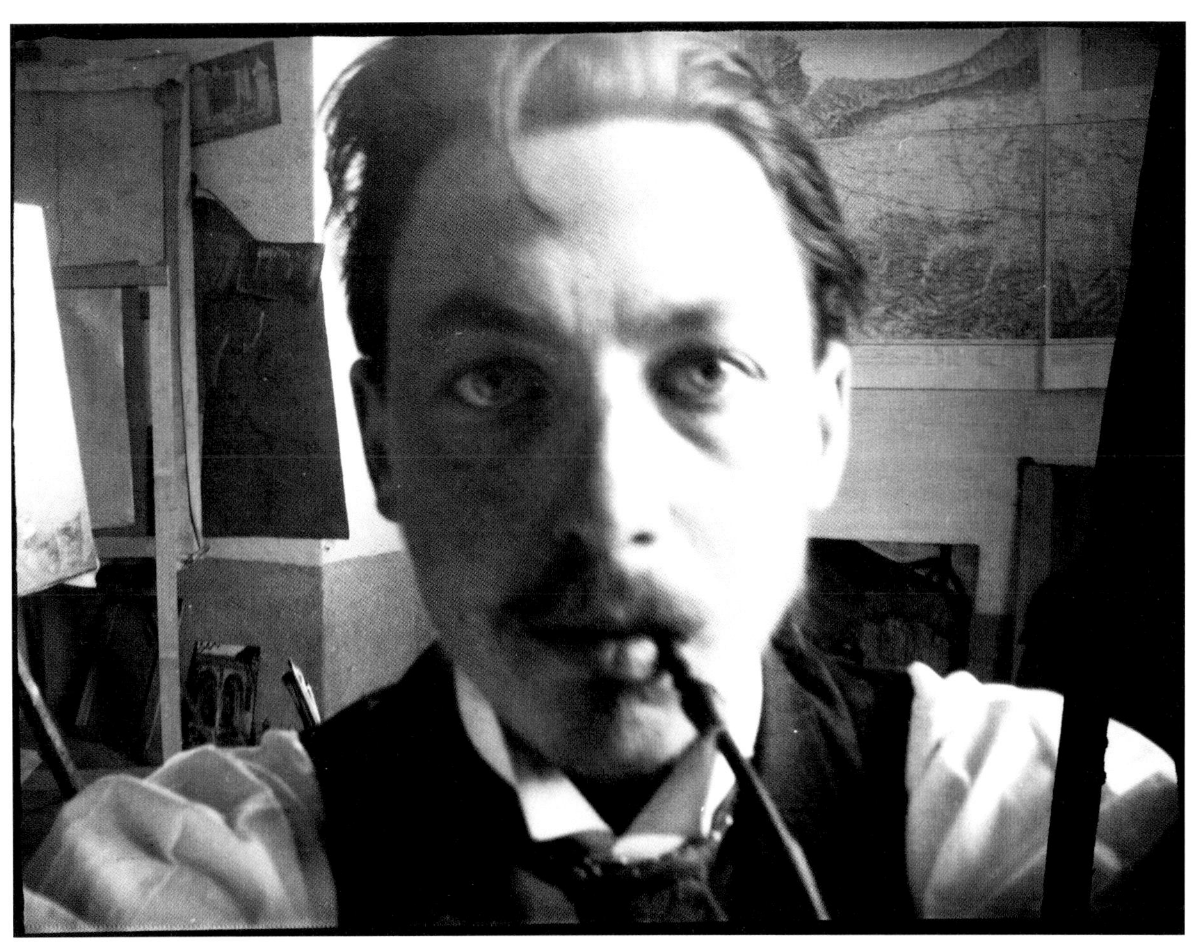

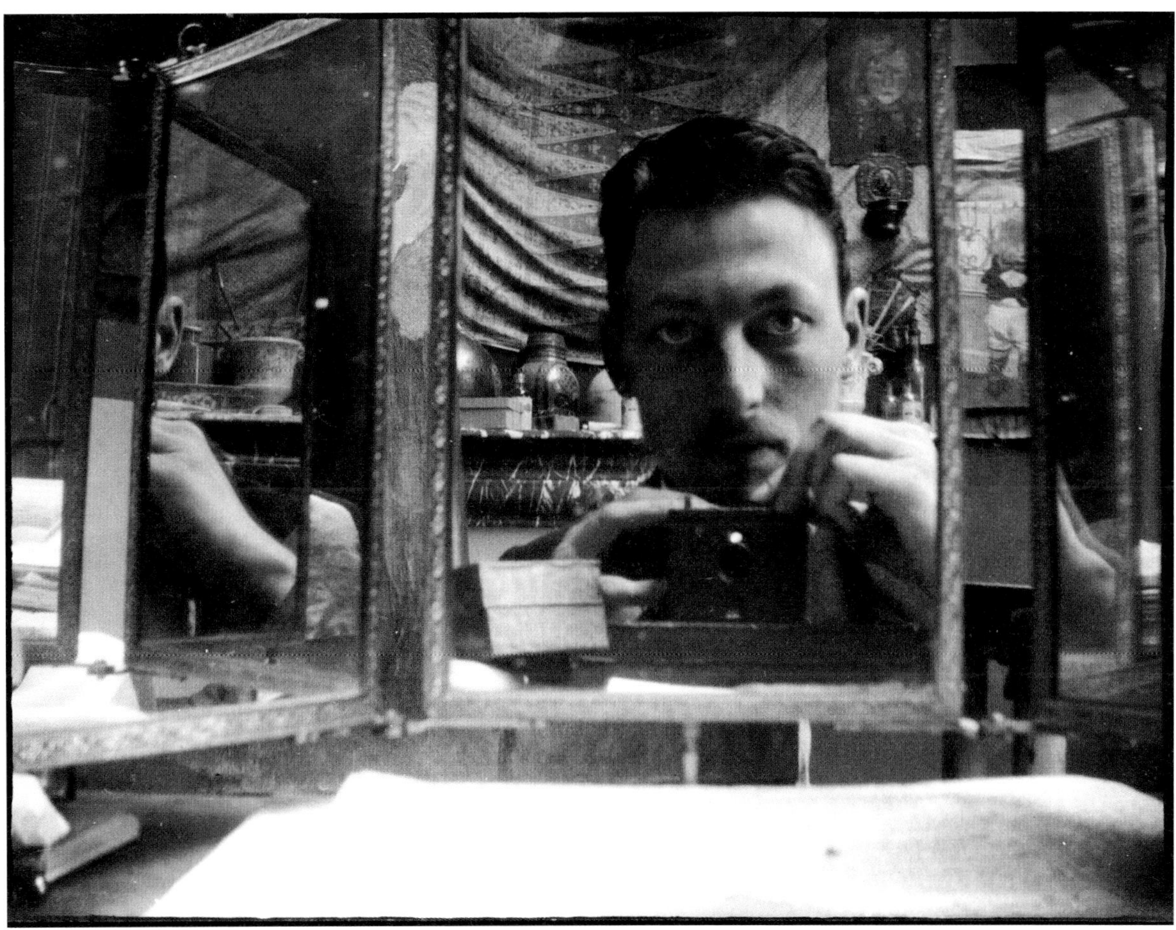

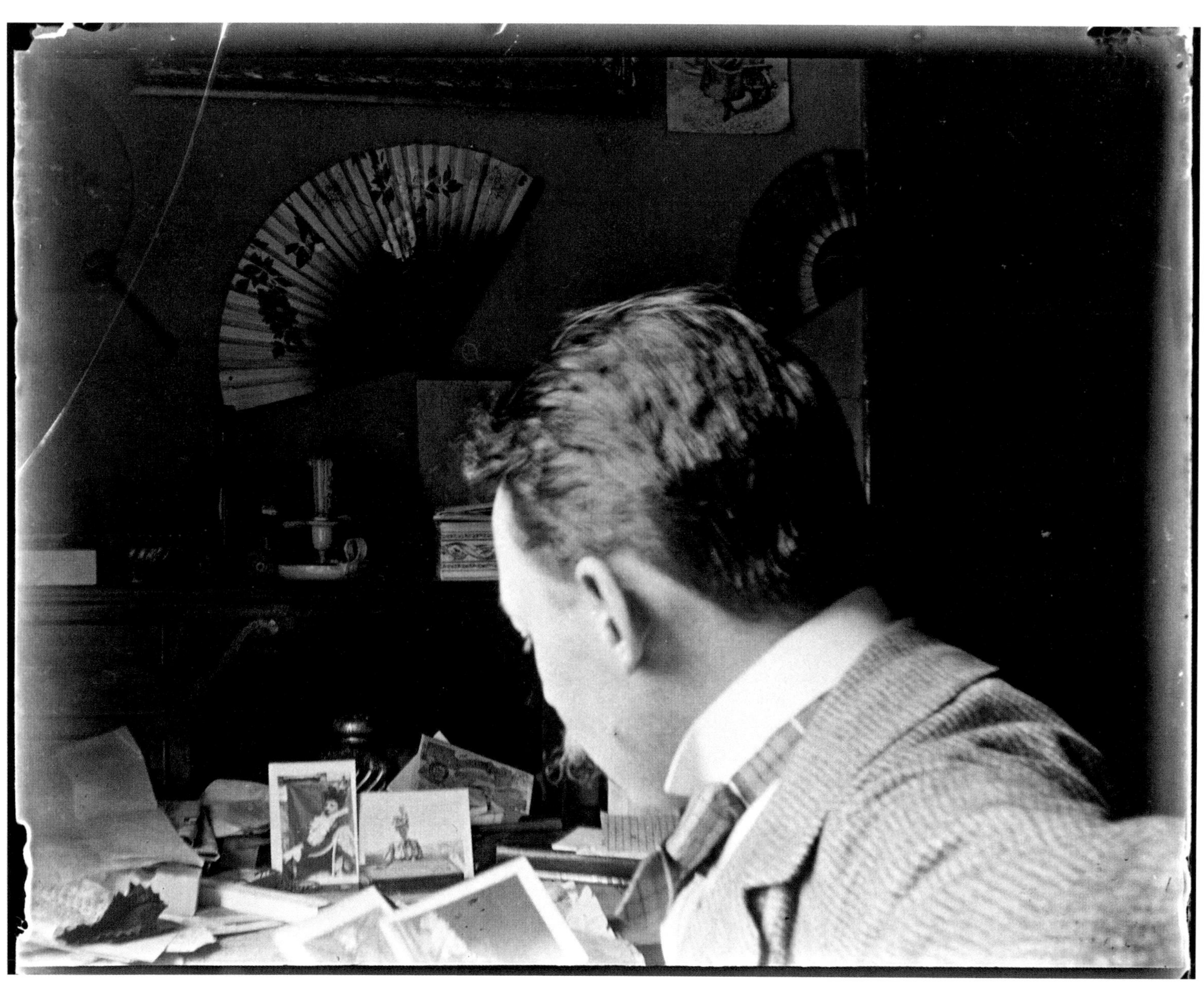

CAT. 95. Henri Evenepoel, Evenepoel studying his photographs, 1897–98. Modern gelatin silver print, 2011, from original negative, 1½ x 2 in. (3.8 x 5 cm). Royal Museums of Fine Arts of Belgium, Brussels, Archives of Contemporary Art in Belgium

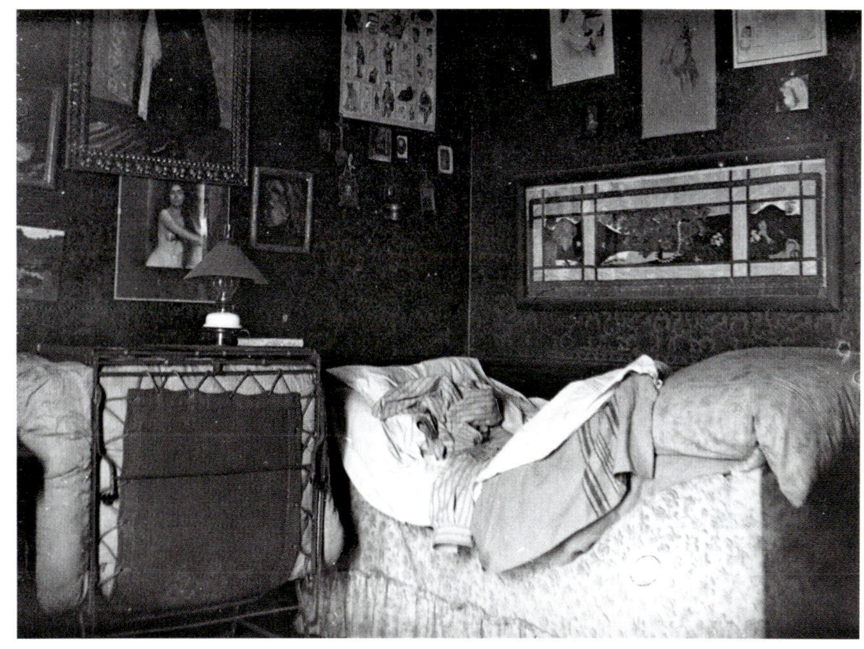

CAT. 96. Henri Evenepoel, The bedroom of Henri Evenepoel—The unmade bed, winter 1898–99. Modern gelatin silver print, 2011, from original negative, 1½ x 2 in. (3.8 x 5 cm). Royal Museums of Fine Arts of Belgium, Brussels, Archives of Contemporary Art in Belgium

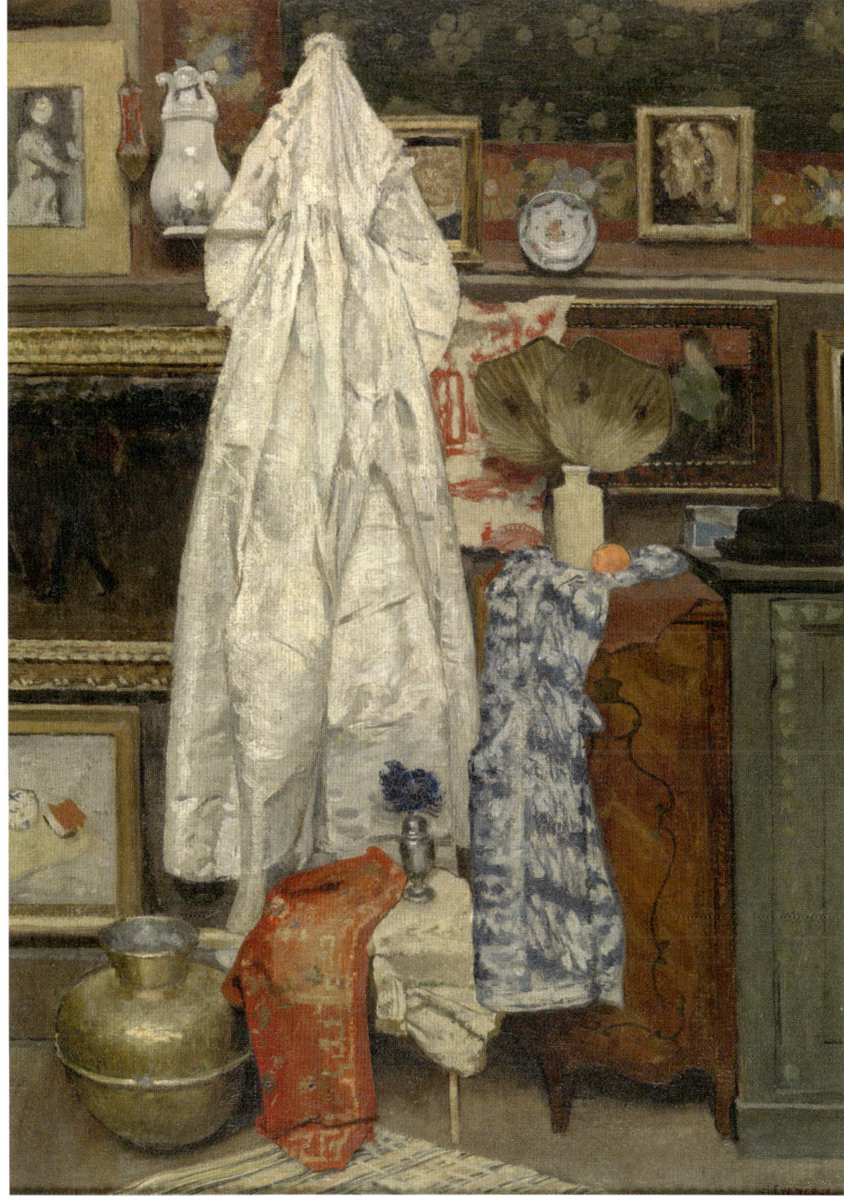

CAT. 97. Henri Evenepoel, *La robe blanche* (The White Dress), 1897. Oil on canvas, 26⅝ x 19⅝ in. (67.5 x 50 cm). Royal Museums of Fine Arts of Belgium, Brussels

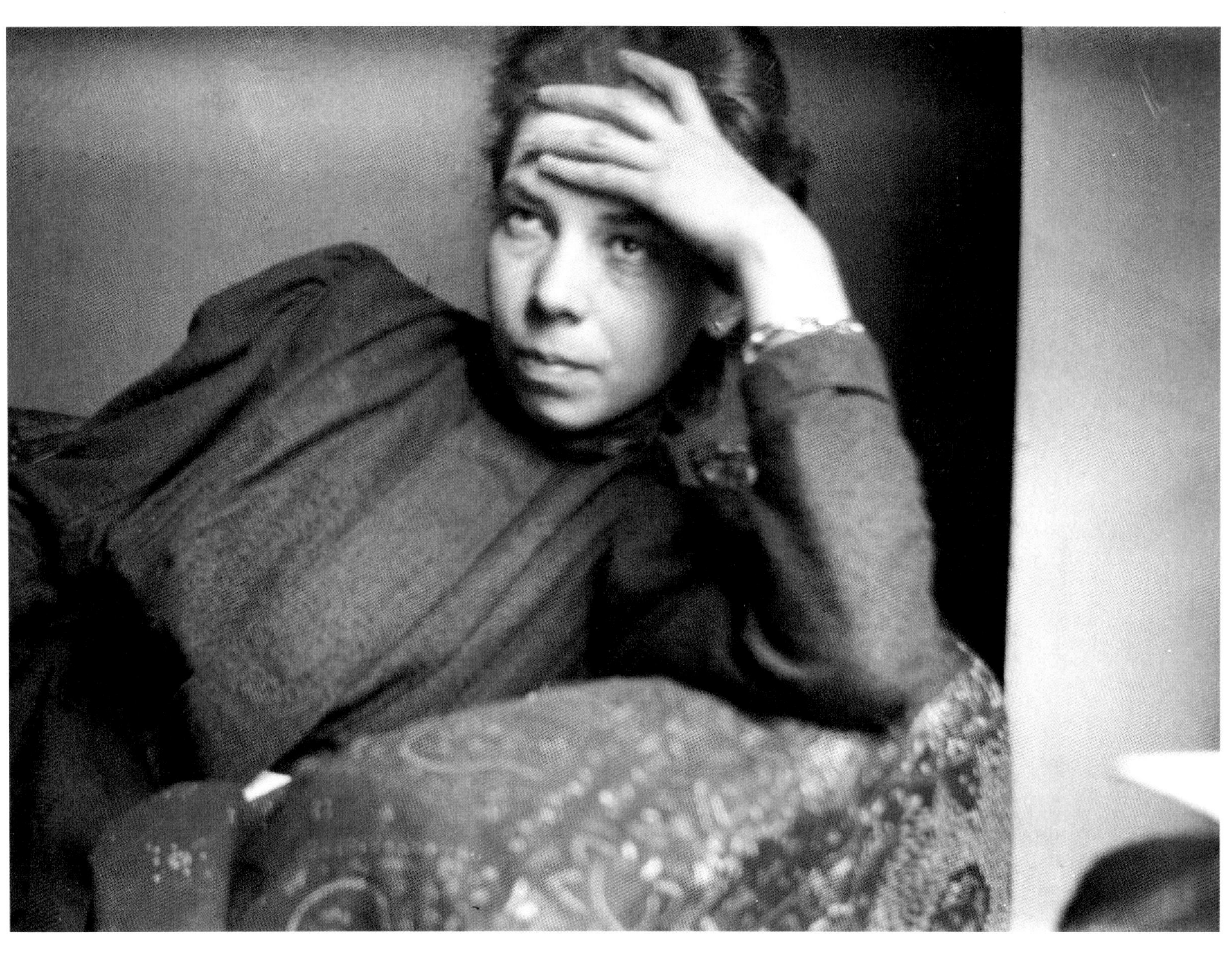

CAT. 98. Henri Evenepoel, Louise de Mey, on bed, Le Trieu-Colin, Wépion, summer 1897. Modern gelatin silver print, 2011, from original negative, 1½ x 2 in. (3.8 x 5 cm). Royal Museums of Fine Arts of Belgium, Brussels, Archives of Contemporary Art in Belgium

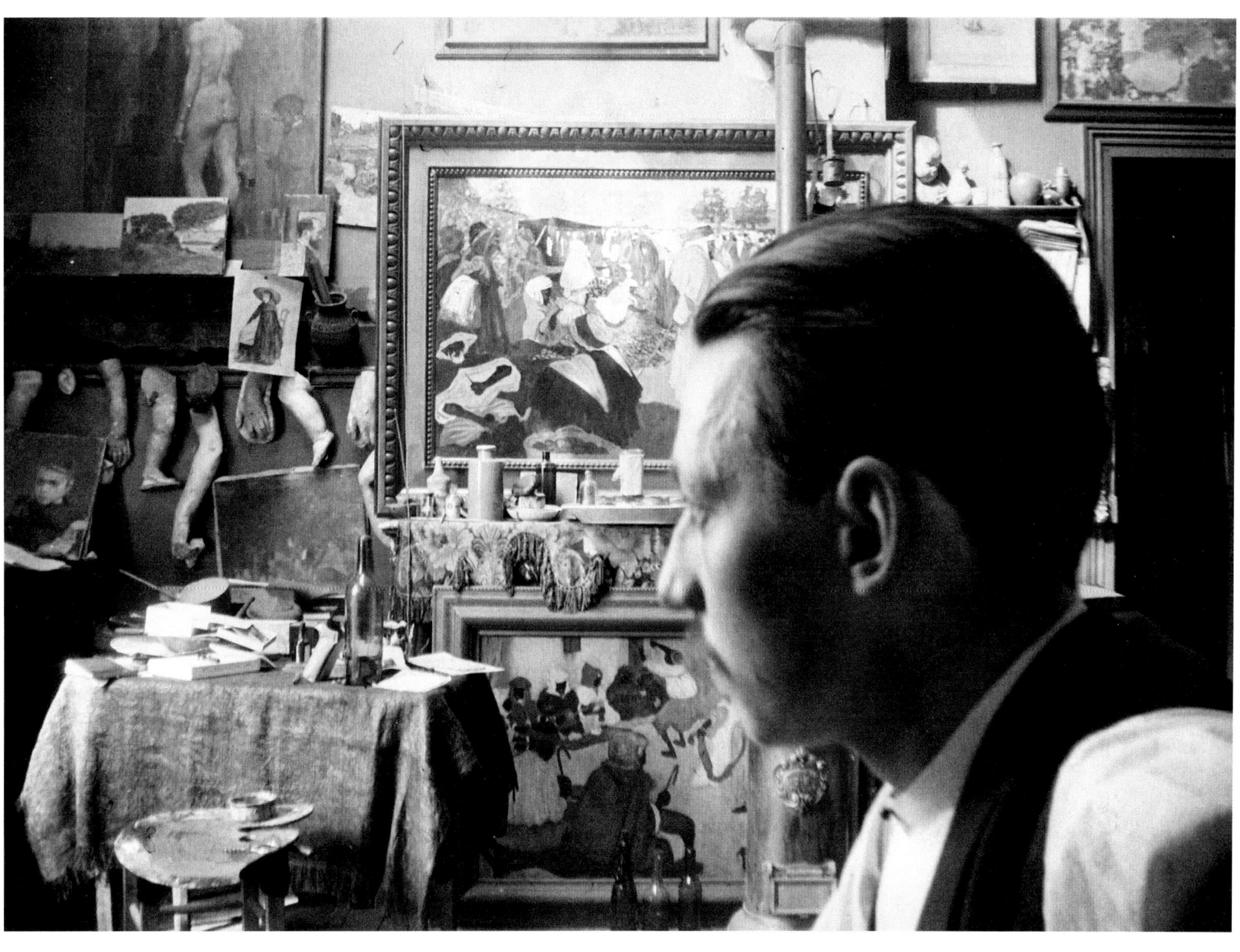

CAT. 99. Henri Evenepoel, Henri Evenepoel, 1898. Modern gelatin silver print, from original negative, 1½ x 2 in. (3.8 x 5 cm). Royal Museums of Fine Arts of Belgium, Brussels, Archives of Contemporary Art in Belgium

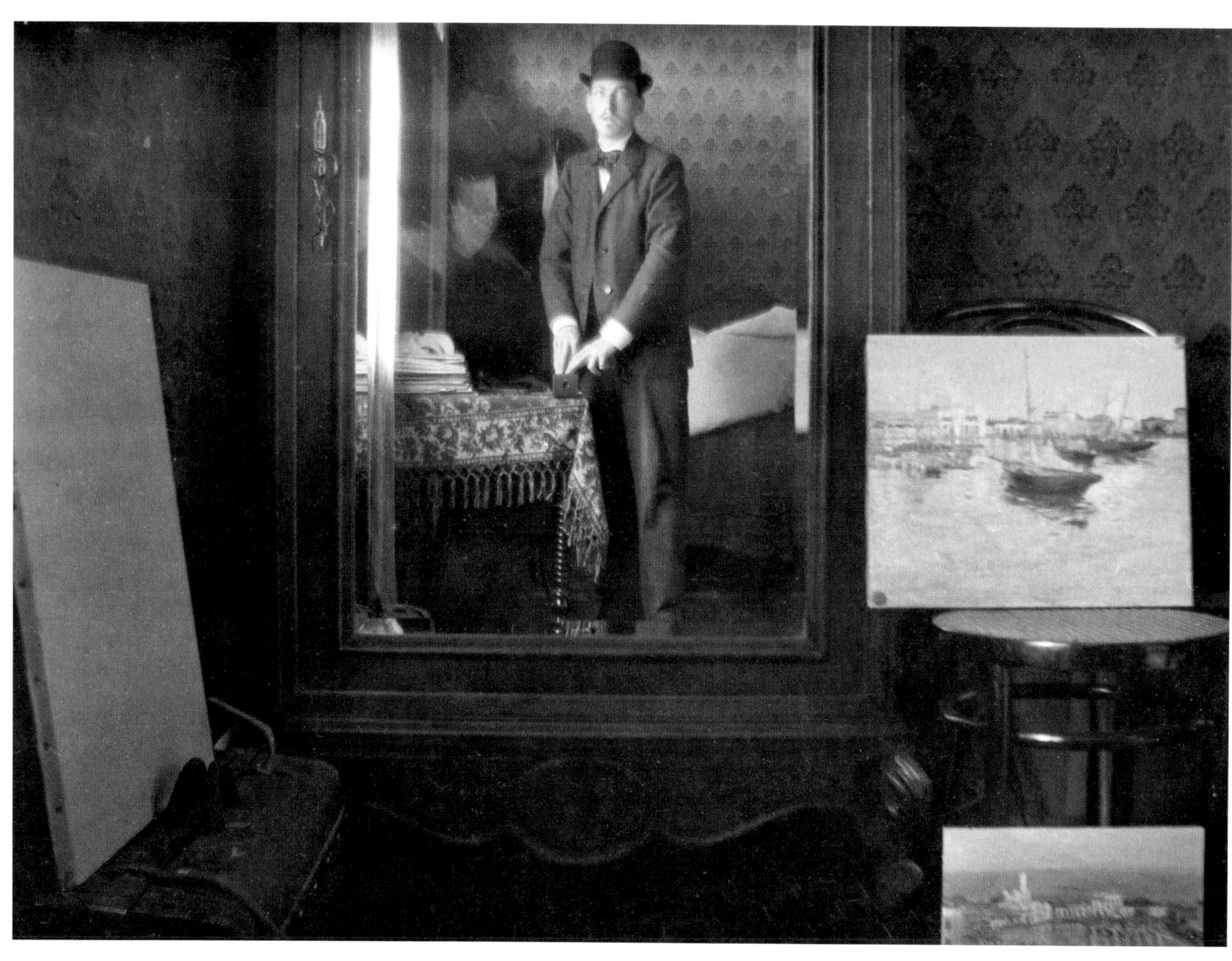

CAT. 100. Henri Evenepoel, Self-portrait in a mirror, in L'hôtel Moderne in Algeria, fall 1897. Modern gelatin silver print, 2011, from original negative, 1½ x 2 in. (3.8 x 5 cm). Royal Museums of Fine Arts of Belgium, Brussels, Archives of Contemporary Art in Belgium

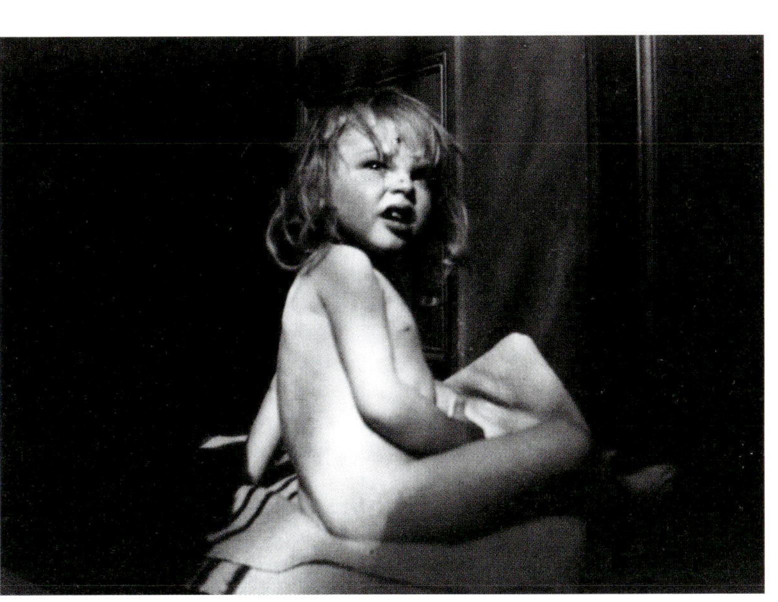

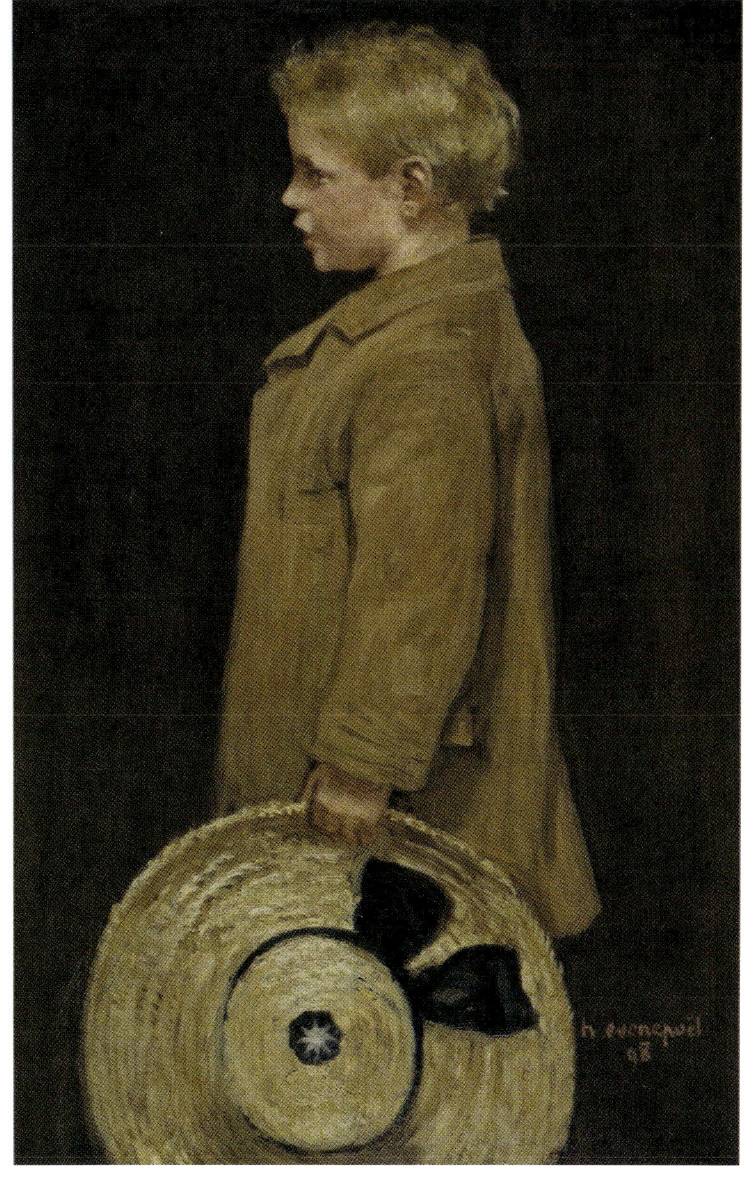

CAT. 101. Henri Evenepoel, Charles de Mey, leaving the bath, 1897. Modern gelatin silver print, 2011, from original negative, 1½ x 2 in. (3.8 x 5 cm). Royal Museums of Fine Arts of Belgium, Brussels, Archives of Contemporary Art in Belgium

CAT. 102. Henri Evenepoel, *Charles au chapeau de paille* (Charles with a Straw Hat), 1898. Oil on canvas, 32⅝ x 21½ in. (83 x 54.5 cm). Private collection, Belgium

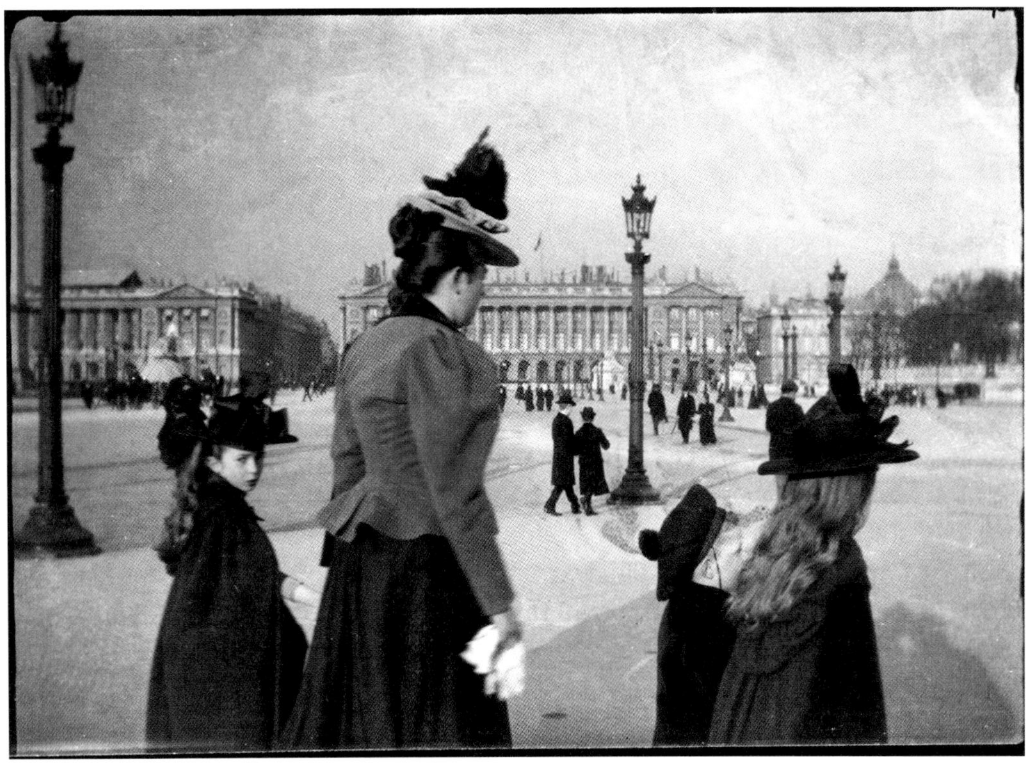

CAT. 103. Henri Evenepoel, Henriette, Charles, Sophie de Mey, and the nanny, Place de la Concorde, Paris, fall 1898. Modern gelatin silver print, 2011, from original negative, 1½ x 2 in. (3.8 x 5 cm). Royal Museums of Fine Arts of Belgium, Brussels, Archives of Contemporary Art in Belgium

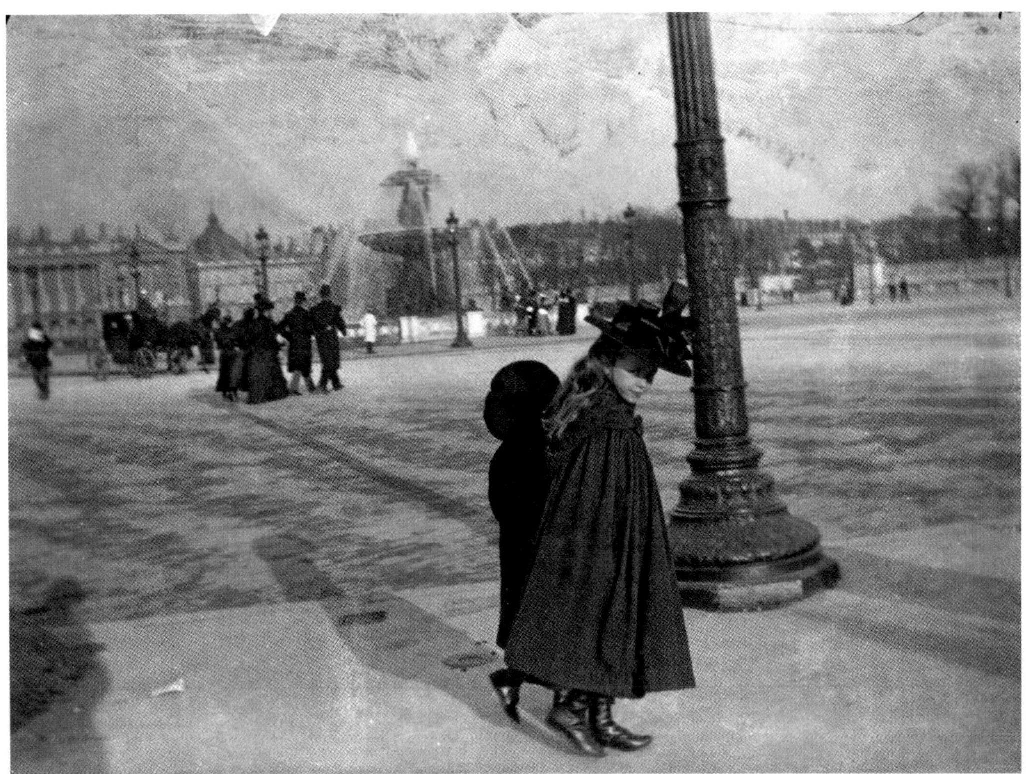

CAT. 104. Henri Evenepoel, Henriette and Charles de Mey, 1898. Modern gelatin silver print, 2011, from original negative, 1½ x 2 in. (3.8 x 5 cm). Royal Museums of Fine Arts of Belgium, Brussels, Archives of Contemporary Art in Belgium

OPPOSITE:
CAT. 105. Henri Evenepoel, Charles, Sophie, and Henriette de Mey with Louise von Mattenburgh on the Place de la Concorde, Paris, fall 1898. Modern gelatin silver print, 2011, from original negative, 1½ x 2 in. (3.8 x 5 cm). Royal Museums of Fine Arts of Belgium, Brussels, Archives of Contemporary Art in Belgium

CAT. 106. Henri Evenepoel, Sophie, Charles, Louise, and the nanny on a walk, fall 1898. Modern gelatin silver print, 2011, from original negative, 1½ x 2 in. (3.8 x 5 cm). Royal Museums of Fine Arts of Belgium, Brussels, Archives of Contemporary Art in Belgium

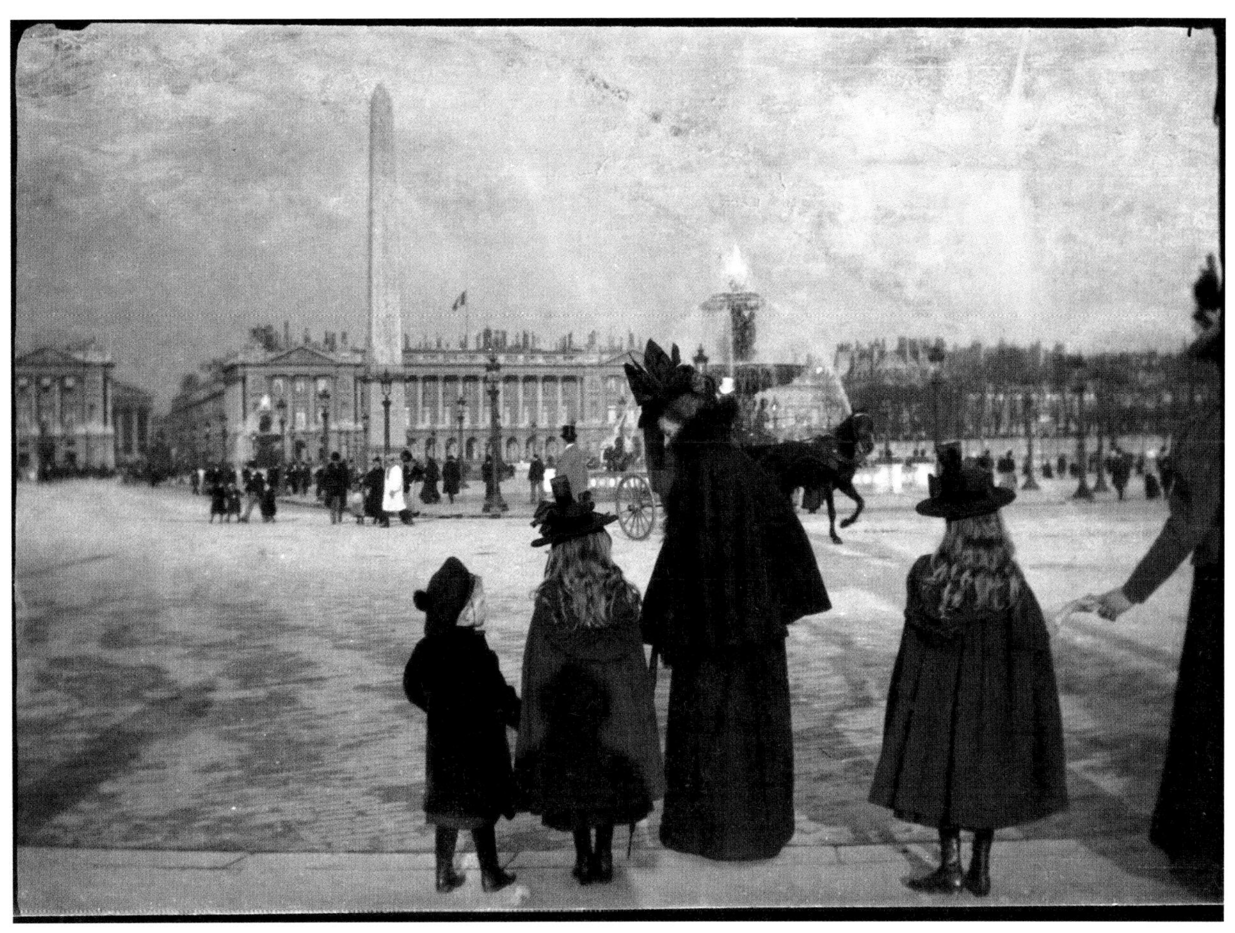

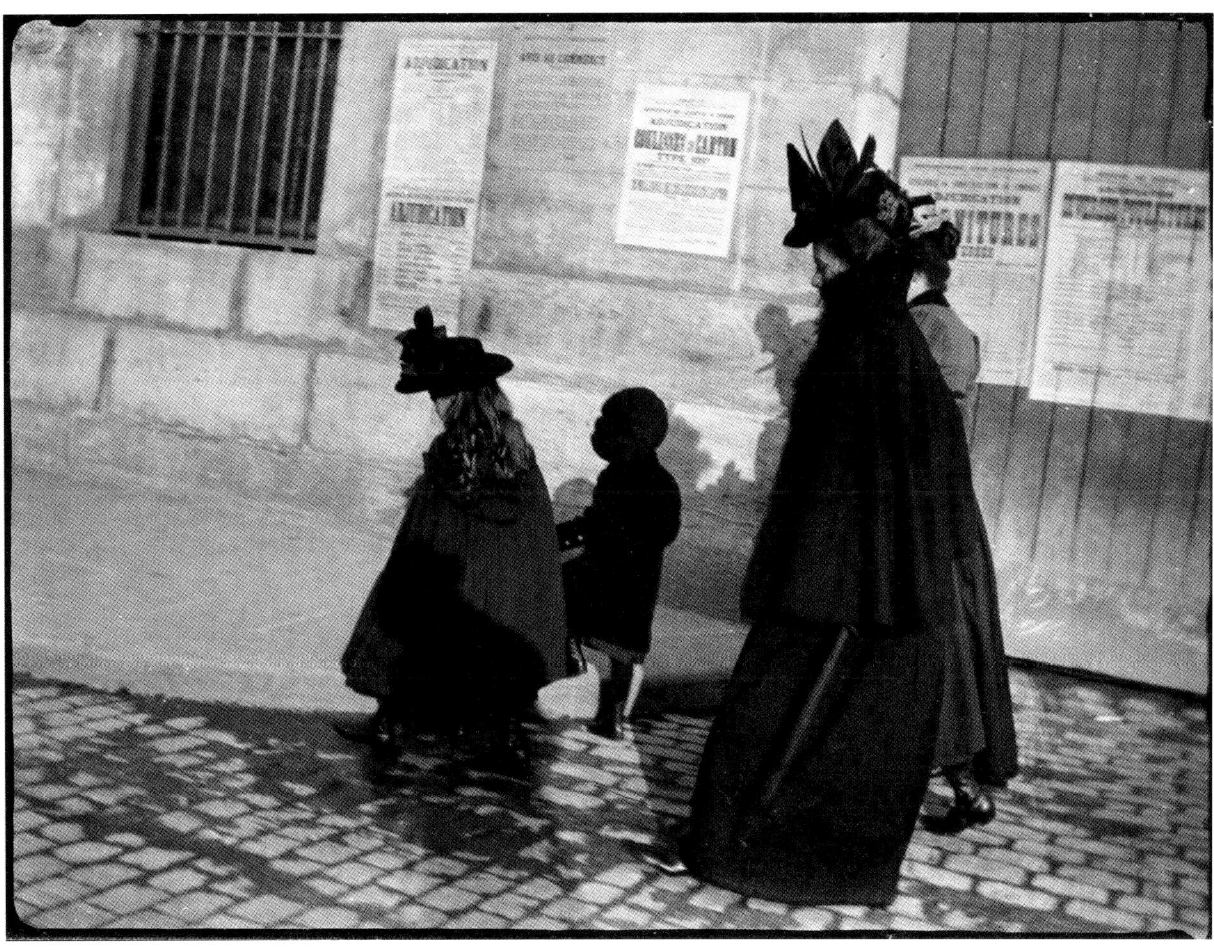
ADJUDICATION
AVIS AU COMMERCE
ADJUDICATION
ADJUDICATION

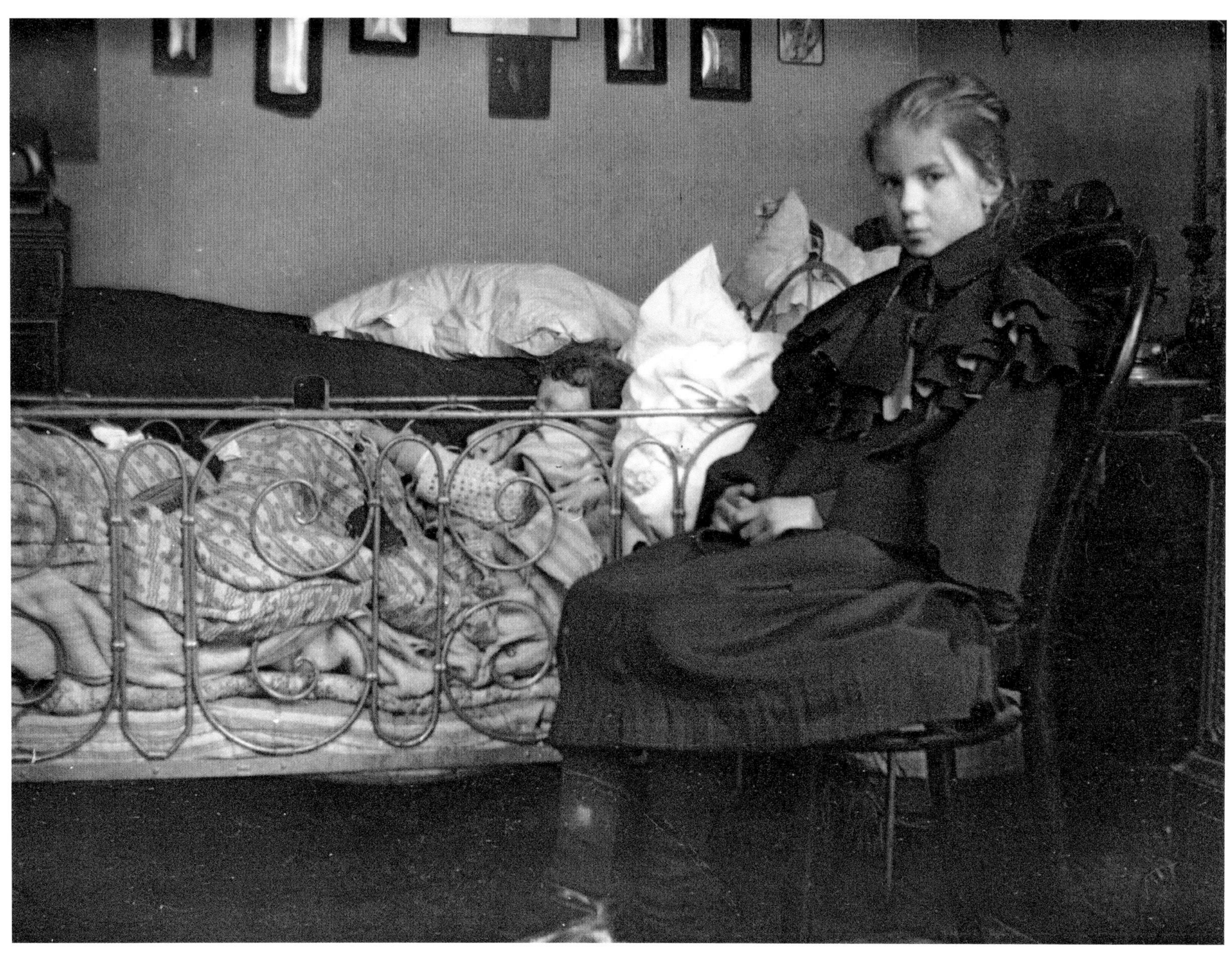

CAT. 107. Henri Evenepoel, Henriette watching over sick Charles, 1899. Modern gelatin silver print, 2011, from original negative, 1½ x 2 in. (3.8 x 5 cm). Royal Museums of Fine Arts of Belgium, Brussels, Archives of Contemporary Art in Belgium

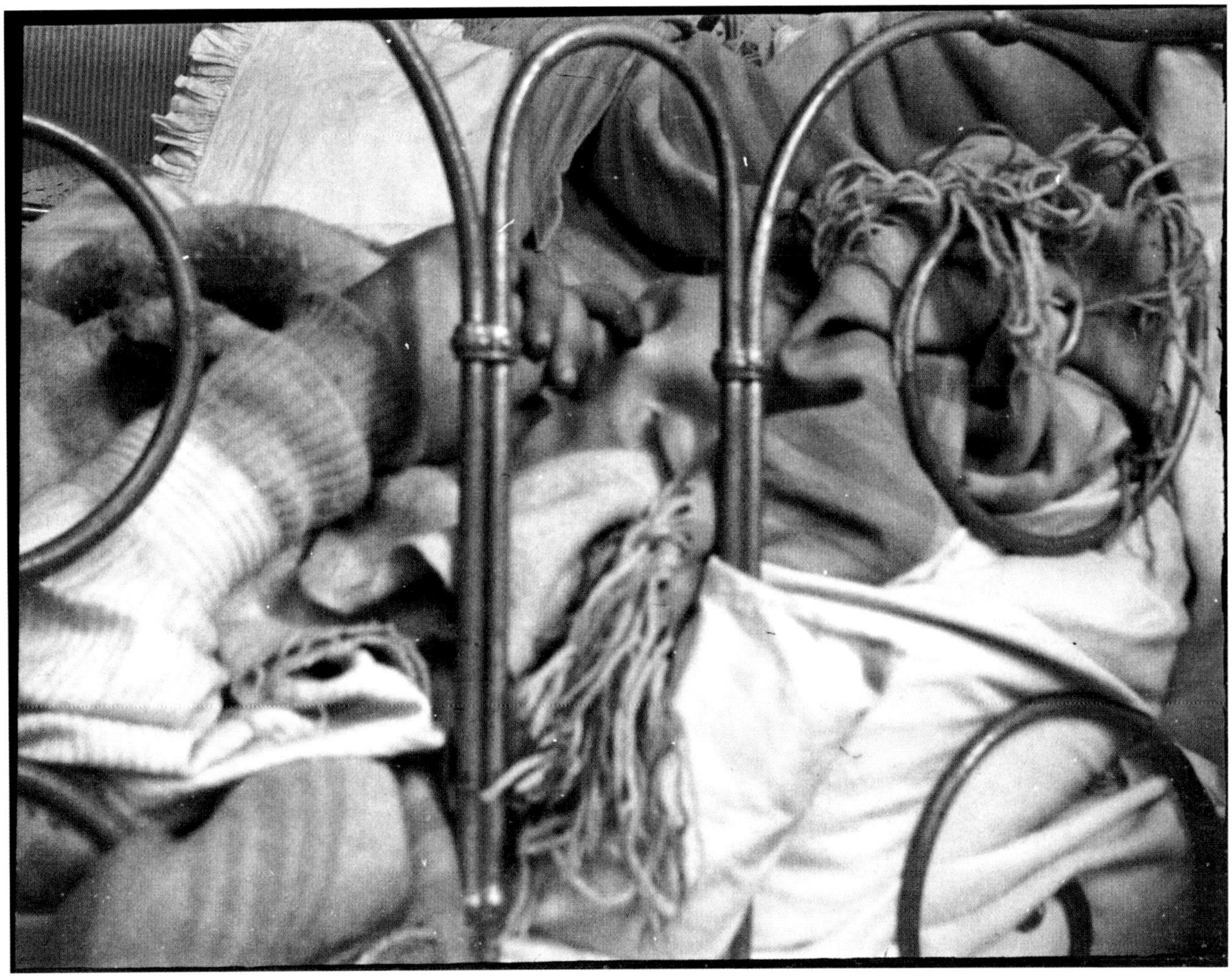

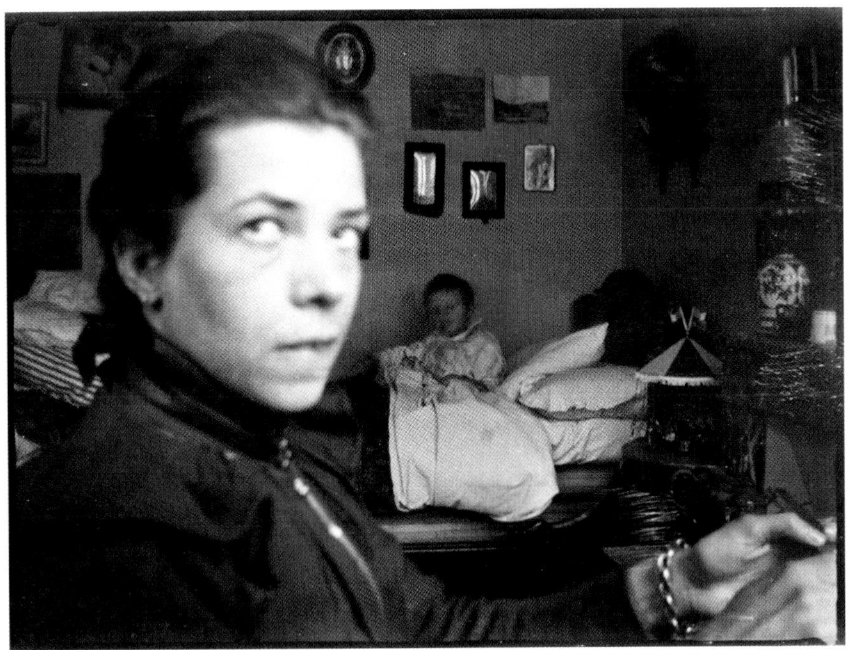

CAT. 108. Henri Evenepoel, Charles asleep in his crib, 1899. Modern gelatin silver print, 2011, from original negative, 1½ x 2 in. (3.8 x 5 cm). Royal Museums of Fine Arts of Belgium, Brussels, Archives of Contemporary Art in Belgium

CAT. 109. Henri Evenepoel, Louise watching over Charles, January 1899. Modern gelatin silver print, 2011, from original negative, 1½ x 2 in. (3.8 x 5 cm). Royal Museums of Fine Arts of Belgium, Brussels, Archives of Contemporary Art in Belgium

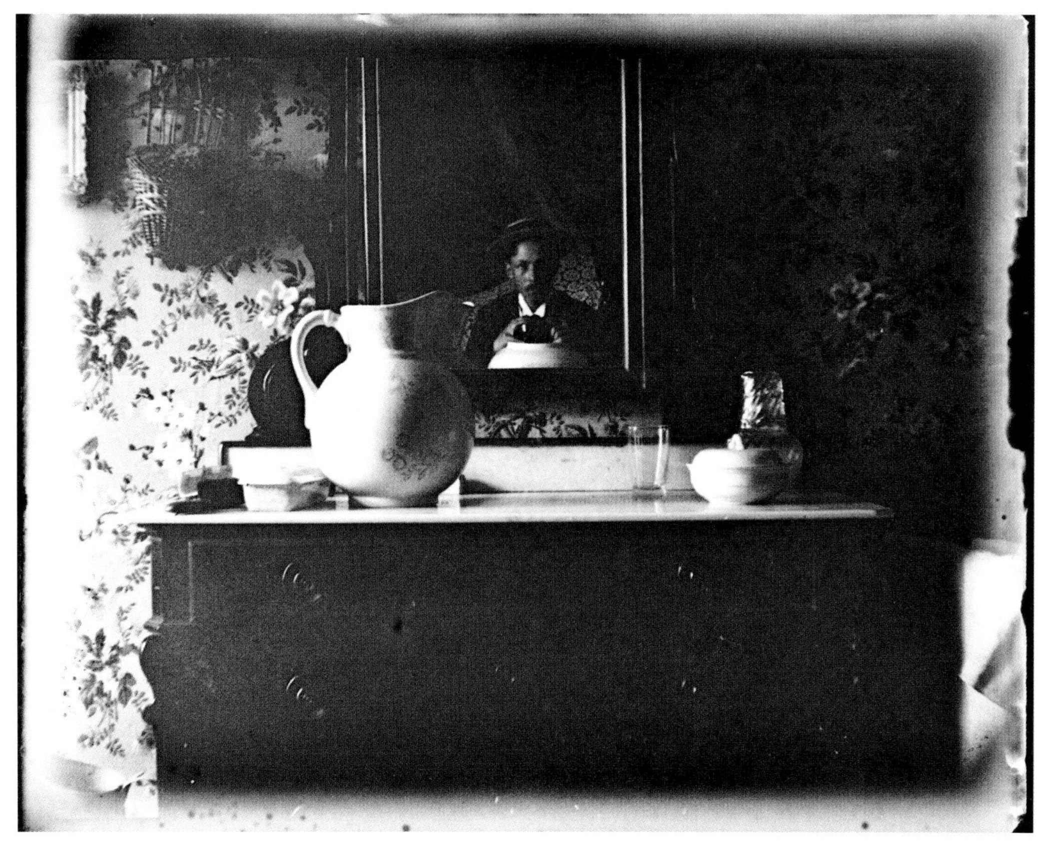

CAT. 110. Henri Evenepoel, Self-portrait in the mirror (Reflection of Henri Evenepoel in a straw hat), 1897–98. Modern gelatin silver print, 2011, from original negative, 1½ x 2 in. (3.8 x 5 cm). Royal Museums of Fine Arts of Belgium, Brussels, Archives of Contemporary Art in Belgium

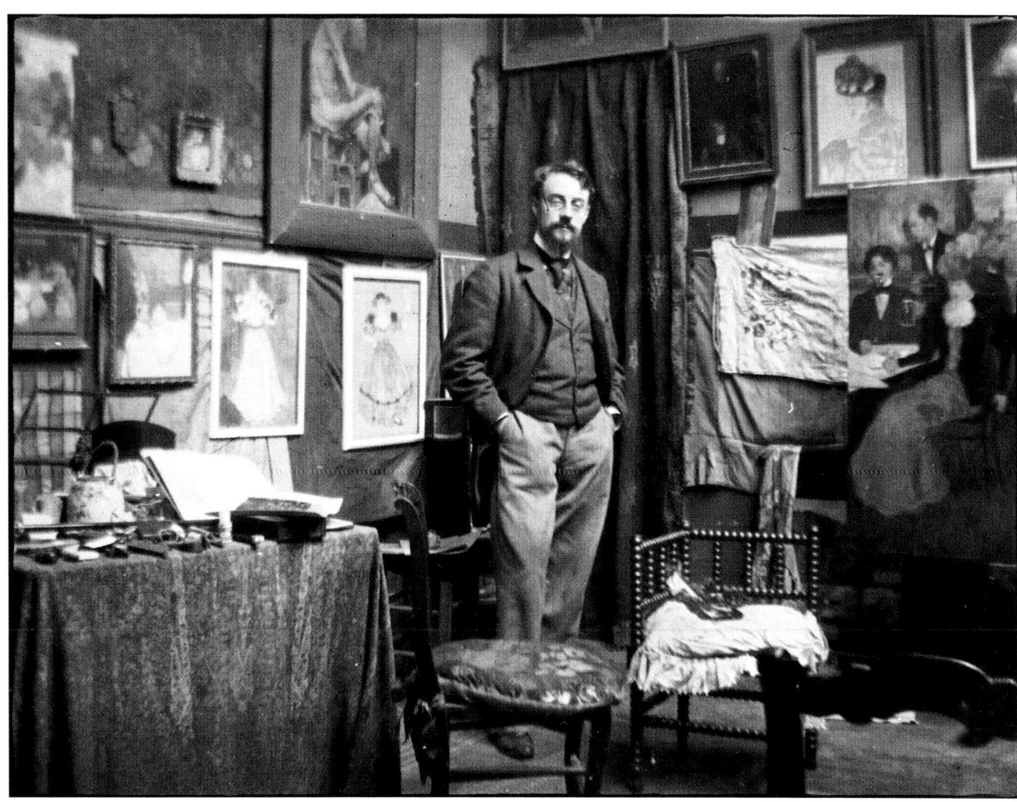

CAT. 111. Henri Evenepoel, Henri Matisse in Evenepoel's studio, fall 1897. Modern gelatin silver print, 2011, from original negative, 1½ x 2 in. (3.8 x 5 cm). Royal Museums of Fine Arts of Belgium, Brussels, Archives of Contemporary Art in Belgium

OPPOSITE TOP: CAT. 112. Henri Evenepoel, Henriette in the studio of Henri Evenepoel, winter 1898–99. Modern gelatin silver print, 2011, from original negative, 1½ x 2 in. (3.8 x 5 cm). Royal Museums of Fine Arts of Belgium, Brussels, Archives of Contemporary Art in Belgium

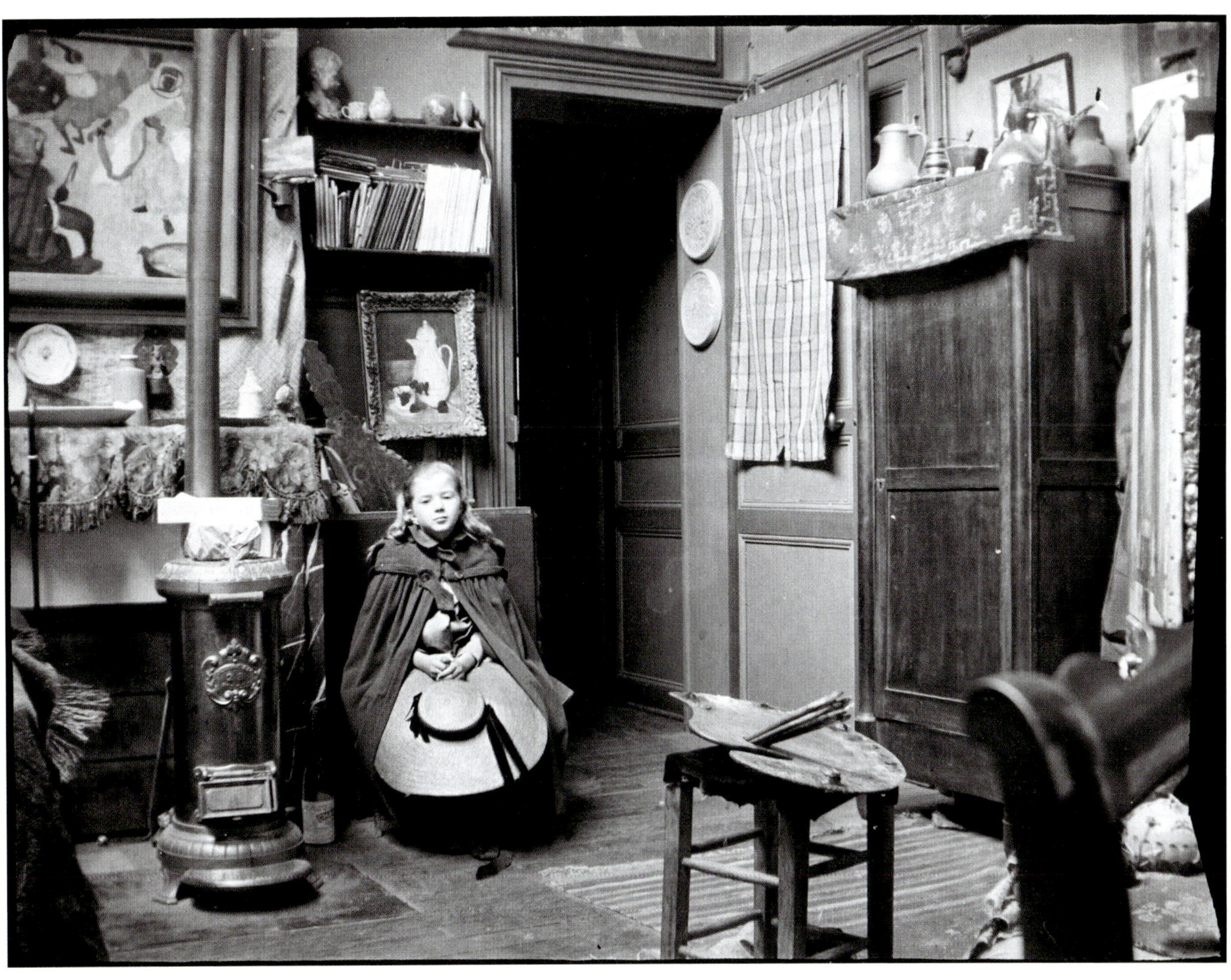

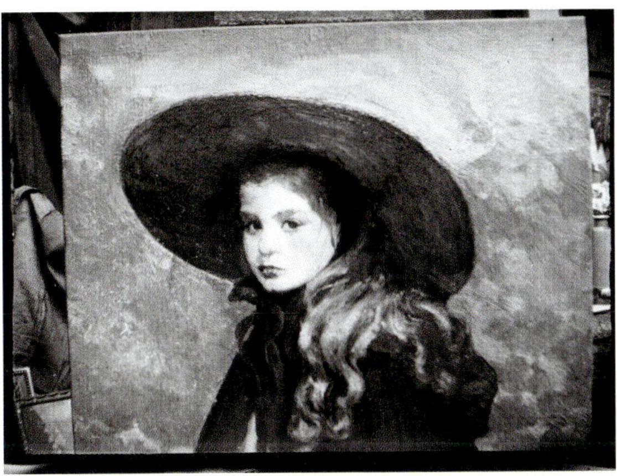

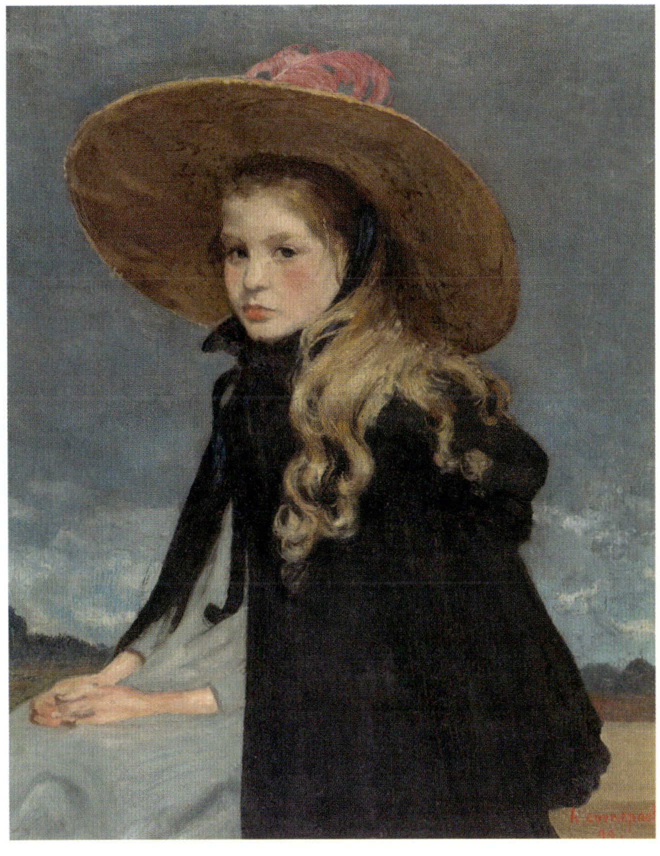

CAT. 113. Henri Evenepoel, Portrait of *Henriette au grand chapeau* in progress, winter 1898–99. Modern gelatin silver print, 2011, from original negative, 1½ x 2 in. (3.8 x 5 cm). Royal Museums of Fine Arts of Belgium, Brussels, Archives of Contemporary Art in Belgium

CAT. 114. Henri Evenepoel, *Henriette au grand chapeau* (Henriette in a Large Hat), 1899. Oil on canvas, 28½ x 23⅞ in. (72.5 x 60.5 cm). Royal Museums of Fine Arts of Belgium, Brussels

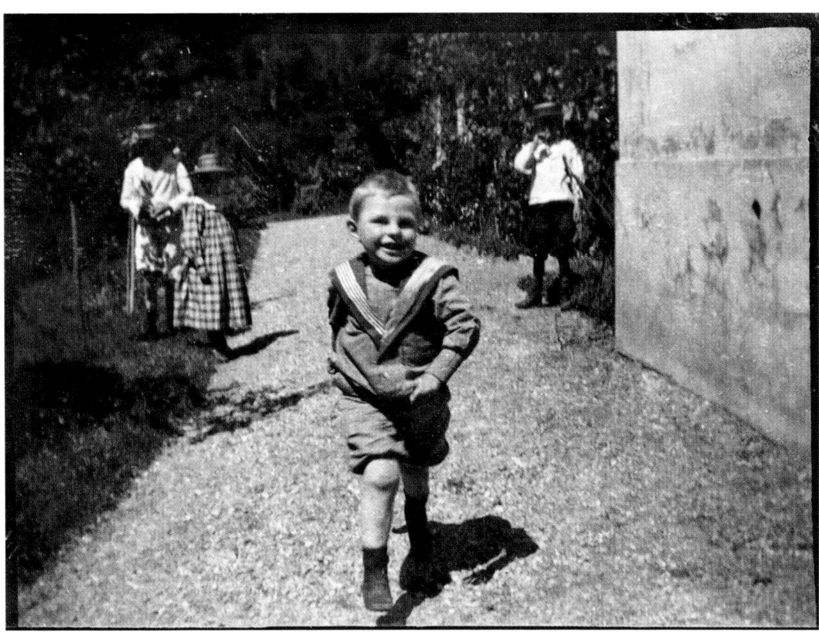

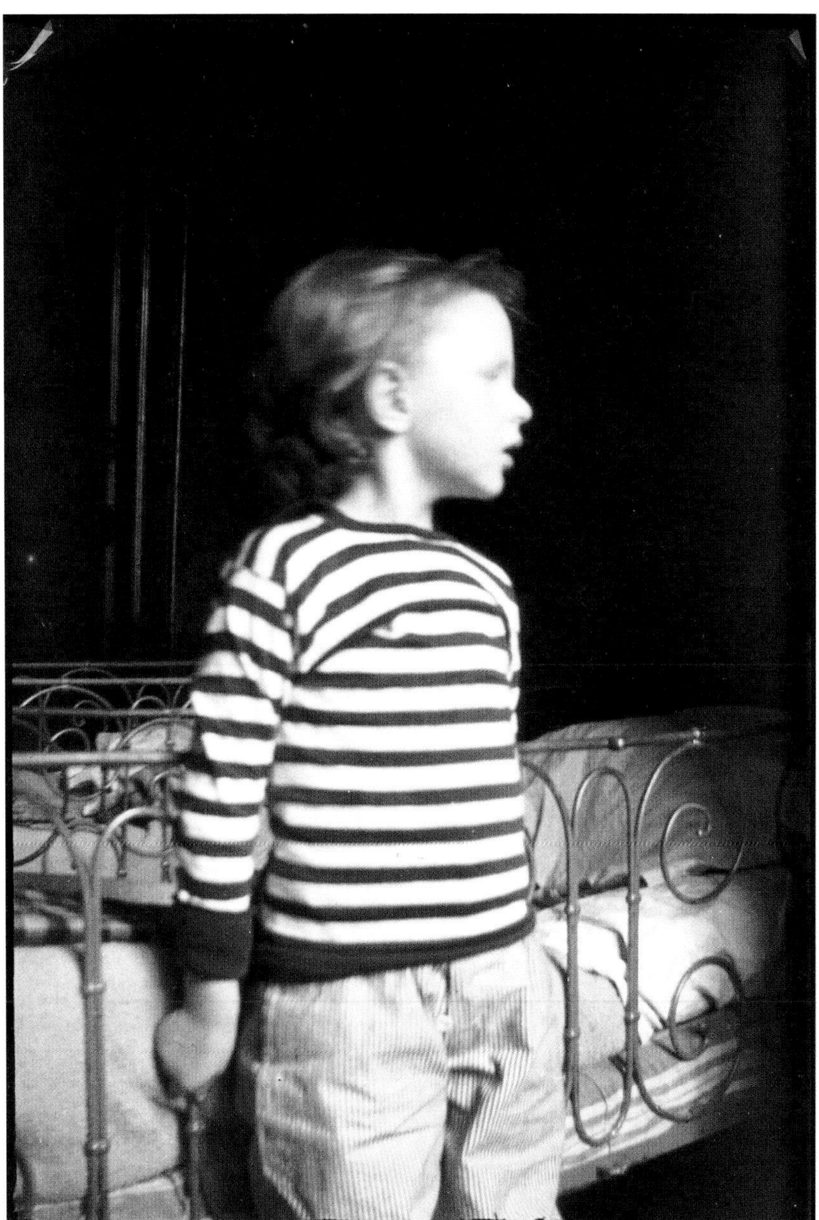

CAT. 115. Henri Evenepoel, Charles de Mey, running toward us, 1899. Modern gelatin silver print, 2011, from original negative, 1½ x 2 in. (3.8 x 5 cm). Royal Museums of Fine Arts of Belgium, Brussels, Archives of Contemporary Art in Belgium

CAT. 116. Henri Evenepoel, Charles standing in his striped jersey, spring 1899. Modern gelatin silver print, 2011, from original negative, 2 x 1½ in. (5 x 3.8 cm). Royal Museums of Fine Arts of Belgium, Brussels, Archives of Contemporary Art in Belgium

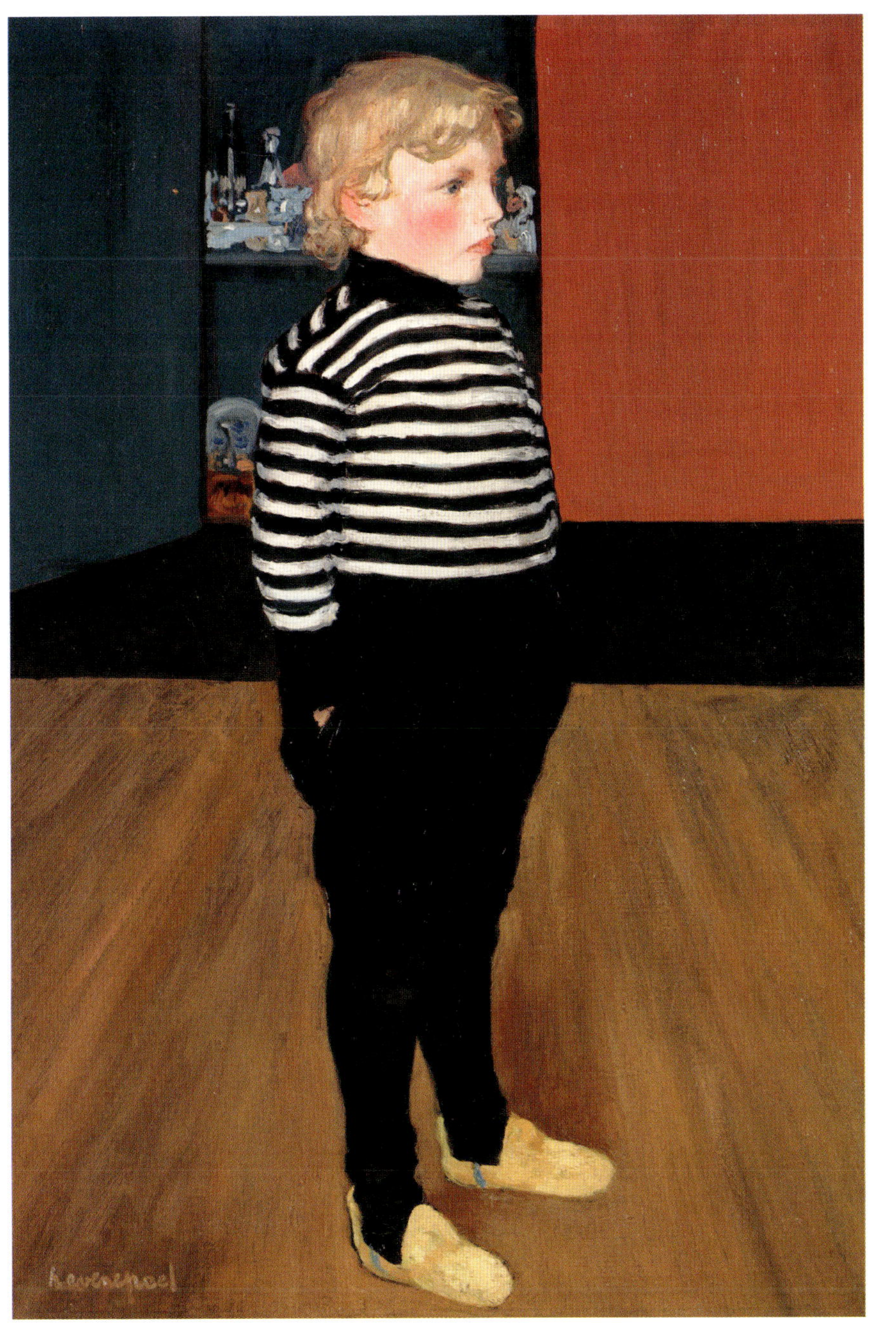

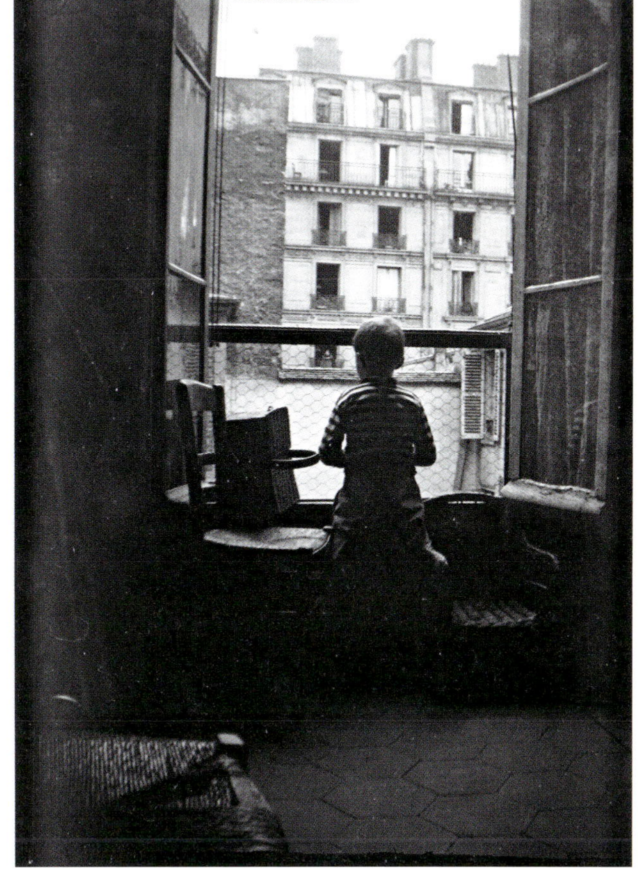

CAT. 117. Henri Evenepoel, *Charles au jersey rayé* (Charles in a Striped Jersey), ca. 1898. Oil on canvas, 28¾ x 19⅝ in. (73 x 50 cm). Fondation Roi Baudouin, Brussels. A gift from Anne and André Leysen

CAT. 118. Henri Evenepoel, Charles at the window, 1899. Modern gelatin silver print, 2011, from original negative, 2 x 1½ in. (5 x 3.8 cm). Royal Museums of Fine Arts of Belgium, Brussels, Archives of Contemporary Art in Belgium

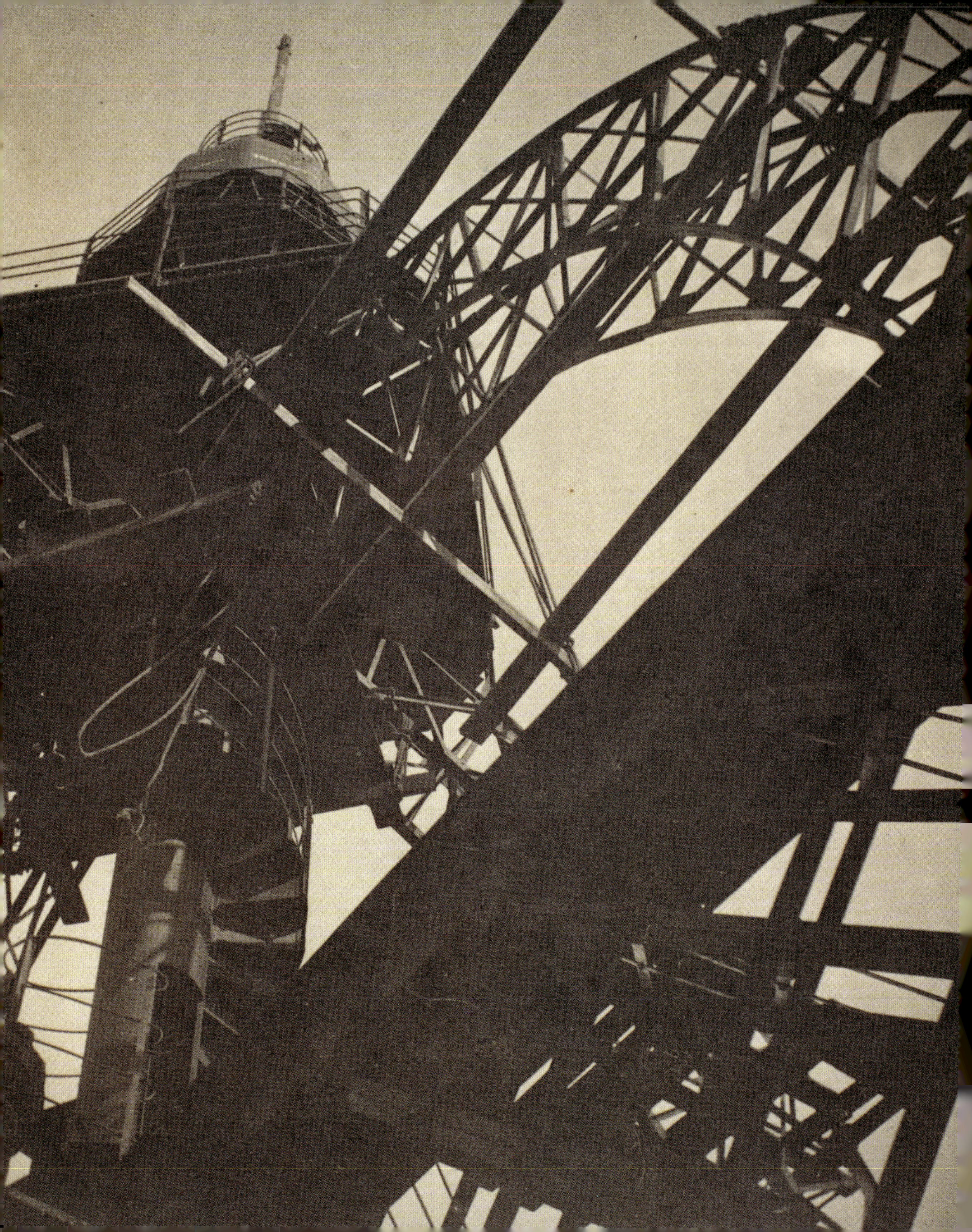

Engineer of Shadow and Light
Henri Rivière as Photographer

Ellen W. Lee

As a pioneering designer of avant-garde theater and the passionate champion of a printmaking revival, Henri Rivière brought an intriguing variety of aesthetic credentials to the dynamic world of turn-of-the-century French art. Over the past twenty-five years, with the discovery of more than three hundred snapshots he made during the 1880s and 1890s, Rivière has also emerged as one of the era's most adept amateur photographers. These images offer fresh insight into the outlook and working methods of an artist who was an ardent student of nature and design, a gifted technician, and a perceptive observer of the world around him.

Rivière's photographs were lovingly preserved by family friends,[1] and many of them are now in the collection of the Musée d'Orsay, where they were exhibited and catalogued in 1988.[2] This cache of pictures reveals Rivière's attraction to the bustle of Parisian boulevards and the beauty of isolated Breton villages, to the novelty of modern engineering and the venerable tradition of manual labor. Like Pierre Bonnard and Edouard Vuillard, painters who also took advantage of the new, more convenient models of the camera, Rivière never exhibited his photographs. His lengthy memoirs, written after World War II and liberally illustrated with sketches and prints, contain no mention of them.[3] Yet a look at the photographs themselves suggests their direct relationships with the artist's "official" work.

DETAIL OF CAT. 124

Unlike many of the nonprofessional photographers who turned to cameras made by the Eastman Company, Rivière did not use a Kodak. He chose instead a simple, lightweight "box" apparatus utilizing glass plates and took advantage of the newly developed, highly sensitive emulsions. The plates, paired with a dry, fast-acting emulsion, eliminated long periods of posing and afforded the photographer the convenience of delayed, rather than immediate, development. The plates, whose metal clips are often visible on the edges of Rivière's prints, measured 3½ x 4¾ inches. His camera also rendered tripods unnecessary, permitting Rivière the flexibility to respond to the serendipity of street life and to take pictures in places that would have been inaccessible with larger or heavier devices.

A native Parisian, Rivière was born in the Montmartre district in 1864 and took an early interest in drawing and reading. He was especially inspired by the illustrated weekly journal *La vie moderne*, one of the many periodicals published in late-nineteenth-century Paris.[4] Almost entirely self-taught, Rivière had just eighteen months of formal artistic study, during 1879 and 1880, in the atelier of the academic painter Emile Bin. There he renewed his acquaintance with

Paul Signac, who introduced him to a pivotal new address in their Montmartre neighborhood, the Chat Noir (Black Cat), just after its opening in November 1881. A vibrant cabaret, the Chat Noir soon became the undisputed center for Paris's most progressive artists, musicians, and poets. Its ambitious impresario was Rodolphe Salis, who built upon the cabaret's success by publishing a weekly four-page journal devoted to the writing and drawing of the Chat Noir habitués. In 1882 Salis offered Rivière an editorial post as assistant secretary of the journal, a tremendous opportunity for an aspiring young artist with no steady income. In addition to the entrée into a sophisticated cultural realm, Rivière gained the tangible fringe benefit of two free meals a day.[5] Before long, he was artistic director of the publication.

As the Chat Noir grew in popularity, the cabaret moved to larger quarters and took on increasingly complex entertainment. In 1886 Rivière became integral to the production of the cabaret's Théâtre d'Ombre (Shadow Theater). As he described it in his memoirs, "the Théâtre d'Ombre was not a child's game as one might imagine, but poems, scenery, and productions that combine to make a truly original and artistic spectacle."[6] The shadow theater called for figures cut from zinc to be seen in silhouette behind a backlit white screen (fig. 1). Rivière not only created drawings for these enormously successful shows, but he also became their highly ingenious director, designing clever choreography for the zinc figures (fig. 2) and inventive set and scene changes. In a powerful demonstration of his prowess as an engineer and tech-

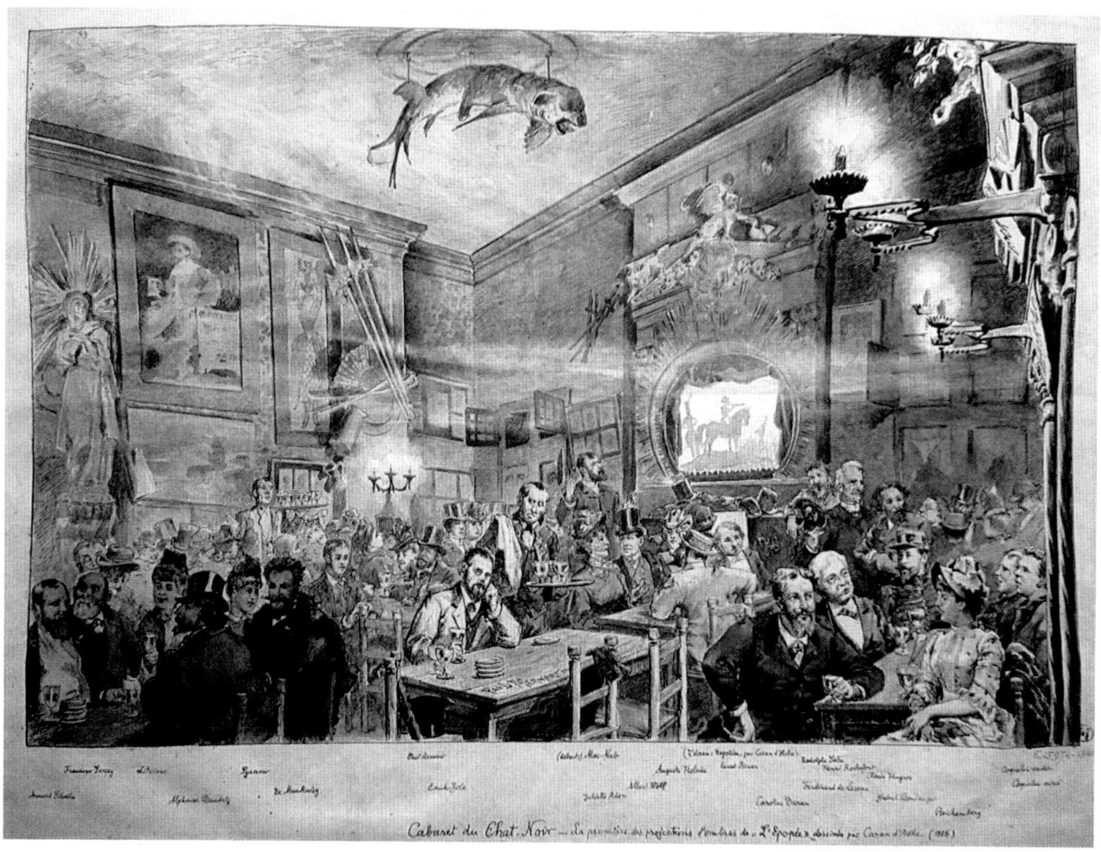

FIG. 1. Caran d'Ache, *L'épopée* (The Epic). Musée Carnavalet, Paris. This was the first shadow projection designed for the Chat Noir.

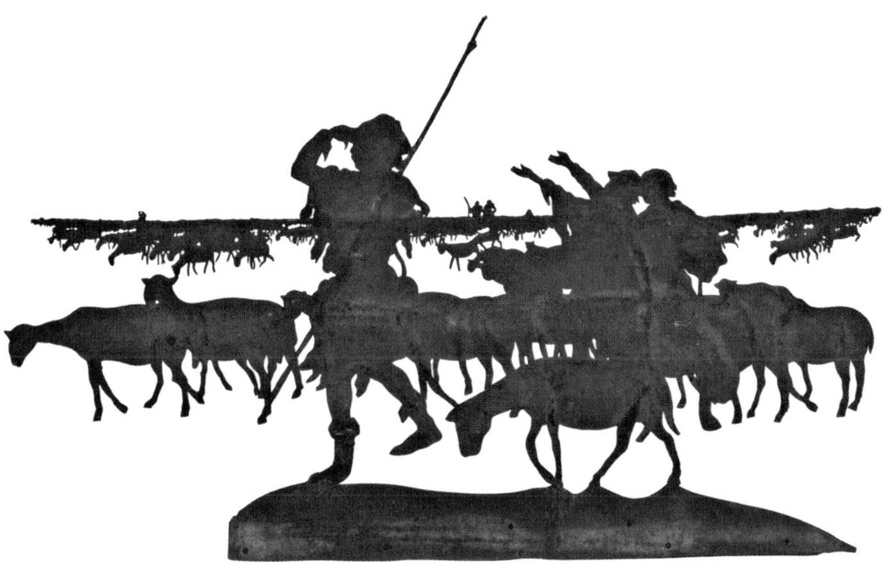

FIG. 2. Drawn by Henri Rivière, *Les bergers* (The Shepherds), from *La marche à l'étoile* (The Journey to the Star), 1890. Cut zinc, 22 x 36¼ in. (56 x 92 cm). Musée des arts décoratifs, Paris

nician, Rivière in 1890 devised a way to use moving colored glass and lights to enhance productions that were originally based on the contrast of light and dark. He and the Chat Noir mounted several shadow plays from 1887 through 1896. This extraordinary entertainment ended in 1897, with the death of Rodolphe Salis and the closing of his cabaret.

Unique documentation of the Chat Noir shadow plays exists thanks to Rivière's foray into photography (cats. 120–23). One can only imagine the artist's delicate moves as he manipulated his camera in the wings, recording the plunging views and tight angles behind the scenes. Costarring in these images are the truncated figures of the men striving to operate the zinc forms and the beams of light that are the medium's animating force. It is not surprising that an artist who designed plays based on light and shadow might appropriate the instrument that allowed him to record those relationships in the world around him. Another legacy of Rivière's mastery of the shadow theater was his reliance as a printmaker on the power of the well-defined silhouette. Many of the artist's lithographs such as *Les bergers* (The Shepherds) from *La marche à l'étoile* (The Journey to the Star) (fig. 3) or *L'aube* (Dawn) from *La féerie des heures* (The Magic of the Hours) (cat. 119) demonstrate his understanding of how to transform a profile into a powerful graphic tool.[7]

Rivière and his colleagues at the Chat Noir were well attuned to *japonisme*, France's enthusiastic assimilation of the characteristics of Japanese art. Japan opened to the West in the 1850s, and by the 1870s European eyes were opened to the beauty of its art. Parisian galleries offered Japanese works to an eager public, and progressive artists such as Edgar Degas, Paul Gauguin, Vincent van Gogh, and Claude Monet assembled collections of Japanese woodblocks, savoring the brilliant colors and novel perspectives of artists such as Katsushika Hokusai and Andō Hiroshige. Rivière became a connoisseur of Japanese art, frequenting the shops and forming a distinguished collection of metalwork, ceramics, and more than eight hundred woodblock prints.

No other European artist of the era absorbed the practice of the Japanese printmakers more fully than Rivière. In his woodcuts and lithographs, he emulated their vibrant colors, asymmetrical compositions, and dramatic cropping and perspective — an approach often in evidence in his photographs. Rivière's devotion to Japanese art meshed perfectly with his zeal for

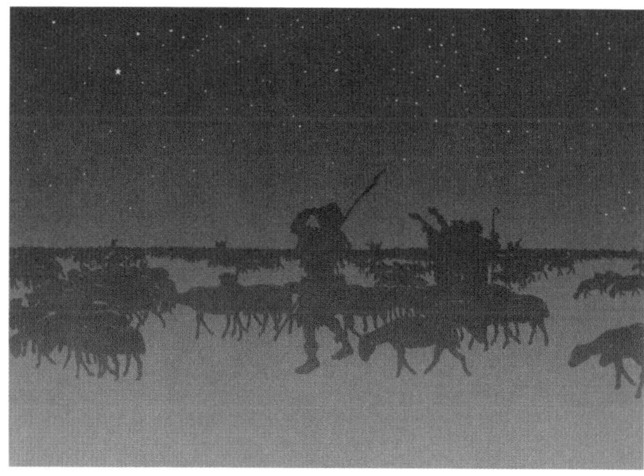

FIG. 3. Henri Rivière, *Les bergers* (The Shepherds), from *La marche à l'étoile* (The Journey to the Star), Tableau II, 1890. Lithograph, 6¾ x 9¾ in. (17.3 x 24.9 cm). Bibliothèque nationale de France

participating in the revival of the color woodblock print. Experimenting intensively, he learned to imitate the Japanese processes, carving his blocks from pear wood cut along the grain, fabricating his own colors, and pulling his prints by hand. He even printed on hundred-year-old Japanese handmade paper and utilized red monogram stamps inspired by those of his Japanese predecessors.[8] From 1890 to 1892 Rivière worked on a series of six woodblocks, *La mer, études de vagues* (The Sea, Studies of Waves), which epitomizes his mastery of Japanese printmaking methods. The woodcuts were a critical success and demonstrated his respect for the artisanal elements of printmaking (fig. 4).

Thanks to Rivière's association with the Chat Noir, he participated in one of the most coveted "photo ops" in the history of Paris. Rodolphe Salis and the staff of the cabaret and journal were invited by Gustave Eiffel to preview his tower a few months before its completion in 1889. The controversial structure was being erected for that year's Exposition Universelle as a symbol of French industrial and engineering prowess. Advised that they were visiting at their own risk and warned of the danger of falling bolts, the bohemian entourage ascended the stairs of the soaring network of iron.[9] Henri Rivière managed to hold onto his camera throughout the climb—and created one of the era's most original suites of photographs.[10]

The thirty-nine images comprising Rivière's Eiffel Tower portfolio suggest that the artist was intrigued by two basic themes: the striking perspectives of lines and angles seen against the backdrop of the city and sky; and the interactions of visitors and workers with this vast, inanimate giant. Several shots have a stunning modernity, as dark girders against the air read as geometric abstractions worthy of the twentieth-century avant-garde (cats. 124, 127, 129, 131). Rivière pointed his camera up, down, and directly outward, framing views that could have been chosen thirty or forty years later by László Moholy-Nagy or Aleksandr Rodchenko. The art historian David Travis described the Eiffel Tower's impact on some twentieth-century photographers, observing that constructions such as the tower and large metalwork bridges were "more than symbols: they were mechanical structures that acquired the dynamic aspect of a new aesthetic if one became a part that moved within."[11]

While Rivière did achieve a new aesthetic with his images of Paris's most familiar silhouette, they are also firmly rooted in his own contemporary vision and

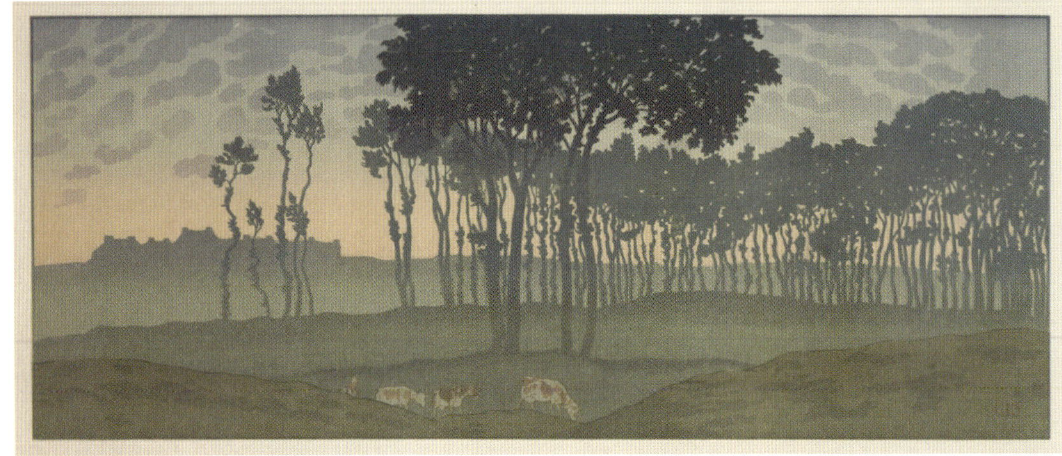

CAT. 119. Henri Rivière, *L'aube* (Dawn), number 1 from the series *La féerie des heures* (The Magic of the Hours), 1901. Lithograph, 9 3/8 x 23 1/2 in. (23.9 x 59.8 cm) image, 12 3/8 x 26 5/8 in. (31.3 x 67.6 cm) sheet. Zimmerli Art Museum at Rutgers University. Gift of Sara and Armond Fields

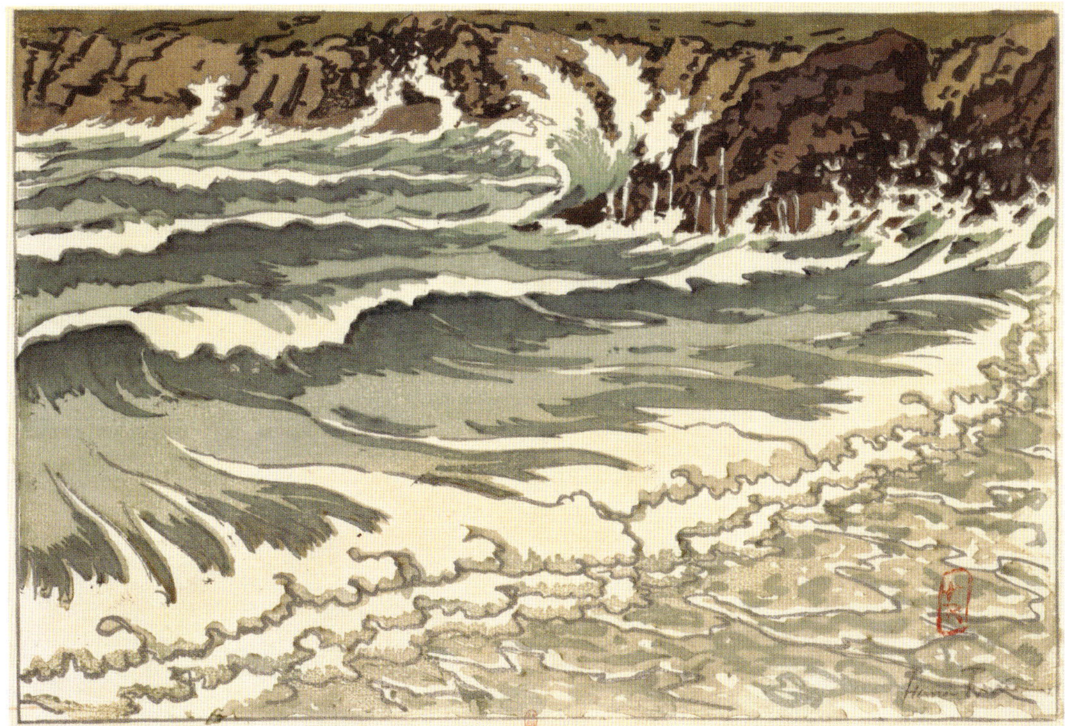

FIG. 4. Henri Rivière, *Surf after the Wave (Tréboul)*, no. 5 from *La mer, études de vagues* (The Sea, Studies of Waves), 1892. Woodcut, 9 x 13¾ in. (23 x 35 cm). Bibliothèque nationale de France

experience. Backlit by boundless sky, perhaps the iron cutouts of Eiffel's tower should be considered the city's largest shadow theater. Also to Rivière's taste are the photographs' abrupt passages from near to far, large to small — an approach favored by Japanese printmakers. And what more powerful sign could there be of the artist's abiding attachment to Japan and the tower than his creation of a bound book of lithographs entitled *Les trente-six vues de la Tour Eiffel* (Thirty-six Views of the Eiffel Tower; cat. 126)? Parodying Hokusai's *Thirty-six Views of Mount Fuji* (1826–33), Rivière at once paid homage to the Japanese master and wittily suggested the omnipresence of Paris's powerful profile through the volume's three-dozen lithographs, created between 1888 and 1902.[12] Four of the views are directly based on photographs from the 1889 preview tour — rare instances of Rivière so literally transferring a camera image to a print (cats. 127–34). Like mighty modernist calligraphy, the powerful lines of *Dans la tour* (Inside the Tower; cat. 128) impose an iron brand upon the gentle curves of the city below. Rivière cleverly removed a distracting plank from the left corner of the photograph, and as Aya Mcdonald noted in her perceptive study of the suite, the artist made slight adjustments in the lithograph to heighten the drama of the perspective.[13] She also observed that he maintained a rather monochromatic palette in this suite, more faithful to the photographs than to his typical practice of choosing vivid hues for his prints.[14] The series's muted colors could also be a reference to the subdued tones of nineteenth-century Japanese books, including volumes by Hokusai.[15] In *En haut de la tour* (At the Top of the Tower; cat. 130), Rivière intensifies the already dizzying sense of suspension by eliminating the sprawling city below, leaving the laborers projected over a cloudy abyss. It cannot be accidental that the last print in the series is *Le peintre dans la tour* (The Painter in the Tower; cat. 132), a flat profile of a man suspended on a rope, painting a beam of the massive structure. Again Rivière based the image on his photograph, sustaining the dramatic contrast in scale and replacing the distraction of the city below with a simplified view of the Seine meandering toward an undefined horizon. Deft designer that he was, in the print Rivière heightened the tension on the rope ever so slightly, creating a gentle curve to contrast with the rigid iron girders. Cast in shadow by the last light of day, Rivière's laborer confronting his task has an anonymity that allows him to be any man and every man.

Other prime subjects for Rivière's camera lay three hundred meters below the tower's summit—on the streets of Paris and along the banks of the Seine. These photographs clearly reflect his abiding interest in workingmen and workingwomen and the pace of everyday life. It is intriguing to picture the artist—at home in the rarefied, nocturnal world of the Chat Noir—spending many of his days recording the bustling shipping activity along the river, the commerce in the markets, and nursemaids promenading with young children.

Riviere's use of a portable camera and plates with highly sensitive emulsion enabled him to respond to fleeting glimpses of Parisian life by making snapshots, or *instantanées*, as they were called in France at the time. Rivière captured some memorable images that suggest he had a droll sense of humor to match his sure sense of design. He seized the opportunity to record the predicament of a worker delivering an armchair, immobilized by pedestrian traffic on the sidewalk (cat. 138). Or, on crossing the Pont du Louvre, Rivière did not fail to note the serendipitous juxtaposition of a family proceeding resolutely toward a horse-drawn streetcar, two small dogs ambling along the bridge, and the generously pleated skirt of a woman walking just in front of him (cat. 139). He caught the energy and animation of the French capital, as in the striking image of a couple walking (cat. 140). The woman strides forward, showing her dress to advantage as she adjusts her parasol, no doubt in preparation for entering the building. Even the profile of the faceless gentleman on the left edge of the snapshot adds to the scene's sense of movement. The asymmetrical composition, the contrast of sunlight and shadow, and the distinction between the curving shapes of the woman's apparel and the strict lines of the architecture display Rivière's gifts as a photographer. The photography historians Françoise Heilbrun and Philippe Néagu characterized the artist's city scenes as "typical of the best snapshot photography of the era."[16] And Michel Frizot wrote that Rivière was without equal in seizing "on the fly" the activity of Parisian street life.[17] Occasionally, these views reveal the presence of the photographer through the shadow that stretches into the foreground; other times, we simply sense his presence, framing the scene and capturing the moment.

Rivière also turned the camera to his personal life, making portraits of his wife, Eugénie, at home. These images, which typically were posed, often feature intricate surface patterns such as the reflection of stained-glass windows in the hallway of the Rivière apartment (cat. 141) or the shadow of ornate ironwork on a maid's white apron (cat. 142). Eugénie Rivière also figured prominently in the many photographs her husband took in Brittany, where the couple vacationed regularly from the 1880s until just before World War I. Two of the finest examples present Eugénie bending down over her knees in a free-flowing gown, playing with her dog (cats. 143, 144). They are taken from vantage points evocative of Rivière's backstage views of the Chat Noir. The dramatic contrast of light and shadow and the isolation of Eugénie on the picture plane have an abstract beauty independent of the appealing subject matter. Like some of the Chat Noir photographs, these two images are cyanotypes rather than gelatin silver prints. Emphasizing the artist's highly developed technical skills, Heilbrun and Néagu have explained that Rivière understood perfectly how to utilize the blue-toned cyanotype to lend vigor and depth to the shadows of highly contrasted images, and how best to use gelatin silver prints on matte paper in order to obtain delicate gray tones.[18]

Another aspect of Rivière's work in Brittany is a group of ravishing photographs showing Eugénie in a pine forest near their small vacation home on the coast (cats. 145, 147, 148). The sense of spontaneity he sought in the urban snapshots was clearly not Rivière's objective here. Rather, he seems to have cast his wife as the human element in a series of elegant tableaux that introduces a lyricism and theatricality not typically found in Rivière's photographs. The dramatic perspective and sinuous silhouettes of trees are reminders of Rivière's attachment to Japanese printmaking. Some years later, he returned to making etchings and produced several landscapes whose incisive lines recall the Breton pine forest imagery first captured with his camera (cat. 146).

This relationship between Rivière's Breton photographs and his printmaking exemplifies how seamlessly camera work is interwoven in his art. Rivière's understanding of shadow theater tempted him to record that milieu through photography and nourished his taste for strong silhouettes and rich contrasts. In turn, he comfortably married the novelty of this theater and its forms to the traditions of Japanese printmaking and to images of contemporary Paris and rural Brittany. And these approaches were all part of Rivière's experience when he picked up a camera. One of his poetic photographs of Brittany might well stand for the intertwined nature of Rivière's art: on a dramatic, jagged outcropping of rock the small figure of a man stands silhouetted against the bright night sky, a willing protagonist in the woodcuts, lithographs, or shadow plays of Henri Rivière (cat. 151).

NOTES

1. Two of Rivière's closest friends were Berthe Langweil Noufflard and her husband, André Noufflard. Their daughters, Henriette and Geneviève, who regarded the artist as a grandfather, made important gifts of Rivière photographs to the Musée d'Orsay, Paris, in 1986. In 1987 the museum acquired additional photographs from the family.
2. The seminal study of Rivière's photography is the catalogue that accompanied the exhibition: Françoise Heilbrun and Philippe Néagu, *Henri Rivière: Graveur et photographe* (Paris: Ministère de la Culture et de la Communication and Editions de la Réunion des musées nationaux, 1988).
3. Henri Rivière, *Les détours du chemin, souvenirs, notes, et croquis, 1864–1951* (Saint-Rémy-de-Provence: Editions Equinoxe, 2004). Although the artist wrote his memoirs just after World War II, this was their first publication.
4. For Rivière's early years, see ibid. and Armond Fields, *Henri Rivière* (Salt Lake City: Gibbs M. Smith, 1983).
5. Rivière devoted two chapters of his memoirs to describing the environment and productions of the Chat Noir. Rivière, *Les détours du chemin*, pp. 28–61.
6. Ibid., p. 52; "le Théâtre d'Ombres n'était pas un jeu d'enfant comme on le pourrait supposer, mais que poèmes, décors et mises en scène concouraient à en faire un spectacle vraiment original et artistique." All translations from French to English are by the author.
7. For an astute study of Rivière's graphic oeuvre, see V. Sueur-Hermel, "Henri Rivière, peintre-graveur et imagier," in *Maître français de l'ukiyo-e: Henri Rivière* (Fondation NHK Service Center, 2009), pp. 185–88.
8. For a thorough analysis of Rivière's assimilation of Japanese printmaking techniques, see J. Bouquillard, "Henri Rivière, un graveur à l'âme japonisante," in *Henri Rivière: Entre impressionnisme et japonisme*, ed. V. Sueur-Hermel (Paris: Bibliothèque nationale de France, 2009), pp. 23–31.
9. Rivière, *Les détours du chemin*, p. 68.
10. For reproductions of all the Eiffel Tower photographs, see Heilbrun and Néagu, *Henri Rivière*.
11. David Travis, "In and of the Eiffel Tower," *Art Institute of Chicago Museum Studies* 13, no. 1 (1987): p. 9.
12. In 2010 the Fine Arts Museums of San Francisco and Chronicle Books copublished a faithful facsimile of the book: Henri Rivière, *Les trente-six vues de la Tour Eiffel* (San Francisco: Fine Arts Museums of San Francisco, Chronicle Books, 2010).
13. Aya Louisa Mcdonald, *Les trente-six vues de la Tour Eiffel par Henri Rivière* (Paris: Philippe Sers Editeur, 1989), p. 66.
14. Ibid., p. 24.
15. Ibid., and James A. Ganz and Karin Breuer, "Afterword," in Rivière, *Les trente-six vues de la Tour Eiffel* (2010), pp. 102–3.
16. Heilbrun and Néagu, *Henri Rivière*, p. 66. "La perception qu'a Rivière de la ville, ou plus exactement de son agitation et de ses bruissements, est typique de la meilleure photographie instantanée de son temps."
17. M. Frizot, "Les nouveaux amateurs," in *La photographie au Musée d'Orsay*, ed. F. Heilbrun (Paris: Musée d'Orsay, Skira Flammarion, 2008), p. 231. "Mais il est tout autant attentif à l'activité de la rue parisienne, et il n'a pas d'égal pour saisir 'à la volée.'"
18. Heilbrun and Néagu, *Henri Rivière*, p. 64.

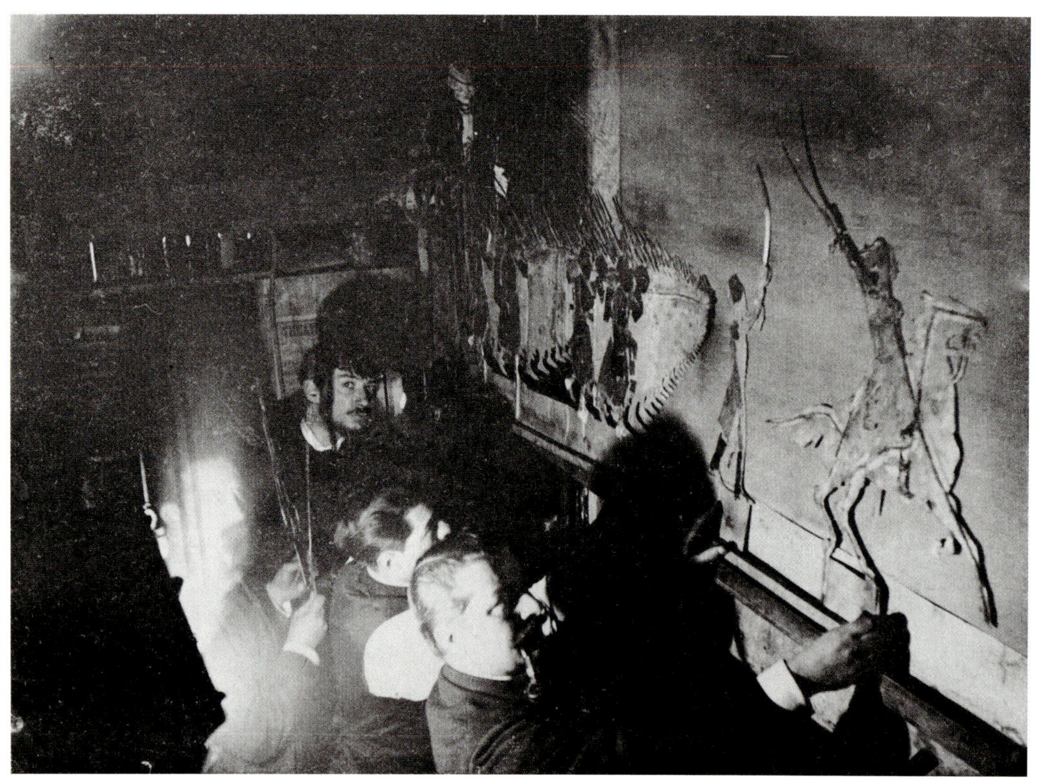

CAT. 120. Henri Rivière, Cabaret of the Chat Noir: Stagehands moving zinc figures behind the screen for *The Epic*, ca. 1887–94. Gelatin silver print, 3½ x 4¾ in. (9 x 12 cm). Musée d'Orsay, Paris. Gift of Mme Henriette Guy-Loé and Mlle Geneviève Noufflard, 1986

CAT. 121. Henri Rivière, Cabaret of the Chat Noir: Moving a set, seen from the first fly, ca. 1889. Cyanotype, 4¾ x 3½ in. (12 x 9 cm). Musée d'Orsay, Paris. Gift of Mme Henriette Guy-Loé and Mlle Geneviève Noufflard, 1986

CAT. 122. Henri Rivière, Cabaret of the Chat Noir: Lighting equipment, ca. 1887–94. Gelatin silver print, 4¾ x 3½ in. (12 x 9 cm). Musée d'Orsay, Paris. Gift of Mme Henriette Guy-Loé and Mlle Geneviève Noufflard, 1986

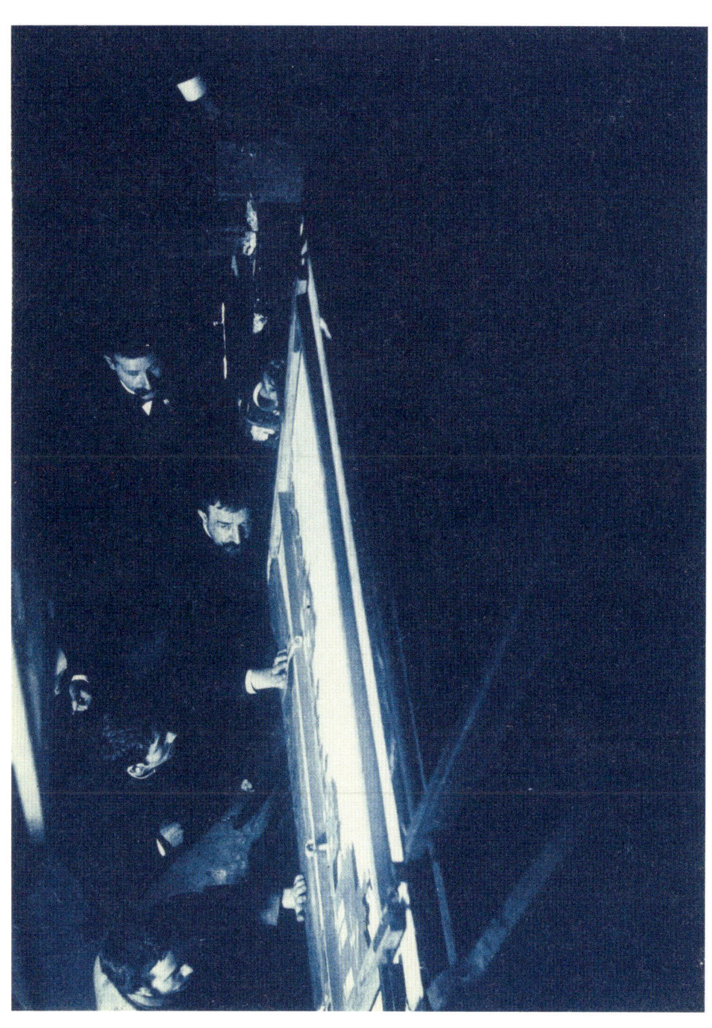

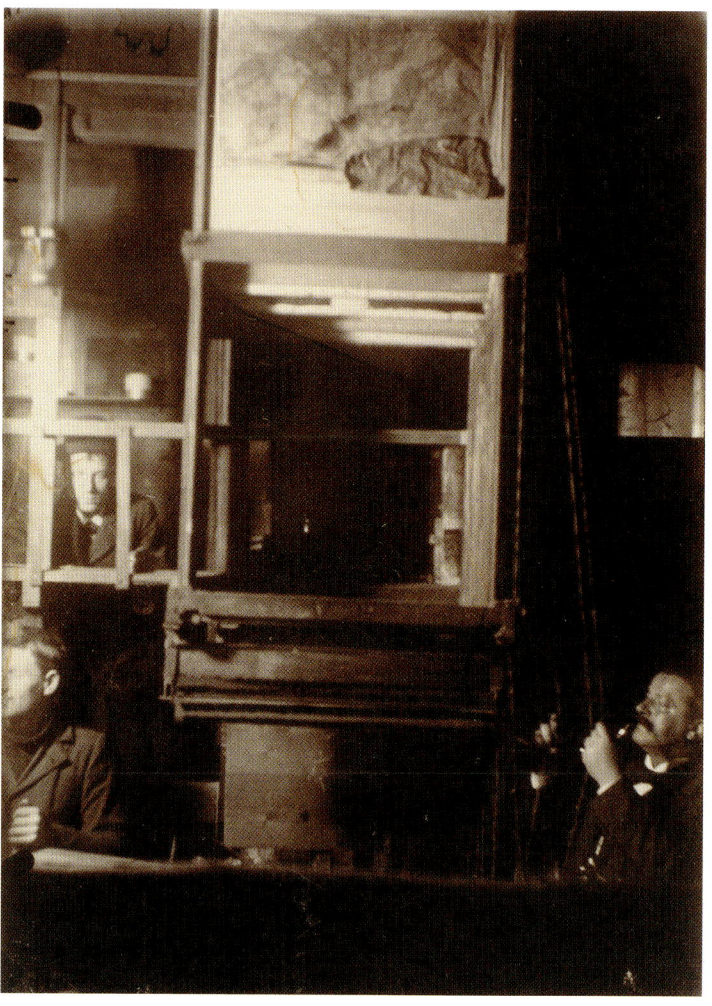

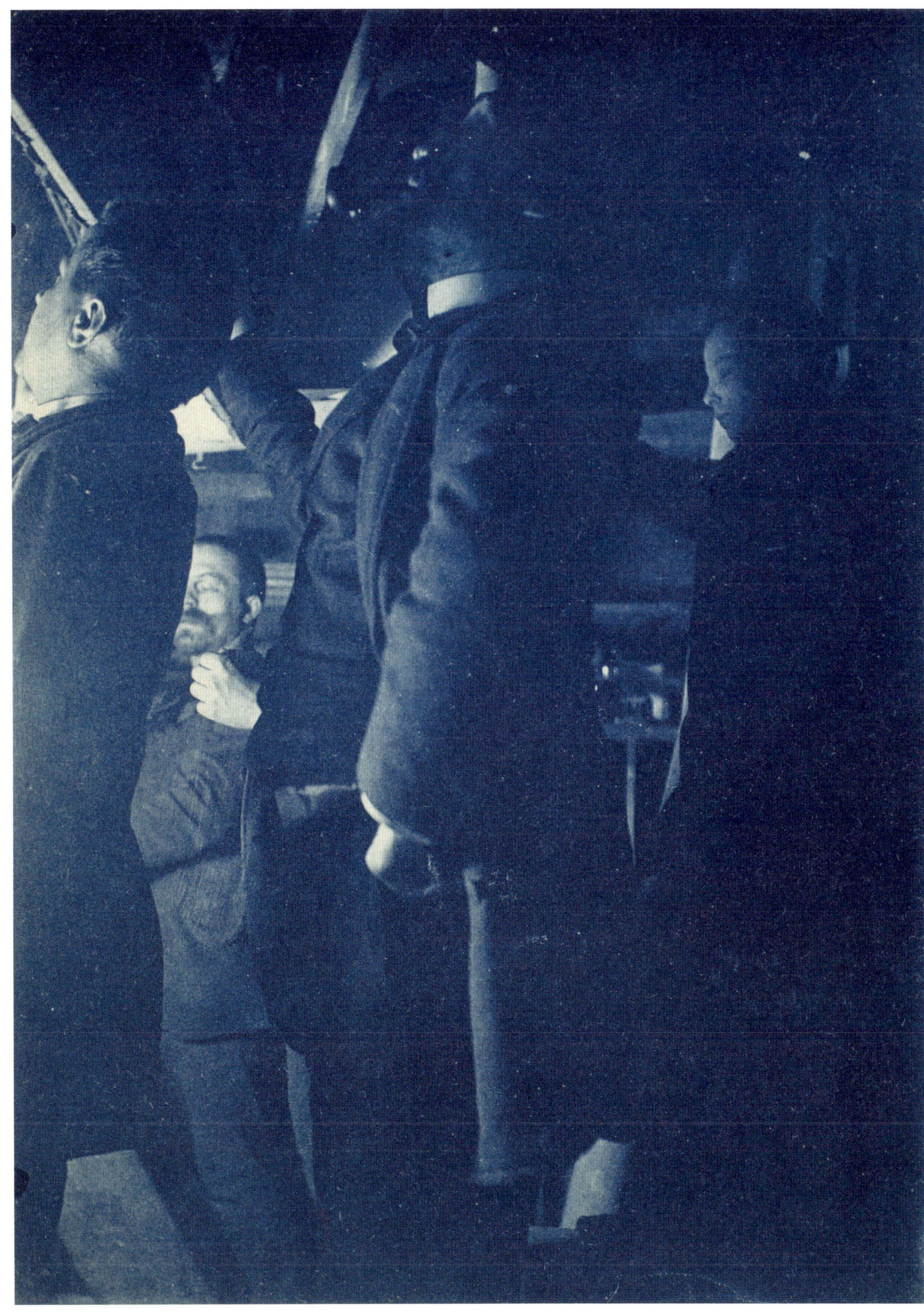

CAT. 123. Henri Rivière, Cabaret of the Chat Noir: Figures during a set change for *Roland*, ca. 1891–94. Cyanotype, 4¾ x 3½ in. (12 x 9 cm). Musée d'Orsay, Paris. Gift of Mme Henriette Guy-Loé and Mlle Geneviève Noufflard, 1986

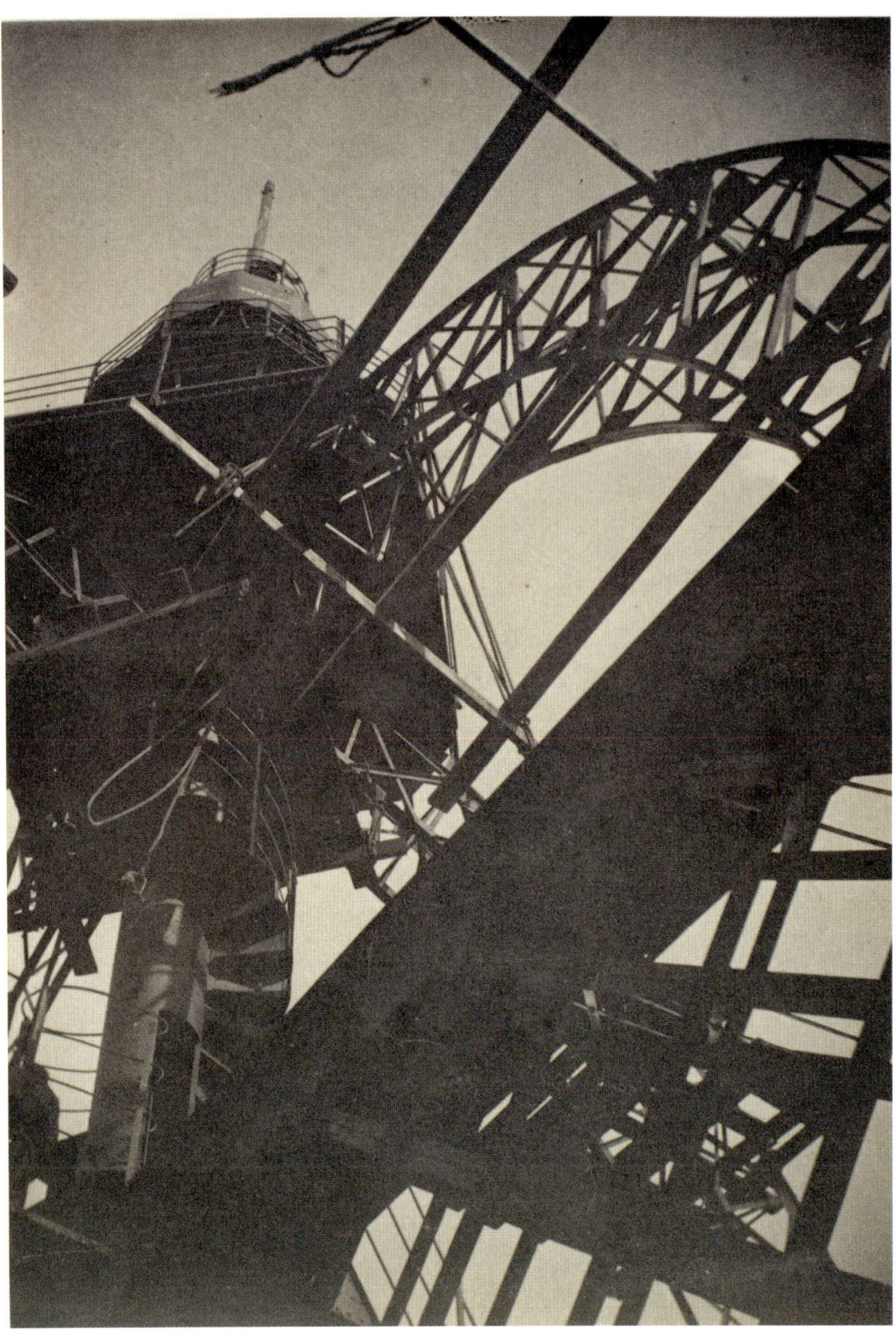

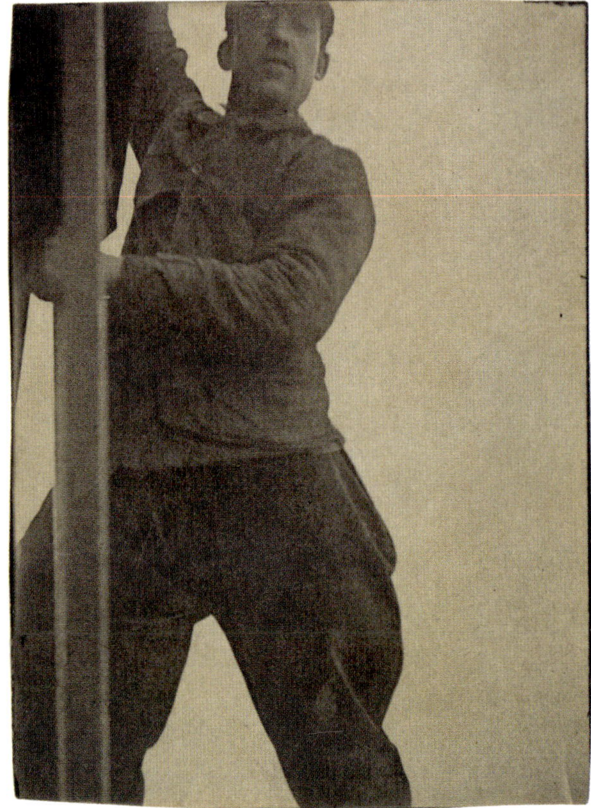

CAT. 124. Henri Rivière, The Eiffel Tower: The "bell tower," light, and lightning conductor (seen from below), 1889. Gelatin silver print, 4¾ x 3½ in. (12 x 9 cm). Musée d'Orsay, Paris. Gift of Mme Bernard Granet and her children and Mlle Solange Granet, 1981

CAT. 125. Henri Rivière, The Eiffel Tower: Workman standing along a girder, 1889. Gelatin silver print, 4¾ x 3½ in. (12 x 9 cm). Musée d'Orsay, Paris. Gift of Mme Henriette Guy-Loé and Mlle Geneviève Noufflard, 1986

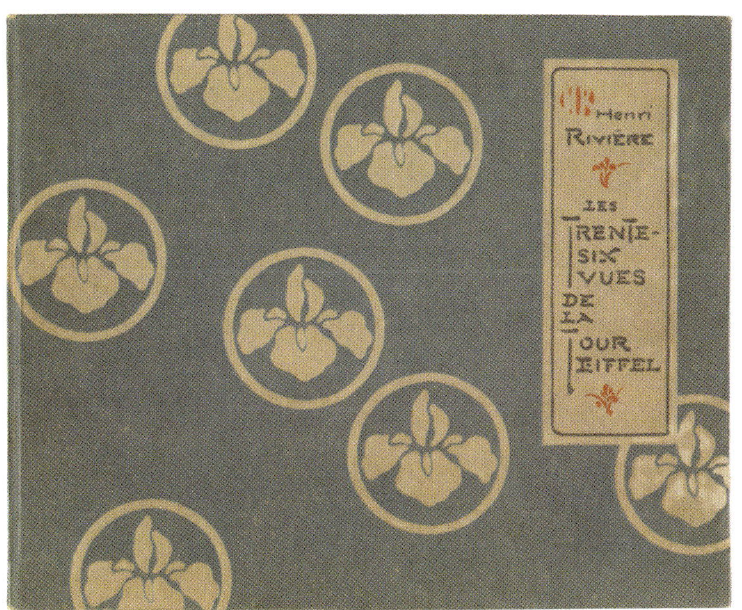

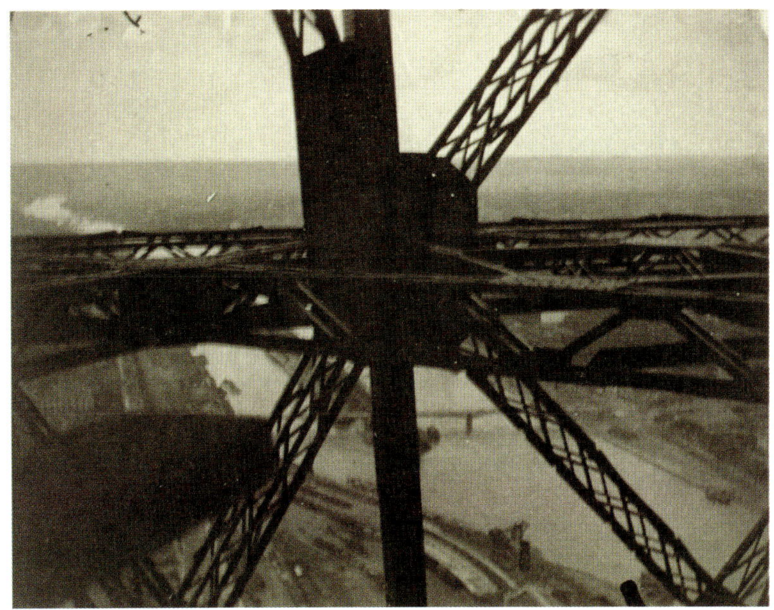

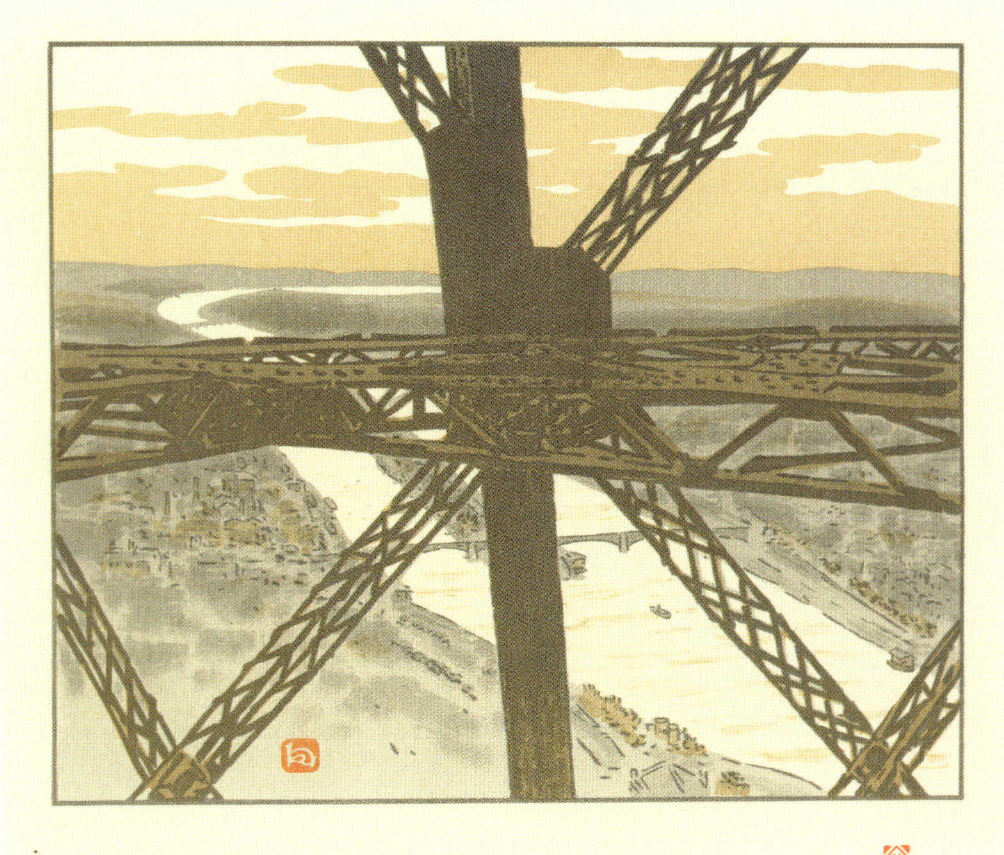

CAT. 126. Henri Rivière, *Les trente-six vues de la Tour Eiffel* (Thirty-six Views of the Eiffel Tower), 1888–1902. Album with 36 lithographs, $9\frac{1}{8}$ x $11\frac{5}{8}$ in. (23.2 x 29.4 cm). Van Gogh Museum, Amsterdam (Vincent van Gogh Foundation)

CAT. 127. Henri Rivière, The Eiffel Tower: An intersection of girders, with the Seine and Île aux Cygnes in the background, 1889. Gelatin silver print, $3\frac{1}{2}$ x $4\frac{3}{4}$ in. (9 x 12 cm). Musée d'Orsay, Paris. Gift of Mme Bernard Granet and her children and Mlle Solange Granet, 1981

CAT. 128. Henri Rivière, *Planche 25, Dans la tour* (Plate 25, Inside the Tower), from *Les trente-six vues de la Tour Eiffel* (Thirty-six Views of the Eiffel Tower), 1888–1902. Lithograph, $6\frac{5}{8}$ x $8\frac{1}{4}$ in. (16.8 x 21 cm). Van Gogh Museum, Amsterdam (Vincent van Gogh Foundation)

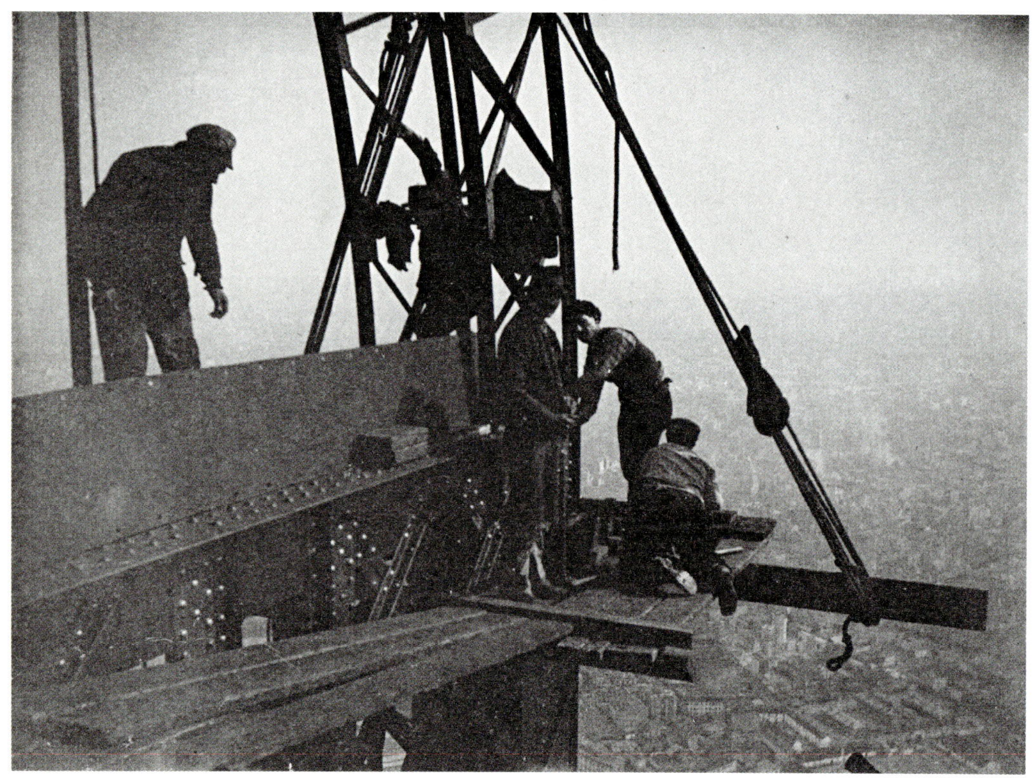

CAT. 129. Henri Rivière, The Eiffel Tower: Five men at work on part of the top floor at the foot of the "bell tower," 1889. Gelatin silver print, 3½ x 4¾ in. (9 x 12 cm). Musée d'Orsay, Paris. Gift of Mme Bernard Granet and her children and Mlle Solange Granet, 1981

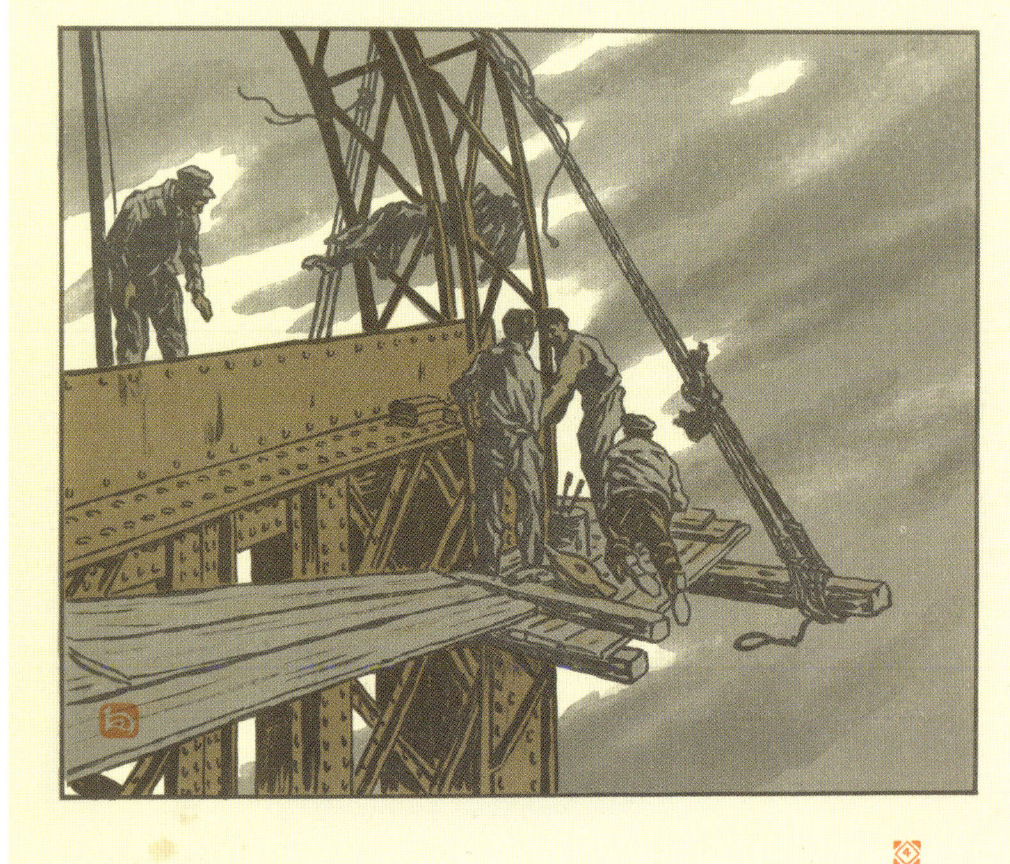

CAT. 130. Henri Rivière, *Planche 4, En haut de la tour* (Plate 4, At the Top of the Tower), from *Les trente-six vues de la Tour Eiffel* (Thirty-six Views of the Eiffel Tower), 1888–1902. Lithograph, 6¾ x 8¼ in. (17.1 x 21 cm). Van Gogh Museum, Amsterdam (Vincent van Gogh Foundation)

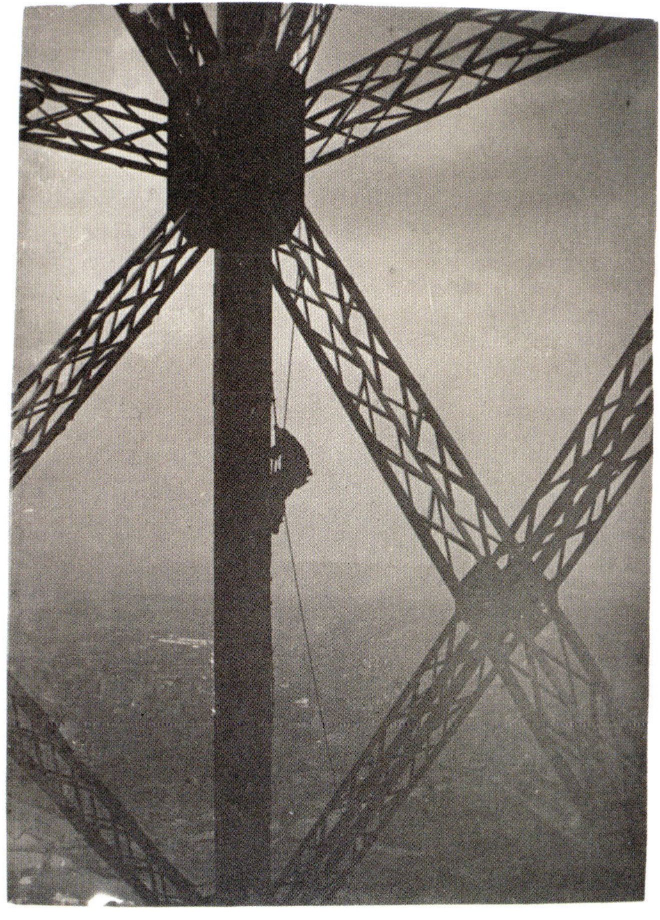

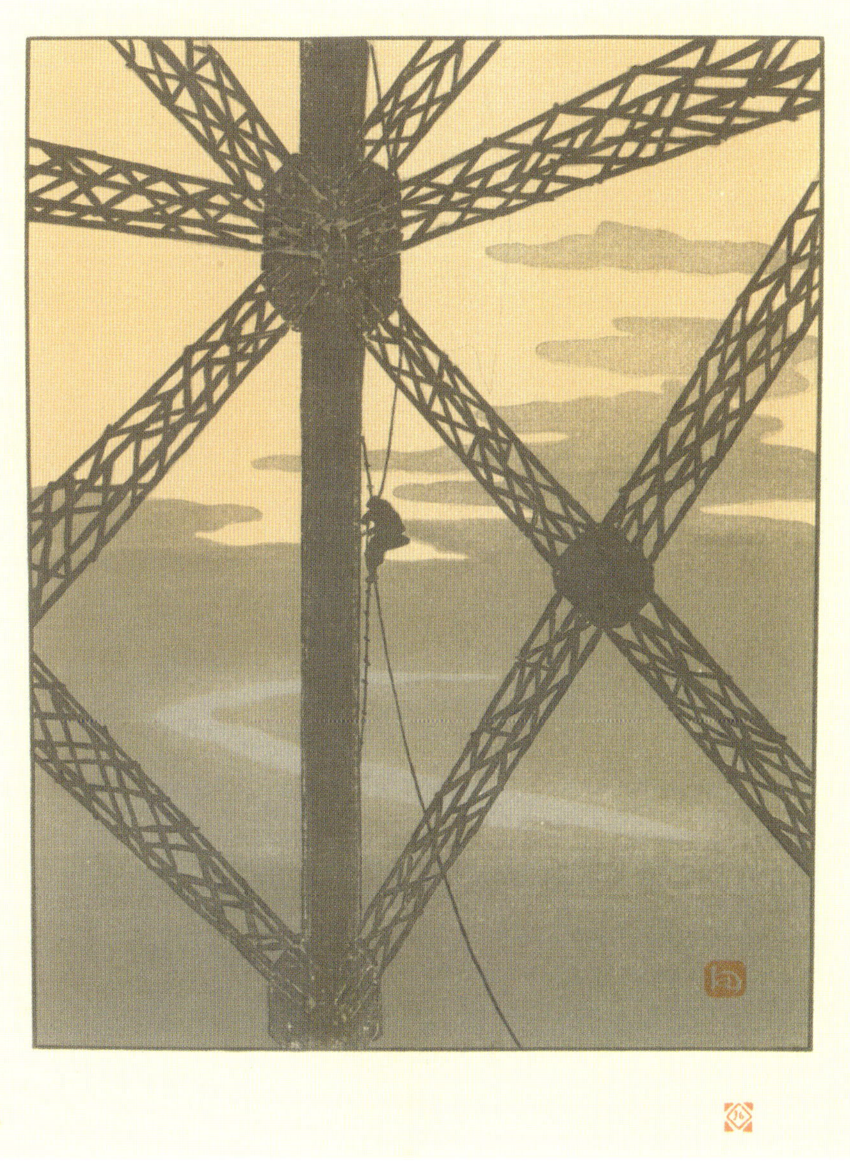

CAT. 131. Henri Rivière, The Eiffel Tower: Painter on a knotted rope along a vertical girder, below an intersection of girders, 1889. Gelatin silver print, 4¾ x 3½ in. (12 x 9 cm). Musée d'Orsay, Paris. Gift of Mme Bernard Granet and her children and Mlle Solange Granet, 1981

CAT. 132. Henri Rivière, *Planche 36, Le peintre dans la tour* (Plate 36, The Painter in the Tower), from *Les trente-six vues de la Tour Eiffel* (Thirty-six Views of the Eiffel Tower), 1888–1902. Lithograph, 8¼ x 6⅝ in. (21 x 16.8 cm). Van Gogh Museum, Amsterdam (Vincent van Gogh Foundation)

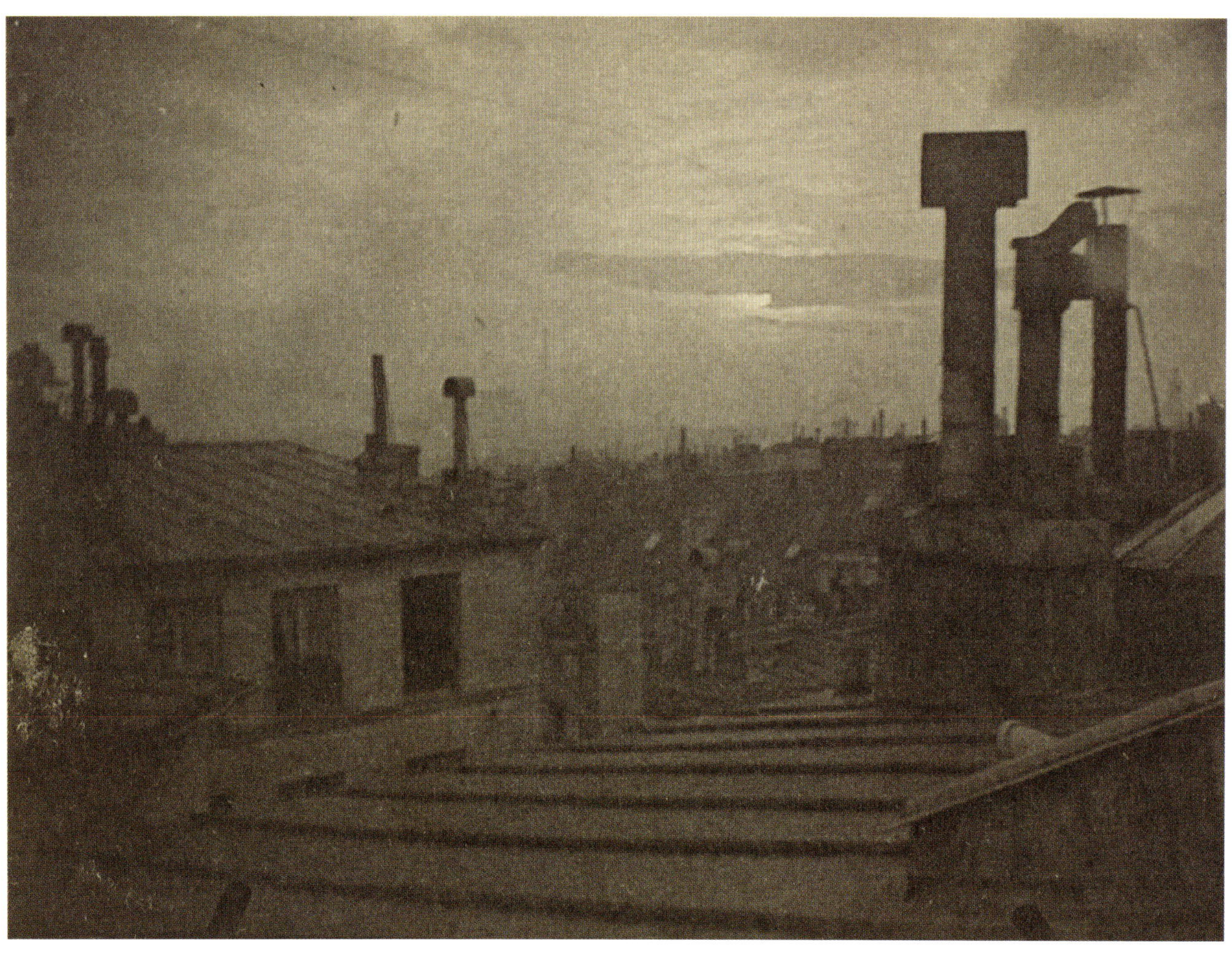

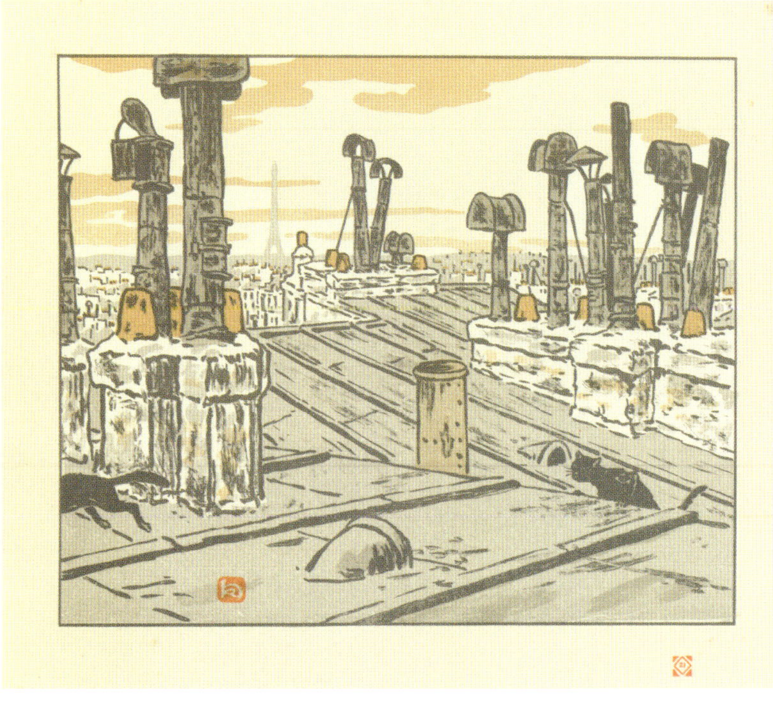

CAT. 133. Henri Rivière, Paris rooftops in the evening with the Eiffel Tower in the distance, ca. 1889–95. Gelatin silver print, 3½ x 4¾ in. (9 x 12 cm). Musée d'Orsay, Paris. Gift of Mme Henriette Guy-Loé and Mlle Geneviève Noufflard, 1986

CAT. 134. Henri Rivière, *Planche 21, Sur les toits* (Plate 21, On the Rooftops), from *Les trente-six vues de la Tour Eiffel* (Thirty-six Views of the Eiffel Tower), 1888–1902. Lithograph, 6⅝ x 8¼ in. (16.8 x 21 cm). Van Gogh Museum, Amsterdam (Vincent van Gogh Foundation)

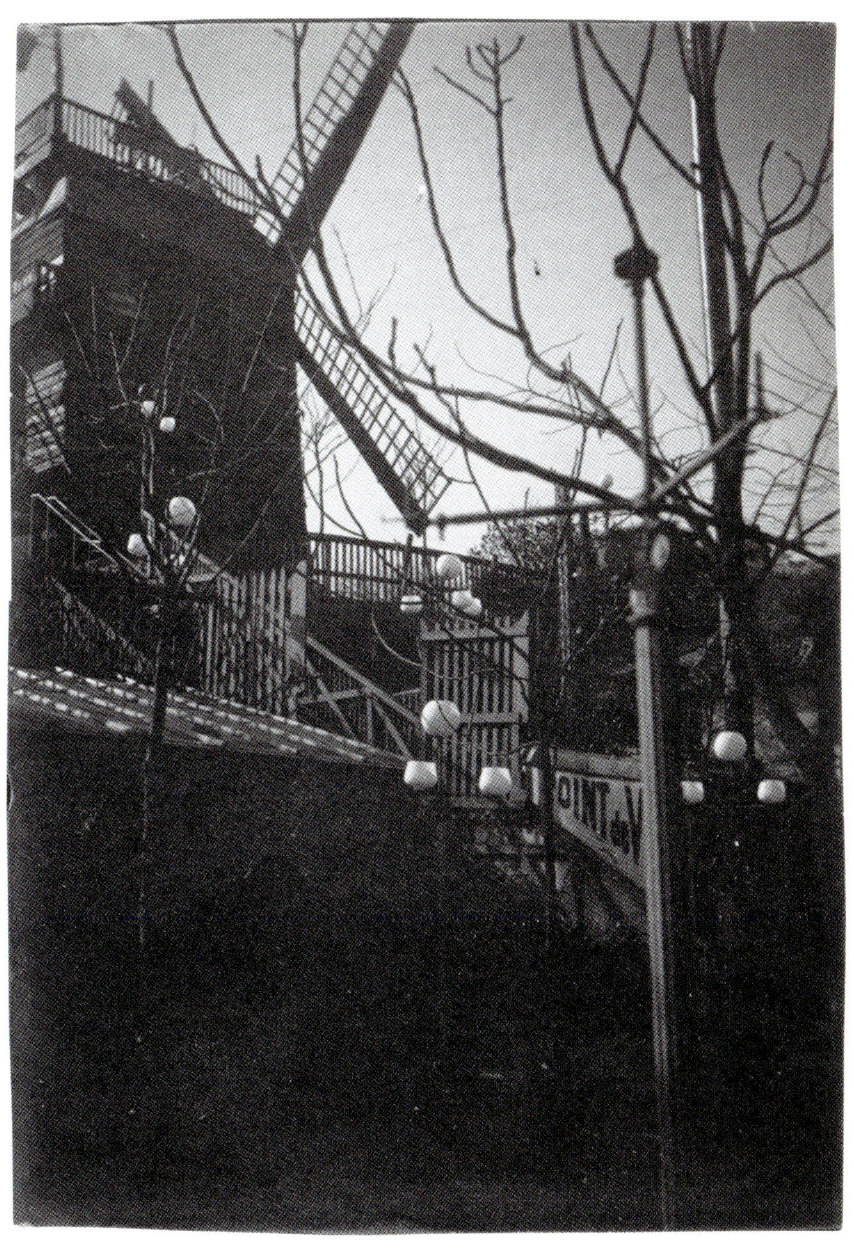

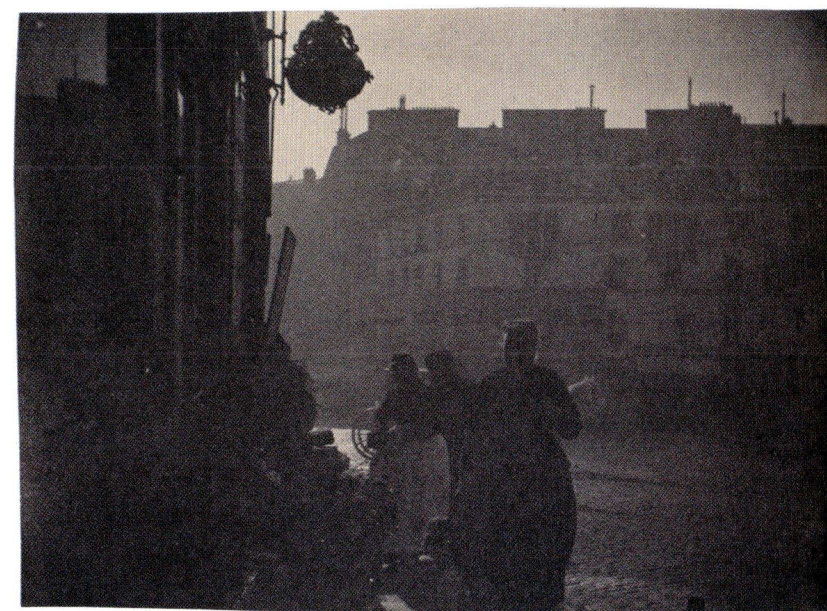

CAT. 135. Henri Rivière, The Moulin de la Galette, ca. 1885–95. Gelatin silver print, 4¾ x 3½ in. (12 x 9 cm). Musée d'Orsay, Paris

CAT. 136. Henri Rivière, Three people in front of a shop, ca. 1885–95. Gelatin silver print, 3½ x 4¾ in. (9 x 12 cm). Musée d'Orsay, Paris

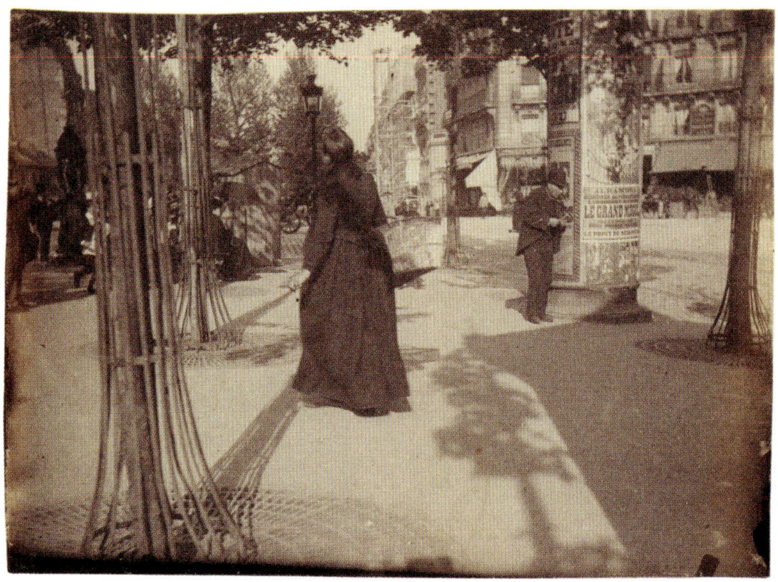

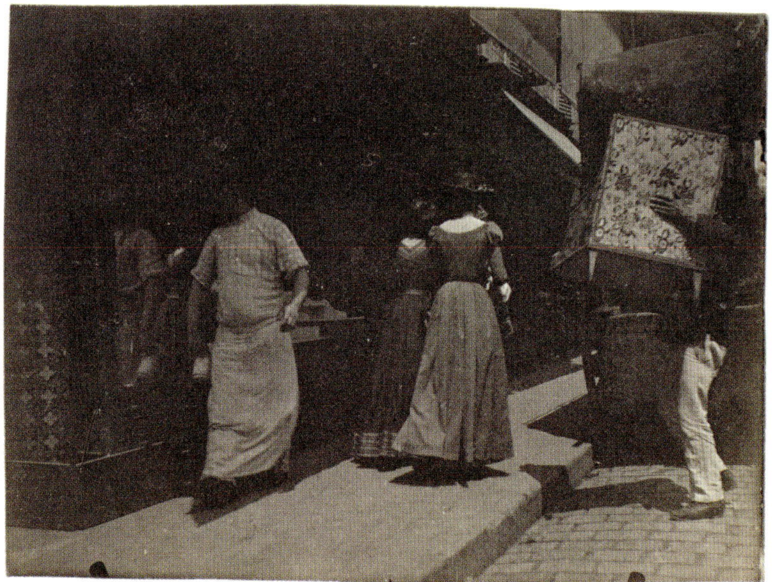

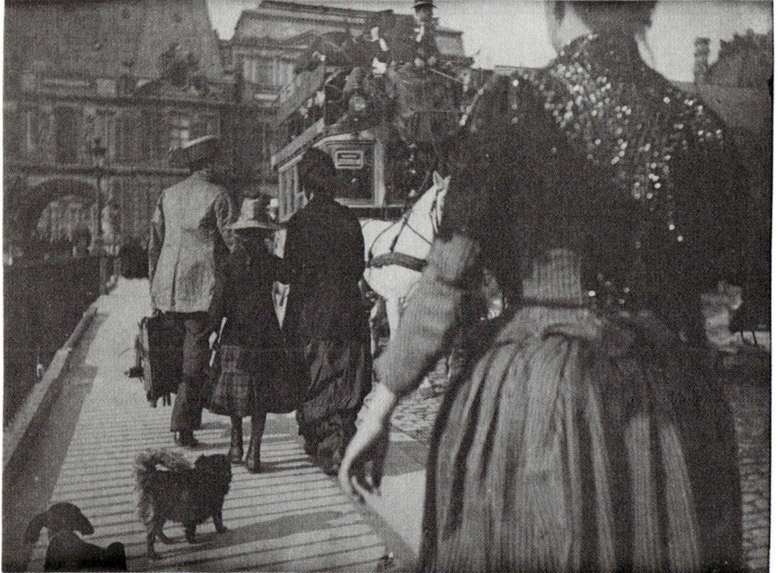

CAT. 137. Henri Rivière, People walking in a public square, ca. 1885–95. Gelatin silver print, 3½ x 4¾ in. (9 x 12 cm). Musée d'Orsay, Paris

CAT. 138. Henri Rivière, People walking in a street, at right a man carrying an armchair, ca. 1885–95. Gelatin silver print, 3½ x 4¾ in. (9 x 12 cm). Musée d'Orsay, Paris

CAT. 139. Henri Rivière, People, two dogs, and a double-decker bus on the Pont du Louvre, ca. 1885–95. Gelatin silver print, 3½ x 4¾ in. (9 x 12 cm). Musée d'Orsay, Paris

OPPOSITE: CAT. 140. Henri Rivière, A couple entering a public building, ca. 1885–95. Gelatin silver print, 4¾ x 3½ in. (12 x 9 cm). Musée d'Orsay, Paris

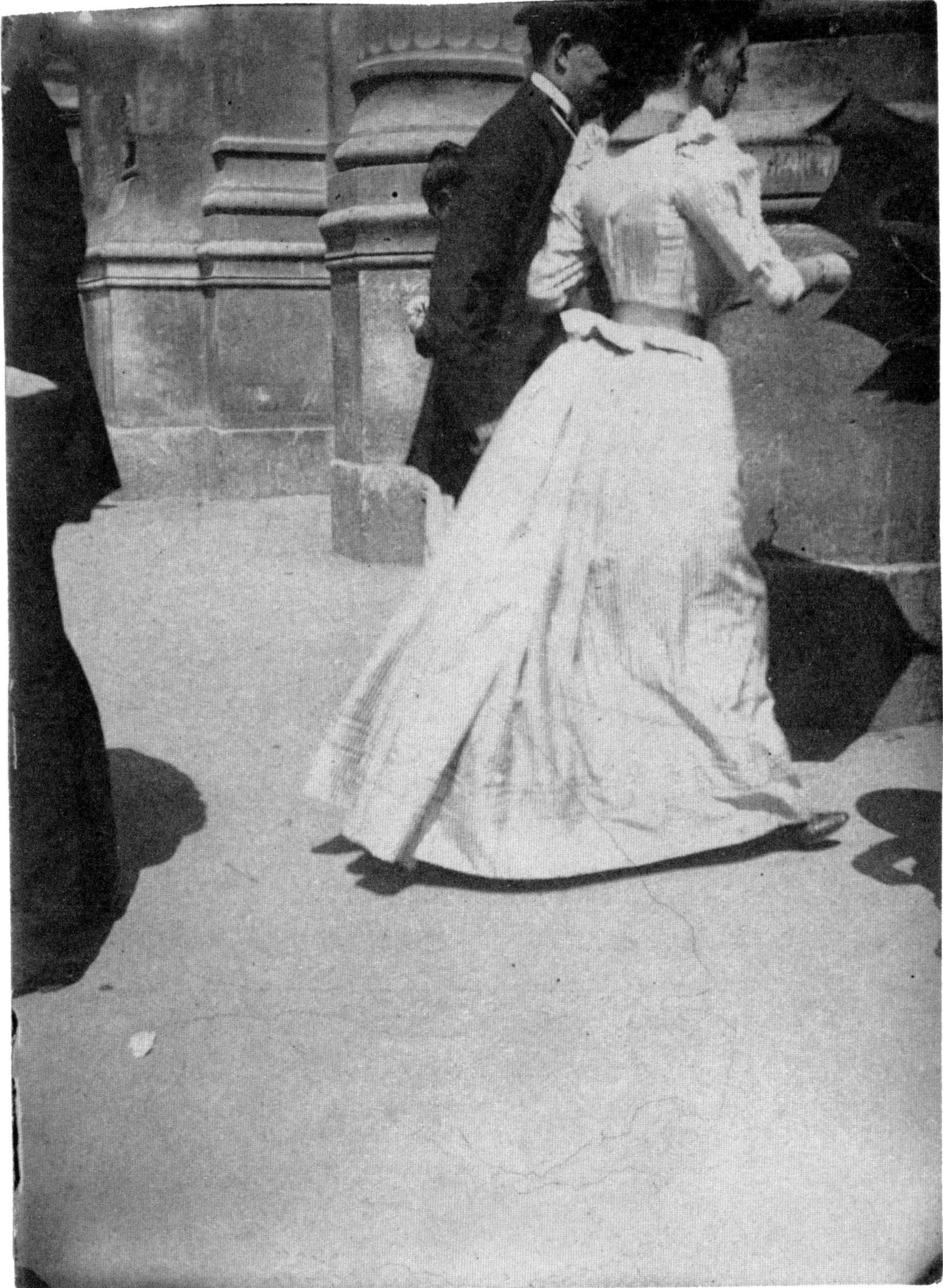

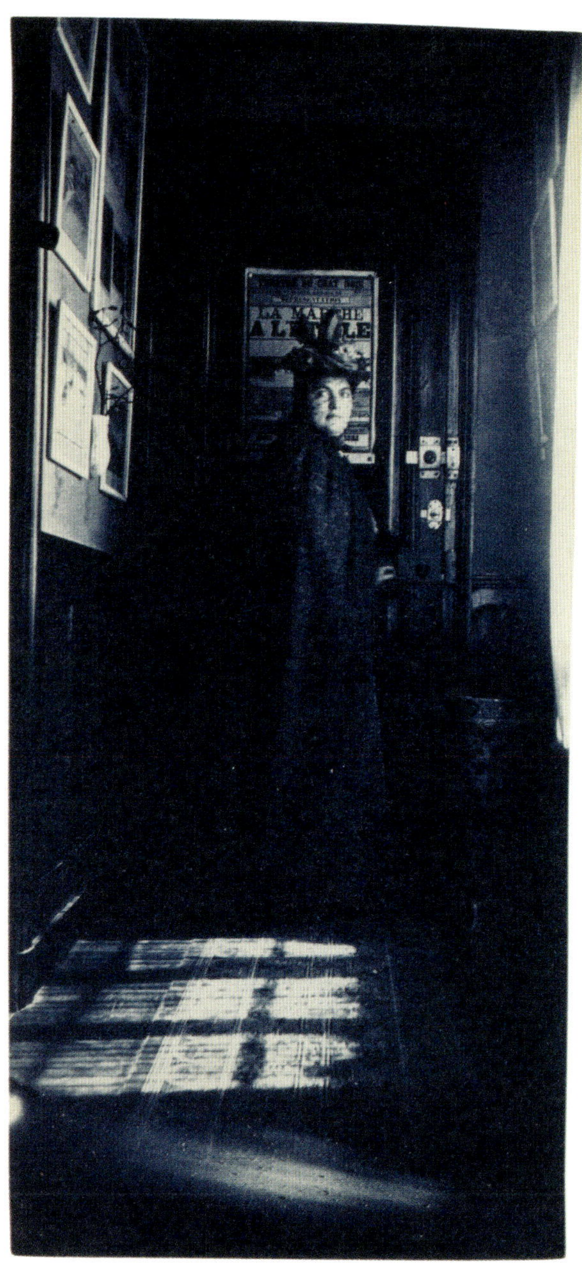

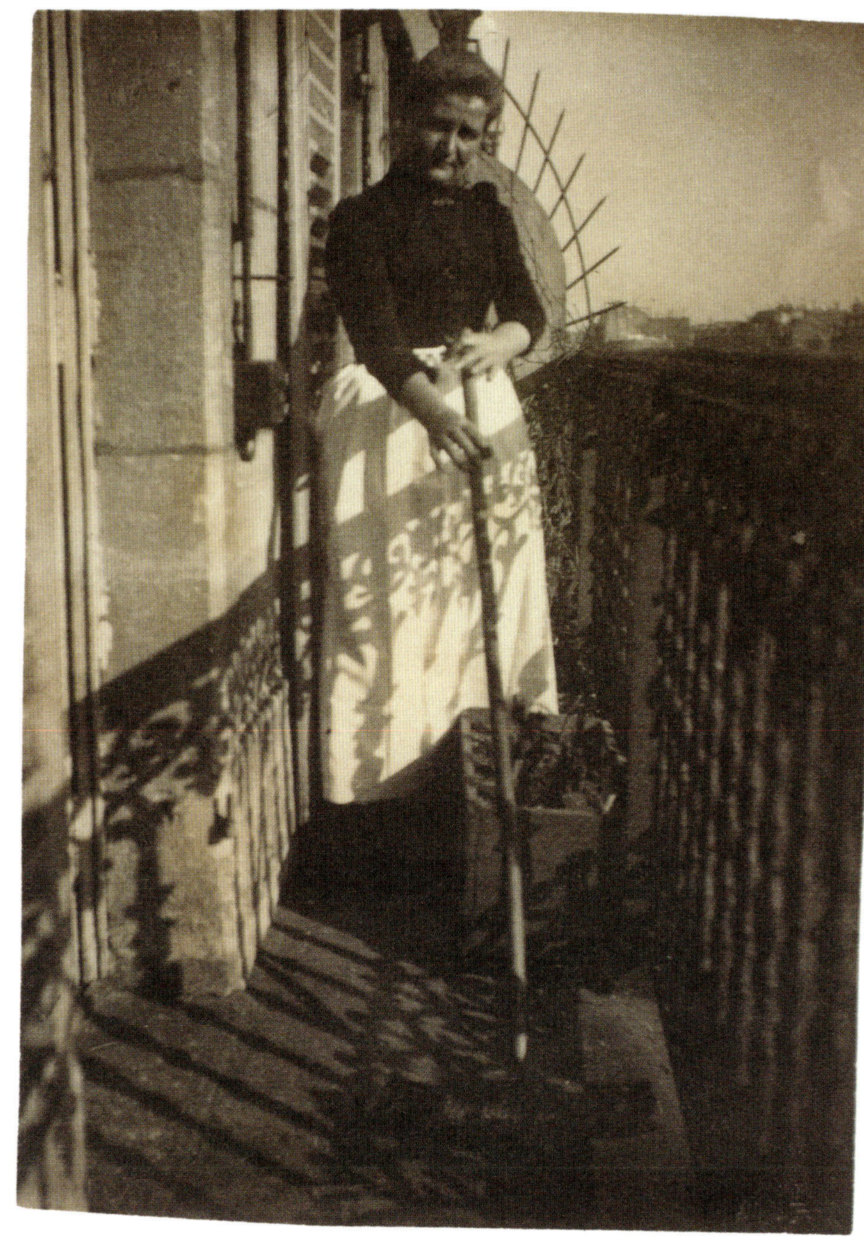

CAT. 141. Henri Rivière, Madame Rivière standing at the hallway door of the apartment on the boulevard de Clichy, ca. 1896. Cyanotype, $4\frac{3}{4} \times 3\frac{1}{2}$ in. (12 x 9 cm). Musée d'Orsay, Paris

CAT. 142. Henri Rivière, Cleaning woman on a balcony, holding a broom, ca. 1896. Gelatin silver print, $4\frac{3}{4} \times 3\frac{1}{2}$ in. (12 x 9 cm). Musée d'Orsay, Paris

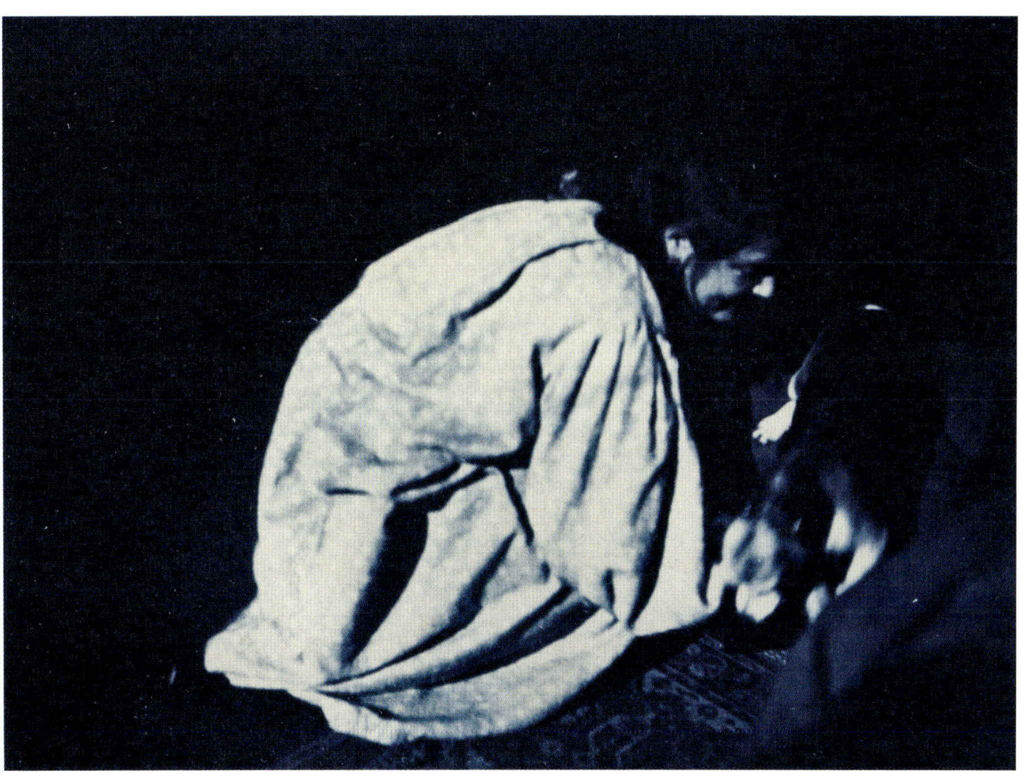

CAT. 143. Henri Rivière, Madame Rivière in profile, crouching on a rug in the apartment, boulevard de Clichy, looking at her dog, ca. 1896. Cyanotype, 3½ x 4¾ in. (9 x 12 cm). Musée d'Orsay, Paris

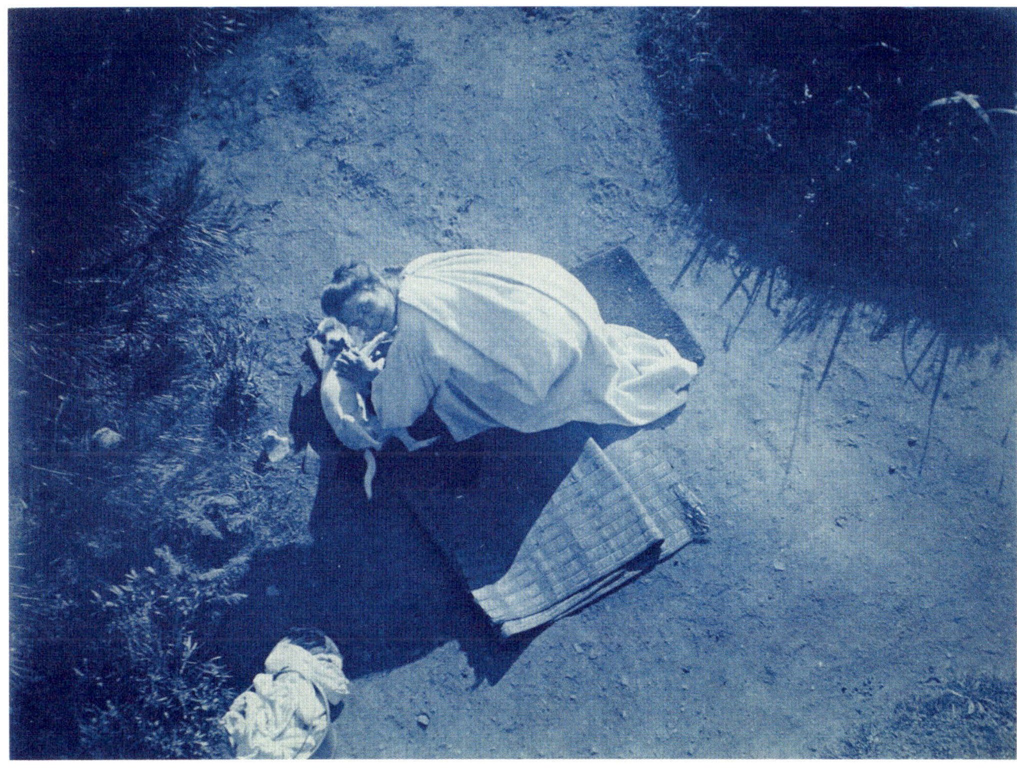

CAT. 144. Henri Rivière, Madame Rivière on her knees, petting her dog, ca. 1890–1900. Cyanotype, 3½ x 4¾ in. (9 x 12 cm). Musée d'Orsay, Paris

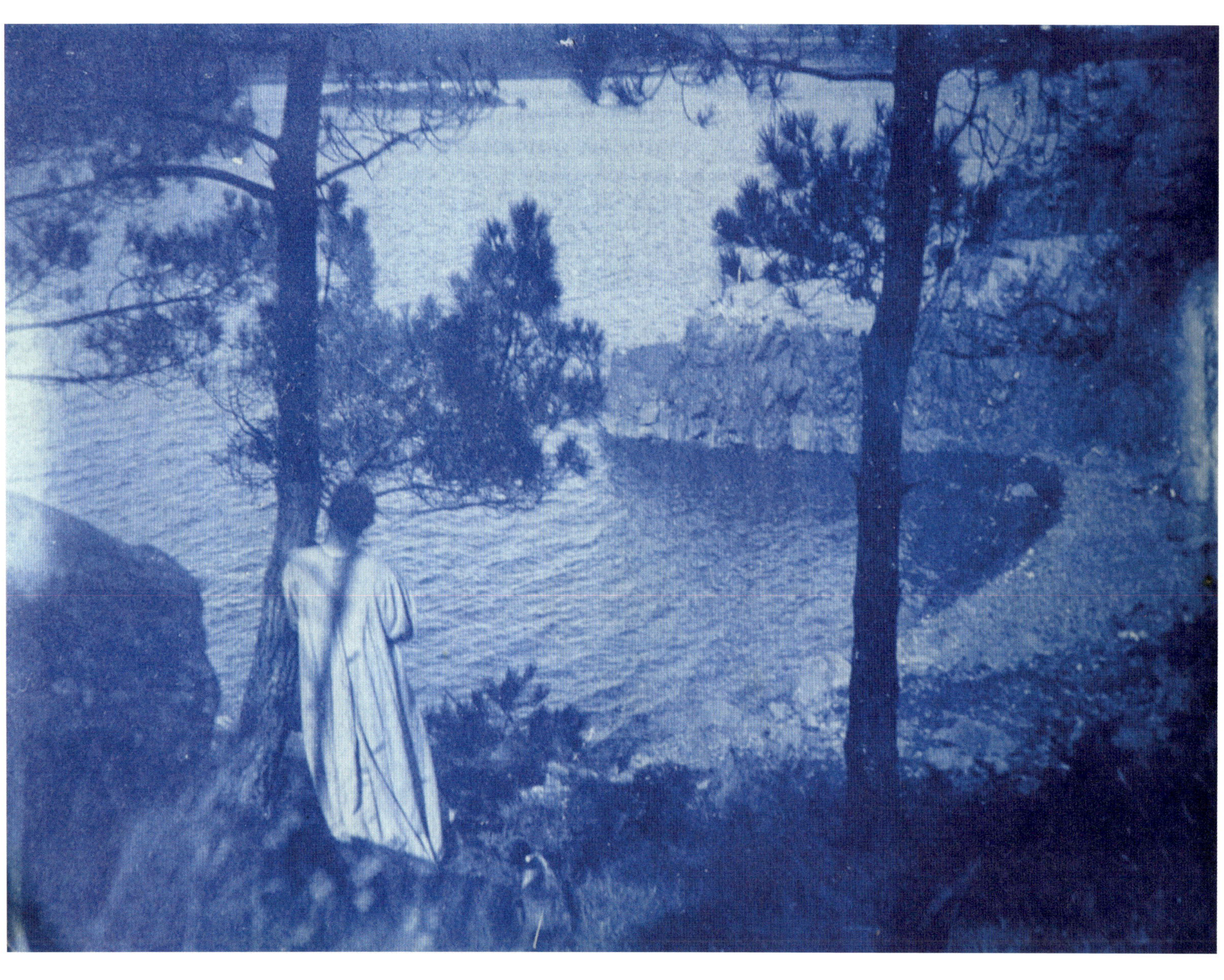

CAT. 145. Henri Rivière, Mme Rivière above the coast, ca. 1890–1900. Cyanotype, 3⅛ x 4¼ in. (8.1 x 10.9 cm). Zimmerli Art Museum at Rutgers University. David A. and Mildred H. Morse Art Acquisition Fund

OPPOSITE:
CAT. 146. Henri Rivière, *Pine Trees in the Rain*, 1907. Etching with white heightening, 9 x 13¼ in. (22.8 x 33.8 cm) image, 12 x 17⅜ in. (30.5 x 44 cm) sheet. Zimmerli Art Museum at Rutgers University. Gift of G. Noufflard and H. Noufflard Guy-Loé

CAT. 147. Henri Rivière, Mme Rivière amidst the pines, ca. 1890–1900. Gelatin silver print, 3⅛ x 4⅜ in. (8 x 11 cm). Zimmerli Art Museum at Rutgers University. David A. and Mildred H. Morse Art Acquisition Fund

CAT. 148. Henri Rivière, Madame Rivière from the front, walking with her dog in a wooded landscape, ca. 1890–1900. Cyanotype, 3½ x 4¾ in. (9 x 12 cm). Musée d'Orsay, Paris

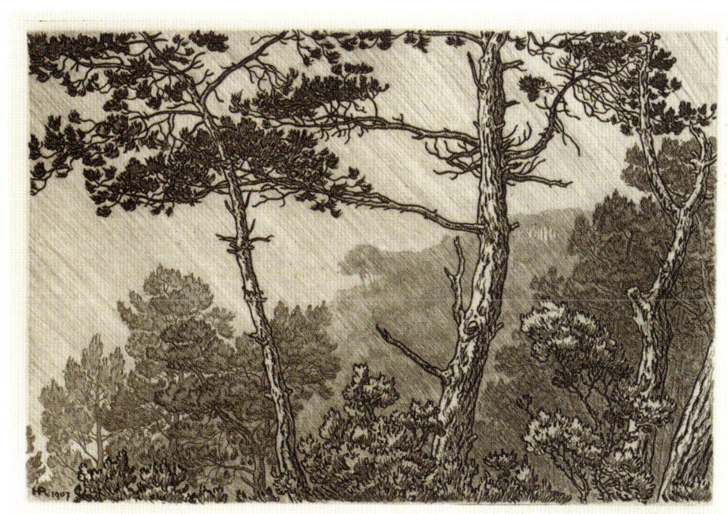

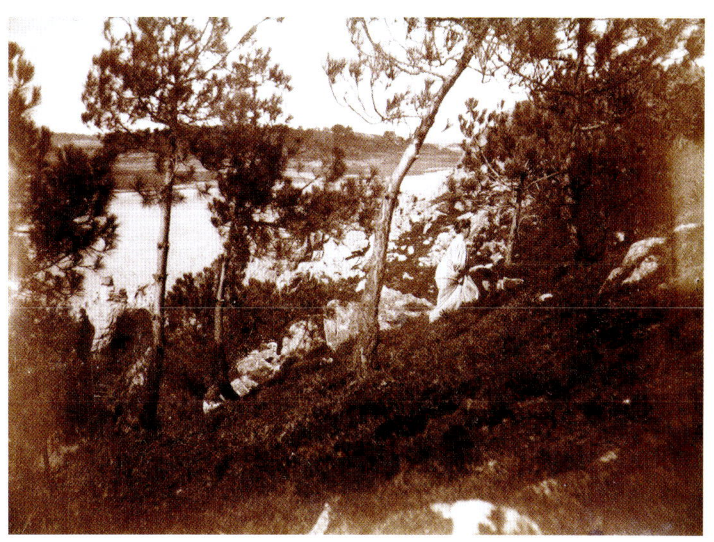

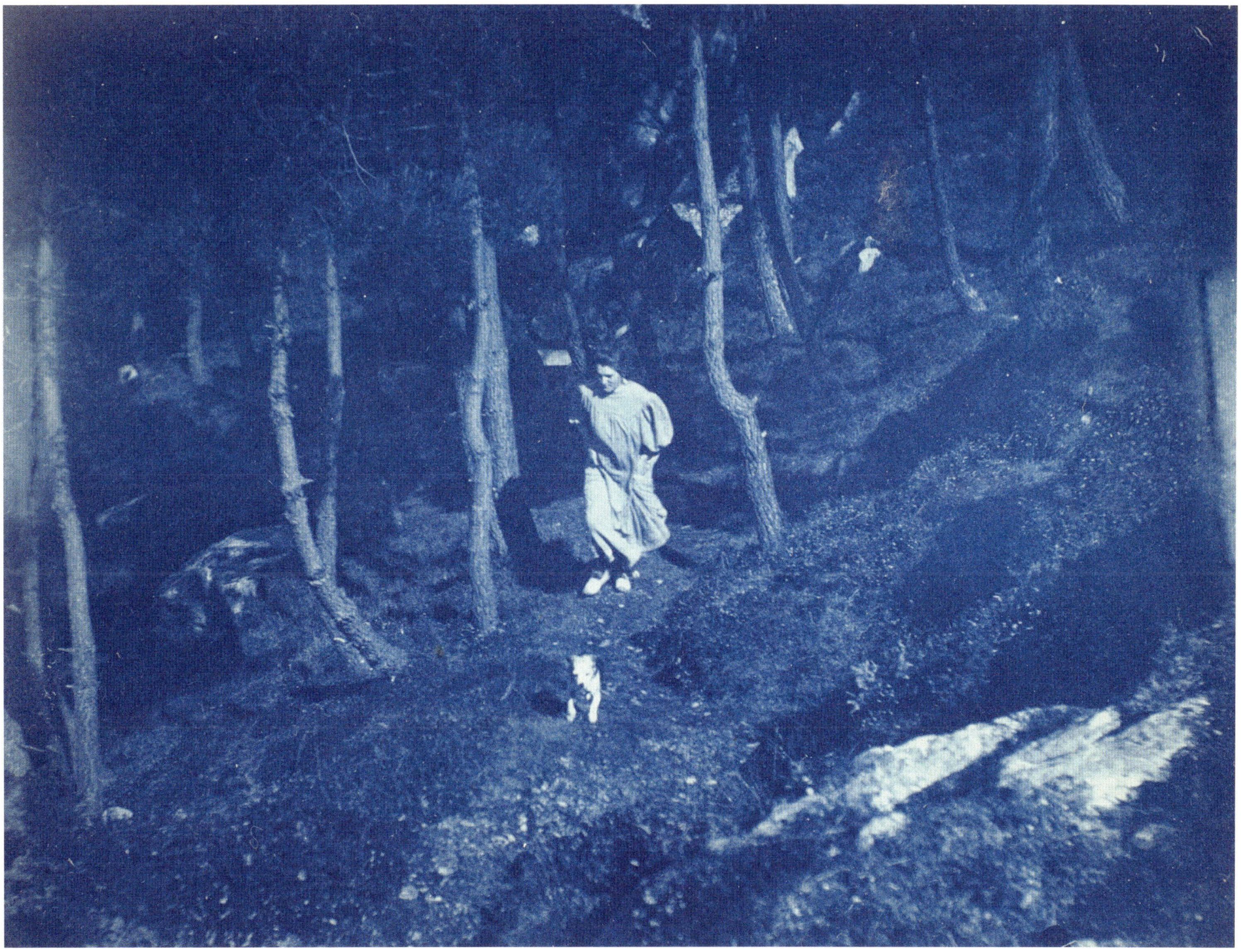

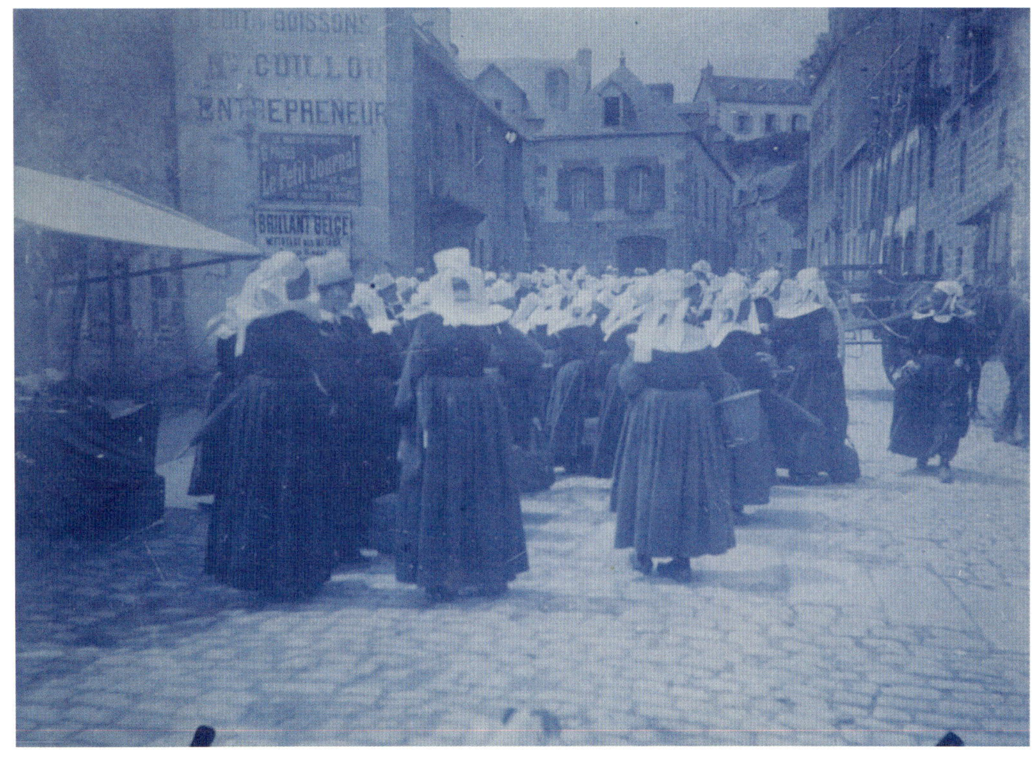

CAT. 149. Henri Rivière, Breton women in the street, ca. 1890. Cyanotype, $3^{1}/_{4}$ x $4^{5}/_{8}$ in. (8.4 x 11.9 cm) image, $3^{1}/_{2}$ x 5 in. (8.8 x 12.7 cm) sheet. Zimmerli Art Museum at Rutgers University. David A. and Mildred H. Morse Art Acquisition Fund

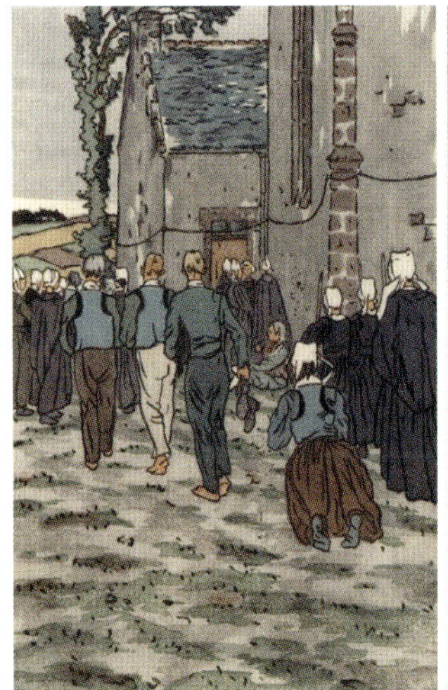
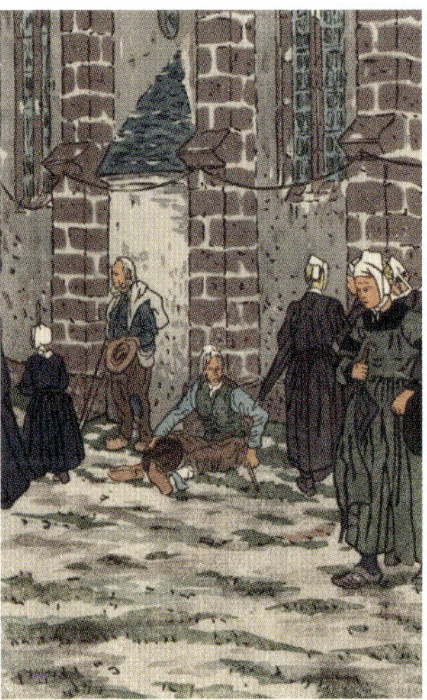
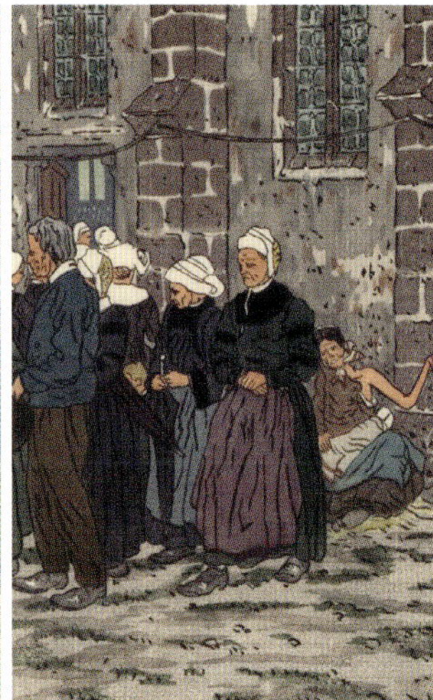
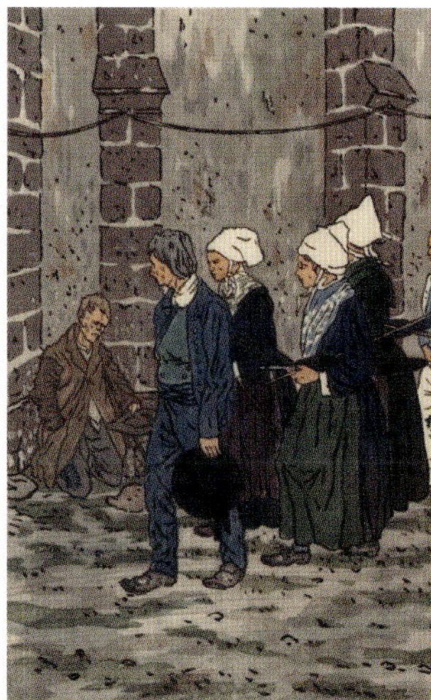
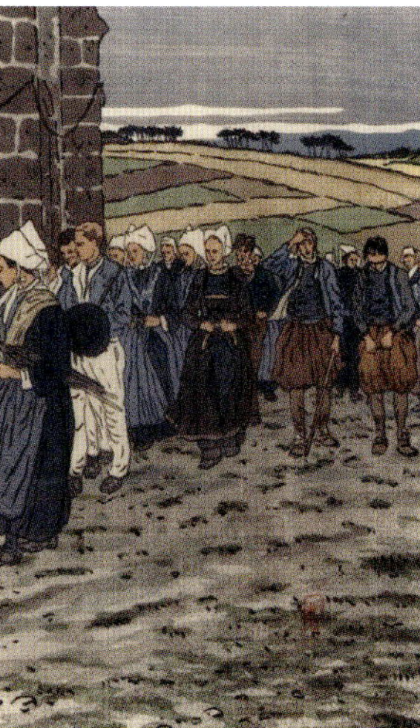

CAT. 150. Henri Rivière, *Le pardon de Sainte-Anne-la-Palud* (The Pardon of St. Anne-la-Palud), number 38 from the series *Paysages bretons* (Breton Landscapes), 1892–93. Five color woodcuts, $13^{1}/_{2}$ x 9 in. (34.3 x 22.8 cm) each sheet. Zimmerli Art Museum at Rutgers University. Gift of Sara and Armond Fields

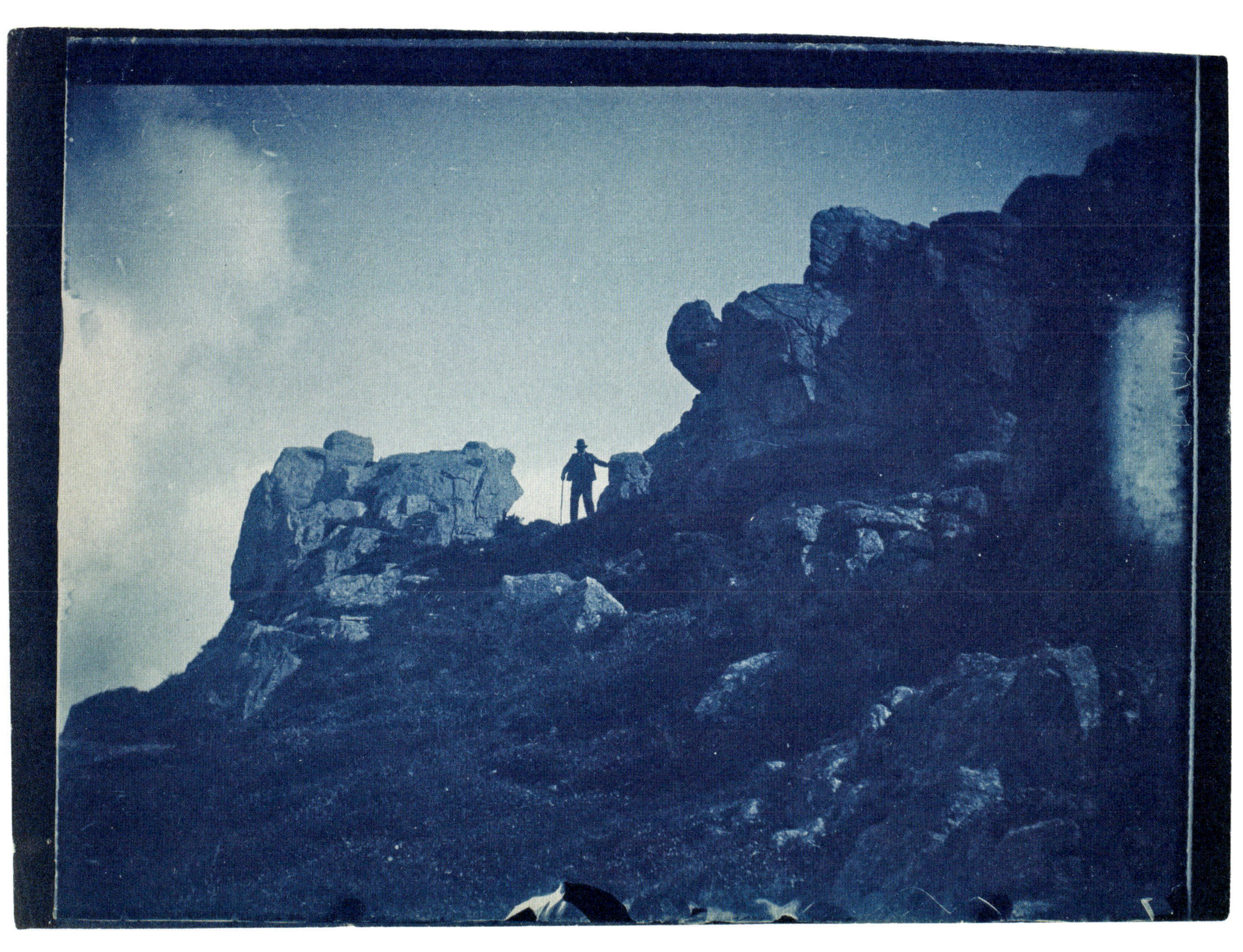

CAT. 151. Henri Rivière, Man walking in a rocky landscape, ca. 1890–1900. Cyanotype, $3^{1/2} \times 4^{3/4}$ in. (9 x 12 cm). Musée d'Orsay, Paris

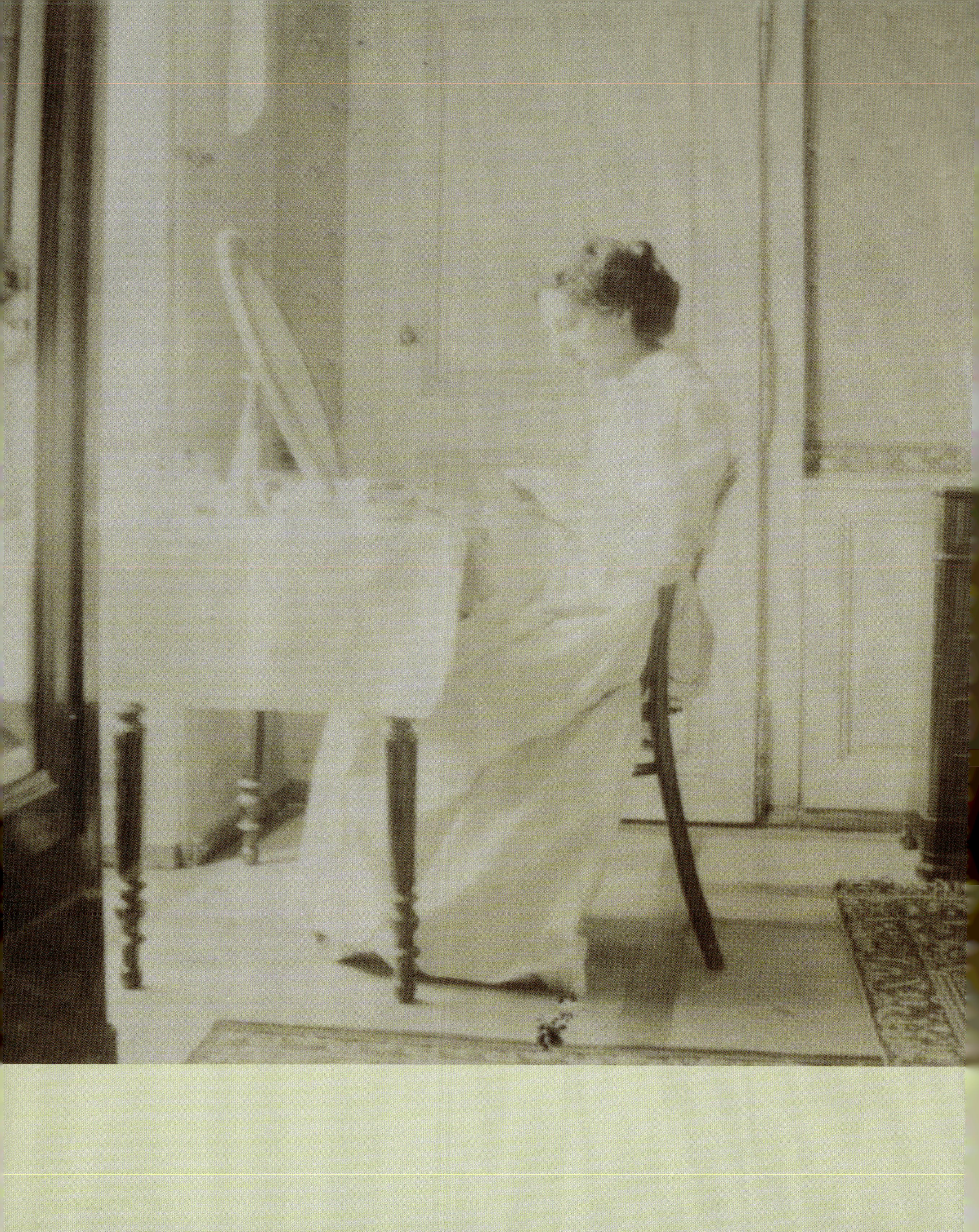

Vallotton and Photography: Freeze Frame

Katia Poletti

The photographic archives of Félix Vallotton are modest indeed, especially when compared to those of his friend Edouard Vuillard. They only include about twenty photographs, offering just a few further parallels with paintings in addition to those pictures already published.[1] Why have so few images been found in the archives of an artist who took up photography in 1899? The scathing criticism he received when it became known that he had painted a nude from a photograph may have driven him to destroy similar items of evidence.[2] In 1916, Vallotton was harshly attacked for borrowing the central figure of his large painting *L'été* (Summer) (1912; Musée cantonal des beaux-arts, Lausanne, Ducrey no. 915) from a photograph that appeared in the bimonthly magazine *L'étude académique* in 1908.[3]

As a portrait artist, Vallotton used photographs in 1901 and 1902, including some taken by Félix Nadar, in a series of eight "decorative portraits" of famous men.[4] Although these pictures reflect a common, indeed traditional, use of photography, in this context, they hearken back to the woodcut portraits and illustrative "masks" of the 1890s, in which Vallotton identified a character with but a few lines and black marks. He generally obtained this effect of synthesis by working from photographs, accentuating their contrasts by eliminating the grays and retaining only the strong opposition between black and white. In 1898, the German art critic and historian Julius Meier-Graefe, who was Vallotton's first biographer, attributed the artist's ability to re-create the facial and psychological traits of a character with such economy of means to his use of photography.[5]

In fact, the artist's most innovative use of photography in his painting coincided with his purchase, in 1899, of a Kodak No. 2 Bullet, Model 1898.[6] With this cube-shaped device, which took 3½ x 3½–inch photographs on No. 101 film, he was able to foreshadow certain pictures with his own photographs. These images were not simply the basis for some of Vallotton's paintings but were also a means of expression whose particular language the painter exploited. In its emphatic two-dimensionality, photography was a medium formally suited to the aesthetics of flatness favored by the Nabis.

The first painting Vallotton made as a Nabi, *Le bain au soir d'été* (Bath on a Summer Evening) (1892–93; Kunsthaus Zürich, Ducrey no. 140), marks a turning point in his approach. Here, he abandoned relief, perspective, details, and any conformity to reality in favor of flat surfaces and arabesques (see also cat. 163). Taking photographs influenced Vallotton's

DETAIL OF CAT. 158

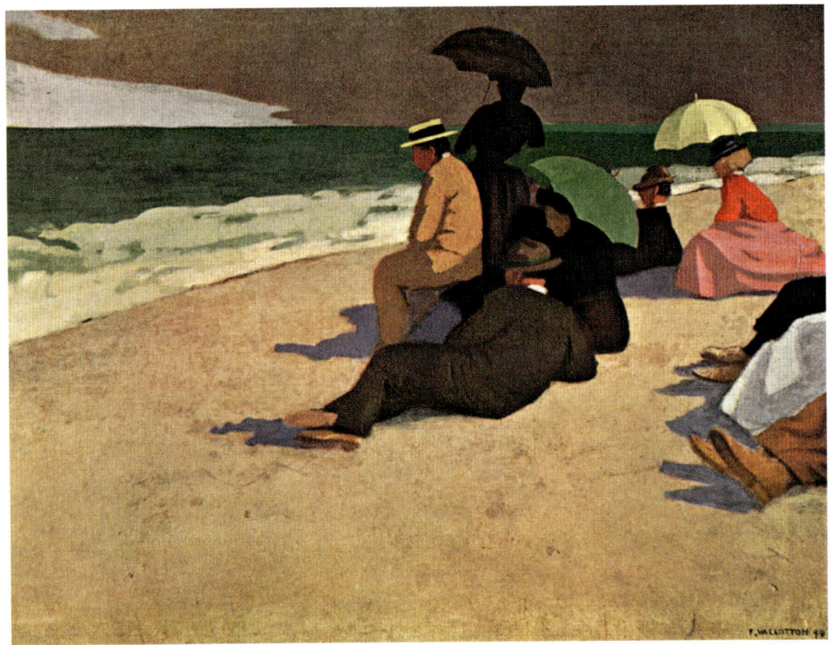

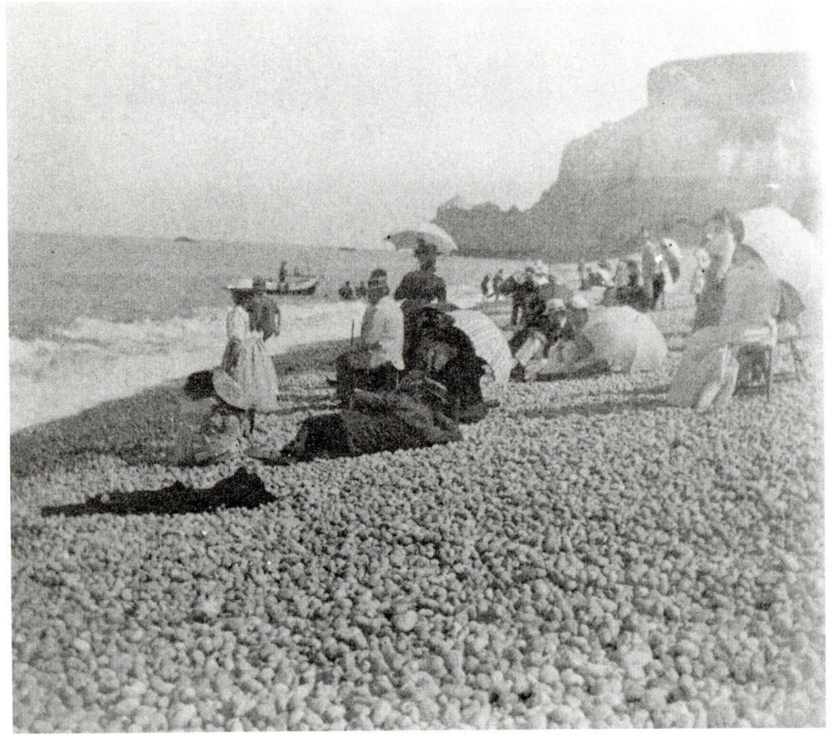

FIG. 1. Félix Vallotton, *Plage d'Etretat* (Beach at Etretat), 1899. Oil on card, 20⅛ x 26⅛ in. (51 x 66.5 cm). Private collection, France

FIG. 2. Félix Vallotton, Beach at Etretat, 1899. Gelatin silver print. Private collection

creative processes by granting him a particular way of seeing that generated new pictorial forms featuring evocative approaches to the framing of elements offscreen (fig. 1), audacious points of view (see fig. 4), and hitherto unseen lighting effects (cat. 157). Between 1899 and 1901, he used backlighting in some interiors; this allowed him to show the figure in silhouette, with an absence of any kind of relief (cat. 159).

Both Vuillard and Vallotton took similar square pictures with their Kodaks. On November 23, 1899, Vuillard wrote Vallotton to thank him for some photographs he had just sent. "They make me very happy," he declared, "and show me even more clearly the vanity of some ideas for paintings."[7] Because the two friends apparently exchanged photographs, it seems likely that some of Vallotton's are in Vuillard's archives and that one or two snapshots in Vallotton's archives were taken by Vuillard; a few identical pictures are in both archives. Like Vuillard, Vallotton took amateur photographs of domestic subjects, capturing moments in his everyday life. He treats the same themes in his paintings — that is, interiors featuring his wife, Gabrielle, overseeing their household or sitting at her dressing table.

Vallotton began taking photographs in the summer of 1899 in Etretat, a fashionable holiday resort on the Normandy coast. He would spend the period from July to late September with Gabrielle and her three children at the local château, where friends such as Thadée and Misia Natanson and Vuillard would visit them.[8] There is no difference between the photographs he shot for personal satisfaction — such as pictures of holiday outings and domestic scenes — and those he intended as prompts for paintings. In his improvised studio in the Château d'Etretat, he painted both *La chambre rouge, Etretat* (Red Room, Etretat; cat. 153) and a series of beach scenes (fig. 1 and cat. 164) on the

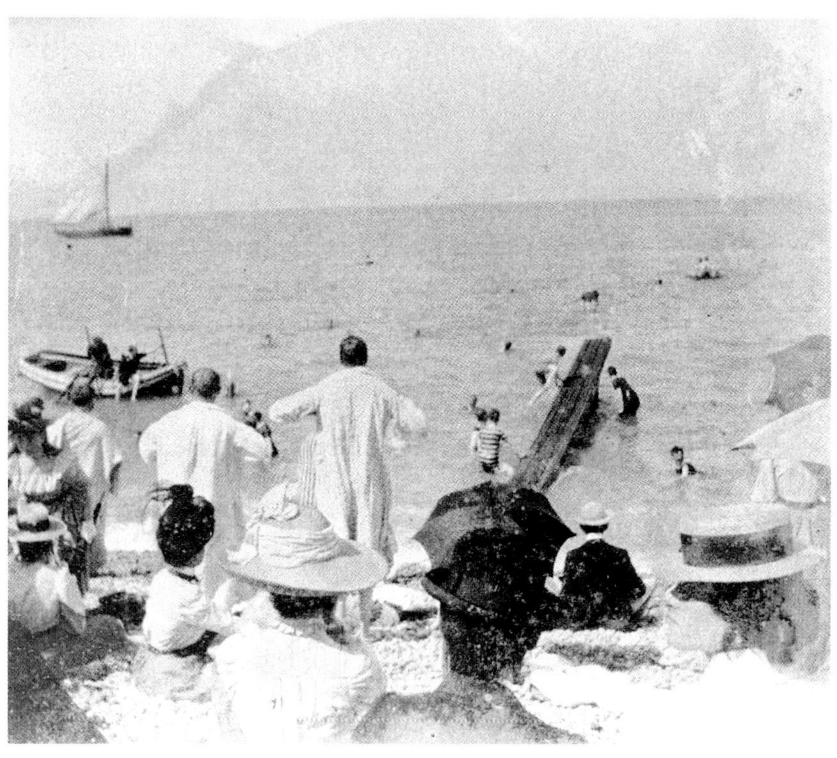

FIG. 3. Félix Vallotton, Beach at Etretat, 1899. Gelatin silver print. Private collection

basis of indoor and outdoor snapshots (cats. 152, 165, 166 and figs. 2, 3).[9]

Rather than true landscapes, the latter are in reality snapshots of daily life by the sea, in the same spirit as the contemporary street scenes and views of Paris parks. The same people appear in two photographs that were taken from different angles within a few minutes of each other. Two little girls seated in the foreground of the first photograph (cat. 165) have moved closer to the water's edge in the second (fig. 2). The grouped figures remain in place: a man lying on his side, a seated woman holding a parasol, a seated man looking at the sea, and a standing woman. Vallotton reproduced the central group of the second snapshot almost exactly in the painting *Plage d'Etretat* (Beach at Etretat; see fig. 1). The additional figures and section of skirt framed by two male legs to the right look as if they were derived from a photograph that remains missing, as is the snapshot that most likely was the basis for *Sur la plage* (On the Beach; cat. 164). In a similar way, Vallotton undoubtedly isolated the scene's three protagonists from the crowd at the water's edge (seen in two photographs, cat. 166 and fig. 3), as either of the dark-haired women wearing boaters visible in both lower corners of the second photograph (fig. 3) could be the lady in a pink blouse on the left. This approach seems to reveal that he manipulated the photographic image to achieve the synthesis he sought in the subsequent painting.

Although Vallotton remained most faithful to his photographic model for *La chambre rouge, Etretat*, even this painting reveals manipulation (cats. 152, 153). The artist respected the snapshot's square configuration but altered a few details of the setting and his wife's expression; in the painting, she looks down at a baby who does not appear in the photograph.

A unique characteristic of photography is that it can capture a moving subject. It is likely that Vallotton based his painting *Le ballon* (The Ball; fig. 4) on a snapshot that caught its subject in mid-leap. Although the identity of the child remains uncertain, the setting is Villeneuve-sur-Yonne, in the garden of Le Relais, home of Thadée and Misia Natanson. It is possible to identify part of the graveled circular esplanade leading to the house and the dense vegetation of the garden. A photograph in Vuillard's archives from a series undoubtedly made by Vallotton, taken from an upper window of the house, shows the same child wearing a straw hat but no longer playing (fig. 5). Vuillard may have received this photograph, shot while both he and Vallotton were staying at Le Relais, in the fall of 1899. Vallotton would have sent this series to Vuillard shortly after finishing the painting *Le ballon*, which is known to be one of the last works he made that year.

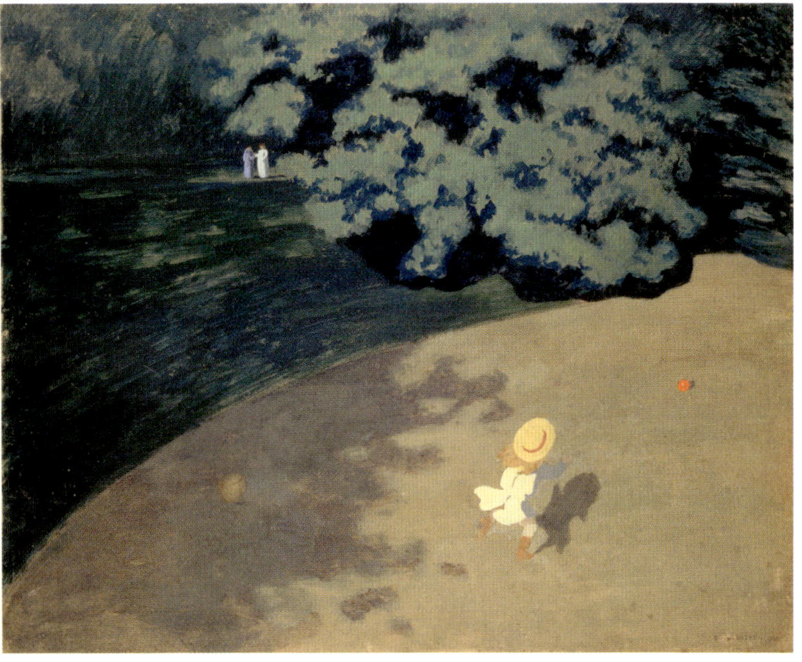

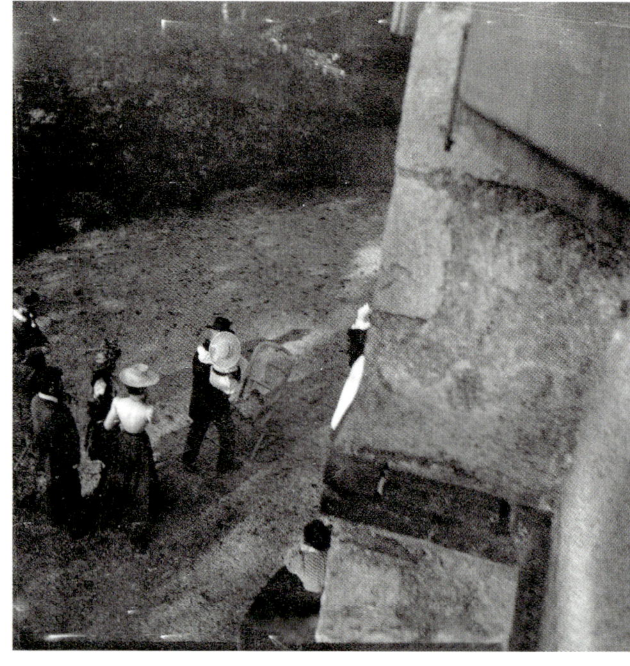

FIG. 4. Félix Vallotton, *Le ballon, ou Coin de parc avec enfant jouant au ballon* (The Ball, or Corner of the Park with a Child Playing with a Ball), 1899. Mineral spirit and gouache on card, 18⅞ x 24 in. (48 x 61 cm). Musée d'Orsay, Paris

FIG. 5. Félix Vallotton, Photo taken from a window of Le Relais, Villeneuve-sur-Yonne, 1899. Gelatin silver print. Archives Edouard Vuillard, private collection

The framing of the photograph of the curved gravel path perfectly intersects the right half of the painting, whose edge marks the end of the visible wall. This unusual perspective, excluding any glimpse of sky, is a formal solution made possible by photography. The similar conjunction of an unusual perspective and moving subjects finds its most eloquent expression in an 1893 woodcut, *La manifestation* (Demonstration).[10] In 1898, Julius Meier-Graefe noted this, writing, "[Vallotton] chooses the visual angle from which his objects most clearly reveal all the particularities of their movements. For example, a running mass gains movement when seen from a very low visual angle, in other words the more the organs of movement are presented to the lens. In 'La Manifestation' the eye is placed as low as possible."[11]

The use of photography in his landscapes with figures in the late 1890s enabled Vallotton to conceive the process of painting at a physical and temporal distance from the motif, a prelude to his later "composed landscapes."[12] He applied this process systematically in 1903, with sketches, but did not abandon photography, at least as a preliminary step to painting landscapes. With his new plate camera, he continued collecting material in the form of photographs.[13] Unfortunately, these have been lost, but sketches annotated with the word *photo* attest to their one-time existence.[14] Perhaps one day these photographs will reappear, along with those Vallotton undoubtedly used for interiors from 1900 to 1904. The snapshot nature of the motifs and absence of preparatory sketches almost certainly indicate the role photography played in the early-twentieth-century interior works of Félix Vallotton.

NOTES

1. See Isabelle de la Brunière and Philippe Grapeloup-Roche, "Vallotton and the Camera: Art and the Science of Photography," *Apollo* 138, no. 388 (June 1994): pp. 18–23, and, using the same examples, Eik Kahng, "Félix Vallotton's Photographic Realism," in Dorothy Kosinski, *The Artist and the Camera: Degas to Picasso*, exh. cat. (Dallas: Museum of Art; New Haven, Conn.: Yale University Press, 1999), pp. 227–35. In the catalogue raisonné of Vallotton's paintings (Marina Ducrey, in collaboration with Katia Poletti, *Félix Vallotton [1865–1925]: L'oeuvre peint*, 3 vols. [Milan: 5 Continents Editions, 2005]), unpublished photographs taken by Vallotton have been linked to the following paintings: *Plage d'Etretat* (figs. 1, 2, see Ducrey no. 272), *Le bain à Etretat* (The Bath at Etretat) (1899; private collection, see Ducrey no. 274), *Le ballon* (figs. 4, 5, see Ducrey no. 286), and *Vieille rue de Marseille* (Old Street of Marseille) (1901; private collection, see Ducrey no. 351). For Vallotton and photography, see also Marina Ducrey, "Vallotton et la photographie: 'Le droit de prendre mon bien où je le trouve,'" in ibid., 1: pp. 82–84.
2. "Je range des paperasses et détruis ce que je puis" (I organize papers and destroy what I can), the artist noted in his journal on April 7, 1919 (Félix Vallotton, *Documents pour une biographie et pour l'histoire d'une oeuvre*, ed. Gilbert Guisan and Doris Jakubec, 3 vols. [Lausanne and Paris: La bibliothèque des arts, 1973–75], 3: p. 237).
3. Regarding this debate, see ibid., pp. 134–35, and Ducrey, 3: pp. 526–29; the incriminating photograph is reproduced in the latter (fig. 915b). *L'étude académique* was published in Paris from 1904 to 1914. Further research would likely help establish that Vallotton used the photographs that appeared in this magazine more frequently than is suggested by the few examples so far known (see Ducrey nos. 236, 842, 915).
4. See Ducrey nos. 367, 368, 369, 394, 395, 397, 404, 405. These portraits are termed "decorative" in the Livre de raison, the record of his works Vallotton maintained from his first appearance at the Salon des artistes français in 1885 until his death. Preserved at the Fondation Félix Vallotton, Lausanne, the manuscript is reproduced in its entirety in Ducrey, 1: pp. 268–311.
5. "Ce procédé de conception, des plus subjectifs, explique le fait que Vallotton fait presque tout—et non seulement les portraits—de tête. Ses portraits naissent souvent de petites photographies très médiocres." (This conception process, of the most subjective kind, explains why Vallotton did almost everything—and not just his portraits—from memory. His portraits were often based on small and very mediocre photographs.) Julius Meier-Graefe, *Félix Vallotton: Biographie de cet artiste avec la partie la plus importante de son oeuvre éditée et différentes gravures originales et nouvelles* (Berlin: J. A. Stargardt; Paris: Edmond Sagot, 1898), pp. 21–22.
6. Vallotton's Kodak camera is preserved in a private collection. See Ducrey, 1: p. 84, fig. 72.
7. "Merci de votre lettre et des photos. Elles font mon bonheur et me font voir encore plus la vanité de certaines idées de peintures." Edouard Vuillard to Félix Vallotton, November 23, 1899, cited in Gilbert Guisan and Doris Jakubec, "Félix Vallotton, Edouard Vuillard et leurs amis de *La revue blanche*," *Etudes de lettres: Revue de la Faculté des lettres de l'Université de Lausanne* 8, no. 4 (October–December 1975): p. 19.
8. Thadée Natanson was co-editor-in-chief of *La revue blanche*, whose most regular illustrator was Vallotton. It ceased publication in 1903, the same year the Nabis group dissolved.
9. Ducrey nos. 265–80.
10. Maxime Vallotton and Charles Goerg, *Félix Vallotton: Catalogue Raisonné of the Printed Graphic Work* (Geneva: Les Editions de Bonvent, 1972), no. 110.
11. "[Vallotton] choisit l'angle visuel sous lequel ses objets révèlent, autant que possible, toutes les particularités de leurs mouvements. Une masse en train de courir, par exemple, gagne en mouvement lorsqu'on la considère sous un angle visuel très bas, c'est à dire plus les organes du mouvement se présentent sous l'objectif. Dans 'La Manifestation' l'oeil est placé aussi bas que possible." Meier-Graefe, *Félix Vallotton*, p. 42.
12. For the composed landscapes, see Marina Ducrey, "Paysages," in Ducrey, 1: pp. 165–93.
13. In a September 24, 1909, letter to his brother Paul, Vallotton suggests that he did the developing himself: "Attached 2 photos you'll like: printed by me. 13–18. clear weather, yellow screen. 13/4 m exposure ordinary plates" (Ducrey, 1: p. 84).
14. See sketch and the notes referring to photographs in Ducrey, 1: p. 172, fig. 175.

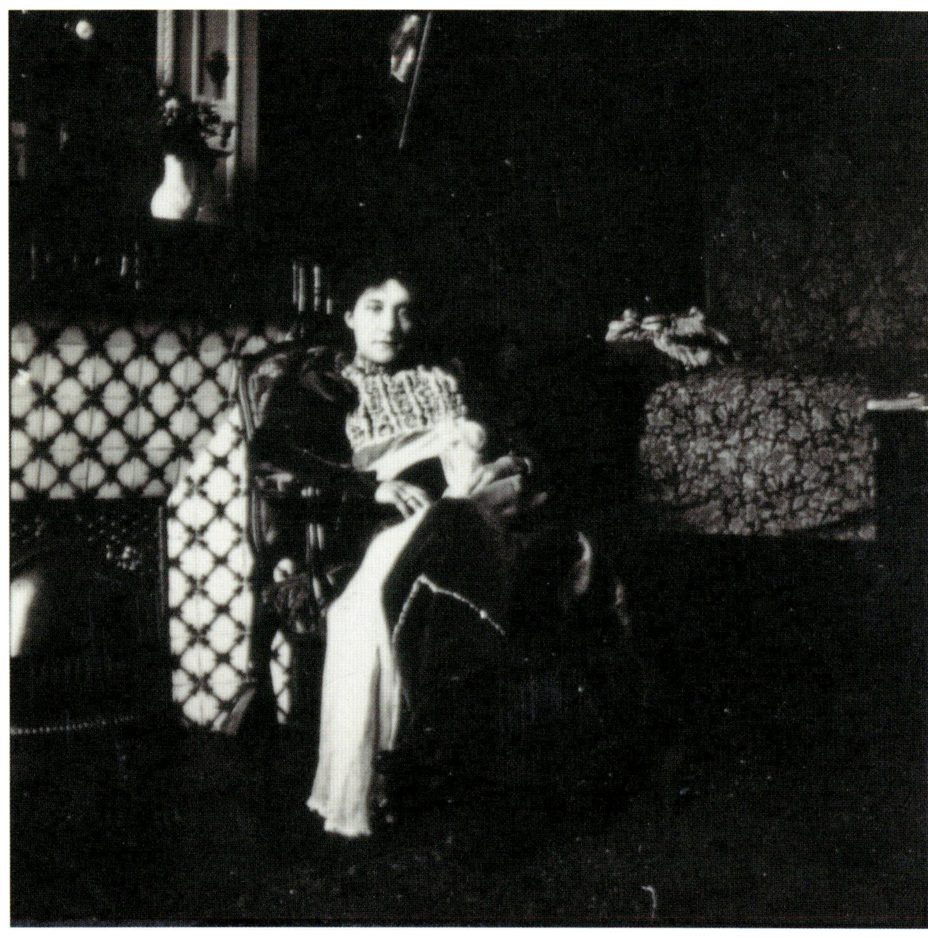

CAT. 152. Félix Vallotton, Gabrielle Vallotton seated before a fireplace, 1899. Gelatin silver print, 3½ x 3½ in. (9 x 9 cm). Isabelle de la Brunière

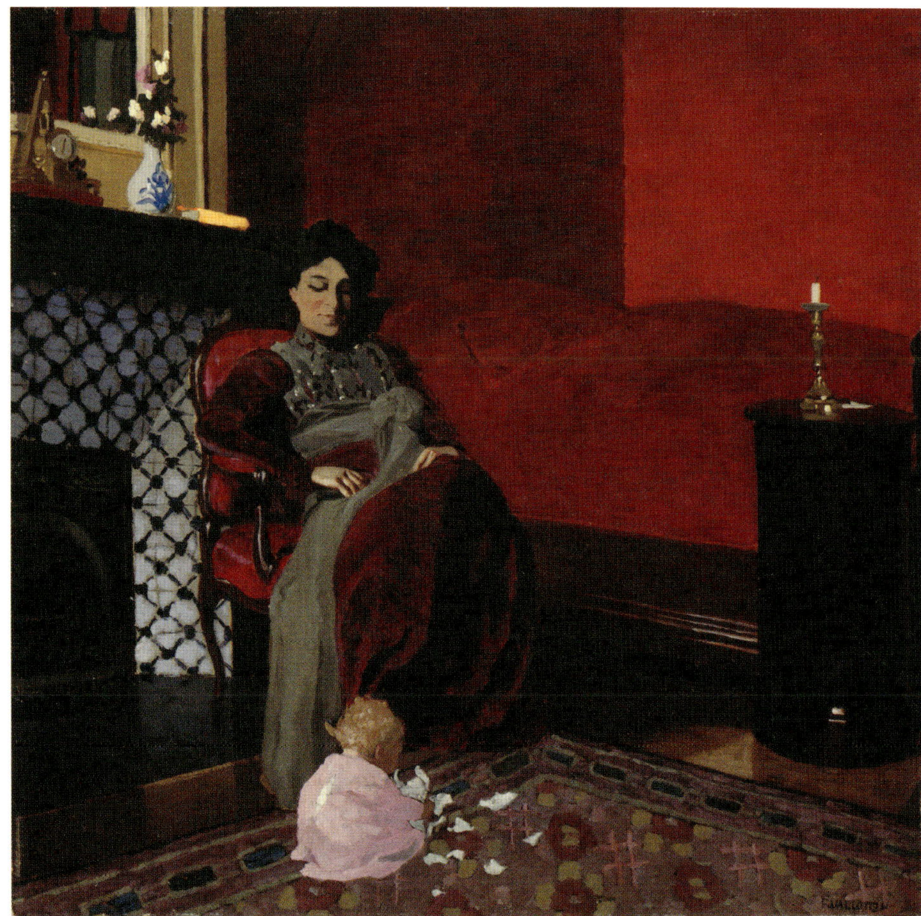

CAT. 153. Félix Vallotton, *La chambre rouge, Etretat* (Red Room, Etretat), 1899. Oil on board, 19⅜ x 20⅜ in. (49.2 x 51.3 cm). The Art Institute of Chicago. Bequest of Mrs. Clive Runnells

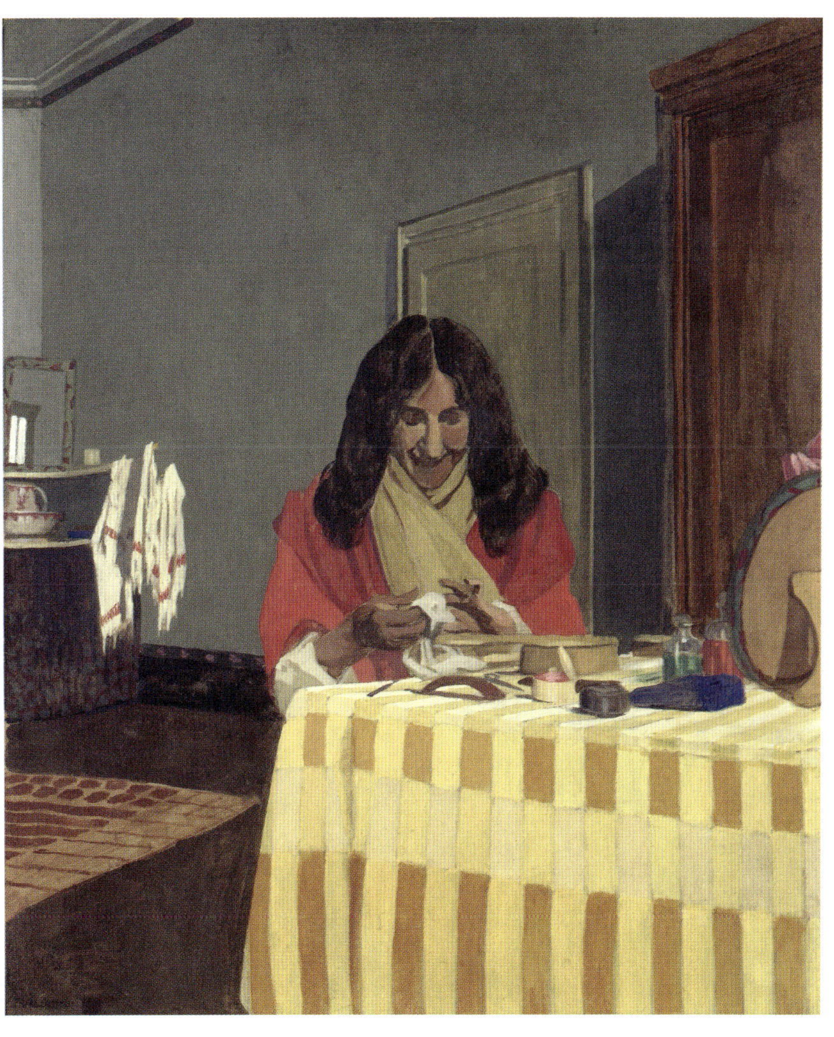

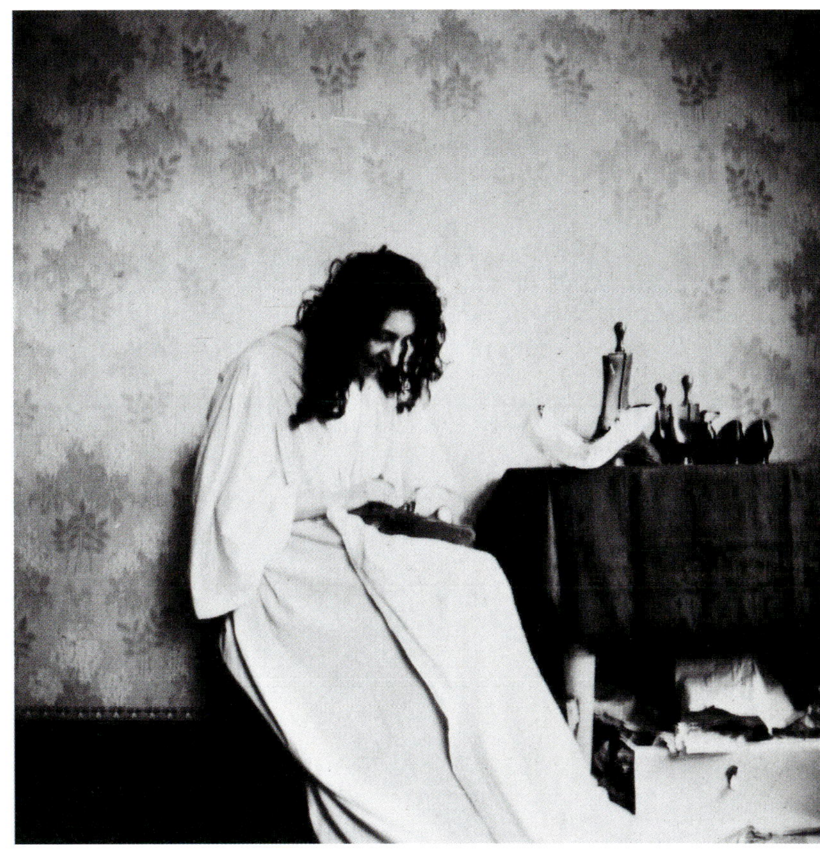

CAT. 154. Félix Vallotton, *Gabrielle Vallotton Doing Her Nails*, 1899. Oil on board, 23 x 19⅝ in. (58.5 x 50 cm). Musée d'Orsay, Paris

CAT. 155. Félix Vallotton, Gabrielle Vallotton at the Villa Beaulieu, 1901. Gelatin silver print, 3½ x 3½ in. (9 x 9 cm). Isabelle de la Brunière

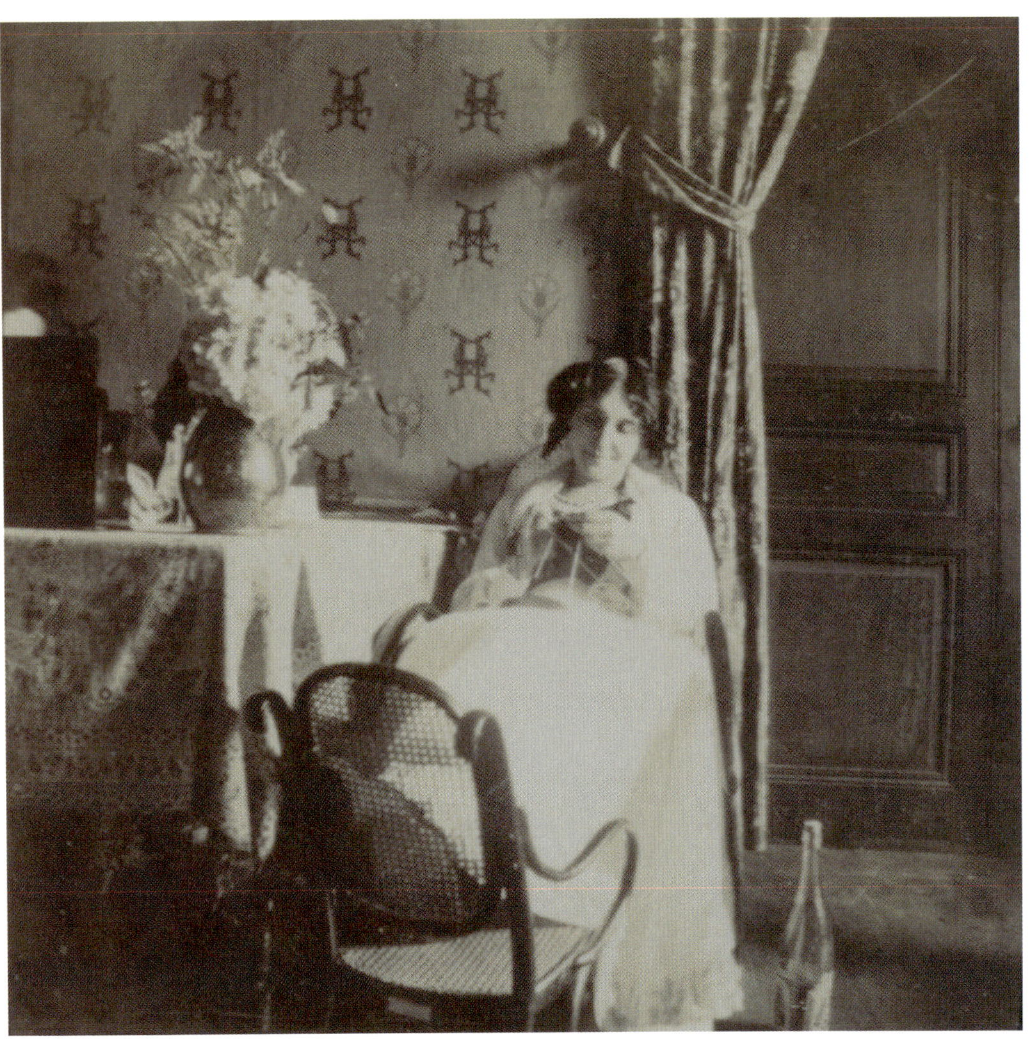

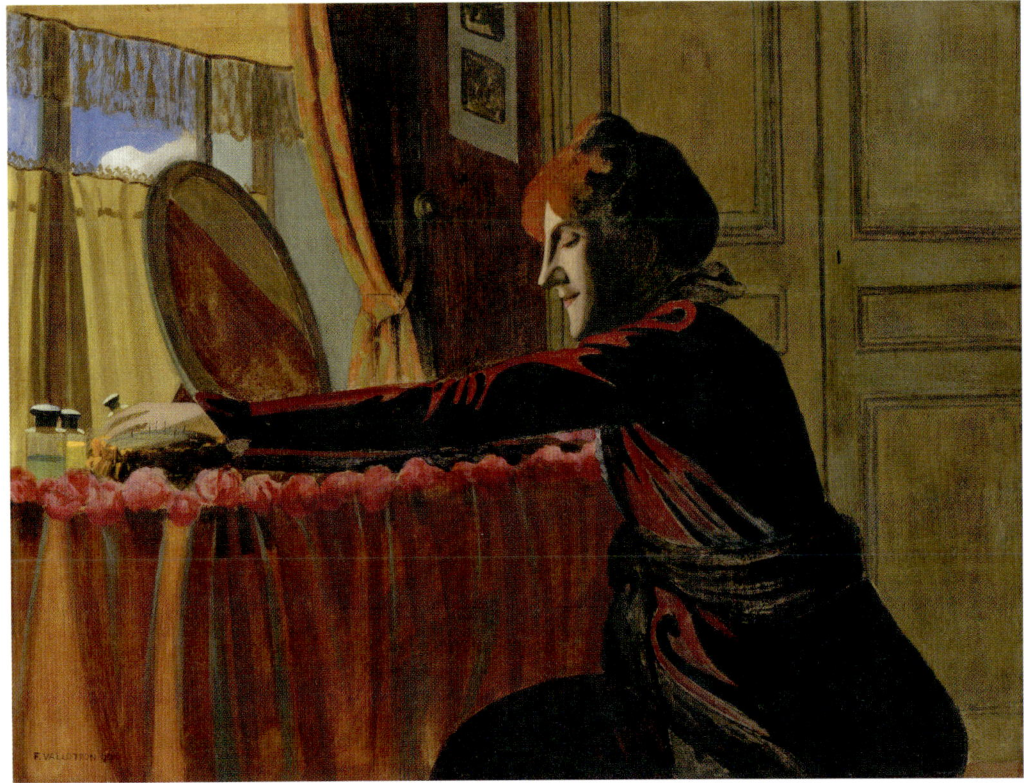

CAT. 156. Félix Vallotton, Gabrielle Vallotton knitting in a rocking chair, Cricqueboeuf, 1902. Gelatin silver print, 3½ x 3½ in. (9 x 9 cm). Isabelle de la Brunière

CAT. 157. Félix Vallotton, *Gabrielle Vallotton at Her Vanity*, 1899. Distemper on board, 22⅝ x 30¾ in. (57.5 x 78 cm). Kunsthaus Zürich

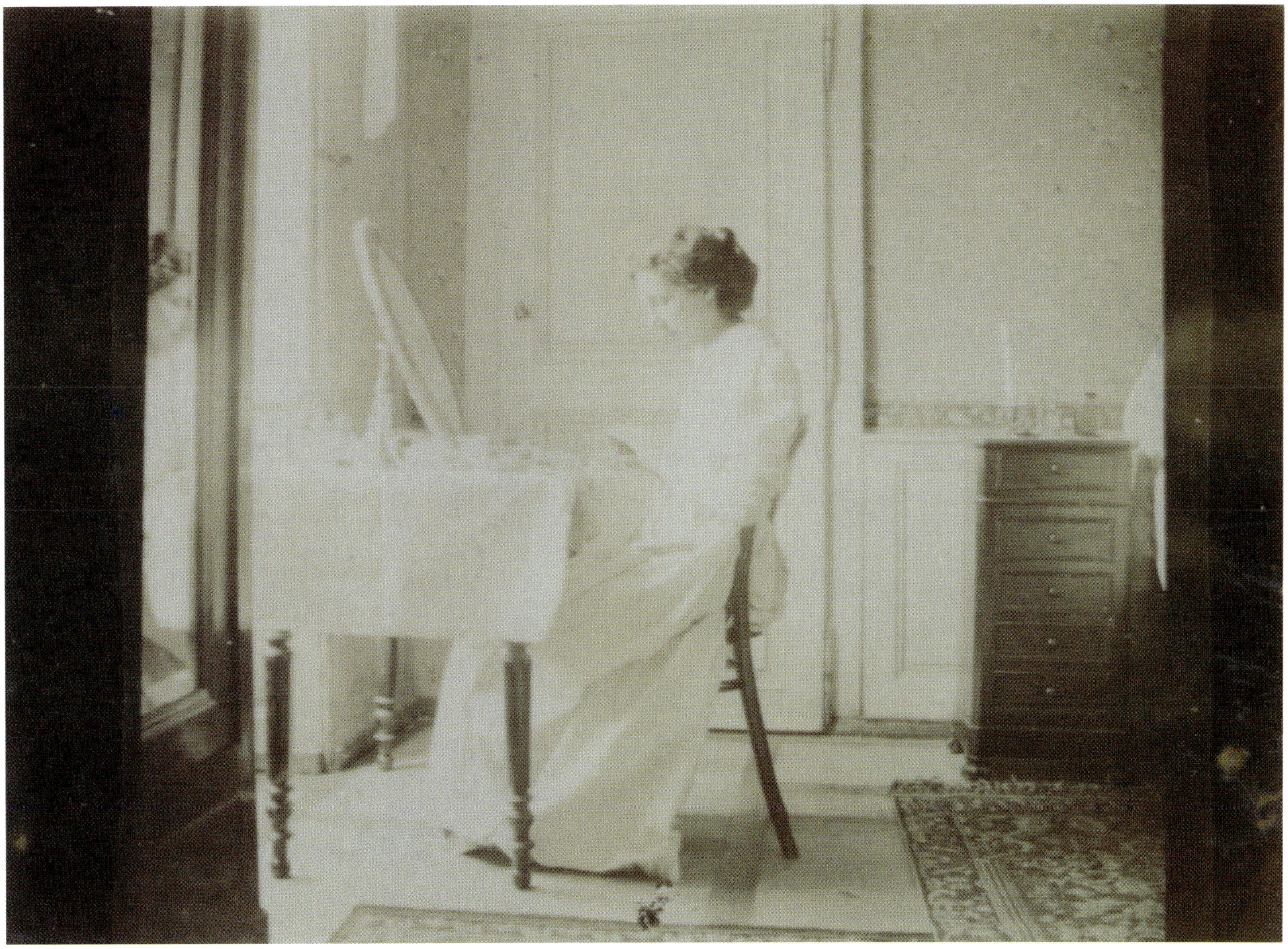

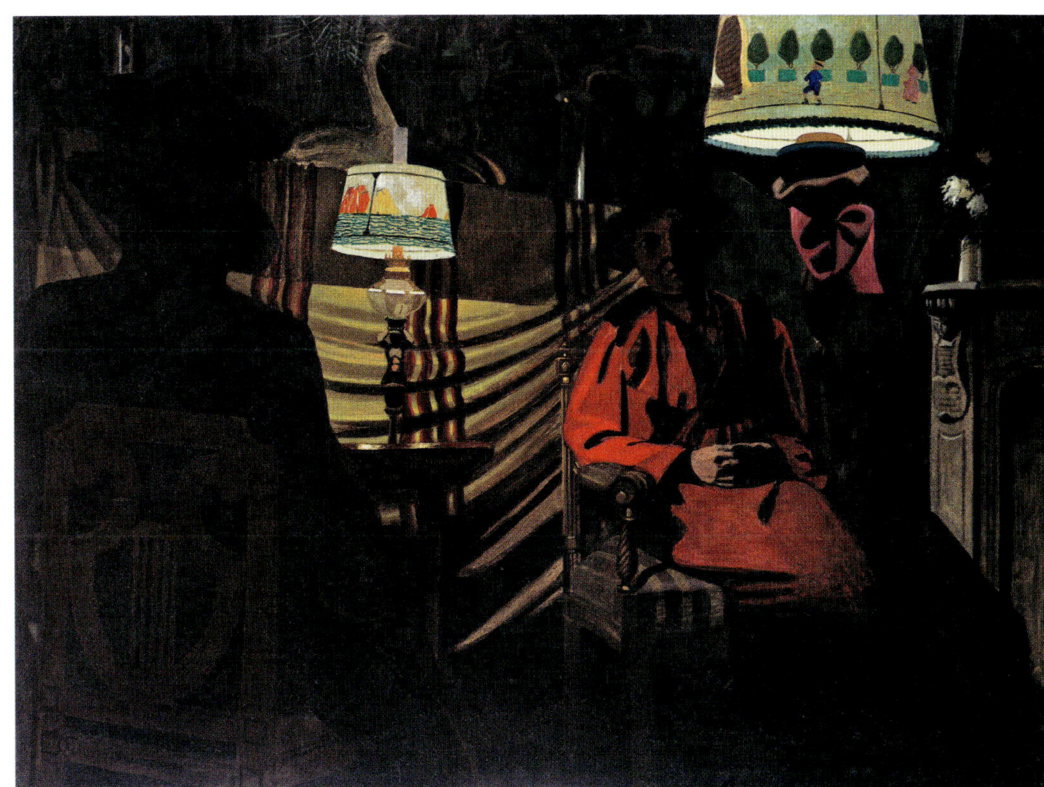

CAT. 158. Félix Vallotton, Gabrielle Vallotton manicuring her nails, ca. 1900. Gelatin silver print, $3^{1}/_{2}$ x $4^{3}/_{4}$ in. (9 x 12 cm). Isabelle de la Brunière

CAT. 159. Félix Vallotton, *La visite, effet de lampe* (The Visit, Lamp Effect), 1899–1900. Oil on board, $31^{7}/_{8}$ x $43^{7}/_{8}$ in. (81 x 111.5 cm). Kunstmuseum Winterthur. Purchase, 1973

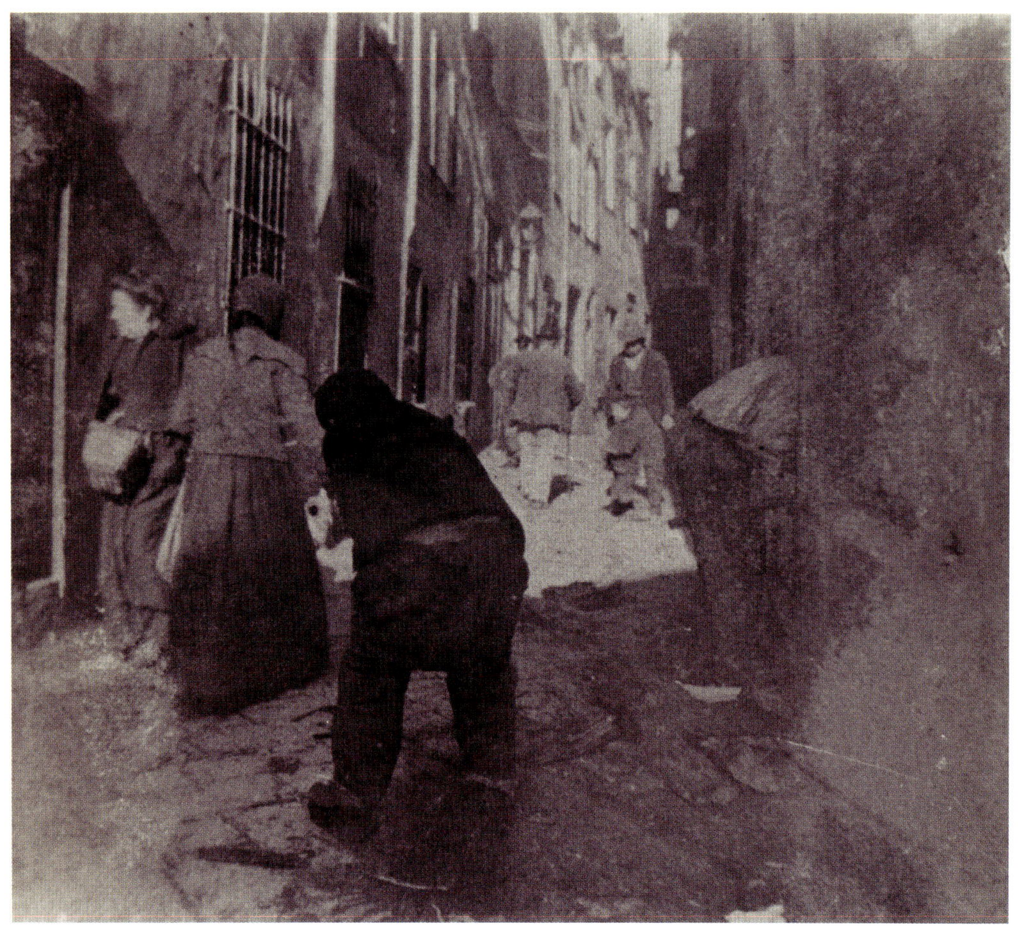

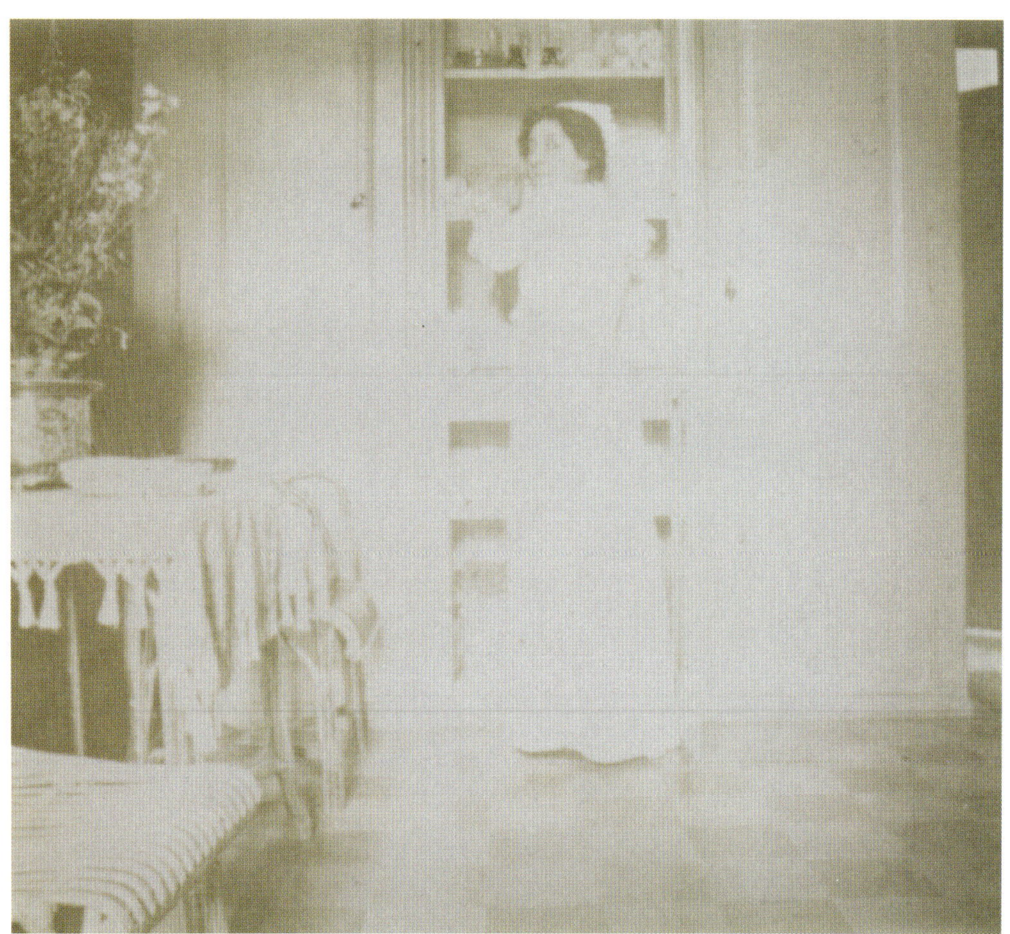

CAT. 160. Félix Vallotton, Alley in Marseille, 1901. Gelatin silver print. Private collection

CAT. 161. Félix Vallotton, Gabrielle Vallotton in a nightgown standing before an open cupboard, 1900. Gelatin silver print, 3½ x 4¾ in. (9 x 12 cm). Isabelle de la Brunière

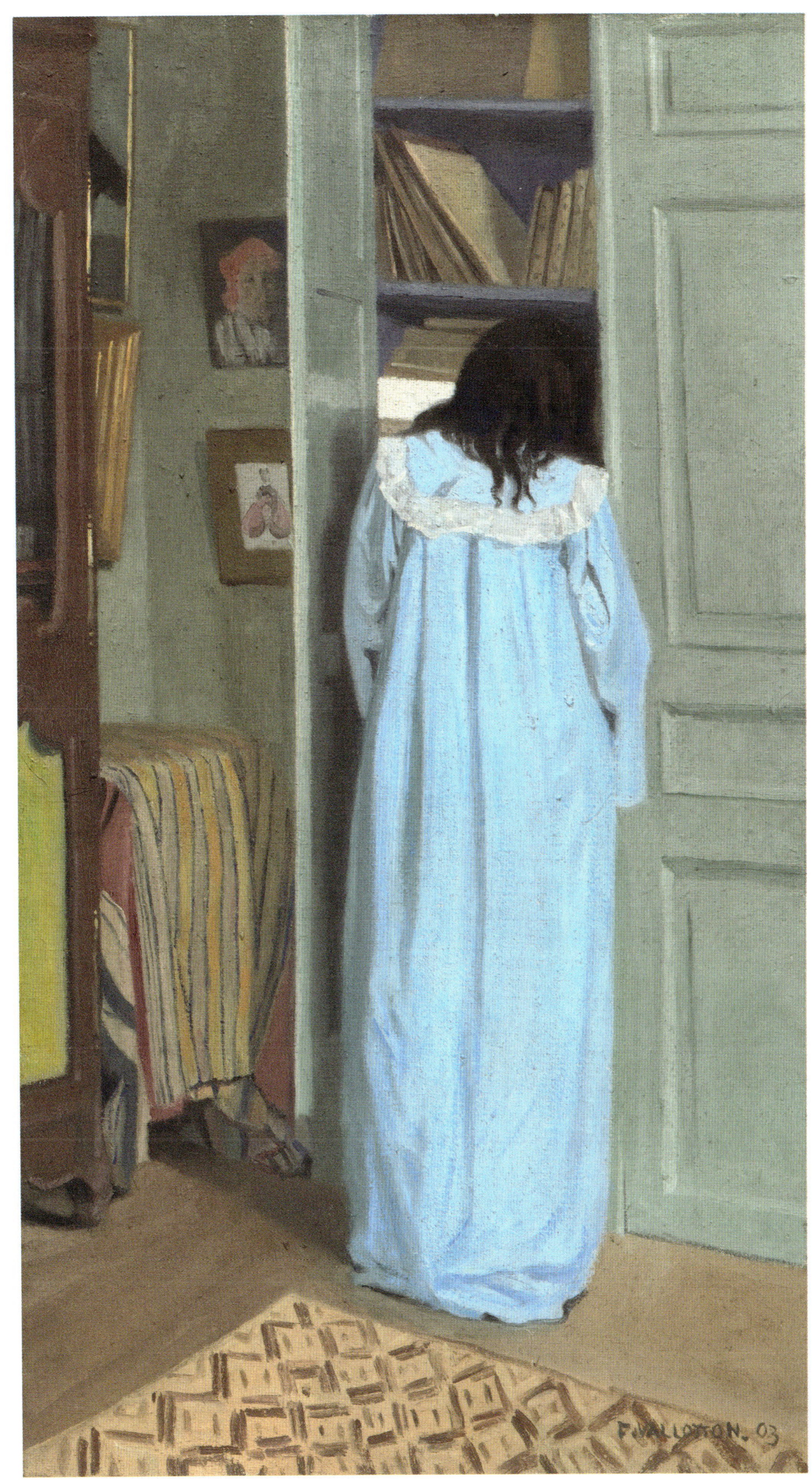

CAT. 162. Félix Vallotton, *Femme en bleu fouillant dans une armoire* (Woman in Blue Rummaging in an Armoire), 1903. Oil on canvas, 31⅞ x 18⅛ in. (81 x 46 cm). Musée d'Orsay, Paris. Acquired with the assistance of Philippe Meyer, 1997

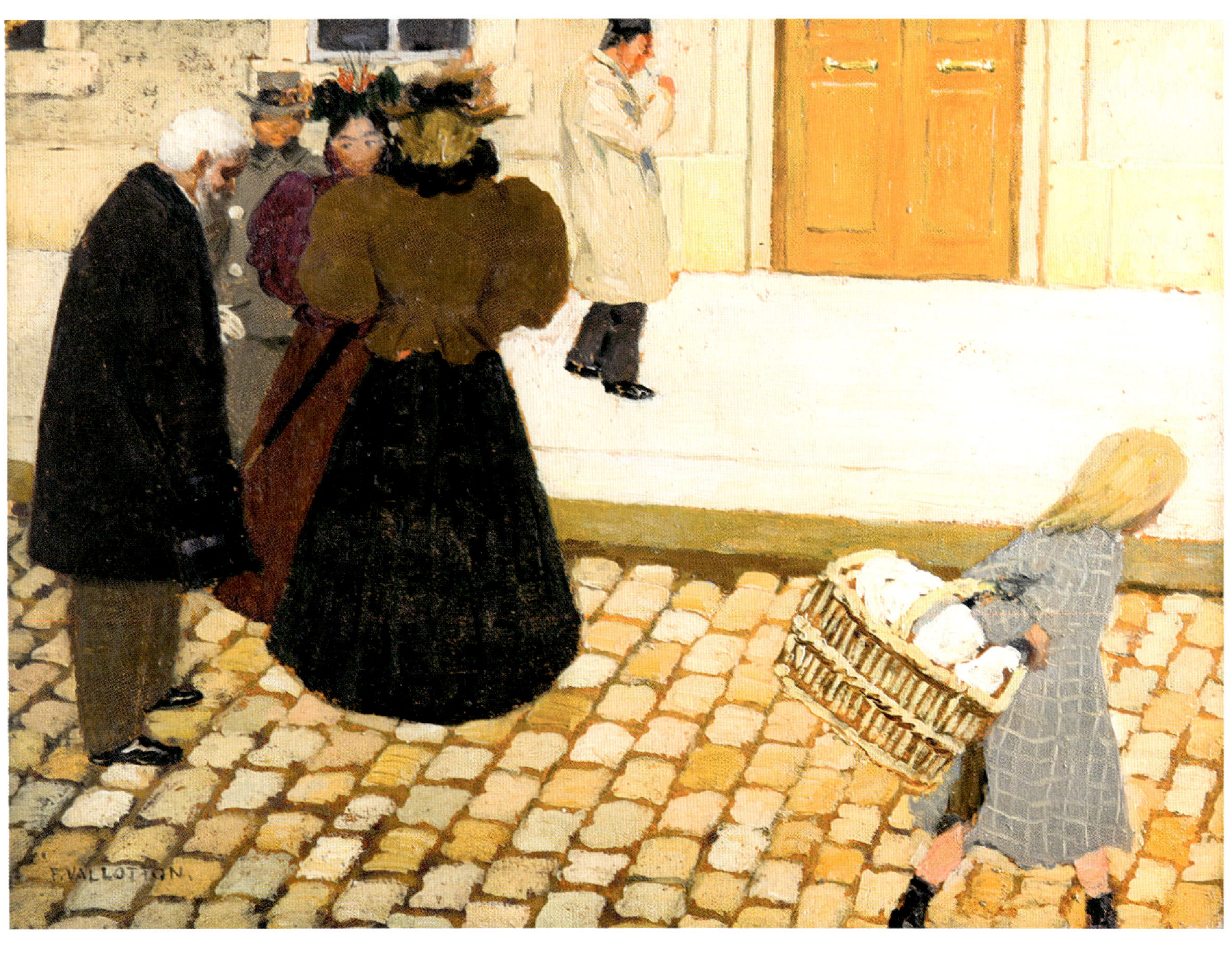

CAT. 163. Félix Vallotton, *Scène de rue* (Street Scene), ca. 1895. Oil on board, 10³/₈ x 13³/₄ in. (26.5 x 35 cm). Private collection

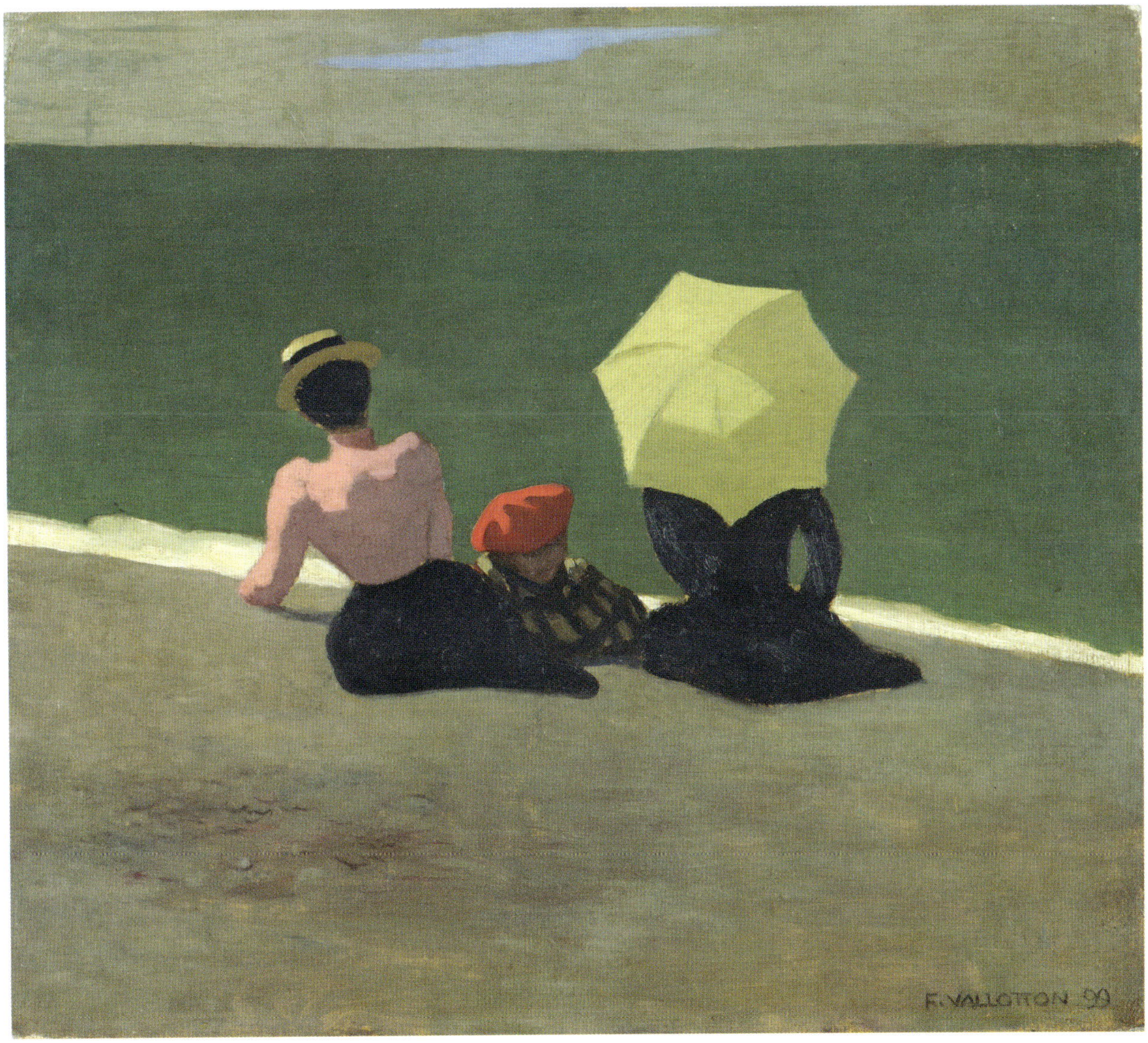

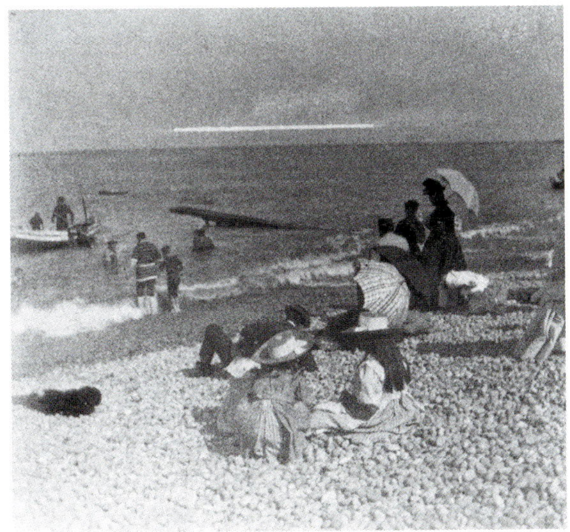

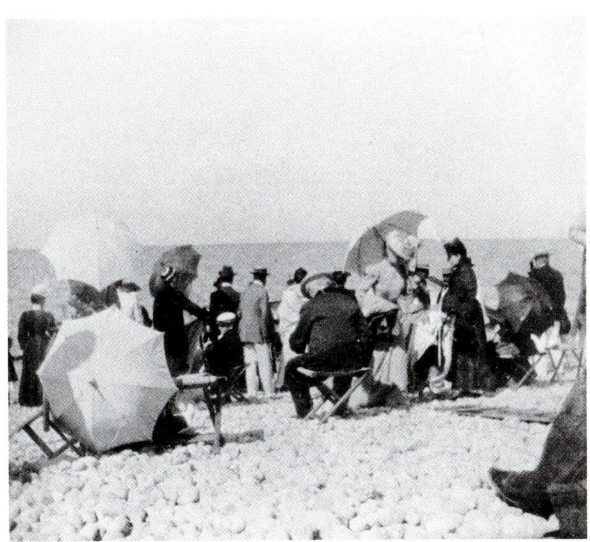

TOP: CAT. 164. Félix Vallotton, *Sur la plage* (On the Beach), 1899. Oil on board, $16\frac{1}{2} \times 18\frac{7}{8}$ in. (42 x 48 cm). Private collection, Switzerland

BOTTOM LEFT: CAT. 165. Félix Vallotton, Beach at Etretat, 1899. Gelatin silver print. Private collection

BOTTOM RIGHT: CAT. 166. Félix Vallotton, Beach at Etretat, 1899. Gelatin silver print. Private collection

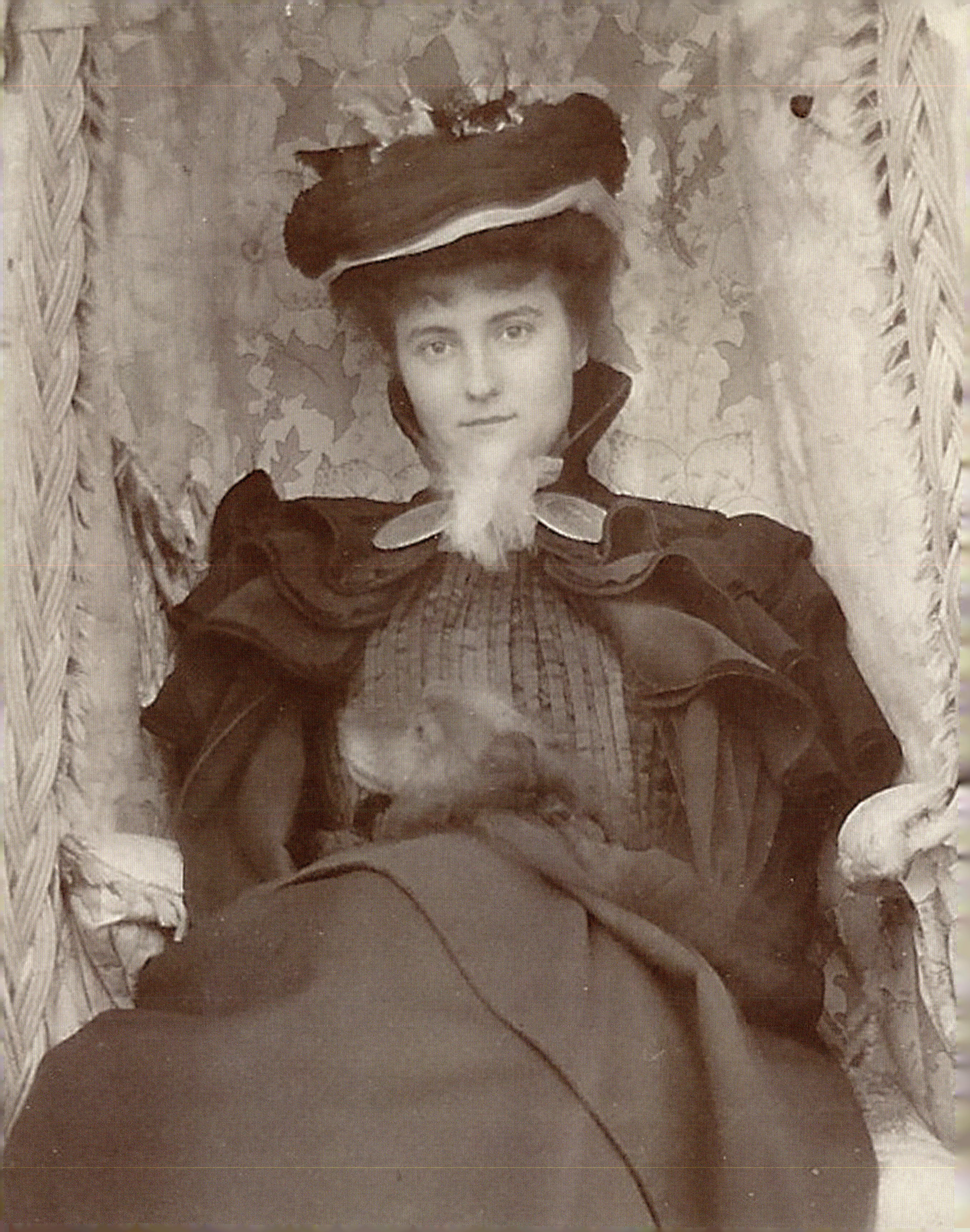

Edouard Vuillard's Photography and the Limitations of Truth

Elizabeth W. Easton

Edouard Vuillard, whose intimate scenes of family and close friends define a whole genre of post-Impressionist painting, densely layered his pictures with pigment and meaning. Carefully composed, with distortions deliberately designed to enhance the drama of the subject, Vuillard's pictures evoke the power of his imagination and craft. Surprisingly, his almost two thousand surviving photographs reveal quite a different approach to image making: Some are rendered with the casualness and rapidity traditionally associated with the snapshot, while others are as studied as his painted compositions.

The many Kodak envelopes that remain in Vuillard's archive (fig. 1) indicate that he would have his rolls of film developed and then print his pictures at home.[1] Comments from his diary such as "take photos to be developed so as not to lose time" suggest that Vuillard was more interested in the resulting printed image than in the process.[2] At the same time, several notes in his journal and in accounts from his intimate circle indicate that either Vuillard or his mother would supervise the printing: "When the number 12 appeared on the little red window of the camera, Vuillard took it to his usual supplier, close to where he lived in the Rue de Clichy, to have it reloaded. The printing of the film was then entrusted to his mother.

DETAIL OF CAT. 174

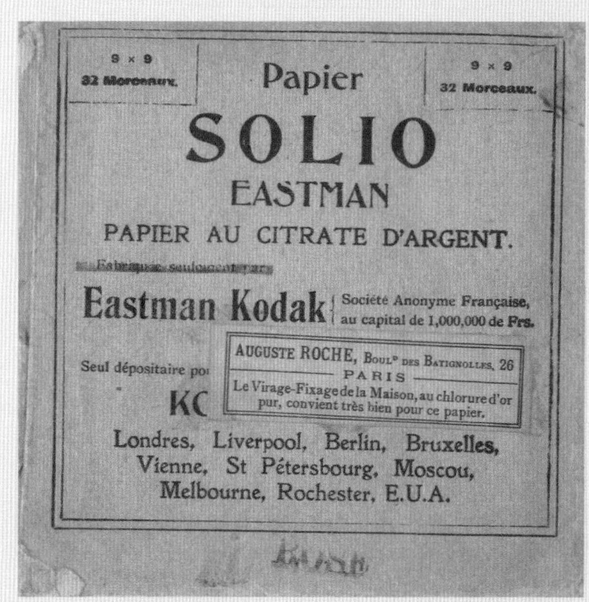

FIG. 1. Eastman Kodak, Solio paper envelope. 3¾ x 3¾ in. (9.5 x 9.5 cm). Private collection, Paris

Sitting by the window overlooking the square, doing some embroidery, she watched the frame exposed to the light and when it was time she proceeded to the 'fixing' in a soup plate."[3]

Vuillard's small canvases of the late 1880s and early 1890s demonstrated an increasing departure from a realistic pictorial rendition, with the artist taking escalating liberties with color, line, and space. Using multiple points of view, enlarging the foreground while minimizing elements of the background, and utilizing a scrim composed of dots of paint that hover on the surface, Vuillard manipulated the picture surface to be alluringly decorative and the space within the composition to be tantalizingly unknowable (cats. 168, 171, 195).

Like his Nabis confrères and other artists of the post-Impressionist generation, Vuillard (much inspired by Gauguin) embraced an aesthetic that was less about appearance and more about portraying his imagination on the canvas. How he reconciled this deliberate departure from objective reality with the vivid recordings of the camera poses an intriguing conundrum which scholars have begun to explore.[4]

Vuillard's photographic oeuvre is diverse. There are pictures that were specifically intended as studies for paintings, or that were used in retrospect as such; pictures whose compositions resemble those of certain paintings post-facto; and many pictures for which there is no equivalent in paint.

Many of his photographs resemble compositions Vuillard painted years before he snapped the shutter. In *The Blue Sleeve* (cat. 169), painted in 1893, he presents a dramatic composition, with his sister, Marie, occupying almost the entire foreground of the canvas, turning toward the viewer over her shoulder; an almost invisible figure in the background is dwarfed by the blue sleeve of her dress. Spatial complexities abound: The transition from foreground to background is achieved by a triangle of light beige (a newspaper) that connects to the darker beige of a table receding at a diagonal into the distance. Similarly, in the photograph of his mother with his friend, the dramatist Romain Coolus (cat. 170), from around 1905, Madame Vuillard dominates in the foreground, making it almost impossible to catch the figure of the artist's friend, who appears as a small element of the dark background; only Coolus's eyes, which gaze directly at Vuillard, draw attention to this elusive figure. The camera's lens exaggerated the distortions of foreground and background, making the foreground appear unusually large and the rear elements seem small. This kind of exaggerated discrepancy is also evident in Vuillard's paintings of a decade earlier.

Vuillard used at least a few of the photographs that have survived as studies for paintings. Sometimes, he would take figures from different photographic

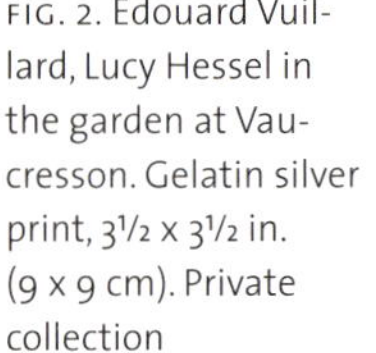

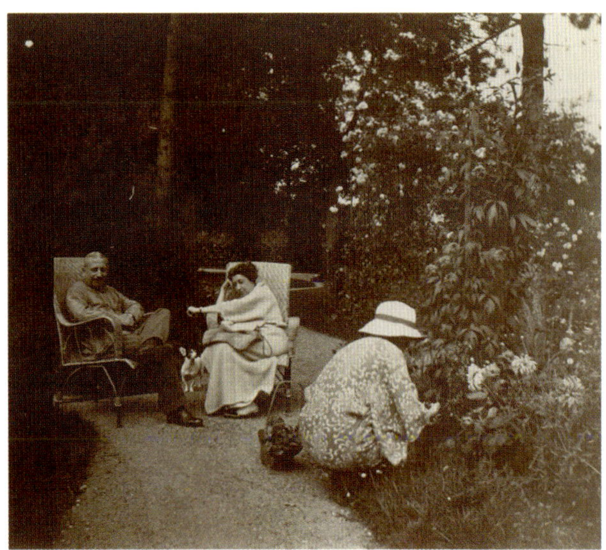

FIG. 2. Edouard Vuillard, Lucy Hessel in the garden at Vaucresson. Gelatin silver print, 3½ x 3½ in. (9 x 9 cm). Private collection

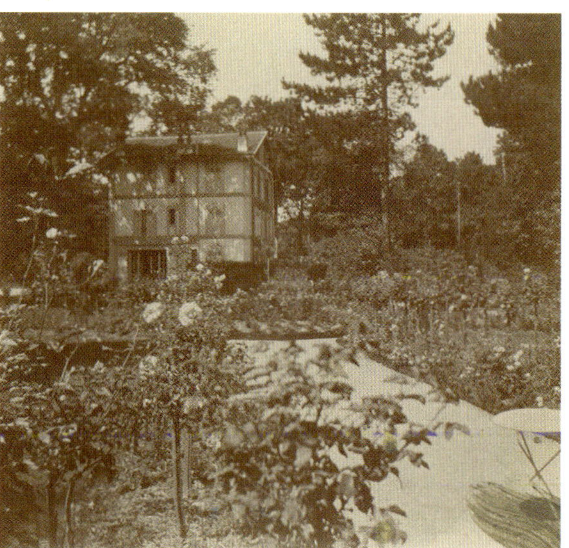

FIG. 3. Edouard Vuillard, The Chateau des Clayes at Vaucresson. Gelatin silver print, 3½ x 3½ in. (9 x 9 cm). Private collection

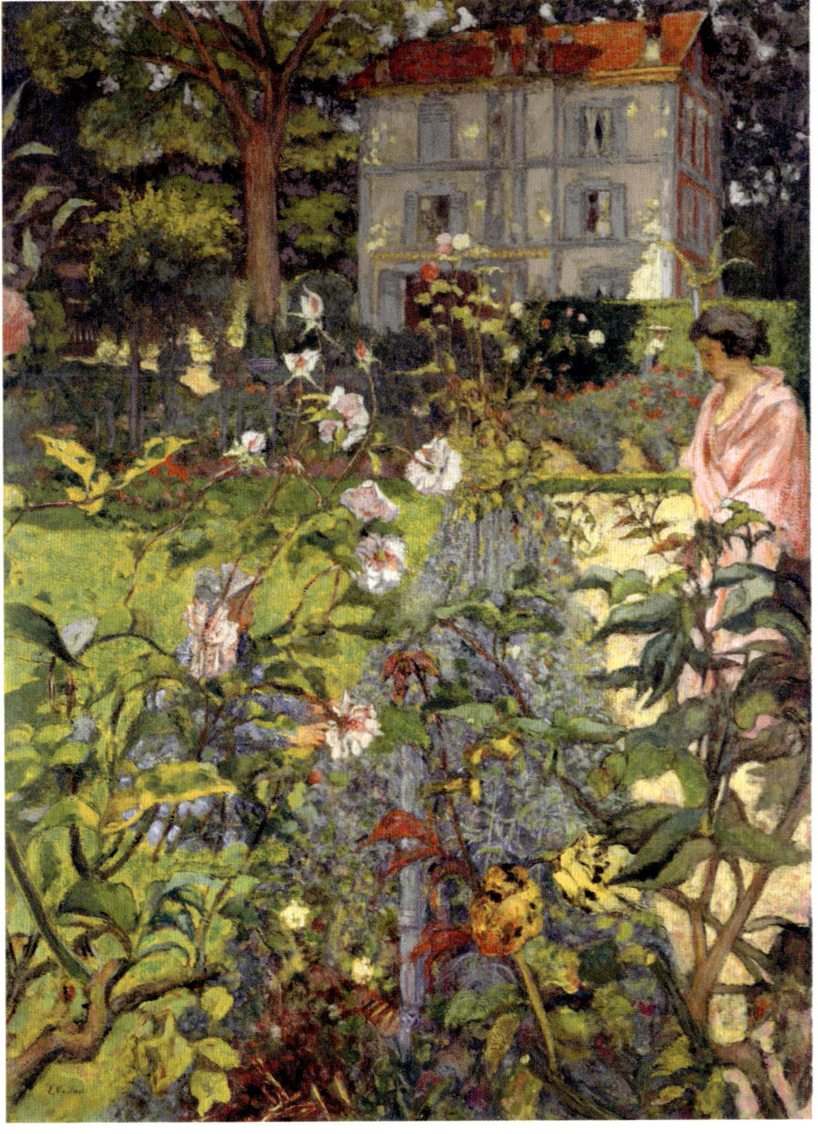

FIG. 4. Edouard Vuillard, *Morning in the Garden at Vaucresson*, 1923. Distemper on canvas, 59½ x 43⅝ in. (151.2 x 110.8 cm). The Metropolitan Museum of Art, New York. Catharine Lorillard Wolfe Collection, Wolfe Fund, 1952 (52.183)

efforts and combine them in a major canvas. Other times, he would take various snapshots of a place he intended to paint (figs. 2, 3) and refer to them while producing his picture (fig. 4). Some photographs closely resemble the paintings—not literally as studies but compositionally, temperamentally, and iconically. In this regard, Vuillard's photographs fall into three main categories, each dominated by one of the three women who consumed his life: Misia Natanson, in the 1890s; Lucy Hessel, after 1900; and his mother, throughout his career.

Vuillard's earliest canvases, from the late 1880s through the first half of the 1890s, are generally either self-portraits or depictions of his own family. The former begin with a Degas-inspired darkness and introspection, and they evolve into a proto-Fauve explosion of color and quasi-abstraction. The latter often convey tense moments of psychodrama enacted at the family dinner table (cat. 192); others are tightly composed portrayals of seamstresses, inspired by his mother's corset-making atelier. Often, his mother and sister, Marie, are seen in small-scale dramas that exaggerate his mother's centrality to the composition and reduce the presence of Marie, who seems to merge with the wallpaper or be crushed by a piece of furniture (cat. 168). Most of these paintings, made between 1888 and 1895, predate Vuillard's use of the camera. Nonetheless, the powerful compositions that dominate the artist's work from this period do inform some of his most arresting photographs taken years later. The distortions of the pictorial space in these canvases prefigure arrangements Vuillard would later adopt, but the subject matter of these early, iconic compositions does not figure in his photographic work.

Apparently, Vuillard began taking photographs around the same time he became involved with the Natanson brothers—Alexandre, Alfred, and Thadée—publishers of *La revue blanche*. This journal included criticism and essays by leading avant-garde cultural figures of the day, including Félix Fénéon, André Gide, Stéphane Mallarmé, and Marcel Proust, and provided an opportunity for artists such as Pierre Bonnard, Henri de Toulouse-Lautrec, Félix Vallotton, and Vuillard to illustrate the publication's covers and essays. As Vuillard became increasingly involved in the Natanson group, he also came under the spell of Thadée's wife, Misia, around 1895. Soon, his feelings for her were infusing all of Vuillard's creative work, from small canvases to large commissioned panels. Writing in his journal on Christmas Eve, 1896, he

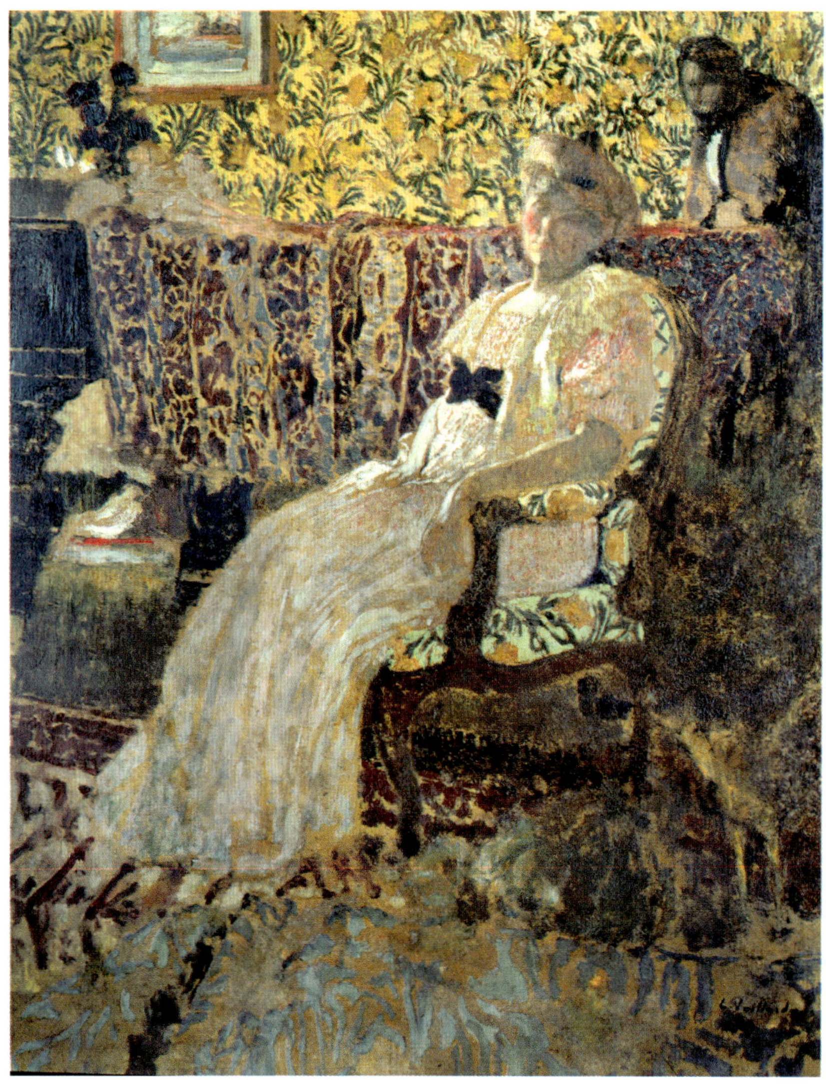

FIG. 5. Edouard Vuillard, *Misia and Thadée Natanson*, ca. 1897. Oil on paper mounted on canvas, 41 x 28 in. (104 x 71 cm). Private collection

acknowledged his feelings for Misia: "Tenderness, desires of work, ambitions and sensualities. . . . Uncertainty and conflicting desires. An abundance of memories."[5] His paintings from this period unabashedly declare the depth of the artist's emotions for this muse to the Parisian avant-garde. Misia unquestionably dominated all the pictures he painted at this time (fig. 5).

Similarly, Misia occupies the center of Vuillard's photographs. Even when there is more than one figure in the picture, it is she who is in focus and the object of Vuillard's gaze. He photographed her as she posed for him (cats. 172, 173)—flirtatiously looking at him with a cocked eyebrow or mimicking him photographing her (cats. 175, 177)—and also caught her unawares—walking up and down stairs, reading, lying down, holding her dog, looking out the window (cat. 178). The sum of these pictures suggests the intensity of their relationship. It is telling that Misia's husband, Thadée, with whom Vuillard worked, appears in only a handful of photos, and even then the center of the composition is Misia (cats. 179, 180). A similar emphasis is evident in Vuillard's paintings of this period. In *Misia and Thadée Natanson*, she appears vulnerable to the artist; her eyes are closed, she seems to join him in a reverie. Thadée, cornered behind the piano, is barely visible, and his face is painted as if to make him blend with the wallpaper. At other times, Vuillard portrayed Misia playing the piano, at which she was a virtuoso. The colors of works such as *In Front of the Tapestry: Misia and Thadée Natanson, Rue St. Florentin* (cat. 181) create a synesthetic explosion of sensual experience.

Toward the end of the decade, as the fortunes of *La revue blanche* waned, Vuillard's social circle changed. In 1900, he met Lucy Hessel, the wife of his dealer, Jos Hessel. She would occupy his affections for the last forty years of his life. Their tempestuous relationship was marked by frequent arguments followed by tearful rapprochements. And though Lucy figured into many canvases, these paintings were never the tour-de-force compositions in which Misia had been the star. His photographs of Lucy do, however, recall those of Misia in both form and tone (cats. 182, 183). Of the hundreds of photographs of Lucy Hessel in the family archive, many depict her at group lunches, picnics, and summer outings to country houses (cat. 184). Many others focus exclusively on her, in unguarded moments when she is not posing for the camera but simply resting her head in her hand with her eyes closed or staring into Vuillard's eyes (cat. 185). Some show her reclining in chairs, in front of windows, in almost the same pose as he had recorded Misia a decade earlier. Others are taken close up, and can only be seen as the record of a private moment. Indeed, in one photograph of Lucy reclining, Vuillard is so close that his own booted foot appears in the picture, at the lower right (cat. 186).

Vuillard snapped photographs of his friend Romain Coolus, of the playwright and journalist Tristan Bernard and his wife, Marcelle Aron, and of Lucy in 1907 at a restaurant in Normandy, creating a narrative that he never captured in paint. By this time, the artist was using photography to express intimacy and immediacy. Pictured at a table in the midst of a meal, three of the four are so close to Vuillard that the lens cannot take in their entire torsos or the tops of their heads. He apparently had placed the camera either flat on the table or slightly tilted, causing the plates, bowls, and glasses occupying the foreground to be completely out of focus. Clearly, a conversation is whirling around the photographer: Coolus raises a finger to emphasize a point (cat. 187), while Bernard scratches his chest as he waits to respond (cat. 188). Aron looks off to the right (cat. 189), and only Lucy, with the light from a window behind her turning the veil of her hat into a kind of halo, looks at the photographer (cat. 190). There is a cinematic connection between the actors in this scene, the continuum of the wooden wainscoting creating a physical link that the characters enact through glances and gestures. Like so much of Vuillard's painted work, in which his presence is felt in the psychological intensity of a scene, this series of images includes Vuillard as the pivotal, but invisible, actor around whom the drama revolves. Only the glance of his mistress acknowledges his presence; and yet once perceived, it changes the impact of the series from something observed to something in which the artist participated.

The woman Vuillard called his muse was neither Misia Natanson nor Lucy Hessel but his mother, with whom he lived until her death, when he was sixty years old. Paintings of her consume the first part of his career, but he photographed her continuously over the years. Some early pictures parallel his painted compositions, but in photographs such as one of the silhouetted figure of Madame Vuillard in the kitchen he shrouded her in a deeper darkness than he ever had in his painted work (cat. 194). As in a drawing by Georges Seurat, the figure is only distinguished by the subtle backlighting that outlines one side of her form. Just as Vuillard's photos of Lucy show that he sometimes abandoned the formal compositions he sought in paint, so too did some shots he took of his mother toward the end of her life. He places her on the bed, in nightgown and cap, bald and toothless, looking out at her son (cat. 198). Only the strong hands resting on her knees recall the authoritative pose they held in his pictures of her twenty years earlier (cat. 196). The photograph of her drying herself after a bath shows her wrapped in a towel and completely bald, bending over her raised foot (cat. 199); her body is out of focus, but the elements of the room behind her are detailed and complex. This is less an homage to a Degas bather than it is Vuillard's evocation of his mother who will soon die and leave the specificity of rooms and objects behind to conjure her memory.

Vuillard's painting and photographs both evolved over the course of his career, but in different directions. The painted work exchanged a private pictorial language, in which iconic pose and spatial complexity expressed highly personal themes for the less psychologically charged imagery of his later, more public work. His photographs, on the other hand, reflect a transition from the compositional approach that characterized his paintings to an innovative use of the camera that emphasized spontaneity and anecdote. In the early photographs, Vuillard orchestrated the compositions as carefully as he did in his paintings. He pointed the camera at unusual angles and framed the compositions in unconventional ways to portray scenes of dark or densely decorated interiors. Later in his career, he chronicled with the camera a world that was no longer the center of his painted universe. The late photographs became the expressive vehicle for a different kind of intimacy where Vuillard bridged the distance between himself and his art.

Like Proust's description of the narrator contemplating a photograph of the Duchess of Guermantes, where the snapshot itself is just the point of departure for an extended reverie, Vuillard's photographs allow the viewer access to the private world of an artist whose universe in paint was completely secret. Vuillard's photographic production substantiates both Roland Barthes's likening of the photograph to a memento mori and Proust's embrace of it as something that conjures the "involuntary memory" of a smell, a sound, a conversation, or a distinct moment: photographs speak both to the instant and to the extended history that precedes and succeeds it.

Because Vuillard never exhibited his photographs, the public only learned of their existence several decades after the artist died. Entries in his journal shed light on his thoughts regarding the relationship between painting and photography. Citing the poet Paul Valéry at one point, he wrote: "It is clear that the 'Good' and the 'Beautiful' have passed out of fashion—As the 'True,' photography has shown us its nature and limitations: registering phenomena as a pure effect of their existence, requiring as *little Man* as possible, that is what our 'True' is."[6] Although he once said that "painting would always have the advantage over photography of being done by hand," Vuillard pushed the limits of the Kodak's dispassionate objectivity to convey a personal, private universe made up of the people who meant the most to him.[7]

NOTES

1. Solio was one of the photographic papers Eastman manufactured in a way that enabled one to print pictures at home. The packages remaining in Vuillard's archive were from Kodak Limited and sold in France.
2. "Porte photos a developer pour ne pas y perdre mon temps." Edouard Vuillard, *Journal*, December 12, 1928. Institut de France.
3. Jacques Salomon's brief preface to the catalogue *Vuillard et son Kodak* remains the only firsthand account of how Vuillard developed his photographs. The preface and Annette Vaillant's "Some Memories of Vuillard," in the same catalogue, comprise the only published documents about his work in the medium. The translation here is taken from the English version of the texts by Salomon and Vaillant accompanying the 1964 exhibition of the same title at London's Lefevre Gallery, "Vuillard and His Kodak," in *Vuillard et son Kodak* (London: Lefevre Gallery, 1964), p. 2.
4. Vuillard's photographic work has been addressed in various publications since it was discovered and first made public. These include: Emilie Daniel, "L'objectif du subjectif: Vuillard photographe," *Les cahiers du Musée national d'art moderne*, no. 23 (Spring 1988): pp. 83–93; Elizabeth Easton, *The Intimate Interiors of Edouard Vuillard*, exh. cat. (Washington, D.C.: Smithsonian Institution Press; Houston: Museum of Fine Arts, Houston, 1989); Easton, "Edouard Vuillard's Photographs: Artistry and Accident," *Apollo*, no. 388 (June 1994): pp. 9–17, and Easton, "The Intentional Snapshot," and Guy Cogeval, "Vuillard and his Photographs," in *Edouard Vuillard*, exh. cat. (Washington, D.C.: National Gallery of Art, 2003), pp. 423–38 and 240–45. Dorothy M. Kosinski, *The Artist and the Camera: Degas to Picasso*, exh. cat. (Dallas: Dallas Museum of Art; New Haven, Conn.: Yale University Press, 1999), contains a chapter by Eik Kahng on Vuillard, "Staged Moments in the Art of Edouard Vuillard," pp. 253–63. Belinda Thompson, *Vuillard*, exh. cat. (London: South Bank Centre, 1991), illustrates many unpublished photographs but does not discuss them specifically. Ann Dumas and Guy Cogeval, *Vuillard*, exh. cat. (Paris: Flammarion, 1990), also reproduces hitherto unknown photographs from the family archive.
5. Edouard Vuillard, *Journal*, I.2, fol. 57v (December 24, 1896).
6. Edouard Vuillard, *Journal*, IV.12, fol. 47 r-v (January 15, 1939).
7. Salomon, "Vuillard and His Kodak," p. 3.

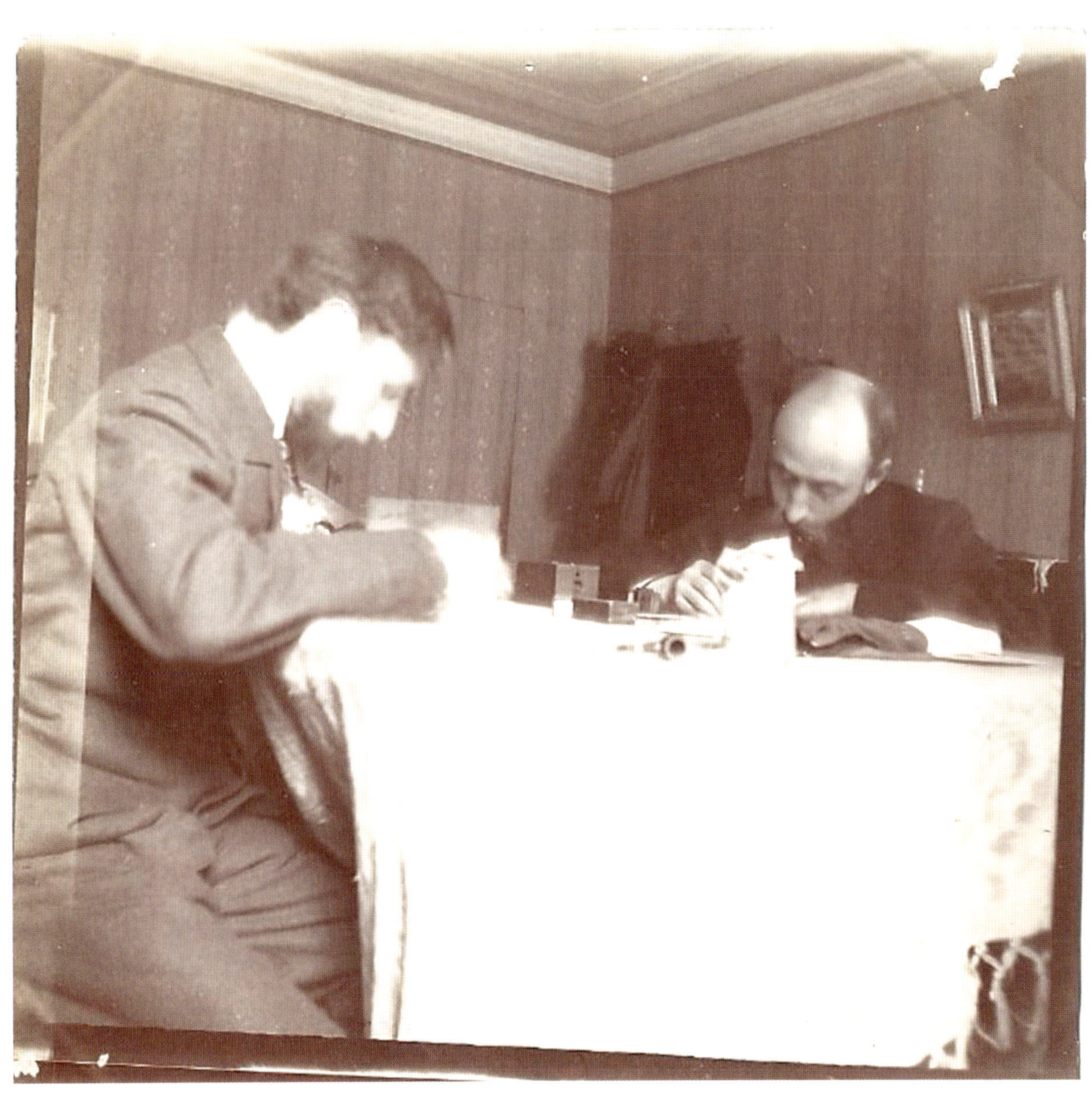

CAT. 167. Edouard Vuillard, Pierre Bonnard and Edouard Vuillard in the dining room, Rue des Batignolles, 1897. Gelatin silver print, $3^{1/2}$ x $3^{1/2}$ in. (9 x 9 cm). Private collection

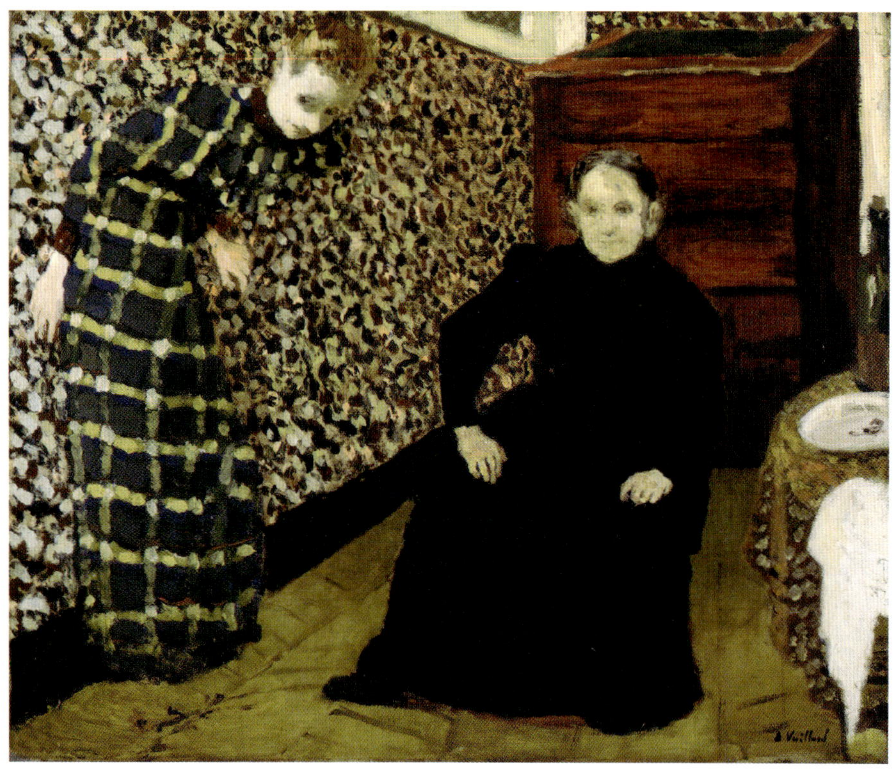

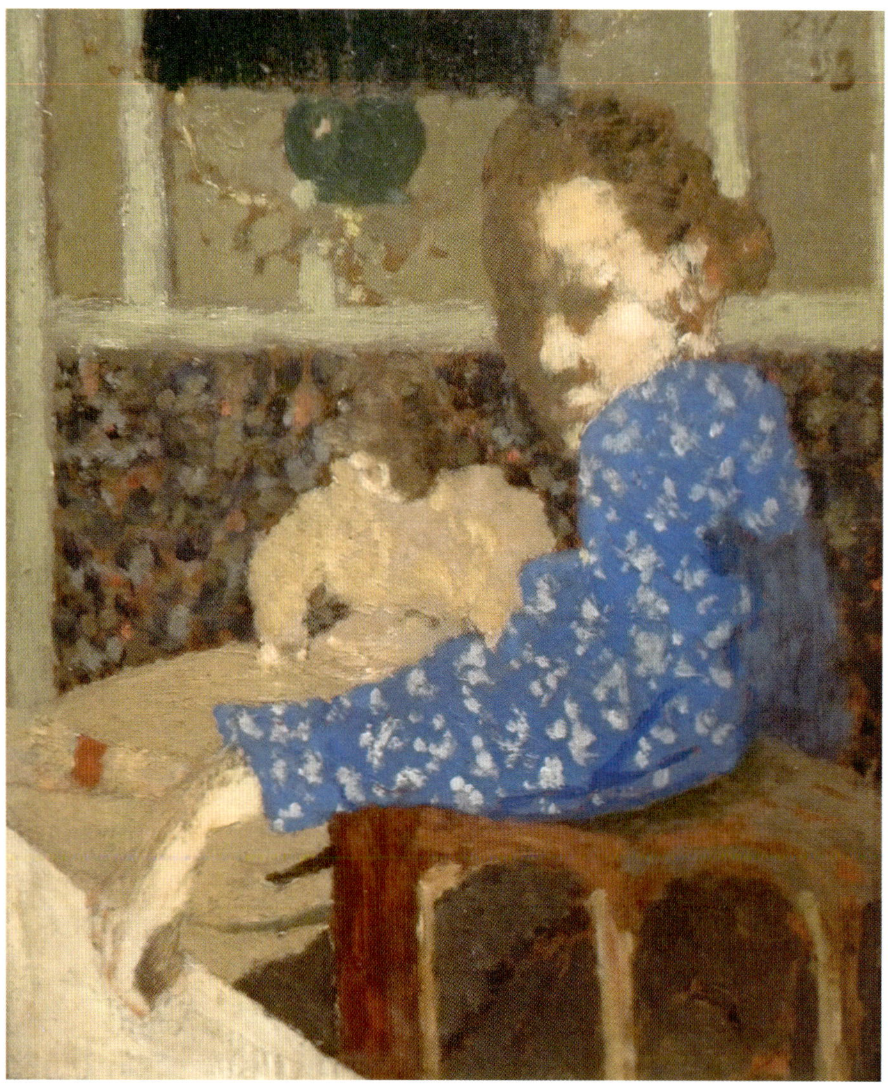

CAT. 168. Edouard Vuillard, *Interior, Mother and Sister of the Artist*, 1893. Oil on canvas, 18¼ x 22¼ in. (46.3 x 56.5 cm). The Museum of Modern Art, New York. Gift of Mrs. Saidie A. May, 1934

CAT. 169. Edouard Vuillard, *The Blue Sleeve*, 1893. Oil on board mounted on cradled panel, 10½ x 8¾ in. (26.6 x 22.3 cm). Collection Malcolm Wiener, New York

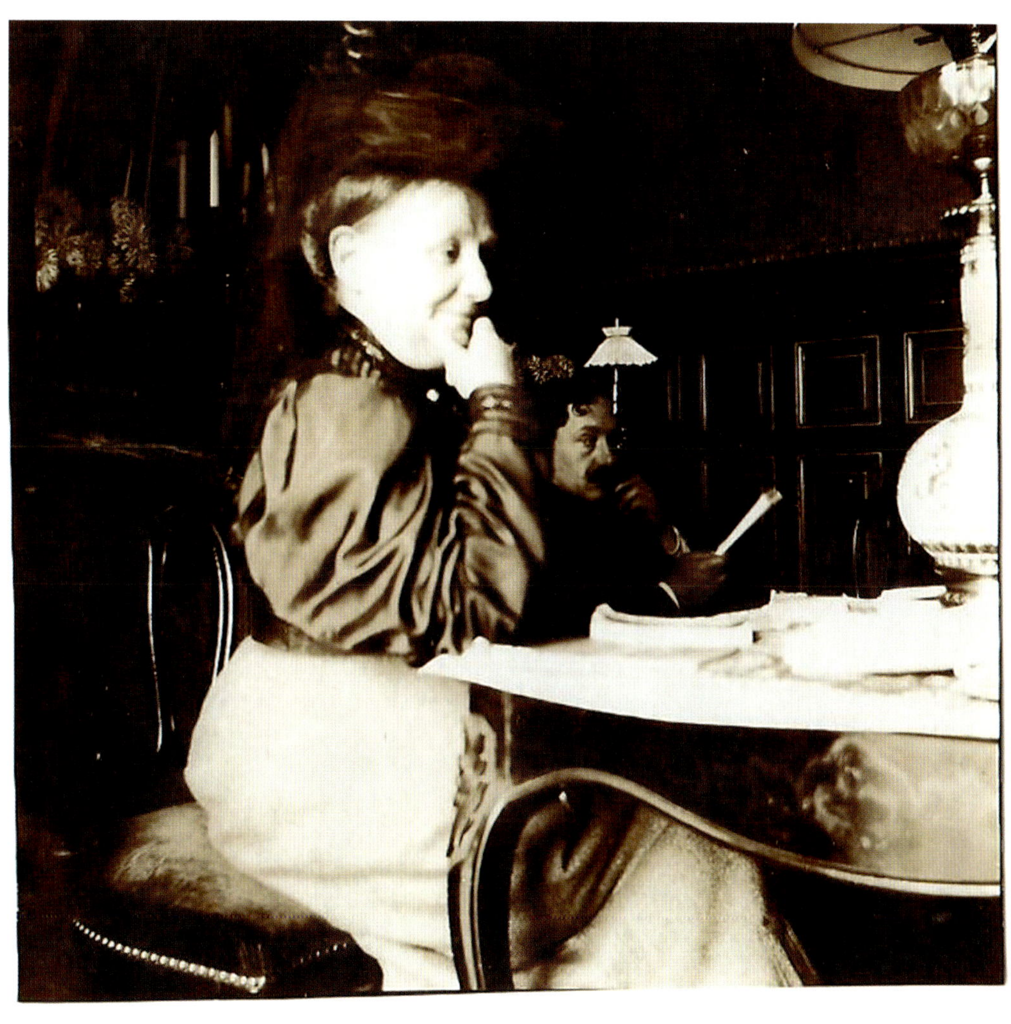

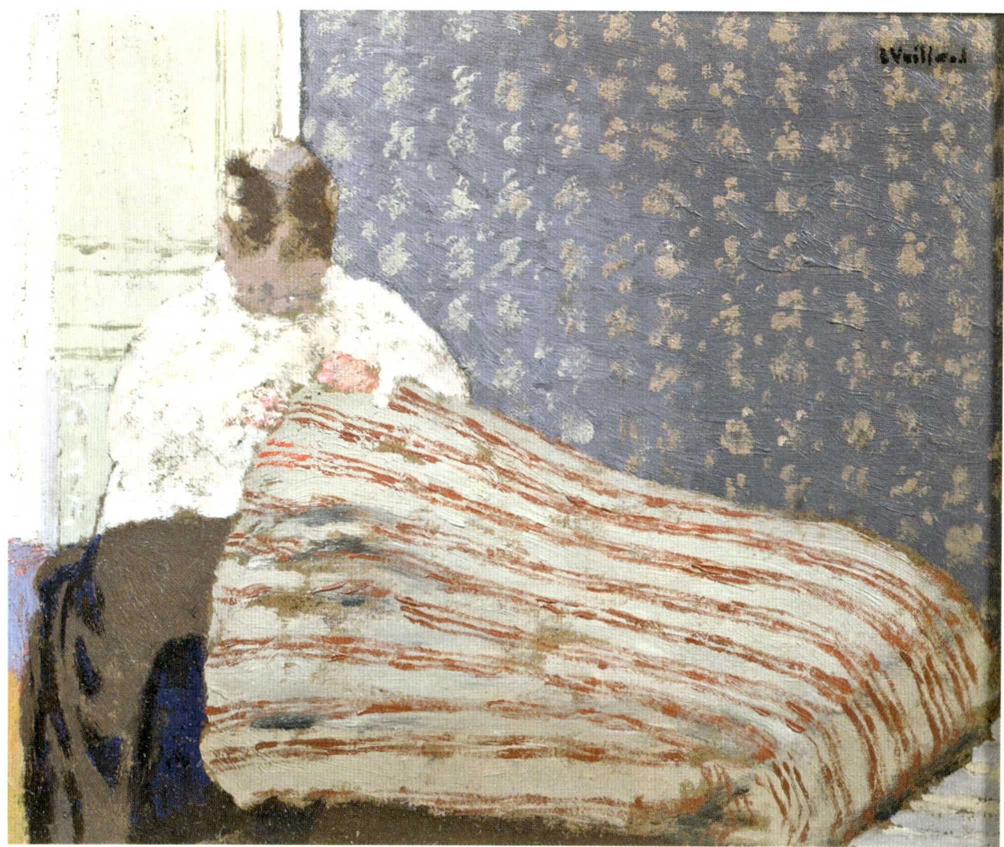

CAT. 170. Edouard Vuillard, Madame Vuillard and Romain Coolus, ca. 1905. Gelatin silver print, 3 3/8 x 3 1/2 in. (8.5 x 8.9 cm). Private collection

CAT. 171. Edouard Vuillard, *Madame Vuillard Sewing*, ca. 1895. Oil on panel, 7 1/2 x 9 3/8 in. (19 x 24 cm). Collection of Kelly Simpson, Katonah, N.Y.

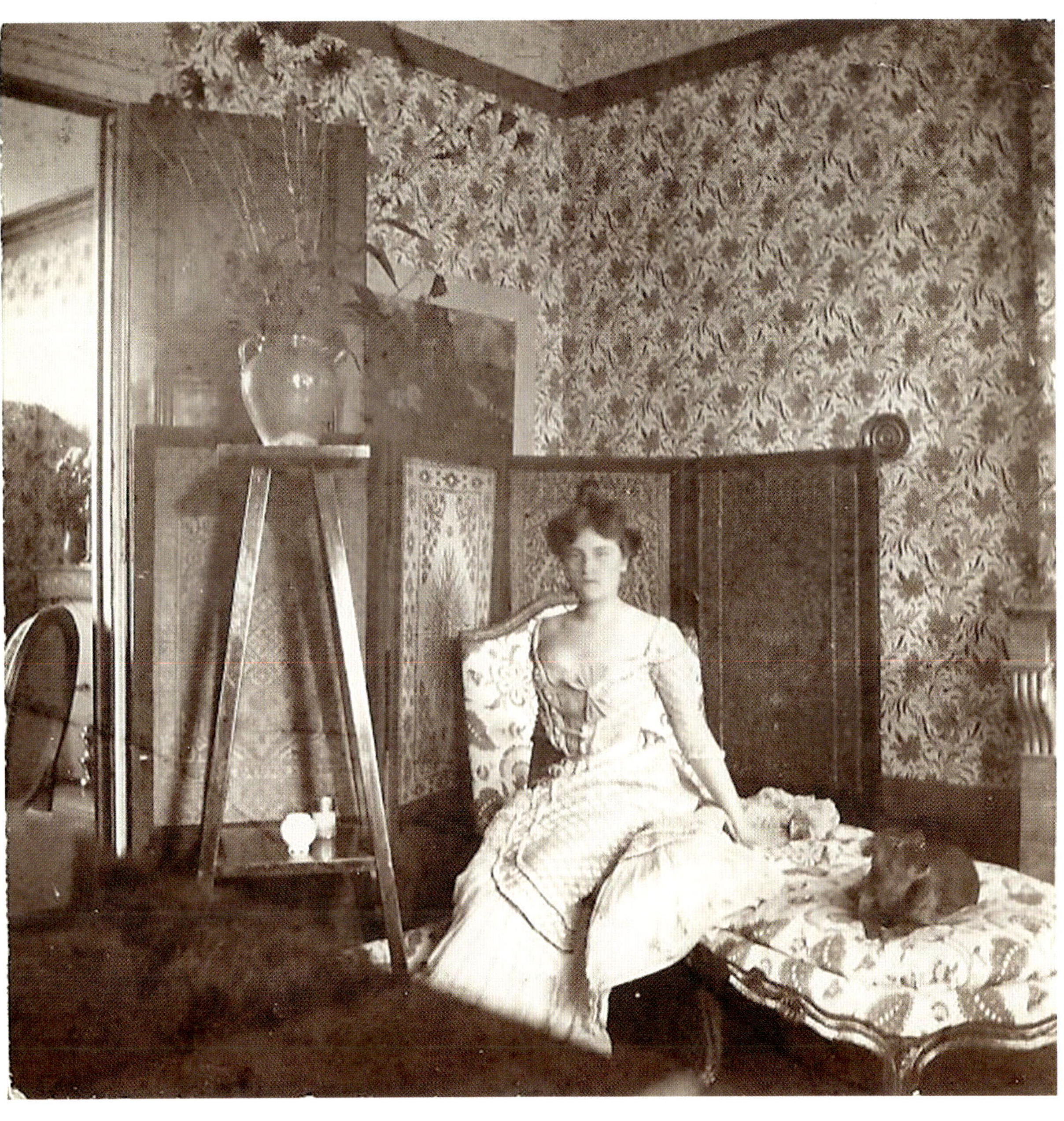

CAT. 172. Edouard Vuillard, Misia Natanson seated on a chaise lounge, Rue St. Florentin, 1899. Gelatin silver print, $3^1/_4$ x $3^3/_8$ in. (8.4 x 8.6 cm). Private collection

OPPOSITE:
CAT. 173. Edouard Vuillard, Misia Natanson seated at the window in the salon of La Croix des Gardes, in Cannes, 1901. Gelatin silver print, $3^1/_2$ x $3^1/_2$ in. (9 x 9 cm). Private collection

CAT. 174. Edouard Vuillard, Misia Natanson in a rattan chair at La Croix des Gardes, in Cannes, ca. 1901. Gelatin silver print, $2^1/_2$ x $3^3/_4$ in. (6.5 x 9.5 cm). Private collection

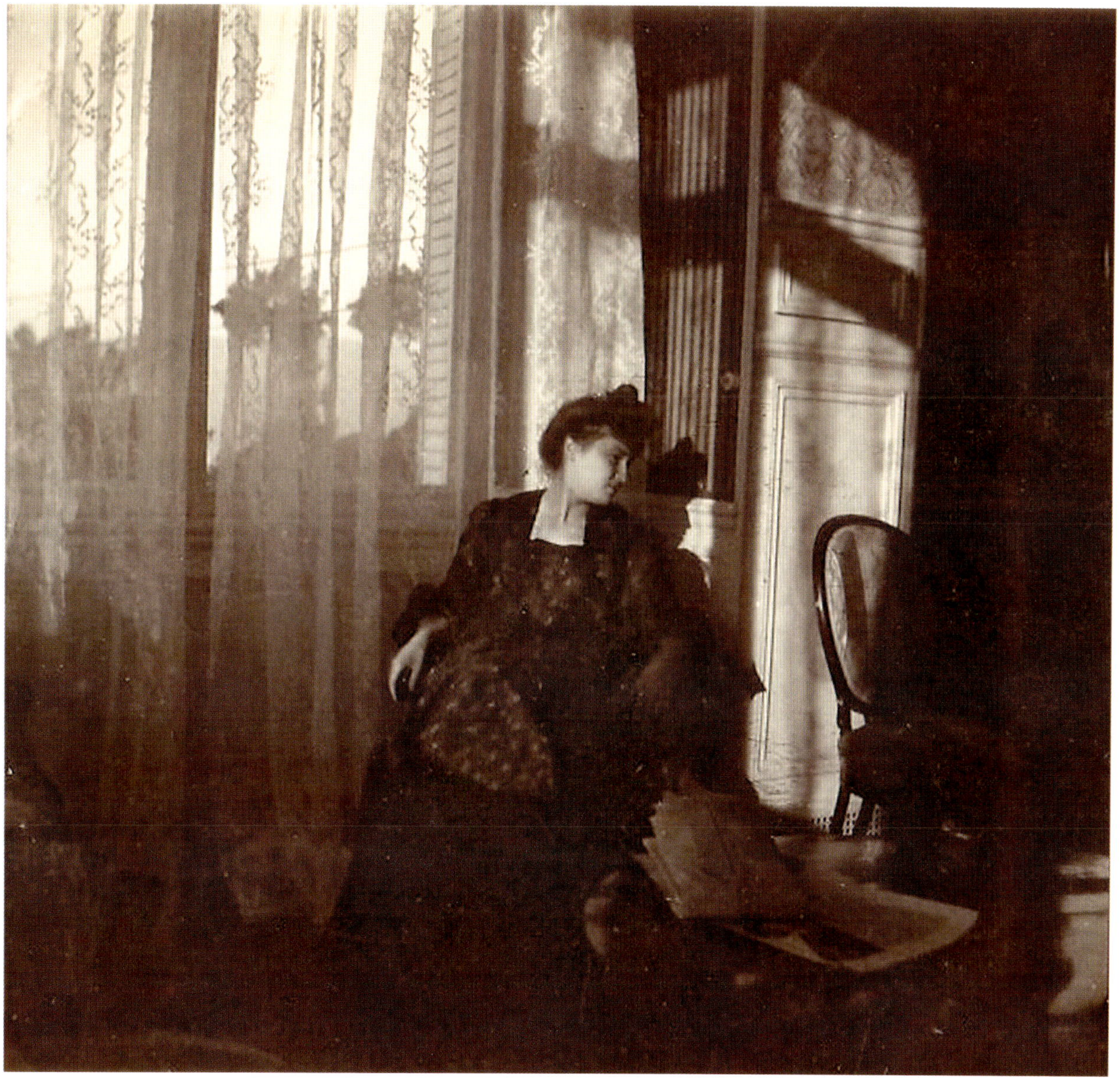

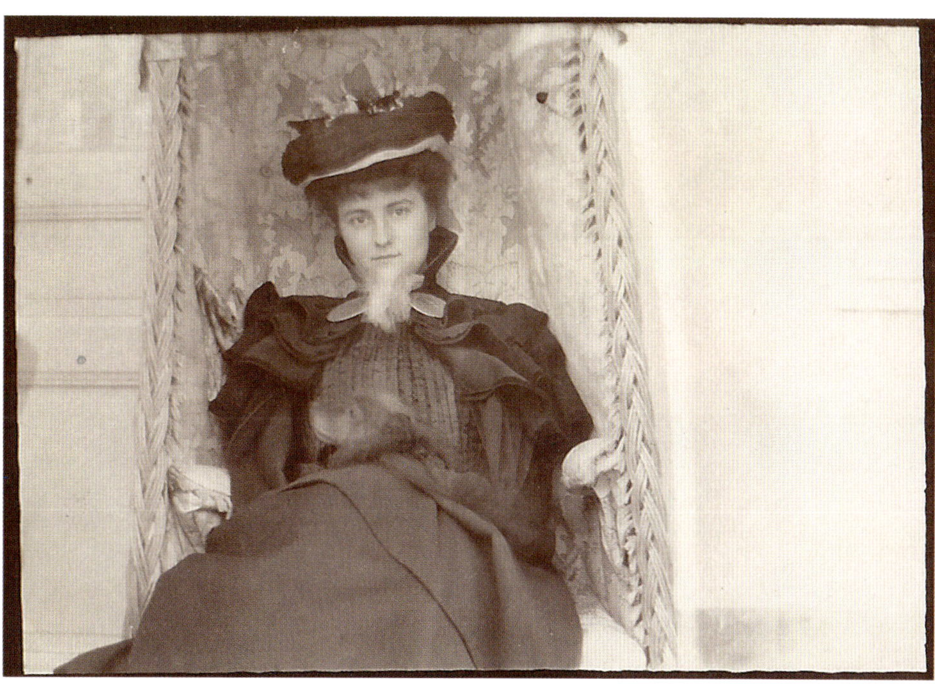

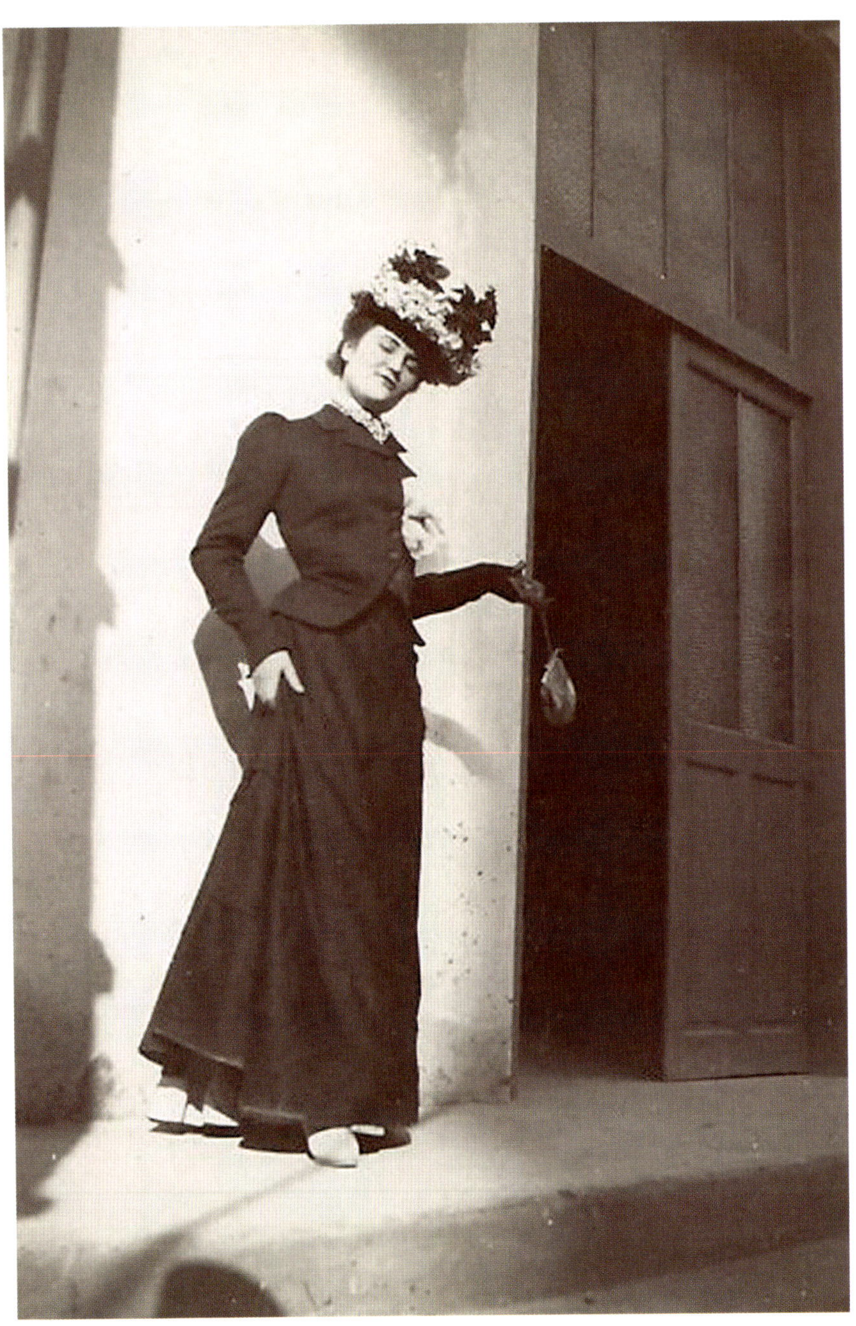

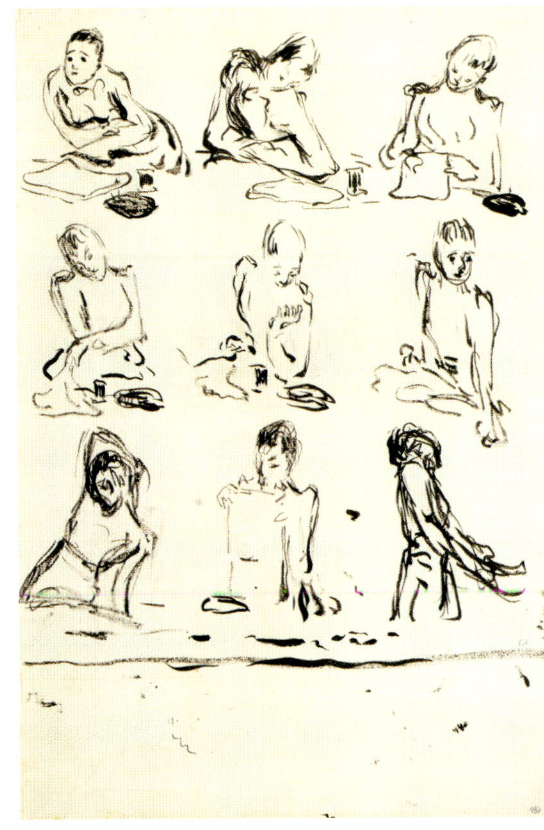

CAT. 175. Edouard Vuillard, Misia Natanson on the steps of La Croix des Gardes, in Cannes, 1901. Gelatin silver print, 3¾ x 2⅝ in. (9.5 x 6.6 cm). Private collection

CAT. 176. Edouard Vuillard, *Neuf silhouettes de femmes, étude de couturieres* (Nine Silhouettes of Women, Study of Seamstresses), n.d. Pen and ink on paper, 18⅛ x 12⅛ in. (46 x 30.9 cm). Musée du Louvre, Paris

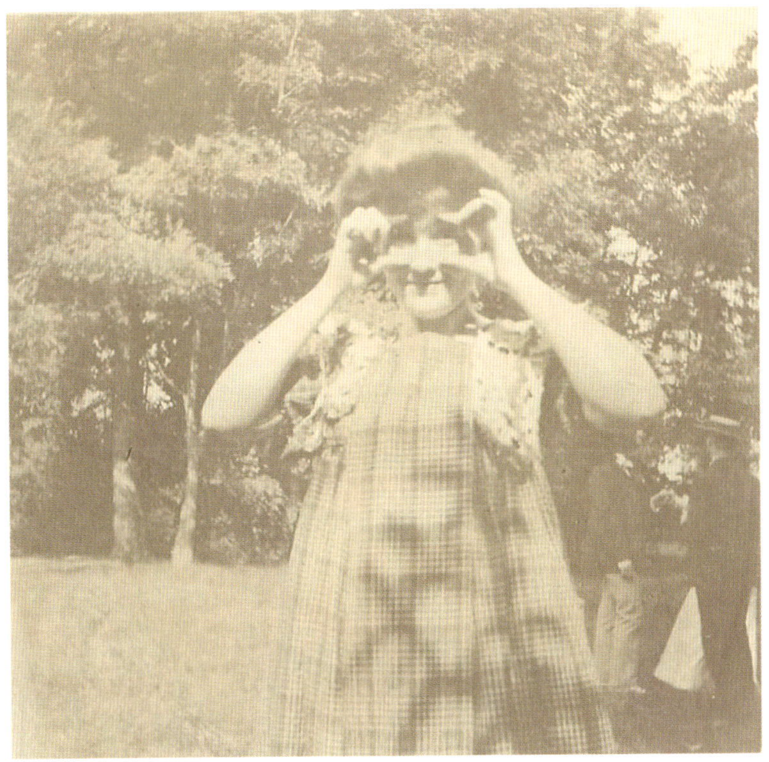

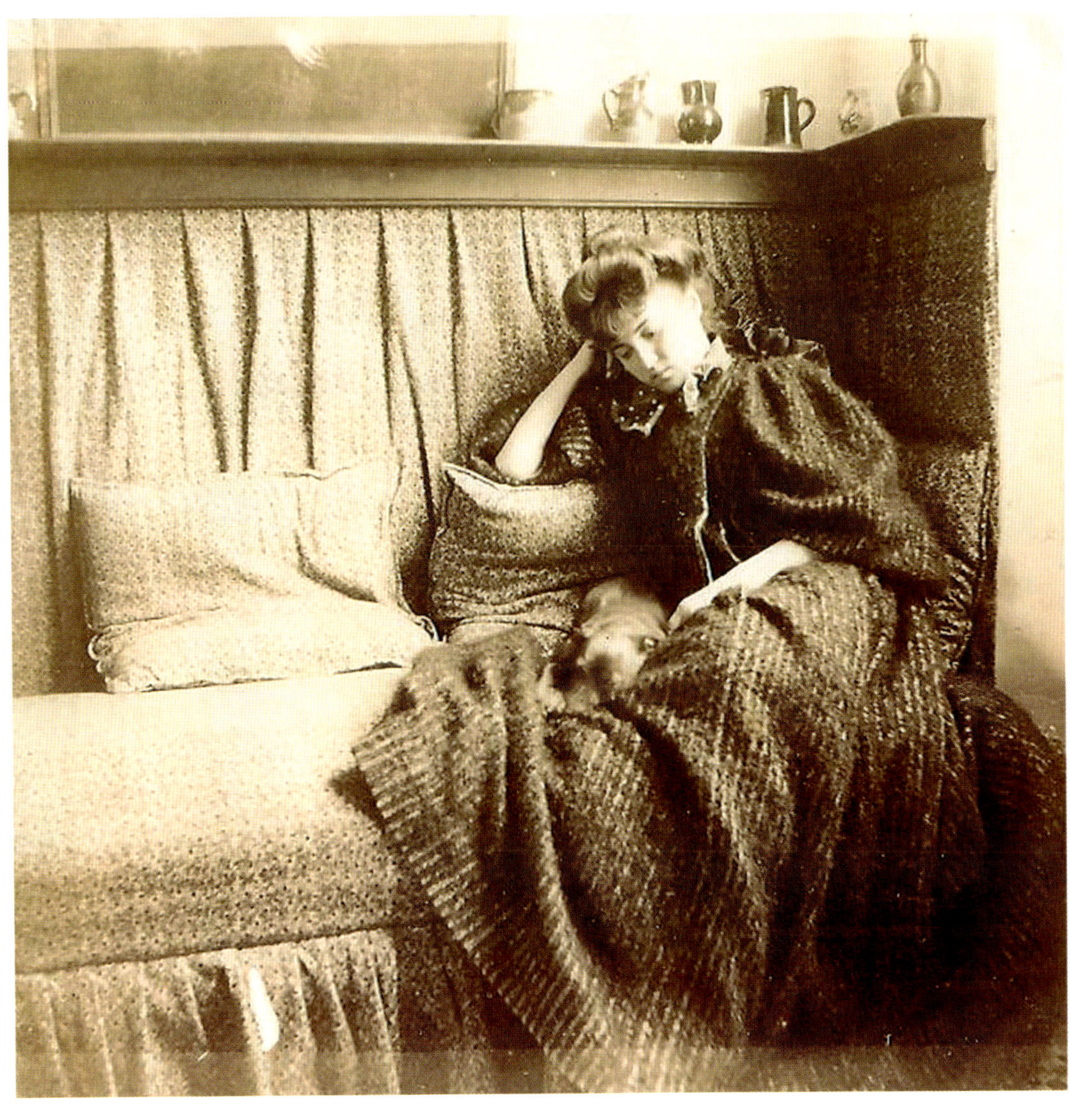

CAT. 177. Edouard Vuillard, Misia Natanson at Villeneuve-sur-Yonne, 1897. Gelatin silver print, 3½ x 3½ in. (9 x 9 cm). Private collection

CAT. 178. Edouard Vuillard, Misia Natanson and her dog at Villeneuve-sur-Yonne, 1899. Gelatin silver print, 3½ x 3½ in. (9 x 9 cm). Private collection

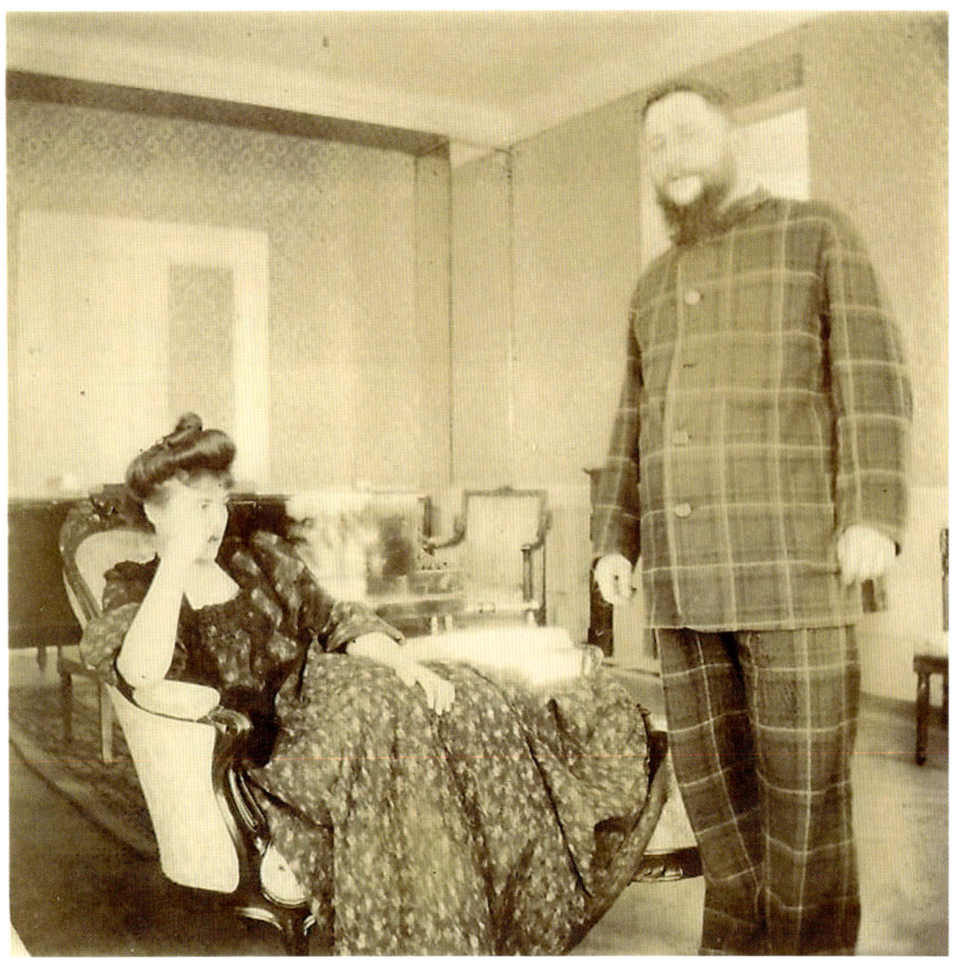

CAT. 179. Edouard Vuillard, Misia and Thadée Natanson in the salon of La Croix des Gardes, in Cannes, 1901. Gelatin silver print, 3½ x 3½ in. (8.9 x 9 cm). Private collection

CAT. 180. Edouard Vuillard, Thadée and Misia Natanson in the salon, Rue St. Florentin, 1898. Gelatin silver print, 3½ x 3½ in. (8.9 x 9 cm). Private collection

CAT. 181. Edouard Vuillard, *In Front of the Tapestry: Misia and Thadée Natanson, Rue St. Florentin*, 1899. Oil on board, 19 x 20 in. (48.3 x 50.8 cm). Private collection

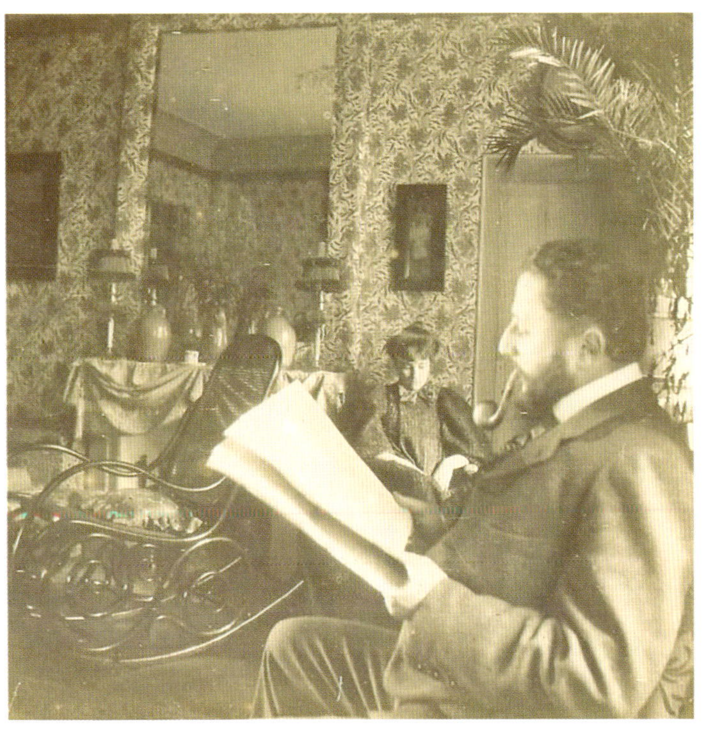

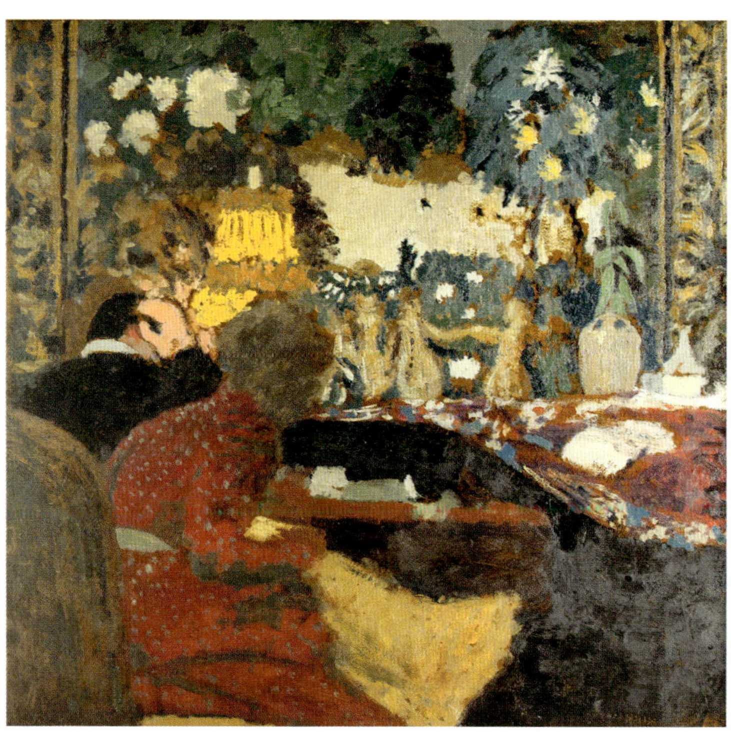

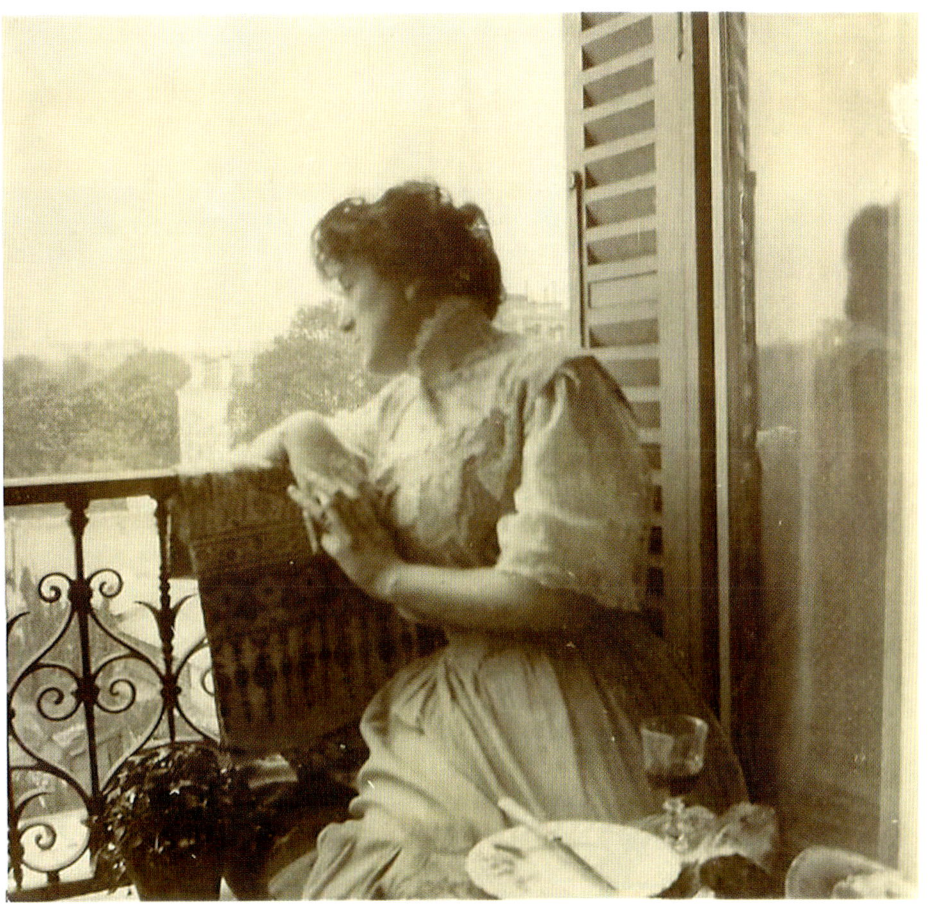

CAT. 182. Edouard Vuillard, Lucy Hessel at the window, Rue Truffaut, ca. 1905. Gelatin silver print, 3 1/8 x 3 3/8 in. (8.1 x 8.6 cm). Private collection

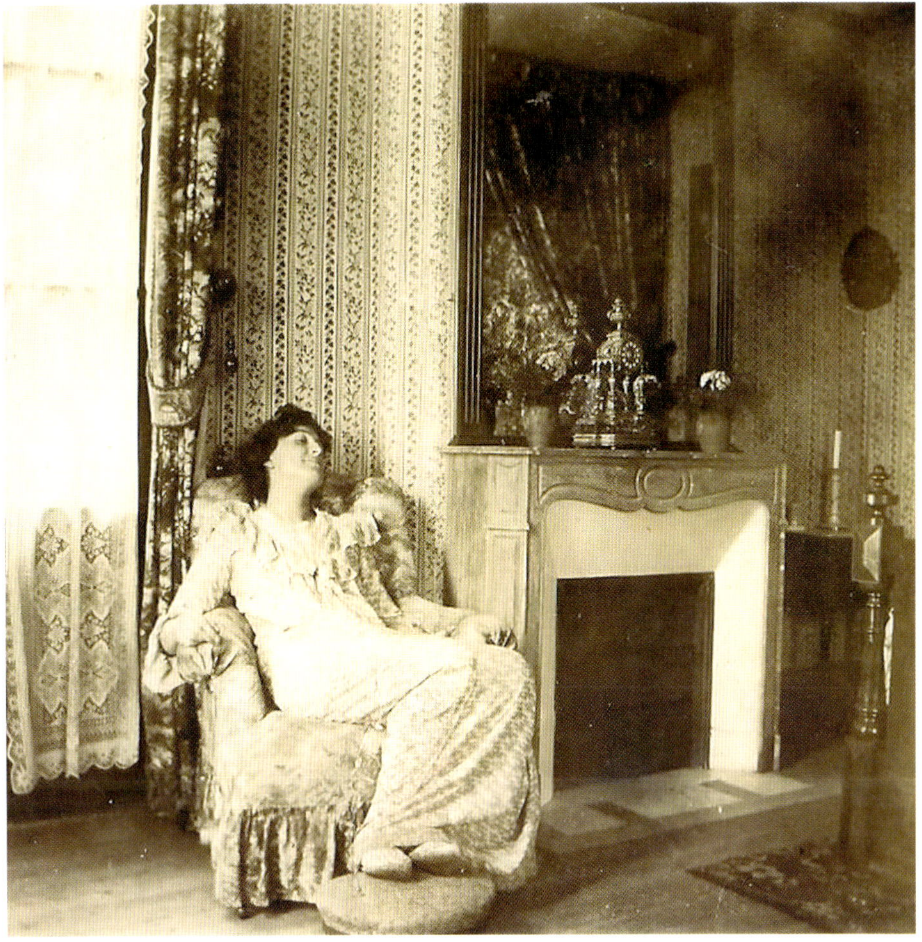

CAT. 183. Edouard Vuillard, Lucy Hessel seated in the salon of La Terrasse, in Vasouy, 1904. Gelatin silver print, 3 1/4 x 3 3/8 in. (8.4 x 8.6 cm). Private collection

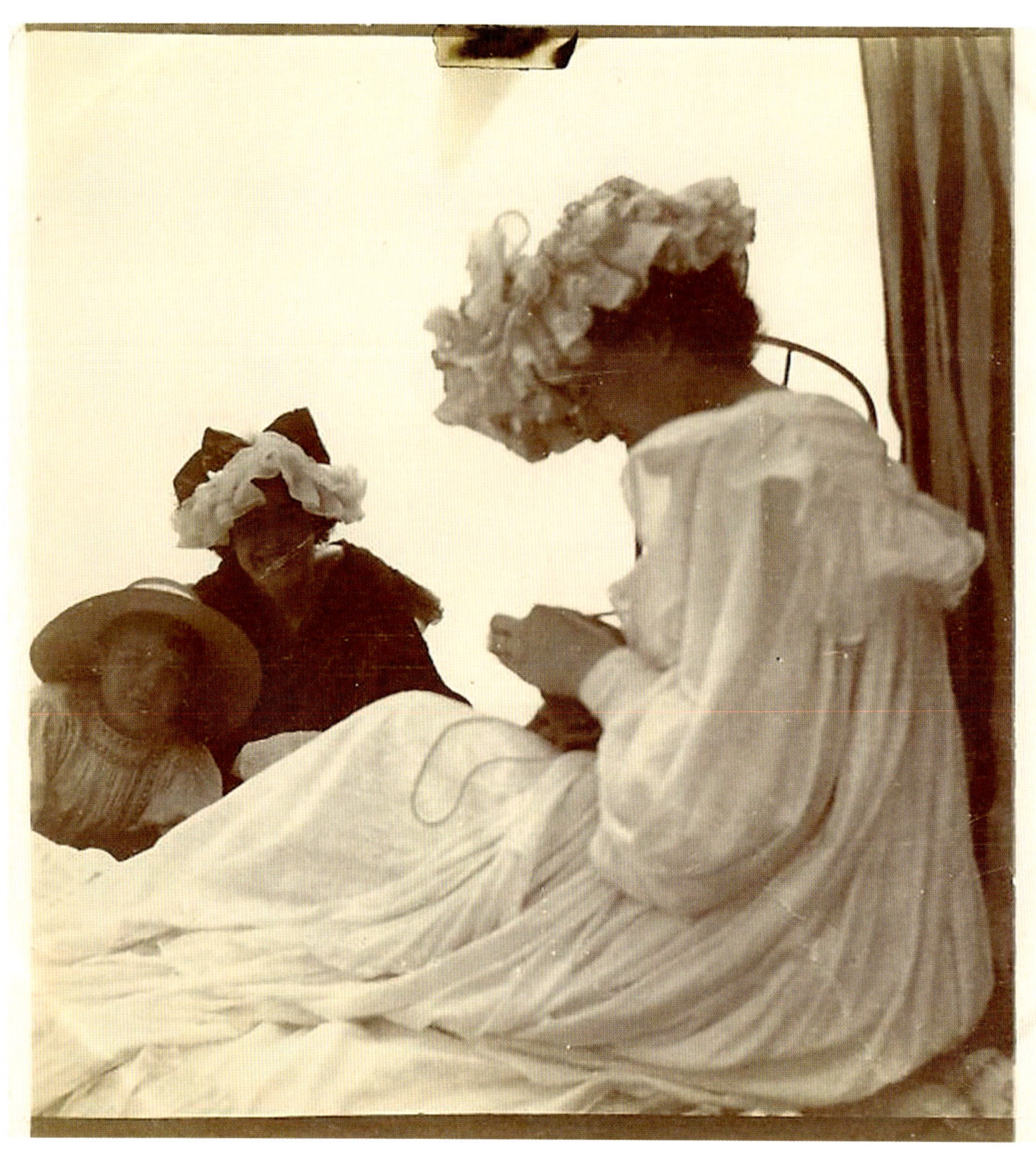

CAT. 184. Edouard Vuillard, Lucy Hessel, Marcelle Reiss, and Pierre Aron at Vasouy, 1904. Gelatin silver print, 3½ x 3½ in. (9 x 9 cm). Private collection

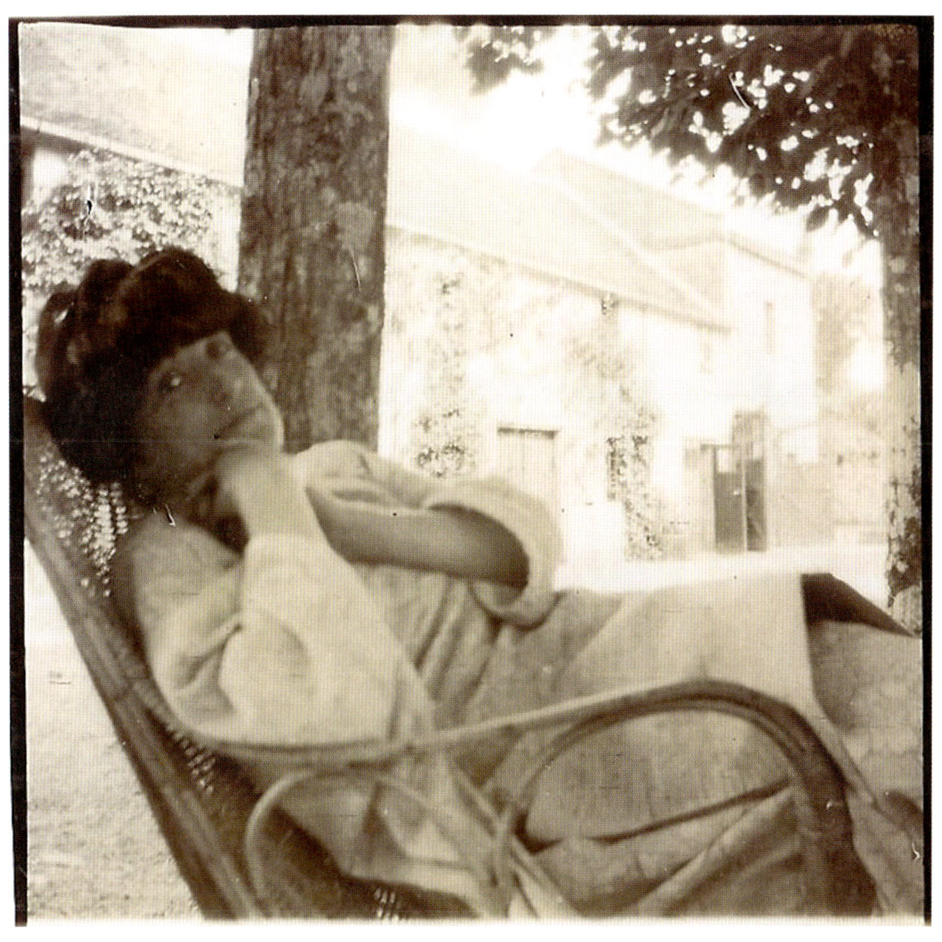

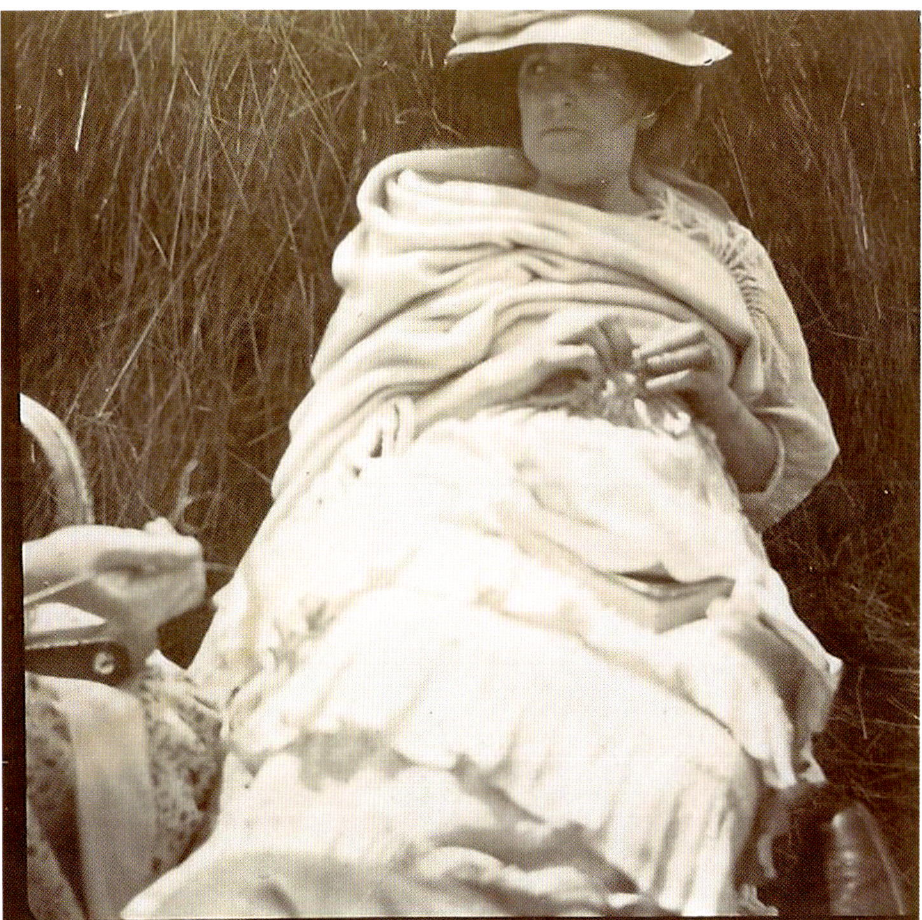

CAT. 185. Edouard Vuillard, Lucy Hessel at Le Chateau Rouge, Amfréville, 1905. Gelatin silver print, 3½ x 3½ in. (9 x 9 cm). Private collection

CAT. 186. Edouard Vuillard, Lucy Hessel leaning against a haystack in Amfréville, 1907. Gelatin silver print, 3½ x 3½ in. (8.8 x 8.9 cm). Private collection

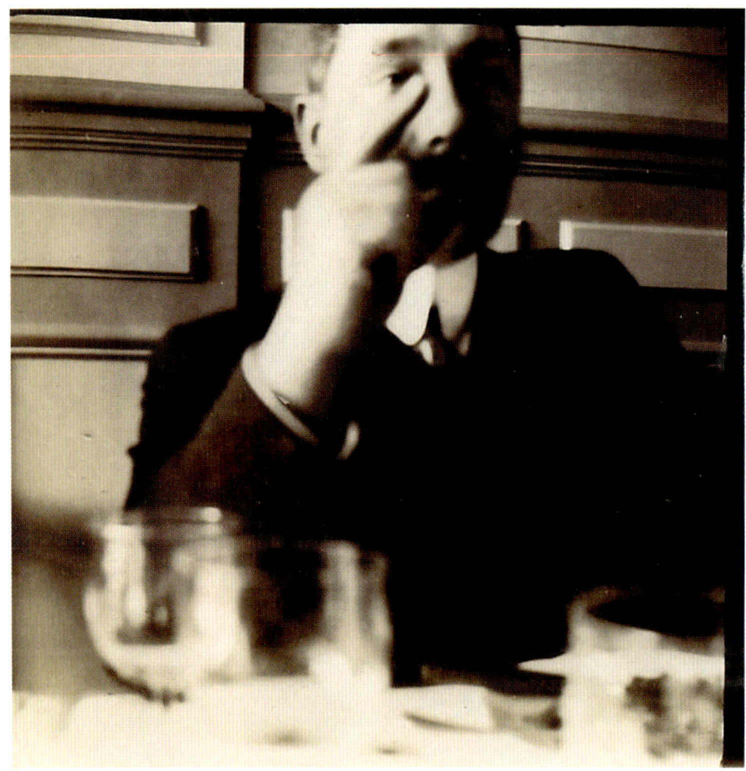

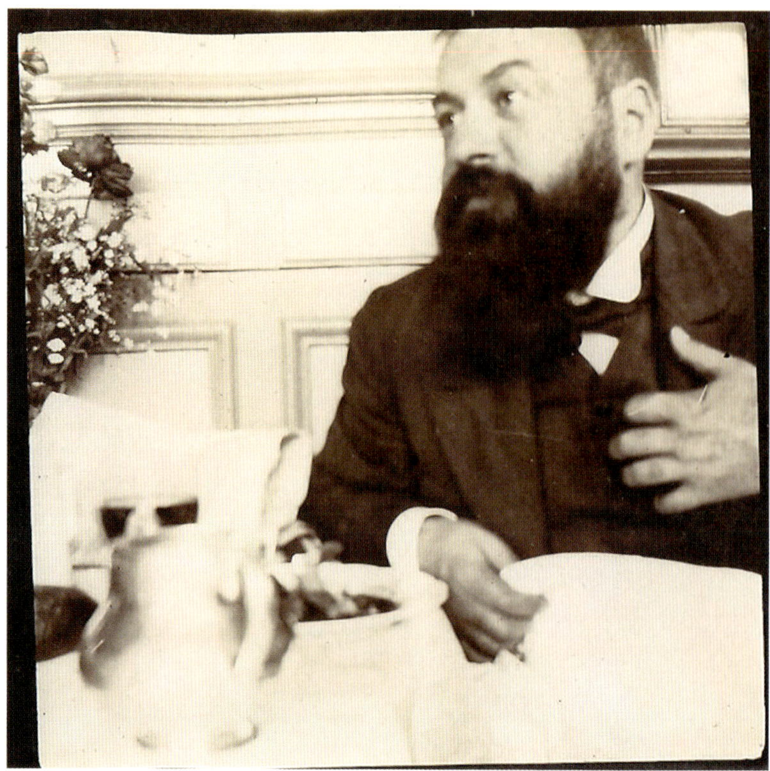

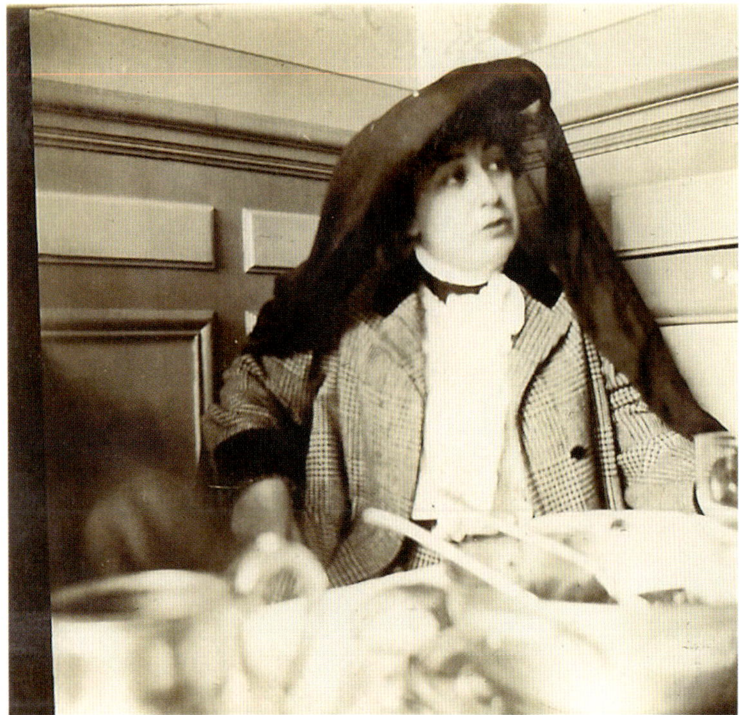

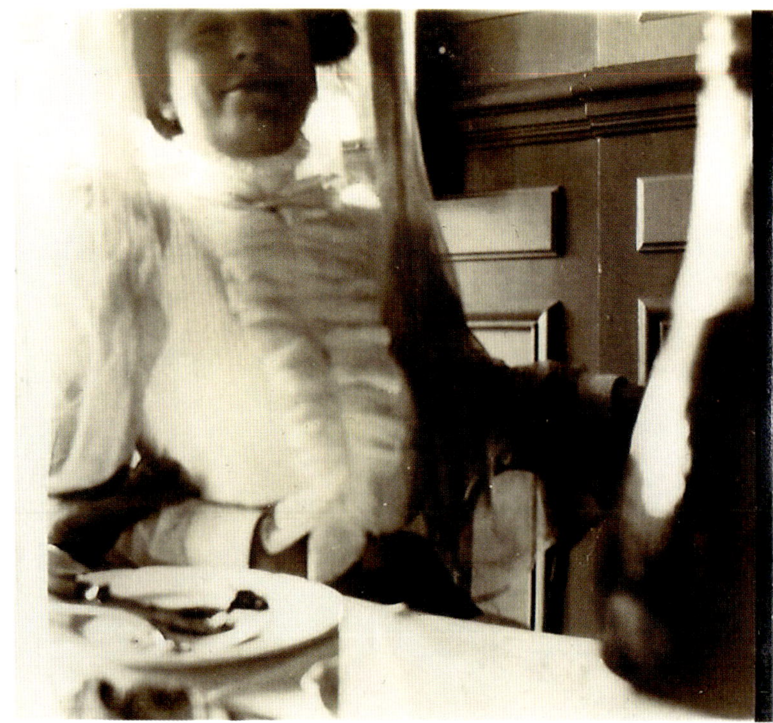

CAT. 187. Edouard Vuillard, Romain Coolus in a restaurant in Normandy, 1907. Gelatin silver print, 3½ x 3⅜ in. (8.9 x 8.7 cm). Private collection

CAT. 188. Edouard Vuillard, Tristan Bernard in a restaurant in Normandy, 1907. Gelatin silver print, 3½ x 3⅝ in. (8.9 x 9.1 cm). Private collection

CAT. 189. Edouard Vuillard, Marcelle Aron in a restaurant in Normandy, 1907. Gelatin silver print, 3½ x 3¾ in. (8.8 x 9.4 cm). Private collection

CAT. 190. Edouard Vuillard, Lucy Hessel in a restaurant in Normandy, 1907. Gelatin silver print, 3½ x 3½ in. (8.9 x 8.9 cm). Private collection

CAT. 191. Edouard Vuillard, Lucy Hessel visiting Madame Vuillard, Rue de la Tour, 1904–8. Gelatin silver print, 3³/₈ x 3³/₄ in. (8.5 x 9.4 cm). Private collection

CAT. 192. Edouard Vuillard, *At Table, Lunch*, 1892. Oil on canvas, 12⁵/₈ x 18¹/₈ in. (32 x 46 cm). Private collection, United States

CAT. 193. Edouard Vuillard, Madame Roussel mère, Marthe Bonnard, Vuillard, Annette Roussel, and Pierre Bonnard around the table at Ker-Xavier Roussel's house, La Jacanette, 1908. Gelatin silver print, 3¹/₄ x 3³/₈ in. (8.4 x 8.6 cm). Private collection

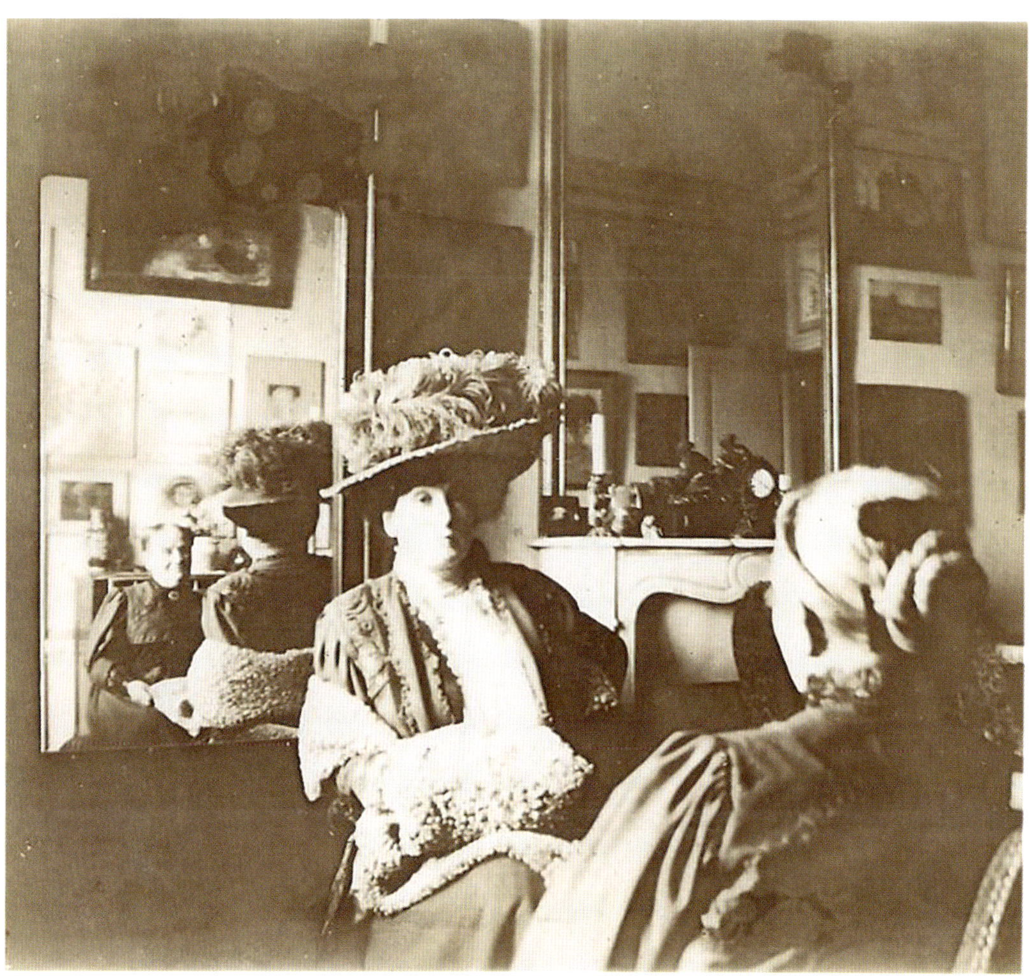

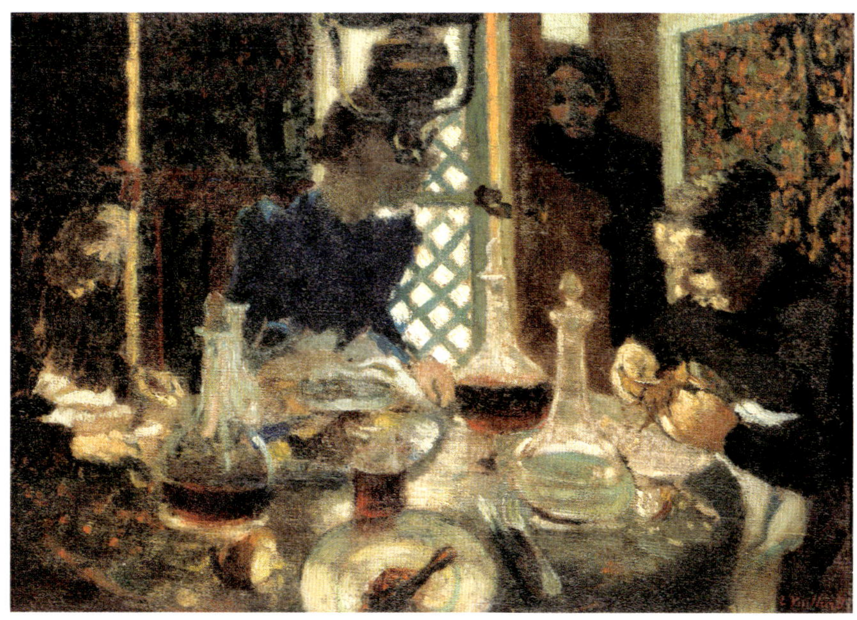

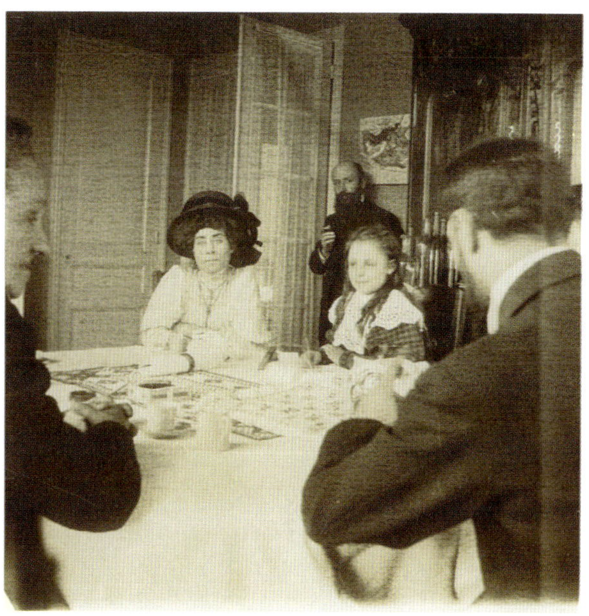

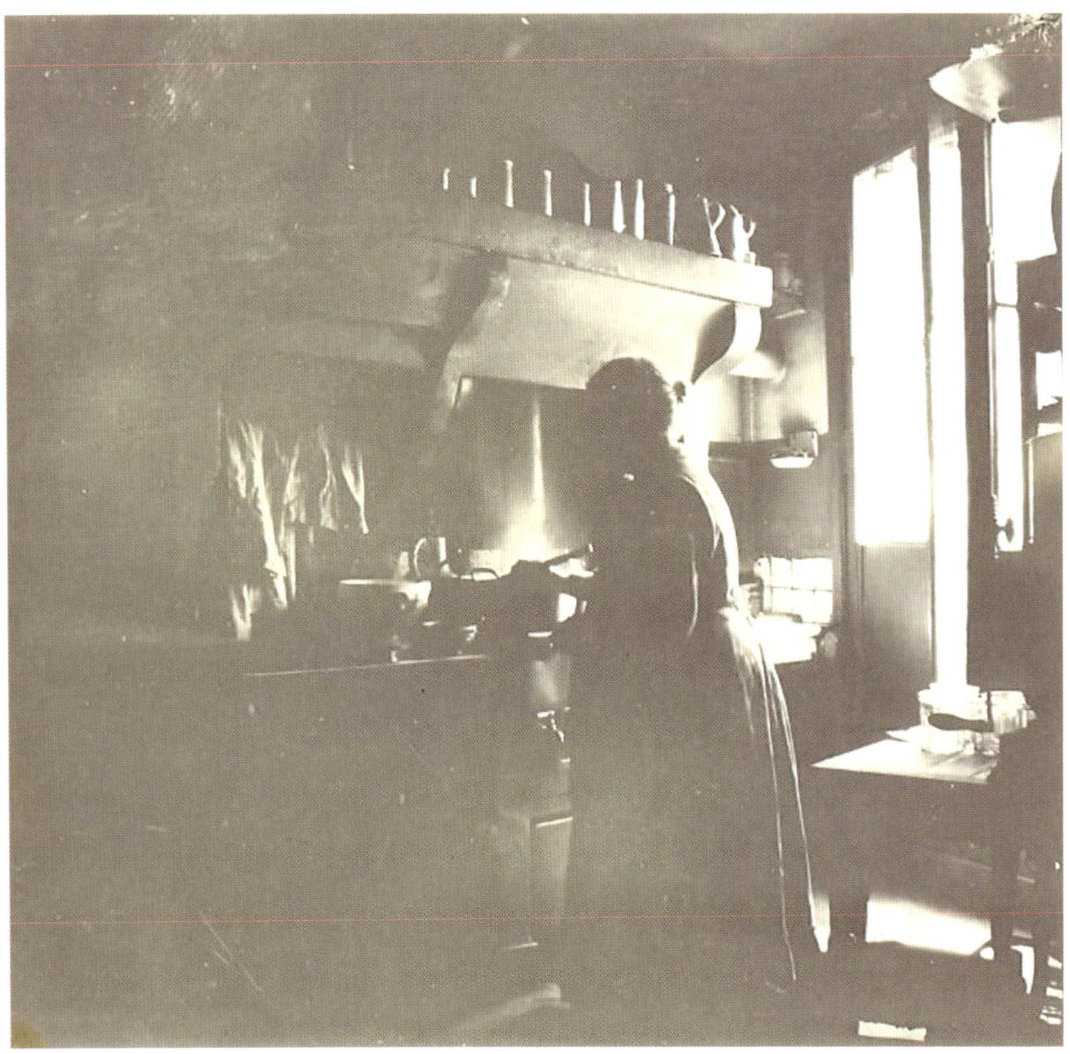

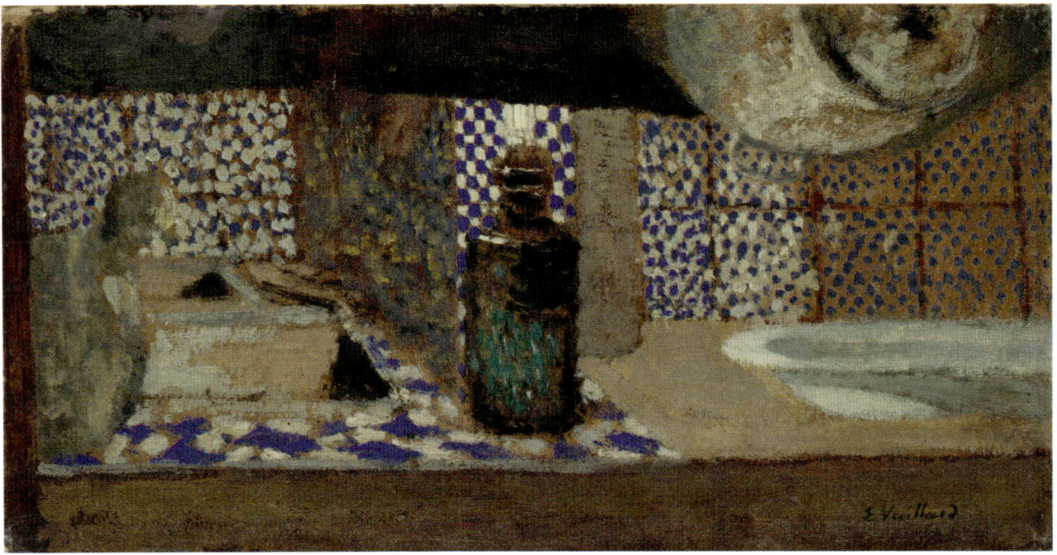

TOP: CAT. 194. Edouard Vuillard, Madame Vuillard cooking, Rue des Batignolles, 1897. Gelatin silver print, $3\frac{1}{2}$ x $3\frac{1}{2}$ in. (9 x 9 cm). Private collection

BOTTOM: CAT. 195. Edouard Vuillard, *The Kitchen*, 1891–92. Oil on cardboard, $6\frac{13}{16}$ x $13\frac{5}{16}$ in. (17.3 x 33.8 cm). Yale University Art Gallery, New Haven, Conn. The Philip L. Goodwin, B.A. 1907, Collection; Gift of James L. Goodwin, 1905, Henry Sage Goodwin, 1927, and Richmond L. Brown, 1907

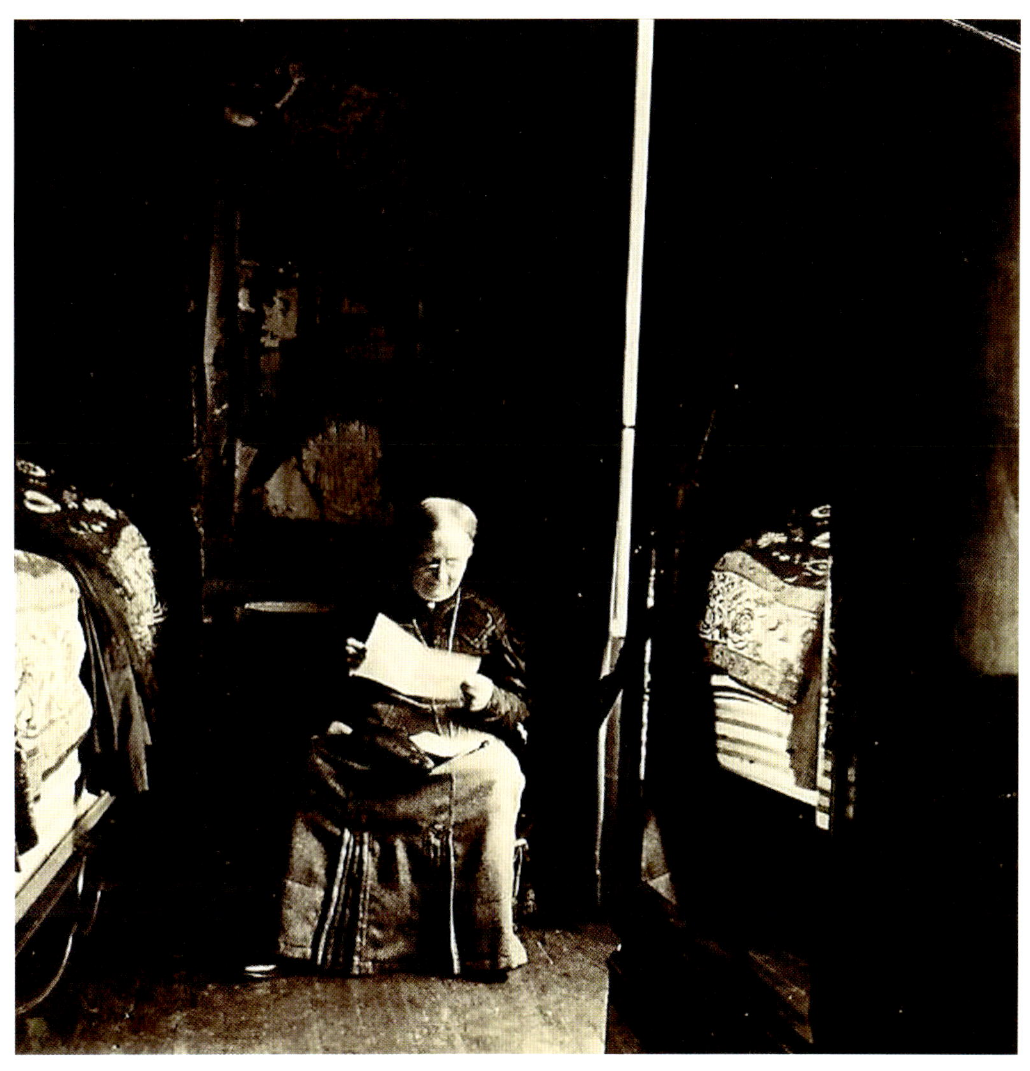

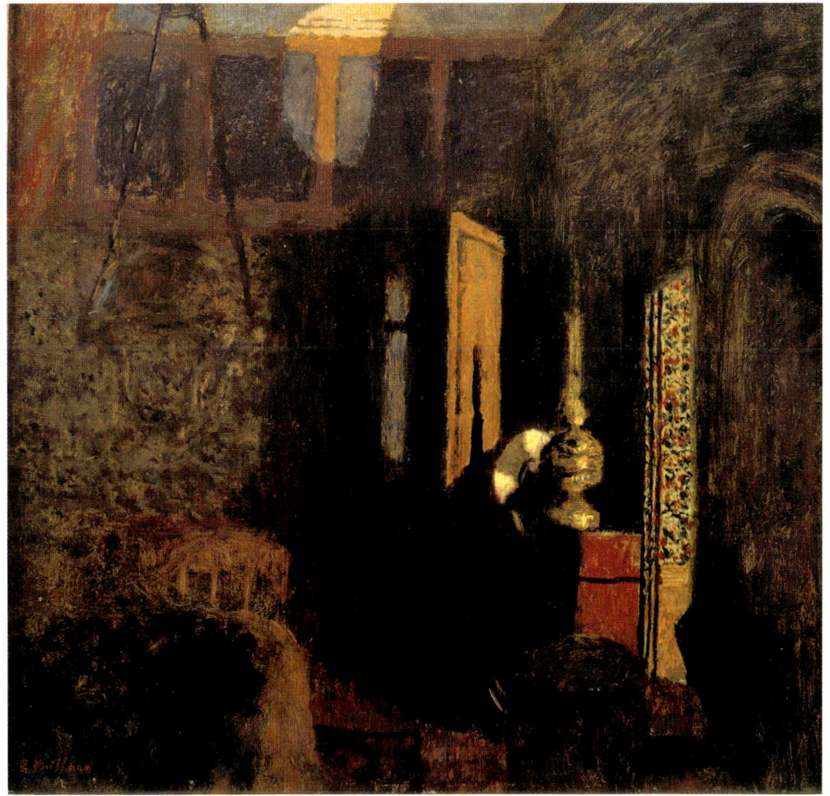

CAT. 196. Edouard Vuillard, Madame Vuillard in her room in Salenelles, 1907. Gelatin silver print, $3^{1}/_{4}$ x $3^{3}/_{8}$ in. (8.4 x 8.5 cm). Private collection

CAT. 197. Edouard Vuillard, *Interior Scene, Mystery*, 1896. Oil on board, $14^{1}/_{8}$ x 15 in. (35.8 x 38.1 cm). Private collection, United States

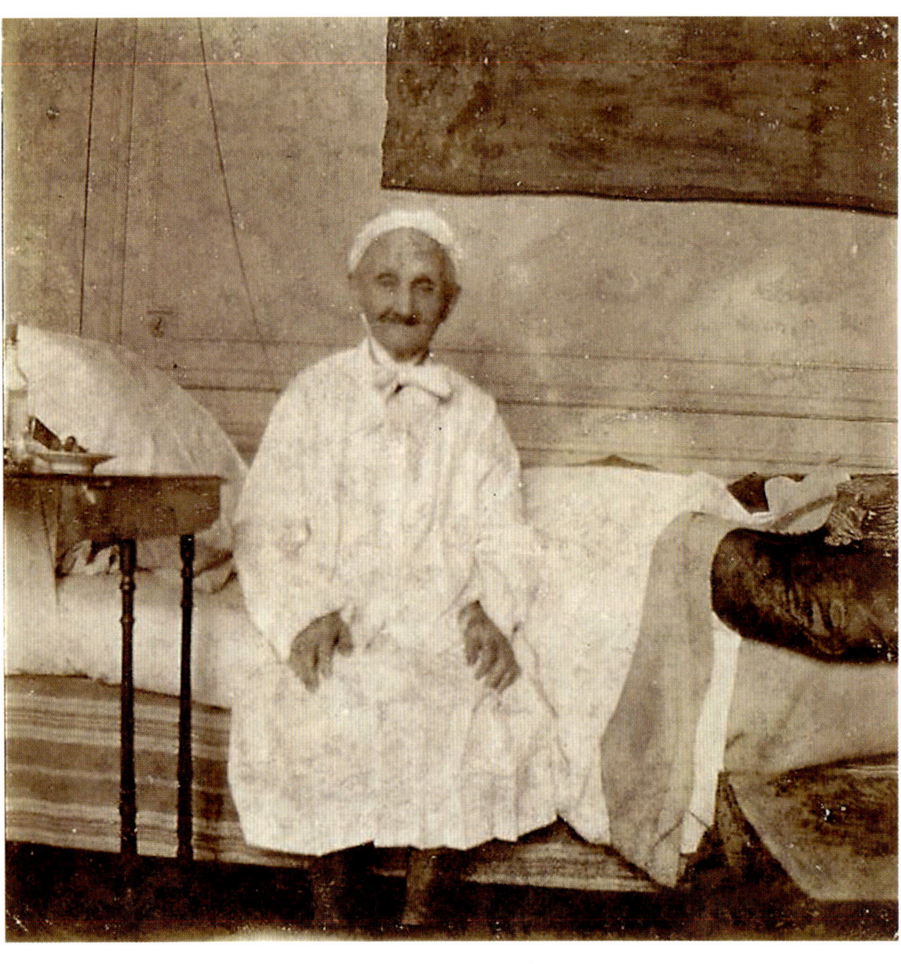

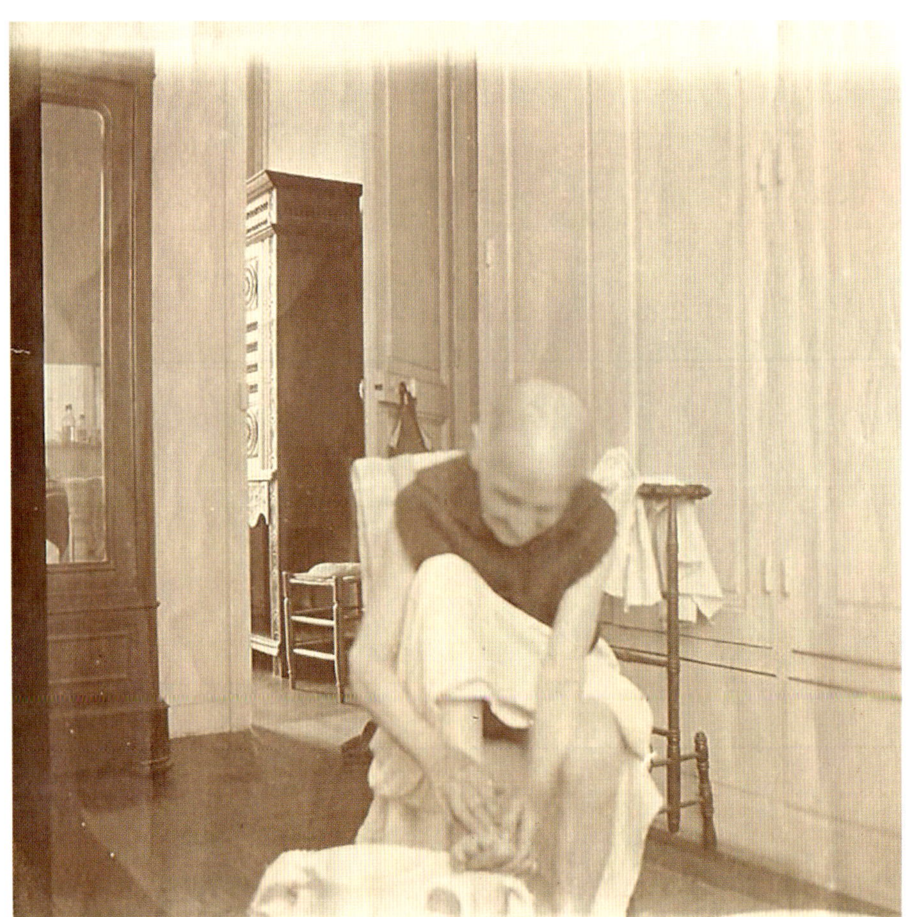

CAT. 198. Edouard Vuillard, Madame Vuillard seated on her bed, Place Vintimille, 1928. Gelatin silver print, 3 3/8 x 3 3/8 in. (8.7 x 8.7 cm). Private collection

CAT. 199. Edouard Vuillard, Madame Vuillard at her toilet, Place Vintimille, 1928. Gelatin silver print, 3 x 2 3/4 in. (7.5 x 6.9 cm). Private collection

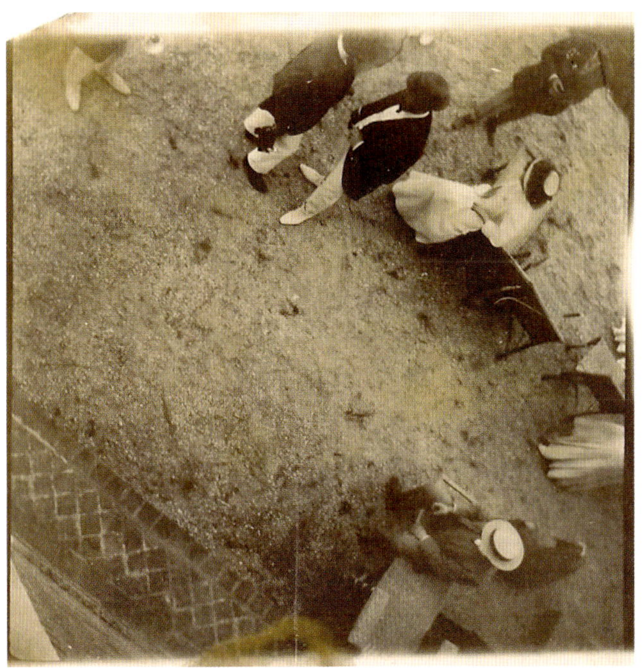

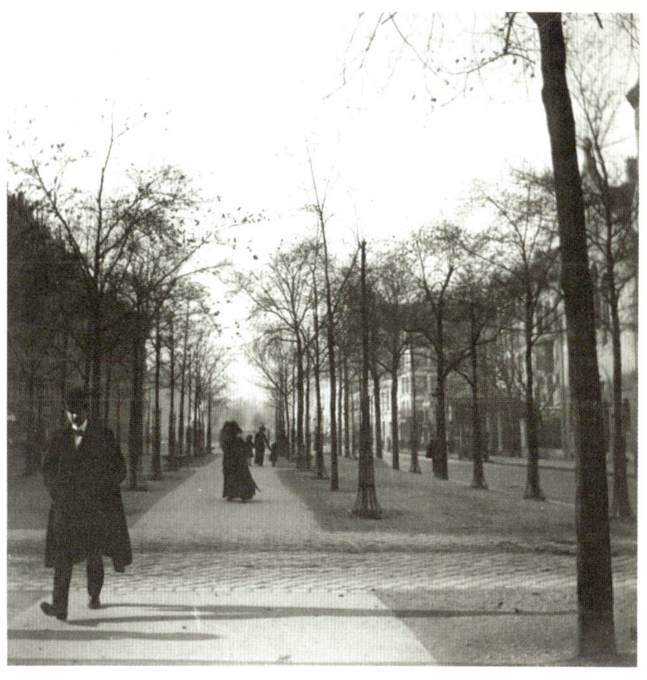

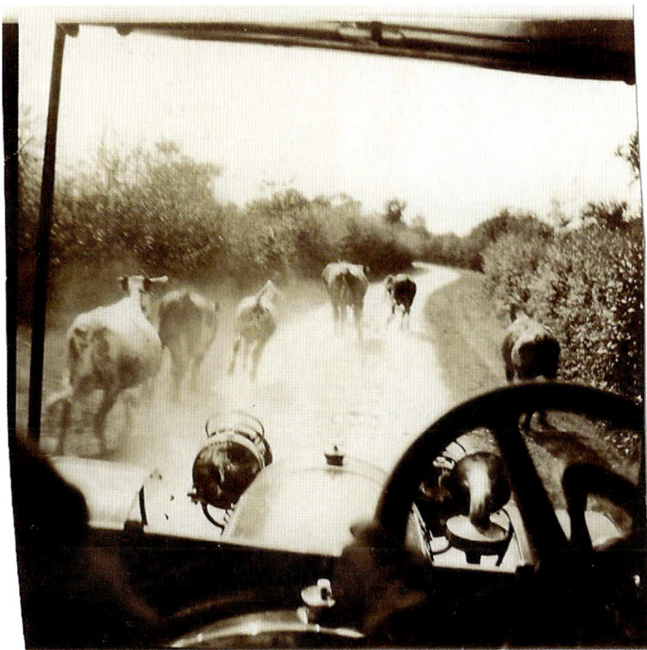

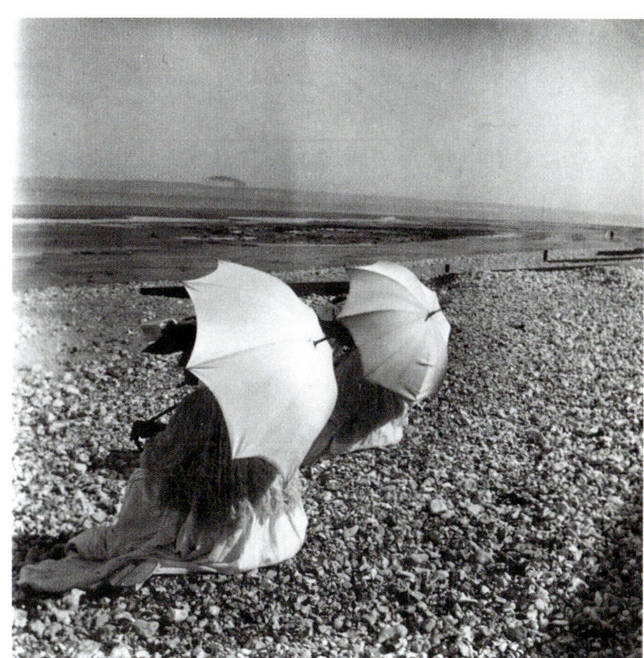

CAT. 200. Edouard Vuillard, Amfréville: View from a window, 1907. Gelatin silver print, 3½ x 3½ in. (8.9 x 9 cm). Private collection

CAT. 201. Edouard Vuillard, Boulevard des Batignolles, 1899. Gelatin silver print, 3½ x 3½ in. (8.9 x 9 cm). Private collection, Paris

CAT. 202. Edouard Vuillard, Cattle in front of the car in Brittany, 1906. Gelatin silver print, 3½ x 3⅜ in. (8.8 x 8.7 cm). Private collection

CAT. 203. Edouard Vuillard, The two sunshades, 1902. Gelatin silver print, 3½ x 3½ in. (9 x 9 cm). Private collection

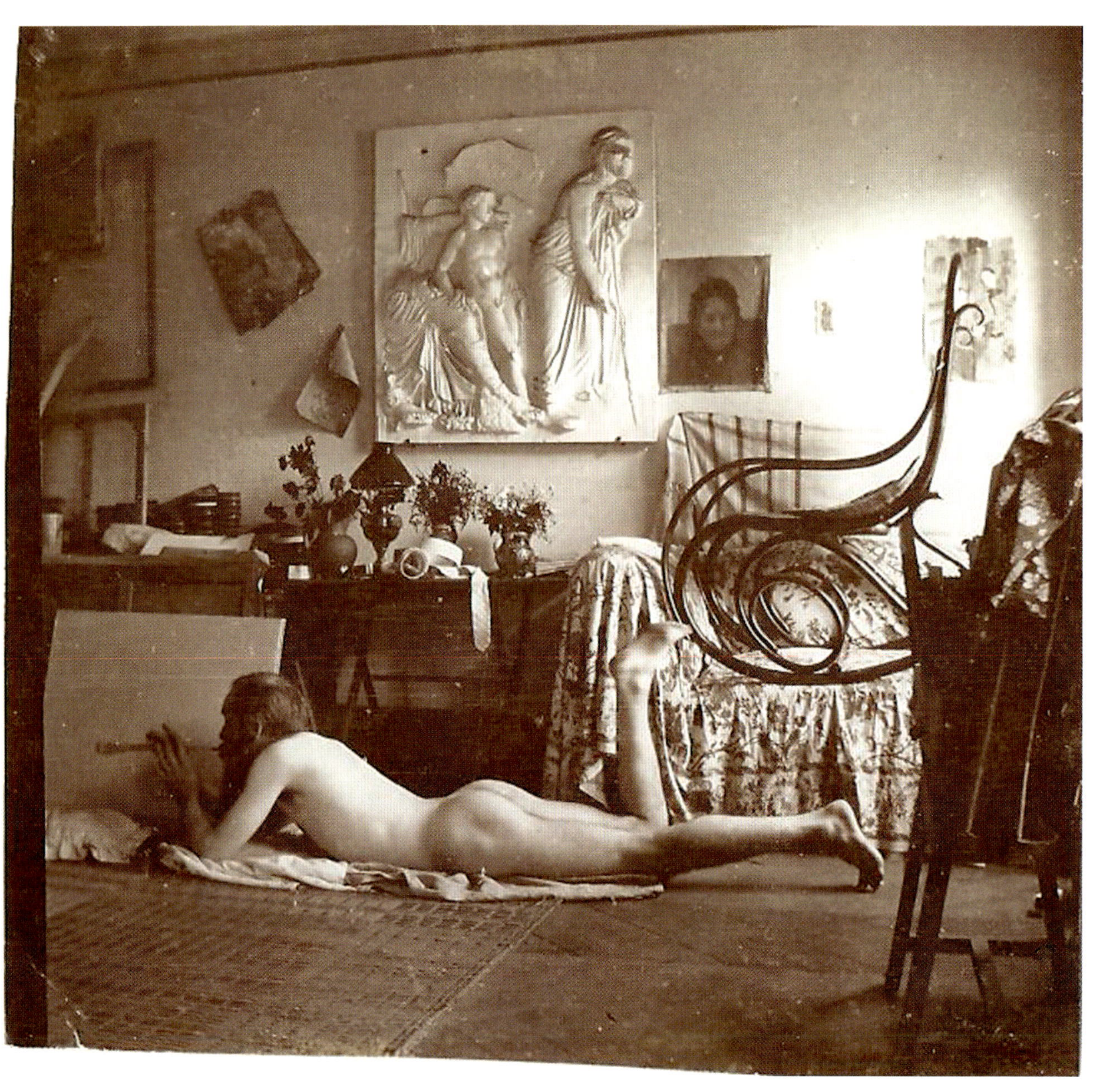

CAT. 204. Edouard Vuillard, Ker-Xavier Roussel nude, Rue Truffaut, ca. 1900. Gelatin silver print, 3 3/8 x 3 3/8 in. (8.5 x 8.7 cm). Private collection

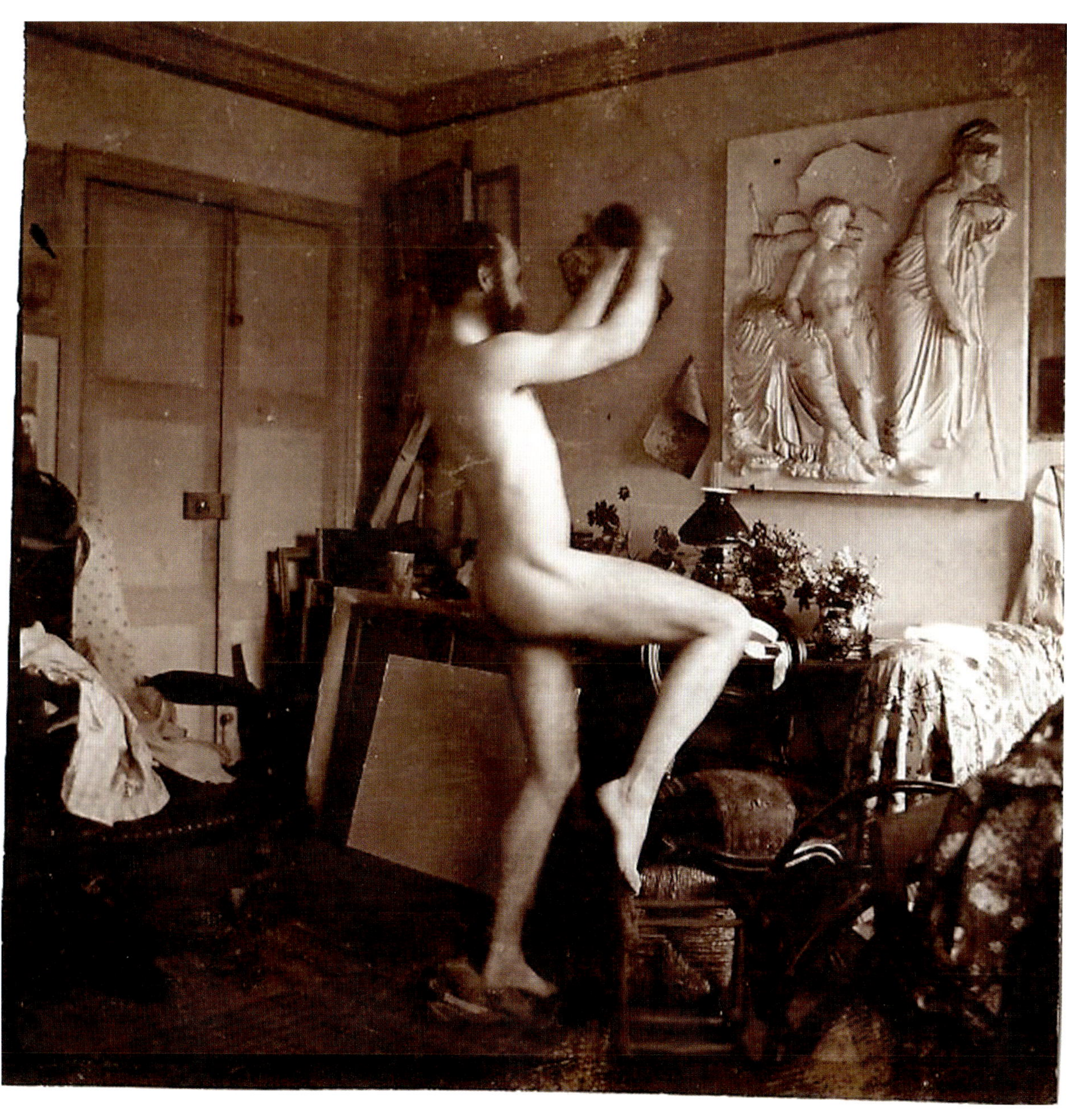

CAT. 205. Edouard Vuillard, Ker-Xavier Roussel dancing nude, Rue Truffaut, ca. 1900. Gelatin silver print, 3³/₈ x 3³/₈ in. (8.7 x 8.5 cm). Private collection

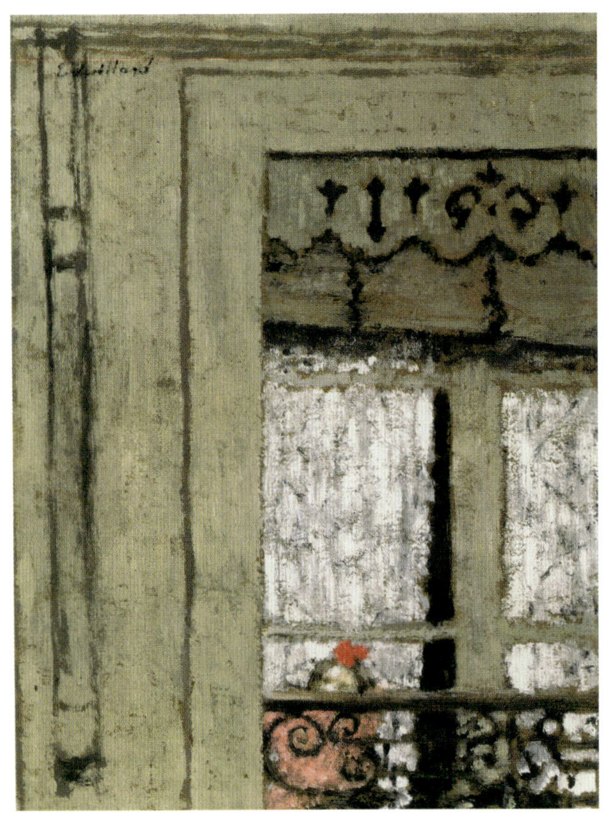

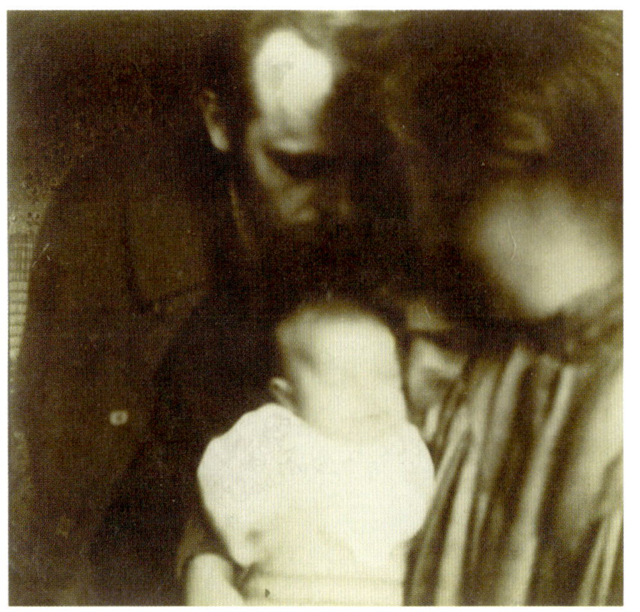

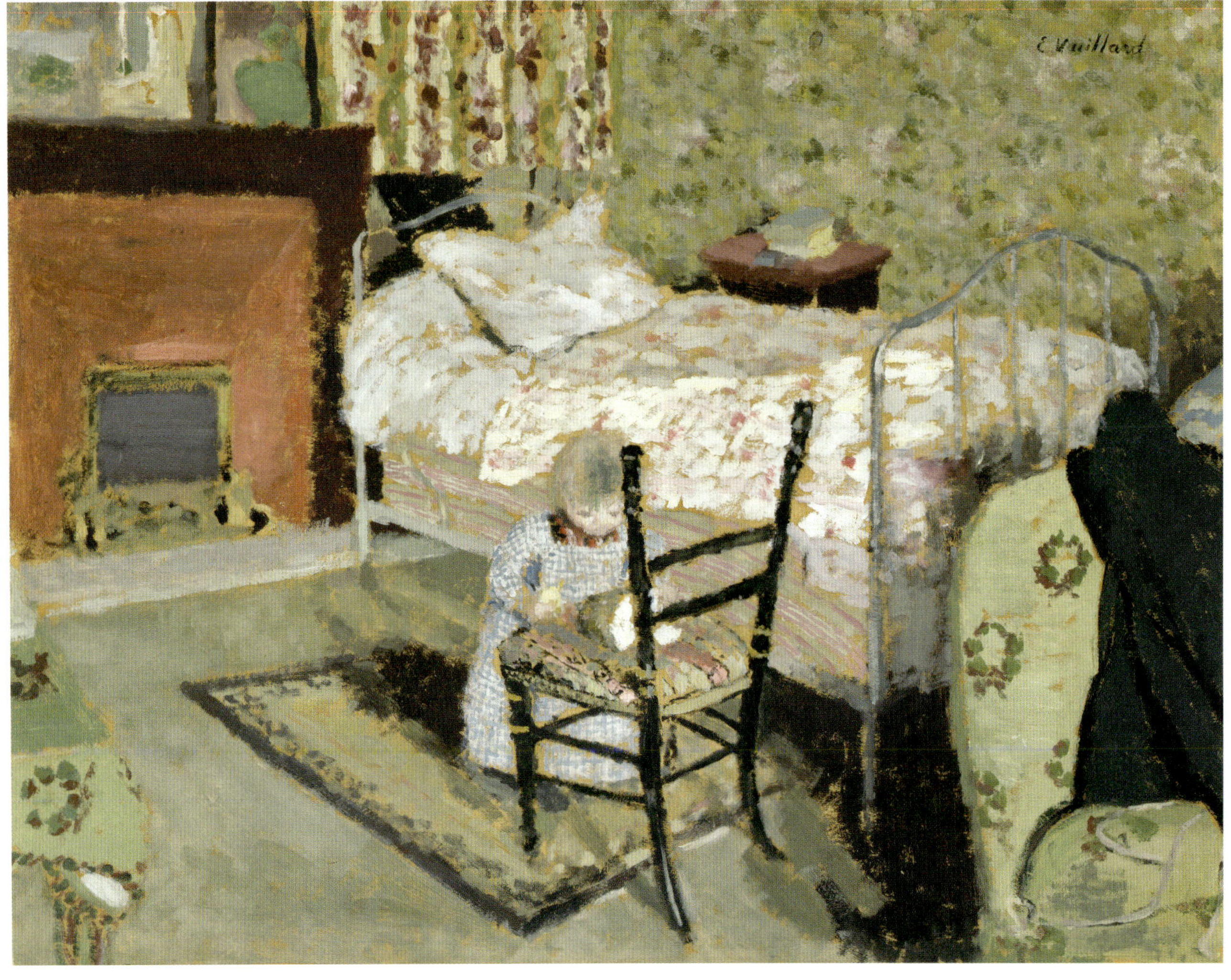
E Vuillard

OPPOSITE:
CAT. 206. Edouard Vuillard, *Child at the Window*, ca. 1901. Oil on cardboard, 13 1/2 x 10 in. (34.3 x 25.4 cm). House Collection, Dumbarton Oaks, Washington, D.C.

CAT. 207. Edouard Vuillard, Ker-Xavier, Annette, and Marie Roussel in Levallois, 1898. Gelatin silver print, 3 3/8 x 3 1/2 in. (8.6 x 8.9 cm). Private collection

CAT. 208. Edouard Vuillard, *Child Playing: Annette in Front of a Wooden Chair*, 1900. Oil on cardboard, mounted on cradled panel, 17 1/4 x 22 3/4 in. (43.8 x 57.8 cm). The Art Institute of Chicago. Mr. and Mrs. A. Ryerson Collection

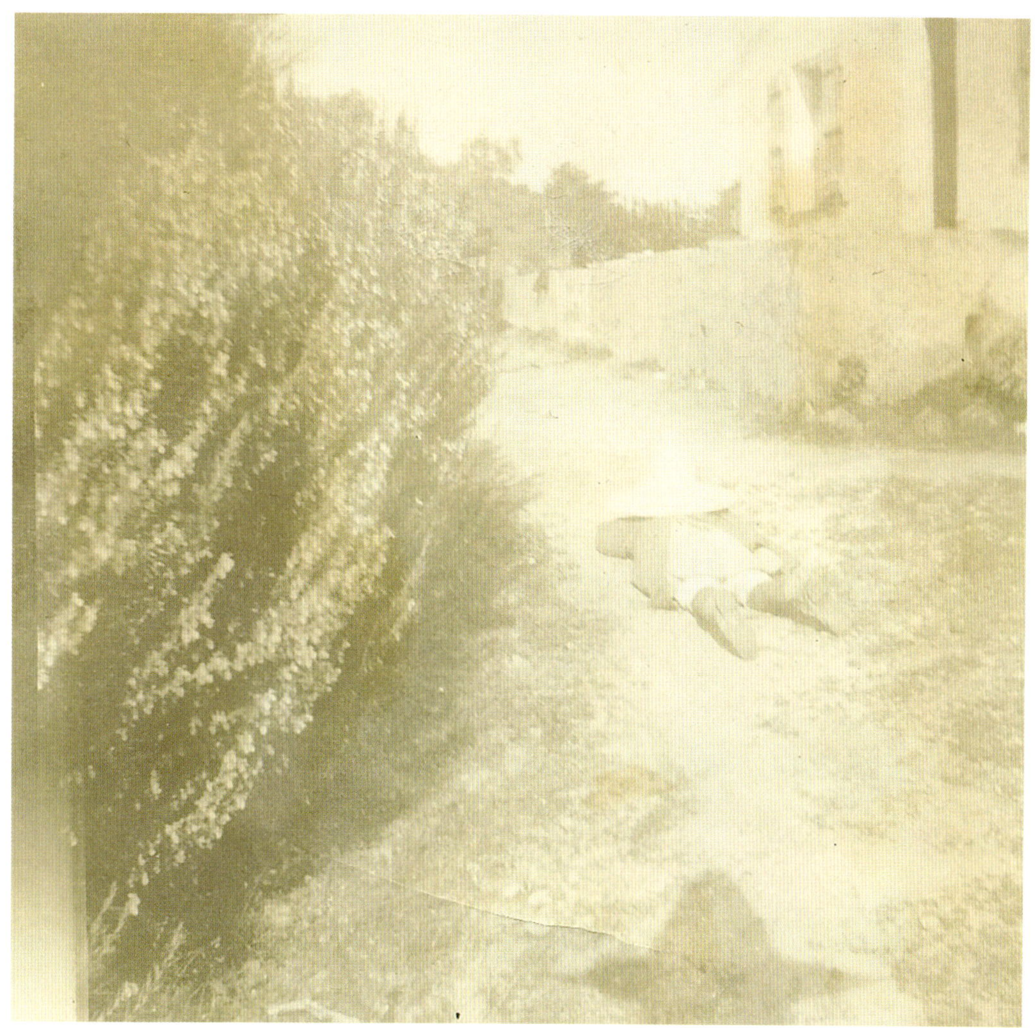

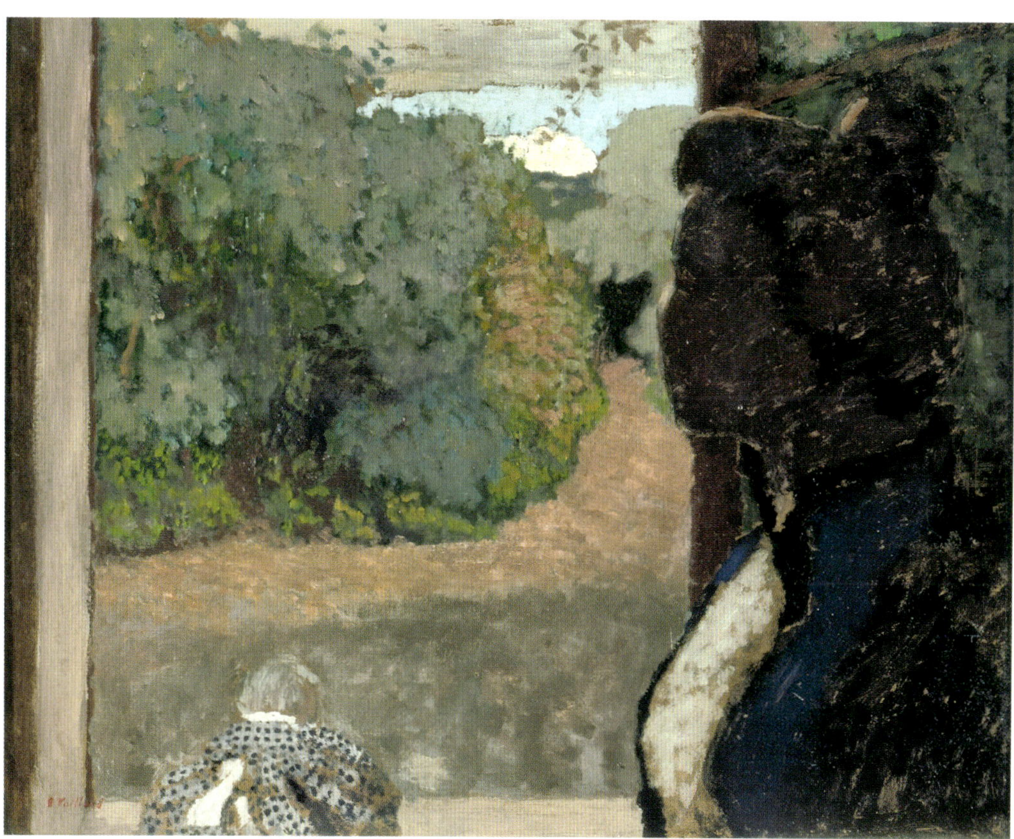

CAT. 209. Edouard Vuillard, Annette Roussel, 1904. Gelatin silver print, 3 3/8 x 3 1/2 in. (8.5 x 9 cm). Private collection

CAT. 210. Edouard Vuillard, *The Lady at the Window*, ca. 1900. Oil on cardboard, 19 1/8 x 24 3/4 in. (48.6 x 62.9 cm). Private collection

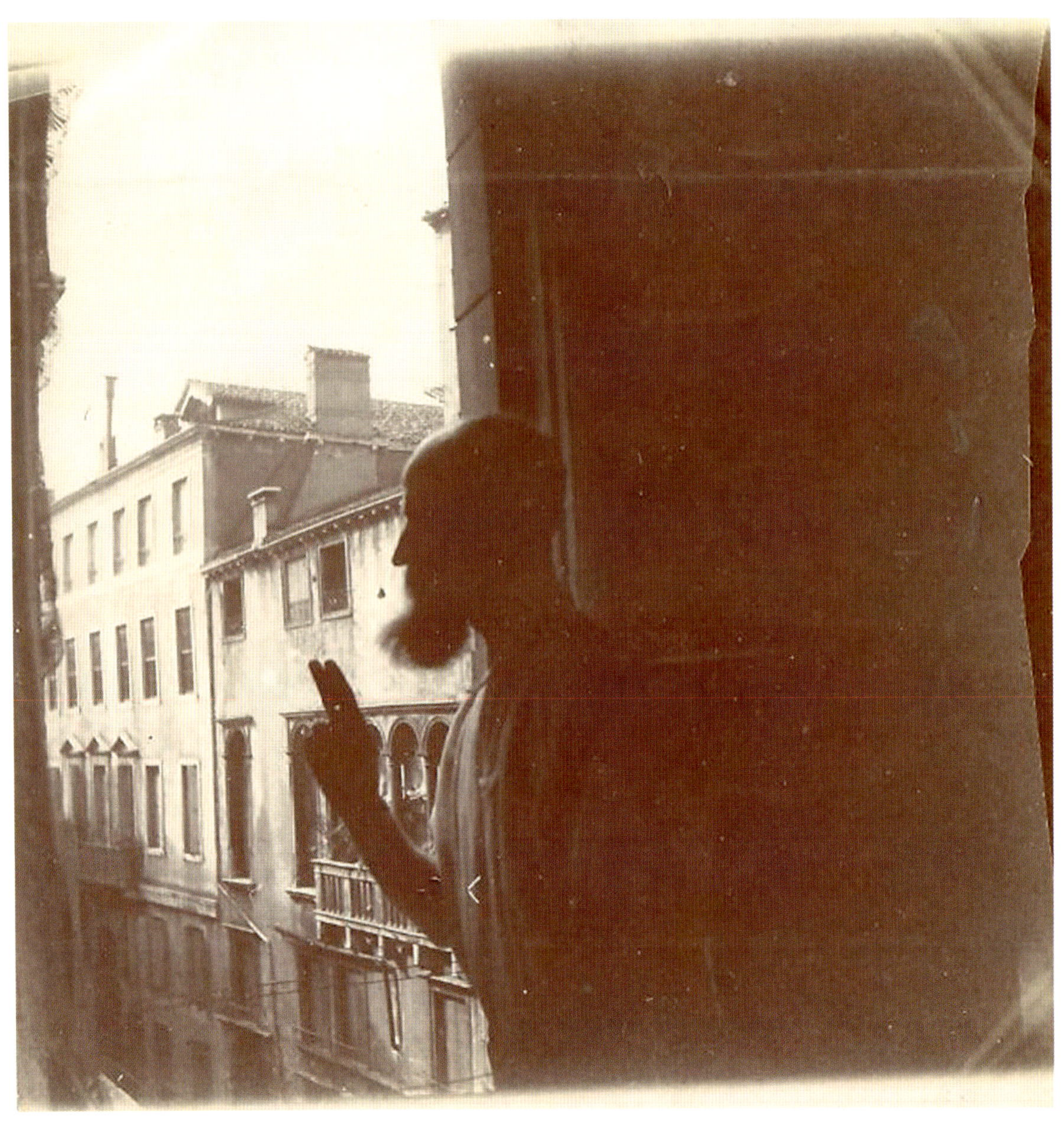

CAT. 211. Edouard Vuillard, Edouard Vuillard at the window in Venice, 1899. Gelatin silver print, 3½ x 3½ in. (9 x 8.9 cm). Private collection

Artist Biographies

Pierre Bonnard

Pierre Bonnard was born October 3, 1867, in Fontenay-aux-Roses, near Paris, the son of Eugène Bonnard, a government official. After studying law for three years, he lost interest in the profession and began taking art classes at the Ecole des Beaux-Arts and the Académie Julian. There, he met the painters Maurice Denis, Paul Sérusier, and Edouard Vuillard, who led these and other artists in the formation of the Nabis group. Bonnard first showed his paintings in the annual Salon des Indépendants exhibition in 1891, and by 1893 was contributing to the prominent avant-garde journal *La revue blanche*. That year, he met sixteen-year-old Marthe de Méligny, who would become his muse and the main subject of his art for the rest of his career. His style, inspired chiefly by Gauguin in the 1890s, used bright lozenges of color and pattern that caused the figures and backgrounds of his compositions to form flat, decorative ensembles. His paint application became looser in the twentieth century, when he gradually shifted his focus from small interiors and portraits to landscapes and began spending more time in the countryside.

In the paintings of this later phase, it is clear that Bonnard was increasingly influenced by the Impressionists. The tragedy of World War I and the growing abstraction and alienation of twentieth-century art did not affect his painting, which remained focused on composition and color. In addition to his canvases, he created stage sets, illustrated books, built painted screens, and designed posters. Bonnard purchased a Kodak camera around 1897 and, over the next two decades, took a few hundred photographs.

After having lived with Marthe de Méligny for years, Bonnard finally married her in 1925. Only then did he learn that her real name was Maria Boursin. He died in January 1947.

George Hendrik Breitner

George Hendrik Breitner was born in Rotterdam on September 12, 1857, and moved in 1876 to The Hague, where he attended the academy until 1880. In the early 1880s, he regularly associated with Vincent van Gogh; the pair roamed the streets "to look for figures and nice scenes," as Van Gogh wrote. Between 1877 and 1887, Breitner was financially supported by the Rotterdam corn merchant A. P. van Stolk, who was not always impressed with the young man's work, and, in later years, by others. In 1886 he settled in Amsterdam, where he remained for the rest of his life (with a break from 1903 to 1906, when he lived in Aerdenhout but kept his studio in Amsterdam). He probably began taking photographs in 1889; the last one that can be dated with certainty was shot in 1915. In spite of the considerable income he earned from his paintings, Breitner had perpetual money troubles, as is evident from many letters devoted to this worrisome subject. Nevertheless, he spent considerable amounts on hobbies such as bicycling and photography, owning several cameras at a time when they were relatively expensive.

Breitner was a solitary individual whose work defies easy classification according to the artistic trends of his time. Although he was influential, he had no committed followers. During the last ten years of his life, he worked little; and after 1914, he did not maintain a studio. He died in Amsterdam on June 5, 1923.

Maurice Denis

Born in Granville, France, in 1870, the painter and critic Maurice Denis lived and worked all his life in Saint-Germain-en-Laye. In 1888, he and his friends Pierre Bonnard and Edouard Vuillard founded the avant-garde Nabis group, which significantly influenced the evolution of modern art. Two years later, he published the group's manifesto in the magazine *Art et critique*, seeking a synthesis between modern and traditional painting. Bold compositions, rhythm, and blocks of color—all imbued the works of the Nabis with decorative power.

Denis married his muse, Marthe Meurier, in 1893; they had seven children. The family often spent holidays in Brittany and Italy, and in 1908, Denis purchased the Villa Silencio in Perros-Guirec in Brittany, where he worked every summer.

Beginning in 1898, a new classicism emerged in Denis's work, particularly in his religious portraits and frescos. In 1914, he bought the former hospital Le Prieuré in Saint-Germain-en-Laye. He moved in and began decorating the chapel, a project on which he worked until 1928. After Marthe's death, in 1919, Denis painted the chapel in her memory. Two years later, he married Elisabeth Graterolle, with whom he had two children. He died in Paris in 1943.

Henri Evenepoel

Henri Jacques Edouard Evenepoel was born October 3, 1872, in Nice to Charles Edmond Armand Evenepoel and Anna Emilie Peppe; they had traveled there from Brussels for a change of climate. His mother died of tuberculosis in 1874, leaving her husband and two sons. Evenepoel's letters to his father, a strict, cultivated man, remain the single most informative source of information about his adult life, artistic experiences, and aspirations. Evenepoel began studying art in Brussels at age seventeen. He departed for Paris in 1892 to enter the Ecole des Beaux-Arts, where in March 1893 he was invited to join the atelier of Gustave Moreau. In Paris, he reestablished contact with his cousin, Louise van Mattenburgh, who was married to Michel de Mey and the mother of two daughters, Henriette and Sophie. Henri and Louise fell in love, and in 1894 she bore him a son, Charles. That same year, Evenepoel produced several poster designs and showed his work at the Salon des Artistes Français. He continued to exhibit in the Salon, and in 1897 was given a one-man show in Brussels. In 1895, he met Henri Matisse, a fellow student of Moreau; the two became close friends.

In 1897, Evenepoel bought a Kodak camera; he would use it constantly over the next two and a half years. His father sent him to Algeria that year, hoping to distance him from Louise and benefit his health. In the brilliant North African sun, his palette brightened considerably. Many photographs he made in Algeria disappointed him, although some became the basis for paintings. He continued to paint portraits of children, especially of Henriette, Sophie, and Charles. All three, and Louise, also appeared in many of his photographs. Showings of his painting *The Spaniard in Paris* (1899; Museum of Fine Arts, Ghent) at the Paris Salon of 1899 and at the Salon of the Libre Esthétique in Brussels in 1900 were highly successful. He died of typhoid in Paris in December 1899.

Henri Rivière

Printmaker, stage designer, watercolorist, collector, and author, Benjamin Jean Pierre Henri Rivière was born in Paris on May 11, 1864. Except for a stay with relatives in the Pyrenees during the Franco-Prussian War, Rivière spent his youth in Paris, living in the Montmartre district. His only formal artistic training took place in the atelier of Emile Bin in 1879 and 1880. In early 1882 Rivière's friend Paul Signac introduced him to the sophisticated world of Parisian culture at the Chat Noir (Black Cat), a cabaret frequented by artists, writers, and performers. Its owner, Rodolphe Salis, hired the eighteen-year-old aspiring artist to work on the cabaret's weekly journal. Rivière became integrally involved with the cabaret's signature entertainment, the Théâtre d'Ombre (Shadow Theater). From 1886 through 1896 Rivière directed several plays there, orchestrating increasingly ambitious productions. During this period he also started making etchings and taking informal photographs.

From the mid-1880s to 1913, the artist and his wife, Eugénie, summered in Brittany, and the Breton landscape became a favored subject. In 1889 Rivière launched his work on woodblock prints and played a leading role in the color printmaking revival. Influenced by the wave of *japonisme* sweeping Paris, Rivière developed his own collection of eight hundred Japanese prints and taught himself to make woodblocks using authentic Japanese methods. In 1890 he produced his first series of woodcuts, *Paysages bretons* (Breton Landscapes). His second series, *La mer, études de vagues* (The Sea, Studies of Waves; 1890–92), set in Brittany but inspired by artists of Japan, was a great critical success. Completed in 1902, Rivière's album of lithographs, *Les trente-six vues de la Tour Eiffel* (Thirty-six Views of the Eiffel Tower), was his homage to Hokusai's *Thirty-six Views of Mount Fuji*.

During the mid-1890s Rivière played a pioneering role in the "democratization" of fine art, creating large "mural prints" in editions of 1,000, which allowed schools and individuals to acquire lithographs inexpensively. In 1906, due to the illness of his trusted printer, Eugène Verneau, etching began to replace lithography in his practice. By 1917 Rivière was focusing almost exclusively on making watercolors of the French countryside, as he seemed to willingly move outside the center of the Parisian art world. His final exhibition, at Paris's Musée des arts décoratifs in 1921, was chiefly composed of watercolors. In the early 1920s he oversaw the publication of a volume of drawings by his friend Edgar Degas and wrote two books on Asian art. After World War II he wrote and designed his memoirs. Rivière died at the home of a family friend in Sucy-en-Brie, outside Paris, on August 24, 1951.

Félix Vallotton

Félix Edouard Vallotton — painter, engraver, draftsman, art critic, and writer — was born in 1865 in Lausanne, Switzerland, became a French citizen in 1900, and died in Paris in 1925. He arrived in Paris in 1882 at the age of sixteen. After an early career as a portrait artist, he began making wood engravings in 1890, reviving a technique that soon brought him international renown. In 1893, he joined the group of painters known as the Nabis brotherhood, which included his friends Pierre Bonnard, Maurice Denis, and Edouard Vuillard as well as several other artists. The 1890s were marked by a major diversification of his activity, including engraving, illustration (he was the main illustrator for *La revue blanche*), art criticism, and painting. For a decade, the main subjects of his pictures were interiors, nudes, landscapes, and lively outdoor scenes. Alongside the street scenes and views of Paris parks, the beach scenes in particular resemble snapshots, and indeed their composition reflects the artist's use of his own photographs. He used photography's ability to erase the three-dimensional aspect of nature to create new pictorial forms suited to the aesthetics of flatness appreciated by the Nabis. His marriage in 1899 to Gabrielle Rodrigues-Henriques, daughter of the art dealer Alexandre Bernheim, marked a turning point in his life and career, after which he concentrated mainly on his original vocation of painting. Vallotton was fiercely independent and, in the space of a few years, he developed a highly personal style, combining discoveries from his woodcuts, lessons learned from the Japanese masters, and the example of illustrious predecessors such as Poussin, Rembrandt, and Ingres. His art does not break with tradition so much as overturn it with powerful decorative effects and a palette of muted tones alternating with very bright colors, often dissonant, sometimes unreal. He was particularly productive — over 1,700 paintings — given that his work was created in the space of only forty years.

Edouard Vuillard

Jean-Edouard Vuillard was born November 11, 1868, in the small Burgundy town of Cuiseaux, but moved at a young age to Paris. After his father died when Edouard was fifteen, he continued living with, and remained close to, his mother until her death in 1928. He attended the Lycée Condorcet on a scholarship, and there met the writer Pierre Véber, the painter Maurice Denis, and his own future brother-in-law, the painter Ker-Xavier Roussel. In 1886, Vuillard enrolled in the Académie Julian; the following year, he was accepted, after three attempts, into the Ecole des Beaux-Arts. There, he joined with fellow students, including Denis, Pierre Bonnard, and Paul Sérusier, in the Nabi brotherhood, taking as its name the Hebrew word for prophet. Despite the stated intention of this group to create a new kind of painting, Vuillard visited the Louvre almost daily and found its vast collection spanning the history of art a continual source of inspiration for the rest of his life. Vuillard began a journal in 1888; the first two volumes, which cover the next decade, contain sketches and notes on pictures and daily life. In the twentieth century, he made daily notations until his death in 1940.

In the mid-1890s, Vuillard became associated with *La revue blanche*, the avant-garde journal published by the brothers Alexandre, Alfred, and Thadée Natanson. Thadée's wife, Misia, became Vuillard's muse, and was the central subject of many of his best works from the second half of the 1890s. Vuillard received several significant commissions from the Natansons and their circle, establishing him as a master of the late 1890s *décoration*. By the end of the decade, as the journal's fortunes waned, Vuillard became involved with a new circle of friends, at the center of which were his dealer, Jos Hessel, and Hessel's wife, Lucy. Vuillard maintained an intimate relationship with Lucy that lasted the rest of his life. Within the *haute-bourgeois* milieu of the Hessels, Vuillard became one of the most sought-after portrait painters of the early twentieth century. He died in June 1940. *Vuillard et son Kodak*, organized by the L'Oeil Gallery in Paris in 1963, was the first exhibition of photographs by any of the Nabis artists.

Exhibition Checklist

This checklist includes all of the works of art featured in the exhibition that accompanies this publication, organized alphabetically by artist. For each artist, paintings, drawings, and prints precede photographs, and photographs are grouped by type. Within each medium, works are ordered chronologically, and when there are multiple works of the same date, in alphabetical order by title.

Titles are provided in languages other than English when those titles have become identified with the pieces through exhibition or publication. Titles for the photographs are descriptive rather than official. For dimensions, height precedes width. A catalogue (cat.) number at the end of the entry indicates that the work is reproduced in this book.

Pierre Bonnard

Afternoon in the Garden, 1891
Oil and pen and black ink over pencil on canvas, 14 3/4 x 17 3/4 in. (37.5 x 45.1 cm)
Private collection (Washington only)
CAT. 4

Intimité (Portrait de Monsieur et Madame Claude Terrasse) (Intimacy [Portrait of Monsieur and Madame Claude Terrasse]), 1891
Oil on canvas, 15 x 14 1/8 in. (38 x 36 cm)
Musée d'Orsay, Paris, acquired with the assistance of Philippe Meyer through the Foundation for French Museums, 1992 (RF 1992-406)
CAT. 3

The Cab Horse, ca. 1895
Oil on wood, 11 3/4 x 15 3/4 in. (29.7 x 40 cm)
National Gallery of Art, Washington, D.C. Ailsa Mellon Bruce Collection (1970.17.4)
CAT. 7

Narrow Street in Paris, ca. 1897
Oil on cardboard, 14 5/8 x 7 3/4 in. (37.1 x 19.6 cm)
The Phillips Collection, Washington, D.C.
CAT. 10

The Mirror in the Green Room (La Glace de la chambre verte), 1908
Oil on paper, 19 3/4 x 25 3/4 in. (50.2 x 65.4 cm)
Indianapolis Museum of Art. James E. Roberts Fund (38.84)
CAT. 21

Jeune femme et enfant (Young Girl and Child, study for a lithograph), 1892
Pencil, 7 7/8 x 4 3/16 in. (20 x 10.6 cm)
Private collection
CAT. 9

The Model and the Artist Reflected in a Mirror (Study for "La Cheminée"), 1916
Pencil and black chalk, 12 1/4 x 9 3/4 in. (31.1 x 24.8 cm)
Private collection
CAT. 20

Crouching Nude in a Tub, 1925
Pencil and gray wash, 8 5/16 x 6 13/16 in. (21.7 x 17.4 cm)
Private collection
CAT. 31

The Little Laundress, 1896
Color lithograph, 11 3/4 x 7 1/2 in. (30 x 19 cm)
Van Gogh Museum, Amsterdam (Vincent van Gogh Foundation) (p 1108V/2000)
CAT. 8

The Vineyard, 1898–99
Lithograph, 13 x 13 3/4 in. (33 x 35 cm)
Van Gogh Museum, Amsterdam (Vincent van Gogh Foundation) (p 1111V/2000)

Square at Night, 1899
Lithograph, 11 x 15 3/8 in. (28 x 39 cm)
Van Gogh Museum, Amsterdam (Vincent van Gogh Foundation) (p 1172V/2000)

Street Corner, 1899
Lithograph, 22 5/8 x 13 3/4 in. (57.5 x 35 cm)
Van Gogh Museum, Amsterdam (Vincent van Gogh Foundation) (p 1168V/2000)

"Eté" (Summer), illustration from *Parallèlement* by Verlaine, 1900
Lithograph with rose-sanguine ink, 11 5/8 x 9 5/8 in. (29.6 x 24.6 cm)
Van Gogh Museum, Amsterdam (Vincent van Gogh Foundation), and private collection
CAT. 29

"Limbes" (Limbo), illustration from *Parallèlement* by Verlaine, 1900
Lithograph with rose-sanguine ink, 11 5/8 x 9 5/8 in. (29.6 x 24.6 cm)
Van Gogh Museum, Amsterdam (Vincent van Gogh Foundation), and private collection
CAT. 27

"Daphnis et Chloé" (Daphnis and Chloé), illustration for *La pastorale de Longus*, p. 69, 1902
Lithograph, 12 x 9 7/8 in. (30.5 x 25 cm) page
Van Gogh Museum, Amsterdam (Vincent van Gogh Foundation) (p 1783V/2000), and private collection
CAT. 23

"Daphnis et Chloé" (Daphnis and Chloé), illustration for *La pastorale de Longus*, p. 185, 1902
Lithograph, 12 x 9 7/8 in. (30.5 x 25 cm) page
Van Gogh Museum, Amsterdam (Vincent van Gogh Foundation) (p 1783V/2000), and private collection
CAT. 24

The Bath, 1925
Lithograph, 13 x 8 7/8 in. (33 x 22.5 cm)
Van Gogh Museum, Amsterdam (Vincent van Gogh Foundation) (p 1149V/2000)

Renée embracing a dog, 1898–99
Gelatin silver print, 1 1/2 x 2 1/8 in. (3.8 x 5.5 cm)
Musée d'Orsay, Paris. Gift of the children of Charles Terrasse, 1992 (PHO 1987-30-4)
CAT. 11

Bonnard with Renée and another little girl, Roussel crouching in the background, 1900
Original negative
Musée d'Orsay, Paris (PHO 1987-29-2)

Marthe nude, seated on the bed with her back turned, 1899–1900
Sepia-toned gelatin silver print, 1 1/2 x 2 1/8 in. (3.8 x 5.5 cm)
Musée d'Orsay, Paris. Gift of the children of Charles Terrasse, 1992 (PHO 1987-31-24)
CAT. 28

Marthe in Montval, seated, her left hand on her right breast, 1900–1901
Sepia-toned gelatin silver print, 1 1/2 x 2 in. (3.9 x 5.1 cm)
Musée d'Orsay, Paris. Gift of M. Antoine Terrasse, 1992 (PHO 1987-31-40)
CAT. 17

Model taking off her blouse in Bonnard's Paris studio, ca. 1916
Original untinted print, 3 1/4 x 2 1/4 in. (8.2 x 5.8 cm)
Musée d'Orsay, Paris (PHO 1985-398)
CAT. 32

Marcel and Robert in a bucket seat, Renée sitting beside them, a fourth child partly visible at the edge of the frame, 1898
Modern print from original negative, negative: 1 1/2 x 2 1/8 in. (3.8 x 5.5 cm) (Sepia-toned gelatin silver print)
Musée d'Orsay, Paris. Gift of the children of Charles Terrasse, 1992 (PHO 1987-30-17)

Robert in profile, walking, 1898
Modern print from original negative, negative: 1 1/2 x 2 1/8 in. (3.8 x 5.5. cm) (Sepia-toned gelatin silver print)
Musée d'Orsay, Paris. Gift of the children of Charles Terrasse, 1992 (PHO 1987-30-16)

Charles and partial view of a nurse, 1899
Modern print from original negative, negative: 1 1/2 x 2 1/8 in. (3.8 x 5.5 cm) (Sepia-toned gelatin silver print)
Musée d'Orsay, Paris. Gift of the children of Charles Terrasse, 1992 (PHO 1987-28-12)

Ker-Xavier Roussel and Edouard Vuillard, Venice, 1899
Modern print from original negative, negative: 1 3/8 x 2 in. (3.5 x 5 cm) (Sepia-toned gelatin silver print)
Musée d'Orsay, Paris. Gift of the children of Charles Terrasse, 1992 (PHO 1987-27-6)
CAT. 1

Andrée Terrasse, a child by her side, and, in the background, Renée, 1899–1900
Modern print from original negative, negative: 1 1/2 x 2 1/8 in. (3.8 x 5.5 cm) (Sepia-toned gelatin silver print)
Musée d'Orsay, Paris. Gift of the children of Charles Terrasse, 1992 (PHO 1987-30-25, original proof)
CAT. 5

Andrée Terrasse and Renée picking fruit in Le Grand-Lemps, 1899–1900
Modern print from original negative, negative: 1 3/8 x 2 in. (3.5 x 5 cm)
Musée d'Orsay, Paris. Gift of the children of Charles Terrasse, 1992 (PHO 1987-30-26)
CAT. 6

Marthe seated in profile on the bed, her left leg hanging down, 1899–1900
Modern print from original negative, negative: 1 5/8 x 2 in. (4 x 5.1 cm) (Sepia-toned gelatin silver print)
Musée d'Orsay, Paris. Gift of M. Antoine Terrasse, 1992 (PHO 1987-31-20a)
CAT. 26

Vuillard holding his Kodak camera, spring 1900
Modern print from original negative, negative: 1 1/2 x 2 1/8 in. (3.8 x 5.5 cm) (Sepia-toned gelatin silver print)
Musée d'Orsay, Paris. Gift of the children of Charles Terrasse, 1992 (PHO 1987-31-18)
CAT. 2

Vuillard holding his Kodak camera, and Renée, 1900
Modern print from original negative, negative: 1½ x 2⅛ in. (3.8 x 5.5 cm)
(Sepia-toned gelatin silver print)
Musée d'Orsay, Paris. Gift of M. Antoine Terrasse, 1992
(PHO 1987-27-16)

Marthe Bonnard, Pierre Bonnard seated in the grass, 1900–1901
Modern print from original negative, negative: 1½ x 2⅛ in. (3.8 x 5.5 cm)
(Sepia-toned gelatin silver print)
Musée d'Orsay, Paris. Gift of the children of Charles Terrasse, 1992
(PHO 1987-30-43)
CAT. 25

Marthe Bonnard, Pierre Bonnard from behind, sitting in the grass, 1900–1901
Modern print from original negative, negative: 1½ x 2⅛ in. (3.8 x 5.5 cm)
(Sepia-toned gelatin silver print)
Musée d'Orsay, Paris. Gift of the children of Charles Terrasse, 1992
(PHO 1987-30-44)

Marthe from behind, holding out her nightdress, 1900–1901
Modern print from original negative, negative: 1½ x 2⅛ in. (3.8 x 5.5 cm)
(Sepia-toned gelatin silver print)
Musée d'Orsay, Paris
(PHO 1987-27-25)

Marthe from the front, bending down, her right hand on the ground, 1900–1901
Modern print from original negative, negative: 1½ x 2⅛ in. (3.8 x 5.5 cm)
(Sepia-toned gelatin silver print)
Musée d'Orsay, Paris. Gift of the children of Charles Terrasse, 1992
(PHO 1987-30-35)

Marthe in Montval, in profile, taking off her nightdress, 1900–1901
Modern print from original negative, negative: 1⅜ x 2⅛ in. (3.5 x 5.5 cm)
(Sepia-toned gelatin silver print)
Musée d'Orsay, Paris. Gift of the children of Charles Terrasse, 1992
(PHO 1987-27-23)
CAT. 14

Marthe in Montval, seated, one hand on the back of her neck, 1900–1901
Modern print from original negative, negative: 1½ x 2⅛ in. (3.8 x 5.5 cm)
(Sepia-toned gelatin silver print)
Musée d'Orsay, Paris. Gift of the children of Charles Terrasse, 1992
(PHO 1987-31-39)
CAT. 16

Marthe in Montval, standing by a chair, 1900–1901
Modern print from original negative, negative: 1½ x 2⅛ in. (3.8 x 5.5 cm)
(Sepia-toned gelatin silver print)
Musée d'Orsay, Paris. Gift of the children of Charles Terrasse, 1992
(PHO 1987-31-37)
CAT. 15

Marthe in profile, drying her leg, 1900–1901
Modern print from original negative, negative: 1½ x 2⅛ in. (3.8 x 5.5 cm)
(Sepia-toned gelatin silver print)
Musée d'Orsay, Paris
(PHO 1987-27-28)

Marthe nude squatting, 1900–1901
Modern print from original negative, negative: 1½ x 2 in. (3.7 x 5.2 cm)
(Sepia-toned gelatin silver print)
Musée d'Orsay, Paris. Gift of M. Antoine Terrasse, 1992
(PHO 1987-31-36)
CAT. 19

Marthe standing in the sun, in Montval, 1900–1901
Modern print from original negative, negative: 1½ x 2⅛ in. (3.8 x 5.5 cm)
(Sepia-toned gelatin silver print)
Musée d'Orsay, Paris. Gift of M. Antoine Terrasse, 1992
(PHO 1987-31-34)
CAT. 22

Little girl wearing a crown of leaves, ca. 1902
Modern print from original negative, negative: 1½ x 2⅛ in. (3.8 x 5.5 cm)
(Sepia-toned gelatin silver print)
Musée d'Orsay. Gift of M. Antoine Terrasse, 1992 (PHO 1987-27-35)
CAT. 12

Bathing: Vivette in the foreground, Robert in the background, and two other children, 1903–5
Modern print from original negative, negative: 1½ x 2⅛ in. (3.8 x 5.5 cm)
(Sepia-toned gelatin silver print)
Musée d'Orsay, Paris. Gift of M. Antoine Terrasse, 1992
(PHO 1987-27-50)
CAT. 13

Marthe in the bathtub, Vernouillet, ca. 1908–10
Modern print from original negative, negative: 3⅛ x 2⅛ in. (7.8 x 5.5 cm)
(Sepia-toned gelatin silver print)
Musée d'Orsay, Paris. Gift of the children of Charles Terrasse, 1992
(PHO 1987-30-47)
CAT. 30

George Hendrik Breitner

Het Oorringetje (The Earring), 1893
Oil on canvas, 26⅜ x 17¾ in. (67 x 45 cm)
Private collection
CAT. 53

The Red Kimono, 1893–94
Oil on canvas, 20¼ x 29⅞ in. (51.5 x 76 cm)
Stedelijk Museum, Amsterdam (A 2214)
(Amsterdam only)

Girl in Red Kimono, Geesje Kwak, 1893–95
Oil on canvas, 24 x 19½ in. (61 x 49.5 cm)
Noortman Master Paintings, Amsterdam, on behalf of private collection, Netherlands
CAT. 50

Bridge over the Singel near Paleisstraat in Amsterdam, ca. 1897
Oil on canvas, 39⅜ x 59⅞ in. (100 x 152 cm)
Rijksmuseum, Amsterdam. Bequest of Mr. and Mrs. Drucker-Fraser (SK-A-3580)
(Amsterdam only)
CAT. 33

On Board, ca. 1897
Oil on canvas, 22⅜ x 23¼ in. (57 x 59 cm)
Stedelijk Museum, Amsterdam (A 2203)

Warehouses, Amsterdam, 1901
Oil on canvas, 32⅛ x 51⅛ in. (81.5 x 130 cm)
The Toledo Museum of Art
CAT. 54

Demolition of Oudezijds Achterburgwal, 1903–4
Oil on board on panel, 30½ x 25 in. (77.5 x 63.5 cm)
Kunsthandel A.H. Bies, Eindhoven
(Amsterdam and Indianapolis only)
CAT. 39

Girl in a White Kimono, n.d.
Oil on canvas
Private collection

Girl in a kimono (Geesje Kwak) at Breitner's studio on Lauriersgracht, n.d.
Gelatin silver print
Collection RKD, The Hague (BR 2031)
CAT. 49

Girl in a kimono (Geesje Kwak) at Breitner's studio on Lauriersgracht, n.d.
Gelatin silver print
Collection RKD, The Hague (BR 2040**)

Girl in a kimono (Geesje Kwak) at Breitner's studio on Lauriersgracht, n.d.
Gelatin silver print
Collection RKD, The Hague (BR 2279)
CAT. 51

Girls in costume, n.d.
Gelatin silver print
Collection RKD, The Hague (BR 2032**)

Singel near Paleisstraat, n.d.
Gelatin silver print
Collection RKD, The Hague (BR 2130)
CAT. 34

Three girls on a bridge, n.d.
Gelatin silver print
Collection RKD, The Hague (BR 2149**)

Woman walking with basket, n.d.
Gelatin silver print
Collection RKD, The Hague (BR 2050**)

Woman with carriage, n.d.
Gelatin silver print
Collection RKD, The Hague (BR 2012**)

Women dancing, n.d.
Gelatin silver, printing-out paper
Collection RKD, The Hague (BR 2158)
CAT. 37

Portrait of Emma and Bé Hermsen, ca. 1905
Modern gelatin silver print, 2011, from original negative
Collection RKD, The Hague (BR 0793)
CAT. 36

Carriage, n.d.
Modern gelatin silver print, 2011, from original negative
Collection RKD, The Hague (BR 0993)

The Dam, n.d.
Modern gelatin silver print, 2011, from original negative
Collection RKD, The Hague (BR 0683)
CAT. 41

Demolition, n.d.
Modern gelatin silver print, 2011, from original negative
Collection RKD, The Hague (BR 0622)

Demolition, n.d.
Modern gelatin silver print, 2011, from original negative
Collection RKD, The Hague (BR 1065)
CAT. 40

Figures walking in snowy landscape, n.d.
Modern gelatin silver print, 2011, from original negative
Collection RKD, The Hague (BR 842)
CAT. 44

Girls holding hands on "Hartjesdag" in Amsterdam, n.d.
Modern gelatin silver print, 2011, from original negative
Collection RKD, The Hague (BR 1291)
CAT. 38

Girls on bridge, n.d.
Modern gelatin silver print, 2011, from original negative
Collection RKD, The Hague (BR 1374)

Horses and a passerby on Cruquiusweg, n.d.
Modern gelatin silver print, 2011, from original negative
Collection RKD, The Hague (BR 1601)
CAT. 46

In London with Marius Bauer, n.d.
Modern gelatin silver print, 2011, from original negative
Collection RKD, The Hague (BR 1454)
CAT. 42

Model in studio, n.d.
Modern gelatin silver print, 2011, from original negative
Collection RKD, The Hague (BR 0904)

Nude before a mirror (Mina Otten?), n.d.
Modern gelatin silver print, 2011, from original negative
Collection RKD, The Hague (BR 914)
CAT. 60

Nude with reflection of Breitner in the mirror, n.d.
Modern gelatin silver print, 2011, from original negative
Collection RKD, The Hague (BR 0911)

On the bridge near Prinseneiland, n.d.
Modern gelatin silver print, 2011, from original negative
Collection RKD, The Hague (BR 1378)

Prinsengracht, n.d.
Modern gelatin silver print, 2011, from original negative
Collection RKD, The Hague (BR 0117)
CAT. 47

Reclining nude, n.d.
Modern gelatin silver print, 2011, from original negative
Collection RKD, The Hague (BR 0909)
CAT. 56

Reclining nude, n.d.
Modern gelatin silver print, 2011, from original negative
Collection RKD, The Hague (BR 0908)
CAT. 57

Reclining nude, n.d.
Modern gelatin silver print, 2011, 3½ x 3⅞ in. (9 x 9.9 cm)
Rijksmuseum, Amsterdam (RP-F-BR1999-7)
CAT. 58

Sand carters at Van Lennepkade, n.d.
Modern gelatin silver print, 2011, from original negative
Collection RKD, The Hague (BR 1241)

Seated nude, n.d. Modern gelatin silver print, 2011, $3^{7}/_{8}$ x $3^{1}/_{2}$ in. (9.9 x 8.9 cm) Rijksmuseum, Amsterdam (RP-F-BR1999-3)
CAT. 55

Singel, n.d. Modern gelatin silver print, 2011, from original negative Collection RKD, The Hague (BR 0693)
CAT. 48

Spui, n.d. Modern gelatin silver print, 2011, from original negative Collection RKD, The Hague (BR 0727)

Spui and walkers in the Kalverstraat, n.d. Modern gelatin silver print, 2011, from original negative Collection RKD, The Hague (BR 1166)
CAT. 43

Street scene, n.d. Modern gelatin silver print, 2011, from original negative Collection RKD, The Hague (BR 1323)
CAT. 45

Two girls in a snowy garden, n.d. Modern gelatin silver print, 2011, from original negative Collection RKD, The Hague (BR 83)
CAT. 35

Two women on bed, n.d. Modern gelatin silver print, 2011, from original negative Collection RKD, The Hague (BR 906)
CAT. 59

Woman at table, n.d. Modern gelatin silver print, 2011, from original negative Collection RKD, The Hague (BR 1736)

Maurice Denis

Forest with Anemones, April 1889 Oil on cardboard, $9^{1}/_{2}$ x 13 in. (24 x 33 cm) Private collection, Saint-Germain-en-Laye

Avril (Anémones) (April [Anemones]), 1891 Oil on canvas, $25^{5}/_{8}$ x $30^{3}/_{4}$ in. (65 x 78 cm) Private collection (Amsterdam only)
CAT. 82

Sur la plage (fillettes à contre-jour) (On the Beach [Two Girls against the Light]), 1892 Oil on board mounted on panel, $8^{1}/_{8}$ x $9^{7}/_{8}$ in. (20.5 x 25 cm) Private collection, Germany
CAT. 68

La capeline rose à Perros (Pink Bonnet), 1893 Oil on canvas, $8^{5}/_{8}$ x $10^{5}/_{8}$ in. (22 x 27 cm) Private collection
CAT. 74

Portrait de Marthe à voilette blanche (Portrait of Marthe in a White Veil), 1894 Oil on canvas, $12^{5}/_{8}$ x $16^{1}/_{8}$ in. (32 x 41 cm) Private collection
CAT. 73

Noële et sa mère (Noële and Her Mother), 1896 Oil on canvas, $13^{1}/_{8}$ x $15^{1}/_{2}$ in. (33.5 x 39.5 cm) Private collection
CAT. 61

Maternité à la fenêtre (au Le Pouldu) (Motherhood at the Window [in Le Pouldu]), ca. 1899 Oil on canvas, $27^{1}/_{2}$ x $18^{1}/_{8}$ in. (70 x 46 cm) Musée d'Orsay, Paris. Paul Jamot bequest, 1941 (RF 1941-42)
CAT. 77

Woman Sewing at the Window (Home Life), 1903 Oil on canvas, $21^{7}/_{8}$ x $19^{1}/_{8}$ in. (55.5 x 48.5 cm) Petit Palais, Musée des Beaux-Arts de la Ville de Paris (PPP02139)

Close-up of Noële in a white collar in her mother's arms at Mercin, Arthur Fontaine's home, November 1896 Gelatin silver print, $4^{3}/_{4}$ x $6^{1}/_{4}$ in. (12 x 16 cm) Musée d'Orsay, Paris. Gift of Mme Claire Denis, through the Société des Amis du Musée d'Orsay, 2006 (PHO 2006-4-4), Druet Album 1.14
CAT. 76

Noële with walker and her mother, hands outstretched, on the balcony of the Villa Montrouge, Saint-Germain-en-Laye, April 1897 Gelatin silver print, $4^{3}/_{4}$ x $6^{1}/_{4}$ in. (12 x 16 cm) Musée d'Orsay, Paris. Gift of Mme Claire Denis, through the Société des Amis du Musée d'Orsay, 2006 (PHO 2006-4-10), Druet Album 1.11.3
CAT. 70

Bernadette, three months old, in Marthe's arms, Saint-Germain-en-Laye, July 1899 Gelatin silver print, $4^{3}/_{4}$ x $6^{1}/_{4}$ in. (12 x 16 cm) Musée d'Orsay, Paris. Gift of Mme Claire Denis, through the Société des Amis du Musée d'Orsay, 2006 (PHO 2006-4-11), Druet Album 3.13
CAT. 63

Noële nude stretched out on the beach, Le Pouldu, summer 1899 Gelatin silver print, $4^{3}/_{4}$ x $6^{1}/_{4}$ in. (12 x 16 cm) Musée d'Orsay, Paris. Gift of Mme Claire Denis, through the Société des Amis du Musée d'Orsay, 2006 (PHO 2006-4-5), Druet Album 1.39
CAT. 69

Bernadette, close-up, Saint-Germain-en-Laye, Villa Montrouge, December 1899 Gelatin silver print, $4^{3}/_{4}$ x $6^{1}/_{4}$ in. (12 x 16 cm) Private collection, Saint-Germain-en-Laye, Druet Album 7.07
CAT. 64

Hortense Denis (1840–1914) and Noële holding the rake in the garden of the Denis grandparents, 1899 Gelatin silver print, $4^{3}/_{4}$ x $6^{1}/_{4}$ in. (12 x 16 cm) Private collection, Saint-Germain-en-Laye, Druet Album 1.35

Bernadette, Anne-Marie, Pornic, August 1903 Gelatin silver print, $4^{3}/_{4}$ x $6^{1}/_{4}$ in. (12 x 16 cm) Musée d'Orsay, Paris. Gift of Mme Claire Denis through the Société des Amis du Musée d'Orsay, 2006 (PHO 2006-4-12)

Bernadette, Noële, and a boy playing with a skipping rope, September 1903 Gelatin silver print, $4^{3}/_{4}$ x $6^{1}/_{4}$ in. (12 x 16 cm) Musée d'Orsay, Paris. Gift of Mme Claire Denis, through the Société des Amis du Musée d'Orsay, 2006 (PHO 2006-4-47), Druet Album 3.34
CAT. 62

Bernadette playing with a stick on the beach, near La Bernerie, 1903 Gelatin silver print, $4^{3}/_{4}$ x $6^{1}/_{4}$ in. (12 x 16 cm) Musée d'Orsay, Paris. Gift of Mme Claire Denis, through the Société des Amis du Musée d'Orsay, 2006 (PHO 2006-4-24), Druet Album 3.47
CAT. 66

Noële and Bernadette sitting on the doorstep, wall of greenery, 1903 Gelatin silver print, $6^{1}/_{4}$ x $5^{7}/_{8}$ in. (16 x 15 cm) Private collection, Saint-Germain-en-Laye, Druet Album 3.40
CAT. 80

Marthe Denis, View of La Place de la Seigneurie, Noële, Anne-Marie, and Bernadette with Maurice Denis, Florence, April 1904 Gelatin silver print, $4^{3}/_{4}$ x $6^{1}/_{4}$ in. (12 x 16 cm) Musée d'Orsay, Paris. Gift of Mme Claire Denis, through the Société des Amis du Musée d'Orsay, 2006 (PHO 2006-4-38), Druet Album 4.36
CAT. 85

Bernadette feeding pigeons in front of the Duomo, Florence, 1904 Gelatin silver print, $4^{3}/_{4}$ x $6^{1}/_{4}$ in. (12 x 16 cm) Musée d'Orsay, Paris. Gift of Mme Claire Denis, through the Société des Amis du Musée d'Orsay, 2006 (PHO 2006-4-36), Druet Album 4.44
CAT. 84

Perros-Guirec, farandole at the Regatta ball, August 1906 Gelatin silver print, $4^{3}/_{4}$ x $6^{1}/_{4}$ in. (12 x 16 cm) Musée d'Orsay, Paris. Gift of Mme Claire Denis, through the Société des Amis du Musée d'Orsay, 2006 (PHO 2006-4-46), Druet Album 5.23
CAT. 65

Marthe nursing Madeleine in front of Noële on the beach, Perros-Guirec, October 1906 Gelatin silver print, $4^{3}/_{4}$ x $6^{1}/_{4}$ in. (12 x 16 cm) Musée d'Orsay, Paris. Gift of Mme Claire Denis, through the Société des Amis du Musée d'Orsay, 2006 (PHO 2006-4-30), Druet Album 5.35
CAT. 78

Madeleine in Marthe's arms, looking down, Saint-Germain-en-Laye, October 1906 Gelatin silver print, $4^{3}/_{4}$ x $6^{1}/_{4}$ in. (12 x 16 cm) Musée d'Orsay, Paris. Gift of Mme Claire Denis through the Société des Amis du Musée d'Orsay, 2006 (PHO 2006-4-17)

Anne-Marie standing behind the carriage of smiling Madeleine, May 1907 Gelatin silver print, $6^{1}/_{4}$ x $5^{7}/_{8}$ in. (16 x 15 cm) Private collection, Saint-Germain-en-Laye, Druet Album 5.51
CAT. 81

Venice, view of the Grand Canal, Bernadette and Madeleine on the balcony, October 1907 Gelatin silver print, $5^{3}/_{4}$ $6^{1}/_{8}$ in. (14.5 x 15.5 cm) Musée d'Orsay, Paris. Gift of Mme Claire Denis through the Société des Amis du Musée d'Orsay, 2006 (PHO 2006-4-34)

Anne-Marie, Bernadette, and Noële under an arcade, Bologna, October–November 1907 Gelatin silver print, $5^{1}/_{2}$ x $5^{1}/_{4}$ in. (14 x 13.5 cm) Musée d'Orsay, Paris. Gift of Mme Claire Denis, through the Société des Amis du Musée d'Orsay, 2006 (PHO 2006-4-43), Druet Album 6.39
CAT. 83

Bella Vista. Madeleine playing under a palm tree, November 1907 Gelatin silver print Private collection, Saint-Germain-en-Laye, Druet Album 6.49

The balcony in Venice: Madeleine and Anne-Marie, 1907 Gelatin silver print, $5^{3}/_{4}$ x $5^{5}/_{8}$ in. (14.5 x 14.2 cm) Musée d'Orsay, Paris. Gift of Mme Claire Denis through the Société des Amis du Musée d'Orsay, 2006 (PHO 2006-4-35)

Marthe nursing Dominique, three weeks after the birth, September 1, 1909 Gelatin silver print, $4^{7}/_{8}$ x $5^{7}/_{8}$ in. (12.5 x 15 cm) Musée d'Orsay, Paris. Gift of Mme Claire Denis, through the Société des Amis du Musée d'Orsay, 2006 (PHO 2006-4-6), Druet Album 7.18
CAT. 79

Two girls, paddling in the sea, swinging little Madeleine, Perros-Guirec, 1909 Gelatin silver print, $5^{7}/_{8}$ x $6^{1}/_{2}$ in. (15 x 16.5 cm) Musée Maurice Denis, le Prieuré, Saint-Germain-en-Laye, Druet Album 11.18
CAT. 67

Dominique and the photographer's shadow by the pebbles of Trestignel, Bernadette, Marthe and Noëlle in the background, August 1910 Gelatin silver print Private collection, Saint-Germain-en-Laye, Druet Album 7.42

Dominique et Bernadette at the window, 59, rue Mareil, n.d. Gelatin silver print Private collection, Saint-Germain-en-Laye, Druet Album 7.54

Marthe in a bonnet, M. and Mme Genêt?, n.d. Gelatin silver print, $4^{3}/_{4}$ x $6^{1}/_{4}$ in. (12 x 16 cm) Private collection, Saint-Germain-en-Laye, Druet Album 1.47
CAT. 75

Noële in a white lace bonnet on the balcony of the Villa Montrouge, n.d.
Gelatin silver print, 4$^3/_4$ x 6$^1/_4$ in. (12 x 16 cm)
Private collection, Saint-Germain-en-Laye, Druet Album 1.60

Noële seated on a balcony, n.d.
Gelatin silver print, 4$^1/_2$ x 6$^1/_4$ in. (11.5 x 16 cm)
Musée Maurice Denis, le Prieuré, Saint-Germain-en-Laye (Album Noëlle 1, pl. 36)
CAT. 71

Noële standing on her father's knees, arms in the air, by the window (Perros-Guirec), Honeymoon House, Rue de Landeval, n.d.
Gelatin silver print, 4$^3/_4$ x 6$^1/_4$ in. (12 x 16 cm)
Private collection, Saint-Germain-en-Laye, Druet Album 1.15

Marthe offering Bernadette a bunch of grapes, Le Pouldu, September 15, 1890
Negative on nitrate cellulose film, 1$^1/_2$ x 2$^1/_4$ in. (3.7 x 5.8 cm)
Musée d'Orsay, Paris. Gift of Mme Claire Denis, through the Société des Amis du Musée d'Orsay, 2006 (PHO 2006-4-1), Druet Album 11.13
CAT. 72

Henri Evenepoel

Albert Devis, 1897
Oil on canvas, 47$^1/_4$ x 19$^5/_8$ in. (120 x 50 cm)
Musée d'Ixelles, Brussels
CAT. 90

Artist in Front of a Window (Self-portrait in Front of a Window), 1897
Oil on board, 16$^1/_8$ x 13$^1/_8$ in. (41 x 33.2 cm)
Collection KBL, European Private Bankers S.A., Luxembourg

La dinette (Charles jouant à la dinette) (The Tea Set [Charles Playing with a Tea Set]), 1897
Oil on canvas, 31$^7/_8$ x 21$^1/_4$ in. (81 x 54 cm)
Stedelijk Museum, Sint Niklaas

La robe blanche (The White Dress), 1897
Oil on canvas, 26$^5/_8$ x 19$^5/_8$ in. (67.5 x 50 cm)
Royal Museums of Fine Arts of Belgium, Brussels
CAT. 97

Le chapeau blanc (The White Hat), 1897
Oil on canvas, 22$^3/_8$ x 18$^1/_8$ in. (57 x 46 cm)
Private collection
CAT. 88

Charles au chapeau de paille (Charles with a Straw Hat), 1898
Oil on canvas, 32$^5/_8$ x 21$^1/_2$ in. (83 x 54.5 cm)
Private collection, Belgium
CAT. 102

Charles au jersey rayé (Charles in a Striped Jersey), ca. 1898
Oil on canvas, 28$^3/_4$ x 19$^5/_8$ in. (73 x 50 cm)
Fondation Roi Baudouin, Brussels. A gift from Anne and André Leysen (Amsterdam only)
CAT. 117

Henriette au grand chapeau (Henriette in a Large Hat), 1899
Oil on canvas, 28$^1/_2$ x 23$^7/_8$ in. (72.5 x 60.5 cm)
Royal Museums of Fine Arts of Belgium, Brussels
CAT. 114

Un noyé au Pont des Arts (A Drowned Man at the Pont des Arts), 1893
Conté crayon and watercolor on paper, 7$^3/_8$ x 4$^1/_2$ in. (18.8 x 11.3 cm)
Royal Museums of Fine Arts of Belgium, Brussels (inv. 7591) (Amsterdam only)

Page from Evenepoel's sketchbook, 1893
Conté crayon on paper, 8$^1/_4$ x 5$^1/_4$ in. (21 x 13.2 cm)
Royal Museums of Fine Arts of Belgium, Brussels (inv. 6389) (Washington and Indianapolis only)
CAT. 86

Filette à la poupée (Little Girl with a Doll), ca. 1894
Conté crayon, India ink, and wash on paper, 11 x 10$^1/_4$ in. (27.8 x 25.9 cm)
Royal Museums of Fine Arts of Belgium, Brussels (inv. 7611) (Washington and Indianapolis only)

At the Square, 1897
Lithograph, 12$^3/_4$ x 9$^1/_8$ in. (32.5 x 23.3 cm)
Van Gogh Museum, Amsterdam (Vincent van Gogh Foundation) (p 1398V/2000)

André Devis, Wépion, summer 1897
Modern gelatin silver print, 2011, from original negative, 2 x 1$^1/_2$ in. (5 x 3.8 cm)
Royal Museums of Fine Arts of Belgium, Brussels, Archives of Contemporary Art in Belgium (inv. 278)
CAT. 89

Louise at Wépion, summer 1897
Modern gelatin silver print, 2011, from original negative, 1$^1/_2$ x 2 in. (3.8 x 5 cm)
Royal Museums of Fine Arts of Belgium, Brussels, Archives of Contemporary Art in Belgium (inv. 236)
CAT. 87

Louise de Mey, on bed, Le Trieu-Colin, Wépion, summer 1897
Modern gelatin silver print, 2011, from original negative, 1$^1/_2$ x 2 in. (3.8 x 5 cm)
Royal Museums of Fine Arts of Belgium, Brussels, Archives of Contemporary Art in Belgium (inv. 121)
CAT. 98

Sophie de Mey, Fooz-Wépion, summer 1897
Modern gelatin silver print, 2011, from original negative, 1$^1/_2$ x 2 in. (3.8 x 5 cm)
Royal Museums of Fine Arts of Belgium, Brussels, Archives of Contemporary Art in Belgium (inv. 231)
CAT. 91

The unmade bed, summer 1897
Modern gelatin silver print, 2011, from original negative, 1$^1/_2$ x 2 in. (3.8 x 5 cm)
Royal Museums of Fine Arts of Belgium, Brussels, Archives of Contemporary Art in Belgium (inv. 489)

Henri Matisse in Evenepoel's studio, fall 1897
Modern gelatin silver print, 2011, from original negative, 1$^1/_2$ x 2 in. (3.8 x 5 cm)
Royal Museums of Fine Arts of Belgium, Brussels, Archives of Contemporary Art in Belgium (inv. 451)
CAT. 111

Self-portrait in a mirror, in L'hôtel Moderne in Algeria, fall 1897
Modern gelatin silver print, 2011, from original negative, 1$^1/_2$ x 2 in. (3.8 x 5 cm)
Royal Museums of Fine Arts of Belgium, Brussels, Archives of Contemporary Art in Belgium (inv. 250)
CAT. 100

Charles de Mey, leaving the bath, 1897
Modern gelatin silver print, 2011, from original negative, 1$^1/_2$ x 2 in. (3.8 x 5 cm)
Royal Museums of Fine Arts of Belgium, Brussels, Archives of Contemporary Art in Belgium (inv. 200)
CAT. 101

Charles in the studio on a stool at right, ca. 1897
Modern gelatin silver print, 2011, from original negative, 1$^1/_2$ x 2 in. (3.8 x 5 cm)
Royal Museums of Fine Arts of Belgium, Brussels, Archives of Contemporary Art in Belgium (inv. 419)

Charles on the potty, 1897
Modern gelatin silver print, 2011, from original negative, 1$^1/_2$ x 2 in. (3.8 x 5 cm)
Royal Museums of Fine Arts of Belgium, Brussels, Archives of Contemporary Art in Belgium (inv. 159)
CAT. 92

Henriette and Sophie playing with a ball, 1897
Modern gelatin silver print, 2011, from original negative, 1$^1/_2$ x 2 in. (3.8 x 5 cm)
Royal Museums of Fine Arts of Belgium, Brussels, Archives of Contemporary Art in Belgium (inv. 233)

Louise with Charles de Mey curled in her lap, 1897
Modern gelatin silver print, 2011, from original negative, 1$^1/_2$ x 2 in. (3.8 x 5 cm)
Royal Museums of Fine Arts of Belgium, Brussels, Archives of Contemporary Art in Belgium (inv. 113)

Evenepoel studying his photographs, 1897–98
Modern gelatin silver print, 2011, from original negative, 1$^1/_2$ x 2 in. (3.8 x 5 cm)
Royal Museums of Fine Arts of Belgium, Brussels, Archives of Contemporary Art in Belgium (inv. 398)
CAT. 95

Self-portrait in the mirror (Reflection of Henri Evenepoel in a straw hat), 1897–98
Modern gelatin silver print, 2011, from original negative, 1$^1/_2$ x 2 in. (3.8 x 5 cm)
Royal Museums of Fine Arts of Belgium, Brussels, Archives of Contemporary Art in Belgium (inv. 394)
CAT. 110

Charles, Sophie, and Henriette de Mey with Louise von Mattenburgh on the Place de la Concorde, Paris, fall 1898
Modern gelatin silver print, 2011, from original negative, 1$^1/_2$ x 2 in. (3.8 x 5 cm)
Royal Museums of Fine Arts of Belgium, Brussels, Archives of Contemporary Art in Belgium (inv. 34)
CAT. 105

Henriette, Charles, Sophie de Mey, and the nanny, Place de la Concorde, Paris, fall 1898
Modern gelatin silver print, 2011, from original negative, 1$^1/_2$ x 2 in. (3.8 x 5 cm)
Royal Museums of Fine Arts of Belgium, Brussels, Archives of Contemporary Art in Belgium (inv. 33)
CAT. 103

Sophie, Charles, Louise, and the nanny on a walk, fall 1898
Modern gelatin silver print, 2011, from original negative, 1$^1/_2$ x 2 in. (3.8 x 5 cm)
Royal Museums of Fine Arts of Belgium, Brussels, Archives of Contemporary Art in Belgium (inv. 31)
CAT. 106

Charles and Louise in the studio, 1898
Modern gelatin silver print, 2011, from original negative, 1$^1/_2$ x 2 in. (3.8 x 5 cm)
Royal Museums of Fine Arts of Belgium, Brussels, Archives of Contemporary Art in Belgium (inv. 408)

Henriette and Charles de Mey, 1898
Modern gelatin silver print, 2011, from original negative, 1$^1/_2$ x 2 in. (3.8 x 5 cm)
Royal Museums of Fine Arts of Belgium, Brussels, Archives of Contemporary Art in Belgium (inv. 28)
CAT. 104

Henri Evenepoel, 1898
Modern gelatin silver print, from original negative, 1$^1/_2$ x 2 in. (3.8 x 5 cm)
Royal Museums of Fine Arts of Belgium, Brussels, Archives of Contemporary Art in Belgium (inv. 400)
CAT. 99

Self-portrait in three-way mirror, 1898
Modern gelatin silver print, 2011, from original negative, 1$^1/_2$ x 2 in. (3.8 x 5 cm)
Royal Museums of Fine Arts of Belgium, Brussels, Archives of Contemporary Art in Belgium (inv. 115)
CAT. 94

The bedroom of Henri Evenepoel—The unmade bed, winter 1898–99
Modern gelatin silver print, 2011, from original negative, 1$^1/_2$ x 2 in. (3.8 x 5 cm)
Royal Museums of Fine Arts of Belgium, Brussels, Archives of Contemporary Art in Belgium (inv. 133)
CAT. 96

Henriette in the studio of Henri Evenepoel, winter 1898–99
Modern gelatin silver print, 2011, from original negative, 1$^1/_2$ x 2 in. (3.8 x 5 cm)
Royal Museums of Fine Arts of Belgium, Brussels, Archives of Contemporary Art in Belgium (inv. 428)
CAT. 112

Portrait of *Henriette au grand chapeau* in progress, winter 1898–99
Modern gelatin silver print, 2011, from original negative, 1½ x 2 in. (3.8 x 5 cm)
Royal Museums of Fine Arts of Belgium, Brussels, Archives of Contemporary Art in Belgium (inv. 429)
CAT. 113

Louise watching over Charles, January 1899
Modern gelatin silver print, 2011, from original negative, 1½ x 2 in. (3.8 x 5 cm)
Royal Museums of Fine Arts of Belgium, Brussels, Archives of Contemporary Art in Belgium (inv. 135)
CAT. 109

Charles standing in his striped jersey, spring 1899
Modern gelatin silver print, 2011, from original negative, 2 x 1½ in. (5 x 3.8 cm)
Royal Museums of Fine Arts of Belgium, Brussels, Archives of Contemporary Art in Belgium (inv. 173)
CAT. 116

Charles asleep in his crib, 1899
Modern gelatin silver print, 2011, from original negative, 1½ x 2 in. (3.8 x 5 cm)
Royal Museums of Fine Arts of Belgium, Brussels, Archives of Contemporary Art in Belgium (inv. 161)
CAT. 108

Charles at the window, 1899
Modern gelatin silver print, 2011, from original negative, 2 x 1½ in. (5 x 3.8 cm)
Royal Museums of Fine Arts of Belgium, Brussels, Archives of Contemporary Art in Belgium (inv. 78)
CAT. 118

Charles de Mey, running toward us, 1899
Modern gelatin silver print, 2011, from original negative, 1½ x 2 in. (3.8 x 5 cm)
Royal Museums of Fine Arts of Belgium, Brussels, Archives of Contemporary Art in Belgium (inv. 228)
CAT. 115

Charles in bed, playing with a carousel, 1899
Modern gelatin silver print, 2011, from original negative, 1½ x 2 in. (3.8 x 5 cm)
Royal Museums of Fine Arts of Belgium, Brussels, Archives of Contemporary Art in Belgium (inv. 134)

Henriette watching over sick Charles, 1899
Modern gelatin silver print, 2011, from original negative, 1½ x 2 in. (3.8 x 5 cm)
Royal Museums of Fine Arts of Belgium, Brussels, Archives of Contemporary Art in Belgium (inv. 184)
CAT. 107

Charles sick in bed, n.d.
Modern gelatin silver print, 2011, from original negative, 1½ x 2 in. (3.8 x 5 cm)
Royal Museums of Fine Arts of Belgium, Brussels, Archives of Contemporary Art in Belgium (inv. 139 or 84)

Self-portrait with pipe, n.d.
Modern gelatin silver print, 2011, from original negative, 1½ x 2 in. (3.8 x 5 cm)
Royal Museums of Fine Arts of Belgium, Brussels, Archives of Contemporary Art in Belgium (inv. 375)
CAT. 93

Henri Rivière

Les trente-six vues de la Tour Eiffel (Thirty-six Views of the Eiffel Tower), 1888–1902
Album with 36 lithographs, 9⅛ x 11⅝ in. (23.2 x 29.4 cm)
Van Gogh Museum, Amsterdam (Vincent van Gogh Foundation) (p 1985S/2002), and private collection
CAT. 126

Planche 4, En haut de la tour (Plate 4, At the Top of the Tower), from *Les trente-six vues de la Tour Eiffel* (Thirty-six Views of the Eiffel Tower), 1888–1902
Lithograph, 6¾ x 8¼ in. (17.1 x 21 cm)
Musée Carnavalet, Paris, and Fine Arts Museums of San Francisco, Legion of Honor, Achenbach Foundation for Graphic Arts (1983.1.2.4)
CAT. 130

Planche 17, En bateau-mouche (Plate 17, On a Riverboat), from *Les trente-six vues de la Tour Eiffel* (Thirty-six Views of the Eiffel Tower), 1888–1902
Lithograph, 6 11/16 x 8¼ in. (17 x 21 cm)
Musée Carnavalet, Paris, and Fine Arts Museums of San Francisco, Legion of Honor, Achenbach Foundation for Graphic Arts (1983.1.2.17)

Planche 21, Sur les toits (Plate 21, On the Rooftops), from *Les trente-six vues de la Tour Eiffel* (Thirty-six Views of the Eiffel Tower), 1888–1902
Lithograph, 6⅝ x 8¼ in. (16.8 x 21 cm)
Van Gogh Museum, Amsterdam (Vincent van Gogh Foundation) (p 1985V/2000), and Fine Arts Museums of San Francisco, Legion of Honor, Achenbach Foundation for Graphic Arts (1983.1.2.21)
CAT. 134

Planche 25, Dans la tour (Plate 25, Inside the Tower), from *Les trente-six vues de la Tour Eiffel* (Thirty-six Views of the Eiffel Tower), 1888–1902
Lithograph, 6⅝ x 8¼ in. (16.8 x 21 cm)
Musée Carnavalet, Paris, and Fine Arts Museums of San Francisco, Legion of Honor, Achenbach Foundation for Graphic Arts (1983.1.2.25)
CAT. 128

Planche 30, Ouvrier plombier dans la Tour (Plate 30, Lead worker in the Tower), from *Les trente-six vues de la Tour Eiffel* (Thirty-six Views of the Eiffel Tower), 1888–1902
Lithograph, 8¼ x 6⅝ in. (21 x 16.8 cm)
Musée Carnavalet, Paris, and Fine Arts Museums of San Francisco, Legion of Honor, Achenbach Foundation for Graphic Arts (1983.1.2.30)

Planche 36, Le peintre dans la tour (Plate 36, The Painter in the Tower), from *Les trente-six vues de la Tour Eiffel* (Thirty-six Views of the Eiffel Tower), 1888–1902
Lithograph, 8¼ x 6⅝ in. (21 x 16.8 cm)
Musée Carnavalet, Paris, and Fine Arts Museums of San Francisco, Legion of Honor, Achenbach Foundation for Graphic Arts (1983.1.2.36)
CAT. 132

L'aube (Dawn), number 1 from the series *La féerie des heures* (The Magic of the Hours), 1901
Lithograph, 9⅜ x 23½ in. (23.9 x 59.8 cm) image, 12⅜ x 26⅝ in. (31.3 x 67.6 cm) sheet
Zimmerli Art Museum at Rutgers University. Gift of Sara and Armond Fields (83.078.017)
CAT. 119

Le pardon de Sainte-Anne-la-Palud (The Pardon of St. Anne-la-Palud), number 38 from the series *Paysages bretons* (Breton Landscapes), 1892–93
Five color woodcuts, 13½ x 9 in. (34.3 x 22.8 cm) each sheet
Zimmerli Art Museum at Rutgers University. Gift of Sara and Armond Fields (83.078.002)
CAT. 150

Pine Trees in the Rain, 1907
Etching with white heightening, 9 x 13¼ in. (22.8 x 33.8 cm) image, 12 x 17⅜ in. (30.5 x 44 cm) sheet
Zimmerli Art Museum at Rutgers University. Gift of G. Noufflard and H. Noufflard Guy-Loé (83.077.001.001)
CAT. 146

Breton Coast, 1911
Etching, 10⅜ x 15¾ in. (26.5 x 40 cm)
Zimmerli Art Museum at Rutgers University. Gift of Sara and Armond Fields (82.056.040)

At the milliner's, ca. 1885–95
Gelatin silver print, 4¾ x 3½ in. (12 x 9 cm)
Musée d'Orsay, Paris (PHO 1987-35-33)

A couple entering a public building, ca. 1885–95
Gelatin silver print, 4¾ x 3½ in. (12 x 9 cm)
Musée d'Orsay, Paris (PHO 1987-35-36)
CAT. 140

Madame Rivière walking two dogs in front of the St.-Lazare train station, ca. 1885–95
Gelatin silver print, 4¾ x 3½ in. (12 x 9 cm)
Musée d'Orsay, Paris (PHO 1987-35-31)

The Moulin de la Galette, ca. 1885–95
Gelatin silver print, 4¾ x 3½ in. (12 x 9 cm)
Musée d'Orsay, Paris (PHO 1987-35-53)
CAT. 135

Paris rooftops in the snow, photographed from a balcony, ca. 1885–95
Gelatin silver print, 3½ x 4¾ in. (9 x 12 cm)
Musée d'Orsay, Paris (PHO 1987-35-55)

People, two dogs, and a double-decker bus on the Pont du Louvre, ca. 1885–95
Gelatin silver print, 3½ x 4¾ in. (9 x 12 cm)
Musée d'Orsay, Paris (PHO 1987-35-26)
CAT. 139

People walking in a public square, ca. 1885–95
Gelatin silver print, 3½ x 4¾ in. (9 x 12 cm)
Musée d'Orsay, Paris (PHO 1987-35-35)
CAT. 137

People walking in a street, at right a man carrying an armchair, ca. 1885–95
Gelatin silver print, 3½ x 4¾ in. (9 x 12 cm)
Musée d'Orsay, Paris (PHO 1987-35-45)
CAT. 138

Three people in front of a shop, ca. 1885–95
Gelatin silver print, 3½ x 4¾ in. (9 x 12 cm)
Musée d'Orsay, Paris (PHO 1987-35-44)
CAT. 136

Cabaret of the Chat Noir: Lighting equipment, ca. 1887–94
Gelatin silver print, 4¾ x 3½ in. (12 x 9 cm)
Musée d'Orsay, Paris. Gift of Mme Henriette Guy-Loé and Mlle Geneviève Noufflard, 1986 (PHO 1986-122-55)
CAT. 122

Cabaret of the Chat Noir: Stagehands moving zinc figures behind the screen for *The Epic*, ca. 1887–94
Gelatin silver print, 3½ x 4¾ in. (9 x 12 cm)
Musée d'Orsay, Paris. Gift of Mme Henriette Guy-Loé and Mlle Geneviève Noufflard, 1986 (PHO 1986-122-34)
CAT. 120

The Eiffel Tower: An intersection of girders, with the Seine and Île aux Cygnes in the background, 1889
Gelatin silver print, 3½ x 4¾ in. (9 x 12 cm)
Musée d'Orsay, Paris. Gift of Mme Bernard Granet and her children and Mlle Solange Granet, 1981 (PHO 1981-124-23)
CAT. 127

The Eiffel Tower: Five men at work on part of the top floor at the foot of the "bell tower," 1889
Gelatin silver print, 3½ x 4¾ in. (9 x 12 cm)
Musée d'Orsay, Paris. Gift of Mme Bernard Granet and her children and Mlle Solange Granet, 1981 (PHO 1981-124-4)
CAT. 129

The Eiffel Tower: Five people on a platform, 1889
Gelatin silver print, 3½ x 4¾ in. (9 x 12 cm)
Musée d'Orsay, Paris. Gift of Mme Bernard Granet and her children and Mlle Solange Granet, 1981 (PHO 1981-124-12)

The Eiffel Tower: Painter on a knotted rope along a vertical girder, below an intersection of girders, 1889
Gelatin silver print, 4¾ x 3½ in. (12 x 9 cm)
Musée d'Orsay, Paris. Gift of Mme Bernard Granet and her children and Mlle Solange Granet, 1981 (PHO 1981-124-21)
CAT. 131

The Eiffel Tower: Scaffolding on the "bell tower," high-angle view over the Seine, 1889
Gelatin silver print, 4¾ x 3½ in. (12 x 9 cm)
Musée d'Orsay, Paris. Gift of Mme Bernard Granet and her children and Mlle Solange Granet, 1981 (PHO 1981-124-10)

The Eiffel Tower: Seen from a riverboat, 1889
Gelatin silver print, 3 1/2 x 4 3/4 in. (9 x 12 cm)
Musée d'Orsay, Paris. Gift of Mme Henriette Guy-Loé and her sister Mlle Geneviève Noufflard (PHO 1986-122-1)

The Eiffel Tower: Spiral staircase between the 2nd and 3rd floors (seen from below), 1889
Gelatin silver print, 4 3/4 x 3 1/2 in. (12 x 9 cm)
Musée d'Orsay, Paris. Gift of Mme Bernard Granet and her children and Mlle Solange Granet, 1981 (PHO 1981-124-19)

The Eiffel Tower: The "bell tower," light, and lightning conductor (seen from below), 1889
Gelatin silver print, 4 3/4 x 3 1/2 in. (12 x 9 cm)
Musée d'Orsay, Paris. Gift of Mme Bernard Granet and her children and Mlle Solange Granet, 1981 (PHO 1981-124-27)
CAT. 124

The Eiffel Tower: Two visitors from the Chat Noir staff, Henri Jouard and Rodolphe Salis on the top platform, 1889
Gelatin silver print, 4 3/4 x 3 1/2 in. (12 x 9 cm)
Musée d'Orsay, Paris. Gift of Mme Henriette Guy-Loé and her sister Mlle Geneviève Noufflard (PHO 1986-122-23)

The Eiffel Tower: Worker on the scaffolding working on a vertical beam, 1889
Gelatin silver print, 4 3/4 x 3 1/2 in. (12 x 9 cm)
Musée d'Orsay, Paris. Gift of Mme Bernard Granet and her children and Mlle Solange Granet, 1981 (PHO 1981-124-11)

The Eiffel Tower: Workman standing along a girder, 1889
Gelatin silver print, 4 3/4 x 3 1/2 in. (12 x 9 cm)
Musée d'Orsay, Paris. Gift of Mme Henriette Guy-Loé and Mlle Geneviève Noufflard, 1986 (PHO 1986-122-57)
CAT. 125

Paris rooftops in the evening with the Eiffel Tower in the distance, ca. 1889–95
Gelatin silver print, 3 1/2 x 4 3/4 in. (9 x 12 cm)
Musée d'Orsay, Paris. Gift of Mme Henriette Guy-Loé and Mlle Geneviève Noufflard, 1986 (PHO 1986-122-13)
CAT. 133

Mme Rivière amidst the pines, ca. 1890–1900
Gelatin silver print, 3 1/8 x 4 3/8 in. (8 x 11 cm)
Zimmerli Art Museum at Rutgers University. David A. and Mildred H. Morse Art Acquisition Fund (1987.0484)
CAT. 147

Madame Rivière from the front, walking with her dog in a rocky landscape, ca. 1890–1900
Gelatin silver print, 3 1/2 x 4 3/4 in. (9 x 12 cm)
Musée d'Orsay, Paris (PHO 1987-35-67)

Cleaning woman on a balcony, holding a broom, ca. 1896
Gelatin silver print, 4 3/4 x 3 1/2 in. (12 x 9 cm)
Musée d'Orsay, Paris (PHO 1987-35-12)
CAT. 142

Cabaret of the Chat Noir: Moving a set, seen from the first fly, ca. 1889
Cyanotype, 4 3/4 x 3 1/2 in. (12 x 9 cm)
Musée d'Orsay, Paris. Gift of Mme Henriette Guy-Loé and Mlle Geneviève Noufflard, 1986 (PHO 1986-122-7)
CAT. 121

Breton women in the street, ca. 1890
Cyanotype, 3 1/4 x 4 5/8 in. (8.4 x 11.9 cm) image, 3 1/2 x 5 in. (8.8 x 12.7 cm) sheet
Zimmerli Art Museum at Rutgers University. David A. and Mildred H. Morse Art Acquisition Fund (1987.0478)
CAT. 149

Mme Rivière above the coast, ca. 1890–1900
Cyanotype, 3 1/8 x 4 1/4 in. (8.1 x 10.9 cm)
Zimmerli Art Museum at Rutgers University. David A. and Mildred H. Morse Art Acquisition Fund (1987.0475)
CAT. 145

Madame Rivière and another woman next to a rock by the sea, ca. 1890–1900
Cyanotype, 3 1/2 x 4 3/4 in. (9 x 12 cm)
Musée d'Orsay, Paris (PHO 1987-35-66)

Madame Rivière from the front, walking with her dog in a wooded landscape, ca. 1890–1900
Cyanotype, 3 1/2 x 4 3/4 in. (9 x 12 cm)
Musée d'Orsay, Paris (PHO 1987-35-64)
CAT. 148

Madame Rivière on her knees, petting her dog, ca. 1890–1900
Cyanotype, 3 1/2 x 4 3/4 in. (9 x 12 cm)
Musée d'Orsay, Paris (PHO 1987-35-60)
CAT. 144

Man walking in a rocky landscape, ca. 1890–1900
Cyanotype, 3 1/2 x 4 3/4 in. (9 x 12 cm)
Musée d'Orsay, Paris (PHO 1987-35-83)
CAT. 151

Cabaret of the Chat Noir: Figures during a set change for *Roland*, ca. 1891–94
Cyanotype, 4 3/4 x 3 1/2 in. (12 x 9 cm)
Musée d'Orsay, Paris. Gift of Mme Henriette Guy-Loé and Mlle Geneviève Noufflard, 1986 (PHO 1986-122-8)
CAT. 123

Madame Rivière in profile, crouching on a rug in the apartment, boulevard de Clichy, looking at her dog, ca. 1896
Cyanotype, 3 1/2 x 4 3/4 in. (9 x 12 cm)
Musée d'Orsay, Paris (PHO 1987-35-57)
CAT. 143

Madame Rivière leaning on the balcony, watching the street, ca. 1896
Cyanotype, 3 1/2 x 4 3/4 in. (9 x 12 cm)
Musée d'Orsay, Paris (PHO 1987-35-6)

Madame Rivière standing at the hallway door of the apartment on the boulevard de Clichy, ca. 1896
Cyanotype, 4 3/4 x 3 1/2 in. (12 x 9 cm)
Musée d'Orsay, Paris (PHO 1987-35-7)
CAT. 141

Félix Vallotton

Scène de rue (Street Scene), ca. 1895
Oil on board, 10 3/8 x 13 3/4 in. (26.5 x 35 cm)
Private collection (Washington only)
CAT. 163

Gabrielle Vallotton at Her Vanity, 1899
Distemper on board, 22 5/8 x 30 3/4 in. (57.5 x 78 cm)
Kunsthaus Zürich (2457)
CAT. 157

Gabrielle Vallotton Doing Her Nails, 1899
Oil on board, 23 x 19 5/8 in. (58.5 x 50 cm)
Musée d'Orsay, Paris (RF 1977-354)
CAT. 154

La chambre rouge, Etretat (Red Room, Etretat), 1899
Oil on board, 19 3/8 x 20 3/8 in. (49.2 x 51.3 cm)
The Art Institute of Chicago. Bequest of Mrs. Clive Runnells (1977.606)
CAT. 153

Sur la plage (On the Beach), 1899
Oil on board, 16 1/2 x 18 7/8 in. (42 x 48 cm)
Private collection, Switzerland
CAT. 164

La visite, effet de lampe (The Visit, Lamp Effect), 1899–1900
Oil on board, 31 7/8 x 43 7/8 in. (81 x 111.5 cm)
Kunstmuseum Winterthur. Purchase, 1973
CAT. 159

Femme en bleu fouillant dans une armoire (Woman in Blue Rummaging in an Armoire), 1903
Oil on canvas, 31 7/8 x 18 1/8 in. (81 x 46 cm)
Musée d'Orsay, Paris. Acquired with the assistance of Philippe Meyer, 1997 (RF 1997-4)
CAT. 162

Gabrielle Vallotton seated before a fireplace, 1899
Gelatin silver print, 3 1/2 x 3 1/2 in. (9 x 9 cm)
Isabelle de la Brunière
CAT. 152

Gabrielle Vallotton in a nightgown standing before an open cupboard, 1900
Gelatin silver print, 3 1/2 x 4 3/4 in. (9 x 12 cm)
Isabelle de la Brunière
CAT. 161

Gabrielle Vallotton manicuring her nails, ca. 1900
Gelatin silver print, 3 1/2 x 4 3/4 in. (9 x 12 cm)
Isabelle de la Brunière
CAT. 158

Gabrielle Vallotton at the Villa Beaulieu, 1901
Gelatin silver print, 3 1/2 x 3 1/2 in. (9 x 9 cm)
Isabelle de la Brunière
CAT. 155

Gabrielle Vallotton knitting in a rocking chair, Cricqueboeuf, 1902
Gelatin silver print, 3 1/2 x 3 1/2 in. (9 x 9 cm)
Isabelle de la Brunière
CAT. 156

Beach at Etretat, 1899
Modern gelatin silver print, 2011, from original negative
Private collection
CAT. 165

Beach at Etretat, 1899
Modern gelatin silver print, 2011, from original negative
Private collection
CAT. 166

Alley in Marseille, 1901
Modern gelatin silver print, 2011, from original negative
Private collection
CAT. 160

Gabrielle Vallotton at the villa Beaulieu, 1901
Modern gelatin silver print, 2011, from original negative
Private collection

Edouard Vuillard

Child Wearing a Red Scarf, ca. 1891
Oil on cardboard, 11 1/2 x 6 7/8 in. (29.2 x 17.5 cm)
National Gallery of Art, Washington, D.C. Ailsa Mellon Bruce Collection (1970.17.90)

The Kitchen, 1891–92
Oil on cardboard, 6 13/16 x 13 5/16 in. (17.3 x 33.8 cm)
Yale University Art Gallery, New Haven, Conn. The Philip L. Goodwin, B.A. 1907, Collection; Gift of James L. Goodwin, 1905, Henry Sage Goodwin, 1927, and Richmond L. Brown, 1907 (1958.21)
CAT. 195

At Table, Lunch, 1892
Oil on canvas, 12 5/8 x 18 1/8 in. (32 x 46 cm)
Private collection, United States
CAT. 192

The Blue Sleeve, 1893
Oil on board mounted on cradled panel, 10 1/2 x 8 3/4 in. (26.6 x 22.3 cm)
Collection Malcolm Wiener, New York (Indianapolis only)
CAT. 169

Interior, Mother and Sister of the Artist, 1893
Oil on canvas, 18 1/4 x 22 1/4 in. (46.3 x 56.5 cm)
The Museum of Modern Art, New York. Gift of Mrs. Saidie A. May, 1934 (141.1934)
CAT. 168

Madame Vuillard Sewing, ca. 1895
Oil on panel, 7 1/2 x 9 3/8 in. (19 x 24 cm)
Collection of Kelly Simpson, Katonah, N.Y.
CAT. 171

Misia at the Piano, ca. 1895–96
Oil on board, 10 1/4 x 9 13/16 in. (26 x 25 cm)
The Metropolitan Museum of Art, New York. Robert Lehman Collection, 1975 (1975.1.224)

Interior Scene, Mystery, 1896
Oil on board, 14 1/8 x 15 in. (35.8 x 38.1 cm)
Private collection, United States
CAT. 197

The Newspaper, ca. 1896–98
Oil on cardboard, 12 3/4 x 21 in. (32.5 x 53.3 cm)
The Phillips Collection, Washington, D.C. (acc: 0957)

The Nape of Misia's Neck, 1897–99
Oil on cardboard mounted on cradled panel, 5 1/4 x 13 in. (13.5 x 33 cm)
Private collection

In Front of the Tapestry: Misia and Thadée Natanson, Rue St. Florentin, 1899
Oil on board, 19 x 20 in. (48.3 x 50.8 cm)
Private collection (Washington only)
CAT. 181

Misia and Vallotton at Villeneuve, 1899
Oil on canvas, 28 3/8 x 20 7/8 in. (72 x 53 cm)
Collection of Kelly Simpson, Katonah, N.Y.

Child Playing: Annette in Front of a Wooden Chair, 1900
Oil on cardboard, mounted on cradled panel, 15 x 21 in. (38 x 53.5 cm)
The Art Institute of Chicago (inv. 1933.1180)

The Lady at the Window, ca. 1900
Oil on cardboard, 19⅛ x 24¾ in. (48.6 x 62.9 cm)
Private collection
CAT. 210

Child at the Window, ca. 1901
Oil on cardboard, 13½ x 10 in. (34.3 x 25.4 cm)
House Collection, Dumbarton Oaks, Washington, D.C. (H.C.P. 1936.40 O)
CAT. 206

Neuf silhouettes de femmes, étude de couturieres (Nine Silhouettes of Women, Study of Seamstresses), n.d.
Pen and ink on paper, 18⅛ x 12⅛ in. (46 x 30.9 cm)
Musée du Louvre, Paris (Fonds Orsay—RF 42665)
CAT. 176

Landscapes and Interiors, 1899
Lithograph, 13⅛ x 17¾ in. (33.5 x 45.2 cm)
Van Gogh Museum, Amsterdam (Vincent van Gogh Foundation) (p 1194V/2000)

Madame Vuillard cooking, Rue des Batignolles, 1897
Gelatin silver print, 3½ x 3½ in. (9 x 9 cm)
Private collection
CAT. 194

Misia Natanson at Villeneuve-sur-Yonne, 1897
Gelatin silver print, 3½ x 3½ in. (9 x 9 cm)
Private collection
CAT. 177

Pierre Bonnard and Edouard Vuillard in the dining room, Rue des Batignolles, 1897
Gelatin silver print, 3½ x 3½ in. (9 x 9 cm)
Private collection
CAT. 167

Vuillard and Misia Natanson under the arch of Les Relais, in Villeneuve-sur-Yonne, ca. 1897–99
Gelatin silver print, 3½ x 3⅝ in. (8.9 x 9.1 cm)
Private collection

Ker-Xavier, Annette, and Marie Roussel in Levallois, 1898
Gelatin silver print, 3⅜ x 3½ in. (8.6 x 8.9 cm)
Private collection
CAT. 207

Thadée and Misia Natanson in the salon, Rue St. Florentin, 1898
Gelatin silver print, 3½ x 3½ in. (8.9 x 9 cm)
Private collection
CAT. 180

Boulevard des Batignolles, 1899
Gelatin silver print, 3½ x 3½ in. (8.9 x 9 cm)
Private collection
CAT. 201

Edouard Vuillard at the window in Venice, 1899
Gelatin silver print, 3½ x 3½ in. (9 x 8.9 cm)
Private collection
CAT. 211

Misia Natanson and her dog at Villeneuve-sur-Yonne, 1899
Gelatin silver print, 3½ x 3½ in. (9 x 9 cm)
Private collection
CAT. 178

Misia Natanson in the Salon at Les Relais in Villeneuve-sur-Yonne, 1899
Gelatin silver print, 3⅞ x 3⅞ in. (9 x 9 cm)
Private collection

Misia Natanson seated on a chaise lounge, Rue St. Florentin, 1899
Gelatin silver print, 3¼ x 3⅜ in. (8.4 x 8.6 cm)
Private collection
CAT. 172

Pierre Bonnard and Ker-Xavier Roussel at the window in Venice, 1899
Gelatin silver print, 3⅞ x 3½ in. (9 x 8.9 cm)
Private collection

Ker-Xavier Roussel dancing nude, Rue Truffaut, ca. 1900
Gelatin silver print, 3⅜ x 3⅜ in. (8.7 x 8.5 cm)
Private collection
CAT. 205

Ker-Xavier Roussel nude, Rue Truffaut, ca. 1900
Gelatin silver print, 3⅜ x 3⅜ in. (8.5 x 8.7 cm)
Private collection
CAT. 204

Misia Natanson in an armchair in the salon of La Croix des Gardes, in Cannes, 1900
Gelatin silver print, 3½ x 3½ in. (9 x 9 cm)
Private collection

Misia and Thadée Natanson in the salon of La Croix des Gardes, in Cannes, 1901
Gelatin silver print, 3½ x 3½ in. (8.9 x 9 cm)
Private collection
CAT. 179

Misia Natanson in a rattan chair at La Croix des Gardes, in Cannes, ca. 1901
Gelatin silver print, 2½ x 3¾ in. (6.5 x 9.5 cm)
Private collection
CAT. 174

Misia Natanson on the steps of La Croix des Gardes, in Cannes, 1901
Gelatin silver print, 3¾ x 2⅝ in. (9.5 x 6.6 cm)
Private collection
CAT. 175

Misia Natanson seated at the window in the salon of La Croix des Gardes, in Cannes, 1901
Gelatin silver print, 3½ x 3½ in. (9 x 9 cm)
Private collection
CAT. 173

Misia Natanson seen in profile in a carriage in Cannes, 1901
Gelatin silver print, 2⅝ x 3¾ in. (6.7 x 9.4 cm)
Private collection

Madame Vuillard cleaning green beans at Myosotis, in Villerville, 1902
Gelatin silver print, 3⅜ x 3⅜ in. (8.5 x 8.7 cm)
Private collection

The two sunshades, 1902
Gelatin silver print, 3½ x 3½ in. (9 x 9 cm)
Private collection
CAT. 203

Annette Roussel, 1904
Gelatin silver print, 3⅜ x 3½ in. (8.5 x 9 cm)
Private collection
CAT. 209

Lucy Hessel, Marcelle Reiss, and Pierre Aron at Vasouy, 1904
Gelatin silver print, 3½ x 3½ in. (9 x 9 cm)
Private collection
CAT. 184

Lucy Hessel seated in the salon of La Terrasse, in Vasouy, 1904
Gelatin silver print, 3¼ x 3⅜ in. (8.4 x 8.6 cm)
Private collection
CAT. 183

Lucy Hessel visiting Madame Vuillard, Rue de la Tour, 1904–8
Gelatin silver print, 3⅜ x 3¾ in. (8.5 x 9.4 cm)
Private collection
CAT. 191

Lucy Hessel at Le Chateau Rouge, Amfréville, 1905
Gelatin silver print, 3½ x 3½ in. (9 x 9 cm)
Private collection
CAT. 185

Lucy Hessel at the window, Rue Truffaut, ca. 1905
Gelatin silver print, 3⅛ x 3⅜ in. (8.1 x 8.6 cm)
Private collection
CAT. 182

Madame Vuillard and Romain Coolus, ca. 1905
Gelatin silver print, 3⅜ x 3½ in. (8.5 x 8.9 cm)
Private collection
CAT. 170

Marcelle Aron reclining on the stairs of the Château-Rouge in Amfréville, 1905
Gelatin silver print, 3½ x 3⅝ in. (8.9 x 9.3 cm)
Private collection

Cattle in front of the car in Brittany, 1906
Gelatin silver print, 3½ x 3⅜ in. (8.8 x 8.7 cm)
Private collection
CAT. 202

Amfréville: View from a window, 1907
Gelatin silver print, 3½ x 3½ in. (8.9 x 9 cm)
Private collection
CAT. 200

Lucy Hessel in a restaurant in Normandy, 1907
Gelatin silver print, 3½ x 3½ in. (8.9 x 8.9 cm)
Private collection
CAT. 190

Lucy Hessel leaning against a haystack in Amfréville, 1907
Gelatin silver print, 3½ x 3½ in. (8.8 x 8.9 cm)
Private collection
CAT. 186

Madame Vuillard in her room in Salenelles, 1907
Gelatin silver print, 3¼ x 3⅜ in. (8.4 x 8.5 cm)
Private collection
CAT. 196

Marcelle Aron in a restaurant in Normandy, 1907
Gelatin silver print, 3½ x 3¾ in. (8.8 x 9.4 cm)
Private collection
CAT. 189

Romain Coolus in a restaurant in Normandy, 1907
Gelatin silver print, 3½ x 3⅜ in. (8.9 x 8.7 cm)
Private collection
CAT. 187

Tristan Bernard in a restaurant in Normandy, 1907
Gelatin silver print, 3½ x 3⅝ in. (8.9 x 9.1 cm)
Private collection
CAT. 188

Madame Roussel mère, Marthe Bonnard, Vuillard, Annette Roussel, and Pierre Bonnard around the table at Ker-Xavier Roussel's house, La Jacanette, 1908
Gelatin silver print, 3¼ x 3⅜ in. (8.4 x 8.6 cm)
Private collection
CAT. 193

Madame Vuillard seated, Rue de la Tour, 1908
Gelatin silver print, 3½ x 3½ in. (8.7 x 8.8 cm)
Private collection

War factory at Oullins, 1917
Gelatin silver print, 3½ x 3½ in. (9 x 9 cm)
Private collection

War factory at Oullins, 1917
Gelatin silver print, 3½ x 3½ in. (9 x 9 cm)
Private collection

Madame Vuillard at her toilet, Place Vintimille, 1928
Gelatin silver print, 3 x 2¾ in. (7.5 x 6.9 cm)
Private collection
CAT. 199

Madame Vuillard seated on her bed, Place Vintimille, 1928
Gelatin silver print, 3⅜ x 3⅜ in. (8.7 x 8.7 cm)
Private collection
CAT. 198

Marcelle Aron ascending the stairs of the Château-Rouge, in Amfréville, 1905
Gelatin silver print, 3½ x 3½ in. (9 x 9 cm)
Private collection

Tristan Bernard and André Picard on the stairs of the Château-Rouge, in Amfréville, 1905
Gelatin silver print, 3½ x 3½ in. (8.9 x 9 cm)
Private collection

Vuillard and Lucy Hessel in Amfréville, 1907
Gelatin silver print, 3⅜ x 3⅜ in. (8.5 x 8.5 cm)
Private collection

Index

Page numbers in *italics* refer to illustrations.

E

F

W

Z

Photo Credits

The photographers and the sources of visual material other than those indicated in the captions are as follows. Every effort has been made to credit the photographers and the sources; if there are errors or omissions, please contact Yale University Press so that corrections can be made in any subsequent edition.

All works by Pierre Bonnard, Maurice Denis, and Henri Rivière © 2011 Artists Rights Society (ARS), New York/ADAGP, Paris
All works by Edouard Vuillard © 2011 Artists Rights Society (ARS), New York

© Archives de l'Art contemporain en Belgique—Royal Museums of Fine Arts of Belgium, Brussels. Photo: L'Atelier de l'Imagier, Brussels (cats. 87, 89, 91–96, 98–101, 103–13, 115, 116, 118)
© Archives Salomon, Paris (Poletti fig. 5)
Photography © The Art Institute of Chicago (cats. 153, 208)
ASOAL/Société française de photographie, Paris (Chéroux fig. 1)
Bibliothèque nationale de France (Lee figs. 3, 4)
The Bridgeman Art Library (Rathbone fig. 1)
Isabelle de la Brunière (Photographic collection of Jacques Rodriques-Henriques) (cats. 152, 155, 156, 158, 161)
© Dumbarton Oaks, House Collection, Washington, D.C. (cat. 206)
© Fondation Félix Vallotton, Lausanne (Poletti figs. 1–3; cats. 160, 165, 166)
Photo by Peter Jacobs (cats. 119, 145–47, 149, 150)
Koning Boudewijnstichting, België © Philippe de Formanoir (cat. 117)
© 2011 Kunsthaus Zürich. All rights reserved (cat. 157)
Photo Les Arts Décoratifs, Paris/Jean Tholance (Lee fig. 2)
The Metropolitan Museum of Art, New York/Scala, Florence (Easton "Edouard Vuillard's Photography" fig. 4)
Copyright photo Mixed Media (cat. 90)
The Museum of Modern Art/Scala, Florence (Easton "Introduction" fig. 1)
RMN (Musée d'Orsay)/Droits réservés (cats. 5, 6, 19, 120, 122, 123, 124, 127, 131, 144, 148, 151, 176)
RMN (Musée d'Orsay)/Gérard Blot (cat. 129)
RMN (Musée d'Orsay)/Hervé Lewandowski (Easton "Introduction" fig. 2; McCauley fig. 3; Rathbone fig. 2; cats. 2, 3, 11, 12, 13, 15, 22, 28, 121, 125, 137, 139, 140, 162)
RMN (Musée d'Orsay)/Jean Schormans (cat. 32)
RMN (Musée d'Orsay)/Jean-Gilles Berizzi (cat. 17)
RMN (Musée d'Orsay)/Jean-Jacques Sauciat (cats. 133, 142)
RMN (Musée d'Orsay)/Michèle Bellot (cats. 141, 143)
RMN (Musée d'Orsay)/Patrice Schmidt (cats. 1, 14, 16, 25, 26, 30, 63, 65, 69, 70, 72, 78, 83, 84)
RMN (Musée d'Orsay)/Preveral (Poletti fig. 4)
RMN (Musée d'Orsay)/Thierry le Mage (cat. 154)
© Royal Museum of Fine Arts, Antwerp/Lukas—Art in Flanders VZW (McCauley fig. 6)
© Royal Museums of Fine Arts of Belgium, Brussels. Dig. photo: J. Geleyns/www.roscan.be (cats. 86, 97, 114)
Société française de photographie, Paris (Chéroux figs. 2–4)
VG Bild Kunst Bonn/Jörg Schanze Düsseldorf (Ooms fig. 2)

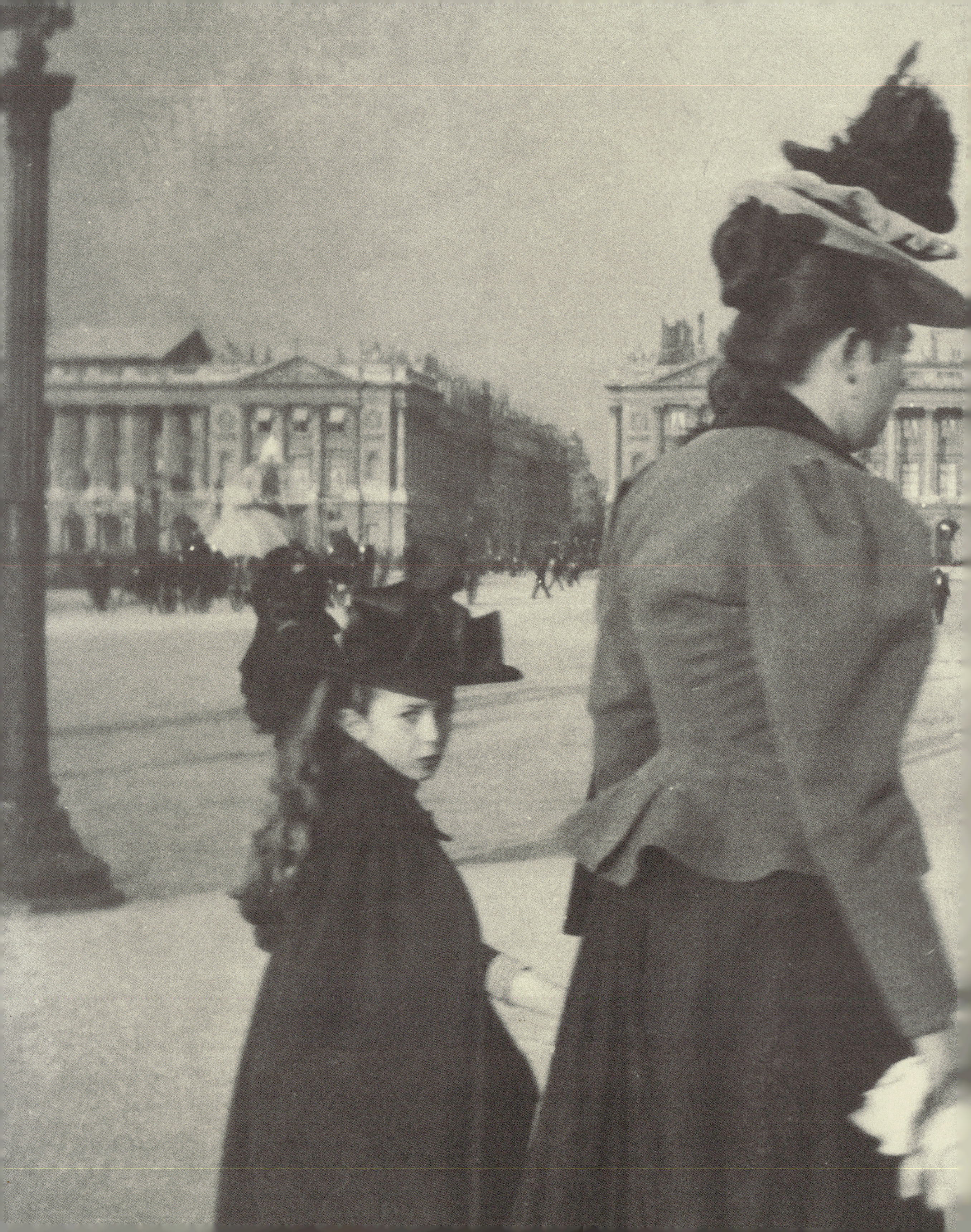